Understanding Optical Communications

ISBN 0-13-020141-3

90000

9 780130 201416

The ITSO Networking Series

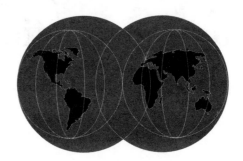

Understanding Optical Communications

HARRY J. R. DUTTON

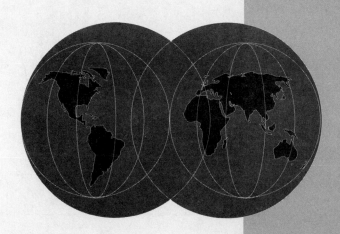

PRENTICE HALL PTR, UPPER SADDLE RIVER, NEW JERSEY 07458
http://www.phptr.com

For information about redbooks:
http://www.redbooks.ibm.com

Send comments to:
redbooks@us.ibm.com

Published by Prentice Hall PTR
Prentice-Hall, Inc.
A Simon & Schuster Company
Upper Saddle River, NJ 07458

Prentice Hall books are widely used by corporations and government agencies for training, marketing, and resale. The publisher offers discounts on this book when ordered in bulk quantities. For more information, contact

       Corporate Sales Department,
       Phone 800-382-3419; FAX: 201-236-7141
       E-mail (Internet): corpsales@prenhall.com
Or Write: Prentice Hall PTR
       Corporate Sales Department
       One Lake Street
       Upper Saddle River, NJ 07458

Take Note! Before using this information and the product it supports, be sure to read the general information under Appendix F, "Special Notices" on page 737.

Printed in the United States of America
10 9 8 7 6 5 4 3 2 1

ISBN   0-13-020141-3

Prentice-Hall International (UK) Limited, *London*
Prentice-Hall of Australia Pty. Limited, *Sydney*
Prentice-Hall Canada Inc., *Toronto*
Prentice-Hall Hispanoamericana, S.A., *Mexico*
Prentice-Hall of India Private Limited, *New Delhi*
Prentice-Hall of Japan, Inc., *Tokyo*
Simon & Schuster Asia Pte. Ltd., *Singapore*
Editora Prentice-Hall do Brasil, Ltda., *Rio de Janeiro*

Contents

Figures

Tables

Preface

The purpose of this book is to educate the reader on the basic science and engineering technology of optical communications. Although reference is made to specific products and technologies, this book is *not* a product manual.

Detailed information about IBM products is given here incidental to objectives of the book, and while every effort has been made to ensure accuracy, such information should not be considered authoritative. Authoritative information about IBM products is contained in the official manuals for the product concerned.

Audience

This book is primarily intended for people who are professionals involved in the fields of data communications or networking. Such people will often be:

Technical planners in user organizations who wish to broaden their understanding of optical communications and the direction product development is taking in the industry.

Corporate network managers who need to understand the basics of optical technology in order to make decisions about its use.

Systems engineers who in the future will plan and install networks involving optical components. These people will find the information here helpful in understanding the basic concepts of the field.

Anyone who has some background and understanding of electronic communications and wishes to expand their knowledge into the optical "world" and who may not have the time to undertake a detailed course.

The information is presented at a "technical conceptual" level and technical detail is only introduced when essential to communicate a particular concept.

About the Author

Harry J. R. Dutton is a Project Leader with the IBM International Technical Support Center, Raleigh NC., USA. Possibly the worlds longest-distance "remote report" he is based in Sydney, Australia. His current responsibilities are for worldwide technical support of ATM and of optical communications architectures and standards.

On joining IBM in January of 1967 as a Systems Engineer, Harry initially specialised in the design and programming of early communication networks. Since then he has worked in communications system design, software design, communications systems programming, product design, customer technical support, project management, consulting and product management. Throughout, his predominant role has been as the interface (on technical matters) between the IBM field companies and product development laboratories.

A frequent speaker at international conferences, he is the author of 18 IBM publications in the areas of X.25, SNA Architecture, Voice/Data Integration, Micro Channel, High Speed Communications and ATM.

Harry is a graduate of the University of New South Wales and a member of the IEEE. He may be contacted by email on:

dutton@au1.ibm.com

By the Same Author

Asynchronous Transfer Mode (ATM) - Technical Overview

by Harry J. R. Dutton and Peter Lenhard. Prentice Hall, 1995.

High-Speed Networking Technology: An Introductory Survey

by Harry J. R. Dutton and Peter Lenhard. Prentice Hall, 1995.

Acknowledgments

This book was written as a project of the IBM International Technical Support Centre, Raleigh.

Producing a book like this is not a task that any mortal can perform in isolation. Thanks are due to the following people for help, advice, technical guidance and review:

Dr Leon Polladian	The University of Sydney, Sydney, Australia.
Mr Denis Kekas	The University of Arizona, Tucson, AZ.
Mr Jon A. Herlocker	The University of Arizona, Tucson, AZ.
Mr James Cleaver	IBM Australia Limited, Sydney, Australia.
Dr Cassimer DeCussatis	IBM Enterprise Systems Division, Poughkeepsie, NY.
Dr Frank Janniello	IBM Research Division, Hawthorne, NY.
Dr Daniel Kuchta	IBM Research Division, Yorktown, NY.

Mr John Kuras   IBM Network Hardware Division, Raleigh, NC.

Mr Ian Shields   IBM Network Software Division, Raleigh, NC.

Mr Gary Steps   IBM Network Hardware Division, Raleigh, NC.

Mr Shawn Walsh   IBM International Technical Support Organisation, Raleigh, NC.

Mr Walter A. Worischek   IBM Austria, Vienna, Austria.

Structure

The book is structured in three sections:

1. Part 1, "Theory and Devices" on page 1 covers some basic optical theory, the propagation of light on fibre, lasers, detectors and devices.

2. Part 2, "Systems" on page 371 is about using optical components to build communications systems. This section also covers advanced devices.

3. Appendices including reference information and background.

Theory and Devices

Chapter 1, "Introduction"

This chapter presents a broad overview of the topics dealt with in detail later in the book.

Chapter 2, "Optical Fibre"

This chapter deals with the nature of light, the propagation of light within a fibre and the characteristics of fibre.

Chapter 3, "Optical Sources"

This chapter describes the phenomena of spontaneous emission and lasing, the basic principles of the semiconductor laser and the different types of lasers available for communications applications.

Chapter 4, "Optical Detectors"

Detection of light using pin-diodes and avalanche photodiodes is described here.

Chapter 5, "Optical Devices"

This chapter covers optical devices such as amplifiers, gratings and couplers etc.

Chapter 6, "Fibre Manufacture, Cables and Connectors"

This chapter covers the basic principles of fibre manufacture as well as the principles of joining fibres with connectors and couplers.

Systems

Chapter 7, "Optical Communication Systems"

Systems engineering is the gentle art of interconnecting devices in such a way that they operate together as a system to perform a useful function for somebody. This chapter covers the basics of setting up an optical communication system.

Chapter 8, "Optical Link Connections in Electronic Networks"

Optical communications is of course very common but it is usually used to form link connections within an electronic network. This chapter describes how optical link connections are used within modern (electronic) communications systems.

Chapter 9, "Wavelength Division Multiplexing"

Wavelength Division Multiplexing is the first step towards full optical networking. WDM involves putting many optical signals onto the same piece of fibre. This chapter describes the challenges in designing an optical WDM system and ways in which these challenges may be met. It also covers optical devices specifically made for WDM applications and systems engineering issues unique to WDM.

Chapter 10, "Lightwave Networks"

This chapter describes various operational optical networking systems from LAN application to the wide area.

Chapter 11, "Fibre In The (Local) Loop - FITL"

Perhaps the biggest potential application of optical networking is for the "last mile" connection between the telephone exchange (central office) and everyone's home. There are many approaches to this and an outline of the application is given here.

Chapter 12, "Research Directions"

Researchers are of course 5-10 years ahead of commercial reality. This chapter describes some interesting areas currently being researched.

Appendices

Appendix A, "An Introduction to Semiconductors"

This chapter offers some background material on the principles behind the operation of semiconductor devices. This is necessary background for the understanding of Lasers, LEDs and detectors.

Appendix B, "An Introduction to Communications Networks"

This chapter describes some basic theory of communications networks - in particular the layering principle as it applies to network structures.

Appendix C, "Laser Safety"

This appendix should be read by everyone.

Appendix D, "Acronyms"

Here is a listing of all the acronyms used within the book.

Appendix E, "Some Useful Facts"

This chapter presents some useful facts and figures.

IBM Redbooks on the World Wide Web

This book is one of a series of "Redbooks" produced by the IBM International Technical Support Organisation. Internet users may find further information about redbooks on the ITSO Web home page. To access the ITSO Web pages, point your Web brouser to the following URL:

```
http://www.redbooks.ibm.com
```

Comments on this book may be sent to:

```
redbooks@us.ibm.com
```

Part 1. Theory and Devices

Chapter 1. Introduction

The use of light to send messages is not new. Fires were used for signaling in biblical times, smoke signals have been used for thousands of years and flashing lights have been used to communicate between warships at sea since the days of Lord Nelson.

The idea of using glass fibre to carry an optical communications signal originated with Alexander Graham Bell. However this idea had to wait some 80 years for better glasses and low-cost electronics for it to become useful in practical situations.

Development of fibres and devices for optical communications began in the early 1960s and continues strongly today. But the real change came in the 1980s. During this decade optical communication in public communication networks developed from the status of a curiosity into being the dominant technology.

Among the tens of thousands of developments and inventions that have contributed to this progress four stand out as milestones:

1. The invention of the LASER (in the late 1950's)

2. The development of low loss optical fibre (1970's)

3. The invention of the optical fibre amplifier (1980's)

4. The invention of the in-fibre Bragg grating (1990's)

The continuing development of semiconductor technology is quite fundamental but of course not specifically optical.

The predominant use of optical technology is as very fast "electric wire". Optical fibres replace electric wire in communications systems and nothing much else changes. Perhaps this is not quite fair. The very speed and quality of optical communications systems has itself predicated the development of a new type of electronic communications itself designed to be run on optical connections. ATM and SDH technologies are good examples of the new type of systems.

It is important to realise that optical communications is *not* like electronic communications. While it seems that light travels in a fibre much like electricity does in a wire this is very misleading. Light is an electromagnetic wave and optical fibre is a waveguide. Everything to do with transport of the signal even to simple things like coupling (joining) two fibres into one is very different from what happens in the electronic world. The two fields (electronics and optics) while closely related employ different principles in different ways.

Some people look ahead to "true" optical networks. These will be networks where routing is done optically from one end-user to another without the signal ever becoming electronic. Indeed some experimental local area (LAN) and metropolitan area (MAN) networks like this have been built. In 1998 optically routed nodal wide area networks are imminently feasible and the necessary components to build them are available. However, no such networks have been deployed operationally yet.

In 1998 the "happening" area in optical communications is Wavelength Division Multiplexing (WDM). This is the ability to send many (perhaps up to 1000) independent optical channels on a single fibre. The first fully commercial WDM products appeared on the market in 1996. WDM is a major step toward fully optical networking.

1.1.1 Optical Transmission System Concepts

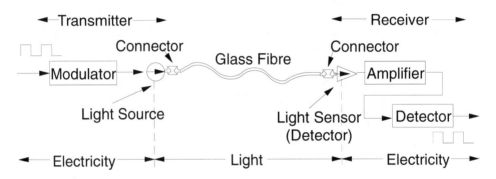

Figure 1. Optical Transmission - Schematic

The basic components of an optical communication system are shown in Figure 1, above.

- A serial bit stream in electrical form is presented to a modulator, which encodes the data appropriately for fibre transmission.

- A light source (laser or Light Emitting Diode - LED) is driven by the modulator and the light focused into the fibre.

- The light travels down the fibre (during which time it may experience dispersion and loss of strength).

- At the receiver end the light is fed to a detector and converted to electrical form.

- The signal is then amplified and fed to another detector, which isolates the individual state changes and their timing. It then decodes the sequence of state changes and reconstructs the original bit stream.[1]

- The timed bit stream so received may then be fed to a using device.

Optical communication has many well-known advantages:

Weight and Size

> Fibre cable is significantly smaller and lighter than electrical cables to do the same job. In the wide area environment a large coaxial cable system can easily involve a cable of several inches in diameter and weighing many pounds per foot. A fibre cable to do the same job could be less than one half an inch in diameter and weigh a few ounces per foot.

> This means that the cost of laying the cable is dramatically reduced.

Material Cost

> Fibre cable costs significantly less than copper cable for the same transmission capacity.

Information Capacity

> The data rate of systems in use in 1998 is generally 150 or 620 Mbps on a single (unidirectional) fibre. This is because these systems were installed in past years. The usual rate for new systems is 2.4 Gbps or even 10 Gbps. This is very high in digital transmission terms.

> In telephone transmission terms the very best coaxial cable systems give about 2,000 analog voice circuits. A 150 Mbps fibre connection gives just over 2,000 digital telephone (64 Kbps) connections. But the 150 Mbps fibre is at a very early stage in the development of fibre optical systems. The coaxial cable system with which it is being compared is much more costly and has been developed to its fullest extent.

> Fibre technology is still in its infancy. Using just a single channel per fibre, researchers have trial systems in operation that communicate at speeds of 100 Gbps. By sending many ("wavelength division multiplexed") channels on a single fibre, we can increase this capacity a hundred and perhaps a thousand times. Recently researchers at NEC reported a successful experiment where 132 optical channels of 20 Gbps each were carried over 120 km. This is 2.64

---

[1] This overview is deliberately simplified. There are many ways to modulate the transmission and the details will vary from this example but the general principle remains unchanged.

terabits per second! This is enough capacity to carry about 30 million *uncompressed* telephone calls (at 64 Kbps per channel). Thirty million calls is about the maximum number of calls in progress in the world at any particular moment in time. That is to say, we could carry the world's peak telephone traffic over one pair of fibres. Most practical fibre systems don't attempt to do this because it costs less to put multiple fibres in a cable than to use sophisticated multiplexing technology.

No Electrical Connection

This is an obvious point but nevertheless a very important one. Electrical connections have problems.

- In electrical systems there is always the possibility of "ground loops" causing a serious problem, especially in the LAN or computer channel environment. When you communicate electrically you often have to connect the grounds to one another or at least go to a lot of trouble to avoid making this connection. One little known problem is that there is often a voltage potential difference between "ground" at different locations. The author has observed as much as 3 volts difference in ground potential between adjacent buildings (this was a freak situation). It is normal to observe 1 or 2 volt differences over distances of a kilometer or so. With shielded cable there can be a problem if you earth the shields at both ends of the connection.

- Optical connection is very safe. Electrical connections always have to be protected from high voltages because of the danger to people touching the wire.

- In some tropical regions of the world, lightning poses a severe hazard even to buried telephone cables! Of course, optical fibre isn't subject to lightning problems but it must be remembered that sometimes optical cables carry wires within them for strengthening or to power repeaters. These wires can be a target for lightning.

No Electromagnetic Interference

Because the connection is not electrical, you can neither pick up nor create electrical interference (the major source of noise). This is one reason that optical communication has so few errors. There are very few sources of things that can distort or interfere with the signal.

In a building this means that fibre cables can be placed almost anywhere electrical cables would have problems, (for example near a lift motor or in a cable duct with heavy power cables). In an industrial plant such as a steel mill, this gives much greater flexibility in cabling than previously available.

In the wide area networking environment there is much greater flexibility in route selection. Cables may be located near water or power lines without risk to people or equipment.

Distances between Regenerators

As a signal travels along a communication line it loses strength (is attenuated) and picks up noise. The traditional way to regenerate the signal, restoring its power and removing the noise, is to use a either a repeater or an amplifier. These are discussed later in 5.10, "Repeaters" on page 328.[2] (Indeed it is the use of repeaters to remove noise that gives digital transmission its high quality.)

In long-line optical transmission cables now in use by the telephone companies, the repeater spacing is typically 40 kilometres. This compares with 12 km for the previous coaxial cable electrical technology. The number of required repeaters and their spacing is a major factor in system cost.

Some recently installed systems (1997) have spacings of up to 120 kilometres.[3]

Open Ended Capacity

The maximum theoretical capacity of installed fibre is very great (almost infinite). This means that additional capacity can be had on existing fibres as new technology becomes available. All that must be done is change the equipment at either end and change or upgrade the regenerators.

Better Security

It is possible to tap fibre optical cable. But it is very difficult to do and the additional loss caused by the tap is relatively easy to detect. There is an interruption to service while the tap is inserted and this can alert operational staff to the situation. In addition, there are fewer access points where an intruder can gain the kind of access to a fibre cable necessary to insert a tap.

Insertion of active taps where the intruder actually inserts a signal is even more difficult.

However, there are some limitations:

---

2 Repeaters have been in use for many years in digital electronic connections.

3 As will be seen later, optical amplifiers are replacing repeaters as the technology of choice in long-line communications.

Joining Cables

The best way of joining cables is to use "fusion splicing". This is where fibre ends are fused to one another by melting the glass. Making such splices in a way that will ensure minimal loss of signal is a skilled task that requires precision equipment. It is particularly difficult to do outdoors in very low temperatures, such as in the North American or European winter.

In the early days of fibre optical systems (the early 1980s) connectors which allowed cables to be plugged and unplugged were unreliable and caused a large amount of signal loss (as much as 3 dB per connector). Of course, the larger the core diameter of the fibre, the easier it is to make a low-loss connector. In the last few years connector systems for fibres with thicker cores (multimode fibres) have improved to the point where the use of a large number of connectors in a LAN system can be very reliable. Typical connector loss for an "SC" coupler (a popular modern type) using 62.5 micron fibre is around .3 dB. It is not this good with single-mode fibres of small core diameter.

One of the major system costs is the cost of coupling a fibre to an integrated light source (laser or LED) or detector on a chip. This is done during manufacture and is called "pigtailing". Although the cost of optical transceivers has decreased rapidly in the last few years, these are still twice the cost (or more) of the same transceivers using electrical connection. For example the current market price of FDDI adapters operating over a copper medium is around half that of the same adapter using fibre. The cost difference is in the optical transceivers and the pigtailing.

Bending Cables

As light travels along the fibre, it is reflected from the interface between the core and cladding whenever it strays from the path straight down the center. When the fibre is bent, the light only stays in the fibre because of this reflection. But the reflection only works if the angle of incidence is relatively low. If you bend the fibre too much the light escapes.

The amount of allowable bending is specific to particular cables because it depends on the difference in refractive index, between core and cladding. The bigger the difference in refractive index, the tighter the allowable bend radius. There is a tradeoff here because there are many other reasons that we would like to keep this difference as small as possible.

Slow Standards Development

This is nobody's fault. Development is happening so quickly, and getting worldwide agreement to a standard is necessarily so slow that standards setting just can't keep up. Things are improving considerably and very quickly, however. Cable sizes and types are converging toward a few choices, although the way they are used is still changing almost daily.

There are now firm standards for optical link connections in LAN protocols (token-ring, Ethernet and FDDI), SDH (for the wide area) and in ATM for both the LAN and the wide area.

Optics for Transmission Only

Until very recently there was no available optical amplifier. The signal had to be converted to electrical form and put through a complex repeater in order to boost its strength. Recently, optical amplifiers have emerged and look set to solve this problem (see 5.2, "Optical Amplifiers" on page 198).

However, optical logic processing and/or switching systems seem to be a few years off yet.

Gamma Radiation

Gamma radiation comes from space and is always present. It can be thought of as a high-energy X-ray. Gamma radiation can cause some types of glass to emit light (causing interference) and also gamma radiation can cause glass to discolor and hence attenuate the signal. In normal situations these effects are minimal. However, fibres are probably not the transmission medium of choice inside a nuclear reactor or on a long-distance space probe. (A glass beaker placed inside a nuclear reactor for even a few hours comes out black in color and quite opaque.)

Electrical Fields

Very high-voltage electrical fields also affect some glasses in the same way as gamma rays. One proposed route for fibre communication cables is wrapped around high-voltage electrical cables on transmission towers. This actually works quite well where the electrical cables are only of 30 000 volts or below. Above that (most major transmission systems are many times above that), the glass tends to emit light and discolor. Nevertheless, this is a field of current research - to produce a glass that will be unaffected by such fields. It is a reasonable expectation that this will be achieved within a very few years.

Some electricity companies are carrying fibres with their high voltage distribution systems by placing the fibre *inside* the earth wire (typically a 1 inch thick aluminium cable with steel casing). This works well, but long-distance high-voltage distribution systems usually don't have earth wires.

Sharks Eat the Cable(?)

In the 1980s there was an incident where a new undersea fibre cable was broken on the ocean floor. Publicity surrounding the event suggested that the cable was attacked and eaten by sharks. It wasn't just the press; this was a serious claim. It was claimed that there was something in the chemical composition of the cable sheathing that was attractive to sharks! Another explanation was that the cable contained an unbalanced electrical supply conductor. It was theorised that the radiated electromagnetic field caused the sharks to be attracted.

Other people have dismissed this claim as a joke and suggest that the cable was badly laid and rubbed against rocks. Nevertheless, the story has passed into the folklore of fibre optical communication and some people genuinely believe that sharks eat optical fibre cable.

Gophers (and Termites) Really Do Eat the Cable

Gophers are a real problem for fibre cables in the United States. There is actually a standardised test (conducted by a nature and wildlife organisation) which involves placing a cable in a gopher enclosure for a fixed, specified length of time. In other countries termites have been known to attack and eat the plastic sheathing.

Most people evaluate the advantages as overwhelming the disadvantages for most environments. But advantages and disadvantages need to be considered in the context of the environment in which the system is to be used. The types of fibre systems appropriate for the LAN environment are quite different from those that are optimal in the wide area world.

1.1.2 Optical Networking

A network may be defined as a collection of transmission links and other equipment which provides a means of information interchange within a group of end users. The concept includes a number of key notions:

1. The objective of the network is to provide a means of information interchange between end users.

2. The network usually contains some shared resources. That is, links and switching nodes are shared between many users.

3. Most networks have a common (often centralised) network management system.

4. Information may be exchanged between any user and any other user. This concept while common in communication networks is far from being universal. Many networks exist for the purpose of connecting a few thousand devices to only

one (or a few) central device(s). For example in a network of cash dispensers there is no communication (and no conceivable need for communication) *between* the cash dispensers - all communication is to/from a central computer.

5. A single user may communicate with multiple other users either simultaneously or serially (one after another) using only a single connection to the network. Again, this is a very common characteristic of networks but it is by no means universal. Some networks provide fixed connections between pre-determined end users with no possibility for quick changes. The characteristic here that qualifies such a system to be called a network would be the sharing of intermediate switching nodes and/or transmission links within the network.

6. The term "network" also usually implies a geographic separation between end users. This is not always true in the sense that communicating end users may be across the room or across the world.

There are many types of networks.

• Perhaps the simplest kind provides a fixed communication path (or rather, a collection of fixed paths) between end users.

• A slightly more complex type is where there is only one connection allowed per user but users may make arbitrary connections at will with other end users. The telephone network is a good example here.

• More complex are so-called "packet switching" networks where information is carried between end users in the form of packets (a.k.a. frames or cells). In these networks a single end user is usually capable of communicating with a large number of other end users at the same time.

• Packet switched networks themselves come in many types. In a "connection-oriented" network paths through the network are defined before information is transferred. Information is always transferred along the predefined path. In a "connectionless" network frames of data are routed through the network based on a destination address carried within the data itself. In this case there is no necessary correlation between the path through the network taken by one particular frame of information and the next frame of data sent by the same user to the same destination.

• Another major distinction between networks comes from the method by which switching is performed.

   – Most networks (especially wide area ones) contain nodal points where information is switched from link to link. The nodes typically consist of a computer-like device.

– Other networks switch information by placing frames onto a shared medium (such as a bus) to which many end users are connected. Each end user filters the information and pays attention to only information addressed to it. This type is typical of Local Area Networks (LANs).

Networks may be further characterised by their geographic extent such as:

- Local Area Network (LAN)
- Metropolitan Area Network (MAN)
- Wide Area Network (WAN)

These names don't only delimit or suggest geographic extent but also denote quite different types of networks which have evolved to meet the requirements of the different environments.

Optical networking is just beginning! In some areas (such as the LAN) quite large experimental (but nevertheless operational) networks have been built. In other areas (such as packet networks) researchers are still wrestling with the problems of applying the concepts in an optical world.

The simplest type of network is where a single link is shared by many different communications between different end users. This is achieved in commercial operation today in Wavelength Division Multiplexing (WDM) systems. A simple extension of WDM allows for long links where channels are tapped off to service individual end users along the way. Networks using this principle (add/drop multiplexing) are possible today and a number of very large networks are planned.

Wide area switched networks (similar to the telephone network) could be built today as all of the required components are available. It is expected that networks of this kind will develop and become common within the next few years. Optical packet switching is a long long way from reality and indeed may not ever be achievable.

However, to realise the benefits of optical technology it will be necessary to build fully optical networks. It is self-defeating to convert the signal from optical to electronic form every time it needs to be routed or switched. It seems likely that fully optical networks will *not* be just optical copies of concepts well explored in the electronic networking world. Over time we can expect new types of networks to evolve which may have some similarities with electronic networks but which will make use of the properties and characteristics of unique optical components.

1.1.3 Optical Interconnects

Over the past ten years optical fibre has been used occasionally to make connections between parts of electronic communication switches and/or computers. Today, the limits of electronic communications are being approached and fibre is being considered as a major means of connection between shelves and frames in major electronic devices.

1.1.4 Optical Computers

There is very strong current research activity in the area of providing "optical computers", that is, computers where the logic is completely optical and the signal is carried optically rather than electrically. Much progress is being made, but it is generally believed that the fruit of this research is many years off yet.

1.1.5 Further Reading

This book is *not* intended as a text on optical communication. It is a very high level tutorial from the perspective of an individual engineer who works in the field.

The author hopes that some readers will come to share the excitement and fascination that the field offers. A large part of this is due to the fact that fibre optics lives at the crossroads of a number of scientific and engineering disciplines. Physics, chemistry, electronics, traditional optics, engineering and mathematics all have a role to play.

The following references are the ones the author has used extensively over the last few years. All of them are good.

In trying to understand the field you will find that the texts often come from different perspectives and have widely different emphases. This is good. But it is extremely important to understand that the field while new is also quite old... Optical fibre research dates back to the 1950's and the first operational systems started in the 1970's. The industry has gone through a number of "generations" of technology already. The most important thing about any book is its *date*. Over the years aspects of technology that once looked important and promising failed to mature or gain acceptance and later became just curiosities.

A good example here is coherent optical transmission systems. In the late 1980's this was a major research focus and looked to many to be the path for future long distance high-speed systems. However, coherent detection has proven to be very difficult indeed. In addition, the advent of the Erbium Doped Fibre Amplifier has delivered most of the performance enhancement that coherent systems might have provided. Despite the fact that many books (including this one) contain much material on coherent systems there is almost no current research in the area and there are no operational systems.

The message is that you will see lots of different devices and techniques described in the literature. Not all of these can be considered in any way current or potential for the future. The only way to make the distinction is to develop an insight into the on-going development of the field. This must *not* be interpreted to mean that all books older than a few years are no longer relevant. To the contrary, the scientific principles involved do not change and this aspect of every book retains its relevance. In addition, there are some books that are considered classics in the field which should be read by every serious student (good examples here are the books by Agrawal (1989) and by Snyder and Love (1983)). Nevertheless, be aware of the date on that book!

1.1.5.1 Texts
Govind P. Agrawal (1989)

> *Nonlinear Fibre Optics*: Academic Press, New York.

Govind P. Agrawal (1995)

> *Nonlinear Fibre Optics - Second Edition*: Academic Press, New York.

Frederick C. Allard (1989)

> *Fibre Optics Handbook for Engineers and Scientists*: McGraw-Hill, New York.

Christopher C. Davis (1996)

> *Lasers and Electro-Optics, Fundamentals and Engineering*: Cambridge University Press, New York, Melbourne.

Casimer DeCusatis, Eric Maass, Darrin P. Clement and Ronald C. Lasky (1998)

> *Handbook of Fibre Optic Data Communication*: Academic Press, London.

Richard P. Feynman (1985)

> *QED - The Strange Theory of Light and Matter*: Penguin Books, London.

Grant R. Fowles (1975)

> *Introduction to Modern Optics*: Dover Publications, Inc., New York.

John Gower (1984)

> *Optical Communication Systems*: Prentice Hall, Englewood Cliffs, New Jersey 07632.

Paul E. Green (1993)

Fibre Optic Networks: Prentice Hall, Englewood Cliffs, New Jersey 07632.

Christian Hentschel (1989)

Fibre Optics Handbook: Hewlett-Packard Gmbh, Boeblingen Instruments Division, Federal Republic of Germany.

Robert J. Hoss (1990)

Fibre Optic Communications Design Handbook: Prentice Hall, Englewood Cliffs, New Jersey 07632.

Gerd Keiser (1991)

Optical Fibre Communications - Second Edition: McGraw-Hill, Inc., New York.

Francois Ladouceur and John D. Love (1996)

Silica-based Buried Channel Waveguides and Devices: Chapman and Hall, London.

Jean-Pierre Laude (1993)

Wavelength Division Multiplexing: Prentice Hall, Englewood Cliffs, New Jersey 07632.

S. G. Lipson, H. Lipson and D. S. Tannhauser (1995)

Optical Physics: Cambridge University Press, New York, Melbourne.

Jacob Millman and Arvin Grabel (1987)

Microelectronics: McGraw-Hill, New York.

B.E.A. Saleh and M.C. Teich (1991)

Fundamentals of Photonics: John Wiley and Sons, Inc., New York.

John M Senior (1992)

Optical Fibre Communications: Principles and Practice, Second Edition: Prentice Hall, Englewood Cliffs, New Jersey 07632.

A. W. Snyder and J. D. Love (1983)

Optical Waveguide Theory: Chapman and Hall, London.

J. Wilson and J. F. B. Hawkes (1989)

Optoelectronics, An Introduction - Second Edition: Prentice Hall, Englewood Cliffs, New Jersey 07632.

1.1.5.2 Educational Web Sites of Interest

There are probably thousands of sites on the Internet that contain useful information. Unfortunately, the addresses change so quickly that publishing them in a book is of doubtful value. However there are two extremely interesting educational sites:

The Light Guide

> This site can be found at:
>
> `www.vislab.usyd.edu.au/photonics`
>
> This is an online tutorial introduction to optical fibre communications. This was developed by the Australian Photonic CRC, (a cooperative including several leading Australian Universities), to introduce senior level high school students to optical communication. It is strongly recommended to anyone wishing to get an introduction to the field.

The Gateway Coalition - Solid State Materials Project

> The address of this site is:
>
> `http://www.cooper.edu/engineering/projects/gateway/ee/solidmat/...`
> `solidmat.html`
>
> This site contains some lecture notes for a university course on solid state materials. Module 4 is titled "Optical Fibres Lecture Notes" and Module 5 is "Manufacture and Physical Properties of Optical Fibres".

Fiber Optic Sensor Technology Handbook

> This is quite a good book with a section on the basics of optical fibre communication as well as its main topic of sensor technology. It is available for download at the following address:
>
> `http://fiberoptic.com/handbook2.html`

1.1.5.3 Industry Magazines

There are a number of industry magazines that are available "free" to people involved in the industry. These magazines often include interesting technical articles but are mainly useful for their advertising. Reading the advertisements can give you an understanding of what products are available and (sometimes) an idea of their costs. Following are details of three of these including their web site addresses.

LaserFocus World is published by PennWell Publishing Co., Tulsa, OK. Their web site is:

> http://www.lfw.com/

Photonics Spectra Magazine is publshed by Laurin Publishing Company, Pittsfield, MA.

http://www.laurin.com/

Fiberoptic Product News is published by Gordon Publications of Morris Plains, NJ. Their web site is:

http:/www.fpnmag.com/

1.1.5.4 Professional Societies

The professional societies make a major and critical contribution to the ongoing development of the field. They are also perhaps the primary source of leading-edge technical information. Their main activities are publishing serious technical journals and organising conferences. In addition, the IEEE is a major standards-making body.

People seriously interested in following any technical career in communications should consider joining one of these societies.

Details of professional society activities may be obtained from their web sites:

The Institute of Electrical and Electronics Engineers (IEEE)

http://www.ieee.org/

Optical Society of America

http://www.osa.org/

The International Society of Photooptical Instrumentation Engineers (SPIE)

- http://www.spie.org/
- http://www.optics.org/

1.1.5.5 WWW Directory

The IEEE Lasers and Electrooptics Society keeps a web page entitled "Sites of Professional Interest along the Information Superhighway". This excellent site is a directory to many sites of interest in the optical communications world. Its url is:

http://engine.ieee.org/society/leos/LEOSweb.html

Chapter 2. Optical Fibre

2.1 The Nature of Light

We all know a lot about light - it is the basis of our most important sensory function. But the question of what light "really is" can be elusive. Light is usually described in one of three ways:

Rays

> In the classical physics that many of us learned at school, light consisted of "rays" that could be reflected and refracted through mirrors and prisms etc. This is a good description as far as it goes but it cannot explain many of the phenomena we make use of in optical communications.

> The problem is that when you try to study "rays" very closely they start behaving like waves. For example, if you pass a beam of light through a small hole or slit about the same diameter as the wavelength the "ray" spreads out at the edges (it diffracts). Also, if you let multiple rays of coherent light (light that is in phase with itself) mix together on a projection screen you get interference effects between the two rays (this forms a pattern of light and dark rings on the screen). Neither of these phenomena (diffraction or interference) are consistent with a ray description.

> In this book we will use the ray model for a number of purposes and in particular to discuss light propagation in multimode fibres. This is the most understandable way. In general the ray model is fine when the distances involved in the device are many times larger than the wavelength.

Electromagnetic Waves

> In the context of optical communications, most of the time it will be found that the best way of regarding light is to think of it as an electromagnetic wave. In this view it is no different from a radio wave except that the wavelength is much shorter!

> In this book we will use this model for most discussions. It is the *only* satisfactory way of conceiving of light propagation in a single-mode fibre, the operation of a Bragg grating or the operation of optical couplers and splitters.

Photons

> In many contexts light behaves as though it consists of tiny particles called "photons".

There are a number of phenomena that the wave model of light can't explain. The best known of these is the "photoelectric effect".

When light falls on a metal plate electrons are dislodged and can be collected on another metal plate nearby. Thus we can generate a current between the two plates. This current can be shown to be proportional to the amount of light that falls on the plate. But if you measure the energy of the electrons dislodged you find a disturbing thing. The electrons dislodged by incident light have a range of energies but these energies are exactly the same regardless of the intensity of the light! The range of energies varies with the wavelength of the incident light but it doesn't change with intensity! If light was made up of waves consisting of an infinitely variable amount of energy this should not be so. The explanation (due to Einstein) is that light consists of tiny particles ("corpuscles" or photons). A single photon dislodges a single electron and gives up all of its energy to the electron in so doing. Greater intensity just means more photons but the energy of each is exactly the same.

This is a useful perspective and is used in many contexts but it too cannot explain many of the observed phenomena.

In our discussion of lasers and LEDs (in Chapter 3, "Optical Sources" on page 99) we will use the concept of light as particles extensively.

It is a fair generalisation to say that light may be looked on as a wave in situations where we are studying transmission or propagation. It may often be regarded as a particle when we are studying its interactions with matter and/or when it is in a confined space (where one dimension of the space is smaller than about 4 times the wavelength).

In the past the question of just what light "really is" has aroused significant controversy among physicists. In 1905 the eminent physicist Max Planck nominated Einstein for membership in the Royal Prussian Academy of Sciences. One section of the nomination letter is as follows: *"that he may sometimes have missed the target in his speculations, as for example in his theory of light quanta, cannot really be held against him."* They didn't hold it against him. In 1921 Einstein was awarded the Nobel Prize for his theory of light quanta (among other things)!

The fact is that rays, photons and waves are all useful analogies that help us to understand what light really is from different viewpoints. Of course, light is all of the above and none of them. The problem is not the enigmatic nature of light but our lack of a more adequate analogy to aid understanding.

This is a little like the famous three blind people examining an elephant. One finds a tree trunk, another a snake the third a rope. It all depends on your point of view.

2.1.1 Light as an Electromagnetic Wave

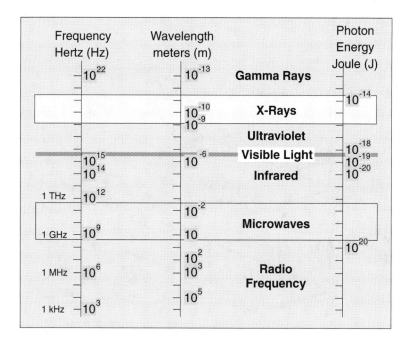

Figure 2. The Electromagnetic Spectrum

There are many excellent textbooks (in Physics, Electronics and Fibre Optics) which deal in depth with the electromagnetic wave nature of light.[4] Indeed, over the years many trees have been assassinated providing paper for the printing of Maxwell's equations. However, some readers may not wish to inquire into this fascinating subject in depth so a very short conceptual introduction is provided here.

One way of thinking about light is to conceive of it as an electromagnetic wave just like a radio wave. Indeed, the word "like" here is a problem. Light and radio waves are not really "like" one another. They are exactly the same thing! The only difference is the wavelength.

An electromagnetic wave consists of two fields. An electric field and a magnetic field. Both of these fields have a direction and a strength (or amplitude). Within the electromagnetic wave the two fields (electric and magnetic) are oriented at precisely

---

[4] A list of some relevant books may be found in the bibliography at the end of Chapter 1.

90° to one another. The fields move (by definition at the speed of light) in a direction at 90° to both of them! In three dimensions you could consider the electric field to be oriented on the y-axis, and the magnetic field on the x-axis. Direction of travel would then be along the z-direction.

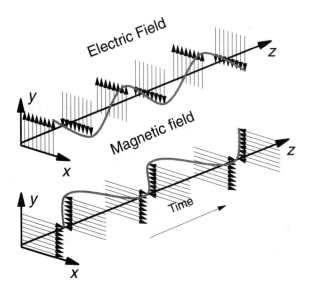

Figure 3. The Structure of an Electromagnetic Wave. Electric and magnetic fields are actually superimposed over the top of one another but are illustrated separately for clarity in illustration. The z-direction can be considered to be either a representation in space or the passing of time at a single point.

It is useful to compare this with wave motion in water which we can see easily. If we look at a twig floating on a pool of water where there are waves we notice that the twig moves up and down in one place. The waves move across the water but the water particles themselves move vertically and have no "forward" motion. Thus wave motion is at 90° (transverse) to the direction of wave travel. This is exactly what is happening with electromagnetic waves. This contrasts with sound waves where the oscillation is in the same direction as wave travel.

As the electromagnetic wave moves the fields oscillate in direction and in strength. Figure 3 shows the electric and magnetic fields separately but they occupy the same space. They should be overlayed on one another and are only drawn this way for clarity. We could consider the z-direction in the figure to represent passing time *or* it could represent a wave travelling in space at a single instant in time.

Looking at the electric field and assuming we are watching time passing, we see that at the start the field is oriented from bottom to top (increasing values of y). Some time later the field direction has reversed. At a still later time the field direction has reversed again and it has now reverted back to its original direction.

The curved line is intended to represent field strength. The field might start at a maximum in one direction, decay to a zero and then build up in the other direction until it reaches a maximum in that other direction. The field strength changes sinusoidally.

The key here is that we have two fields and they oscillate *in phase*. That is the electric and magnetic fields reach their peaks and their nulls at exactly the same time (and place).[5] The rate of oscillation is the frequency of the wave. The distance travelled during one period of oscillation is the wavelength.

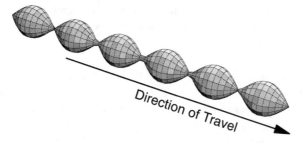

Figure 4. *Amplitude Fluctuation in an Electromagnetic Wave. Here both the electric field and the magnetic field are shown as a single field oscillating about a locus of points which forms the line of travel.*

So we might visualise a "particle" or ray of light travelling through space as two interlocking force fields (electric and magnetic). These fields centre on a point (over time this is of course a line in the direction of propagation) and decay exponentially as we move away from that point (or line).[6]

---

[5] Strictly this is only true for light that is "linearly" polarised.

[6] This description pre-supposes certain boundary conditions on the transmission. It is however appropriate to light travelling (in a bound mode) within an optical fibre.

2.1.2 Polarisation

It is clear from Figure 3 on page 22 that there are two possible ways to orient these fields. In the figure we show the electric field in the vertical plane and the magnetic field in the horizontal plane. We could have drawn the magnetic field in the vertical plane and the electric field in the horizontal. Equally clearly, the axes are perfectly arbitrary and we could draw the fields with any orientation we like between the two. It's just a question of how you choose your axes.

However, if we have an electromagnetic field with the electric field in the vertical position (in relation to some arbitrary axis) then we could have another electromagnetic field with the electric field in the horizontal orientation (in relation to *the same* axes). *When this happens the two electromagnetic waves are orthogonal to one another!* That is, they are independent and do not interfere with each other.

It is also clear that any electromagnetic wave that is oriented between what we have called "vertical" and "horizontal" can be resolved as two components (one in each of the orthogonal directions).

The orientation of the electromagnetic field is referred to as "polarisation". The established convention when discussing polarisation of electromagnetic fields is to refer to the direction of the electric field with respect to some plane or boundary towards which the wave is headed. At any instant in time the fields are oriented in a particular direction (vertical or horizontal or somewhere in between).

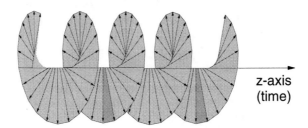

Figure 5. Circular Polarisation. The direction of the electric field vector is represented by the arrows. As time passes (along the z-axis) the electric field rotates by 360 degrees in each wavelength period. Four cycles are illustrated.

However, the field orientations can also change over time and we get what are called "circular" and "elliptical" polarisations. These polarisations occur when the moving fields rotate during their travel. Circular polarisation results when the direction of the electric field rotates through 360° during one wavelength. Of course the associated magnetic field rotates with it. This is illustrated in Figure 5. Elliptical polarisation results when the period of rotation of the fields is not the same as the wavelength.

Actually, circular and elliptical polarisations result when the propagation speed of the two orthogonal polarisations are slightly different (usually caused by the material having a slightly different refractive index in each polarisation). See 2.4.2.1, "Polarisation Mode Dispersion (PMD)" on page 77.

2.1.3 Interference

The phenomenon of interference is one of the most interesting and important aspects of optical engineering. Indeed, interference is *basic* to almost everything we do in fibre optic communications. However, while it can be described very well mathematically a good intuitive description of what it is still eludes us.

2.1.3.1 Young's Experiment

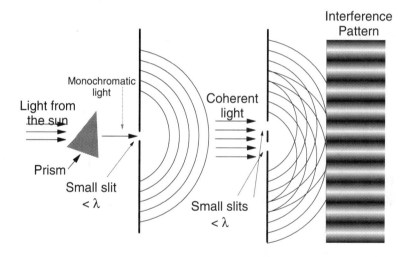

Figure 6. *Young's Experiment*

Historically the most important experiment on optical interference was performed by Thomas Young in 1802.

The set up he used is shown in Figure 6. Sunlight is first passed through a prism to produce light of a single wavelength (monochromatic light). Then it is passed through a narrow slit or pinhole. The resulting "ray" or "beam" illuminates a pair of parallel, narrow slits. After passing through the slits the light is projected onto a screen. The result is the famous pattern of light and dark "interference fringes".

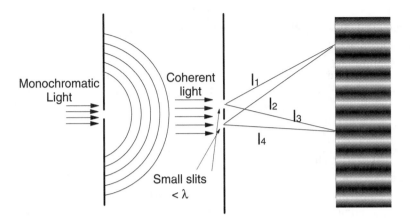

Figure 7. Interference Effects

A number of observations may be made here:

- You don't really need the prism when dealing with sunlight but it heightens the effect significantly. Without a prism you get blurry regions of light and dark as the location of the lines depends on the wavelength.

- By passing the light through the first slit or pinhole we are ensuring that the beam that illuminates the pair of slits is coherent. Coherent light is light in the form of a continuous wave which is in phase with itself over some long period. With the double slit setup you get many parallel waves out of phase with each other but coherent within themselves. Today, you could eliminate the first slit and use a laser for illumination but in 1802 it was to be 160 years before the laser was invented.

- The pattern of light and dark lines is caused by the difference in distance travelled to the screen by light from the two slits. Since the light illuminating both slits is coherent (that is, it is in phase) the waves reinforce one another on the screen when their electric field vectors are in phase. They cancel one another when the vectors are out-of-phase. This is illustrated in Figure 7. Thus when the difference in distance travelled is an exact multiple of the wavelength (l_1 and l_2 in the diagram) we get reinforcement and a bright band. When the difference in path length is an odd number of half-wavelengths (l_3 and l_4 in the diagram) we get destructive interference and a dark band.

- It is important to note here that what has happened is that power has been transferred from the dark bands to the bright ones. The total optical power projected on the screen is the same. No power has been lost. Energy is conserved.

The above described behaviour is very convincing evidence for the wave nature of light. But if we repeat the experiment using extremely low light levels something interesting happens.

- First, we replace the screen with a series of very sensitive electronic optical detectors.[7]

- Next we illuminate the dual slits with a laser through a filter that attenuates the light to such a low level that only individual photons get through.

  As mentioned before, when we get to very low light levels detectors always measure light in quanta (or "clicks" on the detector). When the light intensity is increased you get more clicks - NOT louder ones. This shows that the light is behaving as particles (as photons).

- An interesting effect is observed. Depending on the location of the detector the *number of photons registered (clicks)* is proportional to the light intensity observed at that same place when we illuminate the slits with a bright light. In other words we don't get softer clicks, we get a number exactly (statistically) proportional to the light intensity expected at that point on the screen!

- If you put a detector at one of the slits to detect passing photons the effect disappears!

- If you cover one slit, the effect disappears and you get photons hitting the screen uniformly as we might expect from a uniform source.

- This is very hard to explain! If light travels as "photons" then a photon must go through one slit or the other. If we use a light level sufficiently low so that photons are spaced a long time apart (say a second) there can be no question of wavelike interference. But the interference effect still occurs! Clearly the photon passes through *both* slits!

2.1.3.2 Transmission through a Sheet of Glass

The effects of interference can best be illustrated by observing what happens when a beam of light shines on an interface between glass and air. This is shown in Figure 8 on page 28.

When the incident light is normal (or perpendicular) to such an interface close to 4% of it is reflected. (The reflected percentage is higher if the light is incident at a more oblique angle.) In practice any abrupt interface between two materials of different

---

7 Photomultiplier tubes.

refractive index[8] will cause a reflection. The amount of that reflection depends on the difference in refractive index of the two materials. As shown in the diagram we get the same 4% regardless of whether the light is coming from the air side or from the glass side.

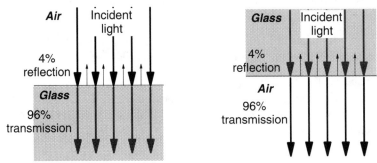

Figure 8. Reflection of Light from a Glass/Air Interface

The interesting part is what happens when a beam of monochromatic light shines at a normal to a thin sheet of glass.[9] It seems obvious that 4% will be reflected from the top junction and 4% from the bottom for a total reflection of 8%. Surprisingly this is precisely what does *not* happen.

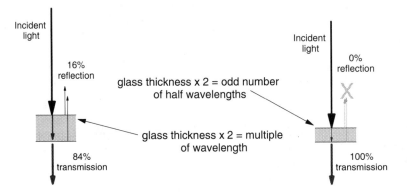

Figure 9. Interference Effects when passing Light through a Glass Sheet

---

8 The refractive index (RI) is the ratio of the speed of light in a vacuum to the speed of light in the substance in question. In this book the abbreviation RI is used in the text. In mathematical formulae the letter "n" is used to designate the RI. See E.3.1.1, "Refractive Index" on page 732.

9 To observe this effect you need to use light of only one wavelength (monochromatic light).

The effect observed depends on the thickness of the glass sheet.

- If the sheet is extremely thin then all of the light passes through without any appreciable loss.

- If the sheet is made just a little thicker then some light is reflected.

- As the sheet is made thicker and thicker the amount of light reflected increases until it reaches a maximum of 16%.

- Of course, the amount of light transmitted through the sheet is the amount of light that is *not* reflected (assuming absorption in the glass to be zero). If 6% is reflected then 94% is transmitted.

- As we continue to make the glass sheet thicker the amount of reflection *progressively reduces* until it reaches zero.

- As we make the glass thicker again it begins to reflect once more and the above process repeats. This phenomenon is illustrated in Figure 10.

This effect can be observed in soap bubbles. You see different amounts of reflectance as the size of the bubble changes (as the thickness of the bubble wall changes). When a bubble gets very thin (about to burst) it becomes completely transparent. The same effect produces the colored bands we see in light reflected off oily water. This is due to refraction by the oil occurring at different angles for different wavelengths.

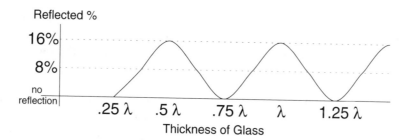

Figure 10. *Variation in Reflectance with Thickness of Glass Sheet. In this case* λ *represents the wavelength of the light being used.*

There are a number of observations we may make about this effect:

1. The maximum reflection (16%) occurs when the round trip distance in the glass (i.e. twice the thickness) is a multiple of the wavelength. The glass is one half wavelength thick. When the reflected ray from the bottom surface reaches the top surface then it is in phase with the reflection being formed on the other side of the

top surface. Thus both reflections (from the top and bottom surfaces) are in phase with one another and constructively interfere.

Both reflected rays are changed 180° in phase by the process of reflection. Because both reflected rays are shifted in phase by the same amount, the phase shift has no affect on the thickness of glass required. In this case waves reflected from the bottom surface are in phase with waves being reflected from the top surface and so reinforce (or constructively interfere with) them.

But why is this 16% of the incident beam? 4% was reflected from the top surface and 4% from the bottom surface. How does 4 + 4 equal 16? Actually, it's not that hard to understand. The percentages we have been referring to are percentages of optical power. Optical power is the square of the strength of the electric field. What we are really adding is electric fields. So on a single surface the reflection is 20% of the electric field strength. Squared this gives 4% of the optical power. If we add 20% from the front surface and 20% from the back surface and then square this (.2 + .2 = .4) we get .4 squared equals .16 or 16%.

2. The minimum reflection (0%) occurs when the round trip distance in the glass is an odd number of half wavelengths! That is, ½λ, 1½λ, 2½λ, 3½λ... This results in the "ray" reflecting from the lower surface having a round trip distance to travel in the glass which is an odd multiple of half the wavelength. When the ray arriving back from the bottom surface is out of phase with the reflected ray at the top surface destructive interference occurs and there is *no* reflection!

But something else has happened here. 100% of the incident light now passes through the glass and can be measured on the other side! So what is this *destructive interference?* No light has been reflected and so clearly no interference has taken place.

Interference doesn't destroy any energy.[10] Energy is always conserved. Indeed perhaps instead of calling it "interference" a better name might be "avoidance". Whenever there is so-called "destructive interference" the energy just appears somewhere else. Whenever there is constructive interference (or reinforcement) energy is lost from some other part of the system.

It's a bit like two people approaching a narrow doorway at the same time. Each sees the other and realises that they can't both fit through the door - so each takes a different route and *nothing* passes through the door. Exceeding strange.

---

10 At times it seems that the principle of the conservation of energy is the only thing classical physics and quantum physics agree on.

The most obvious use of this principle is in "anti-reflection coatings". If you coat the surface of a piece of glass (or the end of a fibre) with a quarter-wavelength thick coating of a material of RI intermediate between that of the glass and that of air, reflections are significantly reduced. This is used in coating lenses of cameras, in spectacle lens coatings and in many fibre-optic devices.

Almost every optical device either uses or is governed or at least affected by interference. The obvious devices are ones such as Fabry-Perot Filters, Mach-Zehnder Interferometers and Array Waveguide Gratings. However, even the simple propagation of light within a fibre is governed by these effects.

2.2 Transmitting Light on a Fibre

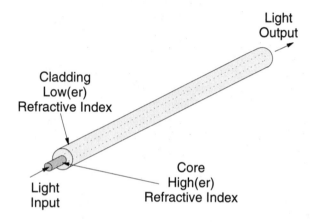

Figure 11. Basic Principle of Light Transmission on Optical Fibre

An optical fibre is a very thin strand of silica glass in geometry quite like a human hair. In reality it is a very narrow, very long glass cylinder with special characteristics. When light enters one end of the fibre it travels (confined within the fibre) until it leaves the fibre at the other end. Two critical factors stand out:

1. Very little light is lost in its journey along the fibre.

2. Fibre can bend around corners and the light will stay within it and be guided around the corners.

As shown in Figure 11, an optical fibre consists of two parts: the core and the cladding. The core is a narrow cylindrical strand of glass and the cladding is a tubular jacket surrounding it. The core has a (slightly) *higher* refractive index than the cladding. This means that the boundary (interface) between the core and the cladding acts as a perfect mirror. Light travelling along the core is confined by the mirror to stay within it - even when the fibre bends around a corner.

When light is transmitted on a fibre, the most important consideration is "what kind of light?" The electromagnetic radiation that we call light exists at many wavelengths.[11] These wavelengths go from invisible infrared through all the colours of the visible spectrum to invisible ultraviolet. Because of the attenuation characteristics of fibre, we are only interested in infrared "light" for communication applications. This light is usually invisible, since the wavelengths used are usually longer than the visible limit of around 750 nanometers (nm).[12]

If a short pulse of light from a source such as a laser or an LED is sent down a narrow fibre, it will be changed (degraded) by its passage down the fibre. It will emerge (depending on the distance) much weaker, lengthened in time ("smeared out"), and distorted in other ways. The reasons for this are as follows:

Attenuation

The pulse will be weaker because all glass absorbs light. More accurately, impurities in the glass can absorb light but the glass itself does not absorb light at the wavelengths of interest. In addition, variations in the uniformity of the glass cause scattering of the light. Both the rate of light absorption and the amount of scattering are dependent on the wavelength of the light and the characteristics of the particular glass. Most light loss in a modern fibre is caused by scattering. Typical attenuation characteristics of fibre for varying wavelengths of light are illustrated in Figure 13 on page 38.

Maximum Power

There is a practical limit to the amount of power that can be sent on a fibre. This is about half a watt (in standard single-mode fibre) and is due to a number of non-linear effects that are caused by the intense electromagnetic field in the core when high power is present.[13]

Polarisation

Conventional communication optical fibre is cylindrically symmetric but contains imperfections. Light travelling down such a fibre is changed in

---

11 Another way of saying this is that light has many frequencies or colours.

12 Depending on the individual the visible limit can vary anywhere between about 700 nm and 800 nm.

13 This of course varies with the diameter of the fibre core as the important factor is really the power density. Fibres with a large core diameter can handle significantly more power than ones with a narrow core diameter.

polarisation. (In current optical communication systems this does not matter but in future systems it may become a critical issue.)

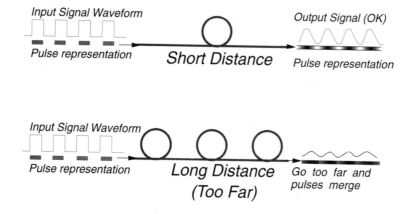

Figure 12. *Effect of Dispersion. The circles in the figure represent fibre loops. This is the conventional way to indicate distance in system diagrams.*

Dispersion

Dispersion occurs when a pulse of light is spread out during transmission on the fibre. A short pulse becomes longer and ultimately joins with the pulse behind, making recovery of a reliable bit stream impossible. (In most communications systems bits of information are sent as pulses of light. 1 = light, 0 = dark. But even in analogue transmission systems where information is sent as a continuous series of changes in the signal, dispersion causes distortion.)

There are many kinds of dispersion, each of which works in a different way, but the most important three are discussed below:

1. Material dispersion (chromatic dispersion)

   Both lasers and LEDs produce a range of optical wavelengths (a band of light) rather than a single narrow wavelength. The fibre has different refractive index characteristics at different wavelengths and therefore each wavelength will travel at a different speed in the fibre. Thus, some wavelengths arrive before others and a signal pulse disperses (or smears out).

2. Modal dispersion

When using multimode fibre, the light is able to take many different paths or "modes" as it travels within the fibre. This is shown in Figure 15 on page 42 under the heading "Multimode Step-Index". The distance traveled by light in each mode is *different* from the distance travelled in other modes. When a pulse is sent, parts of that pulse (rays or quanta) take many different modes (usually all available modes). Therefore, some components of the pulse will arrive before others. The difference between the arrival time of light taking the fastest mode versus the slowest obviously gets greater as the distance gets greater.

3. Waveguide dispersion

Waveguide dispersion is a very complex effect and is caused by the shape and index profile of the fibre core. However, this can be controlled by careful design and, in fact, waveguide dispersion can be used to counteract material dispersion as will be seen later.

Noise

One of the great benefits of fibre optical communications is that the fibre doesn't pick up noise from outside the system.[14] However, there are various kinds of noise that can come from components within the system itself. Mode partition noise (see 2.4.3, "Mode Partition Noise" on page 84) can be a problem in single-mode fibre and modal noise (see 2.3.6, "Modal Noise" on page 64) is a phenomenon in multimode fibre.

None of these effects are helpful to engineers wishing to transmit information over long distances on a fibre. But much can be done about it.

1. If you make the fibre thin enough, the light will have only one possible path - straight down the middle. Light can't disperse over multiple paths because there is only one path. This kind of fibre is called single-mode[15] fibre and is discussed in 2.2.3, "Operational Principles" on page 42.

2. The wavelength of light used in a particular application should be carefully chosen, giving consideration to the different attenuation characteristics of fibre at different wavelengths.

---

14 An exception here is nuclear radiation which can cause light to be generated in fibres and thus cause interference. This effect is minuscule in most environments.

15 In the 1970s this type of fibre was usually called "monomode" but the term has been decreasing in usage and is almost never used today.

Cost considerations are important here too. The wavelength at which a particular light source or detector can operate is determined very largely by the materials from which it is made. Different materials have very different cost structures. In general, the shorter the wavelength the lower the cost.

3. Types of dispersion that depend on wavelength can of course be minimised by minimising the spectral width of the light source. All light sources produce a range or band of wavelengths rather than a single wavelength. This range is usually called the "spectral width" of the light source.

   Lasers are commonly thought to transmit light at one wavelength only. But this is not exactly true. Simple semiconductor lasers built for communications applications typically transmit a range of wavelengths of between 1 nm and 5 nm wide. More sophisticated communications lasers can produce an (unmodulated) spectral width of as little as 0.01 nm. This is discussed further in 3.3.3, "Fabry-Perot Lasers" on page 129.

   It is possible to construct Light Emitting Diodes (LEDs) that emit light within only a narrow range of wavelengths. Typical communications LEDs have a spectral width of between 30 nm and 150 nm.

   The narrower the spectral width of the source the smaller the problem of dispersion.

4. Material dispersion and waveguide dispersion are both dependent on wavelength. Waveguide dispersion can be controlled (in the design of the fibre) to act in the opposite direction from material dispersion. This more or less happens naturally at 1300 nm but can be adjusted to produce a dispersion minimum in the 1500 nm band.

   This is a result of the core profile and refractive index contrast. Achieving this balance at 1300 nm was one reason for the profile of standard single-mode fibre. 1300 nm was a good wavelength because in the late 1980s lasers that operated in the 1310 nm band were relatively easy to make compared to longer-wavelength types. Indeed, this distinction with its concomitant cost difference still exists today.

It is clear from the above that the design of a fibre optical transmission system is dominated by two factors:

1. Signal level (or signal strength). The important aspects here are transmitter power, attenuation in the transmission system, and receiver sensitivity.

2. The control of dispersion.

There is a third factor - that of noise. Noise can become important in many system contexts but in simple point-to-point links it is rarely an issue.

The important features of any fibre transmission system are:

1. The characteristics of the fibre itself: its thickness, its refractive index, its absorption spectrum, its geometry.

2. The wavelength of light used.

3. The characteristics of the device used to create the light (laser or LED). Most important here is the frequency range (or "spectral width") of the light produced.

4. The type and characteristics of the device used to detect the light.

5. How the signal is modulated (systematically changed to encode a signal). This is most important. There are many potential ways to do this and these are discussed in 7.2, "Modulation (Making the Light Carry a Signal)" on page 378.

2.2.1 Characteristics of Glasses

When some solid materials (predominantly compounds of silicon) are melted and cooled again they do not go through any transition from the liquid state to the solid state. That is, there is no defined temperature at which the transition takes place and no "latent heat of fusion" given up. When such materials cool they simply become more and more viscous and never pass through a recognisable transition to a "solid" state. These materials are called "glasses". Many books classify glass as a very viscous liquid rather than as a solid. Molecules within a piece of glass are disordered and randomly distributed.

Ordinary window glass as we know it is made from a mixture of sodium carbonate, calcium carbonate and silicon dioxide. Melted together this forms a mixture of sodium and calcium silicates. Optical fibre is *not* made from window glass!

The predominant material in optical fibre is pure fused silica (silicon dioxide, SiO_2, sand). Pure silica forms a glass when melted but it is not often used in that form outside of the fibre optical world because of the high temperature required to melt it. However, it turns out that pure silica has the lowest absorption of light (in the wavelength bands in which we are interested) of any available material.

To make a fibre we need the core and the cladding to have different refractive indices. So we need to modify the RI of fused silica. One advantage of the liquid-like structure of glass is that we can mix other materials into it in almost any proportion and concentration. We are not limited to fixed ratios as we might be with crystalline structures. Also a very wide range of materials will mix (it is almost correct to say "dissolve") in the glass.

People have been mixing other materials into glass to change the RI for many years! "Lead Crystal" glass (used in chandeliers, vases and tableware) has a high proportion of lead oxide mixed into it in order to increase the RI and make it "sparkle".

We can construct an optical fibre either by doping the core with something that increases the RI or by doping the cladding with something that decreases the RI. However, it is not quite as simple as this. These dopants also change other characteristics of the glass such as the coefficients of thermal expansion. If the core and cladding have significantly different coefficients of expansion they may crack apart after a time - or indeed they may crack apart during manufacture.

In optical fibre we usually mix a proportion of germanium dioxide (4% to 10%) with the silica to increase the RI when required. RI can be decreased by adding boron trioxide (B_2O_3). There are many other materials available that can be used as dopants in this way.[16] There are many other substances that either increase or decrease the RI. Each of these also has an effect on characteristics of the material other than the RI (such as the coefficient of expansion). Other common dopants used to increase the RI are phosphorus pentoxide (P_2O_5), titanium dioxide (TiO_2) and aluminium oxide (Al_2O_3).

Another problem (discussed in 2.2.1, "Characteristics of Glasses" on page 36) is that all dopants increase the attenuation of the silica.

---

[16] In this context the word "dopant" is commonly used although its use is problematic. A dopant in the context of semiconductor materials is usually present in minuscule quantities (one in ten million) but in fibre we are talking up to 10%.

2.2.1.1 Attenuation (Absorption) Characteristics of Glasses

Figure 13 shows the attenuation characteristics of typical modern fibres in the infrared range. Light becomes invisible (infrared) at wavelengths longer than about 730 nanometers (nm).

Note: 1 nm = 10 Å (Angstrom)

There are a wide range of glasses available and characteristics vary depending on their chemical composition. Over the past few years the transmission properties of glass have been improved considerably. In 1970 the "ballpark" attenuation of a silicon fibre was 20 dB/km. By 1980 research had improved this to 1 dB/km. In 1990 the figure was 0.2 dB/km. As the figures show, absorption varies considerably with wavelength and the two curves show just how different the characteristics of different glasses can be.

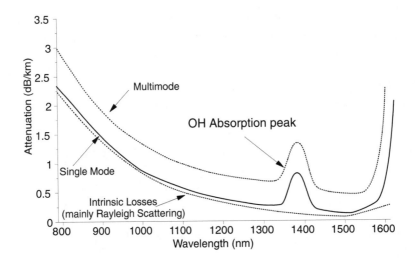

Figure 13. *Typical Fibre Infrared Absorption Spectrum. The lower curve shows the characteristics of a single-mode fibre made from a glass containing about 4% of germanium dioxide (GeO$_2$) dopant in the core. The upper curve is for modern graded index multimode fibre. Attenuation in multimode fibre is higher than in single-mode because higher levels of dopant are used. The peak at around 1400 nm is due to the effects of traces of water in the glass.*

Most of the attenuation in fibre is caused by light being scattered by minute variations (less than 1/10th of the wavelength) in the density or composition of the glass. This is called "Rayleigh Scattering". Rayleigh scattering is also the reason that the sky is blue and that sunsets are red.

In fibre, Rayleigh scattering is inversely proportional to the fourth power of the wavelength! This accounts for perhaps 90% of the enormous difference in attenuation of light at 850 nm wavelength from that at 1550 nm. Unfortunately, we can't do a lot about Rayleigh scattering by improving fibre manufacturing techniques.

There is another form of scattering called "Mie Scattering". Mie scattering is caused by imperfections in the fibre of a size roughly comparable with the wavelength. This is not a significant concern with modern fibres as recent improvements in manufacturing techniques have all but eliminated the problem.

The absorption peak shown in Figure 13 on page 38 is centered at 1385 nm but it is "broadened" by several factors including the action of ambient heat. This absorption is caused by the presence of the -OH atomic bond, that is, the presence of water. The bond is resonant at the wavelength of 1385 nm. Water is extremely hard to eliminate from the fibre during manufacturing and the small residual peak shown in the diagram is typical of current, good quality fibres. In the past this peak was significantly greater in height than shown in the figure (up to 4 dB/km).

In the early days of optical fibre communications impurities in the glass were the chief source of attenuation. Iron (Fe), chromium (Cr) and nickel (Ni) can cause significant absorption even in quantities as low as one part per billion. Today, techniques of purifying silica have improved to the point where impurities are no longer a significant concern.

Some of the dopants added to the glass to modify the refractive index of the fibre have the unwanted side effect of significantly increasing the absorption. This is why single-mode fibre has typically lower absorption than multimode - it has less dopant. The conclusion that can be drawn from the absorption spectrum is that some wavelengths will be significantly better for transmission purposes than others.

2.2.1.2 Fibre Transmission Windows (Bands)

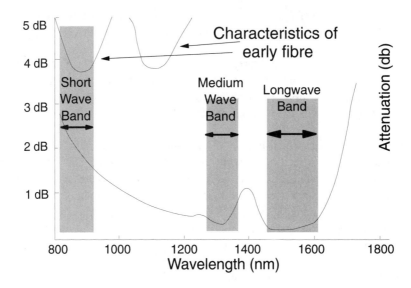

Figure 14. Transmission Windows. The upper curve shows the absorption characteristics of fibre in the 1970s. The lower one is for modern fibre.

In the early days of optical fibre communication, fibre attenuation was best represented by the upper curve in Figure 14 (a large difference from today). Partly for historic reasons, there are considered to be three "windows" or bands in the transmission spectrum of optical fibre. *The wavelength band used by a system is an extremely important defining characteristic of that optical system.*

Short Wavelength Band (First Window)

> This is the band around 800-900 nm. This was the first band used for optical fibre communication in the 1970s and early 1980s. It was attractive because of a local dip in the attenuation profile (of fibre at the time) but also (mainly) because you can use low cost optical sources and detectors in this band.

Medium Wavelength Band (Second Window)

> This is the band around 1310 nm which came into use in the mid 1980s. This band is attractive today because there is zero fibre dispersion here (on single-mode fibre). While sources and detectors for this band are more costly than for the short wave band the fibre attenuation is only about 0.4 dB/km. This is the band in which the majority of long distance communications systems operate today.

Long Wavelength Band (Third Window)

The band between about 1510 nm and 1600 nm has the lowest attenuation available on current optical fibre (about 0.26 dB/km). In addition optical amplifiers are available which operate in this band. However, it is difficult (expensive) to make optical sources and detectors that operate here. Also, standard fibre disperses signal in this band.

In the late 1990s this band is where almost all new communications systems operate.

2.2.2 Transmission Capacity

The potential transmission capacity of optical fibre is enormous. Looking again at Figure 14 on page 40 both the medium and long wavelength bands are very low in loss. The medium wavelength band (second window) is about 100 nm wide and ranges from 1250 nm to 1350 nm (loss of about .4 dB per km). The long wavelength band (third window) is around 150 nm wide and ranges from 1450 nm to 1600 nm (loss of about .2 dB per km). The loss peaks at 1250 and 1400 nm are due to traces of water in the glass. The useful (low loss) range is therefore around 250 nm.

Expressed in terms of analogue bandwidth, a 1 nm wide waveband at 1500 nm has a bandwidth of about 133 GHz. A 1 nm wide waveband at 1300 nm has a bandwidth of 177 GHz. In total, this gives a usable range of about 30 Tera Hertz (3×10^{13} Hz).

Capacity depends on the modulation technique used. In the electronic world we are used to getting a digital bandwidth of up to 8 bits per Hz of analog bandwidth. In the optical world, that objective is a long way off (and a trifle unnecessary). But assuming that a modulation technique resulting in one bit per Hz of analog bandwidth is available, then we can expect a digital bandwidth of 3×10^{13} bits per second.

Current technology limits electronic systems to a rate of about 10 Gbps, although higher speeds are being experimented with in research. Current practical fibre systems are also limited to this speed because of the speed of the electronics needed for transmission and reception.

The above suggests that, even if fibre quality is not improved, we could get 10,000 times greater throughput from a single fibre than the current practical limit.

2.2.3 Operational Principles

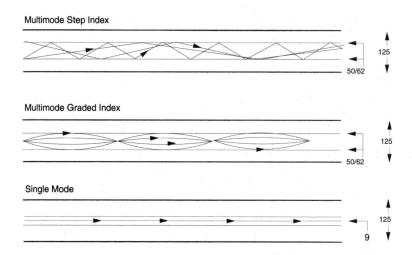

Figure 15. *Fibre Modes*

Figure 15 illustrates the three different kinds of optical fibre.

- Multimode Step-Index

- Multimode Graded-Index

- Single-Mode (Step-Index)

The difference between them is in the way light travels along the fibre. The top section of the figure shows the operation of "multimode" fibre. There are two different parts to the fibre. In the figure, there is a core of 50 microns (μm) in diameter and a cladding of 125 μm in diameter. (Fibre size is normally quoted as the core diameter followed by the cladding diameter. Thus the fibre in the figure is identified as 50/125.) The cladding surrounds the core. The cladding glass has a different (lower) refractive index than that of the core, and the boundary forms a mirror.

This is the effect you see when looking upward from underwater. Except for the part immediately above, the junction of the water and the air appears silver like a mirror.

Light is transmitted (with very low loss) down the fibre by reflection from the mirror boundary between the core and the cladding. This phenomenon is called "total internal reflection". Perhaps the most important characteristic is that the fibre will bend around corners to a radius of only a few centimetres without any loss of the light.

Multimode Step-Index Fibre

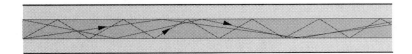

Figure 16. Multimode Step-Index Fibre

The expectation of many people is that if you shine a light down a fibre, then the light will enter the fibre at an infinitely large number of angles and propagate by internal reflection over an infinite number of possible paths. This is not true. What happens is that there is only a finite number of possible paths for the light to take. These paths are called "modes" and identify the general characteristic of the light transmission system being used. This is discussed further in 2.3.4, "Propagation Modes" on page 55. Fibre that has a core diameter large enough for the light used to find multiple paths is called "multimode" fibre. For a fibre with a core diameter of 62.5 microns using light of wavelength 1300 nm, the number of modes is around 400 depending on the difference in refractive index between the core and the cladding.

The problem with multimode operation is that some of the paths taken by particular modes are longer than other paths. This means that light will arrive at different times according to the path taken. Therefore the pulse tends to disperse (spread out) as it travels through the fibre. This effect is one cause of "intersymbol interference". This restricts the distance that a pulse can be usefully sent over multimode fibre.

Multimode Graded Index Fibre

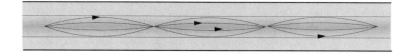

Figure 17. *Multimode Graded index Fibre*

One way around the problem of (modal) dispersion in multimode fibre is to do something to the glass such that the refractive index of the core changes gradually from the centre to the edge. Light travelling down the center of the fibre experiences a higher refractive index than light that travels further out towards the cladding. Thus light on the physically shorter paths (modes) travels more slowly than light on physically longer paths. The light follows a curved trajectory within the fibre as illustrated in the figure. The aim of this is to keep the speed of propagation of light on each path *the same* with respect to the axis of the fibre. Thus a pulse of light composed of many modes stays together as it travels through the fibre. This allows transmission for longer distances than does regular multimode transmission. This type of fibre is called "Graded Index" fibre. Within a GI fibre light typically travels in around 400 modes (at a wavelength of 1300 nm) or 800 modes (in the 800 nm band).

Note that only the refractive index of the core is graded. There is still a cladding of lower refractive index than the outer part of the core.

Single-Mode Fibre

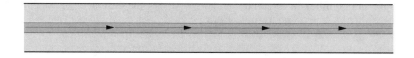

Figure 18. *Single-Mode Fibre. Note that this figure is not to scale. The core diameter is typically between 8 and 9 microns while the diameter of the cladding is 125 microns.*

If the fibre core is very narrow compared to the wavelength of the light in use then the light cannot travel in different modes and thus the fibre is called "single-mode" or "monomode". There is no longer any reflection from the core-cladding boundary but rather the electromagnetic wave is tightly held to travel down the axis of the fibre. It seems obvious that the longer the wavelength of light in use, the larger the diameter of fibre we can use and still have light travel in a single-mode. The core diameter used in a typical single-mode fibre is nine microns.

It is not quite as simple as this in practice. A significant proportion (up to 20%) of the light in a single-mode fibre actually travels in the cladding. For this reason the "apparent diameter" of the core (the region in which most of the light travels) is somewhat wider than the core itself. The region in which light travels in a single-mode fibre is often called the "mode field" and the mode field diameter is quoted instead of the core diameter. The mode field varies in diameter depending on the relative refractive indices of core and cladding,

Core diameter is a compromise. We can't make the core too narrow because of losses at bends in the fibre. As the core diameter decreases compared to the wavelength (the core gets narrower or the wavelength gets longer), the minimum radius that we can bend the fibre without loss increases. If a bend is too sharp, the light just comes out of the core into the outer parts of the cladding and is lost.

You can make fibre single-mode by:

- Making the core thin enough

- Making the refractive index difference between core and cladding small enough

- Using a longer wavelength

Single-mode fibre usually has significantly lower attenuation than multimode (about half). This has nothing to do with fibre geometry or manufacture. Single-mode fibres have a significantly smaller difference in refractive index between core and cladding. This means that less dopant is needed to modify the refractive index as dopant is a major source of attenuation.

It's not strictly correct to talk about "single-mode fibre" and "multimode fibre" without qualifying it - although we do this all the time. A fibre is single-moded or multi-moded *at a particular wavelength*. If we use very long wave light (say 10.6 nm from a CO_2 laser) then even most MM fibre would be single-moded for that wavelength. If we use 600 nm light on standard single-mode fibre then we do have a greater number of modes than just one (although typically only about 3 to 5). There is a single-mode fibre characteristic called the "cutoff wavelength". This is typically around 1100 nm for single-mode fibre with a core diameter of 9 microns. The cutoff wavelength is the shortest wavelength at which the fibre remains single-moded. At wavelengths shorter than the cutoff the fibre is multimode.

When light is introduced to the end of a fibre there is a critical angle of acceptance. Light entering at a greater angle passes into the cladding and is lost. At a smaller angle the light travels down the fibre. If this is considered in three dimensions, a cone is formed around the end of the fibre within which all rays are contained. The sine of this angle is called the "numerical aperture" and is one of the important characteristics of a given fibre.

Single-mode fibre has a core diameter of 4 to 10 μm (8 μm is typical). Multimode fibre can have many core diameters but in the last few years the core diameter of 62.5 μm in the US and 50 μm outside the US has become predominant. However, the use of 62.5 μm fibre outside the US is gaining popularity - mainly due to the availability of equipment (designed for the US) that uses this type of fibre.

2.2.4 Fibre Refractive Index Profiles

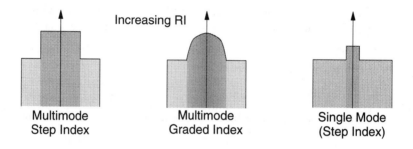

Figure 19. *Fibre Refractive Index Profiles*

Figure 19 shows the refractive index profiles of some different types of fibre.

RI Profile of Multimode Step-Index Fibre

> Today's standard MM SI fibre has a core diameter of either 62.5 or 50 microns with an overall cladding diameter in either case of 125 microns. Thus it is referred to as 50/125 or 62.5/125 micron fibre.

> Usually the core is SiO_2 doped with about 4% of GeO_2. The cladding is usually just pure silica. There is an abrupt change in refractive index between core and cladding.

> The bandwidth.distance product is a measure of the signal carrying capacity of the fibre. This is discussed further in 7.6.1, "Maximum Propagation Distance on Multimode Fibre" on page 420. The bandwidth.distance product for standard step index multimode fibre varies between about 15 MHz/km and 50

MHz/km depending on the wavelength in use, the core diameter and the RI contrast between core and cladding.

RI Profile of Multimode Graded Index Fibre

Graded index fibre has the same dimensions as step index fibre. The refractive index of the core changes slowly between the fibre axis and the cladding. This is achieved by using a varying level of dopant across the diameter of the core. Note the gradations are not linear - they follow a "parabolic" index profile. It is important to realise that GI fibre is relatively difficult to make and is therefore significantly more expensive than step index fibre (either MM or SM).

The usual bandwidth.distance product for 62.5 micron GI MM fibre is 500 MHz/km at 1300 nm. In the 800 nm band the bandwidth.distance product is typically much less at 160 MHz/km. For MM GI fibre with a core diameter of 50 microns the bandwidth.distance product is 700 MHz/km (again at 1300 nm). Recently (1997) MM GI fibre with significantly improved characteristics has become available. A bandwidth.distance product figure for 62.5 micron fibre is advertised as 1000 MHz/km and for 50 micron fibre of 1,200 MHz/km. This is a result of improved fibre manufacturing techniques and better process control. Of course these fibres are considered "premium" fibres and are priced accordingly.

RI Profile of Single-Mode Fibre

Single-mode fibre is characterised by its narrow core size. This is done to ensure that only one mode (well, actually two if you count the two orthogonal polarisations as separate modes) can propagate. The key parameter of SM fibre is not the core size but rather the "Mode Field Diameter". (This is discussed further in: 2.4.1.1, "Mode Field Diameter (MFD) and Spot Size" on page 72.)

Core size is usually between 8 and 10 microns although special purpose SM fibres are often used with core sizes of as low as 4 microns.

The RI difference between core and cladding is typically very small (around .01). This is done to help minimise attenuation. You can achieve the index difference either by doping the core to raise its RI (say with GeO_2) or by doping the cladding (say with fluoride) to lower its RI. Dopants in both core and cladding affect attenuation and therefore it's not a simple thing to decide. There are many different core and cladding compositions in use.

Bandwidth.distance product is not a relevant concept for single-mode fibre as there is no modal dispersion (although there is chromatic dispersion).

The refractive index of fibres is changed and manipulated by adding various "dopants" to the basic SiO$_2$ glass. These can have various effects:

- Some dopants increase the refractive index and others decrease it. This is the primary reason we use dopants.

- All dopants *increase* attenuation of the fibre. Thus dopants are to be avoided (or at least minimised) if attenuation is important for the fibre's application. It is almost always very important.

  We might expect that since the light travels in the core that dopant levels in the cladding may not make too much difference. *Wrong!* In single-mode fibre a quite large proportion of the optical power (electromagnetic field) travels in the cladding. In single-mode fibre attenuation and speed of propagation are strongly influenced by the characteristics of the cladding glass. In multimode graded index fibre the core is doped anyway (albeit at different levels) so (for multimode) it is an issue even in the core.

  In multimode step-index fibre there is an "evanescent field" set up in the cladding every time a ray is reflected. This is an electromagnetic field and is affected by the attenuation characteristics of the cladding.

- If we use a dopant at too high a level not only does it change the refractive index of the glass but it also changes the coefficient of expansion. This means that in operational conditions if we use too much dopant the cladding may crack away from the core.

2.2.4.1 Coating

During manufacture fibre is usually coated with a very thin layer of plastic bonded closely to the cladding. This is often referred to as the "jacket". It is applied as a continuous process as the fibre is drawn. There are two main reasons for this:

1. To prevent water from diffusing into the fibre. Water can cause micro-cracking of the surface. In addition the -OH group is a major source of attenuation due to absorption.

2. If a plastic with a *higher* refractive index than the cladding glass is used this helps to guide unwanted "cladding modes" out of the fibre.

Secondary functions of the coating are that it is usually coloured so that individual fibres can be identified. In loose-tube or gel-filled cables multiple fibres are often packed close together in a common sheath and there is a need to identify which is which. In addition it makes the fibre thicker, easier to handle and less susceptible to damage in handling.

Standard coated fibre has a diameter of 250 microns and thus the coating is 62.5 microns thick. Of course the individual fibre is usually further enclosed in a plastic sheath before integration with other fibres and components into a cable.

2.3 Light Propagation in Multimode Fibre

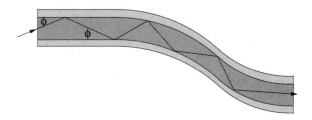

Figure 20. *Light Propagation in Multimode Fibre. Light is bound within the fibre due to the phenomena of "total internal reflection" which takes place at the interface between the core of the fibre and the cladding.*

The key feature of light propagation in a fibre is that the fibre *may bend around corners*. Provided the bend radius is not too tight (2 cm is about the minimum for most multimode fibres) the light will follow the fibre and will propagate *without loss* due to the bends. This phenomena is called "total internal reflection". A ray of light entering the fibre is guided along the fibre because it bounces off the interface between the core and the (lower refractive index) cladding. Light is said to be "bound" within the fibre.

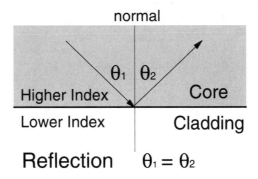

Figure 21. *Reflection*

If we consider the propagation of a "ray" in a multimode step index fibre we can analyse the situation quite easily with the "laws of elementary physics".

"The angle of incidence is equal to the angle of reflection."

This is illustrated in Figure 21 on page 49. This means that $\theta_1 = \theta_2$.

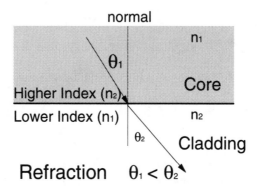

***Figure 22.** Refraction*

The important thing to realise about propagation along a fibre is that *not all light can propagate this way*. The angle of incidence of the ray with the core-cladding interface (the angle ϕ in Figure 20 on page 49) must be quite small or else the ray will pass through into the cladding and (after a while) will leave the fibre.

2.3.1 Snell's Law

In order to understand ray propagation in a fibre we need one more law from high school physics. This is Snell's law. Referring to Figure 22 and Figure 23 on page 51:

$$n_1 \sin \theta_1 = n_2 \sin \theta_2$$

Where n denotes the refractive index of the material.

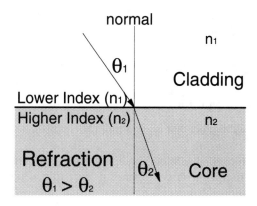

Figure 23. Refraction (2)

Notice here that:

1. The angle θ is the angle between incident ray and an imaginary line *normal* to the plane of the core-cladding boundary. This is counter to intuition but the accepted convention.

2. When light passes from material of higher refractive index to a material of lower index the (refracted) angle θ gets larger.

3. When light passes from material of lower refractive index to a material of higher index the (refracted) angle θ becomes smaller.

2.3.2 Critical Angle

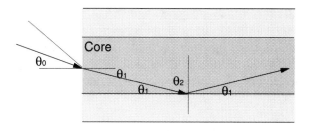

Figure 24. Critical Angle (1)

If we consider Figure 22 on page 50 we notice that as the angle θ_1 becomes larger and larger so does the angle θ_2. Because of the refraction effect θ_2 becomes larger more quickly than θ_1. At some point θ_2 will reach 90° while θ_1 is still well less than that. This is called the "critical angle". When θ_1 is increased further then refraction ceases and the light starts to be reflected rather than refracted.

Thus light is perfectly reflected at an interface between two materials of different refractive index iff:

1. The light is incident on the interface from the side of *higher* refractive index.

2. The angle θ is greater than a specific value called the "critical angle".

If we know the refractive indices of both materials then the critical angle can be derived quite easily from Snell's law. At the critical angle we know that θ_2 equals 90° and sin 90° = 1 and so:

$$n_1 \sin \theta_1 = n_2$$

$$\textit{Therefore} \quad \sin \theta_1 = \frac{n_2}{n_1}$$

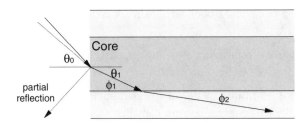

Figure 25. *Critical Angle (2)*

If we now consider Figure 24 on page 51 and Figure 25 we can see the effect of the critical angle within the fibre. In Figure 24 on page 51 we see that for rays where θ_1 is less than a critical value then the ray will propagate along the fibre and will be "bound" within the fibre. In Figure 25 we see that where the angle θ_1 is greater than the critical value the ray is refracted into the cladding and will ultimately be lost outside the fibre.

Another aspect here is that when light meets an abrupt change in refractive index (such as at the end of a fibre) *not* all of the light is refracted. Usually about 4% of the light is reflected back along the path from which it came. This is further discussed in 2.1.3.2, "Transmission through a Sheet of Glass" on page 27.

When we consider rays entering the fibre from the outside (into the endface of the fibre) we see that there is a further complication. The refractive index difference between the fibre core and the air will cause any arriving ray to be refracted. This means that there is a maximum angle for a ray arriving at the fibre endface at which the ray will propagate. Rays arriving at an angle less than this angle will propagate but rays arriving at a greater angle will not. This angle is not a "critical angle" as that term is reserved for the case where light arrives from a material of higher RI to one of lower RI. (In this case, the critical angle is the angle *within the fibre*.) Thus there is a "cone of acceptance" at the endface of a fibre. Rays arriving within the cone will propagate and ones arriving outside of it will not.

In Figure 25 on page 52 there is a partial reflection present when most of the light is refracted. This partial reflection effect was noted earlier in 2.1.3.2, "Transmission through a Sheet of Glass" on page 27. These reflections are called "Fresnel Reflections" and occur in most situations where there is an abrupt change in the refractive index at a material interface. These reflections are an important (potential) source of disruption and noise in an optical transmission system. See 2.4.4, "Reflections and Return Loss Variation" on page 85.

2.3.3 Numerical Aperture (NA)

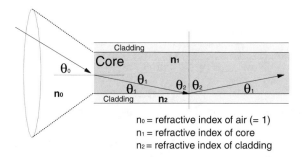

n_0 = refractive index of air (= 1)
n_1 = refractive index of core
n_2 = refractive index of cladding

Figure 26. Calculating the Numerical Aperture

One of the most often quoted characteristics of an optical fibre is its "Numerical Aperture". The NA is intended as a measure of the light capturing ability of the fibre. However, it is used for many other purposes. For example it may be used as a measure of the amount of loss that we might expect on a bend of a particular radius etc.

Figure 24 on page 51 shows a ray entering the fibre at an angle close to its axis. This ray will be refracted and will later encounter the core-cladding interface at an angle such that it will be reflected. This is because the angle θ_2 will be greater than the critical angle. The angle is greater because we are measuring angles from a normal to the core-cladding boundary *not* a tangent to it.

Figure 25 on page 52 shows a ray entering at a wider angle to the fibre axis. This one will reach the core-cladding interface at an angle smaller than the critical angle and it will pass into the cladding. This ray will eventually be lost.

It is clear that there is a "cone" of acceptance (illustrated in Figure 26 on page 53). If a ray enters the fibre at an angle within the cone then it will be captured and propagate as a bound mode. If a ray enters the fibre at an angle outside the cone then it will leave the core and eventually leave the fibre itself.

The Numerical Aperture is the sine of the largest angle contained within the cone of acceptance.

Looking at Figure 26 on page 53, the NA is $\sin \theta_0$. The problem is to find an expression for NA.

We know that $\sin \theta_2 = \dfrac{n_2}{n_1}$ because θ_2 is the critical angle

And $n_0 \sin \theta_0 = n_1 \sin \theta_1$ from Snell's Law

Now, $\cos \theta_1 = \sin \theta_2 = \dfrac{n_2}{n_1}$

We know that $\sin x = \sqrt{1 - \cos^2 x}$ (Rule)

Therefore $\sin \theta_1 = \sqrt{1 - \dfrac{n_2^2}{n_1^2}}$

Since $n_0 = 1$ *then* $\sin \theta_0 = n_1 \sqrt{1 - \dfrac{n_2^2}{n_1^2}}$

Therefore the NA $= \sqrt{n_1^2 - n_2^2}$

Where $n_1 =$ refractive index of the core

$n_2 =$ refractive index of the cladding

Another useful expression for NA is: $NA = n_1 \sin \theta_1$. This relates the NA to the RI of the core and the maximum angle at which a bound ray may propagate (angle measured from the fibre axis rather than its normal).

Typical NA for single-mode fibre is 0.1. For multimode, NA is between 0.2 and 0.3 (usually closer to 0.2).

NA is related to a number of important fibre characteristics.

1. It is a measure of the ability of the fibre to gather light at the input end (as discussed above).

2. Because it is a measure of the contrast in RI between the core and the cladding it is a good measure of the light guiding properties of the fibre. The higher the NA the tighter (smaller radius) we can have bends in the fibre before loss of light becomes a problem.

3. The higher the NA the more modes we have! Rays can bounce at greater angles and therefore there are more of them. This means that the higher the NA the *greater* will be the dispersion of this fibre (in the case of MM fibre)!

4. In SM fibre a high RI contrast usually implies a high level of dopant in the cladding. Since a significant proportion of optical power in SM travels in the cladding we get a significantly increased amount of attenuation due to the higher level of dopant. Thus (as a rule of thumb) the higher the NA of SM fibre the higher will be the attenuation of the fibre.

2.3.4 Propagation Modes

So far our description of light propagation in a multimode fibre has used the classic "ray model" of light propagation. While this has provided valuable insights it offers no help in understanding the phenomenon of "modes".

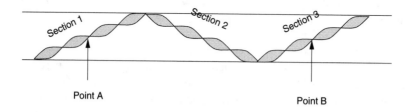

Figure 27. Multimode Propagation. At corresponding points in its path, each mode must be in phase with itself. That is, the signal at Point A must be in phase with the signal at Point B.

When light travels on a multimode fibre it is limited to a relatively small number of possible paths (called modes). This is counter to intuition. Reasoning from the ray model would lead us to conclude that there is an infinity of possible paths. A full understanding of modes requires the use of Maxwell's equations which are very difficult and well outside the scope of this book.

A simple explanation is that when light propagates along a particular path within a fibre the wavefront must stay in phase with itself. In Figure 27 on page 55 this means that the wave (or ray) must be in phase at corresponding points in the cycle. The wave at point A must be in phase with the wave at point B. This means that there must be an integer multiple of wavelengths between points of reflection between the core and the cladding. That is, the length of section 2 of the wave in the figure must be an integer number of wavelengths long. It is obvious that if we have this restriction on the paths that can be taken then there will be a finite number of possible paths.

Figure 15 on page 42 shows the usual simplistic diagram of modal propagation in the three common types of fibre. We must realise however that this is a two dimensional picture and we are attempting to represent a three-dimensional phenomenon! Many modes are oblique and spiral in their paths. In fact the majority of modes *never intersect with the fibre axis at any time in their travel*! This is illustrated in Figure 28.

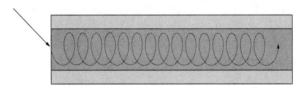

Figure 28. *Spiral Mode. In MM GI fibre most modes have spiral paths and never pass through the axis of the fibre. In much of the literature these modes are also called "corkscrew", "screw" or "helical" modes.*

Perhaps the most important property of modes is that *all of the propagating modes within a fibre are orthogonal*. That is, provided that the fibre is perfect (perfectly regular, no faults, perfectly circular, uniform refractive index...) there can be no power transfer or interference between one mode and another. Indeed this is the basic reason for the restriction (stated above) that corresponding points along the path of a mode must be in phase. If they were not then there could be destructive interference between modes and the wave could not propagate.

2.3.4.1 Weakly Guiding Fibres

Weakly guiding fibres are ones with a low refractive index contrast (refractive index difference between core and cladding). This is true of almost all practical fibres.

It is important to note that "weakly guiding" does *not* mean weak confinement of the light! The light is well confined and guided.

When you do the mathematics of fibre propagation if the RI contrast is less than .045 a simplified set of (scalar) equations known as the weakly guiding approximation may be used. The exact equations involve vectors and are many times more complex. At low levels of RI contrast both sets of equations have essentially the same result.

2.3.4.2 Cladding Modes

When light enters the fibre it is inevitable that some will enter the cladding. Also, when there are bends in the fibre or imperfections in the core-cladding interface then light may leave the core and enter the cladding.

There are many possible modes that light may take in the cladding. Generally these will leave the cladding (and the fibre) relatively quickly but some may propagate for a considerable distance. These modes will add significantly to dispersion and so it is generally desirable to get rid of them.

The principal way of ridding the fibre of unwanted cladding modes is to ensure that the refractive index of the plastic coating on the fibre is higher than that of the cladding. This minimises the reflection between the cladding and coating and minimises guidance at the cladding-coating interface.

2.3.4.3 Leaky Modes

When light is launched into the core of a fibre (in this case either MM or SM) there will be some modes which really don't satisfy the conditions for being guided inside the core but which nevertheless travel there for some considerable distance. This is the marginal case where a mode is borderline between being bound and being a cladding mode. In MM fibres these are usually skew rays of some kind.

Ultimately, these modes leave the core and then the cladding over a distance. However, if distances are short they can travel as far as the receiver. These modes have group velocities slower than the bound modes and so contribute to dispersion of the signal.

In some situations system designers eliminate leaky modes by putting some tight bends into the fibre. The radius of the bend is chosen to pass all legal bound modes and to eliminate leaky ones. This is called "mode stripping".

2.3.4.4 Bends and Micro-Bends

As mentioned above one of the most important characteristics of light propagation within a fibre is that the fibre can have bends in it and the light will be guided *without loss* around the bends.

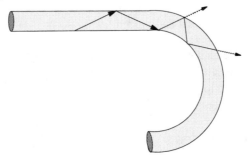

Figure 29. *Propagation around a Bend in the Fibre*

If the radius of a bend is relatively large (say 10 cm or so) there will be almost no loss of light. However, if the bend radius is very tight (say 1 cm) then some light will be lost.

Consider Figure 29. A light "ray" propagating along the straight section of the fibre and reflecting at an angle less than the critical angle will be completely bound within the fibre and will propagate without loss. When a bend is encountered the angle of incidence of that ray with the core/cladding interface may become greater than the critical angle and therefore some light will pass out of the core and into the cladding. Ultimately this light will leave the fibre and be lost.

This applies for both MM and SM fibres (although it is a much more significant effect in MM). As the bend radius is reduced there is a point where loss of light starts to become significant. This is usually of the order of 2 or 3 cm in most fibres. It depends on the refractive index contrast between the core and the cladding.

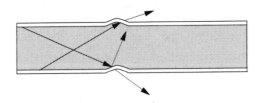

Figure 30. *Effect of a Micro-Bend*

Micro-bends can be an important source of loss. If the fibre is pressed onto an irregular surface you can get tiny bends in the fibre as illustrated in Figure 30. Light (mainly from the higher modes) is lost at these irregularities.

Occasionally when it is necessary to strip the higher order modes (and the cladding modes) from a signal, micro-bends are used intentionally. The fibre is clamped between two rough surfaces (such as pieces of sandpaper) for a short distance (perhaps 5 cm). Higher order modes and cladding modes are "stripped" in this process.

2.3.4.5 Speckle Patterns

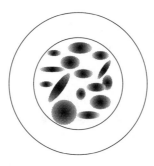

Figure 31. *Typical Speckle Pattern. The speckle pattern is the pattern of energy as it appears at the end of a fibre.*

A speckle pattern is a map of the energy pattern at the end of a multimode fibre. The pattern is a characteristic of laser transmission and does not happen with LED sources. It appears as a number of almost randomly distributed areas of high energy with spaces in between. This is illustrated in Figure 31.

When the observation is made close (within a few metres) to the transmitter you get a very clear pattern where the spots are well defined. When you get further away from the transmitter the spots become less and less well defined and finally the fibre endface becomes almost uniformly illuminated. This change is caused by mode dispersion over the transmission distance. Light from an LED produces almost uniform endface illumination close to the transmitter.

Speckle patterns are caused by interference between modes as they emerge from the end of the fibre. They are a good way to tell how much coherence exists between light in various modes. You often see phrases such as "speckle dependent noise" where (by inference) the speckle pattern is deemed to be a factor in some other effect.

This is of course not true. The speckle pattern is just an easy way of looking at what is happening within the fibre.

2.3.4.6 Phase Velocity

The phase velocity is the speed of propagation of an electromagnetic wave in some medium. In fibre optics it is the speed of the planar phase front of the mode as it propagates along the fibre. It is just the speed of light divided by the "effective index" of the fibre.

$$V_{phase} = \frac{c}{n_{effective}}$$

The effective index is a single number situated between the refractive index of the core and the cladding which summarises the effects of both.

2.3.4.7 Group Velocity

Group velocity is the usual way of discussing the speed of propagation on a fibre. It is the speed of propagation of *modulations* along the fibre. It is generally a little less than the phase velocity.

The reason that group velocity is different from phase velocity is related to the amount of dispersion of the medium. If there is no dispersion in the medium then group velocity and phase velocity are the same.

2.3.4.8 Fibre Parameter or Normalised Frequency - "V"

One often quoted and very useful measure of a fibre is usually called the "V". In some texts it is called the "normalised frequency" and in others just the "dimensionless fibre parameter". V summarises all of the important characteristics of a fibre in a single number. It can be used directly to determine if the fibre will be single-moded or not at a particular wavelength and also to calculate the number of possible bound modes. In addition it can be used to calculate the spot size, the cutoff wavelength and even chromatic dispersion. However it is important to note that V incorporates the wavelength that we are using on the fibre and so to some extent it is a measure of a fibre within the context of a system rather than the fibre alone.

$$V = \frac{\pi d}{\lambda} \sqrt{n_{core}^2 - n_{cladding}^2}$$

$$= \frac{\pi d}{\lambda} NA$$

Where: d = core diameter
$\quad\quad\quad \lambda$ = wavelength
$\quad\quad\quad n$ = refractive index
$\quad\quad NA$ = numerical aperture

If $V \le 2.405$ the fibre will be single-moded at the wavelength used to calculate V.

For the multimode situation the number of modes (N) may be calculated as follows:

$$N \; \frac{V^2}{2} \quad\quad \text{Step Index Fibre}$$

$$N \; \frac{V^2}{4} \quad\quad \text{Graded Index Fibre}$$

Note that these formulae count *both* orthogonal polarisations of one mode as separate modes.

2.3.4.9 Multimode Dispersion (Modal Dispersion)

In multimode fibre, dispersion is usually so large that it dominates other fibre characteristics. In other words, system limitations of multimode fibre systems are usually the result of modal dispersion rather than of attenuation or of other forms of dispersion.

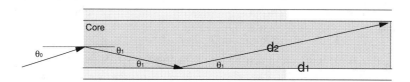

Figure 32. *Multimode Ray Propagation*

The reason for modal dispersion in step index fibre is easily seen from Figure 32. Consider the fundamental mode with a ray propagating straight down the axis of the fibre. This ray will travel distance d_1 in time:

$$t \; = \; \frac{n}{c} \times d_1$$

A ray which entered the fibre at the maximum possible angle (close to the critical angle) will travel the same distance (d_1) in time:

$$t \; = \; \frac{n}{c} \times d_1 \times \frac{1}{\cos\theta}$$

Clearly, for realistic angles there will be quite a large difference in the distance travelled in a given time and thus a significant amount of dispersion.

Using the formula from 2.3.3, "Numerical Aperture (NA)" on page 53:

$$NA = n_1 \sin \theta_1$$

and the knowledge that the sine of very small angles (in radians) is approximately the same as the angle itself we can derive:

$$Dispersion_{time} = NA^2 \times \frac{Length}{2nc}$$

This relates the amount of dispersion in time (ps) to the length travelled, the core index and the NA.

A typical fibre with RI of 1.458 and an RI difference (core and cladding) of .01 has an NA of .2. Such a fibre has an acceptance angle of 12° (measured from the normal to the end interface).

The signal carrying capability of a fibre is usually measured in MHz/km. For MM SI fibre this is usually between about 15 MHz/km and 50 MHz/km. On a fibre of 50 MHz/km bandwidth this means that you can go for 1 km at 50 MHz (analogue sine wave transmission) or 2 km at 25 MHz etc. with acceptable (less than 20%) dispersion.

Graded Index (GI) fibres are much better. Grading the index over the diameter of the fibre is aimed at equalising the group velocities of the various modes and thus minimising multimode dispersion. Of course this is far from perfect! A good quality MM GI fibre with a core diameter of 62.5 microns typically has a transmission bandwidth of 500 MHz/km. A similar MM GI fibre with a 50 micron core diameter will typically have a transmission bandwidth of 700 MHz/km. Because the thinner the core the smaller the NA (other things being equal).

2.3.5 Mode Coupling

Under ideal conditions (perfect fibre) light travelling in one mode on a fibre *cannot* excite (transfer power to) any other mode on the same fibre. That is, each bound (or normal) mode of the fibre is orthogonal to each other bound mode.

However, when there are irregularities in the fibre (the most severe of which being a misaligned connector) light can couple (power can transfer) from one mode to another.

Connector Misalignment

When a connector is badly aligned (or rather whenever it is *not* perfectly aligned) some modes will leave the fibre altogether and be lost. Other modes may transfer some or all of their power into different modes. Power will be lost from some modes and transferred to other bound modes.

If you think of light as rays then you can see how a connector misalignment may cause a "ray" to jump from one mode to another. However, the effects of misaligned connectors cannot be described adequately by the ray model. An electromagnetic field is set up at the irregularity and energy can be transferred from one mode to another in ways quite unexplained by the ray model.

Typically a standing wave will be created and this will transfer energy into other modes in both the forward and the backward directions. Of course a lot depends on the nature of the misalignment.

Material Inconsistencies at a Join or Connector

When two fibres are joined even in a "perfect" fusion splice or with a "perfect" connector there may be differences in the RIs of the two fibres at corresponding points on the interface. This is obviously the case where the two fibres are of different specification. However, it can come about even when fibres are of identical specification but were drawn from different pre-forms.

Whenever such a difference occurs you get some mode transformation across the connection - just how much depends on the amount of the mis-match.

Material Irregularities

These might be the presence of impurities or just variations in density of the glass in the fibre.

Fibre Geometry Irregularities

This covers such things as changes in concentricity of the fibre, variations in circularity or thickness (diameter) of the fibre, local variations in the refractive index of the glass etc. One of the major causes of mode coupling is the presence of imperfections at the core-cladding interface.

Bends and Microbends

Bends in the fibre (especially bends that are very tight) can cause some modes to be lost (mode stripping) and others to couple power into different modes.

Microbends are also an issue. These are bends caused by putting fibre into direct contact with a rough surface of some kind and perhaps putting pressure onto it. An extreme example might be to clamp a piece of fibre between two pieces of coarse sandpaper. The "microbends" so created will cause the fibre to lose power and also to couple power between modes.

Mode coupling is one effect that reduces dispersion! If you have a lot of modes travelling at different group velocities then some will arrive ahead of others. If however there is a lot of random swapping between modes some slower modes will swap to faster ones and vice-versa etc. This is a statistical effect. If there is a lot of mode coupling along the path the signal will tend to arrive with less dispersion than if there was no such coupling.[17] Albeit we only want to do it with a highly incoherent light source such as an LED. With a coherent source (such as a laser) mode coupling can be a source of modal noise.

In some (rare) cases we might want to encourage a lot of mode coupling at particular points in the system. When done intentionally this is called "mode scrambling".

2.3.6 Modal Noise

Perhaps the major problem encountered when using lasers with multimode fibre[18] is the phenomenon of "Modal Noise". Modal noise is unlike most noise in the electronic world in that it does not come from outside the system. Rather, modal noise is a distortion of the signal caused by the channel (the fibre and connectors) itself interacting with the signal in such a way as to produce "random" fluctuations in signal power at the receiver. In many circumstances this can have serious effects for the signal-to-noise performance of the communication link.

The problem is almost exclusively confined to the use of high quality (narrow linewidth, coherent[19], stable) laser sources on multimode fibre. The effect is most pronounced when the conditions that create it arise close to the transmitter (within 20 metres or so). Its effect is felt on links of any length but modal noise is rarely created further than 100 metres from the transmitter. Modal Noise comes from the signal itself so it only happens when there is a signal (when the line is in the "1" state). There is no modal noise in the "0" state. Also, it is more pronounced at low bit rates.

---

[17] This is *only* true if all modes are excited. There is some interesting research under way investigating the transfer of power between modes. It appears that power transfer is not completely random and that there are groups of "fast" and "slow" modes. Power transfer between modes within a group appears to be much more probable than transfer between groups. This is further discussed in 7.6.2.1, "Use of Lasers on MM Fibre" on page 424.

[18] As distinct from using lasers on SM fibre.

[19] For a discussion of laser characteristics see 3.3.2, "Semiconductor Laser Diodes" on page 128.

Modal noise is produced in two stages:

1. Mode coupling, and

2. Mode selective loss

Mode Coupling

When you couple a laser to a multimode fibre the light will travel in many modes along the fibre. If the laser involved is narrow in linewidth and stable (doesn't hop between lasing modes too frequently) the light launched into the fibre will be coherent and in phase in all (or most) of the excited fibre modes. After travelling a very short distance along the fibre the light in each mode will be still at *exactly* the same wavelength but the modes will be out of phase with each other. (Because the group velocity of each mode is different.) This is not much of a problem as when the signal is received each mode will impinge on a different spot on the receiving diode and phase differences will not matter.

However, mode coupling effects (discussed previously in 2.3.5, "Mode Coupling" on page 62) cause light from multiple modes to merge into the same mode. When this happens the phase differences will cause interference in the new mode.

This is a complex process. If two newly mixed signals happen to be about the same amplitude and 180 degrees out of phase then the signals will destructively interfere with one another in the new mode. In this case no power can travel in the new mode. For other phase mismatches the signal loss will be a lot less than total but in most cases the signal power will be significantly reduced. Only in the very unlikely case of the signals being exactly in-phase will all the signal power be coupled into the new mode. However, when "interference" of this kind occurs we never actually lose any power.[20] Power is coupled somewhere else (into other modes).

If the sending laser changes wavelength by jumping to another lasing mode then the effects will change utterly. Mode coupling behavior at an irregularity will change when the wavelength (or the temperature) changes. Of course even the slightest change in laser wavelength will cause very large changes in the phases of the mixed signals. All of this can change the amplitude of the mixed signal significantly and abruptly.

---

[20] Interference was discussed earlier in 2.1.3.2, "Transmission through a Sheet of Glass" on page 27.

Thus we have a picture of power travelling in many modes along a fibre where the distribution of power between the modes is changing abruptly and quite randomly with even very slight variations in lasing wavelength.

It should be emphasised that mode coupling behavior is *not* noise of itself nor is it a direct source of noise. It is the normal way in which laser light travels on a multimode fibre. Noise is created when mode selective loss is present.

Mode Selective Loss

A large irregularity in the fibre (such as a bad connector) causes not only the coupling of modes but also the loss of modes completely from the fibre. If we just think of the loss characteristic, some modes will be completely lost, some will couple their power to other modes but the power will stay in the fibre and other modes may be minimally affected.

So, when the signal described above as changing randomly and abruptly from mode to mode meets a bad connector you get a loss of signal power which varies randomly and abruptly. Even though the signal power loss from each mode at a particular connector is constant, the power arriving moves rapidly from mode to mode. For example, if one particular mode is lost at a connector then no signal is lost when there is no power being carried in that mode and a lot of power is lost when there is a lot of power in the mode. Because the signal power is shifting into and out of that mode quickly and randomly, there is a loss of total signal power which occurs at random (this is noise)!

The result is that "noise" appears in the received signal. A deterioration in signal-to-noise ratio of up to 10 dB can sometimes be seen in this situation.

If we have a relatively uniform fibre with no bad loss points, minor irregularities will nevertheless stimulate mode coupling. As we get further and further from the transmitter the signal becomes more and more mixed and the power present in each mode tends to become the same as the amount of power in each other mode. When such a signal meets a source of mode selective loss (such as the bad connector described above) although power loss occurs there is no "noise" effect because the power loss does not vary.

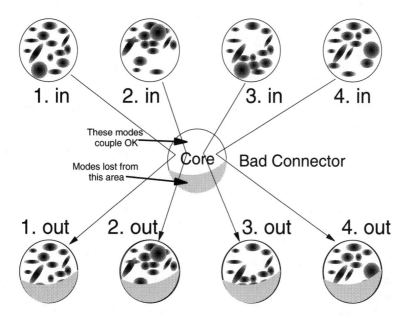

Figure 33. Origin of Modal Noise. The speckle pattern changes rapidly over time, however, energy is conserved and all the power is conserved. When the signal meets a lossy connector, power is lost from some modes and other modes may be unaffected. Since the amount of power in the lost modes changes randomly, the amount of power passing the connector varies randomly.

The process is illustrated[21] in Figure 33. The speckle patterns in the top row of the figure represent the changing power distribution of a signal as it passes a particular point on the fibre. Notice that although the speckles change the total amount of power in the fibre remains constant.

Note: The speckle pattern is used here to illustrate the fact that power is shifting between modes. Speckles are *not* modes. A speckle pattern observed at the endface of a fibre is an interference pattern between arriving modes. It is not a picture of the arriving modes themselves. In this example we have taken some liberties with fact in implying that the shaded areas represent power arriving at the endface. However, the point is that the distribution of power arriving at the endface of the fibre (at a connector) varies randomly and quickly. Power arriving at specific parts of the endface is lost and power arriving elsewhere is coupled into the next section of fibre.

---

[21] exaggerated

Since the amount of power arriving at the parts of the interface where power is lost is *varying* then we lose varying amounts of power.

The "core" in the centre of the figure represents a bad connector where all the modes in a particular (shaded) area are lost from the fibre.

- When the pattern 1-in arrives at the lossy connector its power is roughly evenly distributed and so about 25% will be lost (the grey area).

- When the pattern 2-in arrives at the lossy connector not much power is in the lossy area so perhaps only 10% is lost.

- When pattern 3 arrives a lot of power is in the lossy area so perhaps 40% of the power is lost.

- In the final pattern perhaps 20% is lost.

So in the above example as a constant amount of power passes the lossy connector the output power varies 75%, 90%, 60%, 80%... These variations constitute noise.

It is obvious that this effect will not happen with an incoherent light source (such as an LED). Also, if the laser is multimoded and it hops very frequently between modes[22] then the effect is reduced quite markedly. However, if the coherence time of the laser is long (meaning it has a narrow linewidth) then we can get degradation of the signal.

There are many ways to minimise modal noise effects:

1. Keep connector loss to a minimum. Connectors with a loss of less than 1 dB create very little modal noise. The real issue is with connectors showing losses of around 3 dB close to the transmitter. Mode selective loss of this kind is necessary to produce modal noise. *If there is no loss then there is no noise.*

2. Use a laser that has a relatively large linewidth and hops between lasing modes very frequently. (The very opposite of what we want to do using SM fibre in long distance communication!)

3. Use an ASE (amplified spontaneous emission) laser source with an external modulator. This is cheating as the source is now not really a laser - it is an amplified LED. These are called SLDs (Super Luminescent Diodes) and are really a cross between a laser and an LED. Also, this sometimes requires the use (and added cost) of an external modulator.

---

[22] For many other reasons we don't want this behavior.

4. Do something to the input signal of the laser to destroy its coherence (widen the linewidth).

   One technique is to impose a high frequency "microwave" signal on to the bit stream at the input of the laser. This means that the signal level at the laser input is made to vary sinusoidally over a few cycles in each bit time.

5. Use a short wavelength so that the fibre has a large number of possible modes.

6. Use a large core fibre (to increase the number of modes). We would expect 62.5 micron fibre to have less problem with modal noise than 50 micron.

7. Use a self-pulsating laser diode.

2.3.7 Naming Modes

Detailed discussion and analysis of modal propagation is well outside the scope of this book. However it is useful to understand some of the terminology used in the literature and standard texts. Later it will be seen that multiple modes form in any waveguide situation. This is not limited to fibre propagation but includes, for example, the behavior of light within planar waveguides and within a laser's cavity etc.

Transverse Electric (TE) Modes

TE modes exist when the electric field is perpendicular to the direction of propagation (the z-direction) but there is a small z-component of the magnetic field. Here most of the magnetic field is also perpendicular to the z-direction but a small z-component exists.

This implies that the wave is not travelling quite straight but is reflecting from the sides of the waveguide. However, this also implies that the "ray" path is meridional (it passes through the centre or axis of the waveguide). It is not circular or skewed.

Transverse Magnetic (TM) Modes

In a TM mode the magnetic field is perpendicular to the direction of propagation (z) but there is a small component of the electric field in this direction. Again this is only a small component of the electric field and most of it is perpendicular to the z-axis.

Rather than talk about field components here it might be better to say that the orientation of the electric field is only a few degrees away from being perpendicular to the z-axis.

Transverse ElectroMagnetic (TEM) Modes

In the TEM mode both the electric and magnetic fields are perpendicular to the z-direction. The TEM mode is the only mode of a single-mode fibre.

Helical (Skew) Modes (HE and EH)

In a fibre, most modes actually travel in a circular path of some kind. In this case components of both magnetic and electric fields are in the z-direction (the direction of propagation). These modes are designated as either HE or EH (H = magnetic) depending on which field contributes the most to the z-direction.

Linearly Polarised (LP) Modes

It turns out that because the RI difference between core and cladding is quite small much can be simplified in the way we look at modes.[23] In fibre propagation you can use a single-mode designation to approximate all of the others. Thus TE, TM, HE and EH modes can all be summarised and explained using only a single set of LP modes.

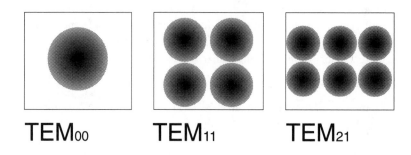

$$TEM_{00} \qquad TEM_{11} \qquad TEM_{21}$$

Figure 34. Energy Distribution of Some TEM Modes. The numbering system used here applies to TE, TM and TEM modes.

It is conventional to number the TE and TM modes according to the number of nulls in their energy pattern across the waveguide. Thus mode TE_{00} would have a single energy spot in the centre of the waveguide and no others. (This would be the same mode as TEM.) Mode TE_{21} would have two nulls (three energy spots) in one direction and a single null (two energy spots) in the other. This is illustrated in Figure 34.

When the subscript numbers are low (0,1,2) the modes are often referred to as "low order" modes. When the subscripts are high numbers the modes are referred to as "high order" modes.

---

[23] Anything that makes this area simpler has got to be good.

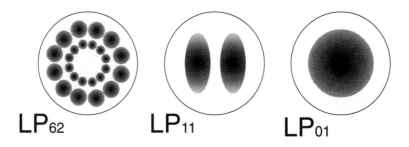

$$LP_{62} \qquad LP_{11} \qquad LP_{01}$$

Figure 35. Energy Distribution of Some LP Modes in Fibre

LP mode numbering is different from TE or TM mode numbering. This is illustrated in Figure 35. LP modes are designated LP_{lm} where m is the number of maxima along a radius of the fibre (note here the number of maxima rather than the number of nulls as before). l here is half the number of maxima around the circumference. Roughly, m is related to the angle of incidence of the ray with the core/cladding interface. l tells us how tight the spiral (helix) is.

The fundamental mode (straight down the centre) is thus referred to in different ways: LP_{01}, HE_{11} or TEM_{00}. In practice, TE and TM designations are usually used when discussing lasers and planar waveguides. LP is used when discussing MM fibre propagation.

2.4 Single-Mode Propagation

The simple way to think about single-mode propagation is to say that the core of the fibre is so small compared with the wavelength of the light that the light is confined to go in one path (or mode) only - straight down the middle. The best way to conceptualise transmission here is to think of light as an electromagnetic wave in a waveguide. This is not the time to think about "rays" of light or even of "photons".

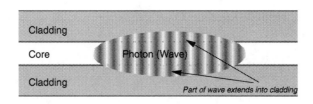

Figure 36. Single-Mode Propagation

Figure 36 shows a schematic of a quantum of light (photon) travelling down a single-mode fibre. The important point here is that the light *must* be thought of as an electromagnetic wave. The electric and magnetic fields decrease exponentially as we move away from the axis of the fibre but nevertheless a significant amount of the optical power travels in the cladding. This does *not* mean that a percentage of the rays or a percentage of the photons travel in the cladding. The electromagnetic wave extends from the core into the cladding and therefore a percentage of *each* electromagnetic wave travels in the cladding.

2.4.1 Single-Mode Characteristics

2.4.1.1 Mode Field Diameter (MFD) and Spot Size

As we have seen optical power (in single-mode fibre) travels in both the core and the cladding. In many situations, not the least being when we join fibre, we need a number that will give us a measure of the extent of the region that carries the optical signal. In single-mode fibre the core diameter is not sufficient.

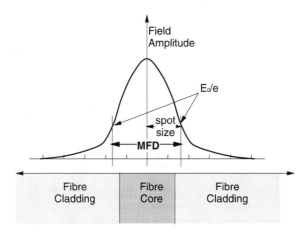

Figure 37. *Mode Field Definition. The mode field is defined as the distance between the points where the strength of the electric field is decayed to 0.37 (1/e) of the peak.*

We introduce the concept of the "mode field". The mode field can be considered the effective core of the fibre although the real core size is typically somewhat smaller. One important point is that there is no abrupt boundary that defines the extent of the mode field. Even though the signal decays exponentially there is no exact cutoff point. Therefore we must choose an arbitrary point as the boundary.

Figure 37 shows the distribution of optical power across the diameter of a typical single-mode fibre. The definition of the mode field diameter is shown. The MFD of standard SMF at 1550 nm is between 10.5 microns and 11 microns depending on the fibre. In the 1310 nm band the MFD of standard fibre is 9.3 microns.

The *spot size* is also sometimes used to characterise single-mode fibre. The diameter of the spot is just the radius of the mode field.

2.4.1.2 *Field Strength at the Fibre End*

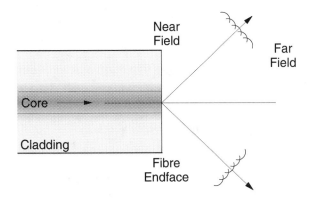

Figure 38. Fields at the End of the Fibre

When the intensity of light is measured at the end of a fibre there are two places at which it can be done - right at the endface itself and some distance away from it.

Near Field

> This is the electromagnetic field at the endface of the fibre itself. In a single-mode fibre this will usually be a profile of the bound mode but if the measurement is made close to the transmitter there may be cladding modes present as well.

> Note that just as described in 2.1.3.2, "Transmission through a Sheet of Glass" on page 27, about 4% of the light reaching the end of the fibre will be reflected (unless an anti-reflection coating is used).

Far Field

> It is extremely difficult to measure the near field directly. Thus the far field is measured and used to calculate the characteristics of the near field such as mode field diameter etc.

The far field consists of a series of lobes spread out away from the axis of the fibre. This is due to the fact that light leaving the endface diffracts in many directions.

2.4.1.3 Bend Loss in Single-Mode Fibre

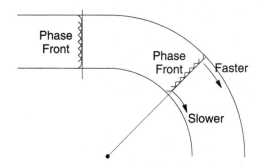

Figure 39. *Reason for Bend Loss in Single-Mode Fibre*

Consider light in SM fibre propagating along the fibre as a wave. There is a phase front which moves along the fibre perpendicular to the direction of travel. The wave front must be in-phase with itself across the diameter of the field. Consider Figure 39. As the phase front moves into a bend the light at the inner radius of the bend *must* move more slowly than the light at the outer radius (considering a single wave occupying all of the mode field). This means that at the outer edge (of the core) the light must experience a lower RI than it would in a straight fibre. If the bend becomes tight enough the apparent RI of the edge of the core will lower to become equal to the RI of the cladding; thus, the wave is no longer confined and will escape from the fibre.

2.4.1.4 Cutoff Wavelength

The cutoff wavelength is the shortest wavelength at which the fibre will be single-moded. Wavelengths shorter than the cutoff will travel in multiple modes whereas wavelengths longer than the cutoff will travel in a single mode.

2.4.1.5 G.652 "Standard" Fibre

The characteristics of single-mode fibre were specified by the International Telecommunications Union (ITU) in the 1980's. The key specifications are as follows:

- Cladding diameter = 125 microns.

- Mode field diameter = 9-10 microns at 1300 nm wavelength.

- Cutoff wavelength = 1100-1280 nm.

- Bend loss (at 1550 nm) must be less than 1 dB for travel through 100 turns of fibre wound on a spool of 7.5 cm diameter.

- Dispersion in the 1300 nm band (1285-1330 nm) must be less than 3.5 ps/nm/km. At wavelengths around 1550 nm dispersion should be less than 20 ps/nm/km.[24]

- The rate of change of dispersion with wavelength must be less than .095 ps/nm²/km. This is called the dispersion slope.

2.4.2 Dispersion in Single-Mode Fibre

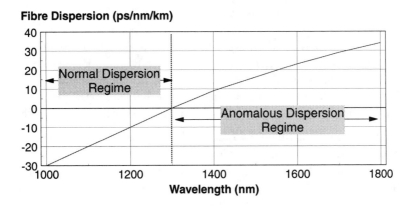

Figure 40. *Dispersion of "Standard" Single-Mode Fibre*

Since modal dispersion cannot occur in single-mode fibre (as you only have one mode), the major sources of dispersion are material (or chromatic) dispersion and waveguide dispersion.

Material (Chromatic) Dispersion

This is caused by the fact that the refractive index of the glass we are using varies (slightly) with the wavelength. Some wavelengths therefore have higher group velocities and so travel faster than others. Since every pulse consists of a range of wavelengths it will spread out to some degree during its travel.

---

24 Picoseconds of dispersion per nanometer of signal bandwidth per kilometer of distance travelled.

All optical signals consist of a range of wavelengths. This range may be only a fraction of a nanometer wide but there is always a range involved. Typically optical pulses used in communications systems range from about .2 nm wide to 5 nm wide for systems using single-mode fibre (with lasers).

Waveguide Dispersion

The shape (profile) of the fibre has a very significant effect on the group velocity. This is because the electric and magnetic fields that constitute the pulse of light extend outside of the core into the cladding. The amount that the fields overlap between core and cladding depends strongly on the wavelength. The longer the wavelength the further the the electromagnetic wave extends into the cladding.

The RI experienced by the wave is an average of the RI of core and cladding *depending on the relative proportion of the wave that travels there.* Thus since a greater proportion of the wave at shorter wavelengths is confined within the core, the shorter wavelengths "see" a *higher* RI than do longer wavelengths. (Because the RI of the core is higher than that of the cladding.) Therefore shorter wavelengths tend to travel more slowly than longer ones. Thus signals are dispersed (because every signal consists of a range of wavelengths).

The good news here is that these two forms of dispersion have opposite signs, so they tend to counteract one another. Figure 40 on page 75 shows the wavelength dependent dispersion characteristics of "standard" single-mode fibre. Notice that the two forms of dispersion cancel one another at a wavelength of 1310 nm. Thus if the signal is sent at 1310 nm dispersion will be minimised.

Dispersion (from all causes) is often grouped under the name "Group Velocity Dispersion" (GVD). On standard single-mode fibre we consider two GVD regimes - the "normal dispersion regime" and the "anomalous dispersion regime".

Normal Dispersion Regime

The normal dispersion regime is represented in Figure 40 on page 75 at the left of the point where the line crosses the zero dispersion point. In this region the long wavelengths travel faster than the short ones! Thus after travelling on a fibre wavelengths at the red end[25] of the pulse spectrum will arrive first. This is called a positive chirp!

---

[25] The use of the terms "red end" and "blue end" here requires some explanation. Any wavelength longer than about 700 nm is either visible red or infra-red. Thus all of the wavelengths in question can be considered "red". However, it is very useful to identify the shorter wavelength (higher frequency) end of a pulse spectrum as the "blue end" and the longer wavelength (lower frequency) end as the "red end".

Anomalous Dispersion Regime

This is represented by the section of the figure to the right of the zero crossing point. Here, the short wavelengths (blue end of the spectrum) travel faster than the long wavelengths (red end). After travel on a fibre the shorter wavelengths will arrive first. This is considered a negative chirp.

Note: The definitions of the words "normal" and "anomalous" given above are consistent with those used in most textbooks and in the professional literature. In some engineering contexts the use of the terms is *reversed*. That is, what we have defined above as normal becomes anomalous and what we defined as anomalous is called normal.

It seems obvious that the wider the spectral width of our signal the more dispersion we will have. Conversely, the narrower the signal the less dispersion. An infinitely narrow signal (a single wavelength) wouldn't disperse at all! Sadly, it couldn't carry any information either! Modulation of a signal widens its bandwidth.

In SM fibre dispersion is usually quoted in picoseconds of dispersion per nanometer of spectral width per kilometer of propagation distance. (ps/nm/km)

The subject of compensation for dispersion is discussed in more detail in 7.5, "Control of Dispersion in Single-Mode Fibre Links" on page 411.

2.4.2.1 Polarisation Mode Dispersion (PMD)

In single-mode fibre we really have not one but two modes (travelling on physically the same path). This is due to the fact that light can exist in two orthogonal polarisations. So we can send two possible signals without interference from one another on single-mode fibre if their polarisations are orthogonal. In normal single-mode fibre a signal consists of both polarisations. However, polarisation states are *not* maintained in standard SM fibre. During its journey light couples from one polarisation to the other randomly.

Birefringence is the name given to the characteristic found in some materials and in some geometries where the ray path exhibits a different refractive index to the different polarisations. This happens in normal single-mode fibre in that there is usually a very slight difference in RI for each polarisation. It can be a source of dispersion but this is usually less than .5 ps/nm/km (for most applications trivial). The effect is to cause a circular or elliptical polarisation to form as the signal travels along the fibre. Dispersion resulting from the birefringent properties of fibre is called "Polarisation Mode Dispersion" (PMD).

More important, it is a source of "Birefringent Noise". This is a form of modal noise (see 2.3.6, "Modal Noise" on page 64). It is also called "Polarisation Modal Noise" in some publications. The mechanism involved is quite similar to the mechanism responsible for modal noise. As the light propagates along the fibre it constantly changes in polarisation in response to variations in the fibre's composition and geometry. Power is not lost but the axes of polarisation and the orientation of magnetic and electric fields in relation to them constantly change. If there is a polarisation sensitive device in the circuit that has significantly higher losses in one polarisation mode than the other, then the effect of meeting with a signal that is constantly changing in polarisation is to produce changes in total signal power. These changes constitute birefringent noise.

2.4.2.2 Dispersion Shifted Fibre

So-called "standard" single-mode optical fibre has its dispersion null point (where waveguide dispersion and material dispersion cancel each other out) at a wavelength of 1310 nm. This was one of the reasons that almost all current long distance fibre networks operate at that wavelength. But there are a lot of very good reasons that we would like to operate in the 1550 nm band. These reasons are principally:

- Fibre attenuation is a lot lower in the 1550 nm band.

- Erbium doped fibre amplifiers (EDFAs) operate in this band. It is true that praseodymium (Pr) doped amplifiers are available which operate in the 1300 band but their quality is not anywhere near as good as the erbium ones.

- WDM systems require a large amplified bandwidth and this means that we want to use the 1550 window and EDFAs.

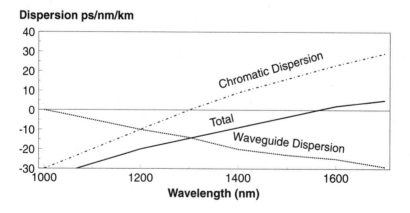

Figure 41. Dispersion Shifted Fibre

Dispersion of standard SM fibre at 1550 nm is very large (Around 17 ps/nm/km). We can mitigate the effects of this quite a lot by using lasers with very narrow linewidths but nevertheless it is a very significant problem.

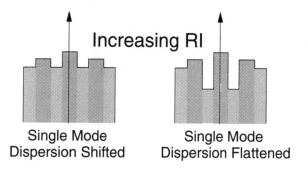

Figure 42. Profiles of Dispersion Shifted and Dispersion Flattened Fibre

This has led to the development of special fibre that has its dispersion minimum at 1550 nm. This is done by manipulating the core profile to introduce dispersion in the opposite direction (with the opposite sign) from the direction in which chromatic dispersion operates. The core profile of this fibre is shown in Figure 42.

Currently dispersion shifted fibre has a number of problems that make it unattractive.

1. It is more prone than standard fibre to some forms of nonlinearity that cause signal "breakup". It has a slightly smaller MFD so electric and magnetic field strengths are greater causing more nonlinearity.

2. The big problem is that it delivers precisely what the name suggests: very low dispersion in the 1550 nm transmission window. But if you are building a WDM system this means that signals on different WDM channels propagate at very nearly the same speed. This should be goodness but so called "four-wave mixing effects" are emphasised because the signals stay in-phase over a relatively long distance. So you get the optical equivalent of near-end crosstalk (NEXT). This is interference between the optical channels!

To overcome this the fibre suppliers have a new (very expensive) fibre that "guarantees" a certain level of dispersion! (About 4 ps/nm/km.) When the price is right it is predicted that this will become the new standard for single-mode long distance cabling.

2.4.2.3 Non-Zero Dispersion-Shifted (WDM-Optimised) Fibre

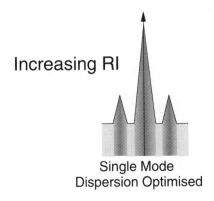

Figure 43. *Non-Zero Dispersion-Shifted Fibre RI Profile*

The major fibre manufacturers now market a fibre specifically designed for WDM systems. Called "Non-zero dispersion-shifted fibre" (NZ-DSF), this fibre has a dispersion of around 4 ps/nm/km in the 1530-1570 nm band. This low but positive dispersion figure, minimises dispersion of the signal while avoiding the unwanted effects of four-wave mixing between WDM channels.

Fibres from different manufacturers have somewhat different characteristics. AT&T calls its dispersion optimised fibre "Tru-Wave" and Corning uses the name SMF-LS.

2.4.2.4 Large Effective-Area Fibres

One of the problems of the dispersion-shifted fibre designs is that they can handle only a relatively low maximum optical power level compared to standard fibre.[26] This limitation in power handling capacity is caused by the fact that the effective cross-sectional area of the core (A_{eff}) is less than that of standard fibre. Standard fibre has an A_{eff} of 80 μm² where NZ-DSF has an A_{eff} of 55 μm².

As described in 2.4.5, "Non-Linear High-Power Effects" on page 87 there are a number of non-linear effects that occur when light is transmitted on a fibre. These effects are almost solely dependent on the *intensity* of light in the fibre core. The smaller the core area the higher will be the power density for any given power level. The smaller effective area of dispersion-shifted fibres therefore limits the power handling capacity of these fibres significantly.

---

[26] Indeed the power handling capacity of standard fibre is quite low enough anyway.

The maximum power handling capabilities of a fibre are extremely important in high bit-rate systems and in WDM systems.

Large effective-area fibres are designed to have an effective area similar to that of traditional (standard) single-mode fibre. For example, Corning's LEAF fibre has an A_{eff} of 72 μm^2.

Because these fibres are designed for use in WDM systems in the 1550 nm band they are NZ-DSF fibres (as described above) and have core profiles similar to that shown in Figure 43 on page 80.

2.4.2.5 Dispersion Flattened Fibre

By using a very sophisticated fibre profile (see Figure 42 on page 79) it is possible to arrange things so that dispersion over the whole range from 1300 nm to 1700 nm is less than about 3 ps/nm/km.

The idea behind this kind of fibre was to install a fibre which would allow people to use 1300 nm systems today and change to the 1550 nm band sometime in the future when needed. It was a good idea in its time (when equipment for the 1550 nm band was not yet available) but has a very significant problem: attenuation experienced in this type of fibre is extremely high (up to 2 dB/km). Dispersion flattened fibre is used in some optical devices but hasn't been used for significant wide area cabling.

2.4.2.6 Dispersion Compensating Fibre

It is possible to construct a fibre profile where the total dispersion is over 100 ps/nm/km in the opposite direction to dispersion caused by the material. This can be placed in series with an existing fibre link to "undisperse" a signal. Dispersion compensating fibre with dispersion of -100 ps/nm/km is commercially available however it has an attenuation of .5 dB/km.

DCF typically has a much narrower core than standard SM fibre. This causes the optical signal to be more tightly confined and accentuates problems caused by "non-linear effects" as described in 2.4.5, "Non-Linear High-Power Effects" on page 87. In addition it is typically birefringent and suffers from polarisation mode dispersion. (See 2.4.2.1, "Polarisation Mode Dispersion (PMD)" on page 77.)

The use of dispersion compensating fibre in operational systems is discussed further in 7.5, "Control of Dispersion in Single-Mode Fibre Links" on page 411.

2.4.2.7 Polarisation Maintaining Fibre

Standard single-mode fibre does not maintain the polarisation state. As the signal travels along the fibre power couples between the polarisation modes more or less randomly as minor variations in the geometry of the fibre dictate. Polarisation maintaining fibres are designed to maintain the signal in the polarisation state that it was in when it entered the fibre.

Polarisation maintenance is usually achieved by making the fibre highly birefringent. That is, it has a large difference in refractive index (and thus group velocity) for the two orthogonal polarisations. This is achieved by making the fibre asymmetric in profile. The difference in group velocity between the modes minimises the possibility of coupling as the modes can't stay resonant long enough for significant coupling to take place.

Figure 44. *Polarisation Maintaining Fibre*

There are many different configurations of PMF. Three of the most popular are shown in Figure 44.

Elliptical Core

Elliptical core fibre is the simplest of the PMF fibres but uses a very high level of dopant in the core.

Bow-Tie

Bow Tie fibre is another popular type which operates by creating stresses within the fibre.

PANDA

Polarisation maintaining AND Absorption reducing (fibre) operates by creating lateral pressures (stresses) within the fibre. The shaded area in the figure is an area of fibre doped to create an area of different coefficient of expansion to that of the cladding. In manufacture, as the fibre cools stresses are set up due to differences in contraction. This modifies the RI without requiring such high levels of dopant. Light does not travel in the stressing cores. This means that the unwanted additional attenuation is minimised.

In addition to their profiles PMF fibres need to be made very carefully to avoid irregularities and in particular twists occurring during manufacture.

There are two other (less well explored) routes to making PMF. These are often referred to generically as "low birefringence" fibres because the way polarisation maintenance is achieved is (partly) through the minimisation of birefringence.

1. The first approach is to attempt to make standard fibre with an almost perfectly circular profile and minimal irregularities. The operating principle for this kind of fibre is that there is no reason for power to couple between the two orthogonal polarisation modes unless there are irregularities. This is not easy but PMF fibres have been made this way.

2. The second way is to twist the fibre during manufacture. The effect can be enhanced by deliberately making the fibre with the core off-centre. In this case the two polarisation modes become circular in opposing directions and coupling of power cannot take place.

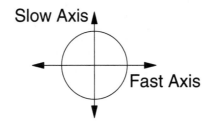

Figure 45. *Axes of Polarisation in PMF*

PMF has two axes of polarisation conveniently named the "fast" and the "slow" axes. Of course the fast axis is the one along which the light experiences a lower RI than on the slow axis. The axes are orthogonal as illustrated in Figure 45.

The objective is that when linearly polarised light is launched into a polarisation-maintaining fibre the polarisation state will remain constant along the fibre. *However, polarisation state remains constant if (and only if) the polarisation at launch matches exactly one of the two polarisation axes of the fibre.* If polarisation state does not match (that is if the axis of polarisation of the launched light is at an angle to the polarisation axes of the fibre) then during propagation the polarisation state will change continuously along the fibre. The polarisation state will rotate. See 2.1.2, "Polarisation" on page 24. Thus in order to use PMF you have to be careful to align the polarisation of the input light with one or other axis of the fibre.

In PMF the birefringence is quoted as simply the difference between the RI experienced by light travelling in the fast mode and the RI experienced by light travelling in the slow mode.

In "high-birefringence" PMF fibres the high levels of dopant needed to achieve high birefringence also cause high attenuation. For this reason polarisation maintaining fibres are not used for long distance communications. (Also, they are expensive and don't offer very much improvement in signal transmission.) However, PMF is used extensively in many situations in interconnecting polarisation sensitive fibre devices. For example the connection between a laser and an external (polarisation sensitive) modulator or the construction of a fibre ring resonator (which relies for its operation on maintaining polarisation). They are also widely used in non-communication fibre optic devices such as sensors.

2.4.2.8 Spun Fibre

This was referred to briefly above. Spun fibre has no polarisation dependence at all! It is made by taking a PANDA fibre pre-form and spinning the pre-form while the fibre is being drawn. This results in a twist in the fibre of about one revolution every 5 mm or so. This is very difficult to do successfully and most times it is made in lengths of only around 200 metres. Spun fibre is not used for distance transmission, however, it is used in many experimental devices.

2.4.3 Mode Partition Noise

As discussed in 3.3.3, "Fabry-Perot Lasers" on page 129, Fabry-Perot lasers do not produce a single wavelength. They "hop" between a number of wavelengths over a band somewhere between 5 and 8 nm in width.

The problem is that fibre dispersion varies with wavelength. When the laser changes wavelength the group velocity changes. Thus instead of getting an even dispersion as we might expect if all wavelengths were produced simultaneously, we get random and unpredictable variations in received signal strength - even during a single bit time. This is a form of noise and degrades the quality of the received signal.

Mode partition noise is a problem in single-mode fibre operation. In multimode fibre modal noise and intermodal dispersion dominate.

2.4.4 Reflections and Return Loss Variation

There are many places in an optical communications system where reflections can occur.[27] In a single-mode fibre link the predominant source of reflections is from connectors and bad fibre joins. Interfaces to equipment can also be a source of reflections.

The most obvious result of reflections is that power is lost from the transmission link. Another problem is that reflections disrupt the operation of some types of lasers (DFB and DBR) causing loss of signal quality and noise although these devices are usually protected by isolators to minimise this problem.

However, in the context of the optical link, reflections can be a source of noise. This is sometimes called "Return Loss Variation". Return loss is defined as the ratio between incident signal power and reflected signal power.

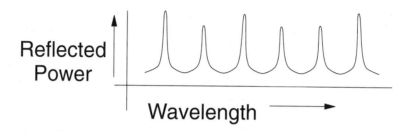

Figure 46. Pattern of Return Loss Variation by Wavelength. Multiple reflections close together on a single-mode link can cause large variations in reflected power between very closely spaced wavelengths. These form a pattern similar to that shown here.

When you measure the amount of reflection in an optical link sometimes you find that the amount of reflected power varies significantly with small changes in the wavelength! This rarely happens with incoherent light but can be significant when high quality lasers are used. These lasers have a "coherence length" of up to 40 metres. Lasers produce coherent, in phase, light for only a short time before shifting to a (very slightly) different wavelength or at least losing phase. Coherence length is simply the distance over which the laser's light travels in a fibre while the source stays in phase with itself. (See Coherence Length and Coherence Time on page 125.) While the coherence length can be up to 40 metres as mentioned above it is typically around 10 metres for good quality communications DFB lasers.

---

[27] See 7.4.4, "Reflections" on page 408.

The effect is caused by interactions between reflections! The basic effect was introduced in 2.1.3.2, "Transmission through a Sheet of Glass" on page 27. Reflections interfere with each other *if they occur within the coherence length of the signal.* Interference can be constructive (reinforcement) or destructive depending on the distance between the reflection sites and the exact wavelength of the signal. Two reflection sites close enough to each other to be within the signal's coherence length act as a Fabry-Perot cavity. (See 5.8.2, "Fabry-Perot Filter (Etalon)" on page 289.) This means that at a very specific set of wavelengths the cavity will strongly reinforce reflections while at other wavelengths the cavity will suppress them. Notice also from the earlier reference that when reinforcement occurs the reflected signal power is greatly increased (it is not just the sum of the reflections). Two 4% reflections can reinforce to give a 16% reflection! This effect depends also on the relative magnitude of the reflections involved. The maximum effect happens when the reflected signal strengths are equal to one another.

The wavelength of even a high quality signal varies very quickly due to things like laser chirp but also due to the modulation itself. Even very slightly different wavelengths can experience very different amounts of return loss. Thus rapid variations in wavelength can result in rapid variations in reflected power. Of course, rapid variations in the amount of power lost from a signal result in rapid variations in the signal's power. This constitutes noise.

Notice that the pattern in Figure 46 on page 85 is repetitive. The distance between peaks here is called the "Free Spectral Range" (FSR) of the Fabry-Perot cavity. There is a very simple formula that relates the distance between reflection sites to the wavelength and the FSR.

$$FSR = \frac{\lambda^2}{2 \times n \times D}$$

Where n equals the RI of the material and D equals the distance between reflection sites.

For example if we have a bad connector giving two reflections one centimetre apart then we have the following:

$$FSR = \frac{1550 \times 1550}{2 \times 1.45 \times 10,000,000} = .0828 \; nm$$

Here the FSR (distance between reflection peaks) is around .08 nm. In this (carefully chosen) example the FSR is of the same order as laser wavelength variations from a good DFB laser modulated at 2 Gbps!

The effect is not limited to locations close to the transmitter but rather can happen at any place in the link where multiple reflection sites exist within a short distance of one another. It is therefore an important systems consideration on single-mode fibre links that reflections should be minimised. This is especially true if the system uses high quality lasers such as are used in long distance or WDM applications.

2.4.5 Non-Linear High-Power Effects

When light travels in a vacuum, individual waves from different sources do not interact with one another. However, when light travels in a material, it can interact with that material in various ways. This interaction can produce changes in the light wave itself and cause interactions between different light waves with the material acting as an intermediary.

The interaction of light with the material in optical fibre is typically very small and thus interactions between different signals on the same fibre are also very small. However, since the signal travels long distances on fibre, very small effects have the opportunity to build up into large ones. Non-linear effects are ones which increase in significance exponentially as the level of optical power in the fibre is increased. At low power levels there is little or no effect. As power is increased the effects appear and can then become very significant. For example in a particular context Stimulated Brillouin Scattering may have no measurable effect on a signal of 3 mW but a significant effect if the power of the signal is increased to 6 mW.

These effects can be grouped into two classes. "Elastic" effects where although the optical wave interacts with and is affected by the presence of matter there is no energy exchange between the two. The prime example of elastic scattering is four-wave mixing. "Inelastic Scattering" is where there is an energy transfer between the matter involved and the optical wave. Stimulated Brillouin Scattering and Stimulated Raman Scattering are examples of this class. These effects are discussed in the following sections.

As far as transmission on fibre is concerned the non-linear effects are nearly always undesirable. After attenuation and dispersion they provide the next major limitation on optical transmission. Indeed in some situations they are more significant than either attenuation or dispersion. However, many optical devices rely on just these same non-linear effects for their basic operation. A lot of research goes into developing special fibre with increased levels of non-linearity to build more effective devices.

2.4.5.1 Four-Wave Mixing (FWM)

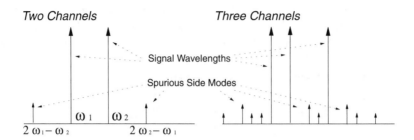

Figure 47. *Four Wave Mixing Effects*

One of the biggest problems in WDM systems is called "Four-Wave Mixing" (FWM). Illustrated in Figure 47, FWM occurs when two or more waves propagate in the same direction in the same (single-mode) fibre. The signals mix to produce new signals at wavelengths which are spaced at the same intervals as the mixing signals. This is easier to understand if we use frequency instead of wavelength for the description. A signal at frequency ω_1 mixes with a signal at frequency ω_2 to produce two new signals one at frequency $2\omega_1-\omega_2$ and the other at $2\omega_2-\omega_1$. The effect can also happen between three or more signals.

There are a number of significant points.

- The effect becomes greater as the channel spacing is reduced. The closer the channels are together the greater the FWM effect.

- FWM is non-linear with signal power. As signal power increases the effect increases exponentially.

- The effect is strongly influenced by chromatic dispersion. FWM is caused when signals stay in phase with one another over a significant distance. The lasers produce light with a large "coherence length" and so a number of signals will stay in phase over a long distance if there is no chromatic dispersion. Here chromatic dispersion is our friend. The greater the dispersion, the smaller the effect of FWM - because chromatic dispersion ensures that different signals do *not* stay in phase with one another for very long.

- If the WDM channels are evenly spaced then the new spurious signals will appear in signal channels and cause noise. One method of reducing the effect of FWM is to space the channels unevenly. This mitigates the problem of added noise (crosstalk) in unrelated channels. However, it doesn't solve the problem of the power that is removed from the signal channels in the process.

Techniques of reducing the effects of FWM are discussed in 7.5.3, "Dispersion Compensating Fibre" on page 415.

2.4.5.2 Stimulated Brillouin Scattering (SBS)

Stimulated Brillouin Scattering is a scattering of light backwards towards the transmitter caused by mechanical (acoustic) vibrations in the transmission medium (fibre). The reflected wave produced is called the "Stokes Wave". The effect is usually trivial but can be very important in situations where a high quality, narrow linewidth laser is used at a relatively high power level.

Stimulated Brillouin Scattering is caused by the presence of the optical signal itself. Even though a signal level of a few milliwatts seems very small, in the tiny cross-section of a single-mode fibre core the field can be very intense. An optical signal is in reality a very strong electromagnetic field. This field causes mechanical vibrations in the fibre which produce a regularly varying pattern of very slight differences in the refractive index. The Brillouin Scattering effect is caused by light being reflected by the diffraction grating created by the regular pattern of RI changes.[28] The reflected light is reflected backwards from a *moving* grating! Hence its frequency is shifted by the Doppler effect. The shift of the reflected wave in standard single-mode fibre is downward in frequency by around 11.1 GHz.[29]

The effect, like Stimulated Raman Scattering (described in the following section), is nonlinear and in practical systems requires a power level of something above 3 mW for any serious effect to be observable (indeed usually its a lot higher than this). It also requires a long interaction length and a very narrow linewidth (long coherence length) signal. In general the signal linewidth must be less than about 100 MHz (around .1 nm) for SBS to become an issue. The effect in the forward direction is experienced as an increase in attenuation. This is rapid and adds noise to the signal. For narrow linewidth signals SBS imposes an upper limit on the usable transmit power.

---

[28] This is a very similar effect to the ones described in 5.7.2, "In-Fibre Bragg Gratings (FBGs)" on page 266 and 5.9.6, "Acoustooptic Tunable Filters (AOTFs)" on page 318.

[29] In fibre there is also a very small forward propagating wave caused by SBS. This is shifted upward in frequency by 11.1 GHz. For all practical purposes this forward propagating wave is so small that it can be safely ignored.

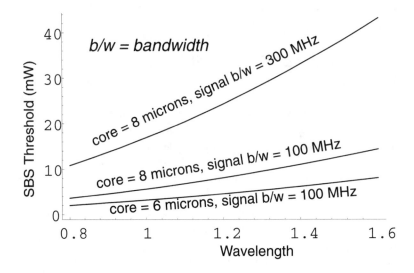

Figure 48. SBS Threshold Variation with Wavelength. *The threshold value is the power level above which SBS causes a significant effect.*

In most current systems SBS has not been much of a problem for the following reasons:

1. Direct modulation of the transmit laser's injection current produces a chirp and broadens the signal. This significantly reduces the impact of SBS.

2. The effect is less in 1300 nm systems than in 1550 nm systems due to the higher attenuation of the fibre.

3. Lasers capable of producing the necessary power level have only recently become available and amplifiers are also a recent innovation.

4. At speeds of below 2.4 GHz it has not been necessary to use either very high power or very narrow linewidth lasers.

5. SBS effects decrease with increase in speed because of the signal broadening affect of the modulation.

In cases where SBS could be a problem the linewidth is often intentionally broadened. This can be done by using an additional RF modulation on the laser injection current, by using an external phase modulator or by using a "self pulsating" laser. Of course increasing the linewidth *mitigates against* long distance transmission because it increases the effect of chromatic dispersion.

However, SBS can be a major problem in three situations:

1. In long distance systems where the span between amplifiers is great and the bit rate low (below about 2.5 Gbps).

2. In WDM systems (up to about 10 Gbps) where the spectral width of the signal is very narrow.

3. In remote pumping of an erbium doped fibre amplifier (EDFA) through a separate fibre. EDFA pumps typically put out about four lines of around only 80 MHz wide. Each of these lines is limited by SBS in the amount of power that can be used.[30] This can significantly limit the potential of remote pumping. Remote pumping is discussed further in 5.2.1.14, "Remote Pumping" on page 216.

2.4.5.3 Stimulated Raman Scattering (SRS)

Stimulated Raman Scattering is caused by a similar mechanism to the one which produces SBS. However, the interactions involved are due to molecular vibrations rather than acoustic ones. Scattered light can appear in both the forward and backward directions. In a single-channel system the "Raman Threshold" (the power level at which Raman Scattering begins to take effect) is very high. Other effects (such as SBS) limit the signal power to much less than the Raman Threshold in single-channel systems.

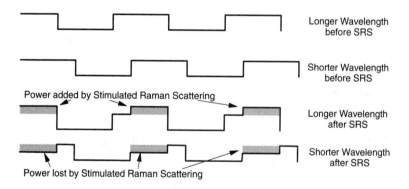

Figure 49. Stimulated Raman Scattering

While Stimulated Raman Scattering is a not an issue in single-channel systems it can be a significant problem in WDM systems. When multiple channels are present, power is transferred from shorter wavelengths to longer ones. This can be a useful effect in that it is possible to build an optical amplifier based on SRS. (See 5.2.7,

---

[30] Just exactly what the limit is varies considerably with the distance involved but in some situations could be as low as 5 mW.

"Raman Effect Amplifiers" on page 229.) But in the transmission system it is a source of noise.

Figure 49 on page 91 shows the principle. Two wavelengths are shown before and after SRS. Notice that power has been transferred from the shorter wavelength to the longer one (from the higher energy wave to the lower energy one). This has resulted in additive noise at the longer wavelength and subtractive noise at the shorter one.

This power transfer is caused by interactions of the light with vibrating molecules. Optical power so transferred is called the "Stokes Wave".

Important characteristics of SRS are:

- *The effect of SRS becomes greater as the signals are moved further and further apart (within some limits).* This is a problem as we would like to separate the signals as much as we can to avoid four-wave mixing effects and when we do we get SRS!

  SRS can take affect over about 40 THz (a very wide range) *below* the higher frequency (shorter wavelength) involved. That is, it can extend over a range of wavelengths of about 300 nm longer than the shortest wavelength involved.

  The effect is maximised when the two frequencies are 13.2 THz apart.

- SRS increases exponentially with increased power. At very high power it is possible for *all* of the signal power to be transferred to the Stokes Wave.

One study concluded that in a 10-channel WDM system with 1 nm channel spacing power levels need to be kept below 3 mw (per channel) if SRS is to be avoided.

2.4.5.4 Carrier-Induced Phase Modulation (CIP)

The presence of light in a fibre causes a (tiny) change in the refractive index of the fibre. This is because the electromagnetic field that constitutes the light acts on the atoms and molecules that make up the glass. This is called the "Kerr Effect". At low intensities the effect is linear; that is, the amount of RI change varies linearly with the intensity of the light. At high intensities the effect is highly non-linear. The RI change caused by a particular amount of intensity change is much greater than the RI change caused by the same amount of intensity change at lower total light levels. This is called the "Nonlinear Kerr Effect".

At very high powers Kerr nonlinearities can be used to balance the effects of chromatic dispersion in the fibre and a "soliton" is formed. (See 12.1, "Solitons" on page 651.)

At medium power levels (below the level needed to form solitons) Kerr effect has been used to construct devices that compress and re-form pulses and hence "undo" the effects of chromatic dispersion.

At low power levels the results of Kerr effect are "self-phase modulation" and "cross-phase modulation".

Self-Phase Modulation (SPM)

As a result of Kerr effects, the RI of the glass experienced by a pulse of light varies depending on the point within the pulse that the RI is experienced. At different points within a single pulse of light in the fibre the RI of the glass is different. So there is a (tiny) difference between the RIs at the leading edge, at the trailing edge and in the middle. This changes the phase of the lightwaves that make up the pulse. Changes in phase amount to changes in frequency. Therefore the frequency spectrum of the pulse is broadened. In many situations the pulse can also be spread out and distorted.

SPM creates a "chirp" (a gradual shift in frequency) over the whole duration of a pulse.[31] This chirp is conceptually like the chirp created by chromatic dispersion in the normal dispersion regime. That is, the chirped pulse has the long wavelengths at the beginning and the short ones at the end. However, unlike chromatic dispersion the chirp produced by SPM is radically different depending on the pulse shape and the instantaneous levels of power within the pulse. Over the duration of a "gaussian" shaped pulse the chirp is reasonably even and gradual. If the pulse involves an abrupt change in power level, such as in the case of a square pulse, then the amount of chirp is much greater than in the case with a gaussian pulse. However, in a square pulse the chirp is confined to the beginning and end of the pulse with little or no effect in the middle.

In single-channel systems where data is sent using Pulse Code Modulation (PCM), SPM usually has a very small effect and in most situations can be ignored. However, in systems where the phase of the signal is significant (such as in phase-shift keyed[32] or coherent systems) SPM can be a serious problem.

Cross-Phase Modulation (XPM)

When there are multiple signals at different wavelengths in the same fibre Kerr effect caused by one signal can result in phase modulation of the other

---

[31] An excellent treatment of SPM (and indeed all of the nonlinear effects) may be found in Agrawal (1989).

[32] See 7.2.9, "Phase Shift Keying (PSK)" on page 393

signal(s)! This is called "Cross-Phase Modulation" (XPM) because it acts between multiple signals rather than within a single signal. In contrast to other nonlinear effects XPM effect involves *no* power transfer between signals. The result can be asymmetric spectral broadening and distortion of the pulse shape. It seems obvious that you can't have XPM without also having SPM. All this of course means added noise.

2.5 Plastic Optical Fibre (POF)

The very first research on optical fibre transmission (in 1955) was done with plastic fibres. Since then the development of silica fibre has all but eliminated plastic from consideration. It survives in niche applications for short distance connections in medical instruments, some industrial instrumentation and in "up-market" consumer hi-fi equipment.

POF is however not dead. It is being actively considered for a number of applications such as networks in the home and small office. In addition new research is opening up a number of other significant possibilities.

The most important characteristic of POF is its thickness. This is because it is the thickness that makes it easy to fit connectors and from this comes low installation cost. Low system cost is the *only* advantage POF has over glass fibres.

Step index POF has a core diameter of 980 microns and a cladding of 20 microns for a fibre diameter of 1 mm. This is a core diameter 100 times larger than single-mode fibre. The total diameter of the fibre is eight times the diameter of typical glass fibre.

While there are many potential plastics that could be considered for use as fibre the one used in current POF systems is called "PMMA" which stands for Poly(Methyl MethylAcrylate).

The result of this is that POF is very easy to fit connectors to. An amateur can add a connector to a POF in about two minutes with minimal training and a special tool that costs around $5. To join or connectorise glass fibre you need a trained person and a special device that can cost up to $20,000. This is the key difference from glass. The fibre itself is about the same cost and tranceivers (for comparable speeds) should cost about the same. However, a major reason that glass fibre is not more extensively used is the cost of installation.

One look at the attenuation characteristics of POF as shown in Figure 50 on page 95 shows that attenuation is very high at all wavelengths. However, wavelengths of 570 nm and 650 nm are feasible for very short distances (up to 100 metres).

An interesting point is that *visible* light is used. At 570 nm only very low power LEDs are available but at 650 nm we can have both low cost lasers and LEDs. Indeed, the red light produced in typical laser pointers used in presentations is 650 nm (although the output power produced by laser pointers is some 10 times higher than the legal "class 1" eye safety limit).

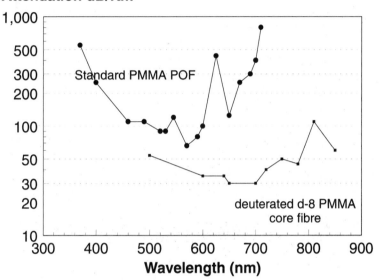

Figure 50. Absorption Spectrum of Plastic Optical Fibre. The upper curve shows typical currently available PMMA POF. The lower curve shows a new type of POF where deuterium has replaced hydrogen in some parts of the molecule. This has the effect of shifting the resonance positions of some chemical bonds and thereby reducing attenuation at the wavelengths of interest.

Both Step-Index (SI) and Graded-Index (GI) forms of POF are available but only the SI is considered commercial at the present time. The specifications of SI POF[33] are as follows:

- Core diameter = 980 microns

- Cladding diameter = 1000 microns (1 mm)

---

[33] It should be noted that there are many different types of POF available. This specification is the one proposed for use with ATM in an office environment.

- Jacket diameter = 2.2 mm

- Attenuation at 650 nm less than 18 dB per 100 metres (180 dB/km!)

- Numerical Aperture = .30

It is claimed that this gives a bandwidth at 100 metres of better than 125 MHz. For GI POF the bandwidth claimed per 100 metres is better than 500 MHz.

Currently proposals are in front of standards bodies suggesting POF in homes at 50 Mbps for a distance of 50 metres and in offices at 155 Mbps over the same distance.

Currently, the major disadvantage of POF is that it cannot be joined by fusion splicing with an acceptable level of signal attenuation. Typical values of 5 dB per join are reported. Much lower figures can be obtained by installing a dry connector. However, there is no easy low loss way of making a join. For the short distances involved this may not matter.

POF has most of the advantages of glass fibre - albeit that it is limited by attenuation to very short distances. As a communications medium glass is *always* significantly better but POF promises to be very much lower in cost to install and to use.

In 1995 early samples of a GI POF were released and also a deuterated POF. These promise longer distances and higher speeds than possible with the current PMMA POF.

2.5.1 POF Research

Currently there is vigorous research activity going on in the use of plastics not only for fibre but for all kinds of optical devices such as lasers, amplifiers, filters etc.

A very promising newer family of plastics are called "amorphous perfluoropolymers". Perfluoropolymers replace the carbon-hydrogen bond in regular polymers with a carbon-fluorine one. These have a lot of highly desirable characteristics but they tend to crystallise easily and are hard to form into useful fibres. Amorphous perfluoropolymers however do not crystallise and form stable glasses. Recent research results suggest that fibres made with amorphous perfluoropolymers can offer at least an order of magnitude better attenuation performance than PMMA and the ability to handle somewhat longer wavelengths (800-900 nm range).

2.6 Hard Polymer (plastic) Clad (silica) Fibre (HPCF)

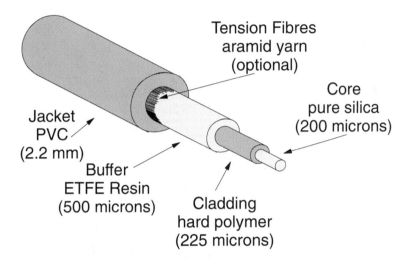

Figure 51. HPCF Structure

Hard Polymer Clad Fibre (HPCF) is the glass fibre industry's answer to POF. The concept is to use a relatively thick glass fibre as a core and a hard plastic coating as the cladding. This has significantly less attenuation than POF and is claimed to cost about the same and to be just as easy to join. It is thinner than POF and therefore suffers from much less modal dispersion.

Of course, many different specifications for HPCF are possible and since (at the time of writing) these are not fully standardised some things may change. The following are the specifications for HPCF as approved by the ATM Forum for use with ATM at 155 Mbps over distances of up to 100 metres.

- Core diameter = 200 microns

- Cladding diameter = 225 microns

- Buffer diameter = 500 microns

- Jacket diameter = 2.2 mm

- Attenuation (at 650 nm) = .8 dB/100 metres

- Numerical Aperture = .3

- Bend radius = 2 cm (loss of 0.05 db at 2 cm)

- Bandwidth = 10 MHz/km

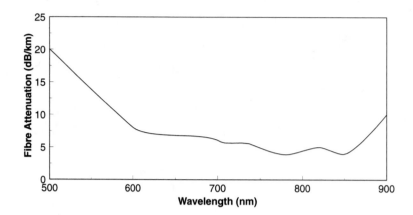

Figure 52. *Attenuation of HPCF in the Short Wavelength Band*

Attenuation is relatively high compared to other types of glass fibre but this is because the wavelength used is in the high-attenuation part of the glass absorption spectrum (650 nm). This wavelength was chosen to be the same as that used for POF. The light sources used are light-emitting diodes (LEDs) rather than lasers partly due to a concern with modal noise if lasers were used. Of course there is no question here of graded index fibre. HPCF is step index with a pure silica core and plastic cladding.

The specifications for HPCF are intentionally very close to those of POF with the exception that HPCF has about 20 times lower attenuation. Also the core diameter of SI HPCF is significantly less than that of POF and therefore the fibre has significantly lower levels of dispersion than POF.

Chapter 3. Optical Sources

There are two kinds of devices that are used as light sources: Lasers and LEDs (Light Emitting Diodes).

3.1 Light Production

Taking the most general view, there is only one way that light can be produced: that is, through the rapid change of state of an electron from a state of relatively high energy to a (more stable) state of lower energy. When this happens the energy has to go somewhere and it is often[34] emitted in the form of light. Of course, this almost always takes place in the context of a particular material and structure. The electron concerned could be bound within a molecule (albeit loosely) or it could be relatively free within the material.

Emission of light, (in the form of a photon) can take place either spontaneously or it can be "stimulated" by the presence of another photon of the right energy level.

Spontaneous emission is really the normal case. When an electron is elevated to a high energy state this state is usually unstable and the electron will spontaneously return to a more stable state very quickly (within a few picoseconds) emitting a photon as it does so. When light is emitted spontaneously its direction and phase will be random but the wavelength will be determined by the amount of energy that the emitting electron must give up.

Stimulated emission is what happens in the operation of a laser.[35] In some situations when an electron enters a high energy (excited) state it is able to stay there for a relatively long time (a few microseconds) before it changes state spontaneously. When an electron is in this semi-stable (metastable) high energy state it can be "stimulated" by the presence of a photon of light to emit its energy in the form of another photon. In this case the incident photon must have the right energy (wavelength)[36] within quite small limits.

---

[34] When light is not emitted, energy is given up in the form of "phonons". Phonons are discrete quantities of kinetic energy which cause mechanical vibrations of the atom concerned.

[35] LASER is an acronym for "Light Amplification by the **Stimulated Emission** of Radiation".

[36] The amount of energy in a photon directly determines its wavelength. See 3.2.2, "Construction and Operation of LEDs" on page 105.

It is of fundamental importance to understand that **when stimulated emission takes place the emitted photon has exactly the same wavelength, phase and direction as that of the photon which stimulated it!**

As mentioned earlier, depending on the particular material in which the electron is found, it could be bound within a molecule or relatively free to move through the material (in the conduction band[37]).

For spontaneous or stimulated emission to occur, energy must be supplied to boost the electron from its low energy state to a higher energy state. The energy can come from many sources:

Heat

One of the most common ways of providing energy to boost an electron into a higher energy state is to apply heat. Of course, most times the electron immediately gives off its energy in the form of a photon and returns to a lower energy state. This is the principle of ordinary incandescent light.

Electrical Discharge

When an electric current is passed through a gas (such as neon), energy from the current "ionises" (breaks the chemical bonds in) the gas. This process injects energy into electrons within the gas and when these electrons are reclaimed into molecules energy is given off in the form of light. (This is often called "fluorescent" light.)

Electric Current

This is different from electrical discharge. This is the principle involved in semiconductor lasers and LEDs. An electric current applied to a semiconductor p-n junction requires that electrons and holes recombine at the junction. This recombination results in electrons going from the high energy "conduction" band to the lower more stable "valence" band. This can result in either spontaneous emission or lasing depending on how the device is constructed.

Chemical Reaction

There are many chemical reactions which result in the emission of light. This is *not* always through a heating effect. During a chemical reaction atoms and molecules are restructured. Often as a result of the restructuring process

---

[37] For a discussion of energy bands see A.1.2, "Why Does a Conductor Conduct?" on page 682

electrons are left in high energy (unstable) states. This excess energy is often given off in the form of heat but it can also be given off in the form of light.

Biological Reactions (Bioluminescense)

Biological reactions are just chemical reactions taking place within living organisms. However, it helps to mention them separately as they appear to be quite different.

There are many biological organisms that use "bioluminescense" for attracting prey or mates or to scare predators. Within these organisms light is generated by initiating chemical reactions that leave electrons in a high energy (excited) state. These excited electrons subsequently make the transition to more stable (lower energy) states by giving up their energy in the form of light. The glow worm and the North American firefly are good examples but there are also many fish and even bacteria that are capable of light generation.

In the firefly, light is emitted by an enzyme called "luciferase" which gives out a green light during the oxidation of its chemical substrate, luciferin.

Absorption of Light

Many substances will absorb light of one particular wavelength, move to a higher (excited) energy state and then (either spontaneously or through stimulation) give off light at a different wavelength.

Of course most substances absorb light but do not exhibit this effect.

A good example here is found in the common fluorescent light. The light produced directly by the electrical discharge within the tube (usually in argon gas) is in the ultra-violet (UV) and invisible! This UV light is absorbed by a coating (called a phosphor) on the inside of the tube and then re-emitted as visible light.

Nuclear Radiation

There are three types of nuclear radiation and each can deliver energy to a substance and cause spontaneous emission.

1. An α (alpha) particle is large and heavy and contains a strong positive charge. (It is the nucleus of a Helium atom.) When an α particle moves through a material it usually does so with a very high energy. It will "knock off" electrons from almost any molecule it encounters along its path. This effect is called ionisation. This transfers energy to electrons and they enter a higher energy state. When the electron transits to a lower energy (stable) state it *may* give out light. Probably the most common and most sensitive radiation detector (the scintillation counter) uses this effect.

2. β (beta) particles are electrons moving with great speed and hence very great energy. They have similar affects on most materials as α particles do.

3. γ (gamma) rays are electromagnetic radiation. They are really just very short wavelength (or very high frequency) light. However they can have extremely high energies. A single γ ray (considered as a high energy photon) can have an energy of around a million times higher than the energy in a photon of visible light.

   γ rays don't get fully absorbed by collision with a single atom as regular light photons do. They act similarly to α and β particles, in that they ionise many atoms along their paths until they lose all their energy and are completely absorbed.

3.1.1 Spontaneous Emission

We use different terms to describe spontaneously emitted light depending on how the energy was supplied:

Incandescent light is any light produced as a result of heating the material.

Fluorescent light is light produced by spontaneous emission from an energy source that is *not* heat. The term fluorescence is used if the emission stops when the external source of energy is removed (or very soon after).

Phosphorescent light is also produced from an energy source that is not heat *but* where the emission continues for some time after the external source of energy is removed.

   Sometimes we use the term (incorrectly) to denote light produced by spontaneous emission when the external source of energy is not immediately apparent. For example, the paint used for the numbers on watch dials earlier this century used a small amount of Radium mixed into the paint as its energy source.[38] At the time this was called phosphorescence when really it was fluorescence. The same is true of light produced in biological systems (by bacteria for example).

It is very important to understand that the ways in which a substance will absorb energy and the ways in which it can spontaneously emit energy are very complex. It is often simpler to think of atoms in isolation and the states of their electron orbits without the effects of adjacent atoms within a material. However, *the context of the*

----

[38] This is no longer legal as it is a severe health hazard.

structure of the material in which the atom is found is critical to its light emitting characteristics.

Electrons *cannot* take arbitrary orbits or states within a molecule. They can take only a quite small (finite) number of states (orbits). When an electron jumps from a high energy orbit to a lower energy one (emitting a photon in the process), the emitted photon has an energy level which represents the difference between the higher and lower energy states of the electron's transition. In A.1.2, "Why Does a Conductor Conduct?" on page 682, electron energy states within a molecule are discussed in more detail.

Thus most substances have characteristic spectra (the light energies they will emit when heated). We all see this effect daily. Copper gives a green light when heated in a flame. Mercury vapour when excited with an electric current gives off a blue (or violet) light (the common mercury vapour lamp). Sodium, when treated in the same way gives off a bright yellow light (the yellow phase of a traffic signal is the same colour as sodium light). The list is endless.

The important thing to notice is that the amount of energy carried by a photon is inversely proportional to the wavelength of the photon. The shorter the wavelength, the higher the energy. This is discussed more fully later in 3.2.2, "Construction and Operation of LEDs" on page 105.

3.2 Light Emitting Diodes (LEDs)

Almost all light sources used in communications today are made from semiconductors. Light Emitting Diodes are simpler than lasers but have a lot in common with them. Therefore LEDs are discussed first.[39]

3.2.1 The Semiconductor Junction Diode

Figure 53 on page 104 shows a p-n junction with an electrical potential applied across it. When the field is applied in one direction the device conducts electricity (called the forward direction), but when the field is applied in the opposite direction (the reverse direction) no current can flow.

---

[39] Background material on semiconductor operation can be found in Appendix A, "An Introduction to Semiconductors" on page 679.

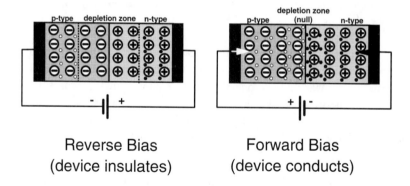

Reverse Bias
(device insulates)

Forward Bias
(device conducts)

Figure 53. Electrical Potentials across a p-n Junction

Forward Bias

When we connect an electrical potential across the junction with the negative pole connected to the n-type material and the positive pole connected to the p-type material then the junction conducts.

On the n-type side free electrons are repelled from the contact and pushed towards the junction. On the p-type side holes are repelled from the positively charged contact towards the junction. At the junction electrons will cross from the n-type side to the p-type side and holes will cross from the p-type side to the n-type side.

As soon as they cross (or perhaps a bit before) most holes and electrons will re-combine and eliminate each other.

> When this happens the free electrons must lose a quantum of energy to fill the available hole. This quantum of energy is radiated as electromagnetic energy with the wavelength depending on the size of the energy "gap" that the free electron crosses when it fills the hole. This phenomenon is called **Injection Luminescence**.
>
> If you choose your materials correctly this emits visible light and you have built an LED.

Some electrons and holes (by chance) don't recombine and continue through the material until they reach the other contact - but this is a very small number. In this context they are called "minority carriers".

The key to operation however is that electrons and holes must be able to leave the contacts and enter the silicon. This is possible because of the ions present in the material. On the n-type side, near the contact, the positively charged ion provides a place for an electron emitted from the contact to enter the silicon lattice. On the p-type side, the negatively charged ions have an electron that is only very weakly held in the lattice. This electron is easily attracted out of the lattice onto the positive contact and thus a new hole in the lattice is born.

Thus electrons enter the n-type material at the contact and flow to the junction. Holes are created at the contact in the p-type material (by loss of electrons to the positive contact) and flow to the junction. Holes and electrons combine and are annihilated at the junction.

Thus electricity flows through the device.

Reverse Bias

When a voltage is applied in the "reverse" direction no current flows at all.

A negative charge is applied to the contact on the p-type side and a positive charge is applied to the contact on the n-type side. In this case the contacts both attract the mobile charges. On the n-type side the mobile electrons are attracted to the positive contact and on the p-type side holes are attracted to the negative charge on the contact. Thus the depletion zone enlarges and there is no conduction.

There is however a small current caused by the random ionisation of covalent bonds within the depletion zone. Heat causes the random breaking of a bond creating both a hole and a free electron. The free electron is attracted by the electric field towards the positive contact and the hole is attracted towards the negative contact. The free carriers can cross the junction if necessary. This process is continuous at room temperature; thus, there is a small current. This current is independent of the applied voltage but varies with temperature.

If you expose the reverse-biased p-n junction to light the light is absorbed and causes ionisation - the creation of a free hole and electron pair. This then creates a current and you have built a light detector.

3.2.2 Construction and Operation of LEDs

As mentioned above in its most basic form an LED is just a forward biased p-n junction. When free electrons from the "conduction band" recombine with holes, they enter the (lower energy) "valence" band[40] and light is emitted.

---

[40] A description of bands and the bandgap may be found in A.1.2, "Why Does a Conductor Conduct?" on page 682.

The wavelength of light emitted by the LED is inversely proportional to the bandgap energy. The higher the energy the shorter the wavelength. The formula relating electron energy to wavelength is given below:

$$\lambda = \frac{h\,c}{\varepsilon_{ph}} = \frac{1.24}{\varepsilon_{ph}\,(Ev)}$$

Where: λ = Wavelength in microns
h = Plancks constant = 6.63×10^{-34} = $4.14 \times 10^{-15} eV.s$
c = Speed of light = $3 \times 10^8 \ metres.sec$
ε_{ph} = Photon energy in eV

This means that the materials of which the LED is made determine the wavelength of light emitted. The following table shows energies and wavelengths for commonly used materials in semiconductor LEDs and lasers:

Table 1. *Bandgap Energy and Possible Wavelength Ranges in Various Materials*

Material	Formula	Wavelength Range λ (μm)	Bandgap Energy W_g (eV)
Indium Phosphide	InP	0.92	1.35
Indium Arsenide	InAs	3.6	0.34
Gallium Phosphide	GaP	0.55	2.24
Gallium Arsenide	GaAs	0.87	1.42
Aluminium Arsenide	AlAs	0.59	2.09
Gallium Indium Phosphide	GaInP	0.64-0.68	1.82-1.94
Aluminium Gallium Arsenide	AlGaAs	0.8-0.9	1.4-1.55
Indium Gallium Arsenide	InGaAs	1.0-1.3	0.95-1.24
Indium Gallium Arsenide Phosphide	InGaAsP	0.9-1.7	0.73-1.35

Notice that for some materials ranges of energies and wavelengths are given. This is because you can mix the materials in different proportions (within some limits) and get different bandgap energies. In addition, the level of dopant used is very important in determining the amount of power that can be produced and also has some affect on the wavelength. Typically the junction area has quite a high level of doping.

Every time an electron recombines with a hole one photon is emitted. This means that the amount of optical energy (power) produced is equal to the number of electrons that recombine multiplied by the energy of the bandgap. The output power is directly proportional to the drive current (multiplied by some efficiency factor < 1).

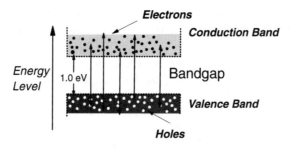

Figure 54. *Bandgap Energy*

It is important to note that the conduction and valence bands are just that - bands. Due to the action of heat, electrons in each band may have many different energies with the proviso that their energies may not occupy the bandgap (call it a banned gap). If we look at the distribution of energy states over a typical bandgap we get a diagram like Figure 54. At ordinary temperatures the majority of electrons and holes are close to the bandgap edges but there is a distribution.

Transitions can take place from any energy state in either band to any state in the other band. This is illustrated by the double arrows. When we use injected carriers (as in a junction diode) the predominant transition is from the conduction band down to the (lower energy state) valence band. Of course the action of heat (or for that matter the absorption of a stray photon of light) can cause electrons to go the other way - from the valence band to the conduction band.

Because of the range of states possible in both bands there is a range of different energy transitions possible. This results in a range of different wavelengths produced in this spontaneous emission. This accounts for the fact that LEDs produce a range of wavelengths. Typically the range is about 80 nm or so. Later, we will see that this also results in lasers producing a range of possible wavelengths.

3.2.2.1 Indirect Bandgap Materials

Some of the energy possessed by an electron in either the conduction band or the valence band takes the form of "lattice momentum". For an electron to jump from the conduction band to the valence band (and give out a photon) the lattice momentum in both bands *must be the same*.

Unfortunately some materials that we would very much like to use to make lasers and LEDs (silicon for example) have *different* amounts of lattice momentum in each of these bands. In order to emit a photon, lattice momentum must first be given up (in the form of a phonon).[41] This requirement for both phonon and photon emission simultaneously means that photon emission is quite an unlikely event. What tends to happen in these materials is that impurity sites in the material offer intermediate states between the conduction and valence bands. Electrons are able to jump between bands *without* radiating a photon by transiting these intermediate states.

This means that light emission from indirect bandgap materials has a very low "quantum efficiency". These materials are sometimes used in special applications but are not efficient enough for practical use. Indirect bandgap materials include silicon, germanium and most alloys of aluminium. Our favorite semiconductor materials!

3.2.3 Heterojunctions (Practical LEDs)

It's easy enough to construct a p-n junction that will emit light of the required wavelength. What isn't easy is getting the light out of the junction and into a fibre.

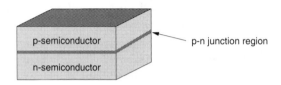

Figure 55. *Simple P-N Junction LED*

As illustrated in Figure 55, p-n junctions are necessarily very thin, flat and need to cover a relatively large area if they are to produce any meaningful amount of light. Further, light is spontaneously emitted in all directions and since the semiconductor material is *transparent* over the band of wavelengths produced,[42] the light will disperse in all directions. It is very difficult to get any meaningful amount of light into a fibre from a regular p-n junction.

What is needed is a way of producing light in a more localised area, with a greater intensity and with some way of confining the light produced such that we can get it (or a lot of it), into a fibre. The heterojunction is the answer to this problem.

A heterojunction is a junction between two different semiconductors with different bandgap energies. A heterojunction is not unlike an ordinary p-n junction. The difference in bandgap energies creates a one-way barrier. Charge carriers (electrons or

---

[41] A phonon is a quantum of energy in the form of mechanical lattice vibration.

[42] It had better be otherwise the light would never get out!

holes) are attracted over the barrier from the material of higher bandgap energy to the one of lower bandgap energy.

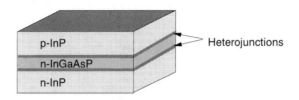

Figure 56. *Double Heterojunction LED*

When a layer of material with a particular bandgap energy is sandwiched between layers of material with a higher energy bandgap a *double heterojunction* is formed. This is called a double heterojunction because there are two heterojunctions present - one on each side of the active material. The double heterojunction forms a barrier which restricts the region of electron-hole recombination to the lower bandgap material. This region is then called the "active" region.

An energy diagram of a double heterojunction is shown in Figure 57 on page 110. The diagram shows the energy levels for the three sections of the double heterojunction.

- On the left is n-InP. The lower dotted line represents the energy level of the valence band in this material. The upper dotted line represents the lowest energy in the valence band for this material. Thus there is a bandgap difference of 1.35 eV.

- In the middle section of the diagram we see n-InGaAsP. Here the valence band is at a higher energy than the valence band of the adjacent n-InP. The conduction band is at a lower energy level.

- On the right we notice that p-InP has higher energy levels than n-InP but the bandgap is the same.

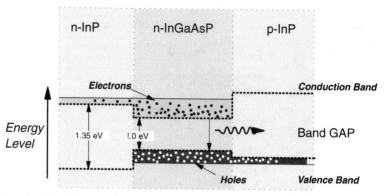

Bandgap boundaries are denoted by dotted lines

Figure 57. Energy Bands in a Double Heterojunction

Electrons are attracted across the left-hand junction from the n-InP to the n-InGaAsP. Holes are attracted across the right-hand junction from the p-InP into the n-InGaAsP. Recombination takes place in the n-InGaAsP and spontaneous emission (or lasing) occurs.

When we discuss semiconductor devices it is very important to realise that they consist of *single* crystals. A heterojunction is a part of the device and the crystal must be continuous across the junction. This means that the natural size of the crystal lattices at the junction must not be too different. If they are more than a few percent different then you either get a chaotic interface between the layers with many incomplete (or "hanging") bonds or the junction may fracture due to stress in the later stages of processing when heat is applied.

The heterojunction allows us to have a small active region where the light is produced. In addition, the material in the active region usually has a higher refractive index than that of the material surrounding it. This means that a mirror surface effect is created at the junction which helps to confine and direct the light emitted.

We are left with four design challenges:

Getting the Light into a Fibre

> This can be accomplished in two ways: by emitting the light on the surface (the Surface Emitting LED or SLED) or by directing the light out the side of the device (the Edge Emitting LED or ELED).

Confining and Guiding the Light within the Device

Within the device the light must be confined and directed to the exit aperture so that it can be directed into the fibre.

It's almost a lucky accident here that the active layer in a heterostructure almost always has a higher refractive index than the adjacent (higher bandgap) material. This junction forms a mirror layer and helps to confine the light to the active layer. For this reason the outer layers are often called "confinement layers".

Getting Power to the Active Region

Power in the form of electrons and holes must be delivered to the active region in sufficient quantity to produce the desired amount of light. This is easier said than done.

This is done primarily by using three different techniques:

1. Careful positioning of the electrical contacts where power is supplied. If you provide a low resistance path through the device to the active region then a large proportion of the available current will follow that path. Emission will take place in the part of the active region where current flows.

2. Using different levels of dopant in the host material. A high level of dopant gives lots of free charge carriers and can deliver a lot of power but there are other reasons why we can't just uniformly dope the host material to a high level. This means that we have different levels of dopant in different parts of the material.

   But every time we get a junction between different materials (even just with different levels of doping) some kind of barrier (junction) is formed and this must be overcome.

3. Using insulating materials to confine the active region and the current path. One method is to use layers of SiO_2 (good old sand) within the device to form the needed barriers. However, SiO_2 is not a good conductor of heat.

   A better (albeit more expensive) method is to use proton bombardment of localised areas. Proton bombardment changes the characteristics of the material increasing its resistance and hence confining the current whilst still providing good heat conduction.

Getting Rid of the Heat

During operation the active region produces a considerable amount of heat. This must be conducted away and dispersed with some form of "heat sink".

Real devices must find a solution to all of the challenges above. Many times improving one aspect of design will make other aspects worse so that compromise between competing requirements becomes necessary.

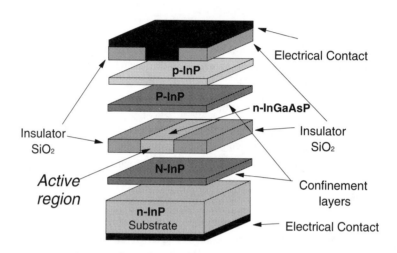

Figure 58. Exploded Structure of an Idealised Double Heterojunction LED

Figure 58 shows the conceptual structure of a double heterojunction, edge emitting LED. Note the convention of using the capital letters N and P to denote high levels of dopant and lowercase n and p to indicate lower levels of doping. The insulating material could be SiO₂ as shown in the picture or a proton bombarded semiconductor material (proton bombardment renders the material insulating). The active region is typically only about 40 microns across.

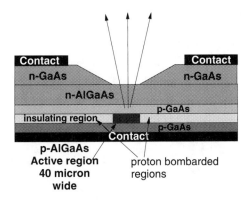

Figure 59. *Schematic Structure of a Burrus LED*

Two configurations of practical LEDs are shown in Figure 59 and Figure 60. This Surface Emitting LED (SLED) operates at 850 nm wavelength and the edge emitter could typically operate in the 1310 nm region. (This is determined by the materials used.) Surface emitting LEDs are often called "Burrus" LEDs because they were first described by Burrus and Miller in a paper in 1971. (See bibliography.)

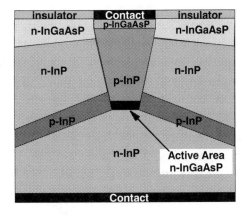

Figure 60. *Schematic Structure of an Edge Emitting LED*

In both types of LED a combination of insulating materials and junctions is used to:

1. Guide the current flow to a small "active region" and

2. Guide the light produced out of the device and into an easy position for coupling to a fibre.

3.2.3.1 Coupling to a Fibre

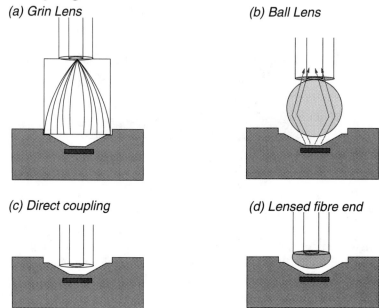

Figure 61. *Coupling to a Fibre*

Coupling light output to a fibre is the most difficult and costly part of manufacturing a real LED or laser device. Four common methods are illustrated in Figure 61.

1. Use of a Graded Index Lens (GRIN lens) is fairly common. A GRIN lens is very similar to just a short length of graded index fibre (albeit with a much larger diameter). The lens collects and focuses the light onto the end of the fibre.

2. A Ball lens is also often used. This is bonded to the surface of the LED with an epoxy resin that has a specific refractive index. However, the RI of the epoxy can't match to both the RI of the fibre and the RI of the semiconductor since the semiconductor will have an RI of around 3.5 and the fibre of around 1.45.

3. The Direct Coupling method is becoming increasingly popular. Just mount the fibre end so that it touches the LED directly. A common way to do this is to mount the LED inside a connector so that when a fibre is plugged in (mounted in the other half of the connector) you get firm mounting in good position. This has the advantage of low cost and low complexity.

4. Another common way is to fix a ball lens to the end of the fibre as shown in the diagram.

3.2.3.2 Partial Reflections

When light encounters a significant difference in refractive index such as at the exit facet of an LED or at the entry to a fibre some of the light is reflected. This is usually only around 4% for rays hitting the surface at 90° (normal to the surface). Reflections are often a problem in coupling to a fibre. They can add significant noise to laser operation especially in the case of narrow linewidth lasers. They can also cause an edge emitting SLED to become a laser!

Both anti-reflection coatings and isolators are used to minimise the effects of unwanted reflections in a system.

3.2.3.3 Anti-Reflection Coatings

Refections can be minimised by coating the surface with an "anti-reflection coating". This is usually a 1/4 wavelength thick coating of magnesium fluoride (MgF_2). Reflection can be reduced in this way to about 1/3 of what it would be without the coating. Ideally the AR coating should have a refractive index half way between the RIs of the two materials between which it is placed.

There are other ways to minimise reflections. Making sure that the surface is relatively rough or cutting the surface at an angle will also reduce immediate back-reflections. Actually this doesn't reduce the reflections - what it does is to prevent reflections returning along the incident path.

3.2.4 Characteristics of LEDs

In communications applications the following characteristics of LEDs are important:

Low Cost

>   LEDs have been very low in cost compared to communication lasers.

>   This is highly controversial. Communication LEDs and lasers are not too different in their structures and are comparable in manufacturing cost. Connecting to single mode fibre (pigtailing) is significantly more costly than connecting to multimode fibre and since lasers are commonly used with single mode and LEDs with multimode there is a cost difference here. However whilst most LEDs can't be used with single-mode fibre,[43] lasers certainly can be used with multimode fibre.

>   In early 1996, people began to use the lasers from CD-ROM players for short distance communications on MM fibre. These are about 1/10 the cost of

---

[43] A special type of LED called an SLD - the superluminescent diode can be used with SM fibre however.

standard communications LEDs (simply because they are made in vast volume - several million per year).

Many people believe that the traditional cost relationship is related much more to the volume of devices produced than to their inherent complexity.

Low Power

The maximum light output of an LED has typically been a lot lower than that of a laser (about 100 microwatts). However, recently a new class of LEDs, with output of up to 75 milliwatts, has become available.

Relatively Wide Spectrum Produced

LEDs do not produce a single light wavelength but rather a band of wavelengths. The range (or band) of wavelengths produced is called the "spectral width" and is typically about .05 of the wavelength (50 to 100 nm).

The spectral width can be reduced (and dispersion reduced) by using selective filters to produce a narrow band of wavelengths. However, this reduces the power of the signal too.

Incoherent Light

The light produced is neither directional nor coherent. This means that you need a lens to focus the light onto the end of a fibre. LEDs are not suitable for use with single-mode fibre for this reason (it is too hard to get the light into the narrow core).

Digital Modulation

LEDs cannot produce pulses short enough to be used at gigabit speeds. However, systems using LEDs operate quite well at speeds of up to around 300 Mbps.

Digital modulation is straightforward. The device "turns on" when the forward voltage applied results in a potential across the junction greater than the bandgap energy required.[44] It extinguishes when the voltage drops below that.

Analogue Modulation

LEDs can also be analogue modulated quite simply by maintaining a forward bias just larger than the bandgap energy (since the device response is linear with current flow). This is one advantage over lasers. While lasers can be

---

[44] This is not the voltage needed across the device as there is a significant voltage drop across the semiconductor between the contacts and the junction.

analogue modulated and are indeed used this way in some commercial situations, this is not an easy thing to do.

3.3 Lasers

LASER is an acronym for "Light Amplification by the Stimulated Emission of Radiation". Lasers produce far and away the best kind of light for optical communication.

- Ideal laser light is single-wavelength only. This is related to the molecular characteristics of the material being used in the laser. It is formed in parallel beams and is in a single phase. That is, it is "coherent".

  This is not exactly true for communication lasers. See the discussion under "Linewidth" below.

- Lasers can be modulated (controlled) very precisely (the record is a pulse length of 0.5 femto seconds[45]).

- Lasers can produce relatively high power. Indeed some types of laser can produce kilowatts of power. In communication applications, semiconductor lasers of power up to about 20 milliwatts are available. This is many times greater power than LEDs can generate. Other semiconductor lasers (such as those used in "pumps" for optical amplifiers) have outputs of up to 250 milliwatts.

- Because laser light is produced in parallel beams, a high percentage (50% to 80%) can be transferred into the fibre.

There are disadvantages, however:

- Lasers have been quite expensive by comparison with LEDs. (Recent development has helped this a lot.) One of the things that causes lasers to have a high cost is that for lasers used in long distance applications temperature control and output power control is needed. Temperature control maintains a stable lasing threshold and power control ensures that the detector can see a stable signal. Both of these require added cost.

  A "peltier effect" cooler/heater is normally used to keep the temperature stable. This also requires a thermistor to measure the device temperature.

---

[45] 10^{-15} seconds.

To control power a p-n diode detector is usually packaged with the laser to measure the power being produced and (via a feedback loop) control the laser's bias current.

Both of these require electronic logic to operate.

- The wavelength that a laser produces is a characteristic of the material used to build it and of its physical construction. You can't just say "I want a laser on x wavelength", or rather you can say it all you like - you just can't have it. Lasers have to be individually designed for each wavelength they are going to use.

  Tunable lasers exist and are beginning to become commercially available but the available tuning range is quite narrow and tuning is quite slow.

- Amplitude modulation using an analogue signal is difficult with most lasers because laser output signal power is generally non-linear with input signal power. That is, the variations in the light produced do not match the amplitude variations of the source signal. However recent developments in laser design have made analogue modulation (with special lasers) a practical technology. It is also possible to modulate the signal after it leaves the laser with a device called an "external modulator". Linear modulation is possible with many types of external modulator.

3.3.1 Principle of the LASER

The key principle in laser operation is the principle of stimulated emission. Figure 62 illustrates the process involved.

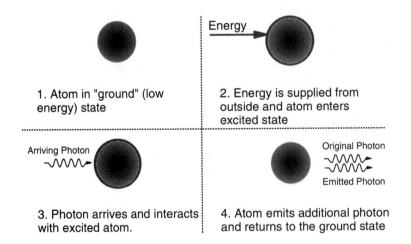

Figure 62. Stimulated Emission

1. An electron within an atom (or a molecule or an ion) starts in a low energy stable state often called the "ground" state.

2. Energy is supplied from outside and is absorbed by the atomic structure whereupon the electron enters an excited (higher energy) state.

3. A photon arrives with an energy close to the same amount of energy as the electron needs to give up to reach a stable state. (This is just another way of saying that the wavelength of the arriving photon is very close to the wavelength at which the excited electron will emit its own photon.)

4. The arriving photon triggers a resonance with the excited atom. As a result the excited electron leaves its excited state and transitions to a more stable state giving up the energy difference in the form of a photon.

The critical characteristic here is that when a new photon is emitted it has identical wavelength, phase and direction characteristics as the exciting photon.

Note: The photon that triggered (stimulated) the emission itself is *not* absorbed and continues along its original path accompanied by the newly emitted photon.

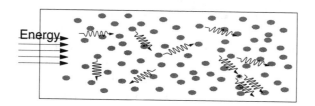

Figure 63. Spontaneous Emission

If we take a material (almost any material), confine it in some space and then bombard it with energy in a form that the material will absorb then something is bound to happen. Usually that something is the spontaneous emission of light (and/or the generation of heat). Most materials will get red hot then white hot as we increase the amount of energy we pour into it.

Materials capable of stimulated emission (or "lasing" are distinguished by the fact that they have a high energy state that is "metastable". That is, it can hold its high energy state for some length of time before decaying spontaneously.

Figure 63 shows a material treated in this way. Excited atoms decay and emit photons randomly in all directions. In the right-hand lower part of the picture a spontaneously emitted photon has met an excited atom and lasing has occurred. This "spontaneous emission" is a far cry from the famous characteristic of lasers that they have parallel highly coherent beams! Spontaneous emission is not lasing!

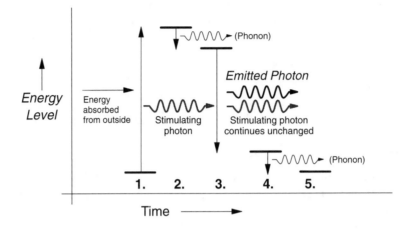

Figure 64. *Energy States of a typical 4-Level Material. A material which has 4 energy levels involved in the lasing process is significantly more efficient than one with only 3 levels. A 4-level system is where the radiative transition ends in an unstable state and another transition is needed to attain the ground state. A 3-level system is where the radiative transition achieves the ground state directly.*

Figure 64 shows the energy transitions involved in stimulated emission. Notice that until now we have been simplifying things a lot. After the atom absorbs energy it typically gives out a small amount of energy (in the form of a lattice vibration called a "phonon" which does not radiate) to reach the metastable state at which lasing is possible. Likewise when the photon emission transition is complete it may still need to emit a small amount of energy to reach its final (stable) state. (This is not always the case. Some materials require this transition, others do not.) Diagrams of the energy states within a material are typically drawn in this way.

In order to have stimulated emission we need another condition to be present. We need a "population inversion" to take place. A population Inversion occurs when there are more electrons in the higher energy state than there are in the lower energy state. Without this condition stimulated emission (lasing) cannot occur. In Figure 64 the radiative transition itself ends in a transient state. Materials that have this "4-level" energy state system are much more efficient at lasing than 3-level· materials (ones where the result of the radiative transition is the ground state itself) because population inversion is relatively easy to attain. Because the lower energy state (after the radiative transition) is itself a transient state it is easier to get a population inversion (more electrons in the high energy state than the low energy one) than if the lower energy state was itself the ground state. There are typically a lot of electrons in the ground state.

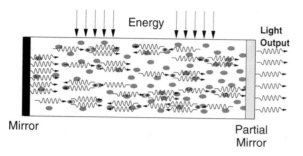

Figure 65. *Lasing*

Need for Population Inversion

The requirement for a population inversion to be present as a precondition for stimulated emission is not at all an obvious one. Electrons in the high energy state will undergo stimulated emission regardless of how many electrons are in the ground state. The condition seems irrelevant.

The problem is that an electron in the ground state will absorb photons at exactly the wavelength at which electrons in the higher energy state will undergo stimulated emission! You must have a greater probability of stimulated emission than absorption for lasing to occur.

It happens that the probability that an electron in the ground state will absorb an incoming photon is usually different from the probability that an electron in the excited state will undergo stimulated emission. So what you really need is not an inversion in the numbers of electrons in each state. Rather you need the probability that an incoming photon will encounter an excited electron and stimulate emission to be greater than the probability that it will encounter an electron in the ground state and be absorbed.

So an inversion takes place when the number of electrons in the excited state multiplied by the probability of stimulation by an incoming photon exceeds the number of electrons in the ground state multiplied by the probability of absorption of an incoming photon.

Figure 65 on page 121 shows how lasing is sustained.

- The space in which the reaction takes place (the cavity) is confined between two parallel mirrors.

- When energy is applied, electrons build up in the high energy state.

- Spontaneous emissions start occurring as soon as some electrons arrive in the high energy state. Most of the spontaneously emitted light doesn't go anywhere near the mirrors and passes out of the chamber.

- Interesting things don't start happening however until sufficient electrons arrive in the excited state for a population inversion to be formed.

- Some spontaneous emissions however result in photons hitting one of the end mirrors. Of course these photons will be reflected back into the material. Again, most of these will pass out of the material relatively quickly.

- A few photons however will be at just the right angle to be reflected back along the path on which they came. These will reach the opposite mirror and continue to bounce back and forth between the mirrors.

- As these photons bounce from one mirror to the other they encounter excited atoms of material. The arriving photons will stimulate emission in the excited atoms which then give out a new photon. The new photons will be *exactly* in the same direction and phase and will have the same wavelength as the photon that excited the emission. Thus these too will bounce exactly between the mirrors. Thus the amount of light bouncing between the mirrors will increase very quickly until it will dominate other emissions.

- The light does have to get out however. This is done by making one of the end mirrors only partially reflective. A percentage of the generated light will leave the laser's cavity through the partial end mirror. Power builds up (very quickly indeed), until the amount of light leaving the end mirror equals the amount of energy being pumped into the cavity (minus losses of course).

The amount of reflectivity needed in the end mirrors is a function of the amount of gain in the cavity. While in some lasers a very high reflectivity (up to perhaps 80% is needed) in many others a quite low level of reflectivity is sufficient. In semiconductor lasers used for communications purposes it is common to allow the relatively low reflectance of the junction between the cleaved end facet and air to form the mirrors. In this case a nominal reflectivity of around 6% is found. However as described before in 2.1.3.2, "Transmission through a Sheet of Glass" on page 27 a nominal 6% reflectance can result in up to 36% of the power (in resonant modes) being reflected.

- Once lasing has commenced, most of the excited atoms encounter a stimulating photon *before* they have a chance to decay (and therefore emit a photon) spontaneously. So spontaneous emission is greatly reduced. It is not eliminated however. Most spontaneous emission (in excess of 99.9%) leaves the cavity and doesn't have much affect on lasing because it isn't in the right direction to be reflected by the mirrors. However, a tiny proportion of spontaneously emitted light happens to have the right direction to bounce between the mirrors and thus trigger lasing. This additional form of lasing is (of course) in the same direction (because of the mirrors) but out of phase with the other modes of light being produced. This is not a major problem with communications lasers. Called *Amplified Spontaneous Emission (ASE)* it is a source of noise in optical amplifiers. It can also be a trigger for the "mode hopping" behavior of some lasers.

The above description has been deliberately very general because of the wide range of materials and conditions under which lasing can occur. Lasing can take place whenever there is an energy gap that electrons must jump to reach a stable state. (Electrons can't take intermediate energy states within the gap.) A wide range of materials can exhibit stimulated emission. Lasing can take place regardless of the state of the material. Solids, liquids and gases can all be used. Also, its not just single atoms that undergo spontaneous emission. Molecules have complex electron orbits and states and typically have different energy levels and lasing characteristics from the elements that make them up. Likewise ions (atoms with missing electrons) can also exhibit stimulated emission and thus be used in a laser.[46]

In summary, to make a laser you need:

1. A material that can enter a high energy metastable state. It should have a bandgap energy of the right magnitude to produce light of the required wavelength. (There must be an available energy transition or sequence of transitions from the high energy metastable state to a lower energy state that will emit light at the desired wavelength.)

2. A way of supplying energy to the material.

3. A suitable method of confinement of the material and of the emitted light.

4. A pair of parallel mirrors at each end of the cavity.

5. It seems obvious but its very important that the material in the cavity of the laser should be transparent (should not absorb light) at the wavelength produced. This is partially the "population inversion" requirement. The lasing medium *does*

---

[46] In fact, in later discussions of the Erbium doped fibre amplifier we will see that the Er^{3+} ion is the active substance.

absorb light at the wavelength produced. To overcome this we need to have more atoms in the excited stated state than in the ground state so that lasing produces more photons than absorption removes. However, it is also very important that other materials (dopants for example) should not absorb light of the required wavelength. This is a non-trivial condition.

Its very important to notice here that the wavelength of light produced is really determined by the characteristics of the lasing material. While we can influence this a little (each material will work within a small range of wavelengths) we can't make a laser that gives off light at (say) 800 nm with materials that lase at 1300 nm. This was previously discussed in the context of LEDs in 3.2.2, "Construction and Operation of LEDs" on page 105.

3.3.1.1 Technical Parameters

Researchers have developed a multitude (perhaps a hundred or so) of different types of communication lasers. The important features of communication lasers are as follows:

Spectral Width

It is a fact that most simple semiconductor lasers do *not* produce a single wavelength of light. They produce instead a range of wavelengths. This range of wavelengths is called the "spectral width" of the laser.

This seems to contradict the basic principle of laser operation. However, it is not so. In a semiconductor laser, a mirrored cavity is used to build up the light. By mechanical necessity, the cavity is long enough for several wavelengths to be produced.

Typically there will be around 8 "modes"[47] and the spectral width is around 6 to 8 nm. It is interesting that these different wavelengths (modes) are not produced simultaneously - or rather their strength varies widely. What happens is that the laser will produce one dominant mode, perhaps for as short a time as a few nanoseconds, and then switch to a different mode and then to another, etc. The total power output of the laser does not vary - just the form of the output.

In both lasers and LEDs power delivered over the spectral width follows a bell shaped curve like that shown in Figure 69 on page 131. It is difficult to determine exactly where such a curve begins and ends. So spectral width is usually quoted as the FWHM (Full Width Half Maximum). FWHM is

---

[47] So named because each frequency resonates on a different path within the cavity.

measured between the points on the curve where power has decayed to one half of the peak. Thus in some contexts it is also called the "3-dB point".

Spectral width is very important because:

1. The wider the spectrum of the light source, the more dispersion the signal will suffer when travelling on the fibre. (This is not too bad for lasers when compared with LEDs, but is still an issue.)

2. In a Wavelength Division Multiplexing (WDM) system it is desirable to pack the channels as closely together as possible in order to maximize the number of channels. The narrower the spectral width the more channels you can have.

3. You can't use frequency or phase modulation techniques or coherent detection methods unless the linewidth (expressed as occupied bandwidth) is significantly less than the bandwidth of the modulating signal. (100 to 1 is a good ratio.) However, enthusiasm for these modulation techniques has waned in recent years. The invention of the fibre amplifier has meant that a regular pin-diode receiver using OOK modulation[48] can give the same performance as sophisticated coherent detection techniques. This is achieved by pre-amplifying the signal immediately before the receiver. This is simpler and lower in cost than proposed coherent detection techniques.

4. Very narrow spectral width signals are subject to a number of non-linear effects which are generally thought to be undesirable. One is Stimulated Brillouin Scattering (SBS) discussed further in 2.4.5.2, "Stimulated Brillouin Scattering (SBS)" on page 89.

Linewidth

Instead of producing a continuous range of wavelengths over their spectral width, semiconductor lasers produce a series of "lines" at a number of discrete wavelengths. This is described more fully in 3.3.3, "Fabry-Perot Lasers" on page 129. Lines themselves vary in width (in different types of lasers) very significantly. The linewidth is inversely proportional to the coherence length of the laser.

Coherence Length and Coherence Time

A particular laser line is emitted at a very specific wavelength corresponding to one mode (light path) in the laser's cavity. Over time this wavelength

---

[48] On-Off Keying

varies somewhat around a center wavelength (the amount of variation is the linewidth). If a sample emission, taken from one line of a laser at a particular time is of exactly the same wavelength and phase as another sample taken at a later time then the laser is said to be coherent over that time.

The length of time that coherence is maintained is called the "coherence time". The length that the signal could travel in a vacuum during that time is called the coherence length.

The coherence time for an LED is of the order of half a picosecond and its coherence length is around 15 microns. A simple laser may have a coherence time of perhaps half of a nanosecond and a coherence length of perhaps 15 centimetres. A very good quality narrow linewidth laser could have a coherence time of perhaps a microsecond and a coherence length of up to 200 metres.

It is relatively obvious that the range of variation of the signal (the linewidth) should be inversely related to the coherence length (and time).

$$\text{Length}_{coherence} \; = \; c \times \text{Time}_{coherence} \; = \; \frac{\lambda^2}{\Delta\lambda}$$

Where $\Delta\lambda$ = Linewidth and λ = Centre Wavelength.

Power

The signal is attenuated as it travels on the fibre and thus the higher the signal power you use the further you can go without needing to regenerate it. In addition, theory tells us that in an optical receiver of a given type you need a certain fixed minimum amount of power per bit transmitted. If you have a working system and want to double the bit rate you must double the power (or double the receiver sensitivity). But transmitters have limits to their power[49] and receivers have limits to their sensitivity. Of course, you can get a higher bit rate by reducing the attenuation (by shortening the distance between stations) thereby increasing the signal power at the receiver.

In some systems, signal power, more than fibre capacity is the limiting factor.

Operating Wavelength (or Range)

Of course, lasers must be able to operate on wavelengths appropriate to the system being designed.

---

[49] Often we want to limit the power somewhat artificially to stay within eye safety limits for example.

The operating wavelength of a laser depends on the materials used for lasing (in exactly the same way as the wavelength of an LED depends on the same materials) and on the geometry of the laser cavity.

Frequency (Wavelength) Stability

In a single-channel system using incoherent detection, a bit of instability (wander) in the laser wavelength doesn't matter too much. However, if the system is using WDM techniques, each laser must keep within its allocated band and wander matters a lot.

Fabry-Perot lasers vary an enormous .4 nm per degree Celsius of temperature variation. Most of the single-mode lasers are significantly better than this, but temperature control is critical.

When most lasers are modulated by OOK[50] (turning them on and off) they produce a "chirp" at the beginning of each pulse (this is a transient frequency shift of as much as several gigahertz). This is a problem in WDM systems and ones using coherent receivers. Chirp is caused by two factors:

1. The depletion of carriers within the active region (cavity) of the laser immediately after inversion is achieved. This causes a shift in RI of the cavity and therefore a shift in the resonant wavelength.

2. By instantaneous heating effects. The cavity itself heats up - after all, the energy ("light") produced is infrared (heat) and this also changes the RI of the material in the cavity. Different types of semiconductor laser react differently to these two effects.

Switching Time and Modulation

A fundamental operational characteristic of any laser is which modulation techniques are possible and how fast they can operate. In general, all lasers can be modulated by OOK (on/off keying) and some by FSK (frequency shift keying). Other modulation techniques require an external modulator to be placed into the light beam after it is generated.

Tuning Range and Speed

In many proposed WDM systems, transmitters, and/or receivers need to be switched between different wavelengths (channels). There are many techniques for doing this. In general, the faster the device can switch, the narrower will be the range of channels over which it can switch.

---

[50] On-Off Keying

Another point is that tunable lasers are seldom capable of continuous tuning over an unbroken range of wavelengths. When they are tuned they "jump" from one wavelength to another (corresponding to the resonance modes of the laser cavity).

3.3.2 Semiconductor Laser Diodes

The most common communication laser is called the "Fabry-Perot" laser. In many situations this type of laser gives good service. However, because it produces a relatively wide spectral width, it is not considered suitable for applications requiring extended distances, coherent reception, or wavelength multiplexing.

The Fabry-Perot laser can be modified by placing something in the cavity that will disperse unwanted frequencies before they reach the lasing threshold. There are a number of alternatives, but a common way is to place a diffraction grating within the cavity. When this is done, the laser can produce a very narrow spectral linewidth (typically today .2 to .3 nm). Lasers using this principle are called Distributed Feedback (DFB) or Distributed Bragg Reflector (DBR) lasers.

Other lasers use a cavity external to the device itself - these are called "external cavity lasers". This allows a long cavity, and if you put a diffraction grating on one of the end mirrors you can get a very narrow linewidth indeed. (The record here is a linewidth of 10 MHz using a 20 cm (yes) long external cavity.)

Modes

In optics, a mode is a path that light may take through a system. Thus multimode fibre is fibre that allows for multiple paths. A multimode laser is one that allows multiple paths within its cavity and hence produces light of multiple wavelengths. Such lasers do not produce multiple wavelengths simultaneously with constant power. Rather, the laser will switch power from one mode to another very quickly (sometimes spending only a few picoseconds in any particular mode), apparently at random, when sending a single pulse. It is important to note that these are power level fluctuations not complete switching between modes. Thus the intensity of a particular mode may fluctuate by as much as 30 dB but it will not disappear altogether.

Thus the word "mode" relates to the path on which light is travelling at a particular instant in time. Light produced in a "multimode laser" is *not* "multimode light". Light produced by a "multimode laser" travels in a single mode along a single-mode fibre perfectly well.

3.3.3 Fabry-Perot Lasers

The Fabry-Perot laser is conceptually just an LED with a pair of end mirrors. The mirrors are needed to create the right conditions for lasing to occur. In practice of course it is somewhat more complex than this - but not a lot. The Fabry-Perot laser gets its name (and its operational principle) from the fact that its cavity acts as a Fabry-Perot resonator (see 5.8.2, "Fabry-Perot Filter (Etalon)" on page 289).

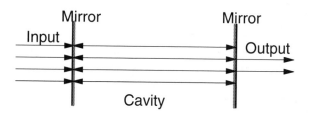

Figure 66. Fabry-Perot Filter. Light enters the cavity through a partially silvered mirror on the left and leaves it through a partially silvered mirror on the right. Only wavelengths that resonate within the cavity are able to pass through. Other wavelengths are strongly attenuated. This is described further in 5.8.2, "Fabry-Perot Filter (Etalon)" on page 289.

To understand the operation of the Fabry-Perot laser it is first necessary to understand the Fabry-Perot filter. The principle of the Fabry-Perot filter is illustrated in Figure 66. When you put two mirrors opposite one another they form a resonant cavity. Light will bounce between the two mirrors. When the distance between the mirrors is an integral multiple of half wavelengths, the light will reinforce itself. Wavelengths that are *not* resonant undergo destructive interference with themselves and are reflected away.

This principle also applies in the FP laser although the light is emitted within the cavity itself rather than arriving from outside.

In some sense every laser cavity is a Fabry-Perot cavity. But when the cavity is very long compared to the wavelength involved we get a very large number of resonant wavelengths all of which are very close together. So the important filtering characteristics of the Fabry-Perot cavity are lost.

We consider a laser to be "Fabry-Perot" when it has a relatively short cavity (in relation to the wavelength of the light produced). Wavelengths produced are related to the distance between the mirrors by the following formula:

$$Cl = \frac{\lambda x}{2 n}$$

Where: λ = Wavelength
              Cl = Length of the cavity
              x = An arbitrary integer - 1, 2, 3, 4...
              n = Refractive index of active medium

This is an extremely simple relationship. Notice here that the only other variable in the equation is the refractive index of the gain medium (dielectric) in the cavity. This is because we always quote the wavelength as what it would be if the wave was travelling in a vacuum.[51] Since the speed of propagation in the cavity is a lot lower than c (the speed of light) the wavelength is a lot shorter than it would be in free space. The adjustment factor is the refractive index.

In practice, we can't make the laser so short that we restrict it to only one wavelength. We need some space for stimulated emission to amplify the signal and we are limited by the density of the power we can deliver to a small area. Typically the cavity length is between 100 and 200 microns (of the order of 400 wavelengths or so) although devices with cavities as short as 30 microns have been made.

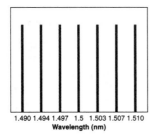

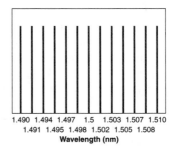

Figure 67. Resonance Examples

Figure 67 shows two examples of typical resonances. On the left we have solved the equation above for a cavity 100 microns long, a wavelength of 1500 nm and a refractive index of 3.45 (InP). We can see that there are 7 wavelengths within 10 nm

---

[51] A wavelength of 1500 nm in free space becomes a real physical distance of 1500/3.45 nm in InP which equals 434.78 nm.

of 1500 nm where resonance may occur. On the right of the figure we can see the same solution but for a cavity 200 microns long. Here there are 13 possible resonant wavelengths. The longer the cavity (and the shorter the wavelength) the more resonant wavelengths we can find within the vicinity of our centre wavelength.

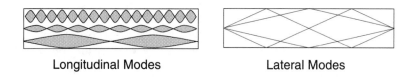

Longitudinal Modes   Lateral Modes

Figure 68. *Resonance Modes in the Cavity of a Fabry-Perot Laser*

Figure 68 (on the left) illustrates the principle of multiple resonant longitudinal modes in the FP cavity. We can get a number of resonant wavelengths provided the cavity length is an integer multiple of the particular wavelength.

On the right of the figure we see another problem. What if the *sides* of the cavity reflect light. What you get here are lateral modes forming which are also resonant and which can also lase! There are various ways of minimising or eliminating these lateral modes and this is discussed later. Transverse modes (vertical paths) cannot exist because the device is too thin in the vertical direction for multiple modes to exist. You could get a lateral mode that was completely side-to-side at right angles to the long axis of the device. You could also get a vertical one of the same kind. However, lateral modes are suppressed as discussed later and there is not enough gain in the vertical direction for lasing to be sustainable.

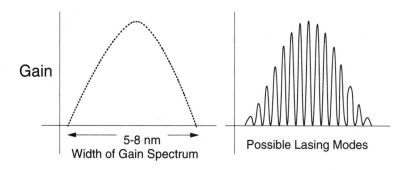

Figure 69. *Modes Produced in a Typical Fabry-Perot Laser*

The lasing medium can only amplify (undergo stimulated emission) over a fairly narrow range because of the characteristics of the material it is made from. A typical gain curve is illustrated on the left-hand side of Figure 69.

Width of Gain Spectrum

From the description of lasing in the previous section one could be excused for thinking that because there is a well defined energy gap between the higher and lower energy states there would only be one possible wavelength over which lasing could take place.

In fact the energy levels we have been discussing are rather "energy bands". Electrons at a particular level have (slightly) different energies within the same band. So transitions from one band to another have some variation in energy (and hence wavelength) because electrons can leave from and arrive into slightly different energy levels within the same band. This varies a lot depending on the material constitution of the active region. Thus when you look at a pattern of spontaneous emission from the particular material you see a band of wavelengths with the strongest emission in the centre.

Of course during lasing, the amount of energy given up during the transition is *identical* to the energy of the stimulating photon.

When we combine the graph of possible resonant wavelengths with the amplifying characteristics of the device we get a pattern of possible modes like that shown on the right of the figure.

Thus an FP laser can produce a range of wavelengths. Each wavelength has to be able to resonate within the cavity and it must be within the gain window of the medium.

The laser output of each possible lasing mode is called a "line". A simple gain guided FP laser produces a number of lines over a range of wavelengths called the "spectral width". Because it is often difficult to determine just where the spectrum or just where an individual line starts or finishes it is usual to quote the width as a "Full Width Half Maximum" (FWHM). This is the point where the amplitude has decayed to half the maximum as shown in Figure 70 on page 133. The linewidth of a laser is closely related to its coherence length; see Coherence Length and Coherence Time on page 125.

As will be seen in the remainder of this chapter, more complex lasers produce fewer lines (often just one). Also, more complex lasers are designed to produce very narrow lines. For most communications applications on SM fibre the fewer the number of lines and the narrower the linewidth the better.

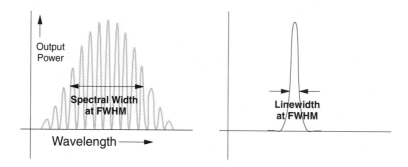

Figure 70. Spectral Width and Linewidth. These are usually measured as the width at half the maximum signal amplitude. That is at FWHM (Full Width Half Maximum).

3.3.3.1 Line Broadening

In the previous section it was noted that a single laser line consists of a narrow range of wavelengths rather than a single wavelength. This is due to the fact that rather than occupy a single energy state electrons may occupy a range of energy states within an energy band. Of course a given electron has an exact energy state at any point in time but a collection of electrons will have a range of (slightly) different energy states within the same band. The mean wavelength of a given transition is determined by the average energy level difference between the two bands involved in the transition.

Thus a laser transition produces a range of wavelengths over a (usually quite narrow) band. The gain curve produced has the typical bell shape of a "standard distribution". There are two mechanisms involved in causing electrons to have different energy states. These are referred to as "homogeneous line broadening" and "inhomogeneous line broadening".

Homogeneous Line Broadening

Sometimes called "natural broadening", this occurs when all of the electrons in the material have the same resonant frequency. Even though all of the atoms in the excited state are equivalent there are differences in energy level due to "uncertainty".

Inhomogeneous Line Broadening

Inhomogeneous Line Broadening takes place when the atoms in the medium have different resonance frequencies. This is the case with "Doppler

Broadening" which is due to the thermal vibration of atoms. It is also the case when impurities are present in the material.

3.3.3.2 Laser Operation

Figure 71. Output Spectrum Changes as Power is Applied. This figure illustrates a good quality Index-Guided FP laser. An unguided FP laser at full power produces as many as seven lines where a gain guided device typically produces three.

When power is applied to the device a number of interesting things occur:

Turn-on Delay

There is an inevitable delay between the time electrical power is applied and when the laser starts to produce coherent light. This is caused by the need to build up the carrier concentration in the cavity to the point of population inversion. The delay can be minimised by operating the device just below the "lasing threshold" (so that it fluoresces a bit in the OFF state). This means that there is already a carrier concentration present in the cavity and less power is needed to reach the inversion state.

Below Lasing Threshold

As the power applied to the device increases there is some fluorescence but lasing does not occur until the "lasing threshold" is reached. This is the power level where the amount of power applied just overcomes losses within the device. It is also the point at which a population inversion is achieved.

Just below the lasing threshold there are weak laser emissions at a range of wavelengths over the whole gain spectrum. This is caused by spontaneous emissions creating short lived laser action but the device has not got enough power for sustained lasing. This is shown in Figure 71.

Just Above Threshold

Just above the threshold lasing gets stronger and (in good index-guided devices) there are only a few strong lines present. This is shown in the centre box of Figure 71 on page 134.

Operational Region (Full Power)

When power is further increased lasing begins to dominate emissions (spontaneous emission is almost eliminated). At this time a small number (in good quality index-guided lasers only one) of the lasing modes will dominate the lasing operation. Typically this will be the strongest mode. So the spectral width of the light produced will narrow substantially.

Hole Burning

After a very short time in operation lasing tends to use up the available excited electrons in the centre (dominant mode path) of the cavity. This happens because we often can't get power to all of the active region at an even rate. Thus a "hole" is burnt in the path taken by the dominant mode. The dominant mode is thereby significantly reduced in power.

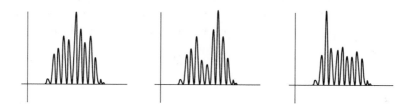

Figure 72. *Typical Mode Hopping Behaviour in an Unguided FP Laser*

Mode Hopping

Hole burning triggers mode hopping. When the strong, dominant mode decreases other modes are able to increase and become dominant.

Thus the laser produces light in one mode for a very short time and then it "hops" to another mode, and then to another and then to another. The whole range of resonant modes within the gain spectrum may be covered. This happens very quickly (a few tens of picoseconds per hop) so you get the effect of the laser producing a band of wavelengths.

It is important to note that when a single mode dominates the others are usually not suppressed entirely but they are strongly attenuated.

When the signal is sent on a dispersive medium mode hopping can become an additional source of noise. This is because each mode is at a different wavelength and each wavelength will travel at a different speed within the fibre. Not only will the pulse disperse but the dispersion will be irregular and random in nature.

Chirp

Immediately after power is applied to a laser there is an abrupt change in the carrier (electron and hole) flux density in the cavity caused by the lasing operation itself. This density of charge carriers is one factor that affects the refractive index. In addition, the temperature in the cavity increases quite rapidly. This temperature increase is too localised to affect the length of the cavity immediately but it does contribute to changing the refractive index of the material in the active region (within the cavity).

These changes in the RI of the cavity produce a rapid change in the centre wavelength of the signal produced. In the case of semiconductor lasers a "downward" chirp is produced. The wavelength shifts to a longer wavelength than it was immediately at the start of the pulse. It is not a large problem in short distance single-channel transmissions but in long distance applications and in WDM systems chirp can be a very serious problem. This is due to the fact that it broadens the spectral width of the signal and interacts with other aspects of the transmission system to produce distortion. Indeed, the chirp problem is the main reason that people use external modulators for transmission rates in excess of 1 Gbps.

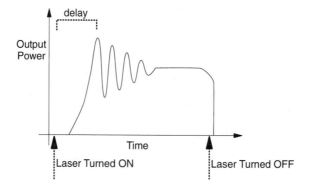

Figure 73. Relaxation Oscillations

Relaxation Oscillations (Ringing or Spiking)

When the laser is turned on you get short term fluctuations in the intensity of the light produced called "relaxation oscillations".

When power is applied to the laser the upper energy state population builds up until an inversion occurs and lasing can commence. However, lasing can deplete the upper energy state very quickly and if pumping isn't quite fast enough lasing will momentarily stop. Very soon afterwards it will start again as the pump builds up a population inversion again.

This effect varies widely between types of laser. Some can turn on with little or no relaxation oscillation, others (if the pump is a little bit weak for example) can produce these oscillations interminably and never reach a stable lasing state.

Most semiconductor communications lasers produce some relaxation oscillation at the beginning of each pulse but stabilise quite quickly.

Relative Intensity Noise (RIN)

RIN refers to a random intensity fluctuation in the output of a laser. The primary cause here seems to be the random nature of spontaneous emissions. As the laser operates new spontaneous emissions occur and some of them can resonate within the cavity and are amplified. This causes some fluctuation in output power.

Phase Noise

The random changes in emissions described above under RIN are by nature different in phase from previous emissions. This causes random changes in phase during laser operation. This variation is a natural consequence of the way lasers operate and cannot be suppressed. However, the effect is not important in amplitude modulated systems.

Intercavity Noise

Intercavity noise is caused by reflections returning a portion of the optical signal back into the laser cavity. When a signal returns into the laser cavity due to a spurious reflection it is at exactly the right wavelength and will be amplified in the cavity. This causes unwanted fluctuations in the light output.

In general there are two kinds of noise here. The first is caused from nearby reflections such as from the laser-to-fibre coupling. This can be minimised by using anti-reflection coatings and lens couplings designed to minimise reflections. The second is caused by reflections from more distant optical components. In some systems (especially long distance systems) an optical isolator is used immediately following the laser to eliminate the problems caused by these far-end reflections.

Drift

After the device has been operating for a while the temperature of the device can change (it will heat up) and this will affect the cavity length and the wavelength will change. Also, there are effects caused by age of the device and the materials it is made from. Some of these effects can cause a slow change in the wavelength over time.

3.3.3.3 Construction of a Fabry-Perot Laser

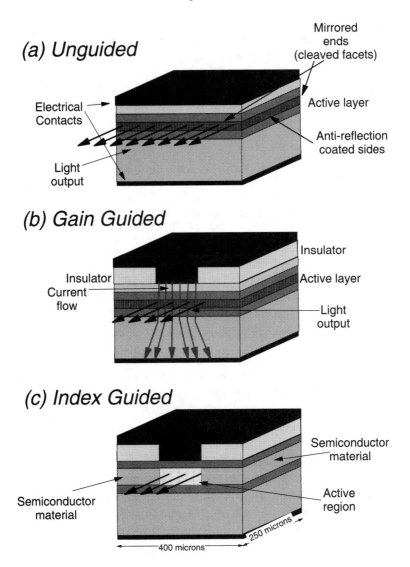

(a) Unguided

Mirrored ends (cleaved facets)

Electrical Contacts

Active layer

Anti-reflection coated sides

Light output

(b) Gain Guided

Insulator

Insulator
Current flow

Active layer

Light output

(c) Index Guided

Semiconductor material

Semiconductor material

Active region

250 microns

400 microns

Figure 74. Directing the Light in a Fabry-Perot Laser

In its basic form an FP laser is just an edge-emitting LED with mirrors on the ends of the cavity.

On the surface of it, an FP laser should be easier than an LED to construct. In an LED you have to give a lot of attention to collecting and guiding the light within the device towards the exit aperture. In an ideal laser you don't have the problem of guiding the light at all. Lasing takes place only between the mirrors and the light produced is exactly positioned. Unfortunately it isn't as simple as this.

A simple double heterostructure laser is shown in part (a) of Figure 77 on page 143. Mirrors are formed at the ends of the cavity by the "cleaved facets" of the crystal from which it is made.

> These devices are made from a *single* semiconductor crystal and the planes of the crystal are exactly parallel. When the device is constructed it is not "cut up" but rather cleaved (cracked) along the planes of the crystal. This results in exactly parallel mirrors at each end of the cavity. The interface of the semiconductor medium (refractive index usually around 3.5) and air (RI around 1.1) forms a mirror.

The active layer is very thin and the refractive index difference between the material of the active layer and the surrounding material is not great. Thus you don't get lasing in the vertical (transverse) mode. You can get lasing in the lateral mode but this is minimised by either coating the sides with an anti-reflection material or just making sure the sides are rough (cut rather than cleaved).

You do however get lasing in the longitudinal mode across the full width of the device. This is a problem as the device will tend to produce many different localised areas of lasing (at different wavelengths). A more significant problem is that it becomes very difficult to guide the light into a fibre! In answer to this problem two general techniques have been developed - Gain guidance and Index guidance.

3.3.3.4 Gain Guided Operation
In order to get lasing on a particular path we need the gain along that path (optical gain) to exceed the loss. We can get quite good control of device lasing if we control the entry of power (current in the form of electrons and holes) to the active region. Lasers using this principle are said to be "gain guided".

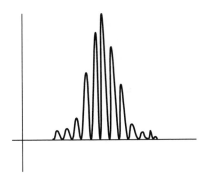

Figure 75. *Emission Profile of a Gain-Guided Fabry-Perot Laser. Note the asymmetry of the line structure. This is caused by Raman Scattering effects within the cavity.*

The typical technique used to guide power into the active region is to limit the area of electrical contact on the surface of the device. In part (b) of Figure 74 on page 139 we see that power is applied along a stripe on the top of the device (in this example). Current will flow predominantly along the path of least resistance (the shortest path) as shown by the grey arrows.

When this happens power is delivered into the active layer in a long stripe. There will easily be sufficient gain along this path (longitudinal mode) for lasing to occur but transverse modes and longitudinal modes outside the region of power delivery may not have sufficient gain to sustain lasing. Thus we get a narrow beam of light issuing from the centre of the active region.

Gain guided FP lasers produce a spectral width of between 5 nm and 8 nm consisting of between 8 and 20 or so lines. Linewidth is typically around .005 nm.

3.3.3.5 Index Guided Operation

Gain guidance can be further improved if we put stripes of semiconductor material (with a high bandgap energy) beside the active region. So we now no longer have a flat layer of active material throughout the whole device but just a narrow stripe through the middle. This is called a "buried heterostructure". Since the active region is now bounded on all sides by material of a lower refractive index (generally about .1 lower) mirrored surfaces are formed and this serves to guide the light much better than gain guidance alone.

An interesting variation on this technique is to use a *lower* RI in the active region than the material surrounding it. In this situation any light that strikes the edges of the cavity is captured and guided OUT of the cavity. Additional modes reflecting from the walls of the cavity are thus eliminated. This is not too much of a power loss since lasing cannot occur in these modes and only spontaneous emissions will leave the cavity by this route. However, while this is an interesting technique the bulk of commercial devices use the former technique of a higher RI within the cavity.

Index guided FP lasers produce a spectral width of between 1 nm and 3 nm with usually between 1 and 5 lines. Linewidth is generally around .001 nm. (Much better than the gain guided case.)

3.3.3.6 Modulating the Signal

The simplest and most common way of introducing modulation into the light beam is simply to modulate the drive current of the laser. There are many forms of external modulators available and these are discussed in 5.9, "Modulators and Switches" on page 300.

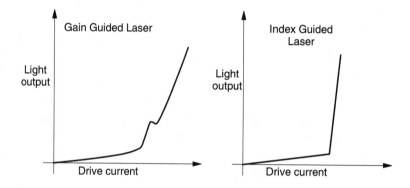

Figure 76. Fabry-Perot laser Output versus Input Current

Figure 76 shows how laser output varies with current input. The kink in both curves is the "lasing threshold" where lasing begins. Notice that the non-linearity of the curve for the gain-guided case makes this kind of laser useless for analogue modulation. However, it will modulate satisfactorily with digital OOK (On-Off Keying).

Operational Characteristics

> For digital modulation it is usual to operate the laser such that a zero bit is represented by a voltage (reflecting a current) at or just above the lasing threshold. This helps the device respond to high frequency modulation. It also means that there is some light output in the zero state. A ones state is usually set at just below the maximum output level.

Extinction Ratio

The extinction ratio is the ratio between the light output at full power and light output when a zero bit is being signaled. As mentioned above this is usually above zero. Extinction ratio is a measure of the difference in signal levels between a one and a zero state. It is usually quoted in decibels (dB).

Temperature Control

For most communications lasers temperature control is critical. The curves shown in the figure above shift significantly to the right as temperature increases. This changes the lasing threshold and the voltage levels needed to operate the device. Some of the lower cost devices can be satisfactorily operated with just good heat sinking. However, most lasers intended for long distance telecommunication applications are packaged with thermoelectric coolers and thermostatic Control.

Power control

One way of ensuring consistent operation over time (and perhaps saving the cost of cooling) is to monitor the light level produced by the laser and to adjust bias currents accordingly. This is often done by using a monitor diode at the back facet of the laser. Provided the back facet lets some light out (it usually does) you can measure the output power produced and control the laser accordingly.

3.3.4 Distributed Feedback (DFB) Lasers

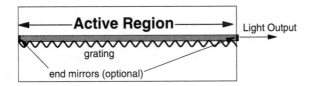

Figure 77. DFB Laser - Schematic

When we want to use lasers for long distance communication we find that standard FP lasers have significant problems:

1. As seen above FP lasers produce many wavelengths over a spectral width of between 5 and 8 nm. Even if we are using the 1310 "zero dispersion" band or "dispersion shifted" fibre in the 1550 nm band there will still be some chromatic dispersion of the signal caused by dispersion being slightly different at the different wavelengths.

2. The "mode hopping" behavior of FP lasers gives rise to "Mode Partition Noise" as described in 2.4.3, "Mode Partition Noise" on page 84.

3. In Wavelength Division Multiplexed (WDM) systems we want to carry many multiplexed optical signals on the same fibre. To do this it is important for each signal to have as narrow a spectral width as possible and to be as stable as possible. Regular FP lasers have too great a spectral width for use in this application.

Distributed FeedBack (DFB) lasers are one answer to this problem. The idea is that you put a Bragg grating into the laser cavity of an index-guided FP laser. This is just a periodic variation in the RI of the gain region along its length.[52] The presence of the grating causes small reflections to occur at each RI change (corrugation). When the period of the corrugations is a multiple of the wavelength of the incident light, constructive interference between reflections occurs and a proportion of the light is reflected. Other wavelengths destructively interfere and therefore cannot be reflected. The effect is strongest when the period of the Bragg grating is equal to the wavelength of light used (first order grating). However, the device will work when the grating period is any (small) integer multiple of the wavelength. Thus only one mode (the one that conforms to the wavelength of the grating) can lase.

Early devices using this principle had the grating within the active region and were found to have too much attenuation. As a result the grating was moved to a waveguide layer immediately adjacent to (below) the cavity. The evernescent field accompanying the light wave in the cavity extends into the adjacent layer and interacts with the grating to produce the desired effect.

In principle a DFB laser doesn't need end mirrors. The grating can be made strong enough to produce sufficient feedback (reflection) for lasing to take place. However, in a perfect DFB laser there are actually two lines produced (one at each side of the Bragg wavelength). We only want one line. A way of achieving this and improving the efficiency of the device is to place a high reflectance end mirror at one end of the cavity and either an AR coating or just a cleaved facet at the output end. In this case the grating doesn't need to be very strong - just sufficient to ensure that a single mode dominates. The added reflections (from the end mirrors) act to make the device asymmetric and suppress one of the two spectral lines. Unfortunately they also act to increase the linewidth.

---

[52] Bragg gratings are described in 5.7, "Diffraction Gratings" on page 260.

A schematic view of a DFB laser is shown in Figure 77 on page 143. DFB lasers are very effective and widely used but they have a problem with chirp. There are two main sources of chirp:

1. When the current is switched on the charge carrier (electron and hole) flux in the cavity changes very rapidly. This causes a change in the refractive index. A change in refractive index (of course) changes the resonant wavelength of the grating and the wavelength of the laser output changes (typically the wavelength gets longer) in well less than a single bit time.

2. During lasing the cavity heats up. This also happens very quickly (in a lot less than a bit time). This heating has two principal effects:

   a. It causes the RI of the cavity to change.

   b. It changes the electron energy gap in the material.

   In an FP laser (as distinct from a DBR or DFB laser) this change in the energy gap dominates other effects and is the predominant cause of chirp. In the DFB laser the energy gap change is irrelevant. This is because the energy gap covers a range of energies and the DFB resonant wavelength is determined by the grating spacing and the cavity RI. So long as the range of energies in the gap extends to cover the resonant wavelength then the device will lase.

This means that a DFB laser will chirp far less than an FP laser. This is because chirp in DFB lasers is caused by the effect of the change in RI. This effect is much smaller than the effect caused by the change in the energy gap (which dominates in FP lasers but doesn't affect DFBs).

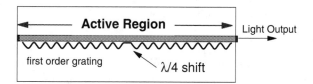

Figure 78. DFB Laser with Phase Shifted Grating - Concept

Sometimes DFB lasers are constructed with a quarter-wave phase shift in the middle section of the grating as shown in Figure 78. This phase shift introduces a sharp transmission "fringe" into the grating reflection band. The fringe acts to narrow the linewidth of the laser significantly.

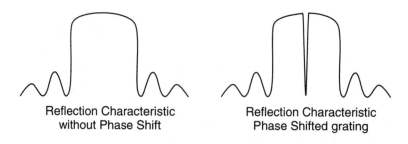

Reflection Characteristic
without Phase Shift

Reflection Characteristic
Phase Shifted grating

Figure 79. Phase Shifted Grating - Reflection Spectrum

Figure 79 shows the reflective characteristics of an unshifted and a shifted Bragg grating structure. Ascending values on the y-axis represent increasing percentage of *reflection*. The x-axis represents wavelength. The axes have not been scaled because the numerical values depend on the period and strength of the grating itself. The phase shifted case (on the right of the figure) shows that a narrow passband exists in the middle of the reflection band. This is caused by the quarter-wave phase shift. What happens is that the reflected waves from each end of the grating will be out of phase with each other and hence will destructively interfere.

DFB lasers have a number of significant advantages over FP types:

1. They can exhibit very narrow linewidths (of the order of 50 kHz).

2. They have quite low chirp as discussed above.

3. They typically have a very low Relative Intensity Noise (RIN).

Nothing however is completely without problems:

1. DBR lasers are extremely sensitive to reflections.

   Any reflection entering the cavity will disturb the laser's stable resonance. This causes a widening of the linewidth. To the extent that reflections returning from the outside vary (see 2.4.4, "Reflections and Return Loss Variation" on page 85) this can also be a significant source of noise. To minimise the effects of this problem DFB lasers are often packaged with an isolator integrated within the assembly. However, these don't always suppress all reflections and additional steps must be taken in system design to minimise the problem.

2. They are sensitive to temperature variations in two ways:

   a. The stable (average) temperature of the device has a very strong influence on wavelength. Wavelength variation on a scale of many seconds or longer doesn't have much detrimental effect on a single channel long distance communication system but it is a critical issue in WDM systems.

The device requires temperature control for stable operation. This is usually provided by including a "Peltier Effect" cooler in the laser package.

b. During transmission (in even one bit time) the cavity heats up. If a long series of "1" bits are transmitted this can cause a significant wavelength shift on a time scale too short to be compensated by the Peltier cooler. This introduces a requirement that higher layer link protocols be "balanced" and spend (on average) as much time in the "0" state as in the "1" state.

3. Varying conditions produce significant fluctuations in laser output power. This is undesirable for many reasons. To counter this a PIN diode is often included in the laser package near the "back facet". This diode picks up a small proportion of generated light from the transmittance of the back facet and provides input to a feedback loop for control of laser drive current.

4. They have a relatively high cost. As seen above, to get stable operation you almost always need temperature control, power control and optical isolation. All this adds to the cost.

3.3.5 Integrated Absorption Modulators

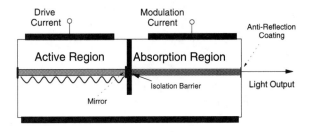

Figure 80. DFB Laser with Integrated Electro-Absorption Modulator

One of the problems with all solid state lasers is the maximum possible speed of modulation. Capacitance effects and effects caused by the (relatively slow) movement of charge carriers within the semiconductor limit the speed of modulation. External modulators are used at high speeds (see 5.9.4, "Electro-Absorption Modulators" on page 312) but this adds cost and complexity. Also signal strength is lost in the additional couplings required.

Figure 80 illustrates a DFB laser with an integrated absorption modulator. Basically, the DFB laser and the modulator are separate devices built together on the same chip.

Note the presence of a mirror between the absorption layer and the laser cavity and the AR coating on the end facet of the device. The laser is run in the on state all the time and modulation is accomplished by varying the absorption in the modulator. The absorption region is reverse-biased and there is only a tiny leakage current. This results in much faster modulation than can be achieved by turning the drive current to the active region on and off. In addition it almost completely removes the problem of chirp because the laser cavity is operating at the same level of output power all the time.

3.3.6 Q-Switching

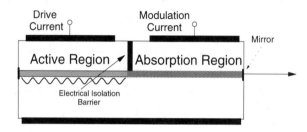

Figure 81. DFB Laser with Electro-Absorption Modulator within the Cavity

In Figure 81 the absorber is shown placed *within* the laser cavity itself. This is similar to the device described in 3.3.5, "Integrated Absorption Modulators" on page 147. All that has happened is we have moved the mirror. However, the device operates in quite a different way now.

When the material is in an absorbent state it prevents lasing. When it is transparent (non-absorbent) the laser can produce light. This laser produces very short high-power pulses. When the laser is in the OFF state (the absorber is absorbing the light) the active medium gets completely pumped up and starts fluorescing. When the laser is then turned ON lasing commences very quickly and produces a short high-power pulse. This method of operation is called "Q-Switching" because the Q of the laser cavity is changed to initiate the pulse.

Lasers switched in this way can be used for generating solitons (see 12.1, "Solitons" on page 651).

3.3.7 Mode-Locking and Self-Pulsating Lasers

Under some conditions some types of laser will produce a very fast sequence of regularly spaced separate pulses. In many cases this pulse stream is a natural result of the construction of the laser. In other cases the behavior can be induced by modulation of the drive current. When a laser produces such a pulse-stream it is said to be mode-locked or self-pulsating. (And sometimes as self-mode-locked.) Mode-locking is not quite the same thing as regular production of pulses by turning the laser on and off. There are two general types of mode-locking: Active mode-locking and passive mode-locking.

In a passive mode-locked device, pulses are produced at intervals corresponding to the round-trip time of the fundamental mode of the laser's cavity. In semiconductor lasers the cavity is generally too short for this type of pulsation to be of much use as a generator of separate pulses. In external cavity lasers and in fibre lasers however the cavity is quite long enough for mode-locked pulses with good separation to be generated. These can be used to produce the very fast streams of short pulses needed in OTDM systems and in Soliton systems.

In a passive device a substance is placed into the optical feedback path which acts as a "saturable absorber". This saturable absorber absorbs light at a fixed maximum rate. At low light levels it absorbs everything and suppresses lasing. At high light levels it saturates and allows high-intensity pulses to pass. Thus after the drive current is switched on, the saturable absorber absorbs light and keeps the cavity Q low. Lasing is suppressed and a large inversion is built up in the active region. At some stage a single photon will happen to be in the right direction and will build up a pulse large enough to pass the absorber. This pulse then oscillates back and forth in the cavity producing output pulses at a fixed interval determined by the cavity length.

In semiconductor lasers you can get similar behavior but the pulses are too close together to be usable as a pulse-train. This is so-called self-pulsating behavior. It is very closely related to "relaxation oscillation" or "ringing" as described in Relaxation Oscillation on page 137.

In an actively mode-locked device there is something placed into the optical path within the cavity that acts as a shutter. Thus the action is very similar to Q-switching with a regular modulated triggering mechanism. The Q-switched laser described in the previous section will do this very well when its absorption modulator is driven with a regular square wavetrain. The usual way this is done is to use only shallow variations in the drive current at the same frequency as the resonant frequency of the laser cavity.

3.3.8 Distributed Bragg Reflector (DBR) Lasers

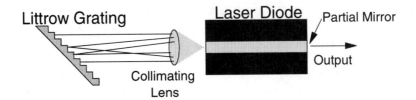

Figure 82. DBR Laser - Schematic

DBR lasers are very similar to the DFB lasers described in the previous section. The major difference is that where DFB lasers have a grating within the active region of the cavity, DBR lasers have a partitioned cavity with the grating in a region that is not active (amplifying).

The reason for this structure is that the refractive index within the cavity of a laser changes during operation due to changes in temperature and electron flux. Change of refractive index in the grating region of course changes the operational wavelength of the device. If you put the grating into an inactive extension of the cavity then there is a lot less wavelength variation from these causes. (Because the characteristics of the material immediately adjacent to the grating are not being changed by the laser's operation.) Figure 82 shows a schematic of this structure.

As in the DFB laser you don't always need end mirrors as the grating can provide sufficient reflection. However, end mirrors are almost always used in an asymmetric configuration. Typically this is 30% mirror on the "back" facet and either just a cleaved facet or a 4% mirror on the front (output) facet.

DBR lasers typically produce a single line only with a linewidth of around .0001 nm. The major problem is that there can be significant absorption in the inactive region near the grating(s). This causes a loss in efficiency.

3.3.9 Quantum Wells

DBR and DFB lasers are often built using a "Quantum Well" structure.

When light is confined into a cavity smaller than its wavelength it behaves as a particle (quantum) rather than as a wave. In the case of semiconductor lasers if we restrict the size of the cavity, quantum behavior changes the operation of the laser in a dramatic and fundamental way.

By their nature, most semiconductor lasers are very thin (20 microns or so) in the vertical direction but this is not thin enough to cause quantum behavior. In QW lasers cavity height is reduced to around 10 or 20 nm. The width of the cavity does not need to be this restricted but of course we want it to be narrow enough to prevent unwanted "lateral" modes from forming. Cavity width is generally from 5 to 20 microns. Of course the cavity has to be many wavelengths long to get sufficient gain. In addition, it is difficult to manufacture lasers with cavities shorter than 50 microns. As with other semiconductor lasers the cavity length is typically 200 to 250 microns. This cavity geometry is called a "quantum well".

The most obvious change in laser characteristic that this brings is that the amount of material in the active region is substantially reduced. This reduces the amount of energy needed to achieve lasing and thus the lasing threshold. The result is a higher gain characteristic but a lower maximum output power than conventional (non-QW) devices. In addition, quantum wells have a much reduced sensitivity to temperature change (compared to DBR and DFB structures). In the very narrow cavity available there is much less space for energy and momentum effects to occur.

The quantum well structure prevents lateral modes forming and ensures that lasing produces only one line. In addition the single line that is produced tends to have a narrower linewidth than for non-QW structures.

As with all DFB and DBR structures, the sides of the cavity are made of a material of lower refractive index than that of the cavity itself. This is the principle of "index guidance" discussed above. In some forms of QW laser the index at the side of the cavity is graded to further confine lateral modes.

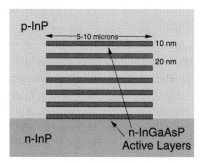

***Figure 83.** Cavity Structure of a Multiple Quantum Well Laser*

Lasers as described above with a single active region are called "Single Quantum Well" (SQW) lasers. Often a number of quantum wells are used one on top of another as shown in Figure 83. These are called "Multiple Quantum Well" structures. Notice that in the figure the separating layers between the cavities are very thin (10 to 20 nm). This means that there is strong interaction between the intracavity fields and a single coherent line is produced. MQW structures retain many of the desirable characteristics of SQW ones (such as reduced lasing threshold) but produce higher gain and greater total power. A disadvantage is that MQW lasers produce a broader linewidth than SQW ones (but still narrower than comparable non-QW structures).

3.3.9.1 Strained-Layer Quantum Wells

Perhaps the most important characteristic of a semiconductor junction is the fact that the crystalline structure of the material *must* be continuous across the junction. That is, the crystal lattices of the different types of material on each side must join into a single crystal. If the spacings of the atoms in the different materials are too different (by more than a few percent) then you get "dislocations" in the crystal structure around the junction which destroy the operation of the device.

However, if we sandwich an extremely thin (about 2 nm) semiconductor layer between much thicker layers of a material with a significantly different lattice constant some exciting things happen. The atoms of the thin material layer conform to the lattice structure of the thicker layers *without* dislocations or cracking! The atoms in the thin layer are pulled apart (or forced together) to conform to the crystalline structure of the surrounding material. This means that the chemical bonds (electron orbits) holding the material together become longer or shorter than their natural length. This has two very beneficial effects:

1. It allows the use of a much wider range of materials in the heterojunction. Usually we are very restricted in the choice of materials used in a junction because of the requirement for lattice matching. The added flexibility allows the design of more efficient lasers.

2. The "strain" in the lattice of the thinner material changes its properties in a number of highly desirable ways. Most obviously, it changes the bandgap energy levels. By engineering the amount of strain we can "tune" the bandgap (laser wavelength) without affecting too much the semiconductor properties of the junction. In addition, the strain allows the device to operate at significantly lower threshold currents than are possible in unstrained MQW lasers.

By their nature Strained-Layer Lasers are a form of MQW laser. They are a very new type which has only been explored since about 1992. Devices have been constructed with very low threshold currents allowing for very high speed modulation. It has proven possible to build devices with output power of up to half a watt. This is extremely high power for semiconductor lasers.

3.3.10 Tunable DBR Lasers

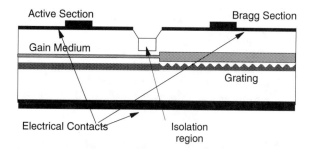

Figure 84. *Tunable 2-Section DBR Laser*

There are several situations where it is desirable to have the ability to change (tune) the laser's wavelength.

- In some WDM systems we would like to tune the laser very quickly (in a few tens of nanoseconds) to a particular wavelength (or channel). A number of proposals for optical LAN and MAN networks require this ability.

- In other WDM situations we may want to establish a path through a wide area network by using wavelength routing. It may be that we only have to do this relatively seldom and that the time taken to do the tuning is not very important. This would be appropriate in a wide area telecommunication backbone network where tuning is used to configure and re-configure routes through the network. A tuning time of around a second in this case would be quite acceptable.

- Still other WDM situations might require the setting up of "calls" across the network (like telephone calls). Set up time in this case can be perhaps a hundred microseconds or so.

- In early fixed channel WDM systems there were two big problems with laser wavelengths:

  1. When lasers are made it is extremely difficult and costly to specify the wavelength exactly. This leads to the process of making a lot of them and measuring them later. Randomness determines that some will have wavelengths we are interested in so we select them and reject the rest. This is expensive.

  2. Over time the materials of which the laser is made deteriorate a bit and the wavelength changes. This is fine in single-channel systems but anathema to WDM systems as wavelengths will start to run into one another.

In both of these cases a laser that can be tuned quite slowly over a relatively narrow range can make a big improvement.

So different systems require different kinds of tunability (range and speed).

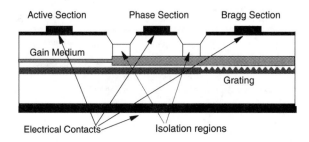

Figure 85. Tunable 3-Section DBR Laser

Figure 84 on page 153 and Figure 85 show two electronically tunable DBR lasers. One is a two-section device and the other has three sections. The device in Figure 84 on page 153 has a discontinuous tuning characteristic over a range of a bit less than 10 nm. The three-section device can be continuously tuned over the same range.

Operation (of the 3-section device) is as follows:

- Current in the left-hand section of the device flows through the gain medium and here lasing (amplification) takes place.

- In the centre and rightmost sections the electron flux within the cavity causes the cavity to change in refractive index within these sections.

- The change in RI causes the wavelength of the light emitted to change also.

- The right-hand section has the grating inside it (or rather immediately adjacent to it) and this is used for broad tuning.

- Fine tuning is accomplished by varying the current in the "phase section" (middle part) of the laser cavity.

A disadvantage of the 3-section device is that it requires relatively complex electronics for control.

3.3.10.1 Sampled-Grating Tunable DBR Lasers

As discussed above the achievable tuning range of DBR lasers is somewhat less than 10 nm. This is not sufficient for many proposed system designs (although it is more than adequate for many others). To extend the tuning range DBR lasers employing a "sampled grating" have been constructed.

Grating Structure

Grating | Blanked sections

Figure 86. Sampled Grating - Schematic

A tunable DBR laser relies on a change in the RI of the cavity adjacent to the grating to change the resonant wavelength. The problem is that the achievable RI change is not very great. A sampled grating consists of a number of short grating sections with periodic blanking between them. Two sampled gratings are used in such a way that the interaction between them causes a small change in RI to produce a large change in wavelength. The major drawback of this approach is that the tuning is discontinuous.

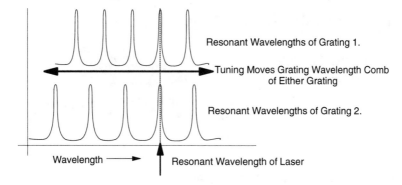

Figure 87. Principle of Operation. Each grating has a different set of possible resonances. One section is tuned until one of its resonances is the same as one of the possibilities of the other grating. This then becomes the lasing wavelength.

Gratings with periodic blanking have the interesting property of producing reflection peaks not only at the Bragg wavelength but at other wavelengths at either side of the Bragg wavelength. Thus you get a grating with multiple (precisely determined) reflection peaks. The separation between these peaks is inversely proportional to the blanking (sampling) period.

If we use two sampled gratings with *different* sampling periods as the opposing end mirrors in a laser we can organise things so that the two gratings have only one reflection peak in common. The common reflection peak will be the resonant wavelength of the laser. When the RI at one of the (sampled) gratings changes then a *different* pair of peaks will be resonant and hence we can achieve a large (albeit discontinuous and abrupt) change in lasing wavelength.

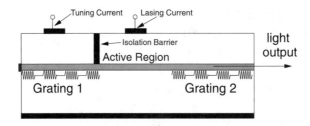

Figure 88. Sampled Grating Tunable DFB Laser - Schematic

This principle works quite well and devices with a tuning range of up to 100 nm have been reported in the literature. Commercial devices (albeit with a more limited tuning range) are currently available. This device is illustrated in Figure 88.

3.3.11 External Cavity DBR Lasers

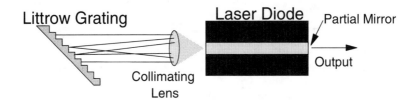

Figure 89. External Cavity DBR Laser Schematic

An interesting form of DBR laser can be constructed where the resonant cavity extends outside the laser chip itself. This runs counter to intuition because as the cavity length is extended so the possible number of longitudinal modes increases exponentially. This would seem to make matters worse.

The key reason for the external cavity is so that we can use a much stronger (more selective) grating. In the configuration illustrated, the "back" mirror of a regular index-guided FP laser is removed and replaced with a lens and Littrow[53] grating assembly. Such lasers produce a single line only with a very narrow line width (a few tens of kilohertz). The major problem here is that these devices are significantly more expensive than other types of high quality laser.

---

[53] More information on Littrow gratings may be found in 5.7.1.1, "Wavelength Selection" on page 263.

A useful feature is that you can mount the grating on a moveable platform (such as a piezoelectric crystal) and mechanically tune the device by tilting the grating. This provides a very wide tuning range but a relatively slow tuning speed.

3.3.12 External Fibre-Cavity DBR Lasers

Figure 90. *Stabilisation of Fabry-Perot Laser with a Fibre Bragg Grating*

One interesting option for providing narrow linewidth, wavelength stable light is to use a simple Fabry-Perot laser diode controlled by an external grating written within the fibre itself. This type of grating is called an "In-Fibre Bragg Grating".[54] It reflects light (is a mirror) at one very specific wavelength. This configuration is shown in Figure 90.

The idea is very simple. You remove the exit mirror from the FP laser and couple it to a fibre containing an FBG at the wavelength you want. This grating should reflect between 50% and 65% of light at the selected wavelength. The laser cavity therefore now extends into the fibre and the laser end-mirror is formed by the grating. The key characteristic here is that the grating *only reflects light at a very specific wavelength.* Thus the cavity cannot resonate at any other wavelength because there will be no feedback at any other wavelength!

This has a number of significant benefits:

1. Cost

   The device is likely to cost a lot less than a semiconductor DBR or DFB laser.

2. Accurate wavelength control

   Wavelength can be controlled very accurately and suffer from minimal drift.

3. Very narrow linewidth

---

[54] Fibre Bragg gratings are discussed in 5.7.2, "In-Fibre Bragg Gratings (FBGs)" on page 266.

By using a strong (highly selective) grating you can have a very narrow linewidth (of the order of 50 kHz).

4. Temperature control is not needed for the laser

You still need to stabilise the grating under conditions of temperature variation. However, this is less of an issue because the grating does not produce heat. In addition, there are ways of compensating the grating for changes in temperature that do not involve active temperature control.

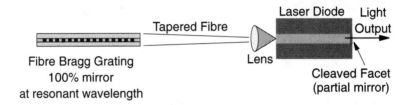

Figure 91. *FP Laser with External FBG - Alternative Structure. The structure here is somewhat easier to fabricate than the device shown in the previous figure. This is due to the mechanical difficulty of having the FBG in the output pigtail.*

The major challenge in making this device is that the grating must be positioned close enough to the laser such that it is within the coherence length. This can be difficult as it means that the FBG needs to be within a centimetre or so of the semiconductor cavity.

As the end of 1998 approaches external fibre-cavity lasers are still in the later stages of research but they are expected to appear on the commercial market by early 1998.

3.3.12.1 Coherence Collapse Operation

Coherence collapse is a very interesting mode. In this case a regular (unmodified) FP laser is used complete with mirrors. The FBG is positioned far enough away from the laser for the signal to lose its coherence (outside its coherence length). This is strictly not an external cavity laser but rather a regular FP diode operated with strong external feedback. Reflection from the FBG injects a very large signal at the FBG resonant wavelength into the laser cavity and competes (conflicts) with the cavity modes. Indeed this reflection dominates the cavity modes.

This has the effect of broadening the laser linewidth but it locks the wavelength on to the FBG so that multiline operation and mode-hopping are suppressed. While the device experiences an *increase* in high frequency noise, low speed operation is very significantly enhanced as instabilities associated with mode-hopping (mode partition noise etc.) are removed.

This is a relatively easy device to build as the laser diode is an ordinary FP laser diode. There is no need to AR coat the facets or to do special processing.

This principle has already found use in stabilising the pump lasers in EDFAs.

3.3.13 Multi-Wavelength Lasers

As these devices are primarily intended for use in WDM systems they are discussed in 9.2.1.1, "Multiwavelength Lasers" on page 520.

3.3.14 Vertical Cavity Surface Emitting Lasers (VCSELs)

VCSELs [55] (also called "microlasers") have been around in various forms since the late 1970's. However in 1991 there was a major development in construction techniques reported and in 1996 the first commercial devices became available.

It seems almost too obvious but when you build a laser you can't just arbitrarily decide on its structure. You are severely limited by material characteristics and available manufacturing technology. In previous sections we have discussed edge emitting lasers where you start with a flat substrate and use the techniques of chip manufacture to build a very thin, flat device that nevertheless has a relatively large area. VCSELs are different. Instead of emitting from the edge they emit from the surface. They are constructed by laying down a very large number (perhaps 500) of relatively thin layers of semiconductor material. The device emits light vertically through the stack of material layers. This is shown in Figure 92 on page 160. As in any laser the overall structure is one of two end mirrors on each side of an "active region" which produces the light. The key points are as follows:

- The mirrors are made of alternating layers of material of different refractive indices with carefully controlled thickness. The stack forms a Bragg grating (see 5.7, "Diffraction Gratings" on page 260) which is a wavelength-selective mirror.

- The sides of the laser are formed by cutting the material out.

- The laser dimensions can be such that no lateral modes are possible. In fact the laser is so confined that it forms a "quantum well" in which light behaves as individual photons rather than as waves or rays. Typical dimensions are about 12 microns in diameter (for single moded operation) and 20 microns (for multimoded

---

[55] pronounced vick-sell

operation). Experimental devices have been made and shown to operate with a diameter of only 3 microns.

- The active region is very short compared to other types of semiconductor laser. This means that the mirrors have to have a relatively high reflectivity. (You need many passes through the amplifying medium to get enough amplification to sustain lasing.)

- One of the big challenges is supplying power to the active region because it must pass through many mirror layers (junctions) first. This problem however has been solved.

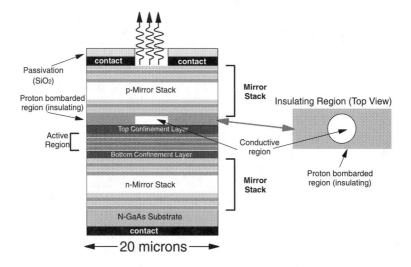

Figure 92. VCSEL Structure

The operational characteristics of VCSELs combine many of the desirable properties of lasers and LEDs.

- Typical coupled output power at present is somewhere around a milliwatt. This is very good for LAN type communications as we only want to transmit up to a maximum power of the (class 1) eye safety limit (-4 dBm).

  Typical LEDs are a lot lower in power and require the use of expensive InGaAs pin diode receivers. VCSELs in the LAN environment can work well with simple, low cost Si diode receivers.

- Current VCSELs on the market offer one of two possible wavelengths: 980 nm or 850 nm. Again this is in the high attenuation window for glass fibre but quite adequate for distances of around 500 metres or less.

- VCSELs with a large diameter (20 microns or so) have multiple transverse modes. This makes the device very suitable for use with multimode fibre.

  The big problem for lasers with multimode fibre is modal noise as discussed in 2.3.6, "Modal Noise" on page 64. The low coherence of output light produced by a multi-transverse mode VCSEL leads to insensitivity to mode selective loss and minimises the problem of modal noise.

- A low divergence circular light beam is produced which allows for easy and efficient coupling to a fibre.

- Typical VCSELs have very low threshold currents (less than 5 mA). Very low power dissipation and low modulation current requirements mean that special driver circuitry is not required.

- VCSELs have very high modulation bandwidths (2.4 GHz has been demonstrated). This is well in excess of what can be achieved with much more expensive LEDs.

- Devices are very stable and generally do not need a monitor photodiode or feedback power control as is conventionally needed for most communications lasers and high-end LEDs.

In 1998 four manufacturers have low priced VCSELs on the market. In the near future we could see them replacing LEDs completely for the LAN communications environment.

3.3.15 In-Fibre Lasers

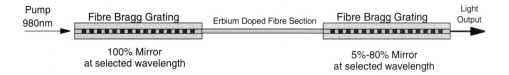

Figure 93. In-Fibre Laser Using FBGs. *Depending on the detailed design the exit mirror might have any reflectivity (at the specified wavelength) between about 5% and 80%.*

Fibre lasers are not as yet in major commercial use but they offer a number of very interesting possibilities and working prototypes have been reported in the literature many times. They are very closely related to fibre amplifiers (described in 5.2, "Optical Amplifiers" on page 198).

The concept is very simple. You use a section of rare earth doped fibre as the gain section (cavity) of the laser. The mirrors can be made in various ways but the use of

In-Fibre Bragg Gratings (FBGs) is very attractive because of their wavelength-selective nature. The laser is pumped with light of a wavelength appropriate to the lasing medium. (This is 980 nm or 1480 nm for Erbium.)

In Figure 93 on page 161 we see a simple example of a fibre laser constructed from two FBGs and a length of Erbium doped fibre. All it is is an optical amplifier with mirrors on the end of the fibre to form a cavity.

- Input light from a pump laser operating at 980 nm enters the cavity through the left-hand FBG. Both FBGs are resonant (reflective) at a very specific wavelength (you choose) in the 1550 band and so the 980 nm light will pass straight through the FBG without attenuation.

- Spontaneous emission will commence in the erbium quite quickly.

- Most of the spontaneous emissions will not be in the guided mode and so will leave the cavity quite quickly.

- Most spontaneous emissions will not be at exactly the right wavelength to be reflected by the FBGs and so will pass out of the cavity straight through the FBG mirrors. But some spontaneous emissions will (by chance) have exactly the right wavelength and will happen to be in the guided mode.

- In this case these emissions will be reflected by the FBGs and amplified in the cavity and lasing has commenced.

Various rare earth dopants can to produce lasers in differing wavelength bands. In addition the type and composition of glass used in the "host" fibre makes an enormous difference to the operational characteristics of the lasing medium. This is because it plays a part in the energy state transitions necessary to support stimulated emission. The exact wavelength however is determined by the characteristics of the grating used:

- Nd^{3+} at 0.9 μm

- Nd^{3+} at 1.08 μm

- Pr^{3+} at 1.06 μm

- Er^{3+} at 1.55 μm

Another factor is the level of rare earth dopant used in the glass. Some glass hosts cannot be doped to very high concentrations. For example, erbium in silica glass can only be used to a maximum of about 1% but it can be used at significantly higher concentrations in "ZBLAN" glasses.[56] If we want the laser to be short (to minimise mode hopping) a high dopant concentration is needed.

The important characteristics of this class of lasers are as follows:

High Power Output

> In communications applications power output of up to 50 mW (very high) is achievable. For other types of applications powers of up to 4W in continuous operation or 10 W in pulsed operation are possible. This is a lot higher than is achievable with semiconductor lasers.

Low Noise

> Fibre lasers have inherently very low levels of Relative Intensity Noise (RIN).

Tunability

> Tunable versions have been constructed with a discontinuous tuning range up to 40 nm or with a continuous range of about 5 nm.

Very Narrow Linewidth

> A 10 kHz linewidth has been demonstrated. (This is about as good as you get.)

Good Soliton Generation

> Fibre lasers create good natural mode-locked solitons.

External Modulation

> You need an external modulator of some kind as you can't control the output by switching the energy source on and off (modulating the pump).

Preselected Wavelengths

> Since FBGs can be manufactured to very accurate wavelength tolerances and do not need active temperature control (heaters and coolers) the device can be manufactured to an accurate wavelength without the need for post-tuning.

Mode Hopping

> Mode hopping is still a problem but can be eliminated if the device is physically short. If this last characteristic is controlled, this type of laser could be a very suitable source for a WDM system.

---

[56] See 12.2, "Advanced Fibres" on page 653.

3.3.16 Fibre Ring Lasers

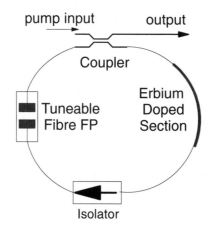

Figure 94. Tuneable Fibre-Ring Laser

A fibre ring structure can also be used to make a very narrow linewidth laser. A conceptual structure of such a laser is shown in Figure 94. The structure is very similar to that of a fibre ring resonator (see 5.8.4, "Fibre Ring Resonators" on page 297). However, in this case the wavelength is controlled by the tuneable FP filter and not by the length of the fibre loop. (Long fibre loops of this kind have resonances spaced very close together and without the FP filter the device would produce multiple lines.) An isolator is necessary to prevent a counter-propagating lasing mode being generated. Such a mode could cause spatial "hole burning" and result in unwanted multimode operation.

The characteristics of this device include:

- Very efficient operation.

- Stable wavelength produced.

- Very narrow linewidth can be produced (less than 10 kHz).

- Output power can be quite high (up to 50 mW). At very narrow linewidths this is limited by SBS.

- The device is tuneable over a range of up to 40 nm.

- Output is already in a fibre so there is no pigtailing involved in connecting to a fibre.

However, an external modulator is required as there is no way to modulate the laser by controlling the pump. Also you need a pump laser to provide necessary energy.

3.3.17 Upconversion Fibre Lasers (Double Pumping)

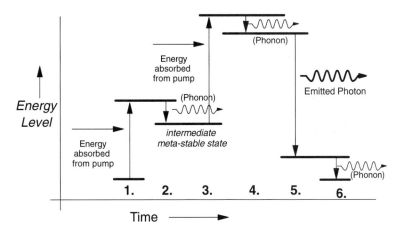

Figure 95. Upconversion Laser Operation

Another very interesting possibility for fibre lasers is for producing wavelengths that are very difficult in other media. The "upconversion" laser is a good example of this. Upconversion is so-called because the photon energy produced is *higher* than the energy of the pump. (That is, the wavelength of the light produced is shorter than the wavelength of the pump.)

For example, a blue laser requires a bandgap energy which is too great for current semiconductors. (The shorter the wavelength the more energy you need.) Some rare earth materials will lase at the desired wavelengths but you need a way of delivering a high energy level from the pump. One answer here is "double pumping". Some materials can be pumped to an intermediate metastable state and then pumped again (with a different wavelength) to reach a high energy state from which they can lase with a blue light. To do this you have to use two pumps (different wavelengths) and mix the pump light at the input of the laser.

A working blue in-fibre laser has been reported in the literature. It uses praseodymium doped ZBLAN[57] fibre. Pumping was at 835 nm and at 1017 nm. Blue light output (at a little over 0 dBm) was demonstrated at a wavelength of 492 nm.

Blue lasers are not a very exciting prospect for communications applications but may have other applications such as in CD-ROM players.

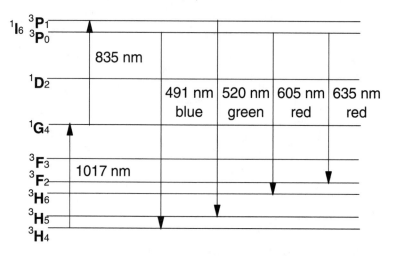

Figure 96. *Some Energy Levels in Praseodymium Upconversion Lasers*

An interesting aspect of fibre amplifiers and lasers is that you often have many potential lasing wavelengths (and you have to do something to suppress the unwanted ones). Figure 96 shows the higher energy levels and lasing possibilities for praseodymium. In operation you get spontaneous emission at all of these levels and the fibre shines with a bright white light!

3.3.18 Gas Lasers

The gas laser is the simplest kind of laser to understand because each atom of the lasing material can be considered to exist in a vacuum. You don't have to consider the influence of the surrounding material.

---

[57] Zirconium Barium Lanthanum Aluminium Sodium Fluoride glass. See 12.2, "Advanced Fibres" on page 653.

Gas lasers are well known for the very high power that can be produced. It is said that they were to be the key weapon in the US "star wars" weapons system. The are commonly used in industry for cutting metal etc.

Low powered gas lasers are also used in more mundane applications. The typical supermarket scanner uses a helium-neon gas laser.

In operation gas lasers are somewhat different from their solid state counterparts. In a gas laser, individual atoms (or ions) interact with their electrons quite unaffected by the surrounding material. In a semiconductor structure the characteristics of the material are all important.

Gas lasers are not used very often in modern communications. However they have a minor use as a transmitter for constructing outdoor optical links. Quite high speed, short distance, line-of-sight connections can be made this way. Unfortunately, heavy rain and smoke cause attenuation and scattering which significantly limit the usefulness of this kind of communication. Carbon dioxide (CO_2) lasers operating at a wavelength in the far infrared (10.6 nm) are often used for this application.

3.3.19 Free Electron Lasers (FELs)

Free Electron Lasers are a laboratory curiosity at this time and are not used for any commercial purpose. However, they illustrate an important thing about the lasing process: *You don't need any atoms present in order to have lasing!* You just need electrons.

In an FEL you use a beam of electrons produced in a particle accelerator. The electron beam is passed through a magnetic field in such a way that electrons are forced to jump from one particular energy level to another. This transition can be stimulated and the electron beam will lase!

An attractive feature of FELs is that they are tunable over a very wide range - from wavelengths of a few millimeters to around 1 micron. So far FELs have not yet produced visible light.

3.4 Further Reading

C.A. Burrus and B. I. Miller (1971)

> *Small Area, Double Heterostructure Aluminium Gallium Arsenide Electroluminescent Diode Sources for Optical Fibre Transmission Lines*: J. of Optical Communication, Vol 4, 1971. p307

Jewell et al. (1991)

Vertical-Cavity Surface-Emitting Lasers: Design, Growth, Fabrication, Characterisation: IEEE J. of Quantum Electronics, Vol 27, No 6, June 1991.

H. Kogelnik and C.V. Shank (1970)

Stimulated Emission in a Periodic Structure: Applied Physics Letters, Vol 18, No 4, February 1971. pp 152-154

H. Kogelnik and C.V. Shank (1971)

Stimulated Emission in a Periodic Structure: Applied Physics Letters, Vol 18, No 4, 15 February 1971. pp 152-154

Tien Pei Lee and Chung-En Zah (1989)

Wavelength Tuneable and Single-Frequency Lasers for Photonic Communications Networks: IEEE Communications Magazine, October 1989. pp 42-52

H. Soda, M. Furutsu, K. Sato, M. Matsuda and H. Ishikawa (1989)

5 Gbit/s Modulation Characteristics of Optical Intensity Modulator Monolithically Integrated with DFB Laser: Electronics Letters, Vol 25, No 5, March 1989. pp 334-335

Chapter 4. Optical Detectors

The predominant types of light detector used in communications systems rely on the principle of ionisation in a semiconductor material. There are a number of different kinds of device but they can all be viewed as variations on a central principle rather than as devices that involve radically different principles. When discussing photodetectors there are four important parameters:

Detector Responsivity[58]

> This is the ratio of output current to input optical power. Hence this is the efficiency of the device.

Spectral Response Range

> This is the range of wavelengths over which the device will operate.

Response Time

> This is a measure of how quickly the detector can respond to variations in the input light intensity.

Noise Characteristics

> The level of noise produced in the device is critical to its operation at low levels of input light.

4.1 Photoconductors

Photoconductors are the simplest conceivable optical detector. The device consists of a piece of (undoped) semiconductor material with electrical contacts attached. A voltage is applied across the contacts. When a photon arrives in the semiconductor it is absorbed and an electron/hole pair is created. Under the influence of the electric field between the two contacts the electron and the hole each migrate toward one of the contacts. The electron to the positive contact and the hole to the negative contact. Thus the resistance of the device varies with the amount of light falling on it.

---

[58] Terrible word but everyone uses it...

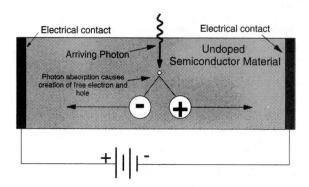

Figure 97. Photoconductive Detector - Principle

Practical photoconductive detectors are usually structured as shown in Figure 98. A flat piece of semiconductor has metal contacts plated onto it. The contact areas are "interdigitised" so that there is only a short distance between the contacts. This is done because the charge carriers drift quite slowly through the semiconductor material and this limits the speed of the device.

An interesting point is that the device exhibits *gain*. This is because electron drift is much faster than hole drift. Electrons tend to arrive at the positive contact before a hole arrives at the other side. This then causes the negative electrode to emit an electron into the semiconductor. This electron in turn may arrive at the positive electrode before the hole arrives at the negative electrode and yet another electron is emitted into the material.

This type of detector is quite useful at longer wavelengths (10 to 30 microns) but has not been used seriously for communications applications. However, there has been renewed research interest in recent times.

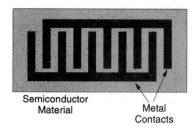

Figure 98. Practical Photoconductive Detector - Schematic

4.2 Photodiodes

Photodiodes convert light directly to electric current. An ideal (p-i-n) diode can convert one photon to one electron of current. (Surprisingly, real devices get very close to this ideal.) This means that the current output from such a device is very small and an external amplifier is needed before the signal can be dealt with by a receiver.

4.2.1 P-N Diodes

The principle involved in a PIN diode is simply the principle of the LED *in reverse*. That is, light is absorbed at a p-n junction rather than emitted.

The characteristics of p-n junctions are discussed in 3.2.1, "The Semiconductor Junction Diode" on page 103.

- A reverse biased p-n junction passes no current unless something happens to promote electrons from the valence band to the conduction band within the depletion zone. At ordinary room temperatures there is a small amount of this due to the action of heat and thus there is a very small current.

- Photons of sufficient energy can be absorbed and cause the promotion of an electron from the valence band to the conduction band (and of course the simultaneous generation of a hole in the valence band).

- The free electron and hole created by the photon absorption now are attracted to their opposite charges at either side of the junction and current flows.

The big problem here is that the depletion zone in a p-n junction is extremely thin. Most light passes through without being absorbed in the junction and instead is absorbed in the doped material at either side of the junction. Ultimately many of the electron-hole pairs created outside the junction do end up being attracted to the junction and creating current. However the process is quite slow and p-n junction devices are not fast enough for current communications applications.

4.2.2 P-I-N Diodes

The answer to the problem created by the extreme thinness of a p-n junction is to make it thicker! The junction is extended by the addition of a very lightly doped layer called the *intrinsic zone* between the p and n doped zones. Thus the device is called a p-i-n diode rather than a p-n diode. This is illustrated in Figure 99 on page 172.

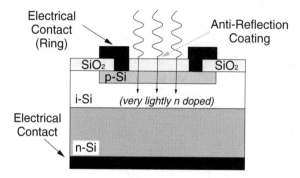

Figure 99. *Typical Silicon P-I-N Diode Schematic*

The wide intrinsic (i) layer has only a very small amount of dopant and acts as a very wide depletion layer. There are a number of improvements here:

- It increases the chances of an entering photon being absorbed because the volume of absorbent material is significantly increased.

- Because it makes the junction wider it reduces the capacitance across the junction. The lower the capacitance of the junction the faster the device response.

- There are two ways of current carriage across the junction: Diffusion and Drift. (See A.1.4.7, "Electrical Conduction in Semiconductor Devices" on page 693.) Increasing the width of the depletion layer favors current carriage by the drift process which is faster than the diffusion process.

The result is that the addition of the "i" layer increases the responsivity and decreases the response time of the detector to around a few tens of picoseconds.

The key to operation of a PIN diode is that the energy of the absorbed photon must be sufficient to promote an electron across the bandgap (otherwise it won't be absorbed!).[59] However, the material will absorb photons of *any* energy higher than its bandgap energy. Thus when discussing PIN diodes it is common to talk about the "cutoff wavelength". Typically PIN diodes will operate at *any* wavelength *shorter* than the cutoff wavelength. This suggests the idea of using a material with a low bandgap energy for all PIN diodes regardless of the wavelength. Unfortunately, the lower the bandgap energy the higher the "dark current" (thermal noise). Indeed but for this characteristic germanium would be the material of choice for all PIN diodes!

---

[59] This just means that it must dislodge an electron from its quasi-stable current state and move it to a higher energy, more mobile, one. It doesn't mean that it must propel the electron across the junction.

It is low in cost and has two useful bandgaps (an indirect bandgap at 0.67 eV and a direct bandgap at 0.81 eV). However it has a relatively high dark current compared to other materials.

This means that the materials used for PIN diode construction are different depending on the band of wavelengths for which it is to be used. However, this restriction is nowhere near as stringent as it is for lasers and LEDs where the characteristics of the material restrict the device to a very narrow range. The optimal way is to choose a material with a bandgap energy slightly *lower* than the energy of the longest wavelength you want to detect.

An interesting consequence to note here is that these crystalline semiconductor materials are *transparent* at wavelengths longer than their cutoff. Thus, if we could "see" with 1500 nm eyes a crystal of pure silicon (which appears dark grey in visible light) would look like a piece of quartz or diamond.

Typical materials used in the three communication wavelength "windows" are as follows:

500-1000 nm Band

Silicon PIN diodes operate over a range of 500 to 1120 nm as silicon has a bandgap energy of 1.11 eV. Since silicon technology is very low cost silicon is the material of choice in this band.

However, silicon is an *indirect* bandgap material (at the wavelengths we are interested in) and this makes it relatively inefficient. (Silicon PIN diodes are not as sensitive as PIN diodes made from other materials in this band.) This is the same characteristic that prevents the use of silicon for practical lasers.

1300 nm (1250 nm to 1400 nm) Band

In this band indium gallium arsenide phosphide (InGaAsP) and germanium can be used. Germanium has a lower bandgap energy (0.67 eV versus 0.89 eV for InGaAsP) and hence it can theoretically be used at longer wavelengths. However, other effects in Ge limit it to wavelengths below 1400 nm. InGaAsP is significantly more expensive than Ge but it is also significantly more efficient (devices are more sensitive).

1550 nm Band (1500 nm to 1600 nm)

The material used here is usually InGaAs (indium gallium arsenide). InGaAs has a bandgap energy of 0.77 eV.

Comparing the wavelength ranges quoted above for detectors and the wavelength ranges for lasers and LEDs quoted in Table 1 on page 106 we see some interesting anomalies. In particular InGaAs is here quoted with a bandgap energy of 0.77 eV and in the table as 0.95-1.24 eV. Other differences also exist for other quoted values.

This difference is *mainly* caused by the fact we are referring to different alloys of the metals. In this case different proportions of In and Ga. In principle you could use any mixture of the two metals and produce any bandgap energy you liked between 0.34 eV (InAs) and 1.42 eV (GaAs). However, within each device we must maintain a continuous, unbroken crystal lattice (otherwise the device won't work).

The range of alloys we can use in a particular application is thus limited by the choice of other materials within the device. The quoted bandgap energies are those used in practical devices.

There are other limiting effects that modify this further.

Operation with reverse bias as described above (called "Photoconductive Mode") has a significant problem. At low light levels the random current produced by ambient heat is a source of noise. At higher light levels however this is not a problem and the device offers the advantages of much higher speeds (than the alternative mode of operation) and linear response characteristics over a wide range. The higher speed characteristics are the result of lowered capacitance caused by the widening of the depletion layer in the presence of reverse bias.

If the device is operated without an externally applied current the natural potentials of the p-i-n junction will cause electrons and holes to migrate across the junction anyway. This is called "Photovoltaic Mode". Thus you get a small voltage (around .15 V) developed across the device. The advantage of this is that there is much less "dark current" caused by ambient heat. Thus in this mode the device is more sensitive but the output requires immediate amplification because of the low voltage levels produced.

The efficiency of p-i-n diodes at long wavelengths can be improved by the use of heterostructures.[60] For example using GaAlAs for the p-layer and GaAs for the i and n-layers. Incident light must pass *through* the p-layer before it enters the i-layer. If it is absorbed by the p-layer then the energy is lost and does not contribute to the current produced. By using a material with a high bandgap energy for the p-layer (higher than the energy of the incident photons) we can prevent incident long wavelength light from being absorbed. This means that there is less light lost before it reaches the i-layer where we want it to be absorbed.

4.2.2.1 Measures of Efficiency in PIN Diodes

There are two common measures quoted when the efficiency of PIN photodetectors is discussed.

1. Quantum Efficiency

   This is simply the ratio of the number of electrons collected at the junction over the number of incident photons. In an idea situation 1 photon releases 1 electron (and its matching hole of course). A perfect quantum efficiency is therefore an efficiency of "1".

   In real devices QE is different at each operating wavelength and so it should always be quoted in association with a wavelength.

2. Responsivity

   Quantum efficiency does not take account of the energy level of the incident photons. Responsivity is a measure that does take photon energies into account. It is simply the output photocurrent of the device (in amperes) divided by the input optical power (in watts). Thus responsivity is quoted in amperes per watt. A typical responsivity for a silicon photodiode at a wavelength of 900 nm is 0.44.

   Of course responsivity is very closely linked to quantum efficiency. It is just quantum efficiency adjusted to account for the variation in energy level implied by different wavelengths.

---

[60] The use of heterostructures in LEDs was described in 3.2.3, "Heterojunctions (Practical LEDs)" on page 108. The principle here is the same.

4.2.3 Schottky-Barrier Photodiodes

In many circumstances the junction between a metal and a semiconductor can display some of the properties of a semiconductor p-n junction.[61] Sometimes called "metal-semiconductor photodiodes", Schottky-Barrier photodiodes make use of this effect. A thin metal layer replaces one half of the p-n junction as shown in Figure 100.

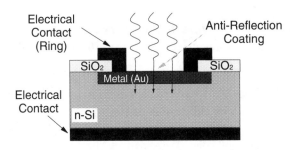

Figure 100. *Schottky-Barrier Photodiode Schematic*

Schottky photodiodes are not often used in current communications products but are the subject of much research as they promise much higher speed, more efficient, operation. This is due to a number of characteristics:

- There are a number of semiconductors available which promise higher efficiency operations but cannot be used in regular p-n or p-i-n configurations because they can't be doped to both p and n characteristics. In addition with normal heterostructure devices you have to match the crystal lattice on both sides of the junction and this severely limits the choice of materials. When one side of the junction is metal you don't have either of these problems.

- The metal layer is a good conductor and so electrons are conducted away from the junction immediately. This means that recombination effects are minimised thus improving the efficiency. In addition it means faster operation.

---

[61] One of the challenges in chip design is to ensure that the electrical contacts do *not* behave in this way.

4.2.4 Avalanche Photodiodes (APDs)

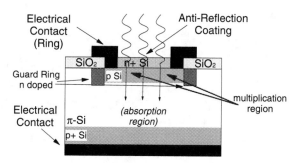

Figure 101. *Avalanche Photodiode (APD)*

APDs amplify the signal during the detection process. They use a similar principle to that of "photomultiplier" tubes used in nuclear radiation detection. In the photomultiplier tube:

1. A single photon acting on the device releases a single electron.

2. This electron is accelerated through an electric field until it strikes a target material.

3. This collision with the target causes "impact ionisation" which releases multiple electrons.

4. These electrons are then themselves accelerated through the field until they strike another target.

5. This releases more electrons and the process is repeated until the electrons finally hit a collector element.

Thus, through several stages, one photon has resulted in a current of many electrons.

APDs are of course different from photomultiplier tubes. Photomultiplier tubes are vacuum tubes with metallic targets arranged in stages down the length of the tube. APDs use the same principle but multiplication takes place within the semiconductor material itself. This process in APDs typically results in an internal amplification of between 10 and 100 times.

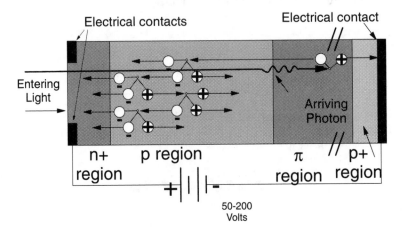

Figure 102. Avalanche (Amplification) Process. The p-region has been enlarged to show avalanche process.

In its basic form an APD is just a p-i-n diode with a very high reverse bias. A reverse bias of 50 volts is typical for these devices compared with regular p-i-n diodes used in the photoconductive mode which is reverse biased to only around 3 volts (or less). In the past some APDs on the market have required reverse bias of several hundred volts although recently lower voltages have been achieved.

The main structural difference between an APD and a p-i-n diode are that the i zone (which is lightly n-doped in a p-i-n structure) is lightly p-doped and renamed the π layer. It is typically thicker than an i-zone and the device is carefully designed to ensure a uniform electric field across the whole layer. The guard ring shown in the figure serves to prevent unwanted interactions around the edges of the multiplication region.

The device operates as follows:

- Arriving photons generally pass straight through the n^+-p junction (because it is very thin) and are absorbed in the π layer. This absorption produces a free electron in the conduction band and a hole in the valence band.

- The electric potential across the π layer is sufficient to attract the electrons towards one contact and the holes towards the other. In the figure electrons are attracted towards the n^+ layer at the top of the device because being reverse biased it carries the positive charge. The potential gradient across the π layer is *not* sufficient for the charge carriers to gain enough energy for multiplication to take place.

- Around the junction between the n+ and p layers the electric field is so intense that the charge carriers (in this case electrons only) are strongly accelerated and pick up energy.[62] When these electrons (now moving with a high energy) collide with other atoms in the lattice they produce new electron-hole pairs. This process is called "impact ionisation".

- The newly released charge carriers (both electrons and holes) are themselves accelerated (in opposite directions) and may collide again.

Both electrons and holes can now contribute to the multiplication process. However now there is a small problem. Looking at Figure 102 on page 178 it is obvious that when an electron ionises an atom an additional electron and hole are produced. The electron moves to the left of the picture and the hole to the right. If the hole now ionises an atom it releases an electron (and a hole) and the electron moves to the left and starts again!

If holes and electrons have an equal propensity for ionisation we can get an uncontrolled avalanche which will never stop! Thus devices are built such that one of the charge carriers has a significantly higher propensity for ionisation than the other. In silicon, electrons are the dominant carrier. In III-V alloy materials holes are often employed.

The result of the above process is that a single arriving photon can result in the production of between 10 and 100 or so electron-hole pairs.

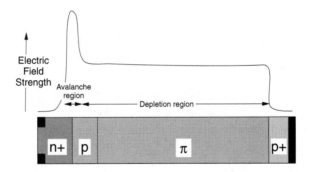

Figure 103. *Electric Field Strengths in an APD. Note the very small avalanche region.*

---

[62] In the illustrated device multiplication of electrons is emphasised in the design although both electrons and holes can cause a multiplicative collision.

The important things to note about the device described above are that the multiplication region is very small and absorption takes place within the π layer rather than near the junction. That is, the absorption and multiplication regions are separated. This is illustrated in Figure 103. There are two important factors here:

1. The strength of the required electric field is extremely high. (Of the order of 10^6 volts/metre.)[63] In the presence of such a strong field, imperfections in the multiplication region (such as lattice mismatches, impurities and even variations in dopant concentration) can produce small areas of uncontrolled multiplication called "microplazmas". To control this effect the multiplication region needs to be small.

   This is the reason for the guard ring mentioned above. Around the edges of the multiplication region you tend to get irregularities and imperfections in the material. Without the guard ring these serve as sites for microplazmas.

   In addition, to create an electric field of the required strength we need an applied bias voltage that increases with the thickness of the multiplication region. (Double the thickness of the region - double the required voltage.) High voltages (indeed voltages above about 12 volts) are expensive and difficult to handle in semiconductor devices and so we aim to minimise the applied voltage.

2. For the above reason the junction region is very thin and therefore it can't absorb many incident photons. The π layer is the absorption layer.

3. Many APDs are designed so that the depletion layer extends through the entire p-region to the π-region boundary.

As with p-i-n diodes different materials are usually employed for each of the three important wavelength bands:

800 nm to 1 Micron Band

> In this band silicon is usually employed although germanium will also work reasonably well. Germanium devices however produce higher noise levels than silicon ones.
>
> As mentioned above for p-i-n structures, silicon has a relatively high bandgap energy and is therefore used only for wavelengths shorter than about 1 micron.

---

[63] This is the field strength you would get if you placed two 100,000 volt high voltage transmission wires only 10 centimetres apart!

In practice, short wavelengths today are only used for very short distance (less than 500 metres) communications. Attenuation over such short distances is generally not great enough to require the sensitivity of an APD (or to justify its cost).

1310 nm Band

This is important as it is the band used by most existing long distance communications systems. Germanium APDs are used extensively but III-V semiconductor alloys are increasing in usage because of the high noise levels in germanium.

1550 nm Band

III-V APDs are used widely in the 1550 nm band. The most common materials system in use is InGaAs/InP where the majority carrier is holes rather than electrons.

4.2.4.1 APD Characteristics

The most important characteristics of APDs are their sensitivity, their operating speed, their gain-bandwidth product and the level of noise.

Sensitivity of APDs

The extreme sensitivity of APDs is the major reason for using them.

Operating Speed

The same factors (such as device capacitance) that limit the speed of p-i-n diodes also influence APDs. However, with APDs there is another factor: "Avalanche Buildup Time". Because (as discussed above) both carriers can create ionisation an avalanche can last quite a long time. This is caused by the to and fro movement of electrons and holes as ionisations occur. Provided the propensity for ionisation in the minority carrier is relatively low, the avalanche will slow and stop but this takes some time.

Avalanche Buildup Time thus limits the maximum speed of the APD.

Gain-Bandwidth Product

The accepted measure of "goodness" of a photodetector is the gain-bandwidth product. This is usually expressed as a gain figure in dB multiplied by the detector bandwidth (the fastest speed that can be detected) in GHz. A very good current APD might have a gain-bandwidth product of 150 GHz.

Noise

APDs are inherently noisy as the multiplier effect applies to all free electrons including those made free by ambient heat. This is especially a problem in longer wavelength devices where the bandgap energy is low.

In the design of devices great care is taken to make sure that the electrical potential gradient is sufficient for multiplication (ionisation) to occur but no greater. Greater levels of bias can cause spontaneous ionisation events.

In many long-distance, wide-area applications where sensitivity is more important than other factors, the APD has been commonly used. However as speeds increase and amplified systems are introduced the noise produced by APDs becomes a limitation. In these systems people today use p-i-n detectors with preamplifiers as you get much higher sensitivity than an APD and much lower noise.

4.2.5 Hetero-Interface Photodetectors

Of available materials, APDs made with silicon have the best response, the highest gain and the lowest noise. However, silicon can't detect at wavelengths longer than about 1 micron because of its bandgap energy. It can't absorb light at longer wavelengths. (If we were able to look at a crystal of silicon with 1500 nanometer eyeballs we would see something that looks like a diamond. Transparent with a high RI.)

The idea of a heterojunction APD is to replace the p-layer silicon material with some material that will absorb light in the long wavelength bands. InGaAs is one such material. The electric fields inside the device are organised such that the detection takes place in the InGaAs material but multiplication is allowed only in the silicon i-layer (this minimises noise). Illumination can be from either side although illumination through the substrate material (silicon) is generally preferred.

The big problem is how to match the lattices of the Si i-layer and the InGaAs material. This has been done using a process called "wafer fusion". The resultant device has been called a Silicon Hetero-Interface Photodetector (SHIP). This structure has been proven to provide a much higher gain-bandwidth product with lower noise than existing APDs. A product of 350 GHz has been reported.

At the present time these devices are in research but commercial products are expected very soon.

4.2.6 Travelling-Wave Photodetectors

When you try to make a p-i-n detector operate at extremely high speeds a serious problem arises. The maximum response frequency is determined by the time it takes for electrons and holes to drift/diffuse across the i-layer. (Both drift and diffusion contribute to the migration of a charge carrier across the i-layer.) Drift and diffusion are slow and it takes a finite amount of time for the device to respond to a pulse of light. To make the device go faster you have to reduce the thickness of the i-layer. But reducing the thickness of the i-layer increases capacitance effects between the p-layer and the n-layer. This increased capacitance acts to slow the device response. To counter the increased capacitance you have to reduce the surface area of the device! So basically as the device gets faster it also must get much smaller. As it becomes smaller it produces less current.

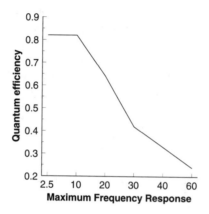

Figure 104. *Variation of Quantum Efficiency with Device Response*

As illustrated in Figure 104, the above effect causes a serious reduction in the quantum efficiency (QE) of p-i-n detectors at speeds above about 10 Gbps. Note that this loss of efficiency is *in addition* to the natural decrease at higher speeds:

> The "natural" loss of efficiency at higher speeds comes about because a detector requires a certain number of photons to reliably detect a bit. When the speed is doubled the number of photons required remains the same. Thus to get the same output level from a detector every time the speed is doubled then the detector halves in its sensitivity! So to get the same BER you need to double the power at the detector every time you double the speed (other things being equal).

The answer to the loss of quantum efficiency is to build the detector as a travelling wave device.

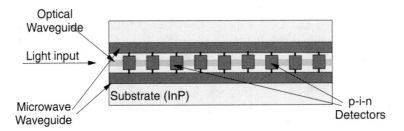

Figure 105. Travelling Wave Photodector - Principle

The principle of a travelling wave detector is illustrated in Figure 105. A number of p-i-n detectors are integrated into an optical waveguide such that light not absorbed in one will travel on to the next. If the outputs were just joined together you wouldn't get a lot of improvement because the outputs come at different times depending on when light arrives at the device. In the TW configuration, light entering the waveguide on the left of the device encounters the p-i-n detectors one after another. Each detector would normally have a simple integrated preamplifier in this configuration. Output of the detectors is placed on an electrical waveguide on which the electrical signal travels in the same direction as the optical signal. The whole idea here is to match the speed of light propagation in the optical waveguide to the speed of electrical propagation in the electric waveguide. Thus the outputs of all the detectors "add-up" in phase as each detector places its output signal onto the waveguide.

It's actually a significant design challenge to match the electronic propagation speed to the optical one but it can be done.

Devices such as this still don't give you as good a quantum efficiency as a regular p-i-n diode at slower speeds. Nevertheless travelling wave devices give a very significant improvement in QE over single-stage p-i-n diodes at extremely high speeds (double or triple).

4.2.7 Resonant-Cavity Photodetectors

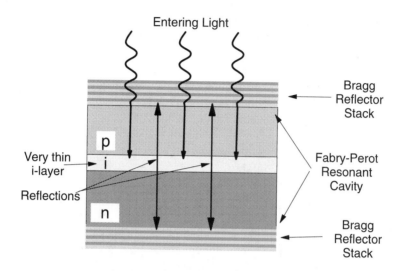

Figure 106. *Resonant-Cavity Photodetector - Principle*

An alternative to travelling wave devices for getting higher quantum efficiency at very high speeds is the Resonant-Cavity Photodetector (RECAP) illustrated in Figure 106.

The principle here is just that you put a p-i-n detector with a very thin i-layer *inside* a resonant FP cavity. The idea is that since the i-layer needs to be very thin to get fast response we can pass the light through it multiple times to give it a bigger chance of being absorbed.

An FP cavity is of course a resonant cavity and is highly wavelength selective - it is a wavelength selective filter (see 5.8.2, "Fabry-Perot Filter (Etalon)" on page 289). Thus this type of detector is highly wavelength specific and could be used in some situations as a WDM demultiplexor.

Devices for the 1550 nm wavelength band are quite difficult to build as the InP/InGaAsP system must be used and this gives very low RI contrast steps with which to build the mirrors. The paper by Murtaza et. al. (1996) describes the construction of a RECAP device with an achieved quantum efficiency of 48%.

4.3 Phototransistors

The fact that traditional transistors (these days called "Bipolar Junction Transistors" or BJTs) are photosensitive has been known ever since they were invented. This is one of the reasons that they are usually sealed in light tight cans - because unwanted light is a source of noise.

Phototransistors are very similar to ordinary BJTs except they are designed for use as detectors. Transistors are amplifiers and in a phototransistor the amplifier gain is controlled by the amount of light striking the device.

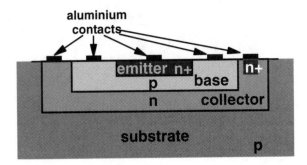

Figure 107. Bipolar Junction Transistor (BJT)

The operation of a BJT is described in A.1.7, "The Bipolar Junction Transistor (BJT)" on page 697. Light arriving in the device is absorbed and creates charge carrier pairs in many different places. The action is different depending on where the charge carrier pairs are created. However, in an intentional phototransistor, absorbtion is intended to take place in the depletion zone between the emitter and the base. Creation of charge carriers here causes a current to flow in the E-B circuit which is then amplified by the transistor action of the device.

These are much lower in noise and have a higher output than APDs, but are significantly less responsive than either APDs or p-i-n diodes. The major problem with phototransistors is materials. We would like to use silicon or gallium arsenide but these have too great a bandgap energy and are limited to detecting wavelengths shorter than about 1 micron. Germanium is usable in the 1300 nm band but while it is easily possible to build transistors with smaller bandgap materials (such as InP) there is no established technology to do so. This takes away much of the potential cost advantage in the 1550 region.

The major use of phototransistors is in non-communications applications using visible (or near visible) light. Alarm systems (light beam detection) and remote controls for TV sets and automobiles are among the most common uses.

Phototransistors are occasionally built as part of an integrated circuit. In this configuration they are referred to as Integrated Preamplifier Detectors (IPDs).

4.4 Further Reading

Joseph Harari, Guanghai Jin, Jean P. Vilcot and Didier Decoster (1997)

Theoretical Study of p-i-n Photodetectors' Power Limitations from 2.5 to 60 GHz: IEEE Transactions on Microwave Theory and Techniques, Vol 45, No 8, August 1997. pp 1332-1336

L.Y. Lin, M.C. Wu, T. Itoh, T.A. Vang, R.E. Muller, D.L. Sivco and A.Y. Cho (1997)

High-Power High-Speed Photodectors - Design, Analysis, and Experimental Demonstration: IEEE Transactions on Microwave Theory and Techniques, Vol 45, No 8, August 1997. pp 1320-1331

S. S. Murtaza et al. (1996)

High-Finesse Resonant-Cavity Photodetectors with an Adjustable Resonance Frequency: IEEE J. of Lightwave Technology, Vol 14, No 6, June 1996. pp 1081-1089

Chapter 5. Optical Devices

In addition to lasers and detectors there are many optical devices that perform useful and necessary functions in an optical communication system. This chapter describes some of these.

5.1 Optical Component Technologies

There are three generic families of technology which are used to build optical devices and components. These are:

1. Optical fibre technology

2. Microoptic technology

3. Planar waveguide technology

Fibre Technology

> Fibre is not only a transmission medium. Many devices such as amplifiers and filters can be made from fibre. Since components usually end up connected to a fibre for transmission, fibre technology tends to be attractive.

Microoptics

> This is where devices are made using traditional optical components (such as lenses, prisms and diffraction gratings) assembled together. This is the obvious technology. However, making very small, very high precision components and assembling them into useful devices to tolerances well less than one micron is very difficult and expensive to accomplish.

Planar Waveguide Technology

> In planar technology devices are constructed on the surface of a flat piece of material such as silica or semiconductor crystal using the techniques of semiconductor chip manufacturing.

Some devices (such as optical amplifiers) can be made in all three technologies albeit that devices constructed in different technologies (for the same general function) are very different. Other devices can only be made in one technology. An example here would be the circulator which is only possible in microoptic technology.

5.1.1 Planar Optical Devices

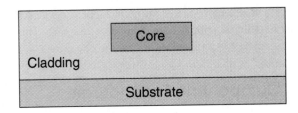

Figure 108. *Planar Waveguide Concept*

The central concept of a planar optical device is to build devices integrated within a block (or "slab") of transparent material. This material could be an optically flat piece of glass (or rather silica), a wafer of silicon (such as we use to make electronic logic devices), a crystal of lithium niobate, block of plastic or one of a number of other materials.

The basic requirement is to guide light on defined paths through the device. To do this we need to use a region of material of higher refractive index than the surrounding material. The light is confined and guided in the same way as it is in a fibre. Figure 108 illustrates the concept. In practice the core area is usually square rather than the rectangular cross-section shown in the figure. A square cross-section has no polarisation sensitivity but a rectangular one is often strongly birefringent. The core is kept at sufficient distance from the substrate to avoid any of the evanescent field entering the substrate. This is because common substrates (like silicon) are strongly absorbent in the wavelength range we are interested in. If the evanescent field was allowed to penetrate the substrate attenuation would be significantly increased.

The concept offers a lot of advantages:

1. You can build a structure of many interconnected devices much more efficiently and with much lower cost than you can with fibre technology. For example the 1x8 splitter illustrated in Figure 109 on page 191 consists of a series of interconnected "Y-junctions". It can be physically quite small and be built with very great precision. Such a splitter might typically measure 1.5 cm x 2.5 cm.

2. Critical dimensions can be controlled much more accurately than you can in fibre technology. For example the coupling length in a resonant coupler or the length of arms in a Mach-Zehnder interferometer are critical to the operation of these devices. You get much greater control in planar technology than in fibre technology.

3. For the above reason (accurate control of dimensions) there are a number of devices that can't be built any other way. For example the devices described in 5.7.3, "Waveguide Grating Routers (WGRs)" on page 280, 5.9.8, "Modulation Using a Mach-Zehnder Interferometer" on page 323 and 9.2.8.1, "Cross Gain Modulation (XGM) in SOAs" on page 542 could not be constructed in any other technology.

4. Many devices can be made together on a single large substrate and later cut up into individual devices. This significantly reduces the cost compared to other technologies where each device must be individually constructed.

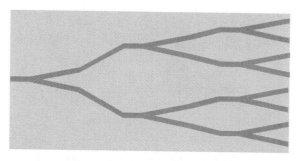

Figure 109. *An 8-Port Splitter Made by Cascading Y-Couplers*

There are however a number of difficulties:

- Planar devices are not as easy to construct as might seem at first. This is really due to the very high precision required. (We need to control dimensions accurately to about .25 of a micron.)

- An attractive approach to making planar devices is to use equipment and technology designed for the manufacture of semiconductor chips. Indeed this is one of the popular techniques. However, when you make a mask it is generally made from a series of dots or squares. This means that diagonal waveguides have regularly occurring steps in their sides. At best this can be a source of loss. At worst, if you happen to chance on a resonant wavelength (if the steps form a grating) bizarre effects are possible.

- Many complex devices (such as circulators) that we would like to construct rely on the characteristics of a number of different materials in the same device, for example, birefringence on specific crystal axes. Obviously we can't do this in planar technology because a planar device is made from a uniform material.

- It is costly and difficult to connect these devices to fibres. Actually this depends very much on the materials used. In LiNbO$_3$ and Si technologies the RI difference between the material and the fibre makes fibre connection complex and expensive. In silica devices the RI is very close to that of the connecting fibre and the connection is much simpler and less costly.

This results in the fact that simple devices made in planar technology are very hard to cost justify compared to similar function devices made in microoptic (discrete component) or fibre technology. Complex devices however are easily cost justified in planar technology.

5.1.1.1 Planar Waveguide Routing and Crossovers

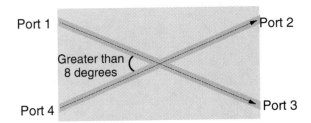

Figure 110. *Planar Crossover*

When many devices are linked together on a common planar substrate the routing of waveguides and the construction of crossovers become critical issues. Waveguides cannot have 90° corners in them! Depending on the dimensions of the waveguide, the RI difference (between waveguide and substrate) and the wavelength in use there is always a minimum radius for bends. Any bend tighter than the minimum radius loses light! This requirement tends to make the devices much larger than we might expect when comparing with electronic integrated circuit devices.

Crossovers are also necessary. Waveguides that cross at angles greater than about 8° (depending on the material RI difference) are needed to ensure that leakage of light in unintended directions does not occur.

5.1.2 Fabrication of Planar Optical Devices

There are three general ways of making planar devices:

1. Diffusion of a dopant into a flat substrate.

2. Deposition/etching techniques similar to those used in making semiconductors.

3. Direct writing of waveguides using a powerful laser beam and photosensitive dopant in the material (such as germanium in silica glass).

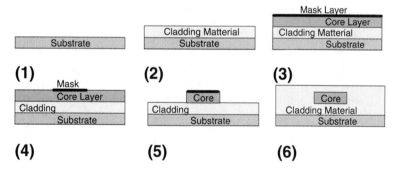

Figure 111. Manufacture of Planar Waveguides by Deposition/Etching

Deposition/Etching

This is essentially the same process as is used to make semiconductor electronic devices. It has very significant advantages over the other methods in that very precise dimensions can be obtained. In addition, devices can (potentially) be three dimensional although this is not yet a commercial technology. Also it is possible to make true hybrid devices with both optical and electronic components included (such as the multiwavelength laser described in 9.2.1.1, "Multiwavelength Lasers" on page 520). However, it is a relatively high cost process because optical devices tend to be orders of magnitude larger than their electronic counterparts and you can only make quite a small number per wafer.

The steps involved in the manufacturing process are illustrated in Figure 111. These are as follows:

1. A silicon wafer (typically about 20 cm in diameter and a few mm thick) is prepared by polishing its surface to make it as flat as possible. This wafer is a single, unbroken, silicon crystal and the polishing can produce a surface that is flat within a variation of one or two atomic diameters! (This is just regular silicon chip production technology.)

2. A layer of silica is deposited on the wafer. This layer is typically 10 to 20 microns thick and will ultimately become part of the "cladding" of the waveguide.

   To do this reactive gasses are mixed at high temperature in contact with the wafer (in a specially designed chamber). The gaseous reaction produces SiO_2 which is deposited onto the surface of the wafer.

3. A second layer of doped silica is deposited by the same process (reaction of gasses) but this time a quantity of dopant is included in the reactive

mixture. This layer is usually around 7 or 8 microns thick and is destined to become the core of the waveguide.

4. The surface of the wafer is then coated with a "photoresist". This is just a layer of photosensitive material specially designed for the purpose. The surface of the wafer is then exposed to light in a process *exactly* like printing a photograph. An image of the pattern wanted on the wafer is projected onto the surface of the photoresist - thus "exposing" it.

   In practice many images of the pattern we want are projected one after another over the surface of the wafer. Each individual device is made on a single exposure but many devices are made on a single wafer. This is done by multiple exposures because the optics involved in projecting the mask have to be very precise indeed and this imposes a relatively small (a few cm) maximum exposure area. Of course this also imposes a maximum size on each device.

   The photoresist is then developed and fixed in a process identical in principle with developing a photograph. This leaves a mask pattern in place on the surface. The mask will prevent the next stage of the process from affecting parts of the surface under the mask and will leave other parts unprotected. The area to become the ultimate waveguide is thus protected by the mask where the area which is to become cladding is unprotected.

5. The wafer is then treated with hydrofluoric acid. This acid dissolves silica and dissolves away all of the "core layer" except that part protected by the mask. (In practice this dissolves some of the cladding layer too but that doesn't matter too much.)

   The areas of photoresist that remain have now served their purpose and are dissolved away.

6. Now another layer of pure silica is deposited over the whole wafer as before and this forms a continuous structure with the previously deposited buffer layer. This is continued until the core layer is covered to the desired depth and the surface is then flat.

7. What we have now is a 20 cm diameter wafer with many devices built on the surface. Another step of masking and etching is now used to create grooves in the final devices to guide the attachment of fibres.

The wafer is then cut up into individual devices, fibres attached and testing performed.

Diffusion and Ion Exchange Techniques

In the diffusion technique a silica or glass substrate (rather than a silicon one) is used. The surface is covered with a mask using the same technique as described above. The mask however now covers the parts of the device that we *don't* want to become waveguiding rather than as above where the mask covers the waveguide areas.

The blank is then subjected to prolonged exposure (usually at a high temperature) to a material which can diffuse its way into the surface and so form a waveguide.

Sometimes we use materials where an additional atom can diffuse by itself into the structure. At other times we use a technique of ion exchange.

An example of the ion exchange technique would be where soda glass (with a high sodium content) is used as the substrate. After masking, the substrate is immersed in molten potassium nitrate. Potassium ions diffuse into the unmasked parts of the glass and sodium ions diffuse out. Thus the ions are exchanged - K replaces Na. this increases the RI and forms a waveguide. The surface may then be coated with more glass or plastic or left uncoated.

Direct Writing with a UV Beam

When you expose silica glass doped with germanium to very high intensity UV light (244 nm) a permanent change takes place that increases the refractive index of the glass. This is mentioned later in this chapter in 5.7.2.10, "Writing the Grating" on page 277. The change in refractive index isn't very great but is enough to create a waveguide.

The principle is very simple:

1. A small sheet of fused silica doped with germanium is used. This is often similar in size and shape to a microscope slide. Alternatively, it can be made a few inches square so that multiple devices can be constructed at the same time. Much higher levels of dopant can be used in planar technology than in fibre so levels as high as 10% are used as this allows for a greater RI change.

2. This "blank" is polished until the surface is very flat (with less variation than one wavelength of light).

3. A UV laser beam (244 nm) at very high intensity is then used to expose the areas on the surface that are to be of higher RI. The beam is very intense and penetrates the material to sufficient depth for a waveguide to be created. The position of the beam is computer controlled and can be operated in two different ways.

- The beam is scanned across the device using the same principle used in laser printers (or for that matter in a regular TV set). The laser beam is turned ON when we want a spot of high RI and OFF when we don't. This is relatively easy to do (the technology is very well established) but it leads to irregularities in the edges of diagonal lines and structures. This is because we are really writing a big square composed of many adjoining points in a square pattern. These irregularities are a source of loss by scattering.

- You can "trace out" the outline of the device you want by precisely controlling the movement of the laser beam. This is potentially the best method but it is harder to control the positioning of the beam precisely.

5.1.2.1 Coupling Planar Devices to a Fibre

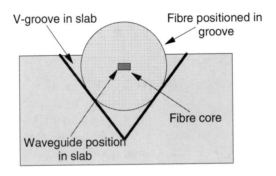

Figure 112. Coupling Fibres to Planar Devices

The most common way of attaching fibres to planar devices is illustrated in Figure 112. Grooves are etched in the device using the same masking and etching techniques described above. These grooves are arranged such that the fibre core and the waveguide within the planar device line up as accurately as possible.

Fibre is placed in the groove and fixed with an epoxy glue. If the fibre is positioned using only the grooves as a guide the coupling gives a typical loss of around .3 dB. If the fibre is aligned actively (by using light in the fibre and device to detect and correct fibre alignment), then the loss is typically only around .1 dB. However, not all devices are amenable to active alignment of the coupling in this way.

5.1.3 Integrated Optical Circuits (Planar Assemblies)

The grand dream of optical researchers is to have the ability to build wholly optical switching nodes as a single assembly. Such a device would include lasers, detectors, WGRs, amplifiers and switches connected by planar waveguides on a single flat piece of material perhaps 50 cm by 30 cm.. Today, the realisation of this objective seems a little far off but leading researchers seem confident that it will be achieved.

Multi-device assemblies produced on a planar substrate are becoming commonplace in the research literature and some have appeared as "standard" commercial components. Some of these devices are:

1. Optical switches where a large number of individual switch elements are integrated onto the same substrate.

2. Laser arrays such as the one discussed in 9.2.1.1, "Multiwavelength Lasers" on page 520. These typically include multiple lasers, external modulators, a combiner and an amplifier.

3. WDM receiver assemblies consisting of AWGs with an amplifier and multiple PIN diode receivers in the same assembly.

The big problems here are practical ones of manufacture. For example, it is difficult to manufacture DFB lasers to a predetermined wavelength. Today when manufacturers want lasers at a specified wavelength they make a lot of them and then measure what they made and classify them accordingly. You can't do this if you are relying on many devices to be accurately made as part of the same assembly. In this case tuneable lasers are perhaps the answer.

Also computer chip making technology (used to make many optical active components) can't currently make a single device larger than a circle with a diameter of about 2.5 cm.

The other problem is faults in manufacture. We do all we can to minimise these but they can't be eliminated entirely. The principle is the same as when making electronic ICs. If you make a wafer containing 100 chips and 10 faults then perhaps you will get 90 good chips and 10 bad ones. If you take the same wafer and make only 4 (much larger) chips then the chances are that each of them will contain one or more faults.

5.2 Optical Amplifiers

As mentioned in the introduction, the recent (late 1980's) advent of practical optical amplifiers has revolutionised communications.

An optical amplifier is a device which amplifies the optical signal directly *without* ever changing it to electricity. The light itself is amplified.

One of the great ironies of the communication world is the move in optical systems from repeaters to amplifiers. In the 1970's carriers around the world adopted digital trunking systems for one overwhelming reason: *In a digital system you can get rid of the amplifiers on long links and use repeaters.* They wanted to use repeaters. Now in the optical communications world we are busy changing back from repeaters to amplifiers.

The reason people wanted to use repeaters in the electrical world was to remove noise. Repeaters receive the old signal, retrieve the digital bit stream, and then generate a new one. Thus, noise and distortion picked up along the transmission path are completely removed by a repeater, whereas, when an amplifier is used, these components are amplified along with the signal.

In an optical communications system we don't have much problem with noise or signal interference. When a signal on a single-mode fibre arrives at its destination it is a lot weaker, but for practical purposes the signal is unchanged. We do have problems with dispersion (and repeaters get rid of dispersion) but there are other compelling reasons for us to use amplifiers:

Reliability of Amplifiers

When a repeater is used the optical signal must be converted to electrical form, passed through the repeater, and then converted to optical form again. The repeater is complex and subject to failure. So a device which just amplifies the signal will do just as well (or better) than a repeater.

Flexibility

A repeater is specialised to a particular signal and its characteristics (speed, code etc.). An amplifier just amplifies whatever it gets so it is not code sensitive. If you want to increase the speed or transmission code format in use on an existing amplified link all you do is change the transmitter and receiver on the ends of the link. You may not (depending on the power level requirements) need to do anything to the amplifiers at all. If you were using repeaters you would have to replace them - something which is a little inconvenient in some environments (such as in undersea cables)!

Wavelength Division Multiplexing (WDM)

In a Wavelength Division Multiplexing system you have many different optical streams on the same fibre. To use repeaters you would have to demultiplex the optical stream and then repeat each individual signal. Amplifiers just amplify the lot regardless. Thus you don't have to demultiplex etc. Really, it is the development of the optical amplifier that has enabled practical WDM systems to be constructed for the first time.

Cost

Optical amplifiers are much simpler than repeaters and should cost significantly less.

There are many possible types of optical amplifiers. Amplifiers can be built in semiconductor technology (like lasers), in planar waveguide technology and in fibres.

Almost any semiconductor laser can be made into an amplifier with a few modifications - You have to add a pigtail to the end facet not already connected to fibre to provide a way for light to enter the device, you need to increase the length of the gain region by about three times and you need to put an anti-reflection coating on both of the laser's end facets. These devices are called "Semiconductor Optical Amplifiers" (SOAs).

The most important type of amplifier is the erbium doped fibre amplifier because it is low in cost (relatively), highly efficient and low in noise.

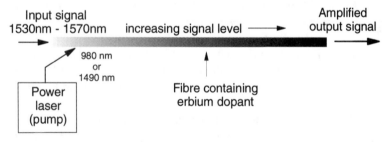

Figure 113. Erbium Doped Fibre Amplifier (EDFA) - Function

In the late 1980s a group of researchers at the University of Southampton in the United Kingdom succeeded in developing a fibre-based optical amplifier which is now firmly established as the preferred means of signal regeneration on long fibre communications links. This was the EDFA - the Erbium Doped Fibre Amplifier. It has become the dominant type of optical amplifier and is illustrated above

(Figure 113). The signal passes along a short length of special fibre and is amplified (by up to 1000 times, 30 dB) during its travel. The signal never becomes electrical and never leaves the fibre.

Today, there is a whole class of optical amplifiers based on the same principles. These are generically called REDFAs (Rare Earth Doped Fibre Amplifiers). The only devices of current commercial interest are doped with erbium or praseodymium but any element from the rare earth section of the periodic table is potentially useful in an optical amplifier.

The above amplifier types (SOAs and REDFAs) both employ the principle of the laser in their operation. Other amplifiers exist which use completely different principles for amplification. One such amplifier is described in 5.2.7, "Raman Effect Amplifiers" on page 229.

5.2.1 Erbium Doped Fibre Amplifiers (EDFAs)

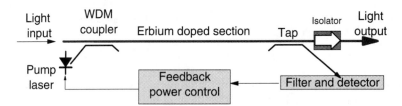

Figure 114. Erbium Doped Optical Fibre Amplifier. Although the device is powered electrically, the amplification process is totally optical and takes place within a short section of rare earth doped, single-mode fibre.

An Erbium Doped Fibre Amplifier consists of a short (typically ten metres[64] or so) section of fibre which has a small controlled amount of the rare earth element erbium added to the glass in the form of an ion (Er^{3+}). This is illustrated in Figure 114.

The principle involved here is just the principle of a laser and is very simple. Erbium ions are able to exist in several energy states (these relate to the alternative orbits which electrons may have around the nucleus). When an erbium ion is in a high-energy state, a photon of light will stimulate it to give up some of its energy (also in the form of light) and return to a lower-energy (more stable) state. This is called

---

[64] Longer lengths up to 200 metres are sometimes used.

"stimulated emission" and was discussed in 3.3.1, "Principle of the LASER" on page 118.

To make the principle work, you need a way of getting the erbium atoms up to the excited state. The laser diode in the diagram generates a high-powered (between 10 and 200 milliwatts) beam of light at a wavelength such that the erbium ions will absorb it and jump to their excited state. (Light at either 980 or 1,480 nanometer wavelengths will do this quite nicely.)

The basic principle of the EDFA is illustrated in Figure 114 on page 200.

Operation is as follows:

1. A (relatively) high-powered beam of light is mixed with the input signal using a wavelength selective coupler. (The input signal and the excitation light must of course be at significantly different wavelengths.)

2. The mixed light is guided into a section of fibre with erbium ions included in the core.

3. This high-powered light beam excites the erbium ions to their higher-energy state.

4. When the photons belonging to the signal (at a different wavelength from the pump light) meet the excited erbium atoms, the erbium atoms give up some of their energy to the signal and return to their lower-energy state.

   This doesn't happen for all wavelengths of signal light. There is a range of wavelengths approximately 24 nm wide that is amplified.

5. A significant point is that the erbium gives up its energy in the form of additional photons which are *exactly* in the same phase and direction as the signal being amplified. So the signal is amplified along its direction of travel only. (This is not unusual - when an atom "lases" it always gives up its energy in the same direction and phase as the incoming light. That is just the way lasers work.) Thus all of the additional signal power is guided in the same fibre mode as the incoming signal.

6. There is usually an isolator placed at the output to prevent reflections returning from the attached fibre. Such reflections disrupt amplifier operation and in the extreme case can cause the amplifier to become a laser!

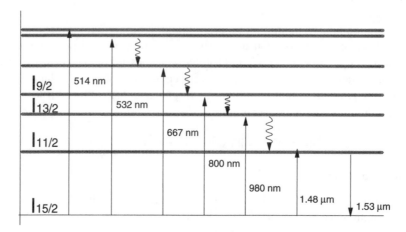

Figure 115. *Energy Level States of Erbium. While the energy states are represented as horizontal lines, they are really "energy bands" centred around a specific energy state. This distribution of energy states is called a "Fermi-Dirac Distribution".*

Operation can be understood with reference to Figure 115. The energy states in the figure are actually groups of sub-states. The $I_{15/2}$ band has 8 sub-states, the $I_{13/2}$ band has 7 sub-states and the $I_{11/2}$ band has 6 sub-states. Electrons can occupy any sub-state within their current band (depending on their energy). In addition each sub-state is "broadened" by thermal energy. This results in each band being relatively wide. Thus when an electron jumps between states there is quite a wide range of energy levels available. Therefore the device will amplify over a relatively wide range.

There are many possible scenarios for operation but the best is when you pump with light at a wavelength of 980 nm.

- A photon at 980 nm interacts with an electron in the $I_{15/2}$ state.

- The electron absorbs the energy from the photon and moves into the $I_{13/2}$ band. The photon ceases to exist.

- The $I_{13/2}$ band is unstable and electrons in this state decay into the band below (the $I_{11/2}$ band) with a half-life of around one microsecond. The energy given off by this decay is absorbed into lattice vibrations (called phonons).

- The $I_{11/2}$ state is metastable. Electrons in this state are able to stay there for a very long time in atomic terms. The half-life for spontaneous emission in this state is around 11 milliseconds! If an electron does decay spontaneously from this state it will emit a photon of light somewhere in the 1550 nm band (most likely around 1553 nm).

- When a photon of signal light arrives and interacts with the excited electron in the $I_{11/2}$ band the electron jumps to the ground state (actually one of the sub-states within the ground state). When this happens it gives out a photon in exactly the same phase and direction and with exactly the same energy (wavelength) as the photon which caused the interaction.

- As with any laser for meaningful amplification to occur you need an "inversion" to be present. This means that there must be more erbium ions in the excited state than in the ground state. This is because the erbium absorbs the signal light (just like it absorbs pump light). The probability that an incoming photon of signal light will encounter an excited erbium atom and be amplified must be greater than the chance that it will encounter a ground state erbium atom and be absorbed. This is further discussed in 3.3.1, "Principle of the LASER" on page 118.

A significant point here is that erbium *only* absorbs light (and jumps to a higher-energy state) if that light is at one of a very specific set of wavelengths. Light in the range of wavelengths between about 1525 nm and 1570 nm will cause the excited erbium to undergo stimulated emission and hence the signal will be amplified. Light at other wavelengths will pass through the device unaffected.

In summary, the device works this way. A constant beam of light (called the pump) at the right wavelength to excite erbium atoms is mixed with the input signal through a wavelength selective coupler. This beam of light constantly keeps the erbium ions in an excited state. (The power level of the pump is often controlled through a feedback loop.) The signal light picks up energy from excited erbium ions as it passes through the section of doped fibre and is amplified.

The process is just the process of lasing as described in 3.3.1, "Principle of the LASER" on page 118 but of course there are no mirrors and no feedback (at least we hope there are no reflections). Just as in any laser an inversion is needed for amplification to commence. This means that there must be more erbium atoms in the upper level excited state than there is in the ground state. Because of the very long upper state lifetime of erbium this is not a significant problem.

5.2.1.1 Technical Characteristics of EDFAs

Perhaps the main characteristic that gives erbium its attractive technical features is that its excited upper state lifetime is around 10 ms. EDFAs have a number of attractive technical characteristics:

1. Efficient pumping

2. Minimal polarisation sensitivity

3. Low insertion loss

4. High output power (this is not gain but raw amount of possible output power)

5. Low noise

6. Very high sensitivity

7. Low distortion and minimal interchannel crosstalk

The quantitative measures of amplifier characteristics are as follows:

Gain (amplifier)

This is the ratio in decibels of input power to output power.

Gain Coefficient

The gain coefficient is a very useful indicator of the efficiency of an amplifier. It is defined as the small signal gain divided by the pump power.

Bandwidth

This is the range of wavelengths over which the amplifier will operate.

Gain Saturation

This is the point where an increase in input power ceases to result in an increase in output power. All of the pump power is used up already and no more power is available. EDFAs are very different to electronic amplifiers in this respect. When gain saturation is reached in an electronic amplifier generally undesirable things (such as crosstalk and distortion) start to occur. When an EDFA saturates the overall gain of the amplifier is lessened but there is no distortion of the signal. It is usual to run EDFAs in "gain saturation".

Polarisation Sensitivity

There is very little sensitivity to polarisation states in EDFAs - this is one of the advantages. Polarisation sensitivity is the difference in gain of an input signal in one polarisation to the gain in the orthogonal polarisation. A typical value here would be between .01 and .1 dB.

Noise

EDFAs add noise to a signal mainly as a result of ASE. The noise figure of an amplifier is expressed in decibels and is defined as the ratio of the signal-to-noise ratio (SNR) at the input to the SNR at the output.

$$Noise = \frac{SNR_{input}}{SNR_{output}}$$

5.2.1.2 Gain Characteristics of EDFAs

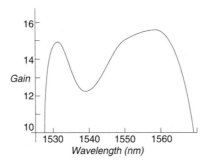

Figure 116. *Gain Curve of a Typical EDFA*

Figure 116 shows the gain curve of a typical commercial EDFA. Note the scale on the y axis is in dB and is therefore logarithmic. Also the origin is not at zero. Gain at 1560 nm is some 3 dB higher than gain at 1540 nm (this is twice as much). In most applications (if you only have a single channel or if there are only a few amplifiers in the circuit) this is not too much of a limitation. However, WDM systems use many wavelengths within the amplified band. If we have a very long WDM link with many amplifiers (say two or three thousand kilometers with 80 or so amplifiers) the difference in response in various channels adds up. This difference in signal levels between channels could become as great as perhaps 100 dB.

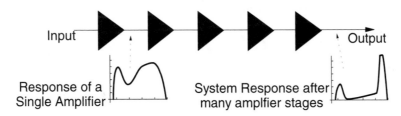

Figure 117. *Response of Cascaded EDFAs*

In other words some channels will be so strong as to be dominant and others will be lost in the noise! This can be so severe that it will easily prevent successful system operation. In less severe cases it means that the SNR varies significantly from channel to channel. Of course the system is only as good as the worst channel. This means that for a WDM system we need each channel to have *the same* amount of gain. That is the amplifier's gain should be "flat" across the range of amplified wavelengths.

A significant complication is caused by the fact that the gain profile of an EDFA changes with the signal power levels. You might get a nice flat response with (say) four channels at full power but when one channel stops (fails or is turned off) the response of the amplifier to the other three becomes uneven (between channels)! That is one channel may now be amplified more than the others.

There is a lot of current research taking place aimed at flattening the gain curve. This can be done by:

1. Operating the device at 77° K. This produces a much better (flatter) gain curve but it's not all that practical.

2. Introducing other dopant materials (such as aluminium or ytterbium) along with the erbium into the fibre core. Depending on the material used this can radically alter the amplifier's response. You can use a series of different co-dopants in sections of fibre along the amplifier. It is widely believed that this approach will in due course result in the development of amplifiers with a completely flat response.

3. Amplifier length is another factor influencing the flatness of the gain curve. This is discussed in 5.2.1.7, "Amplifier Length" on page 210.

4. Controlling the pump power (through a feedback loop) is routine to reduce ASE. This technique also reduces non-linearity in response due to varying input signal levels.

5. Adding an extra WDM channel locally at the amplifier. Power in this circuit is used to soak up excess power and also reduce non-linear variations with power level. This is called "gain clamping".

6. Manipulating the shape of the fibre waveguide within the amplifier. Fibres with dual cores have recently been shown to produce much superior gain flatness characteristics.

At the systems level there are other things that can be done to compensate. For example:

1. Using "blazed" fibre Bragg gratings as filters to reduce the peaks in the response curve. In other words, reduce the response at all wavelengths to that of the worst wavelength. This approach has been reported to work well in field trials.

2. Using channel preemphasis on the signals as they are transmitted. That is, transmit different WDM channels at different power levels to compensate for later amplifier gain characteristics.

Of course in individual systems a combination of the above techniques can be used to achieve an optimal result.

5.2.1.3 Second Gain Window
The usual gain window for EDFAs is from around 1525 - 1565 nm. With careful amplifier design it is possible to have another gain window this time from about 1570 - 1610 nm.

By using co-dopants, principally aluminium and phosphorus, you can get reasonably good gain between 1570 and 1610 nm. This is sometimes called the "second gain window". However, no matter what you do (in a silica host) the gain between 1530 and 1560 nm will still be significantly greater than that at longer wavelengths. Thus to make use of the second window we must avoid putting any signal into the first window.

However, if your signals are situated only in the second window meaningful amplification can be obtained. Some mechanism (such as the integration of a blazed FBG) is needed to cut down on ASE in the first window but this is easily achieved.

Wideband EDFAs have been reported in the literature. These get an amplified bandwidth of around 80 nm. The technique used is to split the incoming signals at around about 1567 nm. The shorter wavelengths are routed to a conventional EDFA section and the longer ones to a section optimised for amplification in the second window. Later, both amplified signals are recombined.

5.2.1.4 Doping the Glass
In silica fibre, erbium can only be introduced at relatively low concentrations (around 1%) due to the fact that higher levels cause faults in the glass. Erbium in the glass is held as an ion Er^{3+}.

From basic chemistry it seems strange that we can mix an ion (an atom minus 3 outer electrons) into glass successfully and leave the electron energy levels relatively undisturbed. In fact, if erbium was an ordinary element then mixing it in glass would change the electron energy levels utterly. The secret is that erbium is a "transition metal". It has a filled outer shell (8 electrons) and a partial shell immediately below. Ionisation causes the loss of electrons from this inner (partially filled) shell. The filled outer shell acts as an electrostatic barrier that prevents too much change in the ionic structure due to the surrounding glass. Other elements in this group (praseodymium, neodymium, ytterbium...) can also be used as dopants in this way. Of course these have quite different energy level distributions from those of erbium.

However, there is some modification of the erbium energy levels by the characteristics of the host glass and this does change the energy level characteristics. In host glasses other than silica the lasing characteristics of erbium are different.

5.2.1.5 Gain Saturation

When the input power of an amplifier is increased you always reach a point where the gain saturates. That is, although the input power is increased the output stays constant.

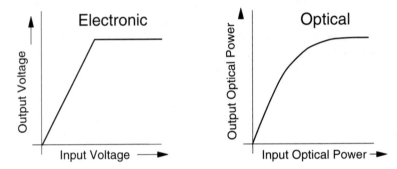

Figure 118. *EDFA Behavior in Gain Saturation*

There are two main differences between the behavior of electronic amplifiers and of EDFAs in gain saturation. These both result from the fact that erbium has a long upper-state lifetime. An erbium amplifier's gain responds to changes in average power (power fluctuations over a few milliseconds). Electronic amplifiers respond to instantaneous changes in power levels.

1. As input power is increased on the EDFA the total gain of the amplifier decreases slowly. An electronic amplifier operates relatively linearly until its gain saturates and then it just produces all it can. This means that an electronic amplifier operated near saturation introduces significant distortions into the signal (it just clips the peaks off).

2. An erbium amplifier at saturation simply applies less gain to all of its input regardless of the instantaneous signal level. Thus it *does not distort the signal*. There is little or no crosstalk between WDM channels even in saturation.

5.2.1.6 Co-Dopants

As mentioned above you can do a lot to change the characteristics of an EDFA by co-doping the fibre with another element. The effects here are complex and not just a simple addition of the characteristics of the two dopants.

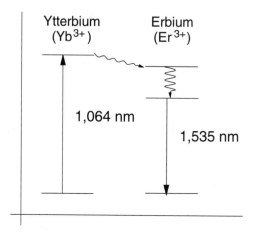

Figure 119. *Energy Levels in Erbium/Ytterbium Co-Doped Amplifier*

Common co-dopants used are aluminium (Al), ytterbium (Yb) and germanium (Ge). These modify the gain spectrum of the amplifier. For example, Ge co-doping produces two gain peaks over the spectrum - one at 1536 nm and the other at 1550 nm. Al broadens and flattens the gain spectrum in the region 1540 nm to 1560 nm.

Yb doping allows the use of very much higher power than obtainable with Er alone. In this case you can pump the Yb and the erbium lases! The energy level scheme for this is illustrated in Figure 119. This is a little like the case in semiconductor lasers where we use a double heterostructure with materials of different bandgaps in close proximity. The Yb can absorb light and boost electrons to a higher energy level. This energy is then transferred to the Er by a rapid non-radiative transition. This is called "Förster energy transfer". We now have excited Er and then these electrons can undergo stimulated emission dictated by the characteristics of the Er. What is really happening is that the Er/Yb material is a new material that has some characteristics of both of its components.

In addition the type of glass used as host also has a critical effect as it significantly modifies the energy spectra and hence the efficiency and gain characteristics of the amplifier.

5.2.1.7 Amplifier Length

As the signal travels along the length of the amplifier it becomes stronger due to amplification. As the pump power travels through the amplifier its level decreases due to absorption. Thus, both the signal power level and the pump power level vary along the length of the amplifier. At any point we can have only a finite number of erbium ions and therefore we can only achieve a finite gain (and a finite maximum power) per unit length of the amplifier. Of course, this is affected by the erbium ion concentration (along with the concentrations of any co-dopants) and the core radius.

In an amplifier designed for single wavelength operation the optimal amplifier length is a function of the signal power, the pump power, the erbium concentration and the amount of gain required.

In an amplifier designed for multiwavelength operation there is another very important consideration - the flatness of the gain curve over the range of amplified wavelengths. As with any laser, signal light is not only amplified (by the excited state erbium) but also it is absorbed by the ground state erbium. So to get meaningful amplification we need to have more excited state atoms than ground state ones (we need an inversion). But there is another factor here. The absorption spectrum of ground state erbium is *not the same* as the gain spectrum of excited state erbium. This is especially true in the presence of co-dopants.

This leads to an important characteristic. *The gain spectrum at any point along the amplifier will be different from the spectrum at any other point along the amplifier.* (Because signal and pump power levels at each point are different and the gain and absorption spectra are different.) The amplifier gain is an integration of the instantaneous gain characteristic at every point along the amplifier.

Actually, this is goodness. It means that with careful design and optimisation of the amplifier's length we can produce a nearly flat amplifier gain curve.

5.2.1.8 Pump Wavelengths

As discussed previously erbium in a silica host can be pumped at either 980 nm or 1480 nm. If a co-dopant is present you can sometimes pump the co-dopant rather than the erbium. For example if Yb is present you can pump at 1064 nm. There are slight differences in amplifier characteristics depending on the pump wavelength.

- The gain spectrum of the amplifier depends somewhat on the wavelength of the pump. This is not a big effect.

- 980 nm is almost twice as efficient, as a pump wavelength, than 1480 nm. This is partly because 1480 is within the gain spectrum of the amplifier and some pump photons will stimulate emission and be amplified rather than absorbed. This is not too great a problem as the resultant photons will probably be absorbed themselves but it does detract from the efficiency of the amplifier.

The other factor is that when you pump at 1480 you have a two-level laser system and it requires more energy to obtain and maintain an inversion than in three-level system operation at 980 nm.

In addition, amplifiers pumped at 980 are relatively insensitive to ambient temperature changes. Amplifiers pumped at 1480 experience significant changes in their gain characteristics with changes in temperature.

- A disadvantage of 980 nm pumping is that the pump bandwidth to which the erbium will respond is quite narrow. You need to control the wavelength of the pump within a relatively narrow range for optimal power transfer. Pumping at 1480 has no such disadvantage.

- Initially, lasers at 980 were not easily available where ones at 1480 were. This meant that the reliability of pumps at 1480 was proven but at 980 there was no data. Thus early operators (especially undersea operators) chose 1480 pumps because they were proven.

Building a good semiconductor laser pump is a very considerable challenge. Pumps need to produce an output of up to 250 mW. This level of power concentrated into the mode field of a single-mode fibre represents a very high power concentration. There is a significant problem with the intense power concentrated on the exit facet of the pump laser. Unless the laser is very carefully designed to protect it you can burn the end facet and erode the device.

5.2.1.9 *Pumping Direction*

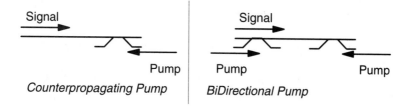

Figure 120. Additional Pumping Options

While EDFAs are very low noise devices they still do create some noise in the form of ASE. This is not a big problem with only a few amplifier stages but if there are many stages then the problem can become significant.

We don't always have to pump in the same direction as the signal (as shown in Figure 114 on page 200). You can pump from the signal output end or from both ends or from the middle as well. You can also (for various reasons) use different pump wavelengths at either end. However, it is very important to keep an inversion present over the whole length of the device.

For example, if you have a low input signal level, pumping from the signal input end might result in too much pump power for the input signal. (Not enough signal to use up all the pump power.) If this happens the erbium at the input end will undergo a lot of spontaneous emission and we will get added noise from ASE.[65] Also it wastes pump power. So in this case we would pump from the other (signal output) end of the amplifier.

5.2.1.10 Cladding Pumps

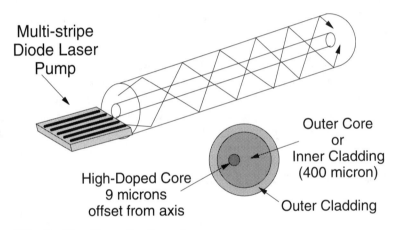

Figure 121. Cladding Pump Configuration

One seemingly obvious way of introducing the pump light into the fibre core is through the cladding! Why not just couple pump light into the cladding and then let it be absorbed when it transits the core. Sadly, it isn't that simple. Pump light if introduced into the cladding would propagate in multiple (several thousand) modes just as the signal does in a multimode fibre. But something over 90% of these modes *never* transit the core (they are spiral and offset) thus they could never be absorbed. Cladding pumping with regular fibre would be very inefficient!

---

[65] Amplified Spontaneous Emission - see 5.2.1.13, "Noise in EDFAs" on page 215

Much research is being done on EDFAs pumped through the cladding. This involves using a very special fibre profile that forces most of the cladding modes to transit the core. The simplest (and it seems to be turning out the best) is just to use a fibre with an offset core! If the core is offset a few microns from the axis of the fibre then most modes will intersect with it at some time. This gives a problem with coupling the signal light into it - because you have to line up the core of the amplifier with the core of a pigtail fibre - but this is possible.

The big attraction of pumping this way is that it allows very high pump power levels. You can't pump at too great a power level into the core because non-linearities in fibre response cause distortion of the signal. The fibre cross-section in the cladding is much larger than in the core so the average power can be kept down while the total power can be relatively high.

Typical diode lasers cannot produce the very high levels of pump power used here. Trials are taking place using multi-stripe diode lasers. These are really multiple lasers situated very close together on the same chip. There is an interesting problem here in pigtailing (connecting the laser output to the fibre).

The configuration shown in Figure 121 on page 212 uses a cladding diameter of 400 microns so that power from the multi-stripe laser can be coupled into it. It's a little unfair to call this the cladding. It is a waveguide for the pump power surrounding the true inner core. So it can be called the inner cladding or the outer core. Surrounding it is another cladding layer with an RI *lower* than that of the inner cladding. This one is to confine the pump light into the inner cladding. So there are three RI levels here: the core (highest), the inner cladding (intermediate) and the outer cladding (lowest).

Both amplifiers and lasers can be made using this technique and devices have been reported with output powers of up to 10 watts!

5.2.1.11 MultiStage EDFAs

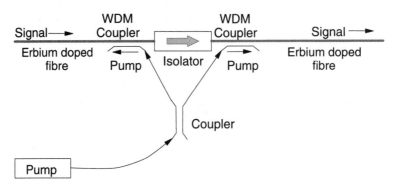

Figure 122. *Two-Stage EDFA Line Amplifier with Shared Pump. Pump power would typically be split in a ratio different from 50:50. The input stage is a lot shorter and requires less pump than the power amplifier stage.*

Some new EDFA designs concatenate two or even three amplifier stages. An amplifier "stage" is considered to consist of any unbroken section of erbium doped fibre. Multistage amplifiers are built for a number of reasons:

1. To increase the power output whilst retaining low noise

2. To flatten the total amplifier gain response

3. To reduce ASE noise

EDFAs with different co-dopants have different gain curves. These can be matched in such a way as to produce a nearly flat response across the whole window. (This is a very important feature when using very long links with WDM.) A total gain of 50 dB is reported for this configuration.

ASE noise in an amplifier can be reduced significantly (by about 6 dB) by placing an isolator within the gain section. This prevents counter-propagating ASE from saturating the gain at the input.

5.2.1.12 Control of Polarisation Mode Dependence (PMD)

Standard EDFAs exhibit two forms of birefringence both of which are usually trivial. These are called polarisation dependent loss (PDL) and polarisation dependent gain (PDG). These effects both result in slightly different gain being exhibited by the amplifier to orthogonal polarisation states. They are discussed further in 9.4.5.4, "Polarisation Effects in EDFAs" on page 560. PDG and PDL are very small effects and are not considered a problem in most systems but in long distance systems with many cascaded amplifiers the effects can be significant.

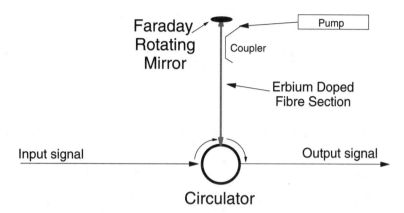

Figure 123. *Polarisation Insensitive EDFA*

One of the ways of combating polarisation mode dependence in EDFAs is to build a polarisation insensitive EDFA.

Figure 123 shows an EDFA design for polarisation independence. Input signal light arrives through the circulator and is amplified. PDL and PDG are introduced in the erbium doped section. The light is then rotated by 90° in polarisation by a Faraday rotating mirror. It then transits the erbium doped section again and the previously introduced PDL and PDG effects are "undone". The PDL and PDG effects re-occur but now operate on the orthogonal polarisation state so that at the exit from the amplifier both polarisation states have had identical amounts of gain. Of course the signal is amplified during its return trip through the erbium doped section.

5.2.1.13 Noise in EDFAs

Wherever there is gain in a system there is also noise. The predominant source of noise in EDFAs is Amplified Spontaneous Emission (ASE). What happens is that some of the excited erbium decays to the ground state (undergoes spontaneous emission) before it has time to meet with an incoming signal photon. Thus a photon is emitted with random phase and direction. A very small proportion of emitted photons will happen to occur in the same direction as the fibre and be captured in a bound mode. These photons will then be indistinguishable from the signal (from the point of view of the amplifier) and be amplified.

ASE is produced over a range of wavelengths exactly corresponding to the gain spectrum of the amplifier. Of course most of this ASE power is then spread over different wavelengths from the signal wavelength and can be filtered out. In WDM systems the demultiplexing operation filters out most of the ASE. However, it is not possible to filter out ASE that happens to be at the same wavelength as a signal.

In most systems ASE is trivial and does not constitute a problem. However, in long links with many stages of amplification ASE can become a limiting phenomenon. This is for two reasons:

1. The noise added to signal channels

2. The effect on amplifier gain of significant amounts of ASE travelling with the signal

There are a few things you can do:

1. Carefully control the amplifier design to minimise the amount of spontaneous emission created in the first place. The most common technique here is to run the amplifier in saturation so that excess pump power doesn't end up as ASE.

2. Place filters either within the amplifier or on the link to filter out wavelengths outside of the channels being transmitted. Spontaneous emission has a strong peak at 1533 nm. This is not a problem if you have a signal there as this wavelength is also a strong gain peak and the signal will be amplified more at this wavelength. If there is no signal at this peak you may need to filter at least this wavelength out.

3. Place isolators between amplifier stages to prevent backward propagating ASE from consuming pump power.

It is important to note that the noise in an EDFA is proportional to the amplifier's gain. In addition to the ASE added by a particular EDFA the EDFA will amplify any noise that was received with the signal just as though it was the signal itself. Design of long links with EDFAs is discussed further in 9.4.5, "Amplifier Issues" on page 557.

5.2.1.14 Remote Pumping

From the basic principle of the optical amplifier it is easy to see that the light source for the pump doesn't need to be very close to the amplifying section of fibre. In some applications (such as undersea systems) it can be very useful to site the pump laser a long way away (many kilometres) from the amplifier. This allows the amplifier to be totally passive and have no electronics or electricity supply. This configuration is shown below:

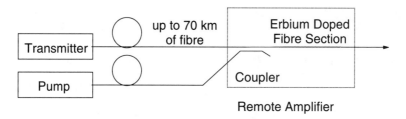

Figure 124. Remote Pumping

Two fibres are used in the connection - one for the signal and one for the pump. It is tempting to consider mixing the pump light and the signal together on the same fibre. However, you have to use a very high power pump signal (around 1 watt!) in order to overcome attenuation of the pump light as it travels to the amplifier. This would cause significant distortion if mixed immediately with the signal light due to fibre non-linearities caused by the extremely high power density in the core. However, if relatively short distances are involved (say less than 20 km) then the power level doesn't need to be so high and pumping on the same fibre may be used. Another point is that you need to pump at 1480 nm because this is the only available pump wavelength that has relatively low levels of attenuation in the fibre. (Attenuation at 980 nm is typically around 3 dB per km.)

Of course the question is always - "why not just amplify the signal to a higher level before transmission?" The problem is that there is a maximum power level you can use in a fibre before other (non-linear) effects (such as stimulated Brillouin scattering) distort, attenuate or add noise to the signal. For narrow linewidth (long coherence length) lasers this can be as low as 10 mW. However, for signals with a bandwidth of over about 100 MHz (or .1 nm) this limit is about 200 mW.

One of the problems is that non-linearities (in this case mainly SBS) impose a practical maximum limit on the pump laser power. Typical 1480 nm pump lasers have 4 lines of around 80 MHz in width each. Because the pump laser is not a modulated signal the linewidth can be less than that of the signal and since it is operated in a CW[66] fashion it doesn't have the broadening effect of laser chirp to assist! Various "broadening" techniques have been suggested which aim to broaden the linewidth of the pump laser to avoid the effects of SBS.

---

66 Continuous Wave - i.e. it is turned on all the time.

In a typical undersea system today amplifiers are sited at spacings of around 100 km. In such a system the remote pumping technique promises to extend the distance between powered amplifiers by about 50 km (to 150 or even 200 km).

5.2.1.15 EDFA System Resilience

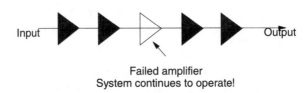

Failed amplifier
System continues to operate!

Figure 125. Amplifier Breakdown Resilience

One interesting characteristic of EDFAs is that when they fail (say from power supply or pump laser failure) the signal passes through the failed amplifier relatively unchanged! (There is some attenuation but this is minor.) If we have a long undersea link with many cascaded EDFAs then we might design the system in such a way as to put the amplifiers a little closer together than strictly necessary. In this case if a single amplifier fails then the signal will carry on to the next amplifier and be boosted there. This is not optimal, but it does work and it can provide a significant level of system resilience. Another way of course is to build EDFAs in multiple relatively independent cascaded sections - when one section fails the others can pick up the load. When electronic repeaters fail they block the signal completely!

5.2.1.16 Using OTDRs in Amplified Links

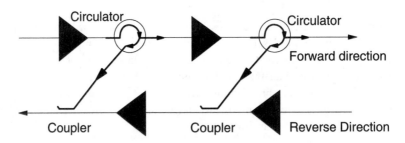

Figure 126. OTDR Path in Link with EDFAs

One of the quoted advantages of EDFAs over repeaters is that you can use an OTDR (see 7.8.2, "Optical Time-Domain Reflectometers (OTDRs)" on page 430) to diagnose link condition right *through* the amplifier. But this is easier said than done. OTDRs send and receive on the same fibre strand and so we would have to allow a bi-directional path through the amplifier. This means that either:

1. You would have to make the amplifier bi-directional and get rid of *all possible* reflections in the system. If you don't the EDFAs will start to lase. In practical terms the danger of lasing makes this systems approach infeasible.

2. You could provide a return path *around* each amplifier (by using circulators) and still stay on the same strand of fibre. This works but has a problem with the distance as the returning signal is not amplified anywhere.

An alternative method using the fibre pair is shown in Figure 126 on page 218. A circulator replaces the isolator at each amplifier's output. This performs the function of the isolator in preventing reflections from getting back into the EDFA and it takes the reflections from the signal path (needed by the OTDR) and couples them into the reverse direction signal path. This provides an explicit return path at the output of each amplifier for OTDR reflections. Of course you now need an OTDR that uses a separate fibre for transmitting and receiving.

Some care is needed in this design to keep the return power levels very low as signal power from one direction can also be coupled into the reverse direction this way and become a source of noise to the signal. In the picture only one direction is shown but it is possible to make the system symmetric and provide a return to allow OTDR use in either direction.

This configuration is actually used in some undersea systems to enable the use of an OTDR on-shore to look at the whole link and locate faults and breakages etc.

5.2.1.17 Amplifier Applications

Optical amplifiers can be employed in many different roles within a communication system. Of course different applications have different requirements and this results in quite large differences in amplifier design.

Preamplifiers

> An optical preamplifier is placed immediately before a receiver to improve its sensitivity. Since the input signal level is usually very low a low noise characteristic is essential. However, only a moderate gain figure is needed since the signal is being fed directly into a receiver.

> Preamplifiers are typically built with a counter-propagating pump to avoid the losses associated with the WDM coupler which introduces the pump light to the system. Typically a preamplifier will not have feedback control as it can

be run well below saturation. However, to maintain a low noise figure it is necessary to maintain a strong inversion from the beginning of the amplifier.

Power Amplifiers

Most DFB lasers have an output of only around 2 mW but a fibre can handle (aggregate) power levels of up to 100 to 200 mW relatively comfortably before nonlinear effects start to occur. A power amplifier may be employed to boost the signal immediately following the transmitter. This is especially useful when an external modulator is used as these can have quite a high insertion loss (between 3 and 10 dB).

Typical EDFA power amplifiers have an output of around 100 mW. Noise is not very important as it is usually many orders of magnitude below the strong input signal level.

Line Amplifiers

In this application the amplifier replaces a repeater within a long communication line. In many situations there will be multiple amplifiers sited at way-points along a long link.

We need *both* high gain at the input and high power output while maintaining a very low noise figure. This is really a preamplifier cascaded with a power amplifier. Sophisticated line amplifiers today tend to be made just this way - as a multi-section amplifier separated by an isolator. If this amplifier is to be used in a WDM system another major concern is to ensure that the amplifier response is flat over the entire range of wavelengths in use.

There are many other factors to be considered in long line link design that concern the amplifiers. These include:

- Polarisation mode dispersion

- Chromatic dispersion

- Noise

These are discussed later in 9.4.5, "Amplifier Issues" on page 557.

5.2.1.18 Second-Generation EDFAs

There is general agreement that amplifier technology has advanced into a "second-generation" but no real agreement as to exactly what constitutes a second-generation amplifier.

However, most people agree that an amplifier with any of the following characteristics is "second-generation":

1. Multi-stage designs

2. Use of co-dopants such as ytterbium

3. Use of multiple pumps

4. Use of gain-equalisation techniques

5.2.1.19 *Summary of EDFA Characteristics*

The EDFA has the following advantages over competing technologies:

- It is significantly simpler than a repeater and will have a much longer mean time to failure.

- It is significantly lower in cost than a repeater.

- It will operate at almost any speed.

- It can be made physically small enough to fit on a printed circuit card.

- It will produce a gain in optical signal of about 25 dB. Some amplifiers can produce a gain of 50 dB or even higher.

- It will amplify many different wavelengths simultaneously (with some small limitations).

- It doesn't need to understand the digital coding. Both amplitude (pulse) modulated and coherent (frequency modulated) light are amplified. Indeed in some applications today light is amplitude modulated in a continuous wave (this is common in cable TV distribution). This too will be amplified without distortion.

    This means that if amplifiers are installed in a long undersea cable for example, at some later time the transmission technique used on the cable may be changed without affecting the amplifiers.

- There is effectively no delay in the amplifier. The delay is only the time it takes for the signal to propagate through a few feet of single-mode fibre.

- It is possible (if the system was planned that way) to use OTDRs (Optical Time Domain Reflectometers) to do end-to-end diagnosis of link faults right *through* an EDFA. This requires careful design (you can't have any isolators in the circuit) but it enables the remote location of line faults over long links containing many amplifiers. This is an enormous operational benefit in some systems (for example in undersea systems).

    OTDRs are further discussed in 7.8.2, "Optical Time-Domain Reflectometers (OTDRs)" on page 430.

- Amplifiers (like their electrical counterparts) can saturate. That is, if the incoming signal is just too big, the amplifier will put out its full power but that will not be enough. However, EDFAs saturate slowly and have a very long time constant. Erbium's "upper state lifetime" is around 11 ms. Therefore when an EDFA saturates it just loses some gain. It doesn't clip signal peaks and distort the signal like an electronic amplifier does. Indeed EDFAs are usually operated in saturation.

If there are multiple wavelength division multiplexed channels on a single fibre then potentially amplifiers can introduce crosstalk between channels. That is, there could be interference with a signal on one wavelength by a signal on another. In fact this effect is minimal in an EDFA due again to the upper-state lifetime of erbium.

There are of course some limitations:

- The amplifier itself adds some noise (and it amplifies the noise received with the signal). This is trivial compared to noise in electrical environments but can be significant if a large number of EDFAs are connected in cascade over a long link.

- At the present time, fibre-based amplifiers do not operate over the entire range of wavelengths of interest. The usual range is about 24 nm (or about 3,000 GHz). Amplifiers have been constructed with a range of up to 80 nm (see 5.2.1.3, "Second Gain Window" on page 207).

- At this stage of development amplifiers give different amounts of gain at different wavelengths. The gain spectrum is not perfectly flat. If a number of WDM channels are present then some are amplified more than others. This can be a problem in long links with many stages of amplification.

- Amplifiers do not re-create pulses. In fact they don't know about pulses - they just amplify whatever happens to arrive. In themselves, amplifiers do not create dispersion but if pulses arrive that are dispersed, then these will be amplified, dispersion and all. In comparison with a repeater, this is a negative for the EDFA. Repeaters re-shape and re-time the signal as well as amplify. In an amplified system you have to do something else to compensate for dispersion.

- In many systems, amplifiers must be placed closer together than repeaters. The signal cannot be allowed to become too weak before reamplification. In some systems in the early 1990s, this resulted in the need to space amplifiers roughly every 30 kilometres where repeaters would have been placed about every 50 kilometres.

Researchers have reported experimental results showing successful (simulated) transmission at 2.4 Gbps over a distance of 21 000 kilometres and higher speeds over shorter distances.

Other types of optical amplifiers (solid-state ones) exist but are nowhere near as good. See 5.2.6, "Semiconductor Optical/Laser Amplifiers (SOAs/SLAs)" on page 227.

5.2.2 Praseodymium (Pr) Doped Fibre Amplifiers

As discussed above, EDFAs operate in the 1550 nm band. Most (indeed almost all) existing transmission systems currently use the 1300 nm band in which EDFAs will not operate. In response to this amplifiers doped with Pr^{3+} which do operate in the 1300 nm band have been developed. However these are nowhere near as good as EDFAs. The gain available in commercial PDFAs is only around 12 dB and the range of wavelengths amplified is not as wide as might be desired. This is adequate in many situations for application as a power amplifier. However, the gain at low signal strength is poor and so they are not useful as receiver preamplifiers.

The technical problem is that non-radiative decay of the excited Pr^{3+} takes place before the Pr has a chance to meet an incoming photon and undergo stimulated emission. This problem is so severe in silica glass that this glass cannot be used for Pr^{3+} doped amplifiers.

Fluorozirconate (ZBLAN) glasses are used instead of silica. The carrier lifetime in flurozirconate glass is only about 100 nanoseconds (in silica it is much shorter still). The result of this is that the quantum efficiency of the amplifier is only around 4%.

However, the characteristics of the host glass are critical here. New research is concentrating on Pr doped chalcogenide fibres where amplifier gains of up to 24 dB have been recently reported. Theory predicts that we "should" be able to achieve up to 60% quantum efficiency in chalcogenide glass.

Praseodymium can be pumped at two (practical) wavelengths:

1. At 1017 nm using a semiconductor InGaAs laser. These are similar to the 980 nm lasers used to pump EDFAs. However the highest power laser available in this class in only 50 mw.

2. At 1047 nm using a Nd:YLF crystal laser. These are available at very high power but are also expensive (by comparison with semiconductor pumps). Pumping at this wavelength is also very low in efficiency. That said, Nd:YLF pumps are the ones used in commercial PDFAs.

Because of the very short carrier lifetime you need to get a high pump light intensity into the core. As a result, current PDFAs use flurozirconate (ZBLAN) fibres with a very narrow (2 micron) core (to concentrate the pump light in the core). The need for a very small core creates significant coupling problems when the amplifier is coupled to standard silica fibre.

The magic formula for designing PDFAs is to "pump hard at both ends" (and hope).

5.2.3 Neodymium (Nd) Doped Fibre Amplifiers

Neodymium is another candidate for the role of active element in fibre amplifiers for the 1300 nm band. Nd will amplify over the range 1310 to 1360 nm in ZBLAN glass and between 1360 and 1400 nm[67] in silica. Efficient pump wavelengths are at 795 and 810 nm.

Quantum efficiency is very low. Small signal gain while adequate in many applications may not be enough for application in high quality preamplifiers. Carrier lifetime in ZBLAN at 390 μsec is quite short and this results in crosstalk problems when operating close to saturation. (However, it seems unlikely that anyone would want to do WDM in the 1300 nm band anyway.) Noise figures are also adequate but not as good as EDFA characteristics (amplified spontaneous emission is a problem).

5.2.4 Plastic Fibre Amplifiers

Recent reported research has suggested that amplifiers using plastic fibre may offer some capabilities not available in glass (or silica) amplifiers.[68]

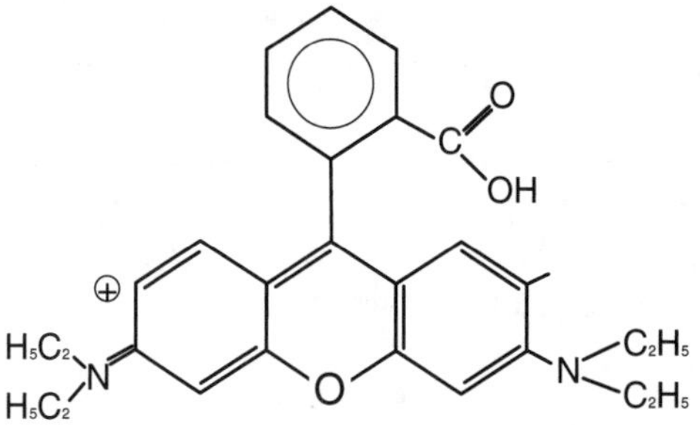

Figure 127. Rhodamine-B

Perhaps the first potential application may be for amplifying signals on plastic fibre. As discussed in 2.5, "Plastic Optical Fibre (POF)" on page 94 plastic fibre has transmission windows at 570 nm and 670 nm but amplifiers are not available at those wavelengths. Some people suggest that instead of using amplifiers on plastic fibre you might as well use glass fibre and in most cases the amplifiers will not be necessary.

---

[67] Useless wavelength range here because of the OH absorption peak at 1385 nm.

[68] See Peng et al. (1996) in the bibliography.

However, a lot of research is going into using plastic in planar optical technology (see 5.1.1, "Planar Optical Devices" on page 190) and a plastic amplifier may be very useful as part of a wider system.

The main interest in using plastic fibre amplifiers lies in the fact that the gain medium can be introduced into the plastic at a relatively low temperature. The gain medium is an organic compound - it "dissolves" in the plastic (like sugar in water).[69] It doesn't become part of the plastic structure. In glass the gain medium dopants tend to be metallic ions. Most organic compounds break down at the 2000° C temperature at which silica melts. In plastic you can use organic dyes as a gain medium. Dye lasers using a liquid medium have been around for many years but the liquids and dyes are difficult (and in some cases dangerous) to handle.

Recently a plastic fibre amplifier using Rhodamine B doped PMMA (PolyMethyl MethylAcrylate) fibre as the host has been developed. The reported gain window was from 610 nm to 640 nm with a pump efficiency of 33% and a gain of 24 dB. This is interesting as the wavelength band is very close to the transmission window for PMMA fibre (but not quite there yet).

Another significant point is that the PMMA fibre can be doped with another material to ensure that its refractive index matches that of glass fibre so that a connection to glass fibre can be made without reflection problems. So potentially we could make amplifiers and other components out of plastic and use them within a glass system.

---

[69] The gain medium is called a "dye" not because it is used to dye anything but because it is usually brightly coloured. Most of the organic compounds used as gain media have a strong absorption in part of the visible range. If you absorb (say) strongly in the red and green then the substance will look bright blue (in reflected sunlight).

5.2.5 Erbium Doped Planar Devices

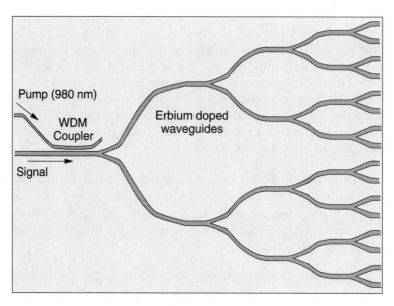

Figure 128. *16-Way Planar Splitter with Amplification*

Planar waveguides can also be used to build erbium doped amplifiers. This would be pointless if all we wanted to do was amplify the signal - EDFAs would do the job much better. However, in complex planar devices there is often a large amount of signal loss and amplification in the device can help to offset it.

In Figure 128 a 16-way planar optical splitter is illustrated. The 16-way split will necessarily cause 12 dB of loss and when you add attenuation in the waveguides and loss in pigtailing you would be lucky if such a device had only 20 dB of loss. However, if we dope the waveguide with erbium and introduce a pump signal as illustrated, the device becomes an amplifier. A useful thing here is that you can dope planar waveguides with erbium at much higher concentrations than you can in fibre - thus you can get a lot higher gain per unit of length.

Of course you could build this device in fibre technology by concatenating a large number of fibre 3 dB couplers and using erbium doped fibre. But such a device would be relatively expensive and quite fragile.

A splitter of this kind might be used in a passive optical network (PON) as described in 11.1.6, "Passive Optical Networks (PONs)" on page 645. In a PON it might well be pumped remotely so that no active equipment was needed in the network itself. In this situation you don't need to overcome all of the splitting losses. It may be that we can tolerate an insertion loss of 6 dB or so and so the amplifier may need a gain per channel of 14 dB. Researchers have built devices of this kind and their characteristics look very promising.

Complex devices have been made in this technology. For example a DFB laser has been constructed with an integrated MZI modulator. In introducing the erbium to the device you can either dope all the lithium niobate before building the waveguides or you can dope only the waveguides (using diffusion techniques). It turns out that if you dope the whole device any areas that you don't want to amplify will absorb so it is considered better to dope only the sections of the waveguides that you want to amplify.

5.2.6 Semiconductor Optical/Laser Amplifiers (SOAs/SLAs)

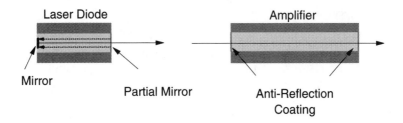

Figure 129. *Semiconductor Optical Amplifier Relationship to Laser*

Semiconductor optical amplifiers (also called Semiconductor Laser Amplifiers) are well known and commercially available. There are basically two varieties.

Simple SOA

> Simple SOAs are almost the same as regular index-guided FP lasers as discussed in 3.3.3.3, "Construction of a Fabry-Perot Laser" on page 139. The back facet is pigtailed to allow the input of signal light. The main problem is that it has been difficult to make SOAs longer than about 450 microns. In this short distance there is not sufficient gain available on a single pass through the device for useful amplification to be obtained. One solution to this is to *retain* the reflective facets (mirrors) characteristic of laser operation. Typical SOAs have a mirror reflectivity of around 30%. Thus the signal has a chance to reflect a few times within the cavity and obtain useful amplification.

However, this is the formula for a laser! An amplifier surrounded by mirrors! The solution here is to operate the SOA below the lasing threshold so that independent lasing doesn't build up.   However it severely limits the characteristics of the amplifier because of saturation effects. In addition the Fabry-Perot resonances of the cavity narrow the passband and provide unequal amplification of WDM channels.

Travelling Wave SLAs (TWSLAs)

The TWSLA is different from the SOA in a number of ways:

1. The cavity is lengthened (doubled or tripled) to allow enough room for sufficient gain (since the amplifier uses a single pass through the device and doesn't resonate like a laser). Devices with cavities as long as 2 mm are available.

2. The back facet is anti-reflection coated and pigtailed to provide entry for the input light.

3. The exit facet of the amplifier is just the same as for a laser except that it is also anti-reflection coated.

4. Because of the absence of feedback the TWSLA can be operated above the lasing threshold giving higher gain per unit of length than the simple SOA. Gains of up to 25 dB over a bandwidth range of 40 nm have been reported.

SOAs have severe limitations however:

- They can't deliver very much power (only a few milliwatts). This is usually sufficient for single channel operation but in a WDM system you usually want up to a few milliwatts *per channel*.

- Coupling the input fibre into the chip tends to be very lossy and hence reduces the effectiveness of the amplifier.   The amplifier must have additional gain to overcome the loss on the input facet.

- SOAs tend to be noisy.

- They are highly polarisation sensitive.

- They can produce severe crosstalk when multiple optical channels are amplified. This is mainly around the power level where the amplifier saturates but this is quite a low power.

This latter characteristic makes them unusable as amplifiers in WDM systems but gives them the ability to act as wavelength changers and as simple logic gates in optical network systems. See 9.2.8, "Wavelength Converters" on page 540. In addition they can be used for pulse compression in Soliton generation and can be effective in single channel OTDM systems.

A major advantage of SOAs is that they can be integrated with other components on a single planar substrate. For example a WDM transmitter device may be constructed including perhaps 10 lasers (at different wavelengths) and a coupler all on the same substrate. In this case an SOA could be integrated into the output to overcome some of the coupling losses.

5.2.7 Raman Effect Amplifiers

Amplifiers using the principle of stimulated Raman scattering were widely researched in the late 1980's but interest waned after the invention of the EDFA. Raman amplifiers are very effective but they had a major problem in that low cost lasers of appropriate wavelength were not available. In 1997 there is a revival of interest in them (at least in part) due to innovations in fibre Bragg grating design.

As described earlier in 2.4.5.3, "Stimulated Raman Scattering (SRS)" on page 91 SRS causes a new signal (a Stokes wave) to be generated in the same direction as the pump wave down-shifted in frequency by 13.2 THz[70] *provided* that the pump signal is of sufficient strength. In addition SRS causes the amplification of a signal if it's lower in frequency than the pump. Optimal amplification occurs when the difference in wavelengths is around 13.2 THz. The signal to be amplified must be lower in frequency (longer in wavelength) than the pump. In regular Ge-doped fibre the effect is very small and it takes a relatively long length of fibre for a significant effect to build up.

In principle it is relatively easy to build a Raman amplifier. All you do is take a long (about 1 km) section of fibre and couple into it a signal and a pump of around 13.2 THz higher in frequency than the signal. A simple device such as this does give quite good amplification.

However, there is a big problem: *Although the pump and the signal don't need to be spaced at exactly the Raman shift apart the closer to this spacing you get the more efficient the amplifier.* But we just can't build very high power (around half a watt or more) pump lasers at any wavelength we desire! Laser wavelengths are very specific and high power lasers are quite hard to build.

---

[70] 13.2 THz is approximately 60 nm in the 1310 band.

5.2.7.1 Wavelength Changing with SRS

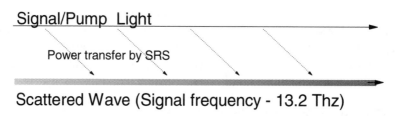

Figure 130. Wavelength Changing Using SRS

One elegant solution to the problem of finding a pump of the right wavelength is to wavelength shift a pump that we *can* get to an appropriate pump wavelength.

Figure 130 shows the principle of shifting an optical pump down by the Raman shift. At the high power level involved some light is shifted by SRS to the new (lower) wavelength (the Stokes wave). Then this shifted light is amplified by SRS. A transfer of power continues progressively from the signal to the Stokes wave. In regular Ge-doped fibre this effect is quite small. In addition the shifted wavelength produced is really quite a wide band of wavelengths when we need a narrow shifted signal.

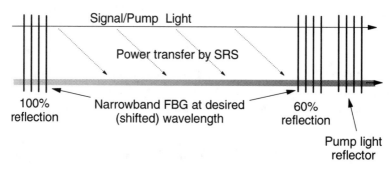

Figure 131. Wavelength Shifter Using FBGs

The effect can be significantly improved by using a configuration as illustrated in Figure 131. Here we have inserted narrowband FBGs to concentrate the shifted light. SRS happens in both directions so the shifted light will reflect between the FBGs and other light (outside the needed wavelength) will exit the device. Efficiency is improved by adding an FBG reflector for the pump wavelength. This is a bit like what happens in a laser but of course it is not a laser because there is no stimulated emission occurring.

If it is set up correctly this wavelength shift can be very efficient converting most of the light to the new wavelength.

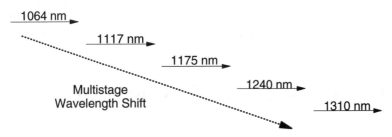

Figure 132. *Multistage Wavelength Shifting*

If we arrange to shift most of the light to a new wavelength then we can shift that light itself again to a new wavelength. Thus shifts can be cascaded in many steps so that very large wavelength shifts may be obtained. In Figure 132 multiple stages are shown to shift a pump wavelength at 1064 nm to 1310 nm. Notice that the wavelength shifts don't need to be exactly 13.2 THz. There is quite a big latitude (a few nm at each stage) in the shifts obtainable.

5.2.7.2 A 1310 nm Band Raman Amplifier

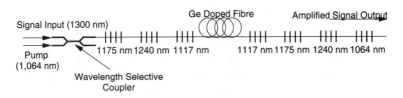

Figure 133. *1320 nm Raman Amplifier Using In-Fibre Bragg Gratings*

Figure 133 shows a most ingenious device. This is a Raman effect 1310 nm band amplifier. It shifts the pump wavelength in four stages down to a wavelength appropriate to pump a 1310 nm signal. Then it uses the developed pump to amplify the signal wavelength by SRS. But all of this happens in the same length of fibre!

Operation is as follows:

1. Signal light and pump light enter the device together through a wavelength selective coupler.

2. The pump light at 1064 nm is shifted to 1117 nm and then in stages to 1240 nm.

3. The 1240 nm light then pumps the 1310 band signal and amplification is obtained.

To gain efficiency a narrow core size is used to increase the intensity of the light. Also, a high level of Ge dopant is used (around 20%) to increase the SRS effect. The surprise is that this is a very effective, low noise process with good gain at small signal levels.

5.3 Second Harmonic Generation (SHG)

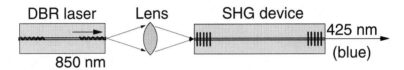

Figure 134. *Generating Blue Light via Second Harmonic Generation. Schematic view from the top.*

Second harmonic generation (SHG), also known as "frequency doubling", is a process which converts light of one particular frequency to light at exactly double that frequency. Another way of saying it is to say that the wavelength is halved. This process only takes place under very specific conditions within a material which has a "second-order non-linear" characteristic. Materials of this kind are sometimes called chi-squared (χ^2) materials.

The energy carried by a photon is a linear function of frequency - if you want to double the frequency you must double the energy. Thus two photons of a particular energy (and frequency) are combined (through interaction with a material) to give out a third photon containing all the energy of the original two (at double the frequency).

Chemical bonds between pairs of atoms (called dipoles) resonate at particular frequencies (wavelengths, energy levels). In some conditions this resonance causes the absorption and re-emission of light at a particular resonant frequency. Normally, light at a different wavelength from the resonant one is unaffected. However, if you get two photons whose total energy *adds up* to the energy required for resonance into close proximity with the dipole, the dipole will absorb *both photons* and re-emit a single photon with the combined energies of the two absorbed ones.

This says that the energies of the two absorbed photons don't have to be the same. This is the general case of "three-wave mixing" where two photons combine through interaction with a material to produce a third photon with the sum of the energies of the original photons. However, in the case of SHG we have two photons with the same energy level combining to produce a third with the sum of the energies of the two original photons.

A few important points:

1. The effect occurs in materials with a so-called "second order nonlinearity". This normally excludes regular optical fibre but it has been discovered that you can obtain the effect in silica fibre if it is heavily doped with Ge and P. The material used must have a dipole which is resonant at the desired (frequency doubled) wavelength.

2. A relatively intense beam of input light is required. This is because you need the simultaneous close proximity of two photons and a dipole. The higher the light level the more chances that this will occur.

3. For a significant effect to occur the phase velocity of both the input and output waves must be the same in the nonlinear material. The longer that the fundamental wave and the generated second harmonic remain in-phase the more efficient will be the conversion.

   This condition is actually quite hard to meet. It is done in crystalline materials by choosing an angle of propagation through the crystal in relation to the crystal axes) where the phase velocities are equal.

The first example of frequency doubling used a ruby laser at 694.3 nm and a crystal of KDP to produce a (very weak) second harmonic at 347.2 nm. Many other examples exist, for instance light at 1060 nm (from a Nd laser) can be frequency doubled in lithium niobate to produce green light at 530 nm. There are also experiments in frequency doubling *within* a laser cavity. An AlGaAs laser at 780 nm is reportedly producing light at 390 nm (by doubling within the laser cavity).

The device in Figure 134 on page 232 has been proposed as a source of blue light for use in high-density digital video recording. The reason for using of a DBR laser in the picture is to produce a very narrow linewidth (hence a long coherence length) for high efficiency conversion.

5.4 Splitters and Couplers

In an optical network there are many situations where it is necessary to combine signals and/or to split them multiple ways. Such devices are in common use. 1x2, 2x2, and 2x1 couplers are commercially available. Furthermore they have very low loss. Of course, they do have some loss.

In proposed WDM network designs, there is often the need for a "reflective star" (a device that accepts many input signals, mixes them, and then splits the combined signal in as many directions as there were inputs). In laboratories these have been built of many 2x2 couplers cascaded together. Many researchers feel that this becomes impractical for devices larger than 100x100. New devices have been designed to perform the "star" function in a single device. These are called "wavelength flattened fused fibre arrays". So far these have not become commercial, but to realize WDM LANs stars of up to 1000x1000 will be necessary.

There are three important characteristics when discussing most optical devices but couplers in particular. These are "Return Loss", "Insertion Loss" and "Excess Loss".

Return Loss

> Most optical devices reflect a part of the signal back down the input fibre. This can vary between a tiny amount and most of the signal! The amount of power that is reflected and thus lost from the signal is called the "return loss".

Insertion Loss

> Insertion loss is just the amount of signal lost in the total transit through the device including any couplings to fibres etc.

Excess Loss

> Excess loss is a measure of practical manufacture versus theory. It is the additional loss of a device over and above the loss required by theory. Of course all real devices are less than perfect.

5.4.1 Resonant Coupling

The vast majority of single-mode optical couplers employ the principle of resonant coupling. Two single-mode fibre cores are placed parallel and close to one another. Notice we are not placing two fibres close together - the claddings are too thick to achieve the effect we want. We must get the cores close together (but not touching). (There are several ways of doing this which will be discussed later.)

Figure 135 on page 235 illustrates the principle. In the figure light enters the device through port 4. As the light travels along the fibre a resonance is set up in the other fibre. Optical power builds up in the fibre at the top of the figure and reduces in the lower one. A reasonable person might conclude that this process would stop when each fibre carries half the power. But physics is often unreasonable. The power transfer continues until *all* of the optical power is travelling in the upper fibre!

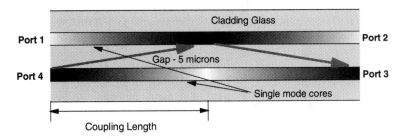

Figure 135. *Principle of Resonant Couplers*

Once all of the power is concentrated in the upper fibre transfer continues and power builds up in the lower fibre once again. This happens until all the power is transferred back to the lower fibre.

In this way power will oscillate from one fibre core to the other until attenuation reduces the signal to a negligible level or until the end of the parallel section of fibres. An important aspect to note is that the total power in the two cores at any place along the coupling section is the same.

It is quite impossible to conceive of this process if we think as light as a "ray" or for that matter as a tiny particle. What happens is that the electromagnetic field centred in one of the cores extends into the other core. This is where the coupling effect comes from. Power from the electromagnetic field in one core causes a resonance in the other and thus the power build up and transfer. Obviously, for this to work properly you have to have fibre cores which are exactly matched and regular in their characteristics. Figure 36 on page 71 illustrates the extent of the electromagnetic field within a single-mode fibre. When we put the cores close enough together we get a coupling effect.

All now depends on the length of the coupling section. For the example in the figure, 100% of the light entering at port 4 will exit the coupler at port 3. This would not have a lot of point. If we made the coupler only half as long as that illustrated, light entering at port 4 would leave at port 2. (Not a lot of point in doing this either!)

If we use a coupling section only 1/4 as long as the one illustrated, we will get an equal power distribution out of ports 2 and 3. This then would be a "3 dB coupler".

Light entering either (or both) of ports 1 and 4 will be evenly distributed on exit to ports 2 and 3 (half of the light will exit at each port).

A Mechanical Resonant Coupler

There is a very simple mechanical device we can build to illustrate the principle of resonant coupling.

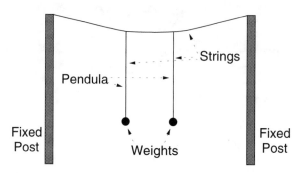

The device consists of two identical pendula as shown above. Two fixed posts are joined by a string at their tops. The two pendula are attached at points along the string equidistant from the posts. (Make the knots relatively loose so this can be tried at various different distances.)

Set one pendulum into motion while the other one is left still. (Motion in relation to the figure is into and out of the page.) What will happen is *exactly* what happens in an optical resonant coupler. Power will gradually transfer from the first pendulum into the second until the first pendulum is still and the second one is in motion. Then power will transfer back again until the original pendulum is moving and the other is stopped.

Observe what happens when the spacing between pendula is varied and/or the masses of the weights made unequal. In this case there will be incomplete power transfer between the two pendula. If the weights are different then the pendulum that you first set into motion never quite stops.

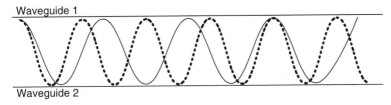

Waveguide 1

Waveguide 2

Figure 136. *Power Transfer in a Resonant Coupler. If two mixed signals (of different wavelengths) are injected into a resonant coupler the power transfer between the waveguides has a different period for each wavelength.*

Important points to note here are:

1. The "coupling length" is formally defined (at a particular wavelength) as the length at which 100% of the power entering at a particular input port is transferred to the other fibre. This is illustrated in Figure 135 on page 235.

2. The amount of coupling and hence the coupling length is strongly dependent on the separation between the two single-mode cores. The further apart they are the greater the coupling length.

3. The coupling lengths are strongly wavelength dependent! Different wavelengths yield different coupling lengths. This is shown in Figure 136. Two mixed signals of different wavelength are shown entering the top left hand port of a coupler. The power transfer between waveguides is shown by the two sinusoids.

This characteristic can be used to construct wavelength selective couplers and splitters as described in 5.4.1.5, "Wavelength Selective Couplers and Splitters" on page 242.

Wavelength sensitivity is not always a convenient characteristic. If you want to transport signals in both the 1300 and 1550 bands you want them to be processed through couplers without separation. Fortunately, by careful design of the coupler (mainly careful choice of coupling length) you can achieve a relatively flat response (no separation of wavelengths) for the whole range between 1300 nm and 1550 nm. Couplers designed in this way are called "wavelength flattened couplers".

4. The effect is symmetric. Light entering one of the "exit" ports will leave the device at one of the "entry" ports.

5. Light exiting the coupler of the opposite fibre from which it entered is 180° shifted in phase. For example in Figure 135 on page 235 light entering on Port 1 and exiting on Port 3 is shifted 180° in phase. Light entering on Port 1 and exiting on Port 2 is unshifted.

6. If the wavelengths are the same (or close together) and the core sizes etc. are also the same then there is *no way to couple all of the power from both input ports to the same output port. We cannot take input on ports 1 and 4 and arrange all the power to exit at port 2*, for example.

5.4.1.1 The Principle of Reciprocity

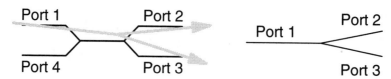

Figure 137. *Reciprocity Principle*

Reciprocity is a principle that applies generally to optical couplers and similar devices. At times it can be a very severe limitation. The principle states that couplers work in both directions (forward and reverse) symmetrically.

In Figure 137 on the left-hand side a resonant coupler is set up to split input from Port 1 equally between Port 2 and Port 3. (Of course this only applies at a particular wavelength or in a specific wavelength band.) Reciprocity states that light entering on Port 2 will be split equally between Port 4 and Port 1. This is hardly surprising since the device is symmetric.

However in the case of a Y-splitter as shown in the right-hand side of the diagram things are not so straight forward. Light entering on Port 1 will be split equally between Port 2 and Port 3 (as we might expect). But light entering on Port 2 will exit on Port 1 *attenuated by 50% (3 dB)*! Thus if we try to combine two input signals by using a y-junction, the signals are combined *but each signal will lose half of its power!*

5.4.1.2 Practical Couplers

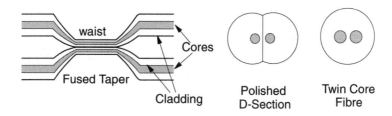

Figure 138. *Some Coupler Configurations*

There are many ways to build these couplers in practice:

Fused Taper Couplers

> To make these you put two regular single-mode fibres into direct contact, heat the section and then apply pulling pressure to the ends of the fibres. The fibres are drawn out and become thinner (both the cladding and the cores). In the process the fibres fuse together. Sometimes the fibres are twisted tightly together before heating and stretching.

> This gives us very much narrower cores and the cores are closer together because of the thinning of the cladding. The narrower cores actually increase the extent of the evanescent field in the cladding and assist in the coupling process! The problem is that it is difficult to control the spacing of the cores or the coupling length with great precision.

> Nevertheless, fused taper couplers are very common commercial devices.

Twin Core Fibres

> This is an extremely attractive idea. You can build fibres with twin cores and control the separation of the cores very precisely indeed. Of course twin core fibre is very low cost to make compared to other available technologies. However, the problem of connecting the twin core section to regular fibres at each port is very difficult. For this reason twin core fibres are of research interest only.

Polishing and Etching

> This technique involves embedding fibres into a solid material such as a piece of plastic. The flat surface is then polished until the cladding of the fibres is removed up to perhaps 4 microns from the core. A D shaped fibre section results. The plastic is then dissolved away. Two pieces of the D sectioned

fibre are then joined longitudinally along the flat areas with index-matching epoxy resin. Sometimes, the cladding on the fibres is thinned out first by etching with hydrofluoric acid (this reduces the amount of necessary polishing).

This is a good technique that is relatively precise but it is more costly than the fused taper method.

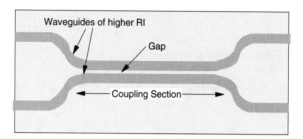

Figure 139. Resonant Coupler in Planar Waveguide Technology

Planar Waveguide Couplers

Couplers are very easy and effective when built in planar waveguide technology. They can be a lot shorter than fibre couplers and if you need to interconnect many in cascade then there is a very large space saving. However, you have to connect the device to fibres for input and output and the cost of this connection makes simple couplers too expensive in planar waveguide technology.

This technology is discussed further in 5.1.1, "Planar Optical Devices" on page 190.

5.4.1.3 3 dB Couplers

A simple 4-port resonant coupler is often called a "3 dB coupler". This is because half of the light entering a particular port on one side of the coupler exits from each of the two ports on the other side of the coupler. Thus the signal is split in half (3 dB = half). Half of the light entering at port 1 will exit at port 2 and half at port 3. Diagrammatically they are usually drawn as shown in Figure 140 on page 241.

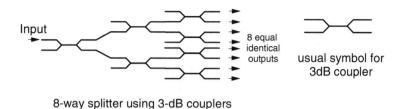

8-way splitter using 3-dB couplers

Figure 140. *Cascaded 3 dB Couplers*

It is often useful to connect many 3 dB couplers in cascade as shown in Figure 140. The configuration shown is a splitter which will divide a single input signal up into 8 separate outputs. As might be expected, if the device is perfect, each output arm will contain one eighth of the input power (loss of 9 dB). What might not be expected is that light entering any of the output ports will appear at the input port *also attenuated by 9 dB*.

5.4.1.4 Asymmetric Couplers and Taps

As mentioned above couplers can be built to split or couple power in many ways:

1. A coupler that splits only a small part of the light into one output and leaves most in the other is often called a "tap". For example light may enter at port 1 and 99% may leave at port 2 and only 1% at port 3. This would be a 99:1 coupler or a 1% tap. (Such devices are often used at the output of an optical amplifier to monitor the output power level and to provide feedback power control to the pump laser.

2. As mentioned above you cannot use a simple coupler to take *all* of the light in two fibres and merge it onto one fibre. Indeed if the light is at the same wavelength then the very best we can achieve is the loss of half of the light in each input fibre! This is not a limitation of mechanical construction technique; it is a law of physics and we can't get around it! However, if the light in the two input fibres is of *different* wavelengths we have an entirely different situation. There are a number of ways to combine light of different wavelengths from separate inputs into the same output fibre with very little loss. The simplest way is with a resonant coupler. This is discussed further in the next section.

5.4.1.5 Wavelength Selective Couplers and Splitters

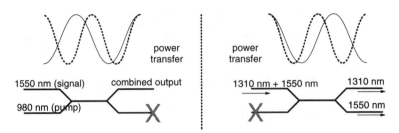

Figure 141. Wavelength Selective Coupling and Splitting

Wavelength selective couplers are used to either combine or split light of different wavelengths with minimal loss. Light of two different wavelengths on different input fibres can be merged (combined) onto the same output fibre. In the reverse direction light of two different wavelengths on the same fibre can be split so that one wavelength goes to one output fibre and the other wavelength is output onto the other output fibre. The process can be performed with very little loss.

As mentioned in previous sections the coupling length is wavelength dependent. Thus the shifting of power between the two parallel waveguides will take place at different places along the coupler for different wavelengths. All we need to do is choose the coupling length carefully and we can arrange for loss free wavelength combining or splitting. Figure 141 shows these functions. The graph of power transfer shows how power input on one of the fibres shifts back and forth between the two waveguides. The period of the shift is *different* for the two different wavelengths. Thus in the left-hand section of the diagram (combining wavelengths) there will be a place down the coupler where all of the light is in only one waveguide. If we make the coupler exactly this length then the signals have been combined. On the right-hand side of the diagram the reverse process is shown where two different wavelengths arrive on the same input fibre. At a particular point down the coupler the wavelengths will be in different waveguides so if we make this the coupling length then we have separated the wavelengths exactly. In fact both the processes described above are performed in the same coupler - the process is bi-directional. Thus the coupler on the left can operate in the opposite direction and become a splitter and the splitter on the right can operate in the opposite direction and become a coupler (combiner). Note that each coupler/splitter must be designed for the particular wavelengths to be used.

Commercial devices of this kind are commonly available and are very efficient. The quoted insertion loss is usually between 1.2 and 1.5 dB and the channel separation is quoted as better than 40 dB. "Wavelength flattened" couplers of this kind operate over quite a wide band of wavelengths. That is a given device may allow input over a range of wavelengths in the 1310 nm band up to 50 nm wide and a range of wavelengths in the 1550 nm band also up to 50 nm wide.

Common applications for wavelength selective couplers are as follows. Figure 141 on page 242 shows the first two of these functions.

Power Input to an EDFA

On the left-hand side of the figure we see an example of coupling two different wavelengths into the same output fibre. At the input of an EDFA you want to mix the (low level) incoming signal light with (high level) light from the pump. Typically the signal light will be around 1550 nm and the pump will be 980 nm. In this case it is possible to choose a coupling length such that 100% of the signal light (entering at port 1) and 100% of the pump light (entering at port 4) leaves on the same fibre (either port 2 or port 3).

A major advantage of this is that there is *very little* loss of signal power in this process.

Splitting Wavelengths for Simple WDM

On the right-hand side of the figure we show an example of sparse WDM demultiplexing. A mixed wavelength stream with one signal in each of the 1300 and 1550 nm bands is separated into its two component wavelengths. A WDM system like this might be used in a system for distributing Cable TV and advanced Video on Demand services to people in their homes. One signal stream might be carried at 1310 nm and the other at 1550 nm. A resonant coupler is shown here operating as a splitter separating the two wavelengths. Note that an identical splitter could also be used to combine the two wavelengths with very little loss.

Adding the Management Channel in Dense WDM

In dense WDM systems where many channels are carried in the 1550 nm band there is often a requirement to carry an additional relatively slow rate channel for management purposes. A convenient way to do this is to send the management information in the 1310 nm band and the mixed "dense WDM" stream in the 1550 band. Wavelength selective couplers are commonly used for this purpose. A management signal (a single wavelength) in the 1310 band is coupled onto a fibre carrying many wavelengths between 1540 nm and 1560 nm. Another similar device is used to separate the signals at the other end of the link.

5.4.2 "Y" Couplers

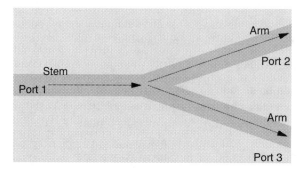

Figure 142. Y-Coupler (Splitter)

Y-couplers are very difficult to build in fibre technology but very easy in planar waveguide technology. A planar Y-coupler is shown in Figure 142. These are extremely efficient at splitting light. Light entering at port 1 will be split equally between ports 2 and 3 with almost no loss.

However light entering at port 2 will lose half its strength (3 dB) before leaving at port 1. This is perhaps surprising, but it is necessary from theory and in practice real devices operate this way (see 5.4.1.1, "The Principle of Reciprocity" on page 238).

Y-couplers are very seldom built as separate planar devices. Connecting the device to fibre is costly and a lot of light is lost in the connections. However, y-couplers of this kind are used extensively as part of more complex planar devices.

5.4.3 Star Couplers

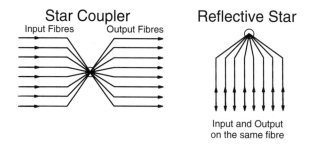

Figure 143. Star Couplers - Concept

A star coupler is just a multi-way coupler where each input signal is made available on every output fibre. There are two generic types as shown in Figure 143. The figure illustrates the *function* being performed rather than the way that function is achieved. The left of the diagram shows an 8-way device where 8 inputs are mixed and made available on 8 outputs. On the right of the diagram is a "reflective star" where input can be on any fibre and output is split equally among all fibres. Star couplers have been the basis of a number of prototype optical LAN and MAN networks.

There are various ways of building star couplers:

Fused-Fibre Star Couplers

Figure 144. *Fused Fibre Star Coupler*

In this technique many fibres are twisted together and heated under tension. The fibres melt together and become thinner as they are drawn out. The light mixes within the fused section.

These couplers are mainly used for multimode operation.

Mixing Plate

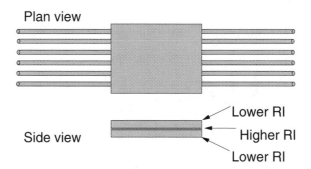

Figure 145. *Mixing Plate Coupler*

The mixing plate technique is illustrated in Figure 145. A fused silica plate is made in the form of a sandwich with a very thin (the same thickness as the fibre's core diameter) layer of higher RI glass in the middle. Fibres are attached to the edge so that the cores line up with the high RI (middle) part of the sandwich.

Entering light travels on a very large number of modes until it leaves through one of the exit fibres. This is essentially the same technique as is used in the planar free-space coupler but realised in fibre technology. It is suitable for either multimode or single-mode operation.

Planar Devices

Figure 146. Planar (Free Space) Star Coupler

A planar star coupler device is illustrated in Figure 146. (The lighter areas of the diagram are those of *higher* refractive index.) The principle of operation is simply a large "free space region" (consisting of material with a relatively high RI) on a planar substrate bounded by material of a lower RI. Light entering the region on one of the input fibres disperses in many modes into this region. Power will couple (more or less equally) from any input to all outputs. Of course operation of the device is bi-directional.

This principle can be used to make both single-mode and multimode star couplers.

Interconnection of Multiple Fibre 3 dB Couplers

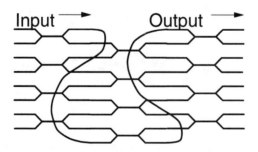

Figure 147. Concatenation of Multiple 3 dB Couplers to Form an 8-Way Star

This is illustrated in Figure 147. This is very easy to construct as it is only a matter of joining fused fibre couplers together (fibre joins). However, the assembly is quite unwieldy as fibres cannot be bent to very tight radii without unacceptable loss of light. Also its cost becomes exponentially greater with the number of required ports. This is linear with the number of couplers but of course the number of couplers needed grows exponentially.

5.4.4 Beamsplitter Prisms

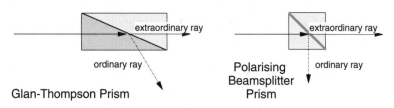

Figure 148. *Polarising Beamsplitter Prisms*

In many situations it is necessary to split an optical signal into its orthogonally polarised components. This is usually done with "Polarising Beamsplitter Prisms" similar to those illustrated in Figure 148.

These devices can be made in a number of ways but two are most popular.

Glan-Thompson Prism

Two prisms made from a birefringent material (usually calcite) are cemented together along their hypotenuses. The thickness of the cementing layer and its index are closely controlled.

A ray incident at the normal to an external surface of this prism is split into two separate rays (an ordinary ray and an extraordinary ray) depending on their polarisations. The extraordinary ray passes through without refraction but the ordinary ray is reflected at the Brewster angle. This is discussed further in 5.4.4.1, "Birefringent Materials" on page 248.

As shown in the figure the device is usually built in a rectangular shape. This allows the incident ray to arrive at 90° to the surface of the prism (for minimum reflection) and yet meet the diagonal surface at the optimum angle.

In real devices of course the entry and exit surfaces of the crystal are anti-reflection coated.

Polarisation Beamsplitter Cubes

These devices perform the same function as the Glan-Thompson prism except that instead of using a birefringent crystal they use a multiple layers of dielectric material at the diagonal interface between the two prisms.

5.4.4.1 Birefringent Materials

Birefringence is a characteristic of some materials such that light of different polarisations experiences a different refractive index within that material. Since an unpolarised ray or beam of light contains waves of both vertical and horizontal polarisations this can be split into two separate (polarised) rays within a birefringent material.[71] The operation of both isolators and circulators is based on birefringent (or at least polarisation) effects.

There are many materials that exhibit birefringent properties. Calcite ($CaCO_3$) and rutile (TiO_2) are commonly used for their birefringent properties. Quartz also has these properties and this can cause a problem in many situations.

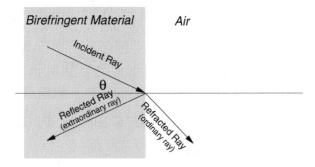

Figure 149. *Splitting of Unpolarised Light into Two Components. An unpolarised ray incident at the Brewster angle is split into two orthogonally polarised components. The ordinary ray is refracted and the extraordinary ray is reflected.*

A birefringent material has a crystal structure. Within this structure there is an "optic axis" (in some materials more than one). When a ray enters the crystal at an angle to the optic axis it is split into two rays. One ray (the ordinary ray) has polarisation perpendicular to the optic axis. The other ray (the extraordinary ray) has polarisation orthogonal to that of the ordinary ray. For the ordinary ray the material exhibits a

---

[71] The phenomena of birefringence in fibres is discussed in 2.4.2.1, "Polarisation Mode Dispersion (PMD)" on page 77.

fixed refractive index (1.66 in the case of calcite). For the extraordinary ray, the material exhibits a *variable* refractive index (between 1.66 and 1.49) depending of the angle of incidence of the original incident ray.

A very useful effect here is that we can find an angle of incidence such that when a ray meets an air-material interface the ordinary ray is refracted *but the extraordinary ray is reflected*. This is shown in Figure 149 on page 248. The angle of incidence at which this occurs is called the "Brewster Angle". This is a good way of separating a single unpolarised ray into two orthogonally polarised ones.

Many ordinary substances exhibit the above effect. When strong sunlight falls on them light of one polarisation is absorbed and light of the orthogonal polarisation is reflected.

For example, a green leaf on a tree looks white in strong direct sunlight - this is because of a strong polarised reflection from the surface. If you are taking a photograph of a brightly lit scene you can use a polarising filter. If you rotate the filter to the correct angle all of the polarised reflections (from the surface) will be blocked but only part of the light radiated from just below the surface (randomly polarised) will be blocked. Thus colours are intensified.

You can see the same effect using polarising sunglasses.

Figure 150 on page 250 shows the different refractions obtained depending on the relationship of the angle of incidence to the optic axis of the crystal. Notice that for rays either parallel to the optic axis or at 90° to it:

- If the ray is normal to the crystal both polarisations are passed through the interface unaffected.

- If the ray is not at a normal to the crystal it is split into two separate rays, the ordinary and the extraordinary polarisations.

For a ray arriving at an angle to the optic axis but nevertheless on a normal to the crystal/air interface, the ordinary ray is not refracted but the extraordinary one is!

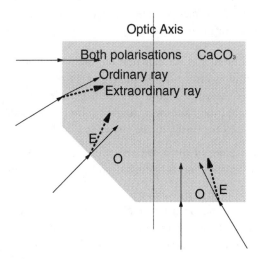

Figure 150. Effect of Optic Axis. An unpolarised incident ray is diffracted in different ways depending on its relationship with the optic axis of the crystal.

5.4.5 Isolators

An isolator is a device that allows light to pass along a fibre in one direction but not in the opposite direction. In function it is quite like a diode in the electrical world. Isolators are needed in optical systems in many roles the most common of which is the prevention of reflections coming back down a fibre from re-entering and disrupting the operations of a laser.

Most optical phenomena are bi-directional and so building an isolator is not as straightforward as we might like. However, one optical phenomenon is not bi-directional. This is the "Faraday Effect". This effect is polarisation dependent so in order to use it you have to take account of polarisation.

5.4.5.1 The Electrooptic Effect

Some materials such as lithium niobate ($LiNbO_3$) have variable refractive index characteristics depending on the strength of an applied electric field. Depending on the orientation of the electric field in relation to the crystal some materials also exhibit variable birefringence. (That is, the RI variations induced are different for different orientations of the electric field.) This effect is used in modulators (see 5.9, "Modulators and Switches" on page 300).

5.4.5.2 *The Faraday Effect*

The Faraday effect is obtained when some materials such as YIG (Yttrium-Iron-Garnet) are placed in a strong magnetic field. Light travelling within the material has its plane of polarisation (electric and magnetic field vectors) rotated by an amount depending on the length and the strength of the magnetic field. This can be useful but the most important aspect is that *the effect is asymmetric*. That is light travelling in one direction might have its polarisation rotated right by (say) 45°. Light travelling in the other direction would have its polarisation rotated *left* by the same amount (in this case 45°). *The rotation is opposite directions in relation to the direction of the ray of light but in the same direction in relation to the rotator!*

5.4.5.3 *A Simple Isolator*

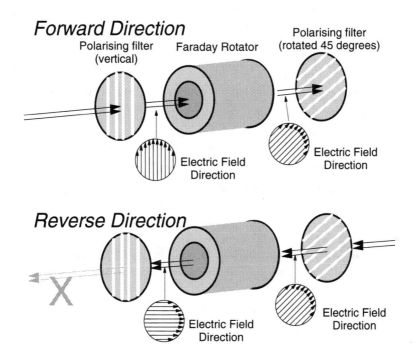

Figure 151. *Isolator Operation*

Isolators are used in may situations to ensure light only passes in one direction. This is necessary for example when coupling a laser to a fibre. Reflected light can cause instability in the laser and cause many undesirable effects.

There are a number of ways of building isolators and most of these rely on one-way polarisation effects.

Figure 151 on page 251 shows the operation of a typical isolator. In the top of the figure light is passing in the "forward" direction from left to right across the page.

- Incoming light first meets a polarising filter which removes all polarisations except those in the direction of the polariser. (This means that if incoming light is randomly polarised we are going to lose 50% of it!) On exit from the filter light is vertically polarised.

- Polarised input light then enters the Faraday rotator. This device (described above) rotates the polarisation (without loss) by 45° to the right.

- The second polarising filter is redundant in the forward direction. Light will pass through this filter now without loss as it is oriented in the same direction as the polarisation of the incoming light.

The reverse direction is shown in the lower half of the figure.

- Light first meets a polariser which filters out any light not oriented at 45° to the vertical. This is necessary as we can't be sure of the polarisation of unwanted reflections.

- The key to operation of the isolator is the Faraday rotator. In the reverse direction this device will rotate the polarisation in the *anti-clockwise direction* (in relation to the direction of propagation). Thus operation of the rotator is asymmetric.

- On exit from the Faraday rotator light is now polarised at 90° from the vertical. When it meets the next polarising filter it will be eliminated (absorbed).

The problem with this type of isolator is that the input polarisation needs to be matched to the orientation of the isolator. If input is unpolarised then we lose half of the signal (3 dB). If the signal is polarised and the orientation is wrong then we can lose all of the signal. Worse than that, if the polarisation varies with time (as it normally does after a long journey on a fibre) the variations will be translated into variations in attenuation. This results in fast random variations in signal level - in other words - serious noise!

This is not quite as bad as it sounds. In many places that we want to use an isolator the light is polarised anyway: for example, at the exit of a semiconductor laser. However, in other situations we need a polarisation independent device.

5.4.5.4 A Polarisation Independent Isolator

In many applications we are unable to control the polarisation of input light. In cases like this a polarisation independent isolator is needed. Such an isolator can be constructed by separating the incoming ray into its two orthogonal polarisations, processing them separately and then re-combining them at the output.

This is an identical process to that used in circulators. It is described in 5.4.6.1, "Circulators - Principle of Operation" on page 254.

5.4.6 Circulators

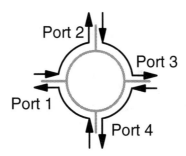

Figure 152. Four-Port Circulator

The basic function of a circulator is illustrated in Figure 152. Light entering at any particular port (say port 1) travels around the circulator and exits at the next port (say port 2). Light entering at port 2 leaves at port 3 and so on. The device is symmetric in operation around a circle.

Circulators are microoptic devices and can be made with any number of ports but 3 and 4 port versions are most common. Also, it is common to build an asymmetric version where the last port (say 4) does not circulate around to port 1. While this saves some cost this is not the most important reason for doing it. If we make sure the last port does not circulate around to the first we can use the device in systems where we don't need (or want) this feature. For example, if the input to port 1 is directly connected to a laser we certainly don't want spurious signals to be returned back into it.

One of the great attractions of circulators is the relatively low level of loss. Typical devices give a port-to-port loss of between .5 dB and 1.5 dB.

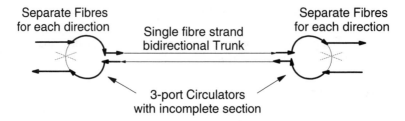

Figure 153. Multiplexing Bidirectional Traffic onto a Single Fibre Strand. Asymmetric three-port circulators are used. The inoperative segment of each circulator is represented by a dashed line.

Circulators are very versatile devices and may be used in many applications. Examples may be found in 9.2.4.2, "Circulators with FBGs" on page 527 and 9.2.5.2, "Circulators with In-Fibre Bragg Gratings" on page 532. A simple example is shown in Figure 153. Here a bidirectional link consisting of two fibre strands (one for each direction) is multiplexed onto a single strand of fibre. This might be done to save the cost of fibre for example. Of course if you did something like this you would need to take particular care to minimise reflections on the link.

5.4.6.1 Circulators - Principle of Operation

By itself there is no single, simple principle behind the circulator. Circulators are made of an assembly of optical components. There are many different designs but the key principle is like that of the isolator.

Light travelling in one direction through a Faraday rotator has its polarisation rotated in one particular direction. Light entering the Faraday rotator from the opposite direction has its phase rotated in the opposite direction (relative to the direction of propagation of the light). Another way of looking at this is to say that light is always rotated in the *same* direction in relation to the rotator regardless of its direction of travel.

This is complicated by the presence of unpredictable polarisation. We could filter the unwanted polarisation out but we would lose (on average) half our light in doing that - and often a lot more. So we separate the incident "ray" into two orthogonally polarised rays and treat each polarisation separately. The two halves of the ray are then re-combined before being output to the destination port.

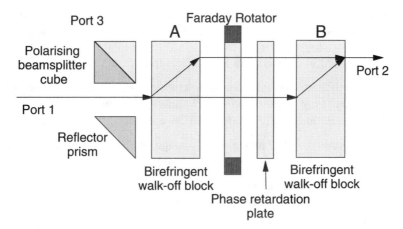

Figure 154. Circulator - Path from Port 1 to Port 2. After Van Delden (1995) by permission PennWell Publishing

Figure 154 shows a basic 3-port circulator. Its components function as follows:

Polarising Beam Splitter Cube

This device separates the input ray into two orthogonally polarised rays. The principles involved were described in 5.4.4, "Beamsplitter Prisms" on page 247.

Birefringent "Walk-off" Block

This is just a block of birefringent material cut at 45° to the optic axis. A ray incident at a normal to the air-crystal interface is split into two rays of orthogonal polarisation. The ordinary ray is not refracted and passes through unaffected. The extraordinary ray is refracted at an angle to the normal.

Faraday Rotator and Phase Plate

This combination passes light in one direction completely unchanged! (In the figure this is the right-to-left direction.) In the opposite direction polarisation of incoming light is rotated by 90°.

In the left-to-right direction the Faraday rotator imparts a phase rotation of 45° (clockwise) and the phase plate rotates the light another 45° (also clockwise). Thus we get a net 90° clockwise rotation.

In the right-to-left direction the phase plate rotates the light in the same direction (in relation to the direction of the ray of light) as before, that is, anti-clockwise at 45°. The Faraday rotator however rotates the phase in the opposite direction (in relation to the direction of the ray) as it did before, that is, clockwise by the same 45°. *That is the phase is rotated in the opposite direction.* Thus there is no net change in polarisation. (Of course in practice there are losses due to reflections and imperfections in device manufacture.)

As shown in Figure 154 on page 255 light travels from Port 1 to Port 2 as follows:

1. A ray input on Port 1 is split into two separate rays of orthogonal polarisations. The "ordinary" ray passes through without refraction but the orthogonally polarised "extraordinary" ray is refracted (upwards in the figure).

2. Both rays proceed from left-to-right through the Faraday rotator and phase retardation plates. Both rays are rotated through 90°.

3. The two rays then meet another birefringent walk-off block (block B) identical with the first. The effect of the phase rotation in the previous stage was to swap the status of the rays. The ray that was the ordinary ray in block A (and was not refracted) becomes the extraordinary ray in block B (and is refracted in block B). The extraordinary ray in block A (the upper path in the figure) becomes the ordinary ray in block B (and is not refracted in block B).

   The light is refracted and re-combined as shown. It is then output to Port 2.

Coupling to fibre on input and output would normally use a lens of some kind. Typically a GRIN lens might be used here.

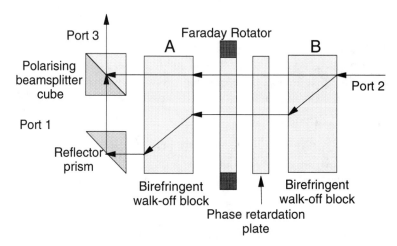

Figure 155. *Circulator - Path from Port 2 to Port 3. After Van Delden (1995) by permission PennWell Publishing*

The path from Port 2 to Port 3 is somewhat more involved:

1. Light entering from Port 3 is split in block B.

2. Travelling in the reverse direction the polarisation of *both* rays is unchanged.

3. Birefringent block A now passes the upper ray unchanged but shifts the lower one further away.

4. The two rays are then re-combined using the reflector prism and the polarising beamsplitter cube.

Notice here that if you only connect Ports 1 and 2 the circulator can be used as an isolator! Indeed if you leave out the beamsplitter cube and the reflector prism you have an excellent (very low loss) *polarisation independent isolator.*

A path from Port 3 to Port 1 can be constructed by adding additional components; however, for most applications this is unnecessary as we don't want the connection from Port 3 to Port 1 anyway.

There are many ways to construct circulators (both 3 and 4 port). All of these ways use combinations of components and similar principles as those described above. The biggest problem with circulators is that the components must be manufactured to very close tolerances and positioned extremely accurately. This causes the cost to be relatively high.

5.5 Polarisation Control

The ability to control and modify polarisation state is important in many applications especially in the testing and characterisation of components.

5.5.1 Fibre Loop Polarisation Controller

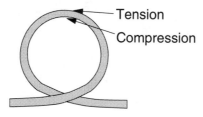

Figure 156. Fibre Loop

One common type of polarisation controller is made with a fibre loop. What we are aiming at is to build a device that receives light in any polarisation state and can convert it without loss into any other polarisation. To do this you need a device that is birefringent but which can have its axes of birefringence rotated.

If you make a loop of fibre with a relatively small diameter (as illustrated in Figure 156 on page 257) then the inner part of the fibre is compressed slightly and the outer part put under tension. Although this is a relatively small effect it induces birefringence in the fibre loop.

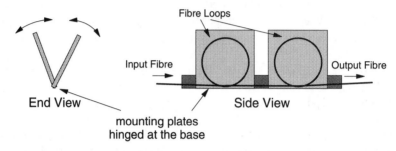

Figure 157. *Fibre Loop Polarisation Controller*

When light arrives on the input fibre it tends to stay in its original orientation (in terms of its polarisation axes) regardless of twists in the fibre. A slight twist in a symmetric fibre isn't noticed by the signal and the polarisation states are not changed in relation to axes in free space regardless of the fibre axes. Thus when the fibre loop is rotated around the axis of the fibre the fast and slow axes rotate in relation to the signal.

This rotation of the birefringent axes has the effect of phase retardation of one component of the signal light in relation to the other. Thus it changes the polarisation of the signal. By rotating the fibre loops you can adjust the device to produce light at any desired polarisation.

Of course you have to take great care that the loop radius is greater than the bend radius of the fibre. If the loop is too tight light will leave the fibre. A typical device might have a loop diameter of about 750 mm.

Real devices have three or four fibre loops rather than two but the effect can be produced with only two loops.

Polarisation controllers of this kind may be used in future coherent communication systems.

5.5.2 Fibre Squeezer Polarisation Controller

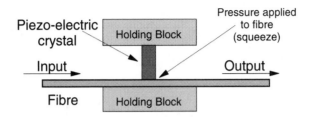

Figure 158. *Polarisation Control by Squeezing the Fibre*

A similar effect to the one described above using fibre loops can be obtained by using devices that squeeze the fibre. Squeezing produces a variable birefringence depending on the amount of pressure applied to the fibre. Pressure is applied using the piezo-electric effect on a crystal. This effect is controllable by varying the voltage applied to the crystal. This can produce very detailed variations in pressure as it is possible to control the movement of the crystal in amounts smaller than the diameter of an atom! In this case you don't rotate (twist) the fibre but instead up to four squeezers are used oriented at different angles in respect to one another.

5.6 Lenses and Prisms

Lenses and prisms are well known in traditional optics and their operation and function is the same in the fibre optical communications application. Lenses are used in many situations such as in coupling a laser or LED to a fibre. Prisms are used in a number of applications such as within a circulator. The only characteristic of these devices that is unusual is that they are often very small indeed!

5.6.1 Graded Index (GRIN) Lenses

GRIN lenses are short cylindrical lengths of glass with a graded refractive index. They are sometimes called SELFOC[72] lenses. Ideally, the index decreases with the square of the distance from the axis of the lens. In this they are very similar to graded index fibre but they are usually quite a lot thicker (1-2 mm). They are made with the same technology used to make GI fibre.

---

[72] Selfoc is a registered trademark of the Nippon Sheet Glass Company.

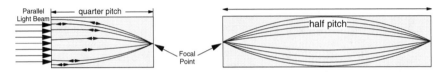

Figure 159. GRIN Lens

The principle is shown in Figure 159. A conventional lens works by refraction at the curved surface of the lens. GRIN lenses operate by internal refraction as light passes through material of varying refractive indices. The length of the lens is of course dependent on the wavelength in use and quite critical (typically varying between 3 and 7 mm).

A "full-pitch" GRIN lens would take the light through a full cycle and would have somewhat limited application. Quarter-pitch and half-pitch lenses are illustrated. A quarter pitch lens focuses a collimated beam onto a single point. This is reciprocal - a point source (such as the end of a fibre) can be converted into a collimated beam. A half-pitch lens takes a point source and focuses it onto another point.

This leads to their most useful features: The focal point of the lens is on the surface and the surface is flat. In addition they are easy to make. The major drawback is that you can't control the grading of the index very precisely so they don't produce quite as sharp a focus as conventional lenses.

GRIN lenses are widely used in couplers, splitters and WDM equipment.

5.7 Diffraction Gratings

A diffraction grating is a device that reflects or refracts light by an amount varying according to the wavelength. For example, if sunlight falls on a diffraction grating (at the correct angle) then the sunlight will be broken up into its component colours to form a rainbow. This function (diffraction) is the same as that of a prism. The device is performing a Fourier Transform and separating a waveform in the time domain into a number of waveforms in the frequency domain.

5.7.1 Planar Diffraction Gratings

Gratings work in both transmission (where the light passes through a material with a grating written on its surface) and in reflection. In optical communications only reflective gratings have a widespread use and so the description is restricted to these. (This is in the context of planar gratings - Bragg gratings are very widely used but they are different.)

A reflective diffraction grating consists of a very closely spaced set of parallel lines or grooves made in a mirror surface of a solid material. Refractive gratings (typically written as scratches in a glass surface) are not used in fibre optical communications and so they are not discussed here. A grating can be formed in almost any material where we vary the optical properties (such as refractive index) in a regular way with a period close to the wavelength (actually the grating period can be up to a few hundred times the wavelength). Reflective gratings are wavelength-selective filters. In optical communications they are used for splitting and/or combining optical signals in WDM systems and as reflectors in external cavity DBR lasers.

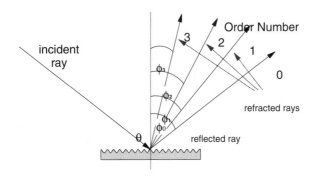

Figure 160. *Grating Principle of Operation*

The basic grating equation is shown below:

$$m\lambda = gs(\sin\theta + \sin\phi_m)$$

Where: gs = groove spacing
m = order of the refracted ray - (integer)
λ = free space wavelength of the incident ray
θ = angle of incidence (measured against the normal)
ϕ_m = angle of refraction (measured against the normal)

A schematic of the operation of a reflective grating is shown in Figure 160. An incident ray (at an angle of θ to the normal) is projected onto the grating. A number of reflected and refracted rays are produced corresponding to different orders (values of m = 0, 1, 2, 3...). When m = 0 we get ordinary reflection $\sin\theta = \sin\phi_0$ which is exactly the same as for any mirror. When m = 1 we get a ray produced at a different angle.

What is happening is that parts of the ray (or beam) are reflected from different lines in the grating. Interference effects prevent reflections that are not in-phase with each other from propagating. Thus we get resultant rays at a series of angles that correspond to points of constructive interference (reinforcement) between the reflections. The number of orders of refracted rays produced depends on the relationship between the groove spacing and the wavelength. We can design the grating to ensure that only the 0 and 1 orders are produced by making the groove spacing smaller than the wavelength.

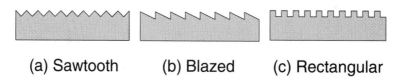

(a) Sawtooth   (b) Blazed   (c) Rectangular

Figure 161. Grating Profiles

The shape of the grooves has no effect on the angles at which different wavelengths are diffracted. However, grove profile determines the relative strengths of diffracted orders produced. This enables us to control the distribution of power into the different orders. For example we will often want to transfer as much power as possible into the first order refracted beam.

Some different groove profiles are illustrated in Figure 161. Profile (b) in the figure is a so-called "blazed" grating. This is perhaps the most popular groove profile because it allows a very high proportion of power to be transferred into the first order mode. However, a particular blazed grating will operate efficiently over only a very restricted range of wavelengths.

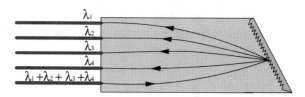

Figure 162. Wavelength Division Multiplexing with a Littrow Grating. Wavelength routing is bi-directional. Separate wavelengths can be combined onto the same output port or a single mixed input may be split into multiple outputs (one per wavelength).

5.7.1.1 Wavelength Selection

There are literally dozens of ways of using a grating to demultiplex (or to multiplex) a number of different wavelengths. Many different wavelengths on a single fibre are separated (or combined) to or from other fibres. Figure 162 on page 262 shows a Littrow configuration for a grating multiplexor.[73] The important characteristic of this setup is that it uses only a single lens (rather than two in other configurations). It is necessary to use a lens of some kind to focus the light onto the ends of the appropriate fibres. To do this conventional lenses, concave mirrors and GRIN lenses have all been proposed. In addition, gratings can be written on the surface of a concave mirror.

In this case a GRIN lens is illustrated. The grating can be bonded (with index matching epoxy) to the GRIN lens or built into the surface of the GRIN lens itself. Practical devices here often use a prism between the grating and the GRIN lens with the grating bonded to one surface of the prism.

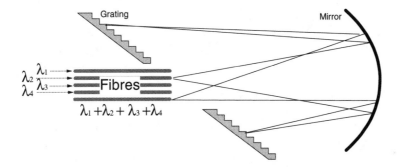

Figure 163. WDM with a Concave Mirror and a Littrow Grating. The lines showing light paths from the fibre to the mirror and thence to the grating should not be understood as narrow "rays" of light. When light arrives on a fibre it diffuses outward and the divergent wave forms a cone. The mirror focuses this divergent beam onto a spot on the grating. The grating reflects at an angle determined by the wavelength of the light. The reflected light is now refocused by the mirror onto a different fibre.

Another configuration is shown in Figure 163. Here a concave mirror is used instead of the GRIN lens to focus the light from the ends of the fibres onto the Littrow grating. This is a very practical principle and grating assemblies can be made with very small wavelength spacings. This type of device is used in the IBM 9729 WDM

---

[73] "Littrow" is a term applied to any reflective grating.

product described in 10.5, "The IBM 9729 - A WDM System for the Metropolitan Area Network" on page 607.

Due to the extreme precision required in manufacture these devices tend to be quite costly. However, commercial devices have outstanding characteristics for WDM systems. Devices with up to 132 channels (wavelengths) are available. The 20-channel device used in the IBM 9729 has a channel-to-channel crosstalk rejection of better than 55 dB (measured).

5.7.1.2 Pulse Compression

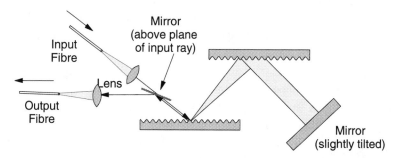

Figure 164. *Double-Pass Grating Compressor*

A pair of parallel gratings such as illustrated in Figure 164 can be used to compress a pulse which has undergone chromatic dispersion. This can be used to compensate for dispersion or to shorten the pulse for other purposes such as in the first stage of soliton [74] formation.

Grating pair devices were considered very promising in the late 1980's but have generally been replaced by in-fibre Bragg gratings. Nevertheless they are interesting and instructive.

Light incident on the first grating is diffracted by differing amounts depending on the wavelength. It is then incident on the second grating of the pair and re-formed into a single ray again. Thus different wavelengths have a different path length within the device and therefore different wavelengths take different amounts of time to travel through it.

---

[74] See 12.1, "Solitons" on page 651.

Unfortunately the second grating does not exactly re-form the ray in the way we would like. One way of compensating (and providing more "chirp") is to reflect the light back through the grating pair. The mirror is very slightly tilted so that the returning ray is not coincident with the input ray. This allows light to be directed out of the device by a mirror positioned a little above the input ray. Thus there is no additional loss in the process of getting the resultant ray out of the device.

The grating pair provides "anomalous dispersion" of the pulse. (See 2.4.2, "Dispersion in Single-Mode Fibre" on page 75.) That is it advances shorter wavelengths to the front of the pulse and retards longer wavelengths towards the back. Of course the amount by which this happens depends on the distance between the gratings. In practice a maximum distance between the gratings tends to be between 10 and 20 centimetres.

As a dispersion compensation device the grating pair is only of limited usefulness.

1. The amount of dispersion compensation it can perform is restricted to quite small amounts by the necessary physical size of the device (distance between the gratings).

2. It provides anomalous dispersion. Therefore it can only compensate for signals that have experienced normal dispersion. Standard fibre operates in the normal dispersion regime only when the wavelength is below 1300 nm. Thus the device can't be used to compensate for dispersion caused by sending at a wavelength of 1550 nm on standard fibre.

3. The loss experienced in the above device is about 6 dB.

However, the device is useful as a pulse compressor both for just shaping laser pulses and for creating solitons (at wavelengths shorter than 1310 nm).

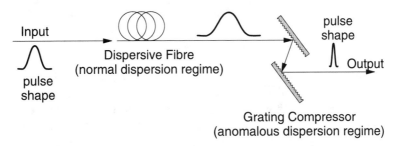

Figure 165. *Pulse Compression with Grating Compressor*

In many ways this device is counter to intuition but nevertheless it works. Illustrated in Figure 165 on entering the device light passes through a section of fibre to disperse the pulse. If standard fibre is used (and the wavelength is less than 1310 nm) this will result in ordering the wavelengths within the pulse so that the longer wavelengths come first. The pulse is therefore dispersed!

When the pulse is passed through the paired gratings it is compressed in the opposite direction from that which the previous journey through the fibre produced. The key here is that the compression process is *not* just a dispersion of the opposite sign. If it was, the best compression we could hope for would be to get the original pulse back! Each wavelength is shifted towards the centre wavelength by an amount proportionate to the difference between that wavelength and the centre. This is caused by the differences in path length experienced by different wavelengths within the pulse compressor device. In the resultant pulse the wavelengths are still ordered as they were before their journey through the compressor.

This process can result in a pulse that is compressed until it is significantly narrower than it was when it entered the device!

5.7.2 In-Fibre Bragg Gratings (FBGs)

In the introduction, the invention of the fibre Bragg grating was nominated as one of the milestone events in the history of optical communication - ranking even with the invention of the Laser. An in-fibre Bragg grating (FBG) is a very simple, extremely low cost, wavelength selective filter. It has a wide range of applications that both improve the quality and reduce the cost of optical networking.

Figure 166. In-Fibre Bragg Grating - Schematic

An in-fibre Bragg grating is just a piece of ordinary single-mode fibre a few centimetres long. The grating is constructed by varying the refractive index of the core *lengthwise* along the fibre. Light of the specified wavelength traveling along the fibre is *reflected* from the grating back in the direction from which it came. Wavelengths which are not selected are passed through with little or no attenuation.

This is the most important characteristic of FBGs - *resonant wavelengths are reflected back toward the source* and non-resonant wavelengths are transmitted through the device without loss. This is certainly not ideal from the point of view of using the device within a system - however this is the way it works!

Figure 166 on page 266 shows the device in schematic form. The grating is written *along the length of the core of the fibre*. Light entering (from the left of the diagram) is reflected if its wavelength is selected (if the grating is spaced such that a resonance condition is set up at that particular wavelength).

The grating consists of regular variations in the refractive index of the core longitudinally along the fibre. Surprisingly, you don't need a big variation in refractive index to produce a good, strong grating. Indeed, a difference of .0001 in the index is quite sufficient to produce the desired effect.

The centre wavelength of the reflection band (for a first-order grating) is given by:

$$\lambda = 2\, n_{eff}\, \Lambda$$

Where: λ = Centre wavelength of the reflection band
n_{eff} = Average refractive index of the material
Λ = Physical period of the fibre grating

5.7.2.1 *Principle of Operation*

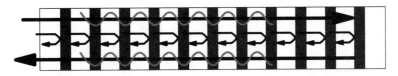

Figure 167. *Principle of Operation of Fibre Bragg Grating*

The principle of the FBG is illustrated in Figure 167. As light moves along the fibre and encounters the changes in refractive index, a small amount of light is reflected at each boundary. When the period of the grating and the wavelength of the light are the same then there is positive reinforcement and power is coupled from the forward direction to the backward direction. Light of other wavelengths encounters interference from out of phase reflections and therefore cannot propagate.

This explanation is not very good if you think of light as rays or as particles. If the non-selected wavelengths are reflected but then destructively interfere with themselves, how and why do these wavelengths pass through the grating with little loss? If we think of light as an electromagnetic wave then the effect becomes quite easy to understand. What is really happening here is that the grating forms an electromagnetic resonant circuit. Power from the forward direction is coupled into the resonant circuit and then reflected back. Non-resonant wavelengths are not affected very much.

5.7.2.2 Characteristics of In-Fibre Bragg Gratings

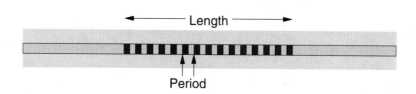

Figure 168. In-Fibre Bragg Grating - Parameters

The most important characteristics of any FBG are:

Centre Wavelength

> This is the wavelength at the centre of the grating's reflection band.

Bandwidth

> This is the width of the reflection band and specifies the range of wavelengths reflected.

Reflectance Peak

> This is a measure of the proportion of incident light reflected at the centre wavelength.

These characteristics are determined by the basic parameters of the grating. These are:

1. The grating period is the distance between modulations of the refractive index in the grating.

2. The grating length.

3. The "modulation depth" (grating strength). The modulation depth or grating strength is determined by the RI contrast within the grating.

4. The RI contrast profile. The modulation depth may be different in different parts of the grating. For example we might have a very small RI contrast at the ends of the grating but quite a large contrast in the middle. The RI contrast profile describes any regular change imposed on the RI contrast (grating depth) over the grating length. The process of making regular changes in the grating strength in

order to influence the characteristics of the grating is called "apodisation" and is described below.

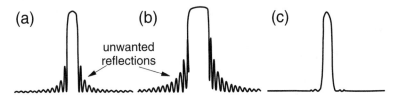

Figure 169. *In-Fibre Bragg Grating - Typical Reflection Spectra. Part (a) shows a typical reflection spectrum of a 1 cm long FBG with relatively low RI contrast. The height of the peak is 100% reflection and the width of the reflection band is .2 nm. Part (b) shows the same grating with a stronger contrast. The reflection band has been broadened. Part (c) shows the same grating as part (a) but after apodisation. Note the reflection peak is now not quite 100%.*

A reflection spectrum for a typical FBG is shown in part (a) of Figure 169. Notice the presence of some relatively strong reflection peaks adjacent to the main reflection band of the grating. The longer the grating the closer these unwanted reflection peaks are to the main reflection band. These peaks are caused as follows:

- The average RI of the grating section is higher than that of the fibre core at either end of it.

- Light at wavelengths unaffected by the grating itself nevertheless "sees" an abrupt change in RI at either end of the grating.

- Thus two partial mirrors are formed at each end of the grating.

- These mirrors act as a Fabry-Perot interferometer and create resonance conditions between them.

- These resonances are also affected by fringe conditions within the grating.

In general the presence of these additional reflection peaks is highly undesirable. They may be removed by "apodising" the grating. Apodisation is a process of tapering the strength of the grating at either end so that the apparent RI change is gradual rather than abrupt. The reflection band of an apodised grating is shown in part (c) of the figure.

The process of apodisation is not always straightforward. The rate at which RI tapering takes place can have a significant affect on the grating characteristics. The simplest form is where the grating is tapered in strength linearly. Tapering can occur however following almost any geometric function such as Sin, Tan, Tanh, Gaussian etc.

The grating parameters can be manipulated to produce desired grating characteristics. For example the strength of the grating and the length of the grating both influence the percentage reflectance and the width of the reflection band.

5.7.2.3 Chirped FBGs

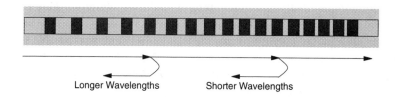

Figure 170. Chirped FBG

A "chirp" is where you get a variation in the period of the grating (and hence a variation in its response to different wavelengths) along the length of the grating. This can be done in two ways:

1. Either you can vary the period of the grating or

2. You can vary the average RI of the grating.

Both procedures have the effect of gradually changing the grating period. When a signal enters a chirped FBG different wavelengths are reflected from different parts of the grating. Thus the grating imposes a wavelength dependent delay on the signal. Some wavelengths are delayed more than others.

There is a major use for chirped gratings - that of equalising the wavelength response of existing fibre networks (designed to operate in the 1300 nm band so that they can be used in the 1550 nm band. This is discussed further in 7.5.6, "Chirped Fibre Bragg Gratings" on page 419.

Chirped FBGs pose an interesting technical challenge which at the time of writing (December 1997) has been almost overcome.

The unwanted reflection side-lobes mentioned above in the case of unchirped gratings appear right across the reflection band of a chirped grating. This appears both in the wavelength domain as an erratic reflected power spectrum and in the time domain as "ripple" on the wavelength dependence of the group delay. This is caused by the fact that the grating resonance at each wavelength appears at a different point along the grating. This means that any particular wavelength will have a grating resonance reflection condition but also a fringe condition from surrounding wavelengths!

As with unchirped FBGs these unwanted variations in response can be strongly attenuated by careful apodisation. However, some ripple still remains in both the reflected power spectrum and in the time domain. This ripple constitutes a noise source added to the optical signal. It has been calculated that this causes a penalty in the SNR of around 3 dB.

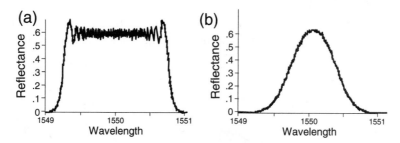

Figure 171. *Reflectance of a Chirped FBG. Part (a) shows the grating without apodisation. Part (b) shows the same grating after apodisation.*

Figure 171 shows the reflectance characteristics of a chirped FBG. Its characteristics are:

- Length 8 cm
- Low grating strength
- Chirp from 1549.25-1550.75 nm

In part (a) of the figure we see the variation in grating reflectance with wavelength. A reflectance spectrum such as this will add noise to a signal as parts of the signal will be reflected in different amplitudes. In part (b) we see the same grating after a low degree of apodisation. Much of the ripple has been removed but the reflectance varies significantly over the reflected band. In both cases the grating strength is low and so the maximum total reflectance at any wavelength is about 60%.

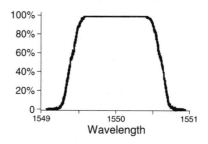

Figure 172. Reflected Power of a Strongly Chirped Grating - Apodised

In Figure 172 we see the same grating as before but this time the grating strength has been doubled. Notice a good 100% reflection over the whole reflected band.

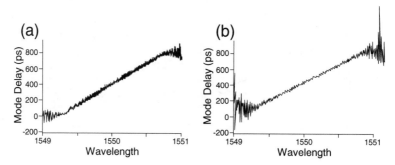

Figure 173. Reflection Profiles of a Chirped FBG. Part (a) shows the grating without apodisation. Part (b) shows the same grating after apodisation.

Figure 173 shows the same gratings in the time domain. The plots are for time delay versus wavelength. In part (a) the grating is not apodised and has a high level of ripple in the response. In part (b) the response is significantly smoother due to apodisation. However, it is important to note that delay ripple has not been removed entirely.

It is important to note that the above figures were produced with a grating simulator (driven by equations). Real gratings have imperfections in their structure which can add very significantly to the ripple (in both reflectance and group delay).

5.7.2.4 Multiple FBGs in the Same Fibre Section

It seems illogical but you can write many different FBGs into the same section of fibre - one on top of the other. Each grating will then respond quite separately and independently to light of its own resonant wavelength. This has been done experimentally and shown to exhibit very little interaction between the different gratings.

This is a very useful feature when writing many chirped gratings to dispersion compensate a WDM system. You don't need to have lots of gratings concatenated one after the other. They can be put on top of one another.

5.7.2.5 Blazed FBGs

Figure 174. Blazed FBG

A blazed grating is constructed when the grating is written at an oblique angle to the centre axis of the core. This is shown in Figure 174. The selected wavelength is reflected *out of the fibre*.[75] If we use a number of blazed gratings we can reflect out unwanted wavelengths and construct a filter to pass only the wavelengths we want.

Another usage is to equalise power across a range of wavelengths for example to "flatten" the response of an EDFA. Here you want to reduce the amount of power over a range of wavelengths so that the overall response of the amplifier-FBG combination is linear. The FBG involved would typically be relatively weak and would be sampled. That is, the grating would be written as a series of short sections each of a different wavelength so that the required band of wavelengths would be covered.

---

[75] Actually into a cladding mode and then out of the fibre

5.7.2.6 Phase-Shifted In-Fibre Bragg Gratings

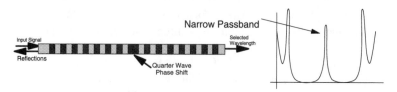

Figure 175. *In-Fibre Bragg Grating - Single Phase-Shift*

A very important characteristic of FBGs is what happens when you shift the phase of the grating in the middle. A "transmission fringe" is created in the centre of the reflection band where light is transmitted through the filter rather than being reflected. A schematic of this is shown in Figure 175. The graph on the right shows the transmittance of the grating. The passband created in the centre of the reflection band is too small to be useful for any practical purpose (at least in WDM systems). However, if we put multiple phase shifts into the grating with very carefully constructed spacing we get a characteristic similar to that shown in Figure 176.

Figure 176. *In-Fibre Bragg Grating - Multiple Phase Shifts*

While the overall reflection band of the filter is not wide enough to be useful in selecting a single wavelength from among many in a WDM system the central passband has excellent characteristics. It is nearly square and its width can be controlled. Further it varies from almost total reflection to almost total transmission. This device has many potential uses in operational systems.

5.7.2.7 Long-Period In-Fibre Bragg Gratings

Most FBGs are constructed as first order gratings. That is the grating period is the same as the centre wavelength of the reflection band. Of course it is possible to use other orders such as a grating period of twice (second order) or three times (third order) the reflected wavelength. *These are not what we mean by long-period FBGs.*

A long-period grating is one where the grating period is many hundreds or thousands of times the resonant wavelength. In a long-period grating power is coupled *forward* rather than backward in the fibre. But in a single-mode fibre there is no forward bound mode available into which the light light may couple. Therefore it couples forward into a cladding mode. Thus after a while the coupled light leaves the system and is lost. A long-period grating then gives much the same effect as a blazed grating - resonant wavelengths are removed from the system.

Long period FBGs are used in the same role as blazed FBGs; for example, to equalise the gain curve of an EDFA. However, many people believe that they are better than blazed FBGs because they don't reflect anything back into the amplifier. A blazed FBG produces a lot of reflected light into the cladding and if it is near the amplifier this can get back into it.

Another example of a long period grating is given in 5.9.5, "Acoustic Modulators" on page 314. In this case the grating is formed by a sound wave in the material but the principles are the same.

5.7.2.8 Temperature Stability of In-Fibre Bragg Gratings

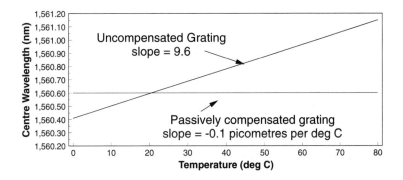

Figure 177. Wavelength Variation with Temperature in FBGs. Temperature dependence of an unpackaged device is compared with that of a commercial "passively compensated" grating. Diagram courtesy of Indx Pty. Ltd.

As with most optical devices the wavelength of an FBG varies with the ambient temperature of the device. This is only partially caused by expansion and contraction of the fibre with temperature and consequent change in the spacing of the RI variations in the core. The dominant effect is a variation in the RI of the fibre itself with temperature.

However, this is not as bad as we might expect. The unpackaged grating is very stable indeed with a total variation of about 1 nm over a temperature range of 80° C! As shown in Figure 177 it is possible to passively stabilise an FBG such that it shows no significant wavelength variation with temperature.

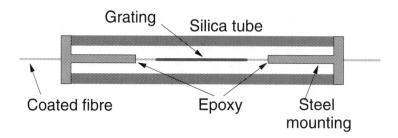

Figure 178. FBG Packaging for Passive Thermal Compensation. Diagram courtesy of Indx Pty. Ltd.

Mechanical strain (stretching) in the fibre also changes the wavelength of the FBG. So if a device is constructed that will put tension onto the FBG at low temperatures and relax that tension progressively as the temperature is increased we can arrange for the two temperature dependent effects to compensate one another.

This is done by packaging the fibre with another material that has different thermal expansion characteristics to that of fibre. A passive stabilisation device is shown in Figure 178. Steel has a much higher coefficient of expansion than the silica of the tube or of the fibre itself.

The fibre is bonded into the steel mounting tubes under slight tension at the lowest temperature at which we want the device to operate. When the temperature rises the expansion of the steel causes the tension in the fibre to be lessened. This variation in tension is arranged to cause wavelength variations in the opposite direction to those caused by normal thermal movement of the fibre itself. Both effects balance out and you get a stable device that does not require active temperature control.

5.7.2.9 Applications of In-Fibre Bragg Gratings

There is a long list of applications for FBGs which seems to grow every day. Some applications have been mentioned already but the most important are:

Wavelength Stable Lasers

> There are a number of ways that an FBG can be used to control (stabilise) a laser to produce a narrow band of a single wavelength. This is discussed in

3.3.12, "External Fibre-Cavity DBR Lasers" on page 157 and 3.3.15, "In-Fibre Lasers" on page 161.

Dispersion Compensation

Chirped FBGs can be used for compensating existing optical transmission networks to allow them to operate in the 1550 nm band. This is a major application which is discussed further in 7.5.6, "Chirped Fibre Bragg Gratings" on page 419.

Wavelength Selection in WDM Systems

WDM systems entered commercial use sometime around about late 1996. Their use is predicted to grow significantly in the next few years. An essential function in a WDM network is separating the incoming stream of many wavelengths into many separate ones. FBGs used in this role are described in 9.2.4.2, "Circulators with FBGs" on page 527.

5.7.2.10 Writing the Grating

The grating is written by exposing the fibre to UV light. UV light (244 nm) is able to make permanent modifications in the refractive index of the core.

At this stage the mechanism involved in the RI modification process is not well understood. It appears to be caused by the breaking of germanium "wrong bonds". In germanium and silicon based glass the vast majority of chemical bonds are between germanium and oxygen or silicon and oxygen. However, sometimes a "wrong bond" is formed for example between two atoms of germanium. The Ge-Ge bond appears to be resonant at 244 nm and will break when exposed to light at this wavelength. This makes irreversible changes in the chemical structure of the glass thus changing the index. Scientists disagree on the precise mechanism involved after the Ge-Ge bond is broken but nevertheless the effect certainly works.

The change in the refractive index is very small indeed. But we don't need a big index change because there are a very large number of periods in the grating (a 1 cm long grating has around 10,000 wavelength periods). An index change of .0001 is sufficient to make an effective grating. Of course the core is unaffected by light in the IR part of the spectrum (where we want our signal).

Much work has been done on ways to make the fibre core more sensitive. The obvious way is to increase the level of germanium dopant. However, you can't do this too far before mechanical effects in the fibre stop you. Co-doping with boron and/or aluminium helps make the core more photosensitive. "Loading" the fibre with hydrogen also helps significantly but hydrogen tends to combine with oxygen to form an OH group which causes added attenuation in the fibre. Loading with heavy hydrogen (deuterium) has the same chemical effect as hydrogen but avoids the absorption resonances.

In some situations it is difficult or impossible to dope the core of the fibre sufficiently. Recently one research group reported the development of a DFB fibre laser. They used a 3-layer fibre structure with an Er doped core and an "inner cladding" layer doped with Ge and B. As the evanescent field of a wave propagating in a single-mode fibre extends into the cladding it was affected and controlled by the periodic grating structure written there.

The ability to write gratings of this kind into the fibre was another of those "accidental" scientific discoveries. A research team headed by K.O. Hill first reported the effect in 1978 (see bibliography). They had transmitted light from an Ar+ laser at 488 nm along a fibre and noticed that the reflectivity of the fibre increased from about 4% to around 90% in about a quarter of a second. What had happened was that the 4% initial back reflection had been sufficient to set up a standing wave pattern. A freak effect (2-photon absorption process) had allowed the 488 nm light to be absorbed by an absorption band that usually is only sensitive to UV light at 244 nm.

Gratings written in the above way (by the propagating wave) are called "internally written gratings". They are not much practical use as their period is determined by the wavelength of the light that wrote them. This wavelength is significantly different from wavelengths that we consider useful in the communications world.

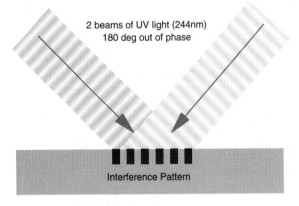

Figure 179. Writing the FBG into a Fibre Core - Interference Pattern Technique

There are many ways to write practical gratings. Two of the most important of these are are shown in Figure 179 and Figure 180 on page 279.

Interference Pattern

Using a beam of light from a single laser, the beam is split and then recombined over the fibre(s) being treated. An interference pattern is generated and this can be arranged such that the period of the grating can be controlled.

This method is well established in laboratories but it is hard to write long gratings with it. (1 or 2 cm is about the limit.) Many potential uses call for gratings to be quite long (20 to 30 cm in some applications) and this technique is not adequate for longer gratings.

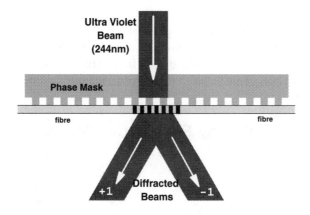

Figure 180. Writing the FBG into a Fibre Core - Phase Mask Technique

Phase Mask

The "phase mask" technique is probably the best current technique. The phase mask diffracts a single beam of incident light. The diffracted beam has interference fringes which can be controlled to produce periodic variations of the type we are seeking. This has an advantage over the dual beam technique in that it allows us to make very long gratings. The mask is long and the beam is scanned along it.

There are many variations of the phase mask technique and some of these are in commercial use.

Surprisingly, all of the above techniques can produce a useful grating in a single exposure of a short pulse from a high power eximer laser. Of course, many fibres can be laid side-by-side and treated at one time. One complication is that you must remove the protective plastic coating (the jacket) from the fibre in order to write the grating.

The fibre used is ordinary single-mode fibre. You can get some improvements by using exotic fibres but these come at the cost of complicating the attachment to standard fibre. Standard fibre will work very well.

Figure 181. Practical FBG

In previous discussions the grating was illustrated as having abrupt changes in the refractive index at every interface. This isn't true. A practical grating is like the one illustrated in Figure 181. The variations in index are quite gradual and approach a sine wave in character. This actually makes very little difference to the effectiveness of the grating.

5.7.3 Waveguide Grating Routers (WGRs)

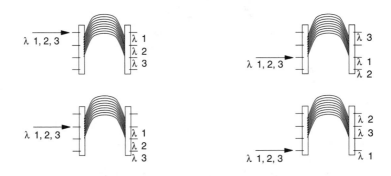

Figure 182. Waveguide Grating Router Basic Function

Waveguide Grating Routers (WGRs) are also called PHASARS or Arrayed Waveguide Gratings (AWGs). These are one of the most important new devices available for WDM systems.[76] Built using planar waveguide technology the WGR has similar functions to those of a Littrow grating. The basic function is illustrated in Figure 182.

----

[76] See Dragone (1991).

- It can take a multi-channel (multi-wavelength) input appearing on a single input waveguide (port) and separate the channels onto different output ports.

- It can combine many inputs (of different wavelengths) from different input ports (waveguides) onto the same output port.

- It can operate bi-directionally.

- It can be connected as an optical add-drop multiplexor.

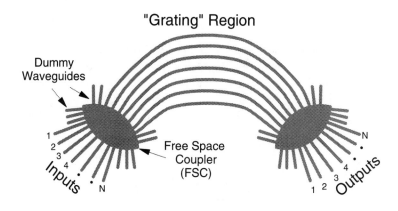

Figure 183. *Waveguide Grating Router*

The conceptual operation of the device is illustrated in Figure 183. It is bi-laterally symmetric and either side could be input or output (or both could take place at the same time).

The input and output stages consist of star couplers called "Free Space Couplers" (FSCs). The inside of an FSC is just a "free space". The "grating region" is just a set of parallel waveguides of different lengths. These waveguides are far enough apart so that the evanescent field in one guide *does not* extend into any other guide. Therefore there is *no* coupling of power between the guides in the grating region.

On the input side, a single-mode input on one of the input waveguides will couple to a very large number of modes in the free space region. These modes then couple to the waveguides in the grating region. Because there are so many modes involved the amount of power coupled from any particular input to each of the waveguides in the grating region is equal. However the distance from any particular input port to each of the grating waveguides is different. This means that at the entrance to the grating region there are phase differences between modes originating at the same input port. Light from different input ports will have different sets of phase relationships.

The central region of the coupler functions like a grating. However it is important to note that it is *not* a grating (it just functions like one). The waveguides in the grating region are sufficiently separated from each other that power *cannot* couple from one to another. The length of each of the guides differs from its neighbour by a fixed delta. This results in phase differences between the signals when they reach the destination star coupler. Interference effects cause the signal at a particular wavelength to be reinforced in one particular output guide and to be extinguished in the other guides. These effects depend on *both* the wavelength and the location of the input port.

The result is that there is destructive interference in *most* of the output waveguides. In just one (at each different wavelength) there will be constructive interference (reinforcement). The particular output guide in which a given wavelength will be output depends on both the location of the input waveguide AND the particular wavelength. N wavelengths on a particular input are spatially separated onto N separate output waveguides.

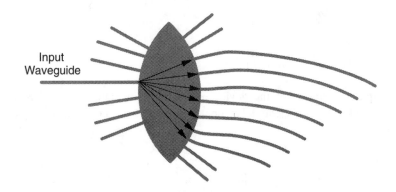

Figure 184. Distribution of Optical Power in the Input FSC. There is no interference here from other input waveguides as no other inputs are coherent with this one.

Another way of looking at it is to consider it as a generalisation of Young's experiment (see 2.1.3.1, "Young's Experiment" on page 25). If we consider a single wavelength signal arriving on just one input waveguide.

- When the signal arrives at the first Free Space Coupler (FSC) it diffracts in many directions and is distributed more or less evenly among the waveguides of the central section. There is no interference here because no other input signal is coherent with this one.

- If there were only two waveguides in the coupling region and they were of the same length the situation in the output FSC would be exactly like Young's double slit experiment. The signal would be reinforced in some of the output waveguides and extinguished in others (depending on their locations).

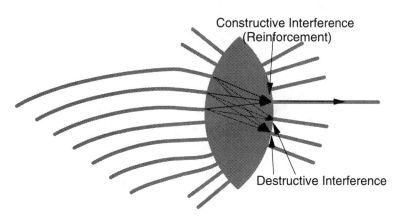

Figure 185. Operation of the Output FSC

- In the real device we have multiple waveguides in the free space region and their lengths are different from one another. In addition the FSCs are shaped in such a way as to influence the interference effects produced. (The distances between different input and output waveguides of the FSC are intentionally different.) As illustrated in Figure 185 a particular wavelength from a particular input waveguide is reinforced in one (and only one) output waveguide and destructively interferes in all other output waveguides.

- In this example (with only one input port in use) multiple wavelengths arriving on the single input port will be directed to *different* output ports.

- If we now disconnect the input from the port we were using and re-connect it to a different input port we get the same effect as described above (the signal is split out by wavelength). However, the output ports now used for particular wavelengths will be different from the first example.

- A given wavelength input on one particular port will be directed to a specific output port. The same wavelength input on a different port will be output on a different port! The output port selected depends both on the wavelength of the input light and the input port it came from.

It is easy to see that if you structure such a device carefully you can arrange different wavelengths to be directed to different output ports.

Another good way of thinking about it is as a generalisation of the Mach-Zehnder Interferometer (see 5.9.8, "Modulation Using a Mach-Zehnder Interferometer" on page 323).

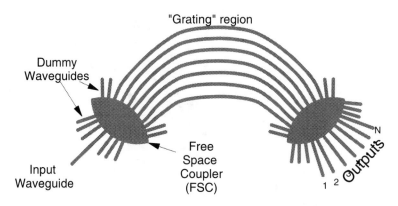

Figure 186. Waveguide Grating Router with Single-Ported Input

As shown in Figure 186 a WGR may be built with only one input waveguide. This configuration is functionally equivalent to the Littrow grating assembly shown in Figure 163 on page 263.

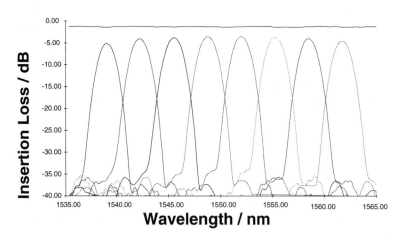

Figure 187. Insertion Loss Characteristics of an Early 8-Port WGR. Each line represents a different optical channel.

Figure 187 shows the transmission characteristics of an early 8-port WGR. Each separate trace represents a different wavelength of input light. This is not really good enough for an operational device. The lines cross over at around -20 dB and peak at around -5 dB or so. For a useful WDM device the place where the lines crossover (this is where we begin to see crosstalk from the device) should be more than 30 dB down from the peak. Today WGR devices with the required characteristics are available.

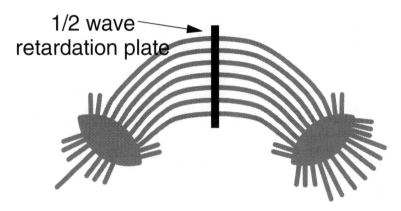

Figure 188. *WGR with Half-Wave Plate for Polarisation Independence*

In their basic form WGRs are strongly birefringent and therefore produce polarisation mode dispersion (PMD). See 2.4.2.1, "Polarisation Mode Dispersion (PMD)" on page 77. This is caused by the rectangular shape of the planar waveguides. They are significantly wider than they are high. There are a number of ways of removing or compensating for this characteristic.

1. The first and most obvious method is to use square waveguides. Square waveguides have similar characteristics to those of fibre and are minimally birefringent.

   This is actually quite hard to do as it is difficult to produce a waveguiding layer thick enough.

2. You can make a cut across the array waveguide region so that the waveguides are cut in half. A polarisation retardation plate (1/2 wave) is inserted into the cut. Thus the polarisation is rotated by 90° half way along the waveguides and PMD acquired in the first half of the waveguide is exactly compensated for by PMD in the opposite direction in the second half of the waveguide. This is a very popular method with researchers and has become the established method of countering PMD.

Its big problem is that it requires that the retardation plate have an RI close to that of the waveguide material. This is fine for silica and lithium niobate based waveguides but it is a problem for devices made in InP.

3. Careful design of the free space coupler at the receiver side of the device can compensate for PMD introduced in the waveguides. However this introduces a severe limit on the total wavelength range over which the device will operate.

4. You can use sectioned waveguides with different PMD characteristics in each section so that a balance is created.

5. It is also possible to split the input signal into its orthogonal polarisations and introduce these into the device at different points in the input free space region.

WGRs are made in planar technology in one of a number of materials such as silica, silicon and InP. A device made in silicon can be much smaller than one made with fused silica and the production technology is very highly developed as we can use standard silicon VLSI production techniques. However, connecting the fibres to a silicon device is lossy due to the large difference in refractive index between silica and silicon. A silica device is larger but much easier to connect fibres to and the connection to fibres is reasonably efficient.

However, the largest cost is still the connection of fibres to the device. A very interesting alternative is to integrate WGRs on the same substrate as lasers, modulators and detectors. This eliminates the cost and losses of pigtailing for connections between different devices. This is discussed further in 5.1.3, "Integrated Optical Circuits (Planar Assemblies)" on page 197.

Typical WGRs can handle a wavelength spacing of .8 nm. Devices with 64 inputs and 64 outputs have been demonstrated and up to 16 channel versions are available commercially. The advertised insertion loss of current commercial devices is less than 6 dB. This compares favorably with other devices performing similar functions. However, currently available WGRs have adjacent channel crosstalk of about -25 dB. This is not as good as current Littrow grating devices and could be a limiting factor in some system designs.

Ways in which this device may be used are discussed further in 9.2.4.5, "Waveguide Grating Routers (WGRs)" on page 528 and 9.2.5, "Add-Drop Multiplexors" on page 531.

5.8 Filters

In current optical systems, filters are seldom used or needed. They are sometimes used in front of an LED to narrow the linewidth before transmission, but in few other roles.

In proposed future WDM networks, filters will be very important for many uses:

- A filter placed in front of an incoherent receiver can be used to select a particular signal from many arriving signals.

- WDM networks are proposed which use filters to control which path through a network a signal will take.

There are many filtering principles proposed and many different types of devices have been built in laboratories. The result is that there are many kinds of active, tunable filters available which will be important in WDM networks. These, like lasers, have the characteristic that the wider you make the tuning range, the slower will be the tuning time.

It is important to note that gratings are filters. Indeed FBGs are probably the most important optical filter in the communications world. Because of their importance they were discussed in a separate section. See: 5.7, "Diffraction Gratings" on page 260.

5.8.1.1 Filter Characteristics

When discussing filters there are a number of concepts that need to be understood. In addition, many devices that are not called filters nevertheless have the characteristics of filters and should be considered along with them. Such devices as switches, modulators, AWGs, grating multiplexors etc. can all be considered types of filter and have many of the characteristics of filters.

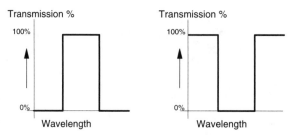

Figure 189. Transmission Characteristics of Ideal Filters. The device on the left would pass a defined range of wavelengths with no attenuation and block all other wavelengths. The device on the right would pass all wavelengths but block (absorb or reflect) a defined range.

In an ideal world filters might have characteristics similar to those shown in Figure 189. However, there is no ideal world. Practical filters almost always are quite different from the ideal. Profiles of two practical filters are shown in Figure 190.

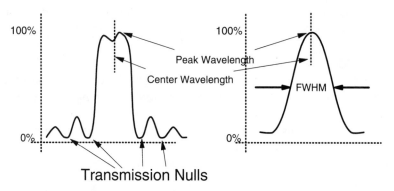

Figure 190. Transmission Characteristics of Two Practical Filters. The left-hand curve is characteristic of acustooptic or electro-optic filters. The right-hand represents the typical shape of a single node of a Fabry-Perot filter with mirrors of only about 40% reflectivity.

The important characteristics of these filters are:

Centre Wavelength

> This is the mean wavelength between the two band edges. It is usually quoted without qualification but sometimes it may be necessary to quote the distance below the peak at which the centre is measured.

Peak Wavelength

> The wavelength at which the filter attenuation is least (as illustrated in the figure).

Nominal Wavelength

> The wavelength of the filter that was intended by the manufacturer. This is usually printed on the outside of the device. The real centre wavelength is sometimes different.

Bandwidth

> It is easy to see from the shape of the right-hand filter that the bandwidth of the filter is going to depend a lot on just where you measure it. Bandwidth is the distance between the filter edges (in nm) at a particular designated distance below the peak. This distance is always quoted in dB. It is common to talk about the 1 dB bandwidth the 3 dB bandwidth or even the 30 dB bandwidth.

Polarisation is also an important factor here. Both the centre wavelength and the bandwidth are often polarisation dependent although these characteristics are usually quoted assuming unpolarised light. Sometimes the centre wavelength and the bandwidth are quoted as maxima and minima indicating the range of variation possible with changing polarisations.

5.8.2 Fabry-Perot Filter (Etalon)

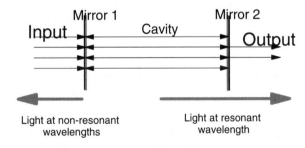

Figure 191. Fabry-Perot Filter

One of the simplest filters in principle is based on the Fabry-Perot interferometer. It consists of a cavity bounded on each end by a partially-silvered mirror. If the mirrors can be moved in relation to each other the device is called an "interferometer". If the mirrors are fixed in relation to each other (such as with spacers) then it is called an "Etalon".[77]

In principle this is just the same as almost every musical wind instrument (organ, flute, oboe...).[78] When we excite the air column within a wind instrument, the column resonates at a frequency (wavelength) determined by the length of the air column and the speed of sound in the air within the column. Wavelengths produced are such that an integral number of half-wavelengths must fit exactly within the column. Other factors such as whether the ends of the column are open or closed complicate the analogy so we will take it no further.

Operation is as follows:

- Light is directed onto the outside of one of the mirrors.

- Most is reflected and some enters the cavity.

- When it reaches the opposite mirror some (small proportion) passes out but most is reflected back.

- At the opposite mirror the same process repeats.

- This continues to happen with new light entering the cavity at the same rate as light leaves it.

If you arrange the cavity to be exactly the right size, interference patterns develop which cause unwanted wavelengths to undergo destructive interference. Only one wavelength (or narrow band) passes out and all others are strongly attenuated.

This is a very interesting process and is just a generalisation of the earlier example of light passing through a sheet of glass in 2.1.3.2, "Transmission through a Sheet of Glass" on page 27. The interesting effects occur on the mirror at *entry* to the cavity:

- When light of a non-resonant wavelength reaches the mirror most of it (depending on the mirror's reflectance) will be reflected. The small amount that gets through into the cavity will bounce around for a while but will ultimately exit through one of the end mirrors or be absorbed by losses.

- When light of the resonant wavelength reaches the entry mirror it passes through into the cavity without loss! This is a very interesting effect.

---

[77] This is really an optical version of the electronic "tapped delay line", "transversal" filter or Standing Acoustic Wave (SAW) filter. In the digital signal processing world the process is performed with a shift register.

[78] Most other instruments too but the analogy isn't quite so clear as it is with wind instruments.

- Assuming there is already light of the correct wavelength resonating within the cavity a proportion (small) of this light will try to exit from the cavity (because the mirror is only partially reflective).

- Arriving light that is at the resonant wavelength and coherent with that in the cavity will try to reflect (or most of it will).

- However, there is destructive interference between light (of the resonant wavelength) leaving the cavity and light coherent with it reflecting from the entry mirror.

- The result here is that 100% of the incident resonant wavelength light passes through the mirror and into the cavity!

- In addition light of the resonant wavelength already inside the cavity cannot exit through this mirror (because of the destructive interference with incoming light). 100% of it is reflected and therefore it can only leave the cavity through the opposite mirror! (Or perhaps be absorbed by losses.)

Thus light of only the resonant wavelength is accepted into the cavity without loss while all other wavelengths suffer significant reflection.

The most important requirement for the functioning of a Fabry-Perot filter is that the reflecting surfaces should be extremely flat (preferably within one hundredth of a wavelength) and absolutely parallel. And of course this is the biggest challenge in building them. It is usual to silver the glass surfaces so that each forms a 99% reflective mirror.

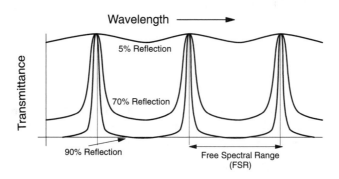

Figure 192. Fabry-Perot Filter Characteristics. Note the narrow passband when the mirror reflectance is relatively high.

The recognised measure of "goodness" of an FP filter is called the "Finesse". This is the ratio of the amount of energy stored within the filter to the amount of energy passing through it. It is much the same concept as the "Q" in electrical circuits. The higher the finesse the narrower the passband and the sharper the boundaries. The major factor influencing the finesse is the reflectivity of the mirrors - the more reflective the mirrors the higher the finesse. Absorption within the device and especially within the mirrors reduces the sharpness of the filter peaks.

This is illustrated in Figure 192 on page 291. Notice that the three lines representing mirror reflectivities of 5%, 70% and 90% respectively all reach 100% transmission (through the filter) at the peak. The peaks are the resonant wavelengths (the lobes of the filter). The distance between the peaks is called the "Free Spectral Range" (FSR) of the FP filter.

$$FSR = \frac{\lambda^2}{2 \times n \times D}$$

Here, n equals the RI of the material between the mirrors and D equals the distance between them.

The finesse of the filter is the ratio of the distance between the transmission peaks (the free spectral range) to the width of each spectral line at the FWHM[79] point.

$$Finesse = \frac{FSR}{FWHM}$$

The resonant wavelengths are given by:

$$\lambda = \frac{2 D n}{m}$$

Where m is an arbitrary integer 1, 2, 3...

If we have a device with an air gap (RI = 1) of 500 microns then the first order (m=1) resonant wavelength would be 1 mm which of course is not light but microwave. Looking at resonances in the wavebands of interest we find (with n = 645) lines at 1,552.8 nm, 1,550.39 nm, 1,547.99 nm etc.

---

[79] Full Width Half Maximum

An FP filter is inherently multi-lobed in the sense that it has multiple passbands but in practice only a single lobe is used. With the spacing between lines (FSR) of only around 2 nm this filter would not be very useful for recovering a signal from a WDM stream (say) 20 nm wide. To increase the FSR we must decrease the spacing between the mirrors.

Energy that is *not* passed through the filter interferes and is reflected back to the source. This must be considered in any system design as reflections can be a source of noise in many systems.

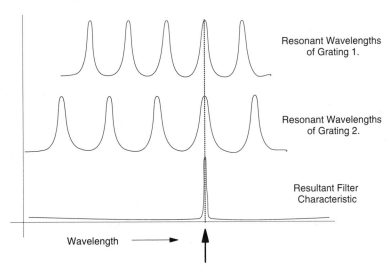

Figure 193. Cascading Fabry-Perot Filters of Different FSR

When filters are cascaded (connected in series) the resultant device operates as a new filter. The new filter has a passband where the passbands of the cascaded FP filters coincide. The passband is always narrowed. Finesse is improved very significantly as the FSR has been widened such that it is the lowest common multiple of the two FSRs of the filters that made it up. So the FSR is increased very significantly.

If two filters of the same characteristics are cascaded then we only get a narrowing of the passband. If the cascaded filters have different FSRs then the FSR of the new filter is much larger. Further discussion of the effects of cascading filters may be found in 9.4.1.1, "Cascading Filters" on page 550.

5.8.2.1 Dielectric Fabry-Perot Filters

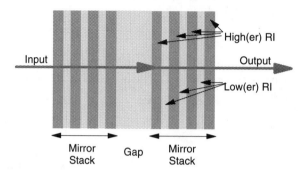

Figure 194. *Fabry-Perot Filter Using Dielectric Mirrors*

In microoptic technology Fabry-Perot filters are often made using a "stack" of materials of different RI as mirrors. Very thin (1/4 wavelength) layers of material with alternating (high and low) RIs are used. Typically these layers are made from SiO₂ (RI 1.46) and TiO₂ (RI 2.3) although other materials are sometimes employed. Each layer of material has a thickness of exactly 1/4 of the longest wavelength which must be handled.

By careful choice of materials and numbers of layers mirrors of any reflectivity we desire can be constructed. In addition, resonator stages (the "gaps" in the figure) may be cascaded. Thus we can control very exactly the passband and filter shape of the device.

A WDM multiplexor/demultiplexor device using dielectric FP filters is described in 5.8.5, "Dielectric Filters for WDM Multiplexing/Demultiplexing" on page 299. The principle is also used widely in semiconductor based devices. The VCSEL is constructed using an identical principle to that described here. See 3.3.14, "Vertical Cavity Surface Emitting Lasers (VCSELs)" on page 159.

5.8.2.2 Tunable Fabry-Perot Filter

The device can be tuned by attaching one of the mirrors to a piezoelectric crystal and changing the voltage across the crystal. Such a crystal can be controlled to the point that you can get accuracy of movement down to less than the diameter of an atom! The only problem is that you usually need quite a high voltage (300-500 volts) to cause the required amount of crystal deformation. Practical devices require about 1 ms to complete tuning which is quite fast for some applications but far too slow for proposed applications such as optical packet switching.

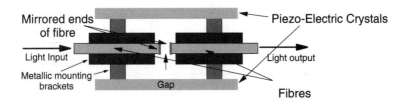

Figure 195. *Tunable Fibre Fabry-Perot Filter*

Figure 195 shows an ingenious variation of the Fabry-Perot filter. Two pieces of fibre are used with their ends polished and silvered. The ends are placed precisely opposite one another with a measured gap (this is the hard part). This avoids the cost of getting the light into and out of a "regular" FP filter - because it arrives and leaves on its own fibre.

The device shown is mounted on two piezo-electric crystals. By applying a voltage across the crystals we can change the distance between the ends of the fibres and hence the resonant wavelength. As mentioned above, piezo-electric crystals can be controlled such that the resulting movement is comparable with the diameter of an atom!

If you want to tune an FP filter then of course there are two alternative approaches. You can physically move the mirrors such that the size of the gap changes or perhaps you could change the RI of the material inside the cavity!

Tunable FP filters can be built by putting a liquid crystal material into the gap. The RI of the liquid crystal material can be changed very quickly by passing a current through the liquid. Reported tuning times for this type of filter are around 10 μsec but in theory sub-microsecond times should be attainable. Tuning range is 30-40 nm. Such filters are expected to be low in cost and require a very low power.

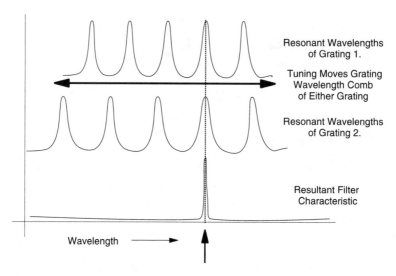

Figure 196. Cascading Tunable Fabry-Perot Filters of Different FSR

If tunable FP filters are cascaded as illustrated in Figure 196, the tuning range is extended very significantly and tuning speed is also improved. As one comb is moved it will line up with the other comb at different peaks. Thus a wide tuning range with relatively small amount of movement can be constructed.

5.8.3 In-Fibre Bragg Grating Filters

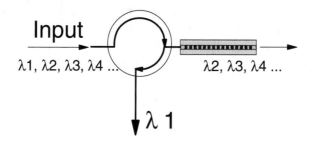

Figure 197. In-Fibre Bragg Grating Used as a Filter

In-Fibre Bragg gratings (see 5.7.2, "In-Fibre Bragg Gratings (FBGs)" on page 266) are near perfect filters. However they have a major defect. They are reflective in their nature rather than transmissive. An FBG will *remove* a particular wavelength from a stream of mixed wavelengths by reflecting it back towards its source. To make use of an FBG as a transmissive filter we need to use a circulator. This is shown in Figure 198 on page 297.

5.8.4 Fibre Ring Resonators

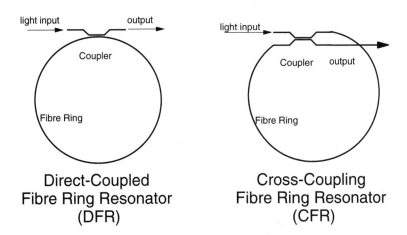

Direct-Coupled Fibre Ring Resonator (DFR)

Cross-Coupling Fibre Ring Resonator (CFR)

Figure 198. Fibre Ring Resonators. The two main types are Direct-Coupling Fibre Ring Resonators (DFR) and Cross-Coupling Fibre Ring Resonators (CFR).

Ring resonators are very similar in principle to Fabry-Perot filters. However, unlike the FP filter, non-resonant wavelengths are passed through rather than reflected back to the source. The resonant wavelengths are absorbed by losses in the device.

Optical power recirculates on the ring if (and only if) the ring length is an integral multiple of the wavelength. The reason you build a fibre ring resonator is so that the ring can be very long (in some instances up to 1 km). A long ring means that the spacings between resonances (that is, the free spectral range) is very small. This close spacing of resonances severely limits the usefulness of the fibre ring resonator in routine signal filtering and WDM applications. However, fibre ring resonators are used for many other purposes:

- Spectrum analysers (The close spacing of resonances is a big benefit here.)
- Sensors
- Narrow bandwidth filters

In slightly different forms fibre ring resonators are also used in:

- Ring lasers

- Interferometers

- Passive fibre gyroscopes

The major difficulty with fibre ring resonators has been that their finesse is limited by the losses in the ring (including the losses in the coupler). These losses can be quite high and the finesse (selectivity) of the device may not be as good as we need.

A single-mode resonator depends for its operation on interference effects in the coupler. For these effects to work properly you need two other conditions:

1. The ring must *maintain* the polarisation state. (Otherwise the interference effects in the coupler will not occur properly.)

2. The ring length must be less than the coherence length of the laser source.

Other types of ring resonators that are very long and do not need these conditions are also used although these are really ring type optical delay lines rather than resonators.

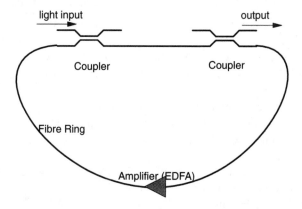

Figure 199. Amplified Fibre Ring Resonator

To get the resonance peaks tuned to where we intend them to be we need some method of changing the refractive index or length of the fibre ring. This is because you can't build a long fibre ring with a length accurate to a few nm. A simple tuning device can be made by using a loop of fibre around a mandrill which can be expanded (very slightly indeed) by a piezo-electric crystal. This stretches the fibre and changes the length of the ring. (The total amount of stretching you need is less than the wavelength and so the effect needed is tiny.) Indeed, in a practical device this mechanism is needed also to compensate for the effects of temperature variations.

One way around the ring loss problem is to place an EDFA in the ring to amplify the signal. This improves the finesse but introduces a major problem:

> A fibre ring with an EDFA in it can be a laser! (Any amplifier with a feedback mechanism can lase.) Spontaneous emission in the EDFA can give rise to lasing (around 1553 nm). This is possible because there is bound to be a resonant wavelength within the ASE band of the EDFA - since the resonances are very closely spaced. To solve this problem you need to put a fibre FP filter at the input wavelength into the ring. Also an isolator is needed to prevent lasing building up in the backward direction.

> Fibre ring lasers are discussed in 3.3.16, "Fibre Ring Lasers" on page 164.

However, their length makes them very sensitive to temperature changes and mechanical vibrations.

5.8.4.1 Planar Ring Resonators

Ring resonators can be made in planar technology. In this case they can be short (a few cm) and thus the passbands can be separated a lot further from one another than in fibre based devices.

5.8.5 Dielectric Filters for WDM Multiplexing/Demultiplexing

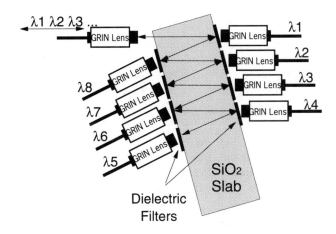

Figure 200. Dielectric Filter based WDM Multiplexor/Demultiplexor

A "dielectric filter" operates on the same principle as a Fabry-Perot filter. The difference is that it is made by depositing a layer of "dielectric" material of controlled thickness. The surfaces of the material form the mirrors of the FP filter. As with all

FP filters the selected wavelength is transmitted and all other wavelengths are reflected.

The above device shows a crystal of transparent material (a crystal is ideal because we need absolutely parallel sides here) on which a series of dielectric filters of different thicknesses have been deposited. Each filter allows a different wavelength to be transmitted and all others are reflected.

Thus a ray of light entering the device will progressively have different wavelengths separated from it. The big problem with these devices is that there is some attenuation at each stage of the filtering process. Thus (in the figure) wavelength 5 is attenuated significantly more than wavelength 1.

Of course the device will operate in reverse and act as a WDM multiplexor.

5.9 Modulators and Switches

Many of the optical sources that we would like to use for fibre transmission are either impossible to modulate or have unwanted bad characteristics when we do modulate them. Fibre lasers for example cannot be modulated by turning them on and off. They are pumped with light from another laser and spend a relatively long time in the high energy "metastable" state before they either spontaneously emit light or lase. This means they can't follow modulations of the pump any faster than a few kilohertz.[80] Semiconductor lasers (even DBR and DFB ones) often "chirp" (change wavelength) when they are modulated and have limits on the speed of modulation imposed by the internal capacitance of the device and the speed of migration of the charge carriers. Both these kinds of lasers are very good fibre light sources. The answer is to have the laser produce a constant beam of light and to modulate the light beam *after* it leaves its source.

The job of a modulator is to replicate variations in an electronic signal onto an optical one. The light intensity should vary with some characteristic of the electrical one (voltage or current). For most applications we need digital modulation so we need the light to be switched ON or OFF and we don't care about states in between. In some applications we do need analogue modulation (where states between ON and OFF matter) and some modulators can achieve this.

---

[80] Gas lasers also cannot be modulated by controlling the energy source.

Modulators consist of a material that changes its optical properties under the influence of an electric or magnetic field. In general three approaches are used:

Electrooptic and Magnetooptic Effects

> There are many materials (such as calcite, quartz, lithium niobate...) that change their optical properties in the presence of either an electric or a magnetic field (or both). This property change is usually a change in refractive index and most often this change is *different* for incident light of different polarisations. Changes in the RI cause changes in phase of the light passing through it. Phase modulation of this kind is not very useful to us. However, other devices (such as a Mach-Zehnder interferometer) may be used to convert the phase change into an amplitude change. Most high speed modulators are built around this principle.

Electro-Absorption Effects

> An ideal simple modulator might consist of a material that had a variable absorption of light depending on the presence of an applied electric field. Unfortunately, there are not too many materials like this. However, a p-n junction in a 3-5 semiconductor (such as Gallium Arsenide) does behave this way and this material is used to build modulators. This is especially useful when you want to build a planar device integrating a laser and modulator in the same device.

Acoustic Modulators

> Acoustic modulators use very high frequency sound travelling within a crystal or planar wave guide to deflect (refract) light from one path to another. By controlling the intensity (volume) of the sound we can control the amount of light deflected and hence construct a modulator.

5.9.1 Switches

Because modulators (in general) turn the signal on and off they make excellent switches. Indeed a digital modulator is just a very fast switch. However, with some types of modulators we may be happy with lesser performance than we may need for switches. For example in some situations we might be prepared to tolerate some light transmission in the "off" state of a modulator (particularly an analogue one). Also we may be prepared to allow significantly more crosstalk in a modulator than in a switch (all depending on the application).

Often we need switches to direct their output to one of two different paths, whereas with a modulator we usually only want to control the light intensity on one particular path.

5.9.2 Optical Switching Elements

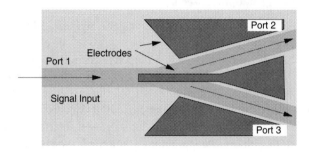

Figure 201. *Digital Optical Switch (DOS) - Schematic*

In almost any network where communications channels are routed or switched within nodes along the path you need a way of switching a single channel from one path to another. Fortunately there are a number of ways to build quite efficient components to do just this.

Figure 201 shows one configuration. A Y-coupler is modified by the addition of electrodes which can impose an electric field on the waveguide material. In this case the material is lithium niobate which changes its refractive index under the influence of an electric field. This element is called a Digital Optical Switch (DOS).

When an electric field is applied the RI of the LiNiO₃ is increased in one arm of the coupler and decreased in the other arm. This action routes the input light (from Port 1) to either one of the output ports depending on the RI of the material in the path (and hence on the electric field direction). Light travels on the path which has the *higher* RI. When the electric field is reversed the RI changes in the opposite direction and the input light is now directed out of the other port of the coupler.

This is quite a low loss operation (1 or 2 dB) and large multi-way switches have been constructed with switching elements such as these as their central switch fabric. These are standard "space division" switches as employed in "crossbar" telephone exchanges etc. This principle is discussed further in 9.2.6, "Optical Space-Division Switches" on page 536.

5.9.2.1 Optical Crossconnects (OXCs)

Figure 202. Crossconnect Switch Element - Function

The crossconnect is a much more versatile switching element than the simple one-input, two-position switch described above. As shown in Figure 202 a crossconnect has two inputs and two outputs. In one state (the "bar" state) the two inputs connect directly to two corresponding outputs. In the cross state each input is directed to the opposite output. A crossconnect can take the place of up to four simple two-position switches.

Crossconnects can be realised in optical technology in a number of ways, two of which are described here:

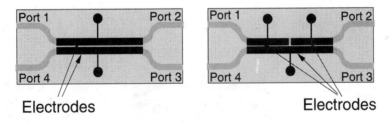

Figure 203. Cross-Connect Using a Resonant Coupler

Resonant Coupler Crossconnect

The device shown in Figure 203 is a resonant coupler implemented on an electrooptic material such as Lithium Niobate. Electrodes placed over the waveguides allow us to apply a voltage across them. Resonant couplers are discussed in 5.4.1, "Resonant Coupling" on page 234.

In the "cross" state there is *no* voltage applied to the electrodes. Coupling length is arranged so that optical power entering Port 1 will cross over and leave at Port 3. Light entering at Port 4 will cross over and leave at Port 2.

When voltage is applied the RI in both waveguides is changed. This changes the speed of propagation of light in each of the waveguides. Because the coupling effect relies on the propagation constants of both waveguides being the same, light cannot couple. Thus when voltage is applied light entering Port 1 leaves at Port 2 and light entering at Port 4 leaves at Port 3. This is the "bar" state.

The major difficulty with this device is that it requires extreme accuracy in device fabrication. Coupling length is critical and has very little tolerance. The RI of the waveguide is likewise critical. In the right hand part of Figure 203 on page 303 a modification of the crossconnect is illustrated which makes the fabrication tolerances significantly less critical. In this case one of the electrodes is built in sections. Each section has an equal but opposite voltage on it.

At first sight this two-section configuration might appear surprising. If the two sections have equal and opposite voltages then the phase of the entering light will be unchanged at the output. Indeed if this were an MZI then the principle wouldn't work but it's not - it's a directional coupler. In this device we don't care about phase changes in the signals. We can treat the two input signals separately as they don't interact. A signal in one waveguide *can't* couple to the other guide if the phase velocity (for that signal) in the two guides is different. This is arranged by making the RIs different at every point along the coupler. It doesn't matter that the overall phase delay of the two waveguides is the same - the phase velocity over the coupler length has always been unmatched.

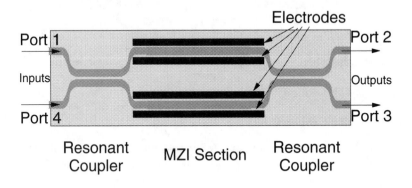

Figure 204. Cross-Connect Using an MZI Configuration

Mach-Zehnder Interferometric Crossconnect

The device shown in Figure 204 on page 304 is basically a Mach-Zehnder interferometer. (See 5.9.8, "Modulation Using a Mach-Zehnder Interferometer" on page 323.) However, instead of using Y-couplers the device uses 3 dB resonant couplers.

When light is input at Port 1, it is split evenly between both arms of the interferometer. If there is no voltage applied the light arrives at the second 3 dB coupler in phase (since the arms of the interferometer are equal in length). The second coupler then acts as a continuation of the first and all of the light is output at Port 3. Likewise light entering at Port 4 will be output at Port 2. This is the "cross" state.

When a voltage is applied across the electrodes the RI in each waveguide is changed. The voltage is arranged to be such that the change in RI results in the light on the two arms arriving at the second coupler 180° out of phase with each other. There is now destructive interference and light which entered at Port 1 will now exit at Port 2. Light entering at Port 4 will now leave at Port 3.

5.9.3 Optically Controlled Switches

5.9.3.1 The Non-Linear Optical Loop Mirror (NOLM)

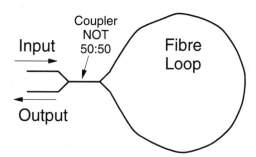

Figure 205. Non-Linear Optical Loop Mirror (NOLM)

The Non-Linear Optical Loop Mirror is a very fast optical switch which may be used for many purposes. In its simplest form it can "clean up" a stream of pulses by removing background noise between the pulses. In a more advanced configuration it can be used for demultiplexing a time-division multiplexed bit stream (see 12.5.4, "Demultiplexing the TDM Signal" on page 668).

The basic function of a NOLM is to attenuate an input pulse by an amount depending (non-linearly) on the intensity of that pulse. Ideally a high intensity signal level is passed without any attenuation but a signal level of lower intensity suffers very high attenuation. Thus high intensity pulses pass unchanged and low intensity background noise is removed.

As shown in Figure 205 on page 305 the basic device consists of a fused fibre coupler (splitter) with two of its arms connected to an unbroken loop of fibre. A signal arriving at the input to the coupler is split and sent both ways around the fibre loop. When it arrives back at the coupler interference effects determine the amplitude of the output. This seems strange because we know that both component parts of the split signal must travel *exactly* the same distance around the loop and therefore arrive at exactly the same time!

The secret is that we make use of the phenomenon of "Nonlinear Kerr Effect". (See 2.4.5.4, "Carrier-Induced Phase Modulation (CIP)" on page 92.) Light at high intensity causes a slight change in the RI of the glass such that the group velocity of the pulse increases. Thus high intensity pulses propagate faster than lower intensity ones. *The key to operation here is that the coupler cannot be just a 50:50 splitter.* The coupler might split in a ratio of (say) 45:55. This results in the pulse in one direction having a higher intensity (and therefore a higher group velocity) than the pulse in the other direction. Thus they will arrive back at the coupler at (very slightly) different times and interfere (either constructively or destructively) with each other.

The conditions above on their own would not produce a useful device. The really important condition is the *nonlinearity* of the Kerr effect. At low light intensity there is no Kerr effect. Thus at low intensity both components of a pulse travel around the loop at the same group velocity and arrive back at the coupler at the same time. At high intensity, Kerr effect comes into play and causes a difference in group velocity and the pulses arrive at (very slightly) different times. What is happening is "Self Phase Modulation" (SPM). The two pulses arrive out of phase with one another and thus interfere.

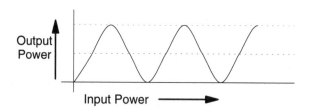

Figure 206. *NOLM Output Power Variation with Input Power*

A graph of output power against input power illustrates device operation. As input power is increased the induced phase shifts cause output power to vary between complete transmission and complete attenuation. As we might expect this effect continues as power is increased still further as power levels cause progressive phase differences.

The effect of a NOLM used as a simple filter is shown in Figure 207. In the input picture there is a significant level of "noise" between pulses. In the output this noise has been removed. A perhaps unwanted side effect of this process is that the pulses have been narrowed somewhat.

The simple device described thus far can be modified to act as an AND gate. This enables it to be used for a number of purposes but especially as a demultiplexor for OTDM data streams. This is further described in 12.5, "Optical Time Division Multiplexing (OTDM)" on page 663.

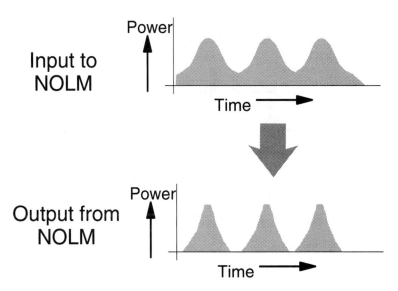

Figure 207. NOLM Filtering Out the Noise from a Stream of Pulses

The major advantage of the device is that it is extremely simple and low in cost. Further it does not need complex alignment of the lengths of the optical path. Alignment is a real problem in many other devices such as fibre-based interferometers.

The disadvantage of the NOLM for pulse switching is the fact that two key effects operate in opposite directions!

1. The "switching ratio" (the ratio of the amplitude of an ON pulse to an OFF condition) cannot be 100%. This is caused by the fact that we must use an asymmetric splitter. The two components of same pulse (in different directions) must be different in amplitude. Therefore interference can never be complete! For this reason we want to use a splitter that is as close to 50:50 as possible.

2. Of course the device won't work if the splitting ratio is exactly 50:50. However, if we use a splitter with a ratio close to 50:50 we have to use a very long fibre loop to get the desired effect. The excessively long fibre loop introduces a number of other undesired effects.

One solution to this dilemma is to place an amplifier into the fibre loop creating the NALM (described next).

5.9.3.2 The Non-Linear Amplifying Optical Loop Mirror (NALM)

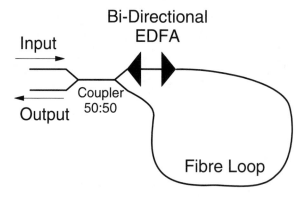

Figure 208. *Non-Linear Amplifying Optical Loop Mirror (NALM)*

The NALM is a modification of the NOLM to allow for a 50:50 splitting ratio and therefore provide complete switching. (NO power transfer occurs in the OFF condition.)

The idea here is to put a bi-directional EDFA into one end of the fibre loop. It is critical that the EDFA be closer to one arm of the splitter than the other. In this case the splitter is now able to be exactly 50:50 (or as close as manufacture will allow).

One half of the pulse will travel around the loop at a low (unamplified) power whilst the other half will travel around the loop at a high (amplified) power. However, both halves of the pulse arrive back at the splitter with exactly the same amplitude!

Of course the presence of an EDFA complicates a simple device and significantly adds to the cost. However, it allows an almost complete switching characteristic.

5.9.3.3 The NOLM as a Logic Gate

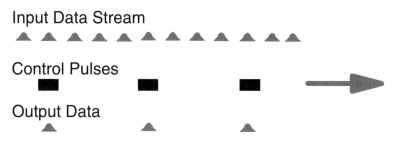

Input Data Stream

Control Pulses

Output Data

Figure 209. Demultiplexing of a TDM Data Stream. A control pulse is used to select a low(er) speed stream of pulses from an incoming high-speed stream of pulses.

In OTDM a high speed stream of pulses is made up of a number of lower speed streams. It is necessary to (optically) "demultiplex" this stream of pulses - selecting out those that belong to the lower speed stream. The logic of this operation is illustrated in Figure 209.

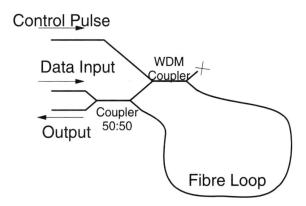

Control Pulse

Data Input

WDM Coupler

Coupler 50:50

Output

Fibre Loop

Figure 210. NOLM Configured as an AND Logic Gate

The device is illustrated in Figure 210. The operation is similar to the basic NOLM described above; however there are a number of crucial differences:

- An incoming data pulse is split 50:50 to travel around the loop.

- At a point close to the end of the fibre loop a clock (timing) pulse synchronised to the incoming data bit stream is coupled into the loop.

- When the control pulse (control pulse) coincides with a data pulse we get cross phase modulation (instead of self-phase modulation as in the basic NOLM). That is, the intense control pulse modifies the RI of the glass and the data pulse travelling in the same direction is speeded up but the data pulse in the opposite direction is not affected.

- This provides a phase difference when the data pulse arrives back at the coupler and the selected pulse is routed to the output.

This is an elegant principle but is quite difficult to implement in practice:

- The control pulse has to be very intense. Practical devices use a control pulse of around 200 milliwatts!

- To ensure the maximum effect a special fibre is needed with a dispersion minimum very close to the wavelength of the data signal.

- The control signal needs to be close in wavelength to the data signal but far enough away for it to be separated out from the data signal in the output (also input) coupler.

- Of course the control pulse needs to be synchronised exactly to the timing of the incoming data stream.

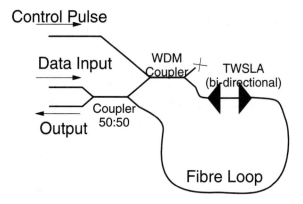

Figure 211. NOLM Logic Gate Using TWSLA

A much improved device can be made by using a TWSLA (Travelling-Wave Silicon Laser Amplifier) in the fibre loop. This is illustrated in Figure 211. The idea here is to use cross-phase modulation in the co-propagating pulses within the TWSLA rather than within the fibre loop. This requires a much shorter loop and much lower power control pulses. This device is a serious contender for the role of demultiplexor in future OTDM systems.

5.9.3.4 Optical ADM for OTDM using Mach-Zehnder Interferometer

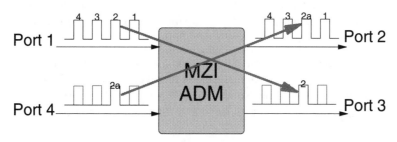

Figure 212. Add-Drop Multiplexor - Functional View

In simple optical TDM systems channels are interleaved with one another at the bit level. See 12.5, "Optical Time Division Multiplexing (OTDM)" on page 663. In order to receive (or replace) a particular channel from among the other channels we need to be able to access every n^{th} bit. For example in an eight-channel system a single channel may comprise every eighth bit. The logical operation to be performed is illustrated in Figure 212.

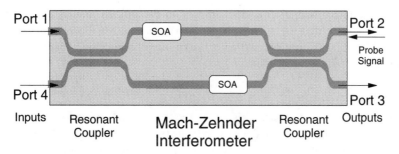

Figure 213. MZI Add-Drop Device

The device shown in Figure 213 is able to replace (add/drop) individual bits within a bit stream *without* affecting the other bits in the stream. As seen in the figure the basic device is a planar MZI with an SOA inserted into each arm. The SOAs are offset from one another by a carefully defined gap.

Operation makes use of the fact that when an SOA saturates the carrier density is fully depleted and this causes a change in the cavity RI and hence a phase shift in the signal passing through it.

The action relies on the presence of a carefully timed, high intensity pulse inserted into the device via Port 2.

- In the "pass through" state (the bar state) the SOAs are powered but there is no power coming from the probe (timing) signal. A data stream arriving on Port 1 will exit unchanged on Port 2. A data stream arriving on Port 4 will leave the device unchanged on Port 3.

- When a pulse arrives on the probe it enters the MZI on Port 2 (counter-propagating). The probe pulse is arranged to be at a significantly higher power level than the signal so that it will saturate each SOA in turn when it arrives. Because of the offset in the location of the SOAs they saturate at different times.

- When one SOA is saturated and the other is not then we get the "cross" state of the switch. A pulse arriving on Port 1 will be switched to Port 3 and a pulse arriving on Port 4 will be switched to Port 2.

- If the probe pulse is synchronised accurately to the data stream this enables a single bit to be switched out of the multiplexed stream and another inserted in its place (the add/drop function).

- If no signal is present on Port 4 then the device becomes a single channel demultiplexor.

Note that the device operation is tied strongly to the offset distance between the two SOAs. This means that the speed of operation is tied to the mechanical construction of the device. It will only operate on a bit stream of predefined speed. Bit streams faster or slower cannot be handled.

5.9.4 Electro-Absorption Modulators

In previous chapters[81] the characteristics of the p-n junction used as an LED or as a laser were discussed. In both devices the junction obtains electrical energy from a current passing through it which results from applying a forward bias.

A reverse-biased p-n junction is a strong absorber of light. At zero bias there is only minor absorption. Electro-absorption modulators make use of this property. Of course the wavelength of light that is absorbed is determined by the bandgap energies of the materials from which the junction is made. Light is only absorbed if it has a *higher* energy than the bandgap energy of the material used. This means that there is a cutoff

---

[81] See 3.2.1, "The Semiconductor Junction Diode" on page 103.

wavelength which depends on the material composition. Absorption will only occur at wavelengths shorter than the cutoff.

It is important to note that the absorption of the junction is controlled by the electric field across it - *not* by any current passing through it. In the absence of incoming light a reverse-biased p-n junction does not pass any current (or rather only minimal current generated by ionisation due to heat). When light is absorbed current flows but this is just a by-product of device operation. The consequence of this is that modulation speed is dependent only on how fast you can change the electric field across the junction. You don't have to wait for the migration of charge-carriers. Hence you can modulate with an electro-absorption modulator at very much higher data rates than you can achieve by controlling the drive current of a laser.

As a separate device the modulator is very simple. It is very similar in construction to an LED, a laser or a semiconductor optical amplifier (SOA). Light enters through a fibre pigtail connected to one facet of the device and leaves through the opposite facet. Response of the device is non-linear and so only digital (on-off) modulation is practical at the moment. Modulation rates of up to 10 GHz are possible. For use at 1550 nm a heterostructure device made from InGaAsP/InP is commonly reported.

Discrete-component (free standing) devices of this kind are *not* considered viable devices for commercial use. This is because of the high loss within the device (between 9 dB and 12 dB of attenuation in the "on" state).

However, this form of modulator is becoming increasingly popular as a part of an integrated device. In this case a laser and a modulator are built together on the same chip with the output of the laser fed directly into the modulator. In this configuration the additional loss caused by the modulator is only of the order of 1 dB or so. The key part of the construction is that you must construct a mirror and electrical isolation barrier between the devices. The mirror is (of course) needed as the exit mirror of the laser. Electrical isolation is needed to minimise unwanted electrical interactions.

Commercial lasers with integrated modulators for the 1550 nm band are available for operation at 2.5 Gbps. This is further discussed in 3.3.5, "Integrated Absorption Modulators" on page 147 and 9.2.1.1, "Multiwavelength Lasers" on page 520.

5.9.5 Acoustic Modulators

When a mechanical vibration is present in a material it causes regular zones of compression and tension within the material.[82] In most materials this causes changes in the refractive index. A regular pattern of changes in RI within a material is a diffraction grating.

Thus if we set up a very high frequency vibration within an optical medium (such as a crystal) we can diffract light from the grating so constructed. We can control the amplitude of these vibrations very accurately (because they are generated electronically). By controlling the amplitude of the sound we can control the amount of light that is diffracted.

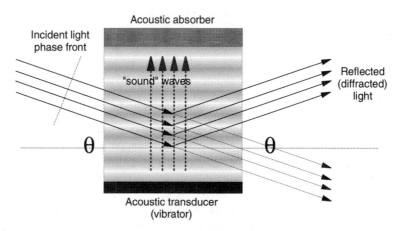

Figure 214. Acoustic Modulator - Bragg Reflection

At first this may seem counter to intuition. A sound wave is a moving wave (as is light). The key is that light travels so very much faster than sound that the sound wave appears to be standing still.[83]

The acoustic frequencies involved are (of course) many orders of magnitude less than the optical frequencies. To form a grating we need the periodicity of the grating to be

---

[82] It seems a little strange to call mechanical vibrations at many megahertz "acoustic" because sound is something we can hear and we can't hear much further than 30 kHz at very best. Nevertheless using extremely high frequency vibrations in electronic devices is an established technology and such vibrations are called "acoustic waves".

[83] The speed of light in quartz is roughly 2×10^8 metres per second. The speed of sound in quartz is roughly 6×10^3 metres per second.

a relatively small multiple of the optical wavelength. In this case a multiple of between about 20 and 200 is appropriate. This is accomplished due to the very great difference in speed of light and sound. Although the frequency of the sound wave is many orders of magnitude lower than the frequency of the light wave the wavelength difference is not that large because the speed of sound is many orders of magnitude lower than the speed of light. In addition very high (for sound) frequencies are employed for the sound wave (50-100 MHz is typical but this can be as high as 3 GHz under some conditions). So we are able to construct an acoustic grating with a period of only a small multiple of the optical wavelength. ("Small" here means a multiple of less than about 100.)

Some Specific Values

In the materials in question the speed of sound varies between about 2 kilometres/sec and about 6 kilometres/sec. In fused silica the speed of sound is 6 km/s. Therefore using an acoustic wave of 100 MHz the wavelength is 30 microns. The wavelength of 1550 nm (free space wavelength) light in fused silica is 1550/1.46 or 1.061 microns. Therefore in this case the optical wavelength is about 30 times the acoustic wavelength. If we increase the acoustic frequency (very difficult in fused silica because of absorption in the material) to 1 GHz then the acoustic wavelength would be only about 3 times the optical one.

There are two important features of Bragg diffraction:

1. The angle of incidence is equal to the angle of diffraction (or reflection).

2. The optical and acoustic wavelengths must have a relationship such that optical waves reflected from the acoustic waves must reinforce one another. This means that the following relationship must hold:

$$\sin \Theta = \frac{n \lambda}{2 \Lambda}$$

Where Θ is the angle of incidence (and reflection) as shown in the figure, λ is the optical wavelength, Λ is the acoustic wavelength and n is any integer.

From the above it can be seen that the angle of diffraction in a typical case will be very small (less than 1 degree).

An interesting property of this device is that you can *modulate a number of different optical wavelengths simultaneously and independently.* If we use only a single acoustic frequency then only one optical wavelength will be diffracted (modulated or switched). If we simply mix *another* acoustic frequency with the first we can arrange things so that a second optical wavelength is modulated by the second acoustic frequency quite independently from the first. In fact we can have a large number of acoustic waves superimposed on one another and modulate a corresponding number of optical wavelengths! This property is not currently used in this type of device but it is very important in the acoustooptic tunable filter described later.

There are two different principles on which an acoustic modulator may operate - Bragg Diffraction and the "Debye-Sears" effect.[84] Bragg diffraction is the form most commonly used in real devices.

These principles are illustrated in Figure 214 on page 314 and Figure 215. The difference between the two modulators is simply the width of the sound wave. If it is very wide we get a single reflection at a specified angle (Bragg diffraction). If it is narrow we get a number of diffracted orders produced as shown in the figure.

In Bragg diffraction, the amount of light diffracted is proportional to the intensity (loudness if you like) of the sound wave. Whatever light is not diffracted passes through in a straight line.

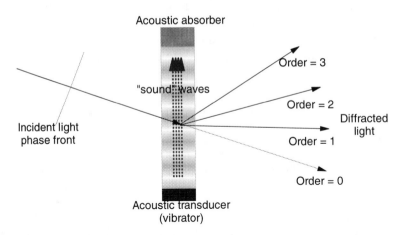

Figure 215. Acoustic Modulator - Debye-Sears Effect

In the Debye-Sears effect the sound wave acts as a *transmissive* diffraction grating. The light is broken up into a number of different output beams. This effect is somewhat more responsive than the Bragg effect because the maximum modulation

---

[84] The Debye-Sears effect takes place in the "Raman-Nath" regime and is sometimes referred to as "Raman-Nath" diffraction.

rate is significantly influenced by the width of the acoustic wave. Nevertheless, the majority of practical modulators and switches use Bragg diffraction.

In both the Bragg effect and the Debye-Sears effect there is a frequency (wavelength) shift in the diffracted (or reflected) light. This is caused by the so-called "doppler effect". When the light beam is in the same direction as the acoustic wave the refracted light (but not the transmitted light) is shifted in frequency. The new optical frequency is the sum of the initial optical frequency and the sound frequency. If the optical beam and the sound beam are in opposite directions the new optical frequency is the initial frequency minus the acoustic frequency. Since in this case we are changing the frequency (wavelength) of the optical signal we are also changing its energy state. To increase the frequency (shorten the wavelength) the optical wave must absorb energy. To decrease the frequency (increase the wavelength) the optical wave must give up energy. This energy is supplied (or absorbed) by the sound wave in the form of "phonons" (lattice vibrations). In many systems applications this frequency shift is not significant enough to cause a problem.

It is important to note that modulation of the acoustic frequency *does not modulate the optical signal*. If the acoustic frequency changes then so does its wavelength. The acoustic wavelength is also the grating period. When the grating period changes then the angles at which the light is diffracted also change. Simply put, if the acoustic frequency changes then the device ceases to work!

Modulation is accomplished by varying the intensity of the acoustic vibrations NOT their wavelength. It is important to remember that when you amplitude modulate any signal you get a broadening of the signal bandwidth itself (by twice the bandwidth of the modulating signal). The sidebands so formed change the shape of the acoustic wave but not its central wavelength. These sidebands are extraneous and do not participate in modulating the optical signal.

The advantages of acoustic modulators may be summarised as follows:

1. They can handle quite high power (a few watts) and are therefore suitable for use with high power gas lasers. An unguided system using a CO_2 laser can be modulated efficiently with an acoustic modulator.

2. The amount of light refracted is linearly proportional to the intensity of the sound wave so analogue intensity modulation is possible.

3. They can modulate multiple different optical wavelengths at the same time.

4. The doppler shift can be used to intentionally shift the wavelength.

There are some limitations in acoustic modulation for communications applications:

- They have a relatively high insertion loss (attenuation).

- They require a relatively high drive current (they are not very power-efficient).

- The maximum modulation rate is significantly lower than other available techniques. The maximum modulation speed needs to be somewhat *slower* than the acoustic frequency used. You can't amplitude modulate a signal faster than its frequency.

(Actually you can modulate at twice the frequency but this won't help in this case. In an acoustic modulator the light is reflected from a number of grating lines - that is from a number of cycles of the acoustic wave.)

So far most available commercial modulators are limited to less than 100 MHz or so although reports in the literature suggest it is possible to go as high as 1 GHz.

5.9.5.1 Acoustic Switches
Acoustic modulators discussed above make excellent switches. These can be used as simple on/off devices - to switch a signal on or off. Alternatively, they can be used to switch an input channel between two possible outputs.

Alternatively, if the incident light contains multiple wavelengths (a WDM stream) then we can select a single wavelength and route it to a different destination without affecting the other WDM channels in the signal. This is because the effect is very wavelength specific.

5.9.6 Acoustooptic Tunable Filters (AOTFs)

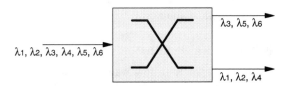

Figure 216. Wavelength Selective Switching Function

The acoustooptic tunable filter has been available for many years but has recently generated a lot of interest for its potential as a wavelength selective switch. In this role it has a very attractive characteristic: *it can switch multiple (arbitrary) wavelengths at the same time.* For example if you had a switch with two outputs and an input stream consisting of six wavelengths (1, 2, 3, 4, 5, 6) the AOTF could direct channels 3, 5 and 6 to one output and the remaining channels (1, 2, 4) to a different output. Any combination can be switched in a single step!

In this device the optical and acoustic waves travel either in the same direction (copropagating waves) or in opposite directions (counterpropagating waves). The basic device is illustrated in Figure 217.

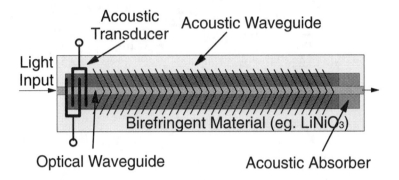

Figure 217. *Acoustooptic Tunable Filter (AOTF) - Basic Structure*

From earlier discussions of the in-fibre Bragg grating we might expect this device to simply reflect the selected wavelength. Indeed this is just what happens when the acoustic wavelength is either the same or a very small multiple (2 or 3 times) the optical wavelength.

Things get much more interesting when the acoustic wavelength is significantly longer (say 30 times) than the optical wavelength. Reflection ceases and the acoustic wave acts to stimulate the optical wave to change modes. In the waveguide configuration illustrated we can stimulate changing to the orthogonal polarisation state! When conditions are right, light in one polarisation can be perfectly changed ("flipped") to the orthogonal polarisation. In this case the "right" conditions include:

- Polarised input light

- A birefringent waveguide medium

  The waveguide medium must present different RIs to the two different (orthogonal) polarisation states.

- The relationship of the optical wavelength and the acoustic wavelength must be exactly correct.

This is because a change in energy is involved in the transition from one polarisation state to the other. During the change the optical wave has either to gain or lose energy from the acoustic wave. The energy levels must match.

- The coupling length (within the device) must be exactly right.

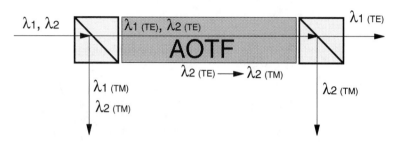

Figure 218. *AOTF Operation (1)*

The basic device is illustrated in Figure 218.

- Unpolarised light (in this example two different wavelengths) enters the device on the left and is split into its two orthogonal polarisations by a beamsplitter prism. The TE (Transverse Electric) mode continues into the AOTF and the TM (Transverse Magnetic) mode is reflected away.

- During its travel through the AOTF the wavelength λ_2 is resonant with the acoustic wave and its polarisation is flipped into the TM mode. Wavelength λ_1 is unaffected.

- When the light reaches the second beamsplitter prism, light of wavelength λ_1 passes through and light of wavelength λ_2 is reflected by the prism.

Thus the wavelengths have now been separated. Of course this is not a very efficient process in an ordinary fibre network because polarisation states in standard fibre change randomly and not only will we lose (on average) 3 dB of signal power we will also introduce polarisation dependent noise effects. So in a practical device we need to process both polarisation states.

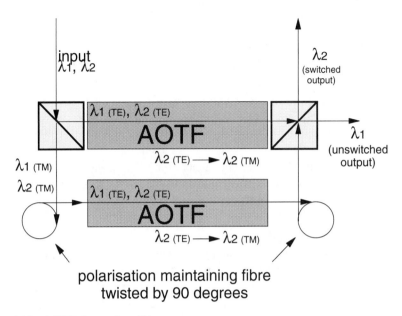

Figure 219. *AOTF Operation (2)*

This is shown in Figure 219. The TM polarisations reflected out of the first beamsplitter prism are carried in polarisation maintaining fibre which is then twisted at 90°. This converts the TM polarisation to a TE polarisation. The light is then sent through an AOTF identical to the other. The same thing now happens and the polarisation of wavelength λ_2 is changed from TE (the new TE) to TM. The output is then fed to the second beamsplitter prism (via a twisted polarisation maintaining fibre) which recombines the polarisation states and separates the channels.

The reason this approach is adopted (shifting the polarisations) is that the TE to TM polarisation flip absorbs energy and (slightly) reduces the wavelength. TM to TE does the opposite. We don't want the problems of re-combining the light at different wavelengths!

The major advantages of AOTFs are their tunability over a wide range of wavelengths and their ability to switch many channels simultaneously (by superimposing acoustic frequencies). The limitations are not too severe:

1. The maximum number of channels that can be switched simultaneously is limited by the maximum power of the acoustic transducer.

2. The shape of the power spectrum actually switched is far from the nice square characteristic we would like. To improve this characteristic the device must be

"apodised". This is simply reducing the strength of the acoustooptic interaction around the edges of the interaction region.

3. The maximum tuning (switching) speed is limited by the time it takes for the acoustic wave to travel from one end of the interaction region to the other. In practice this is about 10 μsec.

4. The best wavelength resolution (WDM channel spacing) that can be achieved (in LiNiO₃) is about 1 nm. This is limited by the maximum interaction length possible.

At this time commercial AOTFs are not suitable for WDM applications; however, it is expected that suitable versions will become available in the near future. For further reading see the paper by Smith et al. (1996).

5.9.7 Phase Modulators

Phase modulation per-se is not common in current optical systems. A phase modulated signal requires a coherent receiver and these are difficult and expensive to build. However, phase modulation is important because it is relatively easy to do and is used as the basis of most practical intensity modulators (described in the following section). A direct application of phase modulation is in creating devices which scramble the polarisation of a signal. See 9.4.5.4, "Polarisation Effects in EDFAs" on page 560.

Some optical materials exhibit the electrooptic effect. That is, they change in refractive index in the presence of an electric field. So, if we make a waveguide from such an optical material and place an electric field across it we can vary the time it takes for the signal to travel through the device simply by varying the electric field. This variation in transit time creates a variation in the phase of the optical signal.

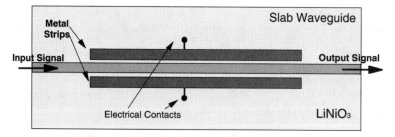

Figure 220. *Electro-Optic Phase Modulator*

A typical direct phase modulator is shown in Figure 220. A lithium niobate crystal is cut in a precise relationship to its crystal axes. A planar waveguide is constructed on the surface of the crystal and areas of the crystal nearby to the waveguide are plated with metal to conduct electricity. A voltage applied across the plated areas creates a variation in the RI of the lithium niobate. Thus a variation in the electric field applied causes a variation in the phase of the optical signal in the waveguide.

If the phase of one polarisation is changed more than the phase of the orthogonal polarisation then we get a change in the polarisation of the signal. Lithium niobate is a birefringent material which (depending on how it is cut it in relation to its crystal axes) exhibits different RIs to orthogonal polarisations. The electro-optic effect in lithium niobate can be arranged to affect one polarisation state more than the other. Thus polarisation can be modulated.

There are no optical communications systems in existence which use polarisation modulation. However, polarisation scrambling of the signal is needed in some long distance systems to overcome the polarisation dependent effects of EDFAs. This is described in 9.4.5.4, "Polarisation Effects in EDFAs" on page 560.

5.9.8 Modulation Using a Mach-Zehnder Interferometer

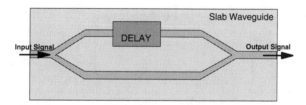

Figure 221. *Mach-Zehnder Interferometer*

Mach-Zehnder Interferometers (MZIs) are used in a wide variety of applications within optics and optical communications. The basic principle is that you have a balanced configuration of a splitter and a combiner connected by a pair of matched waveguides. When something is done to create a phase difference between the signals in the two matched waveguides interference in the recombination process causes differences in the amplitude of the output signal.

Thus an intensity modulator based on an MZI converts changes in phase (which we can create directly) to changes in signal amplitude.

The principle is very simple:

1. The signal entering the device is split through a "Y" splitter into two directions. In a properly constructed device half of the signal goes in each direction and polarisation is not affected.

2. When there is no phase delay (both arms of the interferometer are equal in length) the signal is recombined at the "Y" junction (coupler) immediately before the light exits the device. Since the signals in each arm are coherent with each other they reinforce during recombination and the expected 3 db loss of the recombining Y-coupler is not experienced.

3. When there is a difference in phase at the destination Y-coupler the signals will now be now out-of-phase with one another. When these signals re-combine some (or all) of the optical power will be lost because the signals will interfere with each other. If the phase difference is a full 180 degrees then output will be zero. If there is no phase difference then the light will pass through with very little loss.

4. The phase difference at the destination can be caused either by a real difference in the length of the two arms of the interferometer or by a difference in the optical length. For example, if the RI in one arm is changed the signal will travel at a (slightly) different speed and will thus arrive out-of-phase with the signal in the other arm.

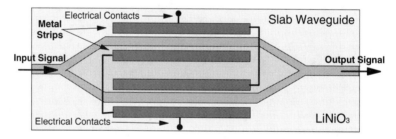

Figure 222. *Modulator Using Mach-Zehnder Interferometer*

Figure 222 shows a Mach-Zehnder interferometer set up as a modulator. In this case there are conductive strips of metal close to each arm of the interferometer. An electric field is used to modulate the phase of the light in either (or both) of the arms of the interferometer. In the figure the electric field is applied to both arms but it is of opposite polarity in each arm.

The interferometer is built from a material which (apart from being transparent at the wavelengths we wish to use) changes its refractive index (slightly) under the influence of an electric field. When current is applied to the conductive plates of the device the refractive index will be changed. A change in refractive index (of course) implies a change in the speed of propagation and this changes the phase of the signal.

In a Mach-Zehnder interferometric modulator we use the small changes in refractive index induced by an electric field to cause large changes in signal amplitude at the output. In one arm the RI will increase and in the other arm it will decrease. This causes the signal in one arm to be retarded in phase and the signal in the other arm to be advanced. When the signal is recombined at the output y-junction the very small phase changes will cause interference effects. These interference effects cause very large variations in the amplitude of the output signal. Thus we have a device that will change the amplitude of the optical signal very significantly according to an applied electric field.

The usual material used to make interferometric modulators is lithium niobate (LiNiO₃). The device requires considerable precision in manufacture as each arm must be identical in length (or only very slightly different). For this reason these are usually made in planar waveguide technology rather than as fibre devices. The effect is very fast in responding to changes in voltage and MZI based modulators are available at speeds up to around 10 Mbps.

5.9.8.1 Travelling-Wave Configuration

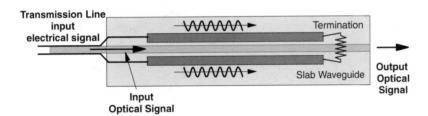

Figure 223. Travelling-Wave Principle

The modulation rate of an MZI can be significantly improved by using a "travelling-wave" configuration. In Figure 222 on page 324 the electrical signal is delivered to the centre of two electrical contact areas plated onto the LiNiO₃ substrate. Distribution of the electrical signal around the contact area becomes a problem when the modulation rate gets into the GHz range.

In Figure 223 the plated contact areas are arranged as part of a transmission line. The electrical input is then impedance matched to the plated contact areas. The electrical signal then travels down the waveguide in parallel with the optical signal. If the propagation speed of both signals can be made the same (or nearly the same) we can have a very long interaction length. This significantly improves the efficiency of the device.

The travelling-wave configuration then:

- Makes the device significantly more efficient.

- Allows for the use of lower voltages.

- Simplifies the electronic connection.

- Makes possible significantly higher modulation rates.

5.9.9 Pockels Cell Modulators

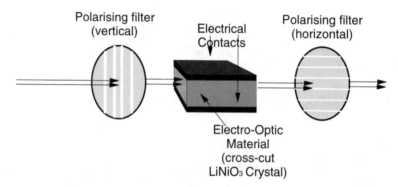

Figure 224. Pockels Cell Modulator

The "Pockels Effect" is a phenomena that occurs in some types of crystals where the refractive index is changed by the presence of an applied electric field. This is a *linear* electrooptic effect because the electric field imposed across a crystal changes the RI linearly with the strength of that field.

In some types of crystal the effect is (slightly) different depending on the orientation of the crystal (the crystal itself is not symmetric). A Pockels effect (cell) modulator makes use of this property to affect the RI of each different polarisation state differently. Light of one polarisation experiences a different RI from light in the other polarisation. This "birefringent" property causes light passing through the device to be rotated in polarisation depending on the strength of the applied electric field.

Figure 224 shows the principle.

- Arriving light is filtered through a polariser so that only light polarised in one particular direction is allowed through.

- The light then passes through a specially cut crystal to which electrical contacts have been attached.

- If there is no applied electric field the light passes through unchanged (except for some minimal attenuation in the material).

  When this light reaches the second polariser it will be absorbed because it is of the opposite polarisation.

- When an electric field is applied, polarisation is changed (rotated) dependent on the strength of the electric field.

  When this light now reaches the second polariser some proportion will be blocked and some will pass through depending on the amount of phase rotation that has taken place. If the phase has been rotated by 90° then all the light will pass through. Lesser amounts will pass through when the phase rotation is less than 90°.

Thus we can modulate the light in direct proportion to the strength of the applied electric field.

It should be noted that this process depends on the way in which the crystal is cut. The "fast" and "slow" axes of the crystal need to be crossed at 45° to the polarisation of the incoming light.

There are a number of different crystalline materials that can be used for constructing effective modulators. These materials include: $LiNiO_3$, ADP ($NH_4H_2PO_4$), and KDP (KH_2PO_4).

The important characteristics of pockels cell modulators are:

1. Input light must be polarised - or at least have an unchanging polarisation state.

   This is fine at the exit point of a laser. You connect your modulator to the laser with polarisation maintaining fibre and align the output polarisation state of the laser to the input state of the modulator.

   However, in normal fibre transmission systems the polarisation state of the signal changes randomly with time (caused by its travel along standard fibre). If a signal like this was fed to a polarisation sensitive device such as this modulator you would get rapid signal "fades" over time (seconds or minutes). Sometimes the input signal would align with the input to the modulator and a strong signal would be input. At other times when the polarisation state changed most of the signal would be blocked. Of course such a system would be unusable.

2. High powers can be handled (higher than you can put into a fibre).

3. A relatively high voltage (around 1000 volts) must be applied to get sufficient modulation effect. This means that during modulation you have some large voltage changes with the result that modulation speed is limited. Also the high voltage requirement contributes to a high cost for the device.

4. The juxtaposition of different crystals of different materials and orientations requires precise manufacture and assembly (another contributor to high cost).

5. Modulators that work at up to 1 GHz (using the "travelling wave" principle are commercially available. This is the same principle that was described earlier in 5.9.8.1, "Travelling-Wave Configuration" on page 325.

5.9.10 Faraday Effect Modulators

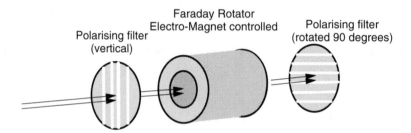

Figure 225. Faraday Effect Modulator

Faraday effect modulators operate on a very similar principle to the Pockels effect modulator described above. The difference is that we make use of the magnetooptic effect to rotate the polarisation rather than the electrooptic effect.

The device is similar in some ways to the isolator described in 5.4.5.3, "A Simple Isolator" on page 251. Of course here we need an electromagnet rather than a permanent magnet to provide a varying magnetic field.

This type of modulator is not in common use as it is slower than the Pockels effect device and somewhat more expensive.

5.10 Repeaters

Until the commercial availability of optical amplifiers in 1992, the only way to boost an optical signal was to convert it to electrical form, amplify or regenerate it, and then convert it to optical form again. See 5.2, "Optical Amplifiers" on page 198.

Boosting the signal electrically either involves a simple amplifier or a more complex repeater. An amplifier just takes whatever signal it receives and makes it bigger. This includes the noise and whatever dispersion of the signal that has already taken place. However, amplifiers are simpler, cheaper, and not sensitive to the coding used on the fibre. They did not become commercially available until 1992 and are only now beginning to be used in new systems (especially undersea systems).

Repeaters have been the method of choice for boosting an optical signal. A repeater is a full receiver which reconstructs the bit stream and its timing. This bit stream and its timing are used to drive a transmitter. This means that the repeated signal has all dispersion and noise removed. It is said that repeaters perform the "three Rs":

- Reamplification
- Reshaping
- Reclocking

"2R" repeaters exist and in this case they only perform reamplification and reshaping but not reclocking.

Repeaters are more complex and more costly than simple amplifiers. They are also very inflexible as they must be constructed for exactly the wavelength, protocol, and speed of the signal being carried. They can't handle multiple wavelengths. In order to carry different wavelengths on the same fibre in a repeatered system, the wavelengths must be separated (with a diffraction grating or a prism) at each repeater and the separate signals separately repeated and then recombined. This process is mechanically complex and requires a separate repeater for each wavelength. Repeaters that handle multiple wavelengths are therefore costly to build and to maintain.

In multimode systems, where dispersion is the main distance limiting factor, electronic repeaters will continue to be the major way of boosting a signal. In single-mode systems over long distances where dispersion isn't so much of a problem, optical amplifiers are rapidly replacing repeaters as the device of choice.

5.11 Further Reading

Amplifiers

I. Baumann et al. (1996)

Er-Doped Integrated Optical Devices in LiNiO₃: IEEE J. of Selected Topics in Quantum Electronics, Vol 2, No 2, June 1996. pp 355-366

J-M. P. Delavaux (1995)

Multi-Stage Erbium-Doped Fibre Amplifier Designs: IEEE J. of Lightwave Technology, Vol 13, No 5, May 1995. pp 703-720

R.J. Mears, L. Reckie, I.M. Jauncey and D.N. Payne (1987)

Low-Noise Erbium Amplifier Operating at 1.54 μm: Electronics Letters, Vol 23, No 19, 1987. p 1026

N. A. Olson (1989)

Lightwave Systems with Optical Amplifiers: IEEE J. of Lightwave Technology, Vol 7, No 7, July 1989. pp 1071-1082

G.D. Peng, P.L. Chu, Z. Xiong, T. Whitbread and R.P. Chaplin (1996)

Broadband Tunable Optical Amplification in Rhodamine B-doped Step-Index Polymer Fibre: Optics Communications, 129, 1996. pp 353-357

L. Reckie, R.J. Mears, S.B. Poole and D.N. Payne (1986)

Tunable Single-Mode Fibre Lasers: IEEE J. of Lightwave Technology, Vol 4, No 7, July 1986. p 956

Hidenori Taga, Noboru Edaqawa, Shu Yamamoto and Shigeyuku Akiba (1995)

Recent Progress in Amplified Undersea Systems: IEEE J. of Lightwave Technology, Vol 13, No 5, May 1995. pp 829-840

Timothy J. Whitley (1995)

A Review of Recent System Demonstrations Incorporating 1.3 μm Praseodymium-Doped Fluoride Fibre Amplifiers: IEEE J. of Lightwave Technology, Vol 13, No 5, May 1995. pp 744-760

A.E. Willner and S.-M. Hwang (1993)

Passive Equalisation of Nonuniform EDFA Gain by Optical Filtering for Megameter Transmission of 20 WDM Channels through a Cascade of EDFA's: IEEE Photonics Technology Letters, Vol 5, No 9, September 1993. pp 1023-1028

Splitters, Couplers and Circulators

Jay S. Van Delden (1995)

Optical circulators improve bidirectional fibre systems: Laser Focus World, November 1995.

William L. Emkey (1983)

A Polarisation-Independent Optical Circulator for 1.3 μm: IEEE J. of Lightwave Technology, Vol LT-1, No 3, September 1983. pp 466-469

Yohji Fujii (1991)

High-isolation Polarisation-Independent Optical Circulator Coupled with Single-Mode Fibres: IEEE J. of Lightwave Technology, Vol 9, No 4, April 1991. pp 456-460

Yohji Fujii (1992)

Polarisation-Independent Optical Circulator Having High Isolation over a Wide Wavelength Range: IEEE Photonics Technology Letters, Vol 4, No 2, February 1992. pp 154-156

Takao Matsumoto and Ken-ichi Sato (1980)

Polarisation-independent optical circulator: an experiment: Applied Optics, Vol 19, No 1, January 1980. pp 108-112

M. Shirasaki, H. Kuwahara and T. Obokata (1981)

Compact polarisation-independent optical circulator: Applied Optics, Vol 20, No 15, August 1981. pp 2683-2687

Littrow (Planar) Gratings

Yohji Fujii and Junichiro Minowa (1983)

Optical demultiplexer using a silicon concave diffraction grating: Applied Optics, Vol 22, No 7, 1 April 1983. pp 975-978

Array Waveguide Gratings

C. Dragone (1991)

An N x N Optical Multiplexor Using a Planar Arrangement of Two Star Couplers: IEEE Photonic Technology Letters, Vol 3, 1991, pp 812-15.

Meint K. Smit (1996)

PHASAR-Based WDM-Devices: Principles, Design and Applications: IEEE J. of Selected Topics in Quantum Electronics, Vol 2, No 2, June 1996.

In-Fibre Bragg Gratings

C. R. Giles (1997)

Lightwave Applications of Fibre Bragg Gratings: IEEE J. of Lightwave Technology, Vol 15, No 8, August 1997. pp 1391-1404

K. O. Hill and G. Meltz (1997)

Fibre Bragg Grating Technology Fundamentals and Overview: IEEE J. of Lightwave Technology, Vol 15, No 8, August 1997. pp 1263-1276

G. W. Yoffe, Peter A. Krug, F. Ouellette and D. A. Thorncraft

Passive temperature-compensating package for optical fibre gratings: Applied Optics, Vol 34, No. 30, 20 October 1995

Remigius Zengerle and Ottokar Leminger (1995)

Phase-Shifted Bragg-Grating Filters with Improved Transmission Characteristics: IEEE J. of Lightwave Technology, Vol 13, No 12, December 1995. pp 2354-2358

Filters

N.J. Doran and David Wood (1988)

Nonlinear-optical loop mirror: Optics Letters, Vol 13, No 1, January 1988. pp 56-58

M.E. Fermann, F. Haberi, M. Hofer and H. Hochreiter (1990)

Nonlinear amplifying loop mirror: Optics Letters, Vol 15, No 13, July 1990. pp 752-754

Haim Kobrinski and Kwok-Wai Cheung (1989)

Wavelength-Tunable Optical Filters: Applications and Technologies: IEEE Communications Magazine, October 1989. pp 53-63

Haruo Okamura and Katsumi Iwatsuki (1991)

A Finesse-Enhanced Er-Doped-Fibre Ring Resonator: IEEE J. of Lightwave Technology, Vol 9, No 11, November 1991. pp 1554-1560

David A. Smith and John J. Johnson (1991)

Low Drive-Power Integrated Acoustooptic Filter on X-Cut Y-Propagating LiNbO3: IEEE Photonics Technology Letters, Vol 3, No 10, October 1991. pp 923-925

K. Smith, N. J. Doran and P. G. J. Wigley (1990)

Pulse shaping, compression and pedestal suppression employing a nonlinear-optical loop mirror: Optics Letters, Vol 15, No 22, November 15, 1990. pp 1294-1296

K. Suzuki, K. Iwatsuki, S. Nishi and M. Saruwatari (1994)

Error-free demultiplexing of 160 Gbit/s pulse signal using optical loop mirror including semiconductor laser amplifier: Electronics Letters, Vol 30, No 18, September 1994. pp 1501-1503

Beatriz Vizoso et. al. (1994)

Amplified Fibre-Optic Recirculating Delay Lines: IEEE J. of Lightwave Technology, Vol 12, No 2, February 1994. pp 294-305

Feng Zhang and John W. Y. Lit (1988)

Direct-coupling single-mode fibre ring resonator: Journal of the Optical Society of America, Vol 5, No 8, August 1988. pp 1347-1355

Modulators and Switches

Janet L. Jackel et al. (1996)

Acousto-Optic Tunable Filters (AOTF's) for Multiwavelength Optical Cross-Connects: Crosstalk Considerations: IEEE J. Lightwave Technology, Vol 14, No 6, June 1996. pp 1056-1066

E. Jahn, N. Agrawal, H. J. Ehrke, R. Ludwig, W. Pieper and H. G. Weber (1996)

Monolithically integrated asymmetric Mach-Zehnder interferometer as a 20 Gbit/s all-optical add/drop multiplexer for OTDM systems: Electronics Letters, Vol 32, No 3, February 1996.

David G. Moodie et al. (1996)

Discrete Electroabsorption Modulators with Enhanced Modulation Depth: IEEE J. of Lightwave Technology, Vol 14, No 9, September 1996. pp 2035-2043

Yukio Noda, Masatoshi Suzuki, Yukitoshi Kushiro and Shigeyuki Akiba (1986)

High-Speed Electroabsorption Modulator with Strip-Loaded GaInAsP Planar Waveguide: IEEE J. of Lightwave Technology, Vol LT-4, No 10, October 1986. pp 1445-1453

M. Renaud, M. Bachmann and M. Erman (1996)

Semiconductor Optical Space Switches: IEEE J. of Selected Topics in Quantum Electronics, Vol 2, No 2, June 1996. pp 277-288

D. A. Smith, J. E. Baran, J. J. Johnson and K. W. Cheung (1990)

Integrated Optic Acoustically Tunable Filters for WDM Networks.: IEEE J. Selected Areas in Communication, Vol 8, 1990. pp 1151-1159.

David A. Smith et al. (1996)

Evolution of the Acousto-Optic Wavelength Routing Switch: IEEE J. of Lightwave Technology, Vol 14, No 6, June 1996. pp 1005-1019

Chapter 6. Fibre Manufacture, Cables and Connectors

6.1 The Technology of Fibre Manufacture

In today's world we take fibre manufacture for granted. Yet it is one of the wonders of the age and its success has made possible the whole field of optical communications. In manufacturing fibre there are two major challenges:

1. Purifying the materials (especially silica) to an extreme degree. Levels of heavy metal impurity of one in a billion are quite sufficient to have an adverse effect on the performance of the fibre.

2. Achieving extreme precision in fibre dimensions and tolerances. The size of the core, its position and the outer dimension of the cladding must be precise to tolerances of one micron or less. Refractive indices must also be precise especially in the case of graded index fibres.

6.1.1 Purifying Silica

Earlier in this book it was pointed out that extremely low levels of impurity in the silica used in fibre can result in very high levels of attenuation. For a good fibre the maximum tolerable level of impurity due to the presence of the "transition metals" (Fe, Cu, Ni, V, Cr, Mn) is about 1 part in 10^9. This is about 1000 times better (more pure) than is usually achieved with traditional chemical purification techniques. The tolerable level of OH (water) impurity is higher than this - it is about 1 part in 10^8 but this is also very hard to achieve.

The extreme levels of purity required are achieved by making use of the same principle we use when we manufacture whisky. When we distill a mixture of alcohol and water (and other things) the alcohol reaches boiling point at a lower temperature than the water. The fermented mixture is heated to a temperature where the alcohol (along with many impurities that impart the flavour) evaporates from the mixture but the water does not.[85] The vapour is collected and cooled and the resulting liquid has a much higher concentration of alcohol than the original mixture.

---

[85] There is a complication here in that alcohol and water form a "constant boiling mixture". Pure alcohol cannot be completely separated from water by distillation. However this is a good illustration of the principles involved.

This is all possible because different chemical compounds have different "boiling points" (different vapour pressures). When you heat other chemical compounds some boil (or vaporise) at lower temperatures than others. You can separate one substance from another by either boiling it off from a mixture of liquids (as in distillation) or by condensing it at a controlled temperature from a mixture of hot gasses.

A very good first stage bulk purification of silica can be achieved by a process very much like making alcoholic spirits. Sand is heated (with an electric arc) to just above the boiling point of silica (2230°C). Silica evaporates and is condensed into a liquid at about 2000°C. Most of the metallic impurities are less volatile and will be left behind. Some impurities are actually more volatile and will not condense at such a high temperature. Thus the silica can be separated in a relatively pure form. This process is difficult however, because of the very high temperatures involved.

Another interesting process is to heat the sand to an extremely high temperature (around 7000°C). Silica is a gas at this temperature but most transition metal compounds decompose. So if you pass sand through a very high temperature electric arc and then condense the silica relatively quickly afterward, most of the impurities decompose and are carried away in the exhaust gasses.

At the input to the fibre manufacturing process chemicals are only pure to about 1 part in a million (1 in 10^6). The fibre manufacturing process itself achieves the necessary additional purification.

In most fibre manufacture the glass material (silica with required dopants) is created at high temperature from reaction between gasses. The following reactions are typical of the ones used in the MCVD[86] process. There are many alternative reactions - for example the chloride form is used here but the fluoride form may be used as an alternative.

$$SiCl_4 + O_2 \rightarrow SiO_2 + 2Cl_2$$

$$GeCl_4 + O_2 \rightarrow GeO_2 + 2Cl_2$$

$$4POCl_3 + 3O_2 \rightarrow 2P_2O_5 + 6Cl_2$$

Gasses are mixed in a carefully controlled way in a chamber. Silicon chloride (in gaseous form) reacts with oxygen to produce silica (silicon dioxide) in solid form and

---

[86] Described later in this chapter.

chlorine. This process is called "vapour deposition" as solid materials (or rather viscous liquids) are formed from the gaseous state and are deposited where we want them. In general most of the impurities are carried away in the exhaust.

The above reactions involve oxidation. In the OVD and VAD processes[87] hydrolysis reactions are used instead:

$$SiCl_4 + O_2 + 2H_2 \rightarrow SiO_2 + 4HCl$$

$$GeCl_4 + O_2 + 2H_2 \rightarrow GeO_2 + 4HCl$$

All current fibre manufacturing techniques make use of vapour deposition in one form or another.

6.1.2 Drawing the Fibre

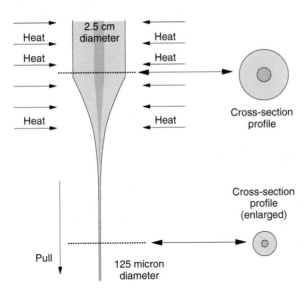

Figure 226. Principle of Drawing a Fibre

The challenge in making a fibre is the construction of a precise cross-section with tiny dimensions. All fibre manufacture is done by "drawing" the fibre from a large cross-section to an extremely small one. The large cross-section can be (usually is) in

---

[87] Also described later in this chapter.

the form of a pre-formed rod of material or it could be in a viscous form fed from a reservoir as described in 6.1.3, "The Double-Crucible Method" on page 339.

The key fact here is that when you draw a fibre as shown in Figure 226 on page 337 *the cross-section of the fibre so-formed is an exact miniaturised replica of the cross-section of the rod from which the fibre was drawn!* That is, the proportions of the fibre profile are exactly the same as the proportions of the rod from which it was drawn. This is only true of course if the rod is uniformly hot (and therefore has a uniform viscosity) through its entire cross-section.

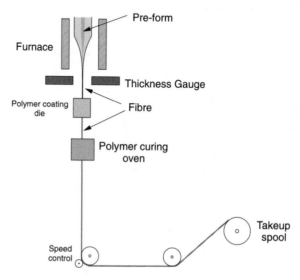

Figure 227. Drawing Tower

Fibre is made using a "tower" illustrated schematically in Figure 227. This tower is usually about 20 feet high to allow the fibre time to cool down before being spooled.

- The process starts with a rod of material called a preform. This rod has exactly the same composition and cross-sectional profile as the fibre we want to produce but is between 1 and 2.5 cm in diameter.

- The end of the preform rod is heated in an electrical resistance furnace until it reaches melting point across its whole cross-section. The required temperature here is typically between 1850°C and 2000°C. This initial heating can take up to an hour because of the need to ensure that the rod is uniformly hot at its end.

- Fibre is drawn from the end of the preform mostly by the force of gravity. A small pulling force is used to enable control of the rate of fibre production (and hence of the fibre's diameter).

- The fibre cools and solidifies very quickly (within a few centimetres of the furnace.

- It then passes through a station which monitors the fibre diameter and controls the pulling speed. This ensures very close control of the fibre's diameter to the desired 125 microns.

  The device used here usually comprises a laser and one or more detectors. The laser produces a very narrow beam which is focused on the fibre itself. A diffraction pattern is produced from interaction of the laser beam and the fibre. This diffraction pattern changes with changes in the diameter of the fibre. The pattern is sensed with an optical detector (or detectors) and monitored for changes. Thus an automatic control is achieved which pulls the fibre a bit faster when it is too thick and a bit slower when it is too thin.

- The fibre is now quite cool and it is passed through a vat of polymer. At the exit point from the vat there is an extrusion die which ensures a uniform coating of polymer onto the fibre. This is done as soon as possible after the fibre is drawn to minimise the absorption of water from the atmosphere.

- The coated fibre then passes through a curing oven where the polymer is cured and set. The fibre is now 250 microns in diameter.

- The fibre is then reeled onto a spool with a diameter of 20 cm or so. This is actually a critical part of the process as the fibre must be evenly spooled. If fibres cross one-another on the spool microbends can result which can do long-term damage to the fibre.

6.1.3 The Double-Crucible Method

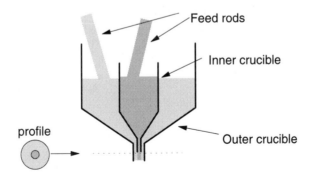

Figure 228. Double-Crucible Method

In the double-crucible method, a pair of platinum crucibles set one inside the other hold molten silica containing the desired dopants etc. Not shown in the diagram, the whole assembly is housed inside a furnace to keep the temperature at the optimum level. This is often done in an inert (nitrogen) atmosphere. The inner crucible holds the core glass and the outer crucible, the cladding. The crucibles are continually replenished by the insertion of feed rods of silica (as shown). Fibre of the desired cross-section is drawn from an outlet in the base of the assembly.

The double-crucible method of fibre manufacture was important in the past but is not in commercial use today. It was very attractive because it is a continuous process and therefore offers potentially very low cost operation. However, it has not been able to deliver the required precision in control of fibre dimensions and characteristics.

6.1.4 Vapour Deposition Techniques

The major methods of fibre manufacture create a solid rod (called a preform) from which the fibre is drawn in a batch process. Preforms are created by depositing silica (including dopants) from reactions between gasses at high temperatures. There are four general processes:

1. Outside Vapour Deposition (OVD)

2. Vapour Axial Deposition (VAD)

3. Modified Chemical Vapour Deposition (MCVD)

4. Plasma-activated Chemical Vapour Deposition (PCVD)

Of the above, VAD and OVD are the most widely used processes for making single-mode fibre although MCVD is also sometimes used. MCVD is used extensively for specialty fibres such as in fibre made for pigtailing and in doped fibres for amplifiers etc. MCVD is also extensively used in making GI multimode fibre. In manufacturing single mode fibre, the VAD process is almost exclusively used in Japan. OVD and MCVD are used in Europe and America.

6.1.4.1 Outside Vapour Deposition (OVD)

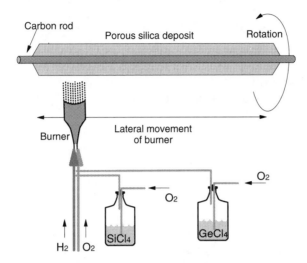

Figure 229. *Outside Vapour Deposition*

The basic process involved in OVD is called "flame hydrolysis". $SiCl_4$ reacts with oxygen to produce silica (SiO_2) and HCl. This reaction takes place *within* an oxy-hydrogen flame.

- At normal temperatures $SiCl_4$ is a relatively volatile liquid.

- Oxygen is passed through the silicon chloride to form a mixture of $SiCl_4$ vapour and oxygen.

- The $SiCl_4$-O_2 mixture is then fed to an oxy-hydrogen burner such that it is introduced into the flame.

- Minute particles of molten silica (called a "soot" are formed in the flame.

- A rod of either carbon or a metal is rotated in a lathe and the silica depositing flame is moved back and forth along it.

- The silica is deposited evenly along the rod.

- Dopants such as germanium are introduced into the flame to create the required variations in the refractive index.

- When sufficient material has built up on the rod the process is stopped and the rod removed. The glass body so formed is a porous conglomerate of silica particles stuck together.

- The preform is then heated (sintered) to coalesce the material into a solid glass tube. The tube is then heated further and collapsed to form a rod.

- In principle you could draw fibre directly from the collapsed silica preform.

- In practice it is a waste of time to deposit all of the cladding in this way. When the preform has built up a sufficient thickness for the core and a small part of the cladding the process is usually stopped. This preform is then sintered and inserted into a silica tube. The assembly is then heated and collapsed together creating a preform with the appropriate profile.

Of course the above process must take place in either a vacuum or an inert atmosphere. Since the process produces HCl and water a mist of hydrochloric acid is also produced which must be neutralised and disposed of.

This process has three problems:

1. It is difficult to remove all the water (OH groups) from the formed glass. Thus the resulting fibre tends to have a large absorption peak around the 1385 nm wavelength region. Considerable success was achieved at removing most of the OH but it was never as good as some competing processes.

2. The fibre produced tends to have a depression in the refractive index along its axis. This is also true for some other processes (such as MCVD) but the effect is bigger in this one.

3. It is a batch process and preforms produced this way are limited in size. This means that the ultimate cost of the process is likely to be high.

OVD was the first of the vapour deposition processes and is important for that reason but is not in commercial use today.

6.1.4.2 Vapour-Phase Axial Deposition (VAD)

VAD is a very important process and accounts for a large proportion of world fibre production. It was originally intended to be a continuous process which would have a lot lower cost than the batch processes. Today it is still a batch process. However it produces large preforms which can be drawn to lengths of up to 250 km of fibre.

The basic mechanism used in VAD is flame hydrolysis (like OVD). It was discovered that if you mix $GeCl_4$ as a dopant into the $SiCl_4$-O_2 feed the proportion of germania (GeO_2) deposited with the silica varies with the temperature of the flame! So if you control the flame temperature you can control the proportion of dopant deposited. Further if a wide flame is used with a temperature gradient across it you can get a graded proportion of germania deposited. This is difficult to do in practice but since it is a very successful commercial process we know that these difficulties have been overcome!

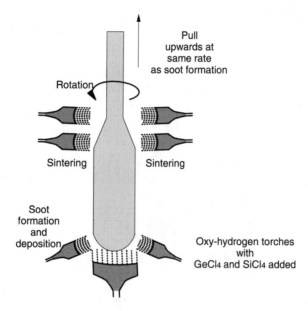

Figure 230. *Vapour Axial Deposition (VAD)*

The process is shown in Figure 230.

- At the bottom of the figure flame hydrolysis torches produce silica soot (including dopants) which are deposited across the base of a relatively wide preform.

- Other dopants can be included instead of or in addition to germanium. POCl₃ and BBr₃ are often used.

- As the soot is deposited the preform is pulled upwards so that the torches themselves do not move.

- Further up the preform other torches (or sometimes an electric furnace) are used to sinter the preform and form a solid glass preform rod.

- The whole process is of course enclosed and an atmosphere of pure oxygen with SOCl₂ vapour is used to capture the water produced by the torches and prevent it from entering the glass.

- The resultant rod is used as the feed for the fibre drawing process.

6.1.4.3 Modified Chemical Vapour Deposition (MCVD)

In the beginning there was a process called Inside Vapour Deposition (IVD). This process was significantly improved and renamed "Modified Chemical Vapour Deposition" (MCVD). Today, MCVD accounts for the majority of world fibre production.

In the MCVD process silica (along with the required dopants) is formed in a gaseous reaction *inside* a silica tube. The reaction takes place in the gas phase. A silica soot is deposited on the inside of the tube as shown in Figure 231.

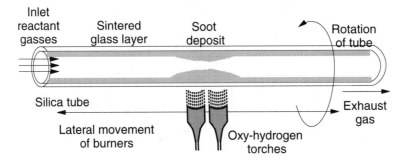

Figure 231. Modified Chemical Vapour Deposition

The reaction between the glass-forming gasses takes place in a hot region of the tube and the silica particles so formed stick to the walls of the tube. The burners traverse the tube many times at temperatures up to 1600°C. This sinters the soot and produces a highly controllable refractive index profile on the inside of the tube. When sufficient material has been built up the burners are moved to one end of the tube, the tube is evacuated and the heat turned up (to around 1800°C). This causes the sides of the tube to collapse on themselves as the burners travel slowly along it.

The big advantages of MCVD are:

1. The gaseous reaction does not produce water so the problem of OH contamination is significantly reduced.

2. You can control the RI profile very accurately.

3. Compared to other processes it is relatively fast (albeit it is still a batch process).

4. If you aren't very careful when using Ge as the core dopant you can get a dip in the refractive index profile along the axis of the fibre. This is caused by the Ge evaporating off at the high temperatures needed to collapse the tube. This RI profile dip is not much of a problem in SM fibres but in some contexts with GI

MM fibre it can be a significant problem. This is discussed further in 7.6.2.1, "Use of Lasers on MM Fibre" on page 424.

6.1.4.4 Plasma-Activated Chemical Vapour Deposition (PCVD)

The PCVD process is very similar in principle to the MCVD process. Instead of heating the outside of the silica tube the energy source is provided by a high power microwave field (the same principle as a microwave oven). The microwave field is provided through a magnetron cavity which surrounds the silica tube. This microwave field can be moved very quickly along the tube as it heats the gas plasma directly and doesn't have to heat up the silica tube itself. This means that you can traverse the tube thousands (instead of hundreds) of times depositing extremely thin layers at each pass. The result is much better control of the RI profile than you get with MCVD.

As it happens the tube is kept hot by another set of heaters but this is only at 1000°C rather than the 1600°C used in MCVD. Heating to create the gaseous reaction comes from the microwave field not from the tube. Silica is deposited on the inside of the tube uniformly without the need to rotate it.

The reaction is nearly 100% efficient and proceeds several times faster than MCVD. In addition the process can produce large preforms capable of producing a few hundred km of fibre.

6.2 Joining Fibres

The diameter of the core in an optical fiber is very small and any irregularity (such as a join) can result in significant loss of power. To get the maximum light transfer from the cut end of one fiber into another, both ends must be cut precisely square and polished flat. They must then be butted together so that there is minimal air (or water) between the butted ends and these ends must match up nearly exactly. In a practical situation outside the laboratory this is very difficult to do.

In the early days of optical data communication (1983), one industry standard specified an optical cable for use in the office environment which was step-index 100/140 μm in diameter. The 100 micron core is very wide and is certainly not the best size for communication. However, at the time it was the best specification for making joins in the field. (This specification is still supported by some systems - including FDDI.)

Joining fibres together is not a trivial task. Light travelling in a fibre is *not* "like" electricity travelling in a wire except in the most superficial way. Light travelling in a fibre is a guided wave and the fibre is a waveguide. Any imperfection or irregularity (such as a join) is a potential source of loss and of noise.

The problem (obvious as it is) is that the dimensions of a fibre are tiny and accuracy of alignment is critical.

A Cable Story

There is a very good story about two telco technicians called to repair a fibre cable in very bad weather. The cable contained over 100 SM fibres and had been accidentally cut.

The story goes that repairing the cable obviously was going to take a very long time (in excess of 12 hours) as each fibre join had to be individually made and tested. So the technicians hauled both the cable ends into their truck to make the repair sheltered away from the bad weather.

It wasn't until the repair was completed that they noticed. Instead of bringing both ends to be repaired into the truck from the back door (as usual) they had brought one end in through a window on one side of the truck and the other end through a window on the other side of the truck! The cable was now threaded through the truck! The telco concerned made the obvious choice - rather than re-cut and re-join the cable - they cut the top of the truck in half!

It's probably not true but it's a good story anyhow.

There are three general ways of joining fibres:

1. By fusion splicing (a type of weld)

2. Use of index matching epoxy glues

3. With mechanical connectors of different types

The common requirement of all three methods is that the cores must be aligned. However, we can't always line the cores up - we line the fibres themselves up. This is not the same. The core is *not always* in the centre of the fibre. The manufacturers try very hard but there is always a variation. Difference between the axis of the core and the axis of the cladding is expressed as the "concentricity" of the fibre. This means that unless you do something to align the cores whilst making the join, there is a random misalignment (and hence loss) imposed by the concentricity error. The major improvement in connector losses observed between the middle 1980's and the 1990's was due generally to better fibre manufacture as much as to better connectors and connection techniques.

6.2.1 Fusion Splicing

A fibre join is a type of weld. The fibre ends are cut, polished, butted up to one another and fused by heat. (Incidentally, with silica fibers you need quite a high temperature - much higher than the melting point of ordinary soda glass.) In practice, a light loss of only .1 dB is the current budget for power loss in a single-mode fiber join. But it should be realised that .1 dB is quite a lot in that it represents the total loss of one half of a kilometer of cable.

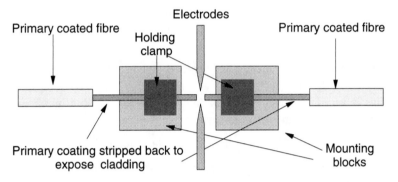

Figure 232. *Fusion Splicing Schematic*

A device setup for fusion splicing is illustrated in Figure 232.

1. Each fibre is stripped of its primary coating and the end cleaved such that it is square.

2. The fibre ends are positioned a few mm from one another and clamped to positioning blocks. There is often a groove provided in the mounting block to aid in correct alignment.

3. The fibre ends are then aligned with one another and brought closer together.

4. When alignment is satisfactory an electric arc is started between the two electrodes and the fibres brought into contact. Heat from the arc melts the glass and the join is made.

There are two major issues here - alignment of the fibre and precise control of the heating arc.

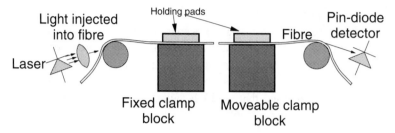

Figure 233. Fibre Alignment Using Optical Feedback

Fibre Alignment

When fibre ends are melted and touched together there are significant effects caused by the surface tension that tend to align the outside of the cladding. This is very convenient when joining multimode fibres but in the case of SM it can cause a number of problems.

A common method of fibre alignment is illustrated in Figure 233.

- The primary coating is stripped from the fibre for several cm from the end.

- When it is mounted in the fusion splicer the fibre is bent tightly around two mandrels (one at each end).

- Light from a laser (or LED) is focused onto a spot on the fibre bend such that some of it enters the core in a guided mode.

- At the other side of the splicer there is an optical detector positioned to capture light radiated from the tight bend.

- One end of the fibre is moved (by moving the mounting block with a piezo-electric actuator) until the output of the detector is at a maximum.

This method works reasonably well but with SM fibres the surface tension effect can change the position as the join is made! Another problem is the fact that the primary coating has to be removed for a long distance either side of the join. This makes the join hard to protect from later damage.

Many current automatic fusion splicers use a visual method of positioning. The fibre ends are examined (magnified) through a digital imaging process. Initially, this is displayed on a screen on the splicer so the operator can check easily for faults in the fibre endfaces. You can clearly see the fibre endface and even the cores this way. Once the operator is satisfied that the ends look okay, a microcomputer in the splicer examines the images of the fibre ends and aligns them automatically.

This method works remarkably well and can produce very low-loss splices. A big advantage is that you don't need to strip the fibre back more than a few cm from the splice.

Control of Heating

Precisely how the fibre is melted and joined is a very important issue. To make a good mechanical join you should melt each fibre end completely and allow for intimate mixing of the glass from the two fibres. However, a join that does this is likely to have a strong perturbation of the refractive index and hence high loss.

If you heat only a very thin layer on the endface of each fibre you get the best optical properties but the mechanical characteristics of the join are not good.

Once the splice is made it must be protected. This is usually done by covering it with a sleeve of heat-shrink material and then applying gentle heat. The material contracts around the fibre and protects the splice. A metal strengthening pin is often integrated into the side of the wrapping to provide additional mechanical strength.

6.2.1.1 Cleaving the Fibre

Before a splice of any kind is made or a connector fitted it is of critical importance that the fibre ends be cut square. (Except for the unusual case where we are making a diagonal splice.) In the case of connectors the ends are often polished to a desired shape later but we need to start off with square cut fibre ends.

The established technique for ensuring a good square fibre end is called "cleaving". This is just the same technique we use when cutting glass to replace a broken window.

1. A scratch or nick is made in the side of the fibre. This destroys the local surface tension and gives the glass a point from which to crack.

2. A stress is applied to the fibre so that it will crack across its diameter. You can apply this stress in many ways. An older technique called for the fibre to be bent around a rod. Unfortunately this had a habit of creating a "lip" on the side of the fibre opposite to the nick.

   In todays world you use a little machine which delivers a short sharp blow to the fibre in exactly the right place. Usually a good square cleave is obtained.

6.2.2 Mechanical Splicing

In this technique the fibre ends are cleaved and polished, aligned with one another and the gap between filled with an epoxy resin which has the same RI as the fibre core.

There are various ways of aligning the fibre ends but we consider the splice to be "mechanical" if the outside of the fibre cladding is aligned without reference to alignment of the cores. There are many ways of aligning the outside of the fibres:

- One common method here is to use a glass tube into which each end of the fibre is pushed. A small amount of the epoxy resin is placed on the end of one of the fibres before insertion. Usually there is a small hole in the tube at the point of the join so that excess epoxy can escape.

- There are many other methods of obtaining mechanical alignment of the outside of the fibres. V-groves, slots and alignment rods are all used. In addition heat-shrink elastomer tubes are also used sometimes.

This splicing technique is the lowest cost but it is also not very good. The quality of the join depends on:

1. The concentricity of the fibre

2. The accuracy of the outside diameter of the fibre

3. The circularity of the outside of the fibre

4. The tolerances and precision of the alignment device used

However, this makes a solid, permanent connection and is used for fibre-to-fibre joins in many situations.

In similar techniques epoxy glues are often used for pigtailing microoptic devices (like circulators). There is a wide range of epoxies available which will meet most requirements. In a recent experimental situation a suitable special purpose epoxy could not be found. However, a dental (uv cured) epoxy was available (made for filling teeth) which had almost exactly the needed RI and a very low coefficient of expansion (you don't want your fillings falling out!).

However, there is significant doubt about the long term stability of epoxy resins. Resins (might) break down and cause scattering over time. We don't know. Recently there has been a major shift in the industry *away* from the use of epoxy resins for just this reason.

6.2.3 Mechanical Splicing with Alignment and Bonding

This process is very similar to straight mechanical splicing but the fibres are actively positioned in the same way as with fusion splicing. The cleaved fibres are inserted into silica sleeves and bonded in place. The sleeve ends with the fibres exposed are then polished to get a very accurate surface. After this the sleeves are actively aligned so that the maximum optical power is transferred. They are then bonded with epoxy and covered with another protective sleeve.

In reality, the role of the inner sleeves is simply to provide rigidity and bulk to the fibre to make handling and positioning easier and gluing of the endfaces mechanically strong.

This technique provides very high-quality splices but it is very time consuming (and hence costly) to perform.

6.2.4 Losses in Fibre Joins

Losses in fibre joins are commonly classified into two kinds:

1. Extrinsic losses are those caused by factors concerned in joining the fibre but are unrelated to the properties of the fibre itself.

2. Intrinsic losses are losses caused by some property inherent in the construction of the fibre.

6.2.4.1 Extrinsic Losses

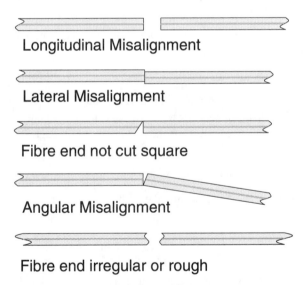

Figure 234. Sources of Loss due to Misalignment in Fibre Joins. Because of the fact that these losses are caused by factors external to the fibre itself they are called "Extrinsic" losses.

As shown in Figure 234 above there are many ways to make a bad fibre join. This applies whether a fused join is to be made or a connector is to be used. Losses and reflections for the different types of mismatches vary but all are to be avoided.

Longitudinal Misalignment

Longitudinal misalignment (or endface separation) has two loss effects. The first is just loss of signal power caused by the fact that light exiting one fibre endface diffuses outwards and (depending on the amount of separation) some of it will not be within the NA of the other fibre and hence cannot enter it in a guided mode. The second effect is that the separated endfaces themselves constitute a Fabry-Perot interferometer. Depending on the wavelength and the exact distance between the endfaces the attenuation can vary between zero and 100%.

Lateral Misalignment

Lateral misalignment is a major potential source of signal loss in all fibres but especially in single-mode fibres. A lateral displacement of one micron in an otherwise perfect join will result in a loss of .2 dB of signal. A displacement of 2.5 microns results in a loss of just more than 1 dB!

Fibre End Not Cut Square

If the fibre end is not cut square then you can't mate the two surfaces closely together.

Angular Misalignment

This problem is worst in single-mode fibres due to the very small mode field and the low RI contrast (low NA). A misalignment of only 1 degree produces a loss of .2 dB. A misalignment of 2 degrees causes a loss of around 1 dB!

Fibre End Irregular or Rough

Rough ends on the fibre scatter the light and prevent close contact between the fibre ends.

Most of the above comments apply to losses when connectors are used rather than when a fused join is made. In the case of a fused join, most of the above faults create a constriction in the fibre itself and a random perturbation of the RI. Losses in this context are hard to predict quantitatively but can be very large.

6.2.4.2 Intrinsic Losses

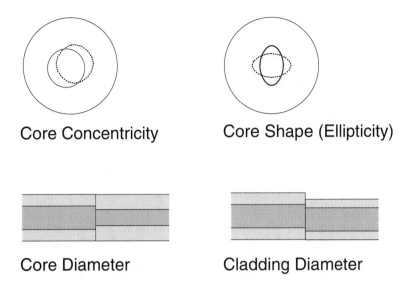

Core Concentricity   Core Shape (Ellipticity)

Core Diameter   Cladding Diameter

Figure 235. Sources of Intrinsic Loss in Fibre Joins

Losses that are caused by factors involving the fibre itself are called "intrinsic losses". The major ones are summarised below:

Concentricity Error

> As mentioned earlier, one of the major causes of loss in fibre joins is concentricity error in the fibre. Concentricity error comes about when the axis of the core and that of the total fibre itself are not exactly aligned. That is, the core is not exactly centred in the fibre. Even assuming that the fibres are lined up *exactly* on the outside, concentricity error will cause the cores to be misaligned.

> Concentricity error is a problem for both SM and MM fibre but it is a significantly greater problem in SM fibres. However, vast improvements in fibre manufacture have been made and major fibre manufacturers have recently (1997) announced big improvements in this area.

Core Shape (Ellipticity)

> No matter how precise the manufacture the core will always exhibit a (hopefully very slight) ellipticity. When a fibre is cut and re-joined the orientation of the core will usually not be the same and some light will be lost. This is not a big problem with MM fibre. With SM fibre, any ellipticity causes the fibre to be birefringent. That is, the fibre will exhibit different RIs

to orthogonal polarisations of light travelling through it. A join in this case can be a source of birefringent noise (see 2.4.2.1, "Polarisation Mode Dispersion (PMD)" on page 77).

Core Diameter

In MM fibre light is obviously lost (some modes escape into the cladding) when a core of a larger diameter is joined to one of a smaller diameter. This happens in the natural situation of every join where the diameter of the fibre core cannot ever be exact. There is always a difference however slight. Note that if the fibres are aligned correctly the loss will occur only when light passes from the larger diameter fibre to the smaller diameter one. Light travelling in the other direction (from smaller to larger) is *not* lost.

In the situation where two fibres of different specifications (with different diameters) are being joined with a connector, then a lot of light is usually lost. This is a common situation, where fibres with a 62.5 μm core can be connected to fibres with a 50 μm core. This happens often because most available data communications equipment is pigtailed using 62.5 micron MM fibre. Some users have installed 50 micron MM cabling and so a mismatch is inevitable. Loss of light in this situation (about 3 dB) is unavoidable. Again, this happens only in the direction where light travels from the larger diameter core to the smaller one.

Mode Field Diameter

In SM fibres the actual core diameter is not very relevant in considering joins. The diameter of the "Mode Field" (generally larger than the core diameter) is the important parameter.

Cladding Diameter

When fibres are joined we line the fibres up with each other using the outside of the fibre (you can't see the core). This means that at some point on the outside of the cladding both fibres must align with each other. If the outside diameters of these claddings are different from one another then the cores cannot be aligned.

Numerical Aperture

When MM fibres of different NAs are joined some modes that were possible in the fibre of higher NA cannot travel in the fibre of lower NA. These will enter the cladding and ultimately be lost. Thus some optical power will be lost. Loss from this source will occur in only one direction (from the *higher* NA fibre to the lower NA one). Light travelling in the opposite direction will be retained.

There is another source of loss and noise here. Fibres with different NAs usually have different RIs in the core or the cladding or both. When you join fibres of different RIs the RI changes at the join. The join then becomes a partial mirror and some light will be reflected back down the fibre. This can cause noise (as well as loss) due to the phenomenon of "Return Loss Variation". This is described in 2.4.4, "Reflections and Return Loss Variation" on page 85.

Refractive Index Profile

Differences in RI profile in the joined fibres can cause the same effects as described above for numerical aperture.

6.2.5 Connectors

In many situations it is highly desirable to be able to change configurations easily. This means that we want to plug a cable into a wall socket and to conveniently join sections of cable. Many different types of connectors are available to do just this. They hold the fibre ends in exact position and butt them together under soft pressure to obtain a good connection. But this all depends on the precision to which connectors can be machined. Most mechanical devices are machined to a tolerance of around one millimetre. Fibre tolerances are around one micron. This means that connectors have to be between 100 and 1000 times more accurately machined than most mechanical "things". Thus, connectors are difficult to manufacture and hard to fit. This all results in a relatively high cost.

Today's connectors are very efficient with typical "off-the-shelf" connectors measuring losses of around .2 dB. However, most manufacturers still suggest planning for a loss of 1 dB per connector.

Connectors are *rarely* fitted in the field. The cost of the equipment needed to fit most current connectors is over US $100,000 and the process is difficult to perform in the field. Thus either you purchase cables with connectors already fitted (the best approach) or you buy connectors already fitted to a short length of cable. In the latter case you splice the pigtail coming from the supplied connector to your cable in order to fit the connector.

There are some types of connector available that are advertised as being easy to fit in the field but these are not the common types used on standard equipment.

The alternative of purchasing a cable with connectors already fitted is a very good one. Connector manufacturers make protective sockets into which the cable connectors can be inserted and locked. These protective sockets have a fitting to allow then to be pulled through a cable duct whilst protecting the fibre cable. Of course cable is purchased in standard lengths but this isn't too much of a problem as excess can be coiled under the floor and gives flexibility when the need arises to move the termination point.

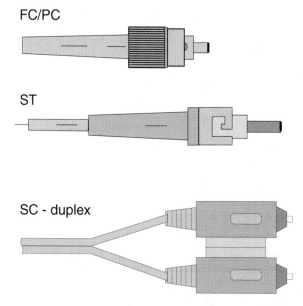

FC/PC

ST

SC - duplex

Figure 236. *Some Typical Connector Types. Most connectors are available in simplex or duplex configurations as shown here.*

There are many different types of connector reflecting development history and country of origin. Connectors for MM and SM fibres are generally different but the most popular connectors come in versions for either type.

In today's world the SC connector is fast becoming the de facto standard. It is interesting that there are SC connector plugs but *not* (in general) SC sockets! The connectors are built to be inserted into a sleeve which accepts one connector at either end. Thus two plugs are connected together with a sleeve. This significantly increases the versatility of the system. Of course sockets are used for direct mounting onto a piece of equipment but in general they are not used on the end of cables. One valuable feature of the SC connector is that the plug comes with a plastic cover over the fibre end. This cover is pushed aside as the plug is inserted into the connecting sleeve or socket. This helps protect the cable end when it is not connected and also it is an excellent aid to eye safety.

Many communications standards specify which optical connector should be used with a particular system.

Table 2. *Connector Characteristics*

Connector Type	Insertion Loss (MM) Typical	Insertion Loss (SM) Typical	Return Loss Typical
ST	0.25 dB	0.2 dB	40 dB
SC	0.25 dB	0.2 dB	40 dB
SMA	1.5 dB		
FSD	0.6 dB		
FC	0.25 dB	0.2 dB	40 dB
D4	0.25 dB	0.2 dB	35 dB
DIN	0.25 dB	0.2 dB	40 dB
Biconic	0.6 dB	0.3 dB	30 dB

Table 2 shows the important characteristics of a selection of connectors.

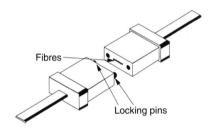

Figure 237. *MT Connector*

The MT connector joins multiple fibres in a flat cable. In the illustrated case there are eight fibres. The connectors plug together and then are inserted into a holding clip which applies pressure to hold the two connectors together.

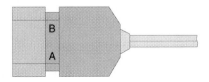

Figure 238. *ESCON Fibre Connector*

Figure 238 illustrates yet another style of optical connector. This was designed for use in computer room environments with multimode fibre. Thus it is somewhat more rugged than other types.

6.3 Fibre Cables

As we have seen, fibres themselves are generally 125 μm in external diameter (very small indeed). While they are very strong under tension (stronger than steel in fact) they break very easily when subject to lateral pressure or any kind of rough handling. To make practical use of fibre for communication the fibre needs to be enclosed in a cable.

Fibre cables vary widely in their characteristics due to the differing environments in which they are installed and requirements they must fulfill. Fibre cables are made to suit the application they are to perform and there are hundreds, perhaps thousands of types. Indeed, if you want to construct an outdoor fibre cable link for a few hundred kilometers you can go to the cable manufacturers and specify anything you want. All details of cable construction are negotiable.

The objective of the cable is to protect the installed fibre from anything that may damage it:

Tensile Stress

> While fibre itself is quite strong under tension, stress causes a significant increase in attenuation and a number of other undesirable effects. We need to protect the fibre from any kind of stress.

Bends

> Bends in the fibre that are too small in radius cause signal loss. Microbends in the fibre caused by crimping of the cable also cause signal loss. One function of the cable is to prevent the fibre being bent to a radius where loss may occur.

> With long distance outdoor or undersea cables this is not a big problem. Such cables often have a minimum bend radius of a few feet!

Physical Damage from Environmental Conditions

> Just what is needed to protect the cable varies with the particular environment. In many indoor environments vermin (rats, etc.) chew cable (they usually find electrical cable unpleasant but fibre is less so). In outdoor ones, gophers and termites also like eating cable. Heavy earth-moving equipment also has very little respect for cable integrity.

One major hazard for outdoor cables is cable-laying machines. In many countries cables are laid along defined cable "rights-of-way". When someone comes to lay a new cable along a route where there are already other cables, the existing ones tend to get cut.

Damage in the Cable Installation Process

Cable doesn't just have to operate satisfactorily in its installed environment but it must withstand the stresses of being installed. In some cases these stresses can be quite severe, for example, being lifted up the core of a multi-story building or dragged through a long conduit.

Water

It sounds illogical, but waterproofing is often more important in the fibre optical environment than it is in the electrical world! Glass immersed in water gradually picks up hydroxyl ions. As mentioned earlier, the presence of hydroxyl ions greatly increases the absorption of light. In addition, the presence of water causes micro-cracking in the glass and this causes the scattering of light. The micro-cracks also weaken the fibre significantly. Water is the worst enemy of an optical fibre system.

Lightning Protection

Lightning is a problem for all outdoor cables containing conductive materials. This, of course, depends on which part of the world you happen to be in. In some places lighting can hit the ground and sever an underground telecommunications cable *up to 10 metres away*!

In addition there are other functions that need to be supported in some environments. For example in some cable situations (especially undersea) it is necessary to provide power for repeaters or amplifiers along a long-distance cable route. One example of this is in submarine cables. Electrical power cabling is often included to deliver power to the repeaters.

6.3.1.1 Cabling Environments

There are many different environments in which we wish to install fibre cable. Cables are specially designed for each environment:

Outdoor Buried Cable (Long Distance)

Typical outdoor buried cables contain a large number of single-mode fibres (up to 100). They contain very extensive waterproofing, strength members and often armouring.

Outdoor Buried Cable (Campus Area)

These are typically lighter than the long distance variety and contain both multimode and single-mode fibres. These usually have good waterproofing and protection but it is often not as strong as long distance varieties.

In some places cable is installed in a conduit such as a 2-inch diameter steel pipe. In this case you don't need strong armouring.

Outdoor Overhead Cable

Cable intended for overhead use needs to have very great tensile strength to prevent the fibres being stressed. Typically they have a separate support member which takes the stress outside of the cable itself.

Outdoor Overhead (High-Voltage Earthwire) Cable

One very popular and creative place to put optical fibre is *inside* the earth wire of a high voltage electrical transmission system. A common system of this kind might operate at 132,000 volts. The earth wire is usually the top wire on the tower (relatively safe from vandalism). You always have to have a name and an acronym. These cables are called "Optical Ground Wire" (OPGW) cables.

Undersea Cable

The undersea environment is the most difficult cabling environment imaginable. Keeping high pressure salt water out of the cable poses a very significant challenge. In contrast to the large numbers of fibres in terrestrial long distance cables there are usually only a small number (6-20) of fibres in an undersea cable. Undersea cables also often carry electric wires to provide power to regenerators (repeaters or amplifiers) in the cable.

Indoor Cabling

Typically indoor cables have a very small number of fibres (most often only two) and these are generally multimode. In the indoor office environment there is less need for waterproofing or armouring than in the outdoor environment. However, you do need some protection from vermin (such as rats) and from accidental damage both during and after installation. In addition, it is often desirable to make the cable from materials that don't give off toxic fumes when they burn. This costs more but may save lives in the case of a fire.

Indoor cables are typically short distance (up to 300 metres or so) and need to be relatively light and flexible for installation in the office environment. They are usually terminated with pluggable connectors.

Jumper Leads and Fly Cables

One of the harshest environments for a fibre cable is as an end-system connector in the office. These often tend to run across the surface of a floor. They get stepped on and desks and chairs occasionally run their wheels over them. These are the best ways known to science of breaking a fibre.

6.3.1.2 The First Stage - Coating the Fibre

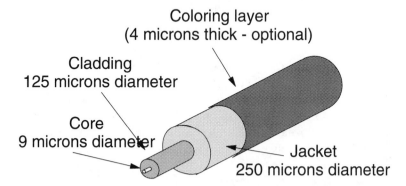

Figure 239. Primary Coated Optical Fibre (PCOF)

The basic form of optical fibre is called "primary coated optical fibre" or PCOF. This is the fibre as it emerges from the drawing tower. You have the core and cladding of course surrounded by a protective plastic jacket. In this form the overall diameter is 250 microns. In many applications (such as in "loose-tube" cables) there is a need to identify the fibre within its cable. To allow this, either the jacket itself is coloured or there is a further very thin coloured coating added immediately prior to building the cable. Since there are no standards for colour coding, cable makers tend to prefer to colour the fibre at cabling time to allow for flexibility in satisfying customer specifications.

In end-user environments PCOF is never used without further encasement in a cable. However, in many optical research and development laboratories it is common to see PCOF running around the laboratory attached to walls and ceilings with sticky tape. This is *not recommended* in normal office environments!

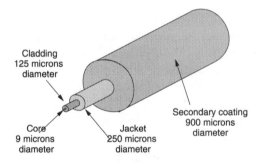

Figure 240. Secondary Coated Optical Fibre (SCOF)

For cabling within office environments, PCOF is usually further coated with a secondary coating as shown in Figure 240. This is called "Secondary Coated Optical Fibre" (SCOF). The secondary coating forms a tight bond with the primary coating so that when you want to strip the fibre to make a join you have to deal with a coating that is 900 microns in diameter. Other levels of cladding within the cable will peel away from the SCOF relatively easily.

6.3.1.3 Basic Cable Construction

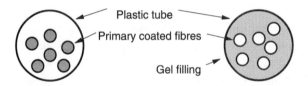

Figure 241. Loose Tube Construction

Cables can be classified into three types depending on how the fibre is encased within them:

Tight Buffered Construction

Tight buffering is where the secondary coated fibre (SCOF) is encased firmly in surrounding material as shown in Figure 240. This is similar to electrical cabling. Construction of this type is usually used for indoor applications where the number of fibres needed in the cable is low and distances are relatively short. However, it is also used for medium distance outdoor applications such as around a campus.

Loose Tube Construction

In loose tube construction a small number of PCOF fibres are carried inside a plastic (PVC) tube of 4-6 mm in diameter. Typically between one and eight primary coated fibres are carried in a single tube. There is plenty of room in the tube for the fibres to move loosely within it.

The idea is that you use somewhat more fibre than cable (5%-10%) in each tube. Fibre coils around inside the tube in a helical pattern. If the cable is stretched or bent then the fibres inside do not experience tension.

Loose Tube with Gel Filler

In most buried outdoor cable today we use a loose tube construction where the tube is filled with a jelly. This prevents the ingress of water from faults in the cable. It also buffers the fibres from one another and helps to prevent losses due to microbends caused by irregularities on the surface of the insides of the tubes.

The composition of the gel used is a significant design issue. Historically, petroleum jelly was used but this exhibits significant changes in viscosity with temperature. Viscosity is very important for a number of reasons:

- The fibre must be free to move within the tube to counter stress caused by temperature changes and/or cable laying.

- The viscosity needs to be high enough to provide some mechanical stability to the tube. And it should allow the cable to be run vertically without the gel settling down to the bottom.

- It needs to be reasonably well-behaved in the field when a cable has been severed and needs to be re-joined. For example, if the gel became very mobile on a hot day and the cable was severed, the gel could run out of the tubes for a long distance.

- Of course the gel needs to be stable during the process of cable manufacture where it may be subject to high temperatures.

Silicone gels are a lot better generally than petroleum ones but today specially designed synthetic gels are used which all but eliminate the early problems with changes in viscosity.

6.3.1.4 Indoor Cables

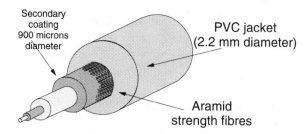

Figure 242. *Single-Core Cable*

The most basic form of indoor optical cable is shown in Figure 242. This is simply a single strand of SCOF with a layer of strengthening aramid (or fibreglass) fibres and an outer PVC jacket added. Single-core cable of this nature is used in short lengths as jumper or fly cables but is almost never used for fixed cabling. This is because it is lower in cost to have a cable with many fibres in it than it is to have many single-core cables. In any case you almost always need two cores anyway.

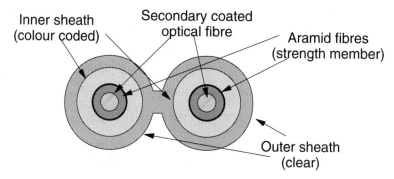

Figure 243. *Dual Indoor Cable*

The construction shown in Figure 243 is a very common low cost indoor cable construction. Two basic single-core cables are carried together in a common "figure-8" sheath.

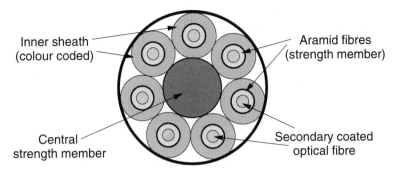

Inner sheath
(colour coded)

Aramid fibres
(strength member)

Central
strength member

Secondary coated
optical fibre

Figure 244. *6-Core Tight Buffered Indoor Cable*

Figure 244 shows the cross-section of a typical heavy-duty, tight buffered indoor cable. Such a cable might be installed vertically in a building riser connecting many floors. Many simple single-cored cables are encased in a common sheath. The central strength member (in this case plastic) supports the weight of the total cable. Tight buffering ensures that individual fibres are not put under tension due to their own weight.

Cables of this kind commonly come with up to 12 fibres each of which is individually sheathed and coloured.

6.3.1.5 Air Blown Fibre (ABF)

In a "blown" fibre installation instead of installing fibre cables you install narrow plastic tubes or conduits. Later, very lightly clad fibre bundles are installed into the tubes (blown in) using a system of compressed air (or compressed nitrogen).

There are various blown fibre systems available but one of the popular ones allows bundles of between 2 and 18 fibre strands (either SM or MM) to be inserted into the already installed tubes. This can be achieved for distances of up to about two kilometers (or about 6000 feet).

The fibre bundles blown into the tube conduits are really very lightweight cables specifically designed for their aerodynamics. In the installation process the fibre floats within the tube and there is very little contact between the bundle and the tube. The installation process is quite fast with drawing speed approaching 50 metres per minute.

The idea of blown fibre originated in the 1980's as a potential solution to the fact that fibre specifications were rapidly changing and people didn't want the expense of installing fibre cable knowing that they would want to replace it in the near future. In today's world, fibre specifications have stabilised significantly and there is less emphasis on the potential need for change later. However, there are some very important advantages in the blown fibre technique.

1. When you install the tubes you can install them in sections as convenient and join them together later. Typical tubes can be joined using very simple "push-fit" connectors within specially designed junction boxes. In some office environments it is very difficult to install a long, unbroken fibre cable. In this situation installation of the conduit tube in sections can save substantial cost.

   When the fibre is "blown in" each single strand is unbroken from end-to-end. Thus you don't have the problem (and cost) of joining the fibre. In addition, because the fibre is installed in long, unbroken lengths you don't get losses or reflection problems from the joins.

   This point is particularly important in the case where some parts of the fibre connection are indoor and other parts outdoor. Once the conduits are connected between the indoor and outdoor sections, the fibre is blown in as a single unbroken cable eliminating the need for making fibre joins (or having connectors) between indoor and outdoor sections.

2. You can install tubes with multiple cavities so that additional fibres can be installed later as the occasion demands. This saves some fibre cost but is more significant in the additional flexibility provided.

3. It is possible to remove fibre from the tubes and re-install it into other tubes on other routes as demands change. Since installing the tube (or regular fibre cable) is the major part of the installation cost, this allows for very low cost changes as the installation evolves.

4. The original reason for blown fibre while perhaps de-emphasised these days has not gone away. As mentioned in other parts of this book, there is a strong difference of opinion among fibre optical engineers on the future of multimode fibre. As speeds increase the bandwidth limitations of GI MM fibre become more and more restrictive. Single-mode fibre itself (just the fibre) is intrinsically lower in cost than multimode fibre but devices that connect to it are very much more expensive.

   It seems generally agreed in the industry that sometime we will have to change from MM fibre in the office to SM and when that happens those with blown fibre installations will be able to effect the change for very significantly lower cost than those with more conventional fibre cabling.

6.3.1.6 Outdoor Cables

A typical outdoor (buried) cable is shown in cross-section in Figure 245 on page 367 above. It consists of six gel-filled loose tubes supported by other cable elements designed to provide strength, mechanical protection and protection against the ingress of water. Note that in addition to the gel filling in the tubes carrying the fibres there is gel surrounding these tubes within the cable. The illustrated cable has six fibres per tube for a total fibre count of 36. This general cable geometry is used with up to twelve tubes supporting as many as eight fibres each for a total of 96 fibres in the cable. If an electrical power supply is needed, copper wires can replace the fibres in one or more of the tubes.

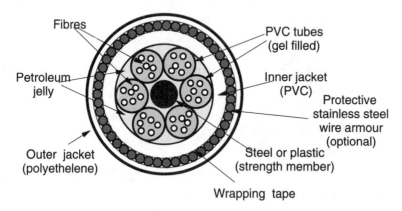

Figure 245. *Typical Outdoor Fiber Cable (Loose Tube - Gel Filled)*

The central strength member is often made from a hard plastic material rather than steel. Indeed the whole cable is often constructed from non-metallic materials. The outer layer of armouring wire is a customer option which is only added to cable destined for use in places where there is a significant danger of damage from the environment. The use of stainless steel is unusual (but optional) as this is a high-cost material. Ordinary steel is much lower in cost but will rust if the outer sheath is penetrated and water gets in. In some locations (such as tropical areas) it is customary to add an outer nylon covering to prevent attack by termites.

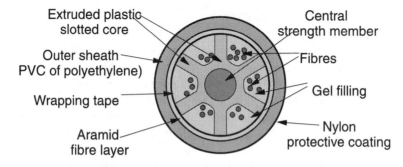

Figure 246. *Segmented-Core Cable Design*

An alternative loose tube construction is shown in Figure 246. Here the cable is formed from an extruded plastic member in the shape of a gear-wheel. Individual primary coated fibres are carried in the indentations (channels) around the outside. In the illustrated case there are six channels for fibres and up to eight fibres may be carried in each. In some geometries up to twenty or so channels are used with as few as one fibre per channel.

Outer elements of the cable are the same as for the regular loose-tube construction. This is a simpler and thus lower cost way of making the cable.

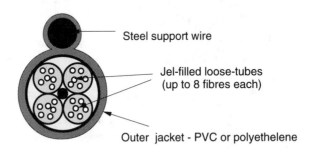

Figure 247. Outdoor Aerial Cable

Aerial cables are designed to be supported from towers and there is a significant problem with stress. One alternative is to have a very strong central strengthening wire. However, if you do this there is often a lot of crushing pressure on the cable at the points of support. The design shown in Figure 247 shows a typical cable designed for overhead installation. It is not very different from underground cable except it is enclosed in a common sheath with a strong separate support wire. The weight of the fibre cable is supported evenly all the way along its length and stresses are minimised.

Figure 248. 12-Core Optical Flat Cable

The basic construction shown in Figure 248 was used extensively in the US in the early 1980's for medium distance communication (up to 10 km or so) with multimode fibre. A flat cable containing 12 fibres is constructed by sandwiching the fibres between two layers of mylar tape with a glue (to hold the fibres in place) in-between. The flat cable is only about 5 mm in width. A stack of 12 of these flat cables forms a square cross-section which is then embedded within a strong protective cable structure.

The key to this construction was the use of a metallic connector which terminated all 12 fibres of one flat cable in one operation. While this worked reasonably well for multimode fibre it didn't have sufficient precision for single mode fibres and the system is no longer used.

6.3.1.7 Undersea Cables

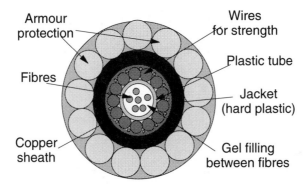

Figure 249. *Typical Undersea Cable Design*

Undersea cables are significantly different from other types of cable.

- They usually have a very small number of fibres (between perhaps 4 and 20). This contrasts with terrestrial cables which often have up to 100 fibres in them.

- At great depths water is under very high pressure and such cables have to prevent water ingress. For this reason all spaces in the cable are filled with very dense plastic or polymer material except for the cavity immediately around the fibres themselves. This is a gel-filled tube as in terrestrial cable construction. The copper sheath shown in the figure is an unbroken tube intended to help keep water out.

- In contrast to what we might expect, under the sea is not a completely safe place. Ship's anchors and fishing trawlers can do significant damage to undersea optical cables.

  Thus the undersea operators commonly make a distinction between "shallow" and "deep" water. Water is considered "deep" if the bottom is more than 1000 metres from the surface.

  Deep water is a relatively safe place to situate a cable and in this environment it is typically laid on the sea floor without special armouring. Thus cable operators plan the cable route to maximise the amount of cable laid in deep water.

  In shallow water it is common to dig a trench in the sea floor and bury the cable. Also, cables laid in shallow water are typically heavily armoured.

Part 2. Systems

Chapter 7. Optical Communication Systems

7.1 Point-to-Point Transmission Systems

7.1.1 Traditional Single-Channel Systems

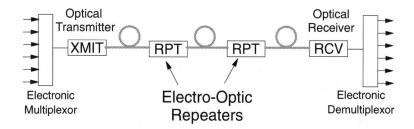

Figure 250. *Conventional Long Distance Fibre Transmission System. These systems typically use electronic repeaters which regenerate the signal at intervals of about 40-50 km. One direction of transmission only is shown.*

Figure 250 shows a typical 1980's long distance communication link structure. Its characteristics are as follows:

- A large number of electronic (digital) signals are combined using time division multiplexing (TDM) and presented to the optical transmission system as a single data stream.

- This single data stream is carried in an optical channel at speeds ranging from 155 Mbps to 1.2 Gbps.

- The wavelength used is almost always 1310 nm.

- Every 30-50 km the signal is received at a repeater station, converted to electronic form, re-clocked and re-transmitted. This completely re-generates the signal (a very small amount of jitter is added to the signal but this is generally not significant). This process removes all distortions caused by noise and signal dispersion etc.

- When such a system needs to be upgraded (to run at a higher speed for example) all of the equipment in the link must be replaced. This is because the repeaters are code and speed sensitive devices.

7.1.1.1 Repeaters

In the world of electronic communications the use of digital transmission revolutionised the technology because we were now able to send information as far as we liked *without* loss or distortion of any kind! This comes about because of the nature of the digital signal. The form of the signal is predetermined and predictable. Therefore we can regenerate it whenever needed and reconstitute it exactly it into its original form.[88] What we do is extract the digital information stream from the old signal and then build a new signal containing the original information. This function is performed by a *repeater*.

As it travels along a wire, any signal (electrical or optical) is changed (distorted) by the conditions it encounters along its path. It also becomes weaker (attenuated) over distance due to energy loss. In the electronic world this loss is caused by resistance, inductance and capacitance in the wire. In the optical world it is caused by absorption and scattering of light in the fibre. In addition the signal will be distorted in many ways and noise may be picked up along the way. After a certain distance the signal threatens to become so weak that we won't be able to receive it. Thus it becomes necessary to boost the signal.

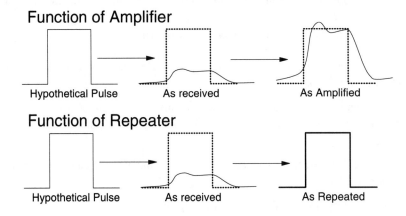

Figure 251. *Repeater Function Compared with Amplification*

The signal can be boosted by simply amplifying it. This makes the signal stronger, *but* (as is shown in Figure 251) it amplifies a distorted signal. As the signal progresses farther down the cable, it becomes more distorted. All the distortions add up and are included in the received signal at the other end of the cable. As will be

---

[88] Provided that the noise level present (signal to noise ratio) allows the signal to be recognised at all.

seen later, this is a severe problem in electronic communication, but much less of a problem in optical communication.

Analogue transmission systems must not allow the signal to become too weak anywhere along their path. This is because we need to keep a good ratio of the signal strength to noise on the circuit. Some noise sources such as crosstalk and impulse noise have the same real level regardless of the signal strength. So if we let the signal strength drop too much the effect of noise increases.

In the digital world things are different. A signal is received and (provided it can be understood at all) it is reconstructed in the repeater. A new signal is passed on (as is shown in the second example of Figure 251 on page 374) which is completely free from any distortion that was present when the signal was received at the repeater.

The result of this is that repeaters can be placed at intervals such that the signal is still understandable but can be considerably weaker than would be needed were the signal to be amplified. This means that repeaters can be spaced further apart than can amplifiers and also that the signal received at the far end of the cable is an exact copy of what was transmitted with no errors or distortion at all.

In the optical world, effects of noise are very much less than they were in the electronic world and optical signals can travel much farther than electrical ones before needing to be boosted. However, dispersion in optical communications meant that in early optical communications systems repeaters were used for signal regeneration instead of amplifiers. This was in part due to the fact that fully optical amplifiers were not yet available.

There is no such thing as a wholly optical repeater![89] Repeaters in optical links receive the signal into electrical form, re-clock and re-shape it, amplify it and re-transmit it. Thus in order to repeat an optical signal it must be converted to electronic form and processed electronically.

It should be noted that the process is both code and timing sensitive. The repeater must be designed to handle the transmission code and speed of the signal. If the signal is changed (for example a faster speed is needed) then the repeaters have to be replaced.

---

[89] YET! - watch this space.

7.1.2 Amplified Single-Channel Systems

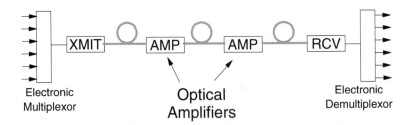

Figure 252. *Amplified Single-Channel Transmission System. These (newer) systems use optical amplifiers (EDFAs) with span lengths from 110 to 150 km. One direction of transmission only is shown.*

Figure 252 shows a newer (amplified) communications link structure.

- The wavelength used is now 1550 nm. This is done for two reasons:

  1. To exploit the low attenuation window of fibre in the 1500 nm "window"

  2. To allow the use of Erbium Doped Fibre Amplifiers (EDFAs)

- The distance between amplifiers is now increased to between 110 and 150 km. (On long distance links this is a very significant cost saving as the cost of maintaining repeater or amplifier "huts" along the route is very high.)

- The speed is generally increased to either 1.2 Gbps or 2.4 Gbps.

While the overall architecture of the system looks much the same as before there are three significant changes:

1. Since we are still using standard fibre which has a large amount of dispersion in the 1550 nm band we need to give some design consideration to the control of dispersion. In older systems, the fibre didn't disperse the signal by very much because we were using the 1310 nm band. The repeaters removed the small dispersion created anyway. Now, by moving to the 1550 nm band, we have brought on a dispersion problem. The amplifiers will cause dispersion to accumulate over the whole length of the link.

2. The link is now both modulation format and speed transparent. It may be upgraded to use higher speeds and the modulation format may be changed (for example from OOK to duobinary or ternary coding) *without* changing equipment in the field. You only have to change the equipment at each end!

3. Provided the link has been planned properly it can now be upgraded to use WDM technology again without change to the outside plant. Some foresight is needed here in planning the amplifier capacity (power) as the addition of WDM will demand significantly higher levels of power. However, it is possible to plan the link in such a way as to enable upgrading to WDM at a future time without change to outside equipment.

There are also a number of other considerations. Noise is not a big problem for optical systems generally as there are not many ways in which noise can enter the system. However, EDFAs do produce some spontaneous emission noise and this tends to get amplified along the way (it is called ASE for Amplified Spontaneous Emission). There are also transmission effects that result in noise being added to the signal and these need to be considered. However, these amplified systems are considered significantly better than the earlier repeatered systems for the following reasons:

- Amplifiers cost less than repeaters and require less maintenance.

- The use of an amplifier enables future upgrades and changes to take place with minimal impact (read cost) on the installed link.

- The use of the amplifier allows for future use of WDM technology with minimal change to the outside plant.

7.1.3 WDM Systems Overview

Figure 253 on page 378 shows a typical first generation long distance WDM configuration. Transmission is point-to-point. This is just logically the superposition of many single-channel systems onto a single fibre. It should be noted that each optical channel is completely independent of the other optical channels. It may run at its own rate (speed) and use its own encodings and protocols without any dependence on the other channels at all. All of the current systems use a range of wavelengths between 1540 nm and 1560 nm. There are two reasons for this: First to take advantage of the "low loss" transmission window in optical fibre and second to enable the use of erbium doped fibre amplifiers. Channel speeds for WAN applications are typically 2.4 Gbps in current operational WDM systems.

In the figure each channel is shown being electronically multiplexed and demultiplexed. In many systems this will be true. However, this is just for illustration purposes. There is no requirement for electronic TDM multiplexing. Each channel is just a clear bit stream with its own unique timing and each may be treated in whatever way is appropriate for its particular role.

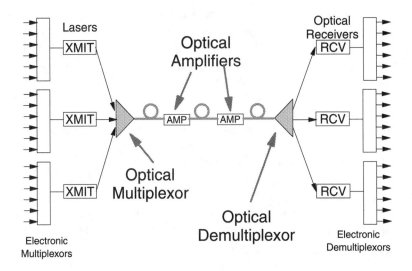

Figure 253. WDM Long Distance Fibre Transmission System. Only one direction of transmission is shown.

When the WDM link is designed it of course is restricted by the characteristics of the most restrictive channel. For example if one channel has a link budget of 15 dB and another of 25 dB then we have to design the WDM link to a budget of 15. System design for WDM is very complex and is discussed further in 9.4, "Systems Engineering in the WDM Environment" on page 547.

7.2 Modulation (Making the Light Carry a Signal)

In order to make light carry a signal, you have to introduce systematic variations (modulation) in the light to represent the signal. Then, when the light is received you must decode it in such a way as to reconstruct the original signal.

7.2.1 On-Off Keying (OOK)

Most current optical transmission systems encode the signal as a sequence of light pulses in a binary form. This is called "on-off keying" (OOK).

Sometimes this is described as amplitude modulation, comparing it to AM radio. In fact, the technique is nothing like AM radio. An AM radio carries an analogue signal. The amplitude of the carrier is continuously varied (modulated) in accordance with variations in the signal. The receiver recovers the signal from the variations of the carrier. But in an optical system, it is much more like a very simple form of digital baseband transmission in the electronic world. The signal is there or it isn't; beyond this the amplitude of the signal doesn't matter.

In fairness, you can call OOK a special case of amplitude shift keying (ASK) in which a number of discrete signal amplitude levels are used to carry a digital signal.

7.2.1.1 NRZ Coding

If the bit stream is to be sent as simply the presence or absence of light on the fibre (or as changes of voltage on a wire), then the simplest coding possible is NRZ. This is illustrated in Figure 254. Here a one bit is represented as the presence of light and a zero bit is represented as the absence of light.

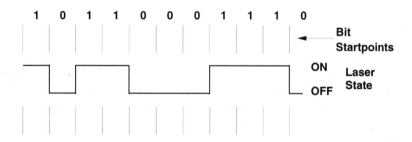

Figure 254. NRZ Coding

This method of coding is used for some very slow speed optical links but has been replaced by other methods for most purposes.

7.2.1.2 Receiving the Data

If a transmitter places a stream of bits on a wire using the NRZ coding technique, how can it be received? This is the core of the problem. Transmission is easy, but re-creating the original bit stream at a receiver can be quite difficult.

On the surface it looks simple. All the receiver has to do is look at its input stream at the middle of every bit time and the state of the voltage on the line will determine whether the bit is a zero or a one.

But there are two important problems:

1. There is no timing information presented to the receiver to say just where the middle of each bit is.

   The receiver must determine where a bit starts and then use its own oscillator (clock) to work out where to sample the input bit stream. But there is no economical way of ensuring that the receiver clock is running at exactly the same rate as the transmitter clock. That is, oscillators can be routinely manufactured to a tolerance of .005% but this is not close enough.

2. The signal will be changed (distorted) during its passage over the wire.

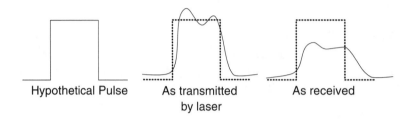

Hypothetical Pulse As transmitted by laser As received

Figure 255. Evolution of an Optical Pulse

The signal we want to send is a sharp "square wave" at the transmitter input. However, the transmitting laser cannot respond exactly and instantly to the signal and the transmitted signal will be much less than our ideal square wave. Particularly there will be some light transmitted during the "0" line state. This is caused by the fact that we want the laser to respond quickly to applied drive current and the laser response is improved significantly when it is biased just below operating threshold. (It is not exactly lasing but it is producing some spontaneous emissions.) During its travel over the fibre to the receiver the signal will be distorted in various ways and will be decidedly fuzzy when it gets to the receiver. The signal will no longer be just a clear presence or absence of light. Instead, the light intensity will change from one state to the other, "slowly" passing through every intermediate amplitude state on the way.

The receiver must now do two things:

1. Decide what line state is a zero and what state is a one.

   The receiver must decide that light amplitude above a certain level represents a one and below that level a zero is represented. This will be adequate in many situations, but this is by no means adequate in all situations, as will be seen later.

2. Decide where bits begin and end.

   As a zero bit changes to a one bit the optical signal amplitude will rise (perhaps quite slowly) from one state to the other. Where does one bit end and the next begin?

3. Decide where a new bit begins and an old one ends even if the line state does not change!

When one bit is the same as the one before then the receiver must decide when one bit has finished and another begun. Of course, in data, it is very common for long strings of ones and zeros to appear, so the receiver must be able to distinguish between bits even when the line state hasn't changed for many bit times.

With simple NRZ coding this is impossible, and something must be done to the bit string to ensure that long strings of zeros or ones can't occur.

A simple receiver might operate in the following way:

1. Sample the line at defined intervals faster than the known bit rate on the line (say seven times for every bit).

   When there is no data being sent, the line is usually kept in the one state.

2. When a state change is detected, this could be the start of a bit. Start a timer (usually a counter) to wait for half a bit time.

3. When the timer expires, look at the line. If it is the same as before then receive the bit. If not then the previous state change detected was noise - go back to 1 (looking for the start of a bit).

4. Set the timer for one full bit time.

5. Monitor the line for a change of state. If a change is detected before the timer expires, then go back to step 2.

6. When the timer expires, receive the bit.

7. Go to step 4.

In the jargon the above algorithm is called a "Digital Phase Locked Loop" (DPLL). Consider what's happening here:

- The receiver is using the change of state from one bit to another to define the beginning of a bit (and the end of the last).

- When there are no changes, the receiver's clock is used to decide where the bits are.

- Whenever there is a state change, the receiver re-aligns its notion of where the bits are.

Successful operation is clearly dependent on:

- How good the receiver is at deciding when a state change on the line has occurred. (Since this is often gradual voltage change rather than an abrupt one, this is a judgement call on the part of the receiver.)

- How accurate the receiver's clock is in relation to the transmitter's.

- How many times per bit the stream is sampled.

  Some practical electronic systems in the past have used as few as five samples per bit time.

  Today's systems, using a dedicated chip for each line, often sample the line at the full clock frequency of the chip. The more frequent the sampling, the more accurate will be the result.

The above technique (the DPLL) is very simple and can be implemented very economically in hardware. But it is also very rough.

Notice here that the bit stream has been recovered successfully but the exact timing of the received bit stream has not. This doesn't matter in the example since the objective was to transfer a stream of bits, not synchronise timing. Later however, there will be situations where accurate recovered timing is critical to system operation.

Frequent state transitions are needed within the bit stream for the algorithm to operate successfully. The maximum number of bits without a transition is determined by the quality of the transmission line and the complexity of the receiver. Typical values for the maximum length of strings of ones or zeros in practical systems are between 3 and 6 bits.

7.2.1.3 Non-Return to Zero Inverted (NRZI) Coding

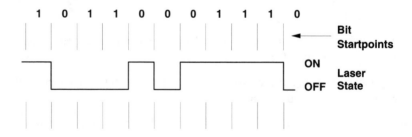

Figure 256. NRZI Encoding Example

In order to ensure enough transitions in the data for the receiver to operate stably, a coding called Non-Return to Zero Inverted (NRZI) is often used.

Most digital communication systems using fibre optics use NRZI encoding. This means that when you have a transition from light to no light or from no light to light, a "1" bit is signaled. When there are two successive pulses of light or two successive periods of dark then a zero bit is signaled. Thus, in NRZI coding, a zero bit is represented as a change of state on the line and a one bit as the absence of a change of state. This is illustrated in Figure 256.

This algorithm will obviously ensure that strings of zero bits do not cause a problem. But what of strings of one bits? Strings of one bits are normally prevented by insisting that the bit stream fed to the transmitter may not contain long strings of one bits. This can be achieved in many ways:

- By using a "higher layer" protocol that breaks up strings of one bits for its own purposes. The HDLC family of protocols for example inserts a zero bit unconditionally after every string of 5 consecutive ones (except for a delimiter or abort sequence).

- By using a code translation that represents (say) 4 data bits as 5 real bits. Code combinations which would result in insufficient numbers of transitions are not used. This is the system used in FDDI (see 8.1.5.2, "Data Encoding" on page 450) for example. Code conversion from 4-bit "nibbles" to 5-bit "symbols" is performed before NRZI conversion for fairly obvious reasons.

7.2.1.4 RZ Coding

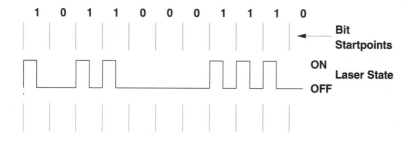

Figure 257. Return-To-Zero (RZ) Coding

In RZ coding the signal returns to the zero state every bit time. As illustrated a "1" bit is represented by a "ON" laser state for only *half* a bit time. Even in the "1" state the bit is "0" for half of the time.

In a restricted bandwidth environment (such as in most electronic communications) this is *not* a coding of choice. The reason is that there are two different line states required to represent a bit (at least for a "1" bit). This means that the communications channel has to be able to handle a much wider analogue "bandwidth" than would be used by other codings such as NRZ. In some environments bandwidth is not a major constraint, for example in the optical fibre environment or in the electronic environment using shielded cables. In this case a number of advantages may be obtained by using RZ or similar codings which use many line state changes (baud) per bit.

RZ coding is proposed as a basis for some Optical Time Division Multiplexing (OTDM) systems described in 12.5, "Optical Time Division Multiplexing (OTDM)" on page 663. This is because there is some time in each bit period to adjust for jitter when synchronising bit streams.

7.2.2 Multi-State Coding

Multi-state codes where a single line state represents multiple bits are normal in the electronic communications world. Some schemes use as many as 16 discrete line states (in this case each state would represent a unique 4-bit group). In electronic systems both signal amplitude and phase are used to create unique line states representing particular bit combinations. In the optical communications world we can't easily use the phase of the optical carrier signal[90] but we can use the signal amplitude.

The use of a multi-level code allows us to get more bits per second onto a connection where the maximum signal frequency is limited. This is the case in most electronic environments such as transmission on Unshielded Twisted Pair (UTP) wire. Past a particular point UTP exhibits an exponential increase in both attenuation and distortion as the signal frequency in increased.

In the optical communications world up to now we have not started to push the boundaries of optical fibre capacity and so far have not needed to resort to special codings. However, there are some problems with dispersion in relation to the maximum modulation frequency.

1. When very narrow linewidths are used (to minimise dispersion or to pack a lot of WDM channels close together) the bandwidth of the modulations becomes significant. Modulation adds twice the bandwidth of the maximum modulating frequency to the signal bandwidth. For example, a 10 GHz signal would add 20 GHz (.12 nm) to the signal bandwidth. If we can reduce the modulation bandwidth we can restrict the maximum signal bandwidth and therefore limit dispersion.

2. Dispersion affects a signal by a fixed amount in time. Therefore if you halve the symbol rate (in simple codes 1 bit = a symbol) you can have twice the amount of dispersion before you have a problem.

---

[90] We can use the phase of the modulations however.

3. Another related issue is that if you halve the symbol rate you just doubled the sensitivity of your receiver. Pin diodes and APDs require a certain amount of power per symbol so when you change the symbol rate you affect the receiver sensitivity.

This doesn't come completely without cost as the system now needs to send a signal at different amplitude levels and to detect these amplitude levels reliably at the receiver.

7.2.2.1 Basic Principle

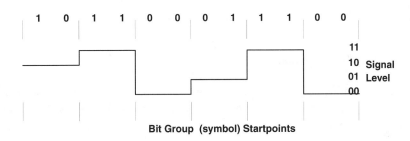

Figure 258. Four-Level Coding Example

Figure 258 illustrates the principle of multi-state coding. Each signaling period on the line (called a symbol or a baud) represents two bits. The frequency of changes on the line is halved compared to NRZ or NRZI coding. However, we now have to send four line states.

The problems here are:

1. To get the same power level difference between line states (and hence the same SNR) that we had in the NRZ case we need four times the signal power. Actually this isn't quite true as the sensitivity of the receiver is increased by 3 dB in the process because of the lowered symbol rate. In this case we probably only lose around 3 dB or so. Nevertheless this can be significant.

2. We need a reliable way of making a laser send 4 discrete signal levels and a receiver discriminate between the four levels. This increases the cost of the tranceivers.

7.2.2.2 Duo-Binary Coding

Duo-binary coding is the simplest of a large family of codes called "partial response" codes. Duo-binary is a three-level code which substantially reduces the bandwidth occupancy of a signal compared to coding with NRZ. To understand DB it is useful to regard a stream of NRZ bits sent to a line as a changing mixture of frequency components rather than a series of square pulses. DB shifts the signal power from high frequency components to low frequency ones.

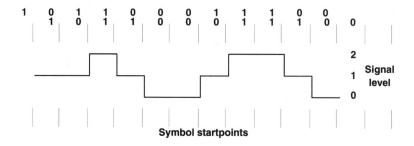

Figure 259. Duo-Binary Code Example

The operational principle is very simple. Every symbol is a combination of the current bit being sent and the previous bit sent. There are three signal levels (here numbered 0, 1 and 2). The rules when combining a bit with the previous one in the stream are:

1 + 1 = State 2
1 + 0 = State 1
0 + 1 = State 1
0 + 0 = State 0

An examination of Figure 259 shows that the number of transitions is significantly less than with NRZ. In this case the added signal power needed is compensated for by the added receiver sensitivity at the lower speed. One problem is that a single bit error can propagate for a long distance and create a multi-bit cluster of errors. A second concern is the bit string 0101010101 which results in an unchanging line signal. Both of these problems can be countered by pre-coding.

Duo-binary code is in use in some high-speed long distance systems because of its spectrum narrowing properties.

You can extend this principle to use longer strings of bits and in this case the system is called "polybinary".

7.2.3 Forward Error Correction (FEC)

Forward error correction is a method of correcting bits within a stream that have been misdetected. That is if a 1 is detected where a 0 was sent or a 0 detected where a 1 was sent.

FEC is a very common system in computer memories where each "word" of memory includes additional bits which are mathematically determined from the data bits. In a typical workstation computer 64 data bits are checked and corrected using 8 additional bits. In this case the algorithms will detect the great majority of multi-bit errors and correct all single-bit errors.

In the communications world FEC is somewhat more challenging than it is in computer memories. In a computer memory each word of data is a fixed length and usually each bit within the word is stored or retrieved using a dedicated separate wire. Thus you can't get words that are longer or shorter than the fixed length. The communications environment is very different. The loss of a bit or the addition of a bit are common error occurrences. FEC coding requires a fixed length block of data with which to work. Thus FEC doesn't easily handle the condition of loss or gain of bits.

To use FEC you have to organise data within fixed frames (a bit like you do in Sonet). Bits are then carried in groups within the frame. A group of bits is checked by a smaller group of additional bits carried at the end. This will usually provide both error detection and error correction.

Using FEC you can afford to have a lower SNR while maintaining a fixed error probability. A lowered SNR requirement means that you might space amplifiers at longer distances or use a faster signal. Of course there is added bandwidth taken up by the additional check bits and additional complexity in both the transmitter and receiver.

FEC is already in use in some undersea systems.

7.2.4 Receiving the Signal

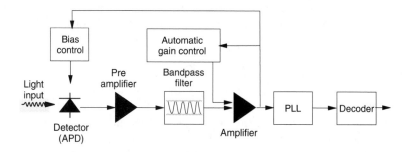

Figure 260. Digital Receiver Functions

The function of the receiver is to accept an optical signal and convert it into an electrical form suitable for use by an end-device. In the case of a digital receiver it must deliver a stream of bits (optionally including timing information) to the device.

The overall process is shown in Figure 260:

1. The incoming optical signal is converted to an electronic one using either a pin-diode or an Avalanche Photo-Detector (APD). These were discussed in Chapter 4, "Optical Detectors" on page 169.

2. The signal is then preamplified and passed through a bandpass filter. There are both low frequency (1000 Hz or so) and very high frequency components here that are not needed. These components both add to the noise and can cause malfunction of later stages in the process. They are best removed.

3. Further amplification with feedback control of the gain is used to provide stable signal levels for the rest of the process. This control circuit usually controls the bias current and thus the sensitivity of the photodiode as well.

4. A phase-locked loop (described in the next section) is then used to recover a bit stream and (optionally) the timing information.

5. At this stage the stream of bits needs to be decoded from the coding used on the line into its data format coding. This process varies depending on the encoding and is occasionally integrated with the PLL depending on the code in use. An example of typical coding used is discussed in 7.2.12, "Character Coding" on page 394.

The important issues for the receiver are:

Noise

Wherever there is gain in a system there is also noise. In the receiver we typically have a very low level input signal which requires a high gain and therefore we have the potential of high noise. Most of the noise in an unamplified optical link originates in the receiver.

Decision Point

The most important parameter of any digital receiver is the decision point. That is, the signal level at which we say that "all voltages below this will be interpreted as a 0 and all voltages above this will be interpreted as a 1".[91]

This is a critical parameter and must be determined dynamically. Some arriving signals might be at -30 dBm for a 1 bit and -50 dBm for a 0 bit. Other signals (for example if the link happens to be short) may be at -5 dBm for a 1 bit and -30 dBm for a 0 bit. In the first example the decision point would be perhaps around -35 dBm (just above the limit of receiver sensitivity). If you used the same decision point for the second signal all you would ever see is a string of "1111111".

This all depends on the extinction ratio of the transmitted signal. The extinction ratio is the ratio of the signal level of a 1 bit to the signal level of a 0 bit. This is illustrated in 7.8.4, "Eye Diagrams" on page 436.

Filtering

Filtering of the incoming signal was described above and is essential. There are a number of very low frequencies that get into the signal and there will be very high frequency harmonics that we don't need. Unwanted harmonics cause the PLL to detect false conditions (called "aliases").

7.2.5 Timing Recovery

There are many situations where a receiver needs to recover a very precise timing from the received bit stream *in addition* to just reconstructing the bit stream. This situation happens very frequently:

- In Sonet/SDH there is a critical requirement for stable timing as exact synchronisation between frames is needed to perform the TDM functions required in the architecture. See 8.6, "Synchronous Optical Network (SONET) and SDH" on page 484.

---

[91] Of course in optical communication we are dealing with optical power levels rather than voltages - but even in optical systems the decision is taken in electronic circuitry. Thus the discussion here refers to the voltage level at the output of the optical detector.

- In Primary rate ISDN a similar but a little less critical requirement exists.

- In token-ring, the all important ring delay characteristic is minimized by maintaining only minimal (two bits) buffering in each ring station. This requires that the outgoing bit stream from a station be precisely synchronized with the received bit stream (to avoid the need for elastic buffers in the ring station).

In order to recover precise timing not only must there be a good coding structure with many transitions, but the receiver must use a much more sophisticated device than a DPLL to recover the timing. This device is an (analogue) phase locked loop.

7.2.5.1 Phase Locked Loops (PLLs)

Earlier in this section (page 381) the concept of a simple "digital phase locked loop" was introduced. While DPLLs have a great advantage in simplicity and cost they suffer from three major deficiencies:

- Even at quite slow speeds they cannot recover a good enough quality clocking signal for most applications where timing recovery is important.

- As link speed is increased, they become less and less effective. This is due to the fact, alluded to earlier in this book, that circuit speeds have not increased in the same ratio as have communication speeds.

  A DPLL needs to sample the incoming bit stream many times per bit. With a link speed of 2,400 bits per second this isn't very difficult to do even by programming. But at multi-megabit speeds it becomes more and more costly and then (as speed becomes too great), impossible.

- As digital signals increase in speed (where speed begins to be limited by circuit characteristics), they start behaving more like waveforms and less like "square waves" and the simplistic DPLL technique becomes less appropriate.

What is needed is a continuous-time, analogue PLL that is illustrated in Figure 261.

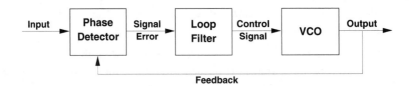

Figure 261. Operating Principle of a Continuous (Analogue) PLL

The concept is very simple. The VCO is a Voltage Controlled Oscillator and is the key to the operation.

- The VCO is designed to produce a clock frequency close to the frequency being received.

- Output of the VCO is fed to a comparison device (here called a phase detector) which matches the input signal to the VCO output.

- The phase detector produces a voltage output which represents the difference between the input signal and the output signal.

  (In principle, this device is a lot like the tuner on an AM radio.)

- The voltage output is then used to control (change) the frequency of the VCO.

Properly designed, the output signal will be very close indeed to the timing and phase of the input signal. There are two (almost conflicting) uses for the PLL output:

1. Recovering the bit stream (that is, providing the necessary timing to determine where one bit starts and another one ends).

2. Recovering the (average) timing (that is, providing a stable timing source at exactly the same rate as the timing of the input bit stream). In many link architectures the secondary device must recover the timing of the received data stream and use it to clock its transmitted stream.

Many bit streams have a nearly exact overall timing but have slight variations between the timings of individual bits.

The net of the above is that quite often we need two PLLs: one to recover the bit stream and the other to recover a precise clock.

7.2.5.2 Jitter

Jitter is the generic term given to the difference between the (notional) "correct" timing of a received bit and the timing as detected by the PLL. It is impossible for this timing to be exact because of the nature of the operation being performed. Some bits will be detected slightly early and others slightly late. This means that the detected timing will vary more or less randomly by a small amount either side of the correct timing - hence the name "jitter". It doesn't matter if all bits are detected early (or late) provided it is by the same amount - delay is not jitter. Jitter is a random variation in the timing either side of what is correct.

Jitter is minimized if both the received signal and the PLL are of high quality. But although you can minimise jitter, you can never quite get rid of it altogether.

Jitter can have many sources, such as distortion in the transmission channel or just the method of operation of a digital PLL. In an optical system the predominant cause of jitter is dispersion.

Sometimes these small differences do not make any kind of difference. In many systems it is sufficient that a correct bit-stream be recovered at the receiver regardless of the timing. In other cases jitter is critical. For example:

1. In the IBM Token-Ring LAN, jitter accumulates from one station to another around the ring and can ultimately result in the loss or corruption of data. It is jitter accumulation that restricts the maximum number of devices on a token-ring to 260.

2. TDM systems such as Sonet/SDH have very strict jitter specifications because of the need to synchronise many different timed data streams to one another. The whole operation of Sonet/SDH depends on exact timing.

7.2.6 Bandwidth Occupancy

There are many situations where we need to know the bandwidth of an optical signal.

- When transmitting on a MM fibre, fibre capacity is quoted as an analogue bandwidth measure, so to determine the maximum distance that can be used we need to know the amount of bandwidth that the signal occupies.

- On SM fibre a modulating signal broadens the spectral width (linewidth, bandwidth) of the carrier signal. In order to calculate effects of dispersion and plan countermeasures we need to know the spectral width of the signal.

- In WDM systems, as in single-channel systems, the modulating signal broadens spectral width. This is more important in WDM as typically we are more concerned with spectral width here. To know how much broadening we need to know the spectral width of the modulating signal.

This is not straight-forward. A square wave signal such as is produced by NRZ or NRZI coding has a fundamental frequency of *half* the bit rate. That is, a 1 Gbps digital signal has a fundamental frequency of 500 MHz. However, this is not the full story. The 500 MHz fundamental frequency is a simple sine wave. A square wave contains many higher frequency harmonics at 3, 5, 7... times (this is an infinite series) the fundamental. From a systems point of view the questions are:

1. Which harmonics are present in the modulating signal? Unnecessary ones can be filtered out electronically before modulation of the signal.

2. Which harmonics are needed at the receiver to recover an adequate signal? This varies from system to system. Two systems at the same bit rate and using the same coding can have very different requirements depending on the jitter requirements of each.

For simple NRZ coded systems we seem to need a minimum of at least twice the bit rate. In many systems we need a lot more (perhaps as much as six times the bit rate).

7.2.7 Analogue Amplitude Modulation (Continuous Wave)

Lasers have traditionally been very difficult to modulate using standard amplitude modulation. This is caused by the non-linear response typical of standard Fabry-Perot lasers. However, some DFB and DBR lasers have a reasonably linear response and can be modulated with an analogue waveform.

The major current use of this is in cable TV and HFC distribution systems. An analogue signal is prepared *exactly* as though it was to be put straight onto the coaxial cable. Instead of putting it straight onto the cable it is used to modulate a laser. At the receiver (often a simple PIN diode) the signal is amplified electronically and placed straight onto a section of coaxial cable. In standard (one-way) cable systems the maximum frequency present in the combined waveform is 500 MHz. In HFC systems this can increase up to 800 MHz or even 1 GHz.

This requires quite precise control of the laser as we have to operate just above the cutoff voltage (so the laser is always transmitting something). In addition, the response of most lasers is very steep with input power and they saturate relatively quickly. So there is a very narrow range over which we can operate. In practice this requires the use of very special DFB lasers which are optimised for analogue modulation. Nevertheless this is a standard, installed technology in cable TV systems.

7.2.8 Frequency Shift Keying (FSK)

It is difficult to modulate the frequency of a laser and this is one of the reasons that FM optical systems are not yet in general use. However, Distributed Bragg Reflector lasers are becoming commercially available. These can be frequency modulated by varying the bias current. For FSK (or any system using coherent detection) to work, the laser linewidth has to be considerably narrower than the signal bandwidth. The real problem in using FM is the need for coherent detection. Coherent detection systems are very complex and hard to build (see 12.8, "Coherent Detection" on page 674).

Coherent detection has a major potential advantage. The receiver "locks on" to the signal and is able to detect signals many times lower in amplitude than simple detectors can use. This translates to greater distances between repeaters and lower-cost systems. In addition, FSK promises much higher data rates than the pulse systems currently in use.

7.2.9 Phase Shift Keying (PSK)

You can't control the phase of a laser's output signal directly and so you can't get a laser to produce phase-modulated light. However, a signal can be modulated in phase by placing a modulation device in the lightpath between the laser and the fibre. Phase modulation has similar advantages to FSK. At this time PSK is being done in the laboratory but there are no available commercial devices. Again, PSK requires coherent detection and this is difficult and expensive.

7.2.10 Polarity Modulation (PolSK)

Lasers produce linearly polarized light. Coherent detectors are very strongly polarization sensitive (it is one of the big problems). Another modulation dimension can be achieved (potentially) by introducing polarization changes. Unfortunately, current fibre changes the polarization of light during transit - but there are techniques to overcome this.

This is not an available technique (not even in the lab) but feasibility studies are being undertaken to determine if PolSK could be productively used for fibre communications.

7.2.11 Directional Transmission

It is "possible" to use a single fibre for transmission in two directions at once. Indeed the IBM 9729 WDM concentrator does just this over distances of up to 50 km. This device however uses *different* wavelengths in different directions. It is also possible to use the same light wavelength bidirectionally at least over short distances. But all this adds cost and complexity to the system (you have to do quite a lot to remove reflections from the system).

In the vast majority of practical fibre optical transmission systems, fibre is a unidirectional medium. Two fibres are needed for bidirectional transmission. Given the size of a single fibre and the number of fibres that can conveniently be integrated into a cable, this looks certain to be the predominant mode of operation for the foreseeable future.

7.2.12 Character Coding

One of the principal activities in the design of a system is that of minimising the cost. There are a number of different electronic technologies available with very different speeds and costs.

1. CMOS (Complimentary Metal-Oxide Semiconductor) technology is the chip technology used in most electronic computers and in all PCs and workstations. It is very low in cost, it has an extremely high circuit density (you can get many millions of logic gates on a single chip), it consumes a minimal amount of power and therefore produces a minimal amount of heat. Unfortunately (compared to other electronic technologies) it is very slow.

2. Bipolar silicon technology is much faster (perhaps 10 times) than CMOS *but* it is less dense and more costly. In addition it consumes more power and in consequence produces more heat.

3. Silicon/germanium bipolar technology is very fast (much faster than silicon bipolar) and about the same cost. However this is a very new technology and not into serious production as yet.

4. III-V alloy chips (such as gallium arsenide) are extremely fast but very low in density and comparatively very expensive. GaAs technology requires still more power and produces still more heat than bipolar silicon.

It is always dangerous to put absolute speeds on any of this as the circuit speeds (of all of the above technologies) improve every day. But the relationships between the technologies stay much the same. In today's world you can handle a serial bit stream for FDDI at 125 Mbps in CMOS but this is about the limit. You can handle serial bit streams at over 10 Gbps in GaAs, but it is very costly.

The above economic reality has a big effect on communications protocol design. We want to design protocols such that they can be processed at minimal cost. This leads to the desire to process our information as streams of characters or "words" rather than as bits. Of course on the fibre you always have a serial bit stream - but you can design the link protocol such that you need *minimal* serial processing of that bit stream.

Thus FDDI is defined such that each half-byte (4 bits) is coded as 5 bits on the line. ESCON and Fibre Channel are coded such that each 8-bit byte is represented by 10 bits on the line. This enables us to receive and synchronise half-bytes or bytes in parallel - minimising the amount of serial (high-speed, costly) circuitry needed.

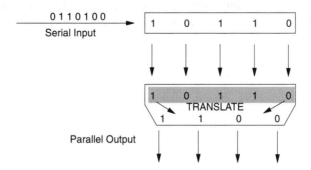

Figure 262. Receiving 4 out of 5 Code. 5-bit groups received in serial mode are synchronised and translated into parallel groups of 4 data bits. This technique is used in FDDI, ESCON and Fibre Channel standards.

The translation process is illustrated in Figure 262. It is important to realise that there is *no necessary relationship* between bit combinations (groups) on the line and the data bit combinations they represent. In the picture the combination on the line is B'10110' which hypothetically represents the data half-byte B'1100'. 8.1.5.2, "Data Encoding" on page 450 describes this operation in relation to FDDI and shows a table of the data encodings.

There are a number of very big advantages in using redundant coding in this way:

1. You can have a unique bit combination that cannot be repeated in regular data which signals the boundaries between characters. This code usually signals the boundary between data blocks or frames when they are present. This allows for fast, unambiguous synchronisation.

2. Because there are many more bit combinations than data characters you can arrange the code such that there is always a good number of bit transitions in the data. This gives three important advantages:

   a. It allows the PLL to lock-on to the data timing easily and reliably.

   b. By ensuring that the laser spends half its time in the ON state and the other half in the OFF state and that it spends (say) no more than 3 bit-times in either state, we are able to ensure that the laser temperature remains relatively constant. This minimises wavelength drift.

   c. Just before the signal is transmitted and just after it is received it is an electronic signal. By making sure that this signal is "DC Balanced" we eliminate the buildup of a DC component in the electronic circuit. This buildup takes power from the signal, upsets the receive threshold and worsens the signal-to-noise ratio.

3. The additional bandwidth required is not much of a problem since with optical fibre bandwidth is not the major constraining factor. (Bandwidth is cheap.)

7.3 Transmission System Limits and Characteristics

The characteristics of various transmission systems are summarised in Table 3.

Table 3. *Optical Fibre State of the Art*

Medium	Source	Technology	Status	Speed	Distance	Product
Copper				2 Mbps	2 km	4 M
Multimode	LED	FDDI	in use	100 Mbps	2 km	200 M
		OC-3		155 Mbps	2 km	310 M
Single Mode	Laser	Long Distance		10 Gbps	50 km	500 G
		Amplitude Modulation		40 Gbps	40 km	1.6 T
		Coherent	in Lab	400 Mbps	370 km	150 G
		Solitons		100 Gbps	4000 km	800 T

A universally accepted measure of the capability of a transmission technology is the product of the maximum distance between repeaters and the speed of transmission. In electrical systems (such as on the subscriber loop) maximum achievable speed multiplied by the maximum distance at this speed yields a good rule of thumb constant. It is not quite so constant in optical systems, but nevertheless the speed × distance product is a useful guide to the capability of a technology. Note that the above table refers to single channel systems only.

Table 4. *Signal Loss in Various Materials*

Material	Attenuation	Regenerator Spacing Max. 35 dB
Coaxial Cable	25 dB/km	1.5 km
Telephone Twisted Pair	12 - 18 dB/km	2 - 3 km
Window Glass	5 dB/km	7 m
Silica - Installed	0.18 - 1 dB/km	50 - 150 km
Silica - Development	0.16 dB/km	250 km
Halide - Research	0.01 dB/km	3500 km

Table 4 shows the attenuation characteristics of various transmission media and the maximum spacing of repeaters available on that medium. Of course, this is very conceptual. Special coaxial cable systems exist with repeater spacings of 12 kilometers. There exist systems capable of operating at very high speed (a few megabits per second) over telephone twisted pairs for distances of four to six kilometers without repeaters. The technology here is called ADSL (Asymmetric

Digital Subscriber Line) or VDSL (Very fast Digital Subscriber Line). This technology makes use of very sophisticated digital signal processing to eke the last bit per second from a very difficult medium. Nevertheless, the advantage of fibre transmission is obvious.

7.4 Optical System Engineering

Putting components (fibres, connectors, lasers, detectors, etc.) together, so that the whole will function as a communication system with desirable characteristics, is no small task.

As mentioned before the two critical factors are:

1. Dispersion
2. Attenuation

Other critical factors are the cost of components and the cost of putting them together. The more complex they are, the more they cost.

7.4.1 System Power Budgeting

Attenuation of both multimode and single-mode fibre is generally linear with distance. The amount of signal loss due to cable attenuation is just the attenuation per kilometer (*at the signal wavelength*) multiplied by the distance. To determine the maximum distance you can send a signal (leaving out the effects of dispersion), all you need to do is to add up all the sources of attenuation along the way and then compare it with the "link budget". The link budget is the difference between the transmitter power and the sensitivity of the receiver.

Thus, if you have a transmitter of power -10 dBm and a receiver that requires a signal of power -20 dBm (minimum) then you have 10 dB of link budget. So you might allow:

- 10 connectors at .3 dB per connector = 3 dB

  See the discussion in 7.4.1.1, "Connector and Splice Loss Budgeting" on page 400.

- 2 km of cable at 2 dB per km (MM GI fibre at 1300 nm) = 4 dB

- Contingency of (say) 2 dB for deterioration due to ageing over the life of the system.

This leaves us with a total of 9 dB system loss. This is within our link budget and so we would expect such a system to have sufficient power. Dispersion is a different matter and may (or may not) provide a more restrictive limitation than the link budget.

The amount of power that we have to use up on the link and in connectors is determined by the characteristics of the components we select as transmitters and receivers.

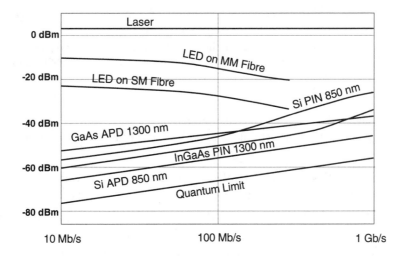

Figure 263. Power Budgeting

Figure 263 shows the characteristics of some typical devices versus the transmission speed (in bits per second). A number of points are interesting here:

1. The power output of a laser doesn't vary much with modulation speed. Every laser has a limit to the maximum speed at which it can be modulated but up to that limit power output is relatively constant.

2. LEDs on the other hand produce less and less output as the modulation rate is increased. In the figure, the difference in fibre types only relates to the amount of power you can couple from an LED into the different types of fibre.

3. All receivers require higher power as the speed is increased. This is more a rule of physics than anything else. To reliably detect a bit a receiver needs a certain number of photons. This depends on the receiver itself but there is a theoretical limit of 21 photons per bit needed. Real receivers require around ten times this but it is a relatively fixed amount of optical power needed per bit. Therefore every time we double the modulation speed we need to also double the required power for a constant signal-to-noise ratio.

4. In addition to the point above there is another important problem when we get to seriously high speeds (above 10 Gbps). Within a pin detector at speeds above 10

Gbps the time taken for electrons to diffuse/drift across the i-layer (in the p-i-n structure) becomes a significant limitation. So if you want the device to respond faster you have to reduce the thickness of the i-layer. But reducing the thickness of this layer *increases* the capacitance between the p and n layers. So you have to reduce the detector surface area to compensate. Both of these actions reduce the volume (size) of the i-layer and hence they reduce the probability that an incident photon will be absorbed and create an electron/hole pair. Thus the quantum efficiency of the detector is significantly reduced. Up to 10 Gbps we expect a (best case) quantum efficiency in pin detectors of around .8. At 20 Gbps this is reduced to .65, at 40 Gbps it reduces again to .33 and at 60 Gbps it becomes .25 or so.

This reduction in quantum efficiency effect operates over and above the doubling of power you need when you double the line speed (as discussed in the previous point).

Current research is under way on the use of travelling wave principles in detectors to increase the quantum efficiency at these extreme speeds. See 4.2.6, "Travelling-Wave Photodetectors" on page 183.

If you look in the figure for a given bit rate (vertical line) there will be a difference between the required receiver power and the available transmitter power. This difference is the amount we have available for losses in the fibre and connectors (and other optical devices such as splitters and circulators). It is also very important to allow some margin in the design for ageing of components (lasers produce less power as they age, detectors become less sensitive etc...).

7.4.1.1 Connector and Splice Loss Budgeting

The signal loss experienced at a connector or splice is *not* a fixed or predictable amount! We know roughly how much loss to expect from a particular connector type or from a particular type of splice in a fibre. The problem is the measured losses in actual splices and actual connectors vary considerably from each other. The good news is that actual measurements form (roughly) a "normal" statistical distribution about the mean (average).

Table 2 on page 357 shows "typical" losses that may be expected from different connector types. This table was complied from specifications obtained from connector manufacturers. However, in the practical world things are a bit more complex than this:[92]

---

[92] The measurement data here was supplied courtesy of Mr Walter A. Worischek.

1. For a connection using almost any modern single-mode connector where *both* connectors (halves of the connection) are from the *same* supplier you can expect a mean loss of .2 dB with a standard deviation of .15 dB.

2. If the manufacturers of the two connectors (halves of the connection) are *different* (the any-to-any case) then you can expect a loss of .35 dB (average) with a standard deviation of .25 dB.

One type of single-mode connector may have an "average loss" of .2 dB but in practical situations this loss might vary from perhaps .1 dB to .8 dB (for the any-to-any case). In budgeting power for a link including multiple connectors we have a real problem deciding how much loss to allow for them.

If a hypothetical link has 10 connectors there *is* a statistical probability (albeit minuscule) that all will be high in loss (in this example .8 dB each) and so perhaps to be safe we need to allocate 8 dB for connector losses. But there is also a probability that each will be .1 dB and therefore we might need to allocate only 1 dB for the loss budget. In fact the probability of each of the above events is smaller than "minuscule" - it is somewhere between about 1 in 10^{10} and 1 in 10^{50} depending on the exact way in which the extreme best and worst case (.1 dB and .8 dB) figures were arrived at in the first place. The same principle applies to fibre splices.

It is possible to get very sophisticated with statistics in predicting the amount of loss but things can be simplified significantly: *If you know the average loss for a single connector and the standard deviation (σ) of the connector loss for a particular situation then you can calculate these figures for any given combination.*

1. The average (mean) of the *total* is just the average loss of a single connector multiplied by the number of connectors. Thus if we have 5 connectors in a link with an average loss of .35 dB per connector then the average loss of the total link will be 5 x .35 or 1.75 dB.

2. It is very important that the term "average loss" in this context be understood. If we fit 5 connectors (pairs) into a single link the total doesn't have an average loss - it has an actual loss. This actual loss will be quite a bit different from the average quoted above.

   If (hypothetically) we were to make a large number of links (say 100) each with five connectors then we could compute the mean (average) loss of a 5-connector link just by averaging over the 100 links. This mean would be very close indeed to 5 times the mean loss of a single connector.

   But we need to take care statistically of the fact that any real 5-connector link will be different from the mean. This is done by quoting not only the mean (for the combination of 5 connectors) but also a standard deviation from the mean.

3. The standard deviation (σ)[93] of the total is just the standard deviation of a single connector multiplied by the square root of the number of connectors $(\sigma\sqrt{n})$ involved. If we have 5 connectors each with a σ of .25 then the σ of the total is $\sqrt{5}$ times .25. That is, 2.235 x .25 which equals .559.

For the above example (5 connectors) then we have a mean of 1.75 dB and a σ of .559. Using a knowledge of the basic characteristics of a statistical "normal distribution" we can now calculate amount of loss to allow for the combination based on the probability we are prepared to accept of our being correct (or wrong!).

- We know that 84.13% of the time the total will fall *below* one standard deviation (σ) above the mean. So, If we allow a loss for the 5 connectors of the mean plus one standard deviation (1.75+.559 = 2.31 dB) then we will be safe 84.13% of the time. That is to say the real value will be *less* than our allowance 84.13% of the time.

- The total will fall below two standard deviations above the mean 97.72% of the time. So if we allow 2.868 dB for the connectors we will be safe 97.72% of the time.

- If we allow 2.32 times the standard deviation then we will be safe 99% of the time.

- In practice, many people like to use the "3-σ" value where we can be confident of being safe 99.87% of the time. For this example the 3-σ value would be 1.75+(3 x .559) which equals 3.427 dB.

We have taken a few shortcuts here. For example we have assumed that the distribution of connector losses is a statistically "normal" distribution. Also we have assumed that all connections are between connectors made by different manufacturers (the any-to-any case). Statistically some of them will really be like-to-like. But while we have taken shortcuts, the result is close enough.

1. If the number of cascaded splices is large (say more than 30) you can safely use the average loss and multiply it by the number of splices involved and ignore the variations.

   There is a statistical law here sometimes referred to as the "law of large numbers". When you add up a large number of variable "things" (with the same

---

[93] It is very easy to become confused about the terminology here. In all statistics literature the Greek sigma (σ) is used to denote the "standard deviation". Another term, the Variance is also often used by statisticians as it is more convenient in some calculations. The variance is σ^2 - that is the square of the standard deviation.

characteristics) the variation in the sum gets smaller and smaller (in relation to the total) as the number gets larger. (This is the effect of the $\sqrt{n}$ term in the standard deviation of a sum as discussed above.)

You can never do this with connectors as you never get a large enough number of them.

2. With a very small number of splices (say two) you can allocate the worst case for each of them. The formula will arrive very close to this anyway.

3. For numbers in between use the calculation method described above.

In long distance links it is common to regard splices as part of the fibre loss. So you might get raw SM fibre with a loss (at 1550 nm) of .21 dB/km. After cabling this will increase to perhaps .23 dB/km. For loss budget purposes you might allocate .26 dB/km for installed cable. Cable is typically supplied in 2 km lengths so in a 100 km link there will be a minimum of 50 splices.

Similarly, in the 1310 nm band, a typical cable attenuation might be .36 dB/km but it is typical to allocate .4 dB/km for fibre losses in new fibre used in this wavelength band.

The same piece of installed fibre cable would then be budgeted at .4 dB/km when used in the 1310 nm band and at .26 dB when used in the 1550 nm band.

7.4.1.2 Power Penalties

There are a number of phenomena that occur within an optical transmission system that can be compensated for by increasing the power budget. In each case the amount of additional power required to overcome the problem is termed the "power penalty".

In all commodity communications products and in most pre-planned systems the effects of power penalties are already included by means of adjustment of the receiver sensitivity. The user systems engineer can usually ignore them quite safely. Nevertheless it is important to understand what they are and get some idea of the magnitude of the penalty. The three most important issues here for digital systems are:

1. System noise

2. Effect of dispersion and

3. Extinction ratio

Signal-to-Noise Ratio (SNR)

The quality of any received signal in any communication system is largely determined by the ratio of the signal power to the noise power - the SNR. Obviously, the SNR is a function of both the amount of noise *and* the signal power. You can always improve the SNR by increasing the signal power (if you can do it without also increasing the noise).

When noise is present the amount of increase in signal power necessary to compensate for the noise and produce the same SNR at the output can be expressed as an amount of power increase in decibels. This is the power penalty due to noise. In simple systems most of the noise comes from within the receiver itself and so is usually compensated for by an adjustment of the receiver sensitivity specification. In complex systems with EDFAs, ASE noise becomes important and to compensate we indulge in power level planning throughout the system.

Inter-Symbol Interference (ISI)

Dispersion causes bits (really line states or bauds) to merge into one another on the link. When this becomes severe it will prevent successful link operation but at lower levels of severity, dispersion adds noise to the signal.

We can compensate for this by increasing the signal power level and thus for certain levels of dispersion we can nominate a system power budget (allowance) to compensate.

Extinction Ratio

If a zero bit is represented by a finite power level rather than a true complete absence of power then the difference between the power level of a 1-bit and that of a 0-bit is narrowed. The power level of the 0-bit becomes the noise floor of every 1-bit. The receiver decision point has to be higher and therefore there is an increased probability of error.

This can be compensated for by an increase in available power level at the receiver. An extinction ratio of 10 dB incurs a power penalty (in either a pin-diode receiver or an APD) of about 1 dB over what it would have been with a truly zero value for a 0-bit. An extinction ratio of 3 dB causes a power penalty of 5 dB in a pin-diode receiver and 7 dB in an APD.

7.4.2 Laser Selection

Depending on the systems environment different lasers are used in different types of systems. As far as SM fibre is concerned the highest quality available laser could be effective in every environment. However, as in most things the higher the precision the higher the cost. So we try to use the lowest cost device that will be adequate in the particular environment.

Factors that need to be considered are:

- Required wavelength
- Required wavelength stability (how important are wander and chirp etc.)
- Spectral width and linewidth
- Required power output
- Modulation rate required

Typical telephone company WAN systems currently use the following types:

155 Mbps - 622 Mbps Systems

Typically index guided Fabry Perot lasers are used at 1300 nm.

622 Mbps Systems

In long distance applications at 622 Mbps, DFB lasers begin to be used. The wavelength used is usually 1300 nm but sometimes 1550 nm is used if a long span is required.

2.4 Gbps Systems (OC 48)

Here people use DBR lasers almost exclusively. This is done at both 1300 nm and at 1550 nm but at the longer wavelength there is usually a need to reduce the linewidth to an absolute minimum. This is caused by the fact that most of these systems (at 1550 nm) operate on standard fibre which has a very high chromatic dispersion.

10 Gbps Systems

These almost exclusively use the 1550 nm band and DBR lasers with external modulators.

Almost all of these systems use avalanche photodiodes (APDs) for detection.

7.4.3 Is There a Speed Limit?

Over the past ten years or so the transmission speeds used in practical wide-area optical systems have at least doubled every two years or so. This has been achieved by improvements in laser sources and detectors and by the shift to the 1550 nm wavelength band. All of this has been with systems that place only a single channel onto the fibre.

However, it seems that there is a real limit on "traditional" single channel optical systems. This limit seems to be approaching very fast (if indeed it hasn't been reached already). The important factors involved are as follows:

Receiver Sensitivity

> As discussed above in 7.4.1, "System Power Budgeting" on page 398 every time we double the transmission speed we must double power at the receiver. This can be achieved in a number of ways:

> - Double the sensitivity of the receiver. This is of course possible but there are limits on receiver sensitivity and presumably we are already using the most sensitive receiver available. Using an optical preamplifier helps a lot here but there are limits.

> - Double the power of the transmit laser or use a power amplifier immediately after the transmitter.

> - Shorten the link by about 15 km. In many situations this is not a practical or economic alternative.

- Use a multi-level encoding technique such that a higher bit rate can be handled with little or no increase in baud rate. This is the traditional technique used in electronic communications systems. This is an eminently practical approach and we are beginning to see trials using 3-level codes. However the receiver must now be able to discriminate between different signal amplitude levels where before it only had to recognise the presence or absence of a pulse. In itself this means that the receiver needs to be somewhat more sensitive or the power levels significantly higher.

Signal Bandwidth

Signal bandwidth (bandwidth of the modulating signal) adds to the bandwidth of the transmitted signal by double its own bandwidth! That is if you modulate a signal at 10 GHz then the broadening of the modulated signal will be 20 GHz. This can result in a significant amount of additional dispersion (if operating on standard non-shifted fibre).

Assuming that the unmodulated laser linewidth is very small we can arrive at an obvious rule of thumb: *double the speed and you double the amount of dispersion*. But there is another effect here. When you double the speed you halve the length of an NRZ or NRZI pulse. Dispersion lengthens a pulse by a fixed amount *in time* - not by a percentage. Thus if you halve the length of a pulse (by doubling the speed) then the same *amount* of dispersion will have twice the effect it had before. So combining the two effects we come to a new rule. **Every time you double the speed you multiply the effect of dispersion by a factor of four! - not two.** (Assuming that the laser linewidth is small in relation to the signal bandwidth.)

An example can be surprising: In an idealised situation (very narrow linewidth laser) at a transmission speed of 2.4 Gbps we are able to go a distance of 1000 km or so on standard fibre before the effects of dispersion prevent system operation. If we keep all the other parameters the same and just increase the speed to 10 Gbps we find that the effects of dispersion prevent system operation at a distance of only *65 km!*

The use of multi-level codes is useful here to limit the modulation bandwidth. The obverse is true here. If you use a multi-level coding scheme to halve the bandwidth of the modulating signal then you lessen the effect of dispersion by a factor of four!

Stimulated Brillouin Scattering (SBS)

Stimulated Brillouin Scattering (SBS) (See 2.4.5.2, "Stimulated Brillouin Scattering (SBS)" on page 89) imposes a limit on the maximum amount of power that the fibre can handle. Thus there is a significant restriction on the maximum amount of signal power that we can use in any particular optical channel. The limit imposed by SBS depends on the signal linewidth, the wavelength and the distance involved but can be as low as 10 mW for a 1550 nm system over a distance of 150 km. This means that we can't increase the signal power at the transmitter by very much to compensate for receiver loss in sensitivity.

We can minimize SBS by using a wide linewidth signal but if we do the effects of dispersion become more significant.

Electronics Cost and Capability

Electronic devices continue to reduce rapidly in cost and increase in speed. However, at the present time, although we can go very fast with electronics, the cost increases exponentially as speed is increased above about 2.5 Gbps.

At the present time 10 Gbps long distance tranceivers are available but extremely expensive. It seems likely that 10 Gbps will be the practical limit of traditional pulse code modulated systems. (Albeit that researchers have demonstrated such systems at up to 40 Gbps.) So to achieve higher throughput we need to use a new technique. WDM (see Chapter 9, "Wavelength Division Multiplexing" on page 513) allows the use of multiple optical signals on the same fibre. Optical CDMA (see 12.4.2, "Code Division Multiple Access (CDMA)" on page 661) also allows the multiplexing of many slow speed optical signals onto a single fibre but this is a long way from becoming practical at this time. Solitons (see 12.1, "Solitons" on page 651) offer the prospect of using ultra-fast optical streams. However, to take advantage of them we will need to use optical TDM (see 12.5, "Optical Time Division Multiplexing (OTDM)" on page 663) to subdivide the optical stream into many different (slower) signals. This is necessary as in the speed range of around 200 Gbps on a single channel the electronics cannot keep up.

7.4.4 Reflections

Control and minimisation of reflections is a key issue in every optical communication system. Of course there are many instances where we create reflections intentionally: for example at the end facets of a laser. The reflections discussed here are unintended ones that occur at connectors, joins and in some devices. These unwanted reflections can have many highly undesirable effects. Among the most important of these are:

- Disruption of laser operation

  Reflections entering a laser disturb its stable operation adding noise and shifting the wavelength.

- Return Loss

Reflections can vary with the signal and produce a random loss of signal power. This is termed "return loss" and is further described in 2.4.4, "Reflections and Return Loss Variation" on page 85.

- Amplifier operation

Reflections returning into an optical amplifier can have two main effects:

  - In the extreme case of reflections at both ends the amplifier becomes a laser and produces significant power of its own. (In a simple EDFA with only Ge as co-dopant this would happen at the "ASE" wavelength of erbium which is 1553 nm. However, with other co-dopants present the lasing wavelength will often be between 1535 nm and 1540 nm.)

  - In lesser cases reflections can cause the amplifier to saturate (by taking away power) and again introduce noise to the signal.

Reflections can be created at any abrupt change in the refractive index of the optical material along the path. The major causes are:

- Joins between high RI material and fibre (such as at the junction between a laser or LED and a fibre or between any planar optical component and a fibre).

- Joins between fibres of different characteristics. This is a bit unusual but there are some cases where this has to happen. For example where a Pr doped amplifier employing ZBLAN host glass is coupled to standard fibre for input and output.

- Any bad connector produces significant reflections. For that matter most good connectors produce some reflection albeit slight.

- Some optical devices such as Fabry-Perot filters reflect unwanted light as part of their design.

Reflections need to be kept in mind and can be controlled by one or more of the following measures:

1. Taking care with fibre connectors and joins to ensure that they are made correctly and produce minimum reflections. This can be checked using an OTDR.

2. The inclusion of isolators in the packaging of particularly sensitive optical components (such as DFB lasers and amplifiers). The use of isolators is important but these devices (of course) attenuate the signal AND are polarisation sensitive. They can also be a source of polarisation modal noise. Their use should be carefully planned and in general, minimised.

3. In critical situations a diagonal splice in the fibre can be made or a connector using a diagonal fibre interface can be employed. The use of a diagonal join ensures that any unwanted reflections are directed out of the fibre core.

Nevertheless, diagonal joins are difficult to make in the field due to the tiny diameter of the fibre and the high precision required.

4. Anti-reflection coatings are very important where the reflection is due to an RI difference. This may be at the edge of a planar waveguide for example. The fibre or waveguide end is coated with a 1/4 wave thick layer of material of RI intermediate between the device material and the air (if air is the adjoining material). The principle involved here was discussed in 2.1.3.2, "Transmission through a Sheet of Glass" on page 27.

In many systems it is critical to ensure that reflections are considered in the system design and that links are tested after installation to ensure that reflections are minimised.

7.4.5 Noise

In single-channel systems the dominant source of noise is the receiver. However, there are many other sources of noise in the system and they need to be considered. This topic is discussed in 9.4.6, "Noise in WDM Systems" on page 563.

7.4.6 Bit Error Rates (BER)

In a digital communication system the measure of system "goodness" is the bit error rate or BER. This is the number of error bits received as a proportion of the number of good bits. It is usually expressed just as a single number such as 10^{-6} which means one in a million. It must be realised that errors are *normal events* in communications systems - there is always the probability of an error (however small).

When an optical communications system is planned the BER is a key objective of the system design and measure of success. It is determined by the link speed, its power, the distance, the amount of noise etc. Detailed calculation is well beyond the scope of this book.

The question of what is an "adequate" BER in a particular situation or what is a good one is purely a judgement call on the part of the people who set the system objectives. However when considering BERs some points should be borne in mind.

- When modern networking systems (such as ATM and Sonet/SDH) were designed it was assumed that they would operate over very low error rate optical links. Errors have a disruptive effect on both of these protocols.

- In the early days, computer networking error rates of 10^{-6} and 10^{-5} on slow speed copper connections were normal and higher level systems were designed to recover and give acceptable throughput. Many modern networking systems will fail entirely if operated over links this bad.

- In current networking technologies an error at the lowest layer has its effects multiply as you proceed up the protocol stack. A single bit error at the physical layer could (in the extreme) cause loss of frame synchronisation in the SDH layer which might cause the loss of perhaps 30 frames. The loss of 30 SDH frames might mean the loss of 100 ATM cells and the loss of these might cause the re-transmission of up to 50 cells for every one lost. So the network could well end up re-transmitting 3000 cells to recover from a single bit error! (This is an extreme and highly unlikely example but the principle is sound.)

- On many public network optical networks today error rates of 10^{-14} are consistently achieved and so user expectation is that errors will be very rare events indeed.

- Public network operators seem to consider the minimum acceptable error rate to be around 10^{-12}.

- In many research reports you find optical network error rates of 10^{-9} quoted. Many people feel that in the context of their use as lowest-layer network within a stack of networks that this figure is just not good enough. This is a judgement call - but...

- The faster the link the lower we need the error rate to be! *But* the harder that low error rate becomes to deliver.

- In many standards (such as the ATM recommendations) the expected error rate performance of links over which the system will be run are specified in the standard.

7.5 Control of Dispersion in Single-Mode Fibre Links

Dispersion broadens a pulse by an amount unrelated to the length of the pulse. Dispersion becomes a problem for a receiver when it exceeds about 20% of the pulse length. Thus, if a pulse at 200 Mbps is dispersed on a given link by 15% then the system will probably work. If the data rate is doubled to 400 Mbps the dispersion will be 30% and the system will probably not work. Hence *the higher the data rate, the more important the control of dispersion becomes*.

- *Modal dispersion* does not exist in single-mode fibre. There is however, a trivial form of modal dispersion caused by birefringent effects separating the two orthogonal polarisation modes in a "single" mode fibre. This is called *Polarisation mode dispersion*. However, the effect is usually trivial.

  In very short single-mode links (less than a few hundred metres) you can get modal dispersion due to additional modes being carried in the cladding. These disappear after a relatively short distance but they can be excited at the laser coupling or in a bad coupler or join.

- *Material dispersion* is significant in both types of fibre.
- *Waveguide dispersion* is significant in both MM and SM fibres but dominates in the SM case because there is no modal dispersion here.

Both material and waveguide dispersion are wavelength dependent effects. If we had a zero spectral width there would be no problem with these types of dispersion. Waveguide dispersion can be manipulated so that it acts in the *opposite direction* (has the opposite sign) to material dispersion. Single-mode fibres (for wide-area applications) of the late 1980s were adjusted such that the two forms of dispersion cancelled each other out at a wavelength of 1310 nm. For this reason, the 1300 nm band was widely used for long distance communication links at that time.[94] However, the attenuation in the 1300 nm band is almost twice that of attenuation in the 1500 nm band. Worse, EDFAs (Erbium Doped Fibre Amplifiers) only work in the 1500 nm band, so if we want to use amplifiers, then we must use 1500 nm.[95]

We can do many things to the fibre to reduce waveguide dispersion (such as varying the refractive indices of core and cladding and changing the geometry of the fibre) and it is now possible to balance the two forms of dispersion at 1500 nm. This type of fibre is called "Dispersion Shifted Fibre". (See 2.4.2.2, "Dispersion Shifted Fibre" on page 78.) Another way of minimizing dispersion (both material and waveguide) is to use a narrow spectral width laser. These techniques combined have meant that almost all new long distance single-mode systems are being installed at 1500 nm.

One important fact to remember is that modulation broadens the bandwidth of the signal (adds to the unmodulated linewidth).

---

[94] And that 1300 nm GaAs (Gallium Arsenide) lasers were readily available.

[95] Recently researchers have succeeded in building praseodymium doped fibre amplifiers which operate in the 1300 nm band but these are inferior to the Erbium doped ones. Early commercial devices which realise a gain of 23 dB at 1310 nm have been reported in the literature. See 5.2.2, "Praseodymium (Pr) Doped Fibre Amplifiers" on page 223.

```
┌─ Calculating Dispersion ──────────────────────────────────────────┐
```

Waveguide dispersion is usually quoted in ps per nm per km at a given wavelength. At 1500 nm a typical dispersion figure is 17 ps/nm/km. That is, a pulse (regardless of its length) will disperse by 17 picoseconds per nanometer of spectral width per kilometer of distance travelled in the fibre. So, in a typical single-mode fibre using a laser with a spectral width of 6 nm over a distance of 10 km we have:

$$Dispersion = 17\text{ps/nm/km} \times 6nm \times 10km = 1020ps$$

At 1 Gbps a pulse is 1 ns long. So if we tried to send data over the above link at 1 Gbps then we would get 102% dispersion - that is, the system would not work. (20% is a good guideline for the acceptable limit.) But it would probably work quite well at a data rate of 155 Mbps (a pulse length of 6.5 ns).

A narrow spectral width laser might produce only one line with a linewidth of 300 MHz. Modulating it at 1 Gbps will add 2 GHz. 2,300 MHz is just less than .02 nm (at 1500 nm).

So now:

$$Dispersion = 17\text{ps/nm/km} \times .02nm \times 10km = 3.4ps$$

So in this example, dispersion just ceased to be a problem.

7.5.1 Control of Spectral Width

Perhaps the most obvious thing we can do about dispersion is to control the spectral width of the signal! Chromatic dispersion is a linear function of spectral width. If you double the spectral width you double the dispersion.

As discussed in 3.3.3, "Fabry-Perot Lasers" on page 129 there is immense variability in the spectral width of available lasers, from over 5 nm for a simple FP laser to less than .01 nm for a DBR laser with an external cavity.

An important factor is that modulation adds to the bandwidth of the signal! Indeed modulation broadens the signal by *twice* the highest frequency present in the modulating signal. Modulation with a square wave implies the presence of significant harmonics up to 5 times the fundamental frequency of the square wave! (Indeed a perfect square wave theoretically contains an infinity of higher frequency components.)

For example, if we want to modulate at 1 Gbps then the fundamental frequency is 500 MHz. A significant harmonic at 2.5 GHz will be present and therefore the broadening of the signal will be 5 GHz or about .04 nm. If we want to modulate at 10 GHz then signal broadening will be perhaps .4 nm. It is easily seen that these amounts are not significant if the laser spectral width is 5 nm but critically significant if the spectral width is .01 nm! This can be controlled by filtering the square wave modulating signal to remove higher frequency harmonics. But this filtering reduces the quality of the signal at the receiver. In practical systems we don't worry about the 5th harmonic and usually can be content with the 3rd. So if we filter a 1 Gbps signal at about 1.5 GHz (at the transmitter) then we can usually build a receiver to suit.

Of course we can reduce the frequency components of the modulating signal by using more complex signal coding rather than simple OOK.

WDM can also help here because (almost by definition) a 2.5 Gbps signal has a quarter of the problem with dispersion as a 10 Gbps signal. (Albeit on a given link both will have the same *amount* of dispersion.) So if you send 4, 2.5 Gbps streams instead of 1, 10 Gbps stream you can go 4 times as far (on a given link) before dispersion becomes a problem.

7.5.2 Dispersion Shifted Fibre

As discussed in 2.4.2.2, "Dispersion Shifted Fibre" on page 78, dispersion shifted fibre is designed with a dispersion zero point at around 1550 nm. For operation in the 1550 nm band this should be ideal. However, it is not always possible or indeed desirable.

1. In many cases we can't have DSF because the fibre we must use is already installed. Digging up a few hundred kilometres of roadway to replace fibre types is an extremely costly exercise.

2. If we are using (or planing to use) WDM technology the problems of four-wave mixing effectively prohibit the use of DSF.

3. If we have a very long amplified link with many cascaded amplifiers we have another problem. The amplifiers will generate a certain amount of amplified spontaneous emission (ASE) noise at wavelengths near to the signal. While this ASE can be filtered out at the receiver it will usually be present on the link. Any ASE within about 2 nm in wavelength of the signal will undergo 4-wave mixing (FWM) with the signal and create significant noise!

   Of course we could filter it out at the output stage of each amplifier but that would mean a long series of cascaded filters which would narrow the signal itself - perhaps into oblivion. See 9.4.1.1, "Cascading Filters" on page 550.

Except in the case of a limited number of amplifier spans DSF is not a good solution to the dispersion problem.

7.5.3 Dispersion Compensating Fibre

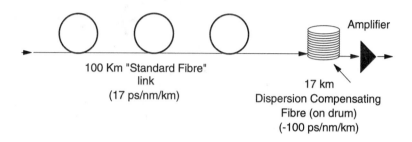

100 Km "Standard Fibre" link (17 ps/nm/km)

Amplifier

17 km Dispersion Compensating Fibre (on drum) (-100 ps/nm/km)

Figure 264. Dispersion Compensation of an Existing Standard Fibre Link

As discussed earlier in 2.4.2, "Dispersion in Single-Mode Fibre" on page 75 we can control the core profile of a fibre to produce just the amount of dispersion we want. In order to equalise an installed link with dispersion at 1550 nm of 17 ps/nm/km (standard fibre) we can connect a (shorter) length of compensating fibre in series with it. The compensating fibre typically has a dispersion of -100 ps/nm/km in the 1550 nm wavelength band. Because the dispersion acts in the opposite direction to the dispersion of the standard fibre the compensating fibre "undisperses" the signal.

You might compensate a 100 km length of standard fibre for operation at 1550 nm by connecting it to 17 km of shifted fibre. However, almost by definition you are not installing the fibre new. So the added length of fibre sits at one end of the link *on a drum*. This adds to attenuation and additional amplification may be needed to compensate for the compensating fibre! DCF has a typical attenuation of .5 dB/km. In addition the narrow core of DCF makes it more susceptible to non-linear high power effects than standard fibre and it is also polarisation sensitive.

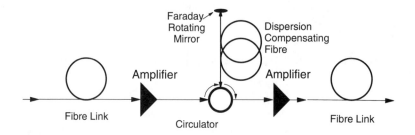

Figure 265. *Dispersion Compensation Using a Mid-Span DCF. The Faraday rotating mirror is used to rotate the polarisation of the reflected signal. Thus any PMD introduced in the DCF section is "undone" in the transit in the opposite direction.*

When installing a new optical fibre link we have the ability to plan for dispersion and the necessary compensation. Thus we might end up with a design such as the one illustrated in Figure 266 on page 417. This is very efficient and effective but relies on installing new fibre.

Figure 265 shows a link configuration with "lumped" dispersion compensation at the mid-span point of the link. In this case you only need half the length of DCF that you might need otherwise (because the light transits the DCF twice). The lumped DCF compensates for dispersion over the whole length of the link. This configuration has the advantage that you can use a Faraday rotating mirror to rotate the polarisation of the signal. Thus any unwanted polarisation dependencies introduced in the DCF are undone by the fact that the light has to transit the same section of DCF again with rotated polarisation. In addition, unwanted polarisation dependencies in the long link itself can be offset somewhat (to the extent that they are the same over the two halves of the link). Indeed this last point is the reason for siting the DCF at mid-span. The major problem with this configuration is that you need access to the link at mid-span. This may not be easily possible in an installed link.

7.5.4 Balancing Dispersion on a Link

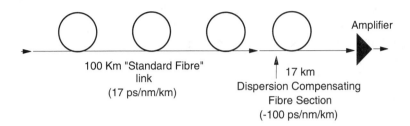

Figure 266. Dispersion Compensation of a New Link with DCF

Of course, if we are planning to operate in the 1550 nm band we could install Dispersion Shifted Fibre (DSF). This has a dispersion of zero at 1550 nm. However, as mentioned elsewhere in this book, WDM systems have a severe problem if the fibre dispersion is really zero! This problem is called 4-wave mixing and is discussed in 2.4.5.1, "Four-Wave Mixing (FWM)" on page 88. It turns out that for WDM operation you really want some dispersion to minimise 4-wave mixing. We could use fibre with a dispersion of 4 ps/nm/km to mitigate FWM but in very long amplified links (such as many undersea cables) even this minimal level of dispersion is a limitation.

In this case the system architects sometimes employ a balanced structure where sections of dispersive fibre with different dispersion characteristics are joined to form the span. The idea here is that no section of fibre has zero dispersion but that different sections have dispersion of opposite sign so that the total at the end of the link (span) is zero. An example is shown in Figure 266.

In a new link designers tend not to use such strongly dispersive fibres and instead might use a fibre with a dispersion of -2 ps/nm/km (see 2.4.2, "Dispersion in Single-Mode Fibre" on page 75) for the majority of the link. To compensate for this at intervals they insert a section (or sections) of standard (17 ps/nm/km) fibre in the link. There are a number of very long undersea links currently in operation which use this dispersion management technique. An undersea link with four WDM channels each operating at 2.4 Gbps over a distance of 4000 km has been reported as an operational system.

In a WDM system it is quite hard to balance dispersive properties of fibres in this way. This is because the range over which the WDM signals are spread may be of the order of 30 or 40 nm. The dispersion characteristics of each fibre used will be *different* at different points over the wavelength range. Matching dispersion characteristics over a range of wavelengths can be very difficult. This may well result in one channel of the WDM spectrum having zero dispersion (total at the end of the link) and other channels having significant finite dispersion!

7.5.5 Mid-Span Spectral Inversion

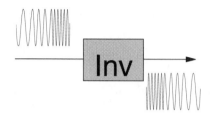

Figure 267. Spectral Inverter - Schematic

The concept here is to use a device in the middle of the link to invert the spectrum. This process changes the short wavelengths to long ones and the long wavelengths to short ones. If you invert the spectrum in the middle of a link (using standard fibre) the second half of the link acts in the opposite direction (really the same direction but the input has been exactly pre-emphasised). When the pulse arrives it has been re-built exactly - compensated for by the second half of the fibre.

Mid-span spectral inversion is a bit difficult to implement in all situations because you have to put an active device into the middle of the fibre link. This may or may not be practical (you might not be able to get access to the mid-point of the fibre link). However, as well as very good compensation for dispersion this technique "undoes" the effect of stimulated Raman scattering in WDM links.

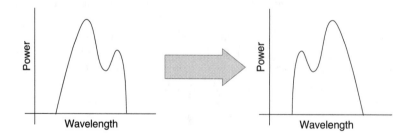

Figure 268. Spectral Inversion - Wavelength (Frequency) Domain

Figure 268 shows a dispersed pulse before input to a phase conjugation process and then at output. The wavelength spectrum has been completely inverted.

This spectral inversion is performed by a process called "optical phase conjugation". This is described in 9.2.8.3, "FWM and DFG" on page 543. Devices that change the wavelength using either 4-Wave Mixing or Difference Frequency Generation invert the spectrum as a biproduct of their wavelength conversion function. These can be used as spectral inverters if we can tolerate the wavelength shift involved.

Although there are devices that can perform phase conjugation (the spectral inversion function) in reality what is often used here is just a section of dispersion compensating fibre on a drum. Several kilometers are typically used. So this can reduce to just another configuration option of dispersion compensating fibre.

7.5.6 Chirped Fibre Bragg Gratings

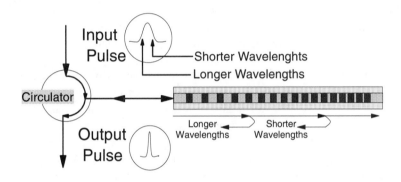

Figure 269. Dispersion Compensation with a Fibre Bragg Grating

FBGs are perhaps the most promising technology for dispersion compensation. A "chirped" FBG is used where the spacings of the lines on the grating vary continuously over a small range. Shorter wavelength light entering the grating travels along it almost to the end before being reflected. Longer wavelength light is reflected close to the start of the grating. Thus short wavelengths are delayed in relation to longer ones. Since the pulse has been dispersed such that short wavelengths arrive before the long ones, the grating can restore the original pulse shape. It undoes the effects of dispersion.

The configuration requires a circulator to direct the light in and out of the grating as shown in Figure 269.

Chirped FBGs need to be quite long (for a simple single-channel application up to 20 cm is commonly required). In a WDM system a fully continuous chirp would require a very long grating indeed. To compensate for 100 km of standard (17 ps/nm/km) fibre the chirped grating needs to be 17 cm long for every nm of signal bandwidth! In this instance a WDM system with channels spread over (say) 20 nm would need a chirped FBG (20 x 17) 340 cm long! Long FBGs are very hard to construct! The current technological limit is about 1 metre in length. However, researchers expect to be able to construct gratings of any desired length in the near future. One current (1997) project is aiming to produce a grating 100 metres long.

It has been discovered that a "sampled" FBG is almost as effective as a continuous chirp and is much easier to construct. In a single-channel application you build the grating as a concatenated series of fixed wavelength gratings rather than as a continuous variable grating. This means you don't need to maintain phase continuity between the different sections. You can write the grating in a number of separate operations and of course this means that it can be as long as you like.

In a WDM system you can use a number of separate chirped or sampled sections. One section for each individual WDM channel. This way you don't have to provide any grating space for the wavelength gaps between the channels.

The major problem with chirped FBGs is that they have a ripple characteristic in the Group Velocity Dispersion (GVD) they produce. This is discussed in 5.7.2.3, "Chirped FBGs" on page 270. (The aim of a chirped FBG is to produce GVD in the opposite direction from that produced on the fibre link.) This ripple can be a source of transmission system noise. The longer the grating the larger the problem with ripple and its resultant noise. In addition short FBGs are filters. When you process a signal through many stages of filtering you get a very narrow signal as a result and this can also distort and add noise to the signal.

7.6 Control of Dispersion in Multimode Fibre

On multimode fibre, modal dispersion usually dominates the other forms of dispersion, so these can be safely ignored in most cases. Fibre manufacturers do *not* quote dispersion on MM fibre in the same way as they do for single-mode fibre.

7.6.1 Maximum Propagation Distance on Multimode Fibre

MM fibre is normally quoted as a frequency response figure per kilometer. Standard (62.5/125) GI MM fibre has a frequency response of 500 MHz per kilometer.[96] This means that an *analogue sine wave signal* of 500 MHz can be expected to travel 1 km

---

[96] In 1997 it is possible to buy 62.5 micron GI MM fibre with a manufacturer certified frequency response figure of 1,000 MHz per km.

without significant dispersion. To go 2 km, you would have to reduce the signal frequency to 250 MHz. It is common to quote this frequency response figure as a "bandwidth". This is fair enough provided we understand that what is being referred to is analogue bandwidth. Many other factors combine to determine the digital bandwidth capacity of the fibre.

There is one subtlety in the quotation of fibre frequency response or bandwidth. That is, the bandwidth × distance product is not really a constant for all lengths of fibre. There is a parameter called the "cutback gamma" which is used to give the real variation of bandwidth versus distance. The problem arises when you use short pieces of fibre to measure the bandwidth and attempt to extrapolate to long distances. You end up predicting a bandwidth that is too low. Conversely if you measure the bandwidth at really long distances (which is what the fibre manufacturers do) and try to extrapolate back to short distances you will predict a bandwidth that is actually much higher than it is in reality.

There is an interesting reason for this effect. The higher order modes are attenuated more than the lower order ones. In simple terms they have farther to travel in the fibre and therefore are attenuated more. This has the effect of attenuating the dispersed "tail" of the pulse in relation to the rest of it. In addition mode coupling (if the fibre allows a lot of it) can randomly mix light from many modes as the signal travels through the fibre. Both of these effects actually improve the transmission characteristics.

The simple formula is that BW is proportional to 1/length. The refined formula is BW is proportional to $1/(\text{length}^{\text{gamma}})$. Typical numbers for gamma are about 0.7-0.8. To take proper account of this, many fibre suppliers give a table of available bandwidth for each of many typical distances.

7.6.1.1 Maximum Digital Bit Rate on a Practical MM Link

The maximum bit rate that can be used on MM fibre is determined by the coding of the data and by the frequency response of the fibre. Data encoding and bandwidth (frequency response) requirements are discussed in 7.6.1.3, "Bandwidth Requirements of the Signal" on page 423. The fibre frequency response is determined by four factors:

Modal Dispersion

> For the purposes of studying modal dispersion, modes can be considered in groups rather than individually. Individual modes within a group tend to travel at very close to the same velocity as other modes within the group. The difference between the speed of mode groups is called "*Differential Mode*

Delay" (DMD). DMD is usually expressed in picoseconds per metre ps/m similarly to the way dispersion is treated on SM fibre.

During travel on the fibre there is much coupling of power between modes within a particular group but little coupling between modes in different groups.

Modal Weighting

This is the relative amount of power coupled into a particular mode group compared to the power coupled into other mode groups. If all the power is coupled into only one mode group then we might expect that we wouldn't get very much dispersion.

Frequency Response of the Receiver

One of the unwanted effects of modal dispersion happening in groups is that in many situations single pulses tend to break up into multiple shorter pulses. If the frequency response of the tranceiver is only just fast enough to receive the original pulse stream, the unwanted higher frequency components (resulting from the break up of the pulse) are filtered out.

Effects Caused by Transmission on the Fibre

Modes couple into other modes, some modes can be stripped out either intentionally or as a result of a bad connector, bad join or too tight bend. The amount and kind of mode coupling depends very strongly on the detailed characteristics of the fibre itself.

The quality of the pulse after transmission then depends on:

1. Which mode groups are excited in what amounts

2. What delays apply to each mode group

3. How much coupling or loss occurs during travel on the fibre

7.6.1.2 Fibre Concatenation

When a number of short sections of MM fibre are joined (fusion spliced) to form a longer length of fibre the fibre frequency response is often observed to *increase*! This means dispersion becomes less. The effect is caused by the stripping of high-order modes. These are often either forced from the fibre or coupled to lower order modes.

Because of the big difference in group velocity between low order and high order modes, this process tends to shorten the pulse and mitigate the effects of dispersion - albeit at the penalty of higher attenuation. The effect can be as great as to improve the characteristics of step-index MM fibre links by as much as 40% over what it would have been on a single unbroken fibre strand. With MM GI fibre at 850 nm you get between 25% and 10% improvement and at 1300 nm you get between 15% and none.

Unfortunately, you can't plan on getting this type of improvement in every situation. It is prudent therefore to use the manufacturer's specifications.

7.6.1.3 Bandwidth Requirements of the Signal

The critical issue is to look at what *bandwidth the signal requires*. Remember that the cable is being quoted as an *analogue* bandwidth and the signal is a digital "baseband" signal. The correct thing to do here is to find the bandwidth requirement of the signal you are using. What some people assume is that for NRZ data you need a bandwidth that is 0.5 of the data frequency. So, FDDI would be 1/2 of 125 Mbaud = 62.5 MHz. Indeed this is the theoretical limit (the best possible case).

This is not a very accurate way because it ignores the difference between the frequency requirements of the pulsed (square wave) signal and the sine wave analogue signal by which the cable was measured. The requirement here is determined by the characteristics of the receiver. For FDDI a practical system might require 0.8 of the data frequency (baud rate) as a rule of thumb. It is conceivable that a system might require up to 3 times the baud rate but this seems quite unlikely.

In fact, the bandwidth requirement heavily depends on the characteristics of the receiver and the details of the protocol (for example how much jitter is acceptable in this protocol).

7.6.1.4 Source Spectral Linewidth

Another characteristic affecting the overall dispersion is the spectral linewidth. Using a spectral linewidth of 50 nm, this is not a problem since modal dispersion dominates, but if the linewidth is very wide then material dispersion should be taken into account. For a 170 nm linewidth LED then a material dispersion constant of 6 or 8 ps/nm/km (picoseconds of delay per kilometer of transit per nanometer of spectral width) for the 1.3 μm LED would be a good rule of thumb. The 170 nm spectral width will end up dominating the fibre bandwidth. If you use 6 ps/nm/km and assume that the 500 MHz/km number from the fibre manufacturers is strictly modal dispersion and does not include chromatic dispersion, then your fibre ends up at 326 MHz/km for your 170 nm wide LED. A 2 km distance would then have about 163 MHz and will easily support 125 Mbaud data without any penalties.

7.6.2 Light Sources for Multimode Systems

In 1997 almost all WAN systems are SM and the use of MM is confined to the campus and office LAN environment. There are three general groups of standards (or de facto standards) in use:

1. A band centered on 850 nm using LED light sources and PIN receivers. This is used mainly for relatively "slow" applications (such as interconnecting token-ring or Ethernet LANs). This is now mainly of historic interest.

2. A band centred on 1310 nm (with a nominal spectral width of around 50 nm). Typical use is with LED transmitters and PIN detectors for distances of up to 2 km.

   This is used by FDDI, ATM (100 Mbps and 155 Mbps protocols), Fibre Channel, IBM ESCON (short distance) etc...

3. A band at 780 nm or 800 nm. This allows the use of very low cost "CD-ROM" lasers over MM fibre. These lasers are much lower in cost than communication LEDs and can be modulated quite satisfactorily at speeds of up to 1.2 Gbaud (1.2 Gbps in the systems proposed).

   Currently this is used by the ATM 622 Mbps on MM Fibre recommendation from the ATM Forum and in the "Fibre Channel" specification. It is also proposed as an alternative for the developing "Gigabit Ethernet" system. Some proprietary systems have been using this band for a number of years, for example, the "OptiConnect" system used in the IBM AS/400 computer systems.

7.6.2.1 Use of Lasers on MM Fibre

Traditionally LEDs have been used for transmission on MM fibre and lasers on SM. However, as mentioned above, there is an increasing use of lasers with MM fibre over short distances.

In the early 1980's people wanted to use lasers on MM fibre for quite long distance (10-20 km) and met with a serious technical problem. The problem was "modal noise" (see 2.3.6, "Modal Noise" on page 64). Modal noise was such a big problem that the use of lasers on MM fibre was all but abandoned.

However modal noise happens when you use a very narrow linewidth laser and a relatively low transmission speed (such as 155 Mbps) and there are some bad (high loss) connectors in the system. This is because modal noise gets worse as the coherence length is increased. A relatively low quality laser (large chirp, wide spectral width, more than one line) actually has much less of a problem with modal noise because the coherence length is very short. High modulation speeds (such as 622 Mbps and 1 Gbps) reduce the effect of modal noise significantly as well. In addition the technology of connectors and splices has improved significantly recently so another of the conditions giving rise to modal noise is removed.

It has been found that lasers developed for CD-ROM players (with some minor changes) can be used for short distance communication on MM fibre very reliably. These can be modulated by controlling the drive current at speeds up to 1 Gbps. With the industry producing around 20 million of these lasers a year the cost is very low. They have recently been specified for use in ATM (622 Mbps) and Fibre Channel. They are also considered to be the leading option for Gigabit Ethernet.

Recently, there has been a lot of study into the idea that perhaps we could launch a reduced set of modes into a MM GI fibre with a laser. The idea is that modes travel in groups and while there is a lot of coupling between modes within the groups there is relatively little coupling between groups. Radial modes (ones that pass through the axis of the fibre) and spiral modes (ones that never pass through the fibre axis) are examples of such groupings. The objective here is/was to find a way of extending the distance capability of MM fibre to allow it to be used at higher speeds for longer distances. One kilometer on GI MM fibre for Gigabit Ethernet would be very nice indeed.

When power is coupled into a MM fibre from an LED we normally see all possible modes excited. This is called an "Overfilled Launch" (OFL). If we use a device such as that shown in Figure 270 we can excite only the radial modes. A launch of this kind is called a "Radial Overfilled Launch" (ROFL).

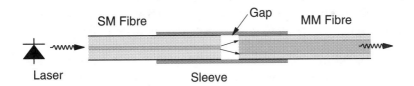

Figure 270. *Radial Overfilled Launch (ROFL). The laser is pigtailed into a SM fibre. The SM fibre is set into a tube opposite the end of a MM fibre with a specific separation (designed to follow the rules for ROFL) between them.*

To achieve a ROFL you need the following conditions:

1. Light from a laser is focused onto the end of the core of a multimode fibre.

2. The optical axis of the laser beam and the fibre core are aligned.

3. The focused spot of light is symmetrical about the fibre axis.

4. The light arrives at an angle within the cone of acceptance of the fibre.

5. The spot is slightly larger in diameter than the MM fibre core.

If the above conditions are satisfied then a ROFL is achieved. In this case most of the power is concentrated along the axis of the fibre and the amount of power across the core decreases exponentially towards the edge.

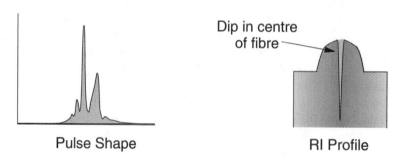

Figure 271. Pulse Breakup and the Fibre RI Profile that Causes It

With many samples of MM fibre using ROFL launch conditions we observe significantly improved fibre bandwidth. The objective of extending the distance is clearly possible. However, with other samples it appears that usable distance is in fact shorter than one might expect from the fibre specification!

On further examination of these "bad" fibres we see behavior similar to that illustrated in Figure 271. The optical pulse breaks up into a number of shorter pulses. This can be improved as suggested earlier by filtering the higher frequency components out of the received signal but nevertheless you don't get a lot of performance improvement.

It turns out that this breakup of the pulse is caused by the fact that some fibres have a reduced RI (a "dip") along the axis of the fibre. In the MCVD process of fibre production, when all the silica and dopants have been deposited on the inside of the tube, it is then heated past the melting point of the silica and collapsed to produce the preform. However, if you are not very careful, this heating process causes some of the dopant material (usually germanium) to be evaporated off the inner surface of the tube. Thus you get a lowered RI right on the fibre axis. The lowered RI region will now form an inner core which will reflect light away from itself rather than guide. By careful control of the process it is possible to eliminate this even using MCVD - however much currently installed GI MM fibre has this characteristic. The problem doesn't occur with fibre made by the VAD process.

An alternative for using lasers on this bad fibre is to excite all the modes - a traditional overfilled launch (OFL). This doesn't give you increased distance but it does allow us to use lasers up to the specified bandwidth of the fibre. There are several ways of achieving OFL with lasers but two are being investigated:

1. Pigtailing the laser with SM fibre and then directly coupling this SM fibre to a MM fibre but offsetting the SM axis from the MM axis by about 20 microns.

2. Pigtailing with a step index MM fibre and (after a predetermined length) joining this to a GI MM fibre.

Both of these techniques result in an approximation to an OFL.

At the time of writing, all of the above techniques are still being investigated by relevant standards committees. Just what they might decide in this case is not yet determined... but the result in any event is problematic.

7.7 Fibre Optics in Different Environments

Optical systems are built to be optimal for the particular environment in which that system is to be deployed. The point here is that the local data communications environment and the wide area telecommunications environment are very different in their character and requirements. Hence we might expect that the systems built for each environment will themselves be different.

Wide Area Telecommunications Systems

In the wide area environment, carrying very high capacity over long distances is the primary requirement. There are relatively few sources and receivers and few connectors. There is very little need to change a system once it is installed.

- Cable cost is very important (though the cost of burying it in the ground is many times higher than that of the cable itself).

- The cost of transmitters, receivers, repeaters, connectors, etc. is much less important because that cost is only a tiny proportion of the total.

- High power is very important to achieve maximum distance between repeaters/amplifiers.

- Component reliability is also very important because these systems are typically multiplexed and a single failure affects many users.

Local Area Data Communications Systems

The most important thing about this kind of system is its need for flexibility.

- The cost of transmitters and receivers, etc. is most critical (because there are a large number of these and they form a large proportion of the total).

- Cable cost is still important but much less so than in the wide area environment. Compared to electrical cables, fibre cables are much easier to install around a building (they are lighter and more flexible).

- The critical thing in this environment is joining the cable and the performance of connectors and patch cables.

- High power is still important so that losses incurred in connectors and patch cables can be accommodated. Also the attenuation of MM fibre is relatively high. However, we don't need power levels as high as are typically used in the wide area world.

- Reliability is also very important because a single failure can disrupt the entire system.

So, in both types of application it is important to have high power and reliability. These requirements lead to different system choices:

- For wide area telecommunications, single-mode fibre and long-wavelength lasers constitute the system parameters of choice. In the 1980s, this meant 1300 nm wavelength lasers were predominant. In the 1990s, these have been replaced by 1500 nm systems (in new plant) almost universally. The remaining 1300 nm systems exist because the fibre that was installed has its dispersion minimum at 1300 nm and changing to 1500 would have meant digging up the ground and replacing the fibre. There are several ways of compensating for wavelength-dependent dispersion effects as discussed earlier in this chapter. These can be used to equalise a fibre designed for operation in the 1300 nm band to the 1500 nm band.

- For local data communications, the choice is for shortwave lasers (or LEDs) and multimode fibres. In the 1980s, this meant wavelengths in the 850 nm range because GaAs LEDs operate in this range and devices appropriate to the 1300 nm band had not been developed at the time. In the 1990s, there has been a general move to 1300 nm (still with LED transmitters and MM fibre). FDDI and the new ATM local area connections have been standardized at 1300 nm.

However, we are about to witness a switch back to shorter wavelengths for short-distance, high-speed connections. "CD lasers" are the kind of lasers used in compact disk players and laser printers, etc. These lasers are very low-cost (less than US $10) and are made by some 20 or so manufacturers. Total industry volume of these lasers is about 20 million per year (1998). These operate typically around 780 nm (for the CD player application, the shorter the wavelength the better). The new standardised Fibre Channel (for interconnecting computers within a machine room) allows for transmission at 1 Gbps over a few hundred meters using these lasers.

7.7.1.1 *Custom Engineering or Commodity*

Another big difference between the wide area environment and the local area environment is the ability to "engineer" optimized solutions for a given situation.

In the WAN, when a user (almost always a telephone company) wants to install a link, then they do a full study of the characteristics of the link involved, design and analyze a solution, and custom-build it. To do this requires an army of skilled people but the cost is easily justified by the fact that the cost of installing links of this kind is extremely high.

In the local area world, the user typically wants to install a system which works with "off-the-shelf" components. This means that you need a very few "rules-of-thumb" for interconnection of standardized components. In this situation components are over-specified to allow for extreme situations. For example, using FDDI (100 Mbps) over MM fibre (62.5 micron GI) the standard says that the maximum distance allowed is 2 kilometers. In fact, if you use good-quality cable and not too many connectors you can go to 5 kilometers safely with most available equipment. But suppliers generally will not warrant their equipment for use outside the guidelines inherent in the standard. This is because the cost of people to do optimal design exceeds the amount saved through optimization.

Optical engineering is significantly more complex than this short chapter might suggest - designing optimal networks outside of manufacturers' guidelines is a highly skilled job. Be warned.

7.8 Test Equipment and Techniques

Experience tells us just what happens when you install a new communications system of any kind. Nothing. You turn it all on and wait and *nothing* happens! (This is actually quite a good outcome - sometimes you get smoke from one or other piece of equipment!) Then you have the task of tracking down just what is and is not happening and where the problem is. Experience also tells us that the most likely problem is that someone plugged a cable into the wrong socket!

Perhaps the biggest irony of optical communications is that you can't *see* anything! So if we want to find out what's going on in the system in order to make it work then we appropriate test equipment on hand.

In many situations a simple optical power meter is quite sufficient but in others very sophisticated equipment is essential.

7.8.1 Optical Power Meters (Optical Multimeter)

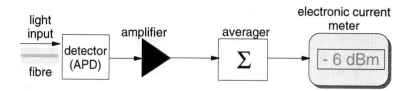

Figure 272. *Optical Power Meter - Logical Structure*

The simplest and most basic piece of equipment used in the field is the optical power meter. This is shown in Figure 272 and requires very little explanation.

Different models have different connector types and are specialised to either multimode or single-mode fibre. There is always a wavelength switch to adjust the power readings for the particular wavelength being received. Also there is usually a range switch which determines the range of signal power expected - although this last function can be automatically determined by the meter itself.

7.8.2 Optical Time-Domain Reflectometers (OTDRs)

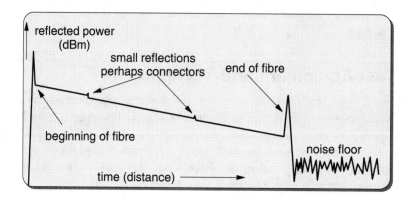

Figure 273. *OTDR Display - Schematic*

The Optical Time-Domain Reflectometer enables us to look at a fibre link from *inside the fibre*. In reality it is just a radar system for looking at fibre. High intensity pulses are sent into the fibre from a specialised laser and when the pulse returns its strength is displayed on an oscilloscope screen in the form of a trace. A schematic of such a display is shown in Figure 273. Important considerations are as follows:

Reflections from within the Fibre

In the trace you see reflections coming from all along the fibre itself. This is the result of Rayleigh scattering. Rayleigh scattering was mentioned in the chapter on optical fibre as the major limiting factor in fibre attenuation. This scattering occurs backwards towards the transmitter and we can receive it and display the result.

Faults and Joints etc.

Every time there is a discontinuity or imperfection in the fibre the effect can be seen in the trace. Such events can be the presence of a connector or a splice or some more serious imperfection such as a crimp in the cable due to poor installation.

In the schematic above we can see the reflections from the beginning and end of the fibre as well some imperfections in between.

Noise Floor

At the end of the fibre you see a characteristic large (4%) reflection followed by the signal dropping to the noise floor.

Measurable Parameters

From an OTDR you can quickly determine the following characteristics of the fibre link under test:

- The length of the fibre

  This is not as precise as it sounds. What you can calculate is the length of the fibre itself. Most long distance cables employ "loose tube" construction and the fibre length is between 5% and 10% longer than the cable itself.

- The attenuation in dB of the whole fibre link and the attenuation of separate sections of fibre (if any).

- The attenuation characteristics of the basic fibre itself.

- The locations of connectors, joints and faults in the cable

  These locations are measured from the beginning of the fibre and can be as accurate as a few metres.

Usually you can't see the fibre close to the instrument. A "dead zone" extends from the connector at the instrument itself for about 20 metres into the fibre. So if the trace in the figure above was real we would need to have a piece of fibre about 20 metres long connecting from the OTDR to the end of the fibre under test. Often you don't have this luxury in the field. In which case many OTDRs come equipped with a red laser source which you can use to illuminate the fibre. When you look at a fibre illuminated in this way (from the side) bad joints and fibre faults will scatter the red light and you can see it. But beware YOU MUST NOT LOOK AT THE SOURCE OR AT THE END OF THE FIBRE DIRECTLY. This can damage your eyes. Before using a feature like this read the manufacturer's instructions carefully.

Advantages

The major advantage of the OTDR is that tests can be done from one end of the link and you don't need access to the other end. This means you don't need two people to do the test and you save the problem of coordinating between people. Also the testing is much quicker. So even simple tests which could be performed with a basic optical source at one end of the link and a power meter at the other are often performed with an OTDR.

Characteristics

OTDRs today are extremely sophisticated devices and come with many options. They can be large fixed laboratory instruments or small portable ones about the size of a laptop computer. Different models are available for multimode and single-mode fibres. Of course different models have different levels of sensitivity (and price). There is always a range of options for the user to control such as wavelength used for the test, timescales, pulse duration etc.

Many modern OTDRs come with additional functions such as optical power meter or laser source so that a good OTDR often has all of the function needed by a technician in the field. In addition many OTDRs offer computer output so that you can collect OTDR data in the form of digital readings and analyse it later on a computer.

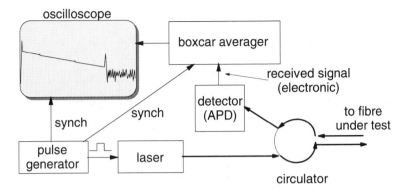

Figure 274. OTDR Operational Logic

The principle of operation of a typical OTDR is shown in Figure 274. In the figure a circulator has been used to enable transmission and reception of the pulse from the single strand of fibre under test. Other means of signal splitting/combining are used but circulators offer the least attenuation.

As might be expected the big problem with an OTDR is that the returning signal is *very low level* especially on long distance fibre sections. We can't use signal pulses of too high a power for many reasons and so pulses of 10-20 mW are typically sent. The problem of low return power is addressed in two ways:

1. A very sensitive APD detector is used. As noted elsewhere in this book detectors double in sensitivity every time you halve the digital bit rate. Thus an APD becomes very sensitive indeed at the very low pulse rates used. The penalty for using APDs is additional noise but this is mitigated by the averaging process.

2. A "boxcar averager" circuit is used to average many thousands of returning pulses. The averaging process removes a large amount of noise. (Most of the noise comes from the APD and its associated circuitry.) In some (very sensitive, long distance) OTDRs the averaging time can be of the order of several minutes! The averager provides logarithmic scaling of its output so that the vertical scale on the display can be displayed in dBm.

The pulse rates used are quite slow! Since the optical signal propagates at approximately 5 microseconds per kilometer we have to allow 10 microseconds per kilometer of fibre length. So for 20 km of fibre we need to wait at least 200 microseconds between pulses and so a pulse rate of 5000 pulses per second would be the maximum possible.

7.8.3 Spectrum Analysers

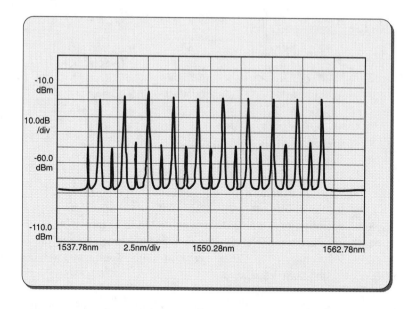

Figure 275. Spectrum Analyser - Display Schematic

There are many occasions where we want to look at the wavelength spectrum of the signal(s) on a fibre. One such occasion would be to examine the wavelength spectrum of a WDM system to help understand system operation and to diagnose faults. A spectrum analyser scans across a range of wavelengths and provides a display showing the signal power at each wavelength.

Figure 275 shows a simplified example of the kind of display produced by a typical spectrum analyser. The figure is a drawn copy of an actual measurement of a WDM link connecting two IBM 9729s. (The 9729 is described in 10.5, "The IBM 9729 - A WDM System for the Metropolitan Area Network" on page 607.) The 9729 uses 20 wavelengths on a single strand of fibre - 10 wavelengths in one direction and 10 in the other interleaved. The signal was extracted from the link using a "10 dB splitter".[97] The signals in the reverse direction are significantly lower in power than the forward direction (as measured). This is due to the fact that the signals we are seeing in the reverse direction are really reflections from the grating.

---

[97] A resonant coupler with a 90:10 coupling ratio

From this display we can calculate:

1. The power levels of each channel.

2. The spectral width of each channel.

3. Any interference between channels such as crosstalk possibilities.

4. By connecting it in different places through the system we can track many potential problems such as laser drift etc.

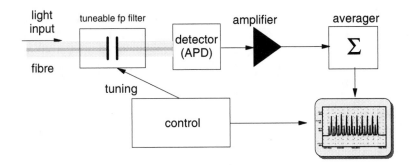

Figure 276. *Spectrum Analyser - Logical Structure*

The logical structure of the device is shown in Figure 276.

- Light input from the fibre is passed through a tunable Fabry-Perot filter.

- The filter is scanned at quite a slow rate (perhaps 10 times per second) through the range of wavelengths that we want to examine.

- Optical output of the FP filter is fed to an APD to convert it to electronic form.

- The output of the APD will contain rapid variations due to modulation of the signal in each channel etc. These modulations are averaged out electronically so that the electrical signal level now represents the average power level of the optical signal (average over a few milliseconds).

    The electronic signal now needs to be scaled logarithmically as we need the y-axis scale to be in dBm.

- The electronic signal is now fed to the y-axis control of an oscilloscope.

- The x-axis is swept across in synchronism with the wavelength setting of the FP filter.

- This results in a display similar to that in the figure.

Like OTDRs, spectrum analysers vary widely in their capabilities and prices. They range from large, very accurate and expensive laboratory instruments to small, much less expensive devices about the size of a laptop computer. You can even buy one that does not have a display and instead connects to your laptop computer.

In using one you need to be aware of the resolution (minimum width) of each wavelength measured and also of the accuracy of the instrument.

7.8.4 Eye Diagrams

When you think about it there is a paradox involved in much of the testing we would like to do. You have a signal that is varying extremely quickly - so quickly that we need sophisticated receiver circuitry to detect its changes of state. Yet we expect to be able to measure and display the signal very accurately - much more accurately than we could ever possibly receive it.

The secret is that we receive the signal many times (indeed millions of times) and display the aggregate. Signals when they carry information vary and therefore we can never get a good solid picture of a particular state or change of state. However we can get an excellent idea of the aggregate.

The eye-diagram has over the years become the recognised way of looking at an electronic signal and determining its "goodness" as a carrier of information. It consists of many (from hundreds to millions) of instances of the signal displayed over the top of one another. In extremely fast equipment you might get only one or two points on a trace at a single sweep. But displaying them together allows us to assess the quality of the received signal very well indeed.

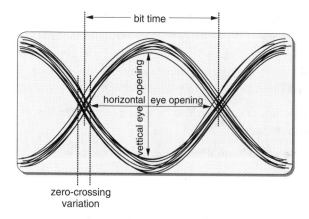

Figure 277. Eye Diagram - Schematic

The diagram is produced by feeding the result of the analogue section of the receiver circuit to the y-axis control of an oscilloscope. The sweep is set to display one full cycle (2-bit times) and is usually triggered from the receiver's PLL circuit (the receiver's derived clock).

The following aspects of the eye are important:

1. The vertical eye opening indicates the amount of difference in signal level that is present to indicate the difference between one-bits and zero-bits. The bigger the difference the easier it is to discriminate between one and zero. Of course this is affected significantly by noise in the system.

2. The horizontal eye opening indicates the amount of jitter present in the signal. The wider the eye opening is on this axis the less problem we are likely to have with jitter.

3. The thickness of the band of signals at the zero-crossing point is also a good measure of jitter in the signal. However, you need to be careful here as the sweep is usually triggered from the receiver PLL and variations here are as much an indicator of the quality of the PLL as they are of the signal itself!

4. The best indication of signal "goodness" is just the size of the eye opening itself. The larger it is the easier it will be to detect the signal and the lower will be the error rate. When the eye is nearly closed it will be very difficult or impossible to derive meaningful data from the signal.

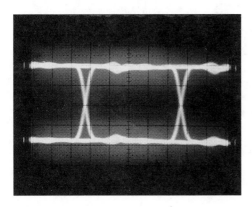 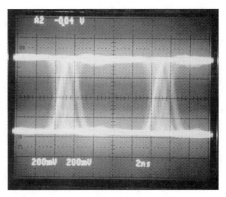

Figure 278. Real Eye Diagrams

Figure 278 shows two real eye diagrams of a modulated signal (actually 100 Mbps FDDI code). On the left is a very good situation with a wide open eye and very little jitter. On the right we have an example of a signal which will be relatively easy to detect but which contains a significant amount of jitter.

The real pictures look significantly different from the hypothetical diagram of Figure 277 on page 436. The real ones look like a pair of joined horizontal H'es rather than 8's. This is because we are looking at a real signal. Sometimes it has two 0 bits in a row and sometimes it has two 1 bits in a row. Hence at top and bottom there are two horizontal tracks in the summation.

7.9 Further Reading

Andrew R. Chraplyvy (1990)

> *Limitations on Lightwave Communications Imposed by Optical-Fibre Nonlinearities*: IEEE J. of Lightwave Technology, Vol 8, No 10, October 1990. pp 1548-1557

D. M. Kuchta and C. J. Mahon (1994)

> *Mode Selective Loss Penalties in VCSEL Optical Fibre Transmission Links*: IEEE Photonics Technology Letters, Vol 6, No 2, February 1994. pp 288-290

Dietrich Marcuse (1991)

> *Calculation of Bit-Error Probability for a Lightwave System with Optical Amplifiers and Post-Detection Gaussian Noise*: IEEE J. of Lightwave Technology, Vol 9, No 4, April 1991. pp 505-513

Chapter 8. Optical Link Connections in Electronic Networks

This chapter discusses the physical layer specifications, standards and protocols used in common networking systems applications of point-to-point optical links.

Up until the present time optical communications has been confined to the operation of point-to-point links. Today with the advent of WDM and add/drop multiplexing we are just beginning to see the dawn of real optical networking. Optical link connections now dominate wide area communications. They have a strong presence in local area communications for inter-building links and in other connections where the distance is greater than about 100 metres.

However, it is a major mistake to assume that the influence and effect of fibre optical communication stops at the link connection! Today's high speed electronic networking systems (Sonet/SDH, ATM...) are designed to operate on fibre connections and in fact often cannot operate effectively over copper. The characteristics of fibre connections are very different from those of copper and this influences fundamentally the whole way in which networks are built.

Networks of the 1970's and early 1980's were built on a number of firm ground rules:

1. Links were very slow - much slower than the computers to which they were attached.

2. Bandwidth was very expensive (due to the fact that the links were slow).

3. Error rates were high (by today's standards very high). A typical copper link connection was considered "good" if it had an error rate of 1 in 10^6 (one error per million bits sent).[98]

Although increasing processing speeds of computers have allowed us to use better and significantly more efficient ways of transferring data on copper, the above rules-of-thumb still hold.

As a result of these technical conditions communications networks of the 1970's and 1980's emphasised efficiency of data transfer. Bandwidth (bits-per-second) was expensive so people tried to optimise in such a way as to maximise the amount

---

[98] Error rates are often expressed as a single number with a negative exponent. An error rate of 1 in 10^6 would be expressed as "an error rate of 10^{-6}".

available. Since errors were relatively common good error control and recovery (using minimal overhead) was critical.

Fibre optics changes this fundamentally:

1. Links are fast - very fast - much faster than the computers to which they are attached.

2. Bandwidth is very low in cost. The cost of having a link is still much the same as before but the speed has increased by four orders of magnitude.

3. Error rates are very low indeed. Typical error rates on today's long line telecommunications networks are around 10^{-12}.

   In fact there is nothing inherent in either copper wire transmission or fibre optical transmission that determines these error rates. When designing copper connections we simply increase the speed of the link until we get to an error rate of 10^{-6}. Copper would give us error rates very similar to those of fibre if (and only if) we decreased the speed of the connection by an order of magnitude or two. Conversely if we increase the speed of any given optical link we just keep increasing the error rate. We could compare the two using links of the same error rate and all this would do is make the link speed gap between the two technologies even greater. Of course, in copper technology we need every bit-per-second we can get. In fibre technology connections are usually faster than the immediate need. So part of the added capability of fibre is taken (by choice) as an improvement in the error rate rather than as an increase in the speed.

When people began to use the old (1970's) networking protocols over the new fibre optical links an interesting effect occurred: *As the link speed was increased all of these protocols continued to "work" but there came a point (usually quite quickly) where the network throughput stopped increasing regardless of increases in link speed!* This point is key. With all the changes in technology one critical factor had not changed - the speed of light! (Sad that, the physicists have let us down!) Electricity in a wire and light in a fibre travel at roughly the same speed - 5 microseconds per kilometre. Propagation delay - the time it takes for a signal to get from one end of a connection to the other had not changed.

A related (if obvious) point is that when communication links get faster they *don't* get any faster. High speed communications links simply pack bits closer together on the link. The bits still travel at the same speed. The time it takes for a given bit to travel from end-to-end across the system is the same as it always was!

In order to actually be able to deliver high network throughput to the end user new networking architectures had to be devised. These networking technologies are based on a new set of ground rules:

1. Link level error recoveries of the traditional kind must be got rid of! In traditional networking architectures (for example X.25) the link level sends a small number (called a "window") of data blocks and then waits for a response saying that one or more of them has been received OK. When the response comes then more blocks of data are sent.

   This is fine on high error rate low speed connections. On a high speed long distance connection (say between New York and Los Angeles) it is quite possible to have over a megabyte of data "in flight" at any particular moment in time. Windowed link control protocols would require very large buffers at each end of the line AND would be very inefficient in operation.

2. Flow and congestion control in networks is still absolutely necessary. However, flow and congestion controls that use protocols similar to the windowed form of link error recovery protocols suffer from the same problems. New methods of flow and congestion controls must be found.

3. Because bandwidth is now very low in cost we can afford to use some of it for administrative purposes.

4. Link speeds are now so fast that switching data at transit nodes cannot be effectively performed in software. Available computers are just not fast enough. So the switching function must be performed in hardware logic. This means that the design of the protocols should be such as to allow a very simple switching process implemented in hardware logic.

5. We still want to minimise the cost of switching hardware. Many (if not most) existing communications protocols require the serial processing of bits. This means that hardware doing the processing must operate at full link speed. To do this we would require very fast (and expensive) hardware technologies. Lower speed technologies (such as CMOS) are significantly lower in cost. Therefore protocols must be designed to enable processing of data in characters, bytes or words rather than as individual bits. In this way as data is received (in fast expensive logic) it can be converted into parallel form and further processing can proceed using slower (lower cost) technology.

6. At higher layers too, network protocols need to be simplified and designed such that processing can operate on groups of bits in parallel rather than on individual bits. Error detection and recovery (which is still *critical*) must be performed end-to-end between end users rather than stage-by-stage within the communications system.

8.1 Fibre Distributed Data Interface (FDDI)

FDDI was developed by the American National Standards Institute (ANSI). It was originally proposed as a standard for fibre optical computer I/O channels but has become a generalised standard for operation of a LAN at one hundred megabits per second. Ironically, FDDI can run very well on copper cabling and in fact today is more often installed using copper wire than fibre. The important characteristics of FDDI are as follows:

Optical LAN at 100 Mbps

>   FDDI is primarily intended for operation over optical fibre but has found greater acceptance in operation over standard copper wire (shielded twisted pair).

Dual Token Rings

>   There are two token rings operating in opposite directions. The primary ring carries data. The secondary ring is used to "wrap" the ring should the ring be broken. The secondary ring is not normally used for data traffic.

Ring Characteristics

>   Using multimode optical fibre for connection, an FDDI ring (segment) may be up to 200 km in length attaching a maximum of 500 stations up to two kilometers apart.

Frame (Packet) Switching

>   Like many other types of LAN (token-ring, ethernet...) data transfer takes place in frames or packets. In FDDI the maximum frame size is 4500 bytes. Each frame has a header which contains the physical address of the destination FDDI station.

Guaranteed Bandwidth Availability

>   In addition to the "equality of access" characteristic of token-ring, FDDI offers a form of "guaranteed" bandwidth availability for "synchronous"[99] traffic.

---

[99] In FDDI the word "synchronous" is used to mean "traffic which has a real-time requirement". That is, to transmit synchronous traffic a station must gain access to the ring and transmit its frames within a specified time period. This is *not* the usual meaning of the word synchronous. The usual meaning is that the timing of something (usually a bit stream) is identical over the length of the connection. Also that it is synchronised to something else (such as a system clock). Thus it usually implies regular, exactly timed, delivery of information. The meaning in FDDI is not quite the same.

Token-Ring Protocol

The ring protocol is conceptually similar to the token-ring (IEEE 802.5) LAN but differs significantly in detail. FDDI ring protocol is dependent on timers, whereas, TRN operation is basically event driven.

Ring Stations

An FDDI station may connect to both rings or to only the primary ring. There may be a maximum of 500 stations connected to any one ring segment.

Ring Monitor

Like token-ring, there is a ring monitor function. But unlike token-ring this function is performed cooperatively by all stations rather than by a single active monitor. During operation all stations monitor for errors and if any are found the finder requests re-initialisation of the ring.

Different from token-ring, each station does *not* need to have the ring monitor function.

8.1.1 Structure

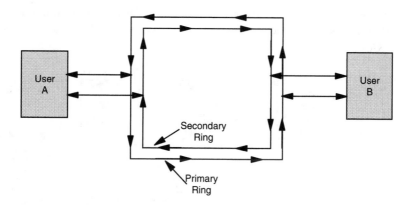

Figure 279. FDDI Basic Structure

Figure 279 shows the basic structure of an FDDI LAN. This consists of counter-rotating rings with the primary one carrying data.

Should there be a break in the ring, the stations can "wrap" the ring through themselves. This is shown in Figure 280 on page 444. The secondary ring is used to complete the break in the primary ring by wrapping back along the operational route.

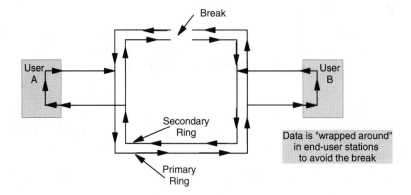

Figure 280. FDDI Ring Healing

There are two classes of station:

Class A Stations connect to both the primary and secondary ring and have the ability to "wrap" the ring to bypass error conditions. These are sometimes called Dual Attachment Stations (DAS).

Class B Stations connect only to the primary ring. This is to allow for lower cost (lower function) attachments. These are called Single Attachment Stations (SAS).

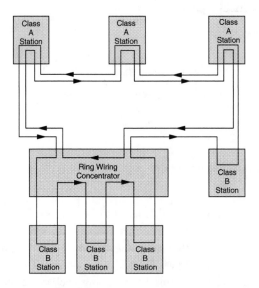

Figure 281. FDDI Ring Configuration

Figure 281 shows class A and B stations connected to a backbone FDDI ring. In addition a Ring Wiring Concentrator (RWC) is present which allows the connection of multiple class B stations in a "star wired" configuration.

The ring wiring concentrator could be a simple device which performs only the RWC function or it could be quite complex containing a class A station with the ring monitor function as well.

Some users choose to attach some SAS stations to the secondary ring. This allows the secondary ring to be used for data transport and of course gives higher aggregate throughput. However, unless there is a bridge between primary and secondary rings, an SAS station on the primary ring cannot communicate with an SAS station on the secondary ring.

8.1.2 Access Protocol Operation

Ring access in FDDI is controlled by a special frame called a token. There is only one token present on the ring at any time. In principle when a station receives a token it has permission to send (place a frame of data onto the ring). When it finishes sending, it must place a new token back onto the ring.

FDDI is a little more complex than suggested above due to the need to handle synchronous traffic. There are three timers kept in each ring station:

Token Rotation Timer (TRT)

> This is the elapsed time since the station last received a token.

Target Token Rotation Timer (TTRT)

> This is a negotiated value which is the target maximum time between opportunities to send (tokens) as seen by an individual station. TTRT has a value of between 4 milliseconds and 165 milliseconds. A recommended optimal value in many situations is 8 milliseconds.

Token Holding Timer (THT)

> This governs the maximum amount of data that a station may send when a token is received. It is literally the maximum time allocated to the station for sending during each rotation of the token.

When a station receives a token it compares the amount of time since it last saw the token (TRT) with the target time for the token to complete one revolution of the ring (TTRT).

- If TRT is less than the target then the station is allowed to send multiple frames until the target time is reached. This means the ring is functioning normally.

$$TTRT - TRT = THT$$

- If TRT is greater than TTRT it means the ring is overloaded. The station may send "synchronous" data only.

- If TRT approaches twice TTRT there is an error condition that must be conveyed by the ring monitor function to the LAN Manager.

- This implies that each station may observe delays to traffic and thus must be able to tolerate these delays - perhaps by buffering the data.

When a station attaches to the ring, it has a dialogue with the ring monitor and it indicates its desired Token Rotation Time according to its needs for synchronous traffic. The ring monitor allocates an Operational Token Rotation Time which is the minimum of all requested TTRT values. This then becomes the operational value for all stations on the ring and may only be changed if a new station enters the ring and requests a lower TTRT value.

Within the asynchronous class of service there are eight priority levels. In token-ring a token is allocated a priority using three priority bits in the token - a station with the token is allowed to send frames with the same or higher priority. In FDDI the priority mechanism uses the Token Rotation Timers rather than a specific priority field in the token.

The sending station must monitor its input side for frames that it transmitted and remove them. A receiving station only copies the data from the ring. Removal of frames from the ring is the responsibility of the sender.

When a station completes a transmission it sends a new token onto the ring. This is called "early token release". Thus there can only be *one* station transmitting onto the ring at one time.

In summary:

- A token circulates on the ring at all times.

- Any station receiving the token has permission to transmit synchronous frames.

- If there is time left over in this rotation of the token the station may send as much data as it likes (multiple frames) until the target token rotation time is reached.

- After transmission the station releases a new token onto the ring.

- Depending on the latency of the ring, there may be many frames on the ring at any one time but there can be only one token.

- The transmitting station has the responsibility of removing the frames it transmitted from the ring when they return to it.

8.1.3 Ring Initialisation, Monitoring and Error Handling

In an FDDI ring there is no single "ring monitor" function such as in an IEEE 802.5 token-ring. This is because all stations on the ring perform part of the function cooperatively.

- The elastic jitter compensation buffer that exists in the active monitor of 802.5 does not exist, because every node regenerates the clock and there is no jitter propagation around the ring.

- All stations monitor the ring for the token arriving within its specified time limit.

- When the ring is initialised all stations cooperate to determine the TTRT value.

- When a break in the ring occurs all stations beacon but give way to any received beacon on their inbound side. In this way the beacon command that circulates on the ring identifies the immediate downstream neighbor of the break in the ring.

8.1.4 Physical Media

There are four types of media currently used for FDDI:

- Multimode Fibre

  This is the originally defined mode of operation and the predominant mode of adapters on the market in 1991.

- Single-Mode Fibre

  This has been included in the standard by ANSI but as yet has only minor usage.

- Shielded Twisted Pair (STP) copper wire

  The use of FDDI over STP cable, while it doesn't have the electrical isolation advantages of fibre, is significantly less than the cost of using FDDI on fibre. This makes FDDI an economic alternative for the desktop workstation.

  In 1992, when a proposal was put to the ANSI committee for a standard that would work on STP but not on UTP it was rejected in favor of the (hoped for) development of a standard that would work on both types of cable. Subsequently, a group of manufacturers, concerned that a standard that would work on UTP was some time away announced products using a specification called "SDDI".

  In 1994, the ANSI committee approved a standard which will work on STP or UTP-5. Most manufacturers are moving to use this standard instead of the previous SDDI implementation.

- Unshielded Twisted Pair-5 (UTP-5)

  In 1994 a standard was established for using FDDI over UTP-5 but *no standard exists for operating over UTP-3*. The UTP-5 standard involves using a changed data encoding scheme from the simple encoding used on fibre.

The ANSI committee is still studying other media:

- Unshielded Twisted Pair-3 (UTP-3)

  There are many problems with the use of UTP-3. Nevertheless, many users have installed low grade Telephone Twisted Pair (TTP) cabling for Ethernet connections. Many of these users now wish to use the same cable for FDDI.

  This problem has been solved but at the cost of very complex tranceivers. However, you have to be very careful in ensuring that the UTP has been installed in accordance with the standard. If it has not, then the link may either have a very high error rate or produce significant EMI (or both)

- SDH/Sonet links

  An FDDI structure could be operated over a wide area using channels derived from the public network. Channels derived from SDH/Sonet can be used[100] to construct an FDDI ring over a wide area using public network facilities. The full 125 Mbaud rate is mapped into into an STS-3c channel.

8.1.5 Physical Layer Protocol

The basic functions of the physical layer are:

1. To transport a stream of bits around the ring from one station to another.

2. Provide access to the ring for each individual station.

To do this the physical layer protocol must:

- Construct a system of clocking and synchronisation such that data may flow around the ring.

- Receive data from a station and convert it into a form suitable for transmission.

- Receive data from the ring and convert it into the form expected by the node access protocol.

- Provide a transmission system that allows the station to send and receive any arbitrary bit stream (transparency).

---

[100] See 8.6, "Synchronous Optical Network (SONET) and SDH" on page 484.

- Signal the station (node access protocol) at the beginning and end of every block of data.

- Keep the ring operational and synchronised even when there is no data flowing.

8.1.5.1 Ring Synchronisation

In FDDI, each ring segment is regarded physically as a separate point-to-point link between adjacent stations. This means that the exact timing of data received at a station *cannot* be the same as the timing of data transmitted. Since it is not possible to build (at an economic cost) oscillators that are exactly synchronised there will be a difference between the data rate of bits received and that of bits transmitted! This is solved by the use of an "elasticity buffer" ten bits wide.

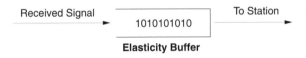

Elasticity Buffer

Figure 282. *Ten-Bit Elasticity Buffer Operation*

Most of the time a station simply passes data on around the ring. The need is to pass this data with minimal delay in each station. This means that we need to start transmitting a block towards the next station *before* it is completely received. The received signal arrives at the rate of the upstream station's transmitter. When data is sent onward to the next station in the ring it is sent at the rate of this station's local oscillator. So data is being received at a different rate from the rate that it is being transmitted!

This discrepancy is handled by placing an "elastic buffer" between the receiver and the input port to the ring station. The ring station is then clocked at the rate of its local oscillator (that is, the transmit rate).

The FDDI specification constrains the clock speed to be ± .005% of the nominal speed (125 megahertz). This means that there is a maximum difference of .01% between the speed of data received and that of data transmitted.

When a station has no data to send and is receiving idle patterns the elasticity buffer is empty. When data begins to arrive the first 4 bits are placed into the buffer and nothing is sent to the station. From then on data bits are received into the buffer and passed out of the buffer in a FIFO manner.

If the transmit clock is faster than the receive clock then there are (on average) 4.5 bit times available in the buffer to smooth out the difference. If the receive clock is faster than the transmit clock there are 5 bit positions in the buffer available before received bits have to be discarded.

This operation determines the maximum frame size:

`(4.5 bits / .01%) = 45,000 bits = 9,000 symbols = 4,500 bytes`

A 16-bit idle pattern is sent after the end of every frame (between frames) so that the receiver has time to empty its elasticity buffer if necessary before the arrival of another frame.

While this mechanism introduces additional latency into each attached station, it has the advantage that it prevents the propagation of code violations and invalid line states.

8.1.5.2 Data Encoding

Each group of four data bits is encoded as a five-bit group for the purpose of transport on the ring. This means that the 100 Mbps data rate is actually 125 Mbaud when observed on the ring itself. This type of encoding is discussed in 7.2.12, "Character Coding" on page 394.

The bit stream resulting from the above encoding is further converted before transmission by using "Non-Return to Zero Inverted" (NRZI) encoding as described in 7.2.1.3, "Non-Return to Zero Inverted (NRZI) Coding" on page 382. This adds more transitions into the data stream to further assist with timing recovery in the receiver. In NRZI encoding, a "1" bit causes a state change and a "0" bit causes no state change.

A sequence of IDLE patterns (B'11111') will result in a signal of 010101 thus maintaining synchronisation at the receiver. Some valid 4B/5B data sequences (for example X'B0' coded as B'10111 11110') can contain up to 7 contiguous "1" bits and NRZI provides the additional transitions that allow the receiver to synchronise satisfactorily.

The combined effect of 4B/5B encoding and NRZI conversion is that the maximum length of signal without a state change is 3 bits.

Table 5 (Page 1 of 2). FDDI Code Translation Table

Data Encoding	Meaning	Symbol	Line Code
0000	Data	0	11110
0001	Data	1	01001

Table 5 (Page 2 of 2). FDDI Code Translation Table

Data Encoding	Meaning	Symbol	Line Code
0010	Data	2	10100
0011	Data	3	10101
0100	Data	4	01010
0101	Data	5	01011
0110	Data	6	01110
0111	Data	7	01111
1000	Data	8	10010
1001	Data	9	10011
1010	Data	A	10110
1011	Data	B	10111
1100	Data	C	11010
1101	Data	D	11011
	Quiet	Q	00000
	Idle	I	11111
	Halt	H	00100
	Start Del (1)	J	11000
	Start Del (2)	K	10001
	Ending Del	T	01101
	Reset	R	00111
	Set	Q	11001
	Code Violation	*V*	Other

8.1.5.3 Media Specifications

FDDI is specified to use either single-mode or multimode fibre at a wavelength of 1300 nm. The standard multimode fibre specification is 62.5/125 but the other sizes of 50/125, 85/125 and 100/140 are optional alternatives. The mode field diameter for single-mode fibre is 9 microns. This means that an LED, rather than a laser, is usually used as the light source and that the detector is a PIN diode rather than an avalanche photo diode.

The power levels are expressed in dBm.[101] Two different transmitter power ranges and two different receiver sensitivity "categories" are specified. These are:

Transmit Power Cat. 1 = From − 20 dBm to − 14 dBm

Transmit Power Cat. 2 = From − 4 dBm to 0 dBm

Receiver Sensitivity Cat. 1 = From − 31 dBm to − 14 dBm

Receiver Sensitivity Cat. 2 = From − 37 dBm to − 15 dBm

A typical tranceiver may have the following specification:

```
Input:   - 16 dBm
Output:  - 27 dBm
```

(Input and output here refer to the optical cable.) What this says is that this FDDI transmitter transmits at a power level of -16 dBm and that the associated receiver is able to handle a signal of -27 dBm. In this implementation this means that you have 11 dB for loss in cables etc. If this cable loses 3 dB per kilometer then for devices two kilometers apart the cable loss will be 6 dB and there is 5 dB left over for losses in splices and connectors etc.

In practical terms (as discussed in 6.3, "Fibre Cables" on page 358) cables vary in their losses and loss varies with temperature. Calculation of maximum allowable distance is something that needs to be done carefully, in conjunction with the cable manufacturer's specifications. For any fibre link longer than a few hundred metres it is advisable to check it carefully on installation using an OTDR. At this time the attenuation for the link should also be measured.

On another point of practicality. Some devices on the market actually transmit at a higher power level than that specified here. In addition, it is easy to overload a PIN diode receiver if the power level is too high. This means that if FDDI stations are installed close together (for example, in the same room), attenuators may be needed in the cable to cut down the light to a level acceptable to the receiver.

---

[101] This is a measure of absolute power. The signal level in decibels in relation to one milliwatt. Thus 3 dBm is 3 dB above 1 milliwatt or 2 mw. -6 dBm is 6 dB below one mw or .25 mw.

8.1.5.4 Optical Bypass Switch

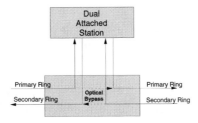

Figure 283. *Optical Bypass Switch*

To maintain connectivity of FDDI rings when power is turned off or when the node fails optical bypass switches may be used, either built into the station or as separate devices

These switches are mechanical devices (switching is mechanical but operation could be electrical) usually operating by moving a mirror. Mechanical operations invariably lack some precision so bypass switches introduce additional loss to the ring even if the station is operating correctly. This limits further the possible distance between nodes.

8.1.5.5 Physical Layer Operation

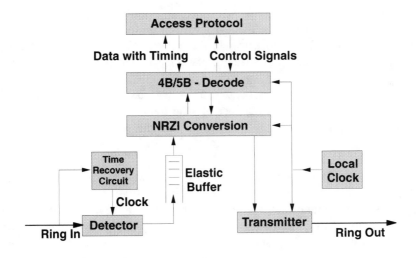

Figure 284. *Physical Layer Structure*

Figure 284 summarises the operation of the physical layer(s) of FDDI.

8.1.5.6 Physical Level Comparison with Token-Ring

In some discussions of FDDI a comparison is drawn with token-ring and the point made that since FDDI uses a data rate of 125 Mbps to send a data stream of 100 Mbps, and token-ring uses two signal cycles per bit (16 Mbps is sent at 32 MHz), that therefore token-ring is somehow "inefficient" by comparison. Nothing could be further from the truth.

Because FDDI is intended primarily to operate over a multimode fibre connection, physical level operation was designed for this environment and is therefore quite different from the electrical operation of token-ring.

In the token-ring architecture, a major objective is to minimise delay in each ring station. This is achieved by having only a single bit buffer in each station for the ring as it "passes by". Operation with such a short delay requires that the output data stream be *exactly* synchronised (both in frequency and in phase) with the input data stream.

There are two problems here:

1. Simple identification and recovery of the data bits

   This requires fairly simple circuitry and usually takes the form of a digital phase locked loop (DPLL).

2. Reconstructing the exact timing of the incoming bit stream

   This means that a new timing signal must be constructed as nearly identical with the signal that was used to construct the received bit stream as possible. To do this requires a very complex analogue phase locked loop.

This then is one of the major reasons for using the Manchester code for TRN. Because of the guaranteed large number of state transitions in the code, the recovery of accurate timing information is much easier and the necessary circuitry is simpler and lower in cost.

On an optical link, data is sent as two states: light or no light. Recovering an accurate clock is more difficult here (especially on multimode fibre). At the speed of FDDI, there is less need to minimise buffering in the node. Also, because of the "early token release" protocol, there is much less loss of efficiency due to node delay. For these reasons, FDDI does not synchronise its output clock to its input clock. The penalty is the need to have the elastic buffer and the added node delay that that implies.

8.1.6 Node Structure

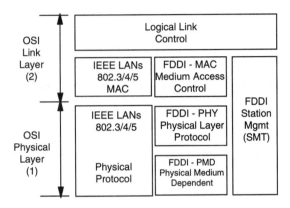

Figure 285. FDDI Node Model

Figure 285 shows the theoretical model of FDDI compared to the IEEE LANs (token-ring, Ethernet...). Their relationship to the OSI model is shown on the left.

It is assumed by FDDI that IEEE 802.2 logical link control will be used with FDDI, but this is not mandatory.

The FDDI standard is structured in a different way to the others. Station management is not a new function. Most of its functions are performed for example by token-ring, but the functions are included in the physical and MAC components. Also, the physical layer is broken into two to facilitate the use of different physical media.

The functions of the defined layers are as follows:

Physical Medium Dependent Layer (PMD)

- Optical link parameters
- Cables and connectors
- Optical bypass switch
- Power budget

Physical Layer Protocol (PHY)

- Access to the ring for MAC
- Clocking, synchronisation, and buffering

- Code conversion

- Ring continuity

Media Access Control

- Use token and timers to determine which station may send next.

- Maintain the timers.

- Generate and verify the frame check sequence etc.

Station Management (SMT)

- Ring Management (RMT)

  This function manages ring operation and monitors the token to ensure that a valid token is always circulating.

- Connection Management (CMT)

  This function establishes and maintains the physical connections and logical topology of the network.

- Operational Management

  This function monitors the timers and various parameters of the FDDI protocols and connects to an external network management function.

8.1.7 High-Speed Performance

Compared with the 16 Mbps token-ring, of course FDDI data transfer (at 100 Mbps) is much faster. Ring latency is, however, another matter. Propagation speed is much the same.

The delay in a TRN node is around two bits. In an FDDI node the delay will depend on the design of the particular chip set but it is difficult to see how the delay could be less than about 20 bits. This means that an FDDI ring will have a longer latency than a 16 Mbps token-ring of the same size and number of stations.

FDDI follows the same "early token release" discipline as 16 Mbps token-ring but still only one station may transmit at any time.

Token Holding Time (THT) is a critical factor. If THT is relatively short, then a station may only send a small amount of data on any visit of the token. If it is set large then a station may transmit a lot of data. Since it can take a relatively long time for the token to go from one station to another, during which no station may transmit, the longer the THT the greater the data throughput of the ring.

A short THT means that "ring latency" can be relatively short so that the delay for a station to gain access to the ring is also short. A short THT therefore is suitable for support of real-time applications. If the THT is very short the system gives better response time but low overall throughput. Setting it very long, gives higher throughput but a relatively poor response time.

The key tuning parameter is the Target Token Rotation Time (TTRT). At ring initialisation all stations on the ring agree to the TTRT by adopting the shortest TTRT requested by any node. Stations then attempt to meet this target by limiting their transmissions. TTRT is a parameter which may be set by system definition in each node.

Work reported by Raj Jain (referenced in the bibliography) suggests that a value of eight milliseconds is a good compromise in most situations.

Of course, there may be only one token on the ring at any time and only one station may transmit at any time. In a long ring (a large number of stations and/or a great geographic distance), this represents some wasted potential.

8.2 Ethernet (IEEE 802.3)

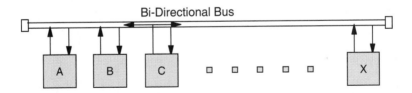

Figure 286. *Ethernet Bus Topology*

The basic topology of an Ethernet network is shown in Figure 286. Many end user devices are connected to a common bus using the same transmission protocol and band. When one station sends all stations receive the data and check to see if it is addressed to them. If it is not then the frame of data is discarded. If two stations transmit simultaneously then garbage is created. It can be seen here that the principal problem is the question of how access to the bus (permission to transmit) is to be managed. The protocol used to control access to the medium is called the "Media Access Control (MAC)" protocol.

8.2.1 Principles of Ethernet

The basic principle used in Ethernet is called "Carrier Sense Multiple Access with Collision Detection (CSMA/CD)".

Using this technique, before a device can send on the LAN it must "listen" to see if another device is sending. If another device is already sending, then the device must wait until the LAN becomes free. Even so, there is always a time during which two devices might start sending at the same time without knowing it. In this case there will be a collision and neither transmission will be received correctly. In CSMA/CD, devices listen to the bus to detect collisions. When a collision occurs the devices must wait for different lengths of time before attempting to retry. It is not always certain that data will get through without error or that the sending station will know about lost data. Therefore, each user of the LAN must operate an "end-to-end" protocol for error recovery and data integrity.

In all CSMA type LANs there is a gap in time between when one device starts to send and before another potential sender can detect the condition. The longer this gap is, the higher the chance that another sender will try to send and, therefore, the higher the possibility of collision. The major determinant of the length of the gap is the physical length of the LAN. Since we can't easily change the timeout conditions the practical efficiency of this kind of LAN is restricted by the maximum allowed physical length of the LAN rather than its actual length in any given situation. The utilization of the carrier medium (usually a bus) is limited more by collision probabilities than by data block sizes. In some situations, 10% is considered quite a good bus utilisation.

Performance:

- As the data transfer speed of the LAN increases, throughput does not increase at the same rate. Faster link speeds do nothing to affect the propagation delays. Thus the length of the "gaps" during which collisions can occur becomes the dominant characteristic.

- There is no way of allocating priorities.

- Fairness of access to the LAN is questionable.

- Low access delay. CSMA techniques have the advantage that if nothing is currently happening on the LAN, a device may send immediately and doesn't have to wait (as it does in some other techniques). A disadvantage is that as LAN utilization increases, access delay becomes highly erratic and (potentially at least) unbounded.

The big advantage of CSMA techniques is one of cost:

- The hardware adapters are very simple and low in cost.

- The cables typically used are low-cost telephone twisted pair or CATV style coaxial cable.

- In the early days, Ethernet usually ran over genuine bus-type networks, which used less cable than ring or star topologies. However, real bus based networks are very difficult to manage and all of today's Ethernet networks are star-wired from hubs.

The principles of CSMA/CD LANs are well understood and described in many textbooks. However, a short overview is presented here as background to the discussion of performance.

Structure

In IEEE 802.3 networks, stations are connected to a bus such as that shown in Figure 286 on page 457. Any station may transmit on the bus and the transmission propagates in both directions and is received by all other stations.

In modern 802.3 networks, the wiring is usually through a hubbing device (each station is wired point-to-point to the hub and the bus is put together by wiring within the hub).

Frame Format

Each transmitted frame is preceded by an 8-byte preamble used for synchronization and delimiting the start of a frame. This is followed by the header including the destination address (6 bytes), the source address (6 bytes) and a 2-byte length field. The user data may vary from 46 to 1500 bytes - if a frame is shorter than 46 data bytes it must be padded out to length. The whole is followed by a 2-byte CRC. Thus a frame on the LAN may be from 70 bytes to 1524 bytes.

Protocol

The CSMA/CD protocol is extremely simple:

- When a station has data to transmit, it listens to the bus to see if any other station is transmitting.

- If no other station is transmitting, the station starts its own transmission immediately.

- If another station is transmitting (the bus is busy), then the station must wait until the bus becomes free.

- As soon as the bus becomes free, the station may start its own transmission.

- Because there is a time delay for electricity to travel down the bus, two stations may start transmission simultaneously. If this happens, a collision will occur and data will be lost.

- In order to recover from the loss of data due to collisions, a transmitting station must listen to the bus while it is sending to monitor for collisions.

- On detection of a collision, the transmitting station sends a short "jamming" signal (to improve the chance that the other transmitting station will also detect the collision) and immediately stops its transmission.

- Each station (that was in the collision) now waits for a random delay before trying to transmit again.

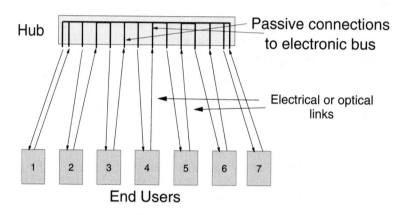

Figure 287. Ethernet Hub Topology

As mentioned above, Ethernet today is always wired radially from a hub device as illustrated in Figure 287. This is done for two basic reasons:

1. Bus cabled networks are exceedingly difficult to manage. Location and correction of faults is difficult. The addition of new workstations and the re-location of old ones is also unwieldy.

2. Today people desire to use unshielded twisted pair copper cable for cost reasons. UTP has too much attenuation and is therefore too limiting in terms of distance for use as a bus.

Although the wiring is a star in topology the system is still a logical bus as the bus connections are made within the hub.

8.2.2 Ethernet on Fibre

Even a superficial glance at the Ethernet protocol shows that it cannot be easily implemented solely on fibre. The problem is that we can't construct an optical bus network in the way that we can construct a copper one.

It would be certainly possible to use Ethernet protocols over a star topology such as that described in 10.2.1, "Network Topology" on page 585. However, it would have severe restrictions on the number of attached stations due to the required equal splitting of the signal at the star coupler.

When Ethernet is run on fibre, the fibre replaces a point-to-point copper link connection. Basic Ethernet runs at a speed of 10 Mbps encoded as 20 Mbaud (2 baud per bit) using Manchester encoding.

The Manchester coding is very important as it is the basis for collision detection. The Manchester code is a balanced code. When two signals collide they OR with one another rather than add arithmetically. The OR of two balanced signals is no longer balanced. The imbalance in the signal gives rise to a direct current (DC) fluctuation on the wire which is detected by the end stations and interpreted as a collision.

Translating this signal to fibre is very easy. The two-state electrical signal is just sent as a two-state optical signal and all is fine. The 20 Mbaud signal requires only around 30 MHz of bandwidth so it cannot tax the capabilities of even the lowest quality MM fibre.

The optical specification of 10 Mbps Ethernet uses LEDs at a nominal wavelength of 850 nm.

8.2.3 CSMA/CD Performance

The central problem for CSMA/CD protocols is propagation delay.

- When a station starts to transmit, it takes time for the signal to propagate down the bus and for other stations to become aware that the bus is busy. During that time a second station may detect that the bus is free and start transmitting itself - causing a collision.

- When some station is transmitting (and the bus is busy), other stations may themselves acquire data for transmission. When the bus becomes free, all the stations that were waiting now try to transmit.

- However, propagation delay has the same effect at the end of a transmission as it does at the beginning. It means that stations become aware that the bus is now free at different times, depending on where they are on the bus in relation to the transmitter that has just stopped.

Propagation speed in this environment is about 5.2 μsec per kilometer (this increases slightly if there are many repeaters involved - because they buffer a few bits). If an average data block ("frame") is 1000 bits long then the average transmission time is 100 μsec (at 10 Mbps). Overall efficiency depends critically on the ratio of these two factors.

The accepted formula for the *absolute maximum* throughput on a CSMA/CD LAN is:

$$\text{Maximum Utilization} = \frac{1}{1 + 6.44\rho}$$

Where:

$$\rho = \frac{\text{end-to-end delay}}{\text{transmission time}}$$

(This formula is *not* absolutely accurate in all situations because it rests on assumptions about the statistical distribution of stations wanting to transmit. It represents the worst case.)

Applying the formula to a regular 802.3 LAN at 10 Mbps, for a block length of 1000 bits (100 μsec transmit time), and a LAN length of 2 km (a delay of 10.4 μsec), we get a maximum utilization of 58%. At 100 Mbps the maximum utilization (from the formula) is 13%. It is important to realize that these percentage figures represent a kind of 100% utilization figure. To achieve this utilization, attached stations would need to have an infinite queue length (and an infinite access delay). Thus when evaluating queueing delays we need to treat this "maximum utilization" as the media speed.

8.2.3.1 Why Does Ethernet Work so Well?

From the above discussion it seems clear that CSMA-CD leaves a lot to be desired as a LAN access method. Clearly, depending on traffic characteristics, it has a maximum useful throughput of between 15% and 40% of the medium speed. Further, access delay (the time it takes for a workstation to get access to the LAN) is random and unpredictable. *Yet Ethernet works. Ethernet equipment forms over 80% of all LAN equipment in existence and in the vast majority of cases it functions very well indeed. The question is why?*

Figure 288 on page 463 shows what happens as more and more load is presented to an Ethernet. By "presented" here we mean that a station on the LAN has the data and is trying to send it. Notice that when load gets too high for the LAN, instead of data continuing to be transported at some maximum figure, LAN operation collapses and nothing at all gets through! Why then does it work so well (*and it does!*)?

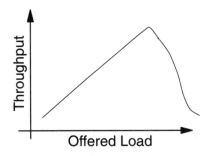

Figure 288. *Relationship between Offered Load and Throughput on Ethernet. As "offered load" increases so does throughput (the network handles the load) until a point is reached where too many stations are trying to send. At this point the network collapses and no traffic gets through.*

There are many answers to this:

- The real problem is that the assumptions upon which Figure 288 is based are false. These assumptions are as follows:

    1. A large number of workstations are connected to the LAN.

    2. Traffic demand from workstations is "random" in nature.

    3. Traffic is any-to-any.

    The fact is that very few LANs, if any, exhibit these characteristics.

- Traffic is almost never any-to-any at random. Traffic is almost always client-to-server and server-to-client. On a typical LAN with 100 workstations there will be only perhaps five servers (for example, two data servers, two print servers and a WAN gateway server).

    When a client sends a request to a data server, it must wait for the server to respond before it sends anything else. In its turn, when the server has sent one data block (out of a file of perhaps 100 data blocks) then the client must respond before the server is allowed to send the next block (to this particular client).

    This has two effects:

1. It provides an elementary "higher-layer" flow control protocol. If the LAN becomes congested and data takes some time to get through, then the rate of requests drops correspondingly.

2. Every operation on the LAN becomes serialized to the speed of the server. If 30 clients try to get data from the server simultaneously, then the server will only be able to service these requests at the (quite limited) speed of its disk access subsystem. Indeed many servers limit the maximum number of requests that can be in progress at any one time.

   This means that the total maximum demand that can be placed on the LAN (in many situations) is the total available throughput of the servers.

- The client/server method of operation described above also has the side effect of ensuring that only a very few stations ever make simultaneous requests! Figure 288 on page 463 assumes that traffic comes from an unlimited (large) number of simultaneous requesters. With only a few simultaneous requests, you do get some throughput and the system does continue to operate without collapse.

- Perhaps one answer is that it doesn't work very well at all! In recent years, LANs have become bigger and workstations faster, so throughput has become a more and more significant problem. Large users have been continually faced with segmenting their LANs and connecting the segments together with bridges or routers to get around severe congestion problems.

Nevertheless, most practical LANs consist of perhaps five PCs sharing a printer or a dozen or so PCs sharing a file server. In these situations Ethernet is cheap, simple, and works very well indeed.

8.2.4 High Speed or "Fast" (100 Mbps) Ethernet (HSE)

The objective of the 100 megabit CSMA/CD development was to provide a natural growth path upward from the existing 10Base-T (10 Mbps on UTP) standard. It was felt (accurately) that there would be significant user demand for a simple, cost-effective upgrade path.

The requirements were as follows:

- It must be low in cost. Otherwise the user would be better off going to FDDI (on copper or fibre).

- It must preserve the existing 802.3 MAC (Medium Access Control) logic. This is needed to allow most existing software to use the system.

- It *must* use UTP (unshielded twisted pair) cabling. This is because most current 802.3 users have UTP cabling.

- It must be capable of easy migration from the existing standard.

The way chosen to meet these requirements was to reduce the maximum physical extent of the LAN, reduce the timeouts accordingly and leave everything else the same. Of course new link encoding protocols had to be designed to work on the various media at the higher speed.

- In standard Ethernet the maximum physical extent of the LAN is 1.6 kilometers. Timeouts were calculated to allow for propagation delays over this distance. In fast Ethernet the maximum physical distance between any two end users in the same "collision domain" is 200 metres. Timeouts were re-calculated to fit these shorter distances.

- All of the other timings and parameters of 10 Mbps Ethernet are maintained with fast Ethernet. This means that the performance characteristics (maximum utilization, etc.) are the same as for 10Base-T.

- All fast Ethernet devices must be connected to a hub. Bus connection as used in traditional Ethernet is not possible.

8.2.4.1 100Base-FX - 100 Megabit Ethernet on MM Fibre

Fast Ethernet uses identical physical layer optical specifications to those of FDDI. This applies to the optical signal specifications, data encodings and even the cable plugs. There are minor modifications to allow for environmental differences caused by the continuous nature of the FDDI stream and the burst nature of Ethernet. See 8.1.5, "Physical Layer Protocol" on page 448.

8.2.5 Gigabit Ethernet (GbE)

Gigabit Ethernet could mark a milestone in the history of local network communications. It looks like being the very first networking system where the cost of implementation on optical media is less than the cost on electrical media!

As the name suggests, gigabit Ethernet is designed to scale Ethernet up again in speed by another order of magnitude. The data transfer rate is 1 Gbps of real data (which means 1.25 Gbaud after encoding). This involves some very real technical challenges!

If we scale Ethernet up in speed again by restricting the geographic size of the network then we would arrive at a maximum network extent of 20 metres! This would not be very useful! However the technological environment and the user requirement has changed quite a lot in the last few years. The role of shared media networks has changed a lot.

Switches versus Shared Media

The basic principle of a shared medium network such as an Ethernet network is that all end users connect to a common medium. When one sends, the others listen and we achieve any-to-any connectivity. But this means that only one device can send at any one time. From a throughput point of view we can say that "on average" every device on the LAN gets an equal share of the LAN capacity. Further every device on the LAN must connect to it at the common speed of the LAN.

The consequence of this is that every end user gets (on average) 1/n th of the capacity of the LAN (n = the number of connected users). But each end user must pay the cost of a LAN attachment adapter that runs at the full speed of the LAN! Up to a certain speed this doesn't matter but when you get to very high speeds (whatever "very high" means at the time) you get a problem. Each end user gets only a relatively low throughput from the LAN but they must pay for a very high speed adapter to do it. If you look at the total cost it becomes quite high.

If we replace the network hub with a switch (where the MAC protocol stops) we can get higher throughput per end user with much lower speed (lower cost) end user adapters. There is now a trade-off between the cost of the switch and the extra cost of the end-user adapters.

It turns out that for high-throughput LANs you get better throughput per end user and lower total network cost using switches rather than shared media! In addition, the use of switches allows networks to use different speeds for different end-users. For example:

- PCs doing text applications may be connected to a switch over a shared segment at 10 Mbps.

- Technical workstations might be connected directly to the switch at 10 or 100 Mbps.

- High function servers might be connected at 1 Gbps directly to the switch.

- Switches may be connected to each other at either 100 Mbps or 1 Gbps.

In this example all of these connection types may be on the same switch thus optimising the throughput and cost of the system.

User Requirement

In light of the above economic considerations it is felt that users will want gigabit Ethernet to perform a different role from the one historically played by "regular" Ethernet. Thus it is likely that GbE will be used in two roles:

1. Point-to-point connection

   This may be between pairs of switches (or routers) or between end users and a switch (or router). Point-to-point connections do *not* have timing restrictions and therefore these can be as long as the physical protocol allows.

2. Collision domain

   It is felt that it is important to retain collision domain type operation with a LAN extent of 200 metres. This is needed to give users flexibility. However there are things we can do to make this a bit more efficient.

8.2.5.1 Protocol Modifications

Gigabit Ethernet is just the same as regular Ethernet with some changes to the MAC layer protocol and completely new physical layers.

Collision Domain Environment

The Ethernet MAC protocol is maintained and the maximum extent is the same as for HSE.

Minimum Frame Size

It is very important that GbE have the same minimum frame size as the other two major Ethernet systems because we must have software compatibility. However, the minimum frame size is not arbitrary. The sender of a frame must be sure that a collision has not occurred on a frame it has sent. The minimum frame must be long enough so that the sender is still transmitting when it is notified of a collision. Thus it must be a multiple of the maximum propagation delay across the LAN.

GbE needs a minimum frame size of 512 bytes! For frames shorter than 512 bytes the sender must continue to send idle characters after completion of the data frame up to 512 byte times. This is called "carrier extension". This means that the shortest frame you can send in a collision domain is 512 bytes (point-to-point links are different).

Maximum Frame Size

The maximum frame size of 1524 bytes is the same as before. However, for increased efficiency the MAC protocol allows a station to send multiple frames in bursts rather than just a single frame. This is similar in principle to what FDDI does in the same situation - for the same reasons.

8.2.5.2 Gigabit Ethernet Media

At the time of writing this is a highly controversial issue. The five media types involved are:

Unshielded Twisted Pair Class-3 (UTP-3)

> At the present time there is no proposal to use UTP-3 for GbE because it is felt to be outside the capability of this medium.

Unshielded Twisted Pair Class-5 (UTP-5)

> This is a high-quality balanced cable. At this time there is a firmly proposed protocol. Basically, you use all four pairs in the cable to carry 250 Mbps each bi-directionally. This is a big ask. Many people are very enthusiastic about it and believe it will perform well. Some others believe that it cannot work at the current state of technology. In this regard we mean "cannot keep within the legal radio frequency emission limits".

Shielded Twisted Pair (STP)

> GbE will work fine on STP for distances of up to about 500 metres.

Single-Mode Fibre

> No problems here. GbE will work very well indeed on SMF for as great a distance as we like.

Multimode Fibre

> Herein lies both a controversy and a genuine problem. It is generally agreed that we would like to use MM fibre for distances of up to 2 km. Many users have cable runs already installed like this. However, some people believe that it cannot work reliably for further than about 250 metres. See the discussion in the next section and in 7.6.2.1, "Use of Lasers on MM Fibre" on page 424.

8.2.5.3 Optical Specifications

The physical layer encoding uses 8/10 code in the same way as Fibre Channel and ESCON.

There are two proposed optical physical layers:

Single-Mode Fibre

> GbE on SM fibre uses a wavelength of 1310 nm and is planned to operate at distances up to 2 km.

Multimode Fibre

This specification is still under development. However, it is planned to use CD-ROM lasers at a wavelength of 780 nm on MM fibre or VCSELs at a wavelength of 850 nm. On 62.5 micron MM GI fibre specified for FDDI the allowed distance is 200 metres. It is hoped that by implementing a restricted launch (as discussed in 7.6.2.1, "Use of Lasers on MM Fibre" on page 424) the available distance may be able to be extended up to at least 1 km and perhaps 2 km.

8.3 Fibre Channel

Fibre channel is a standard developed by the American National Standards Institute (ANSI) Committee X.3 to address problems with existing computer channel interfaces such as HIPPI, IPI and SCSI.

It specifies the point-to-point physical interface, transmission protocol and signalling protocol for a high-speed serial link connection that has small-footprint connectors and is scalable in terms of cost, distance and speed. Many different "higher layer" protocols may use this link connection.

It may be thought of as a hybrid between a channel and a network, having enough network capability to support distributed processing over considerable distances using serial interfaces while maintaining the simple, reliable interfaces usually associated with channel connections. Recently fibre channel has also been promoted as an alternative LAN protocol.

In addition to passive topologies, fibre channel allows for a self-managed "fabric" functioning as a crosspoint switch and capable of controlling the topology dynamically.

8.3.1 Structure

Fibre channel allows for the interconnection of computers and peripheral devices using point-to-point, crosspoint switch or arbitrated loop technologies. Each such device is called a "node" and each node connects to the fibre channel through an N_Port (or NL_Port for an arbitrated loop). The N_Port design is symmetric for both computers and peripherals allowing common connectors to be used. The three types of connectivity are:

Point-to-Point

This topology, illustrated in Figure 289 on page 470, connects two nodes directly and neither fabric nor fabric services are involved.

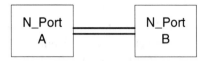

Figure 289. Fibre Channel Point-to-Point Topology

Crosspoint Switch

The crosspoint switch, illustrated in Figure 290, allows interconnection of any two attached nodes and contains a fabric that controls the topology, handling connection requests from attached nodes. Attachment to the fabric is through F_Ports (or FL_Ports if the fabric is attached to an arbitrated loop).

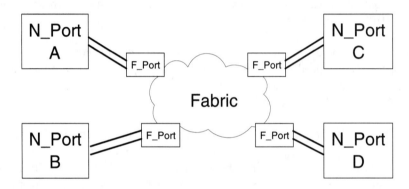

Figure 290. Fibre Channel Crosspoint Switch Topology

Arbitrated Loop

The arbitrated loop, illustrated in Figure 291 on page 471, provides for low cost attachment of 3 to 126 nodes in special environments such as a string of disk drives. Devices are connected to the loop through an NL_Port. Fabric elements may also be connected to the loop through an FL_Port.

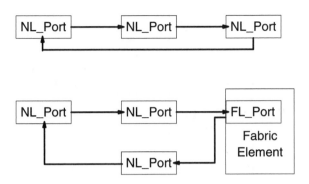

Figure 291. *Fibre Channel Arbitrated Loop Topologies*

Fibre channel is structured as a set of layers:

FC-0   defines media and interfaces (receivers and transmitters)

FC-1   defines the transmission protocol

FC-2   defines the signalling protocol and link services

FC-3   defines the common services

FC-4   defines the mapping to the upper layer protocols

ULP   are the upper layer protocols such as IPI3, SCSI, IP and SBCCS that use the fibre channel services

FC-0, FC-1 and FC-2 together constitute the fibre channel physical layer FC-PH.

8.3.2 Physical Media

The FC-0 specification allows several physical variants depending on speed, media, transmitter type and range. Each variant is described by a symbol with one code from each of these four characteristics as shown in Figure 292 on page 472.

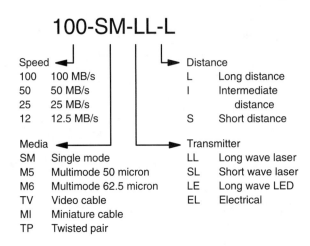

100-SM-LL-L

Speed
100	100 MB/s
50	50 MB/s
25	25 MB/s
12	12.5 MB/s

Distance
L	Long distance
I	Intermediate distance
S	Short distance

Media
SM	Single mode
M5	Multimode 50 micron
M6	Multimode 62.5 micron
TV	Video cable
MI	Miniature cable
TP	Twisted pair

Transmitter
LL	Long wave laser
SL	Short wave laser
LE	Long wave LED
EL	Electrical

Figure 292. Fibre Channel Physical Nomenclature

The transmission uses an IBM patented 8B/10B encoding so the above speeds use 1062.5 Mbaud for 100 MBps data transfer, 531 Mbaud for 50 MBps, 266 Mbaud for 25 MBps and 132 Mbaud for 12.5 MBps.

Table 6 (Page 1 of 2). Fibre Channel Media Capabilities

Media variant	Fibre type	Transmitter Type	Wavelength	Data Rate (MBps)	Bit Rate (Mbaud)	Distance
100-SM-LL-L	SM	Longwave laser	1300nm	100	1062.5	2m-10km
100-SM-LL-I	SM	Longwave laser	1300nm	100	1062.5	2m-2km
50-SM-LL-L	SM	Longwave laser	1300nm	50	531.25	2m-10km
25-SM-LL-L	SM	Longwave laser	1300nm	25	265.625	2m-10km
25-SM-LL-I	SM	Longwave laser	1300nm	25	265.625	2m-2km
100-M5-SL-I	MM 50 micron	Shortwave laser	780nm	100	1062.5	2m-500m
50-M5-SL-I	MM 50 micron	Shortwave laser	780nm	50	531.25	2m-1km
25-M5-SL-I	MM 50 micron	Shortwave laser	780nm	25	265.625	2m-2km
25-M6-LE-I	MM 62.5 micron	LED	1300nm	25	265.625	2m-1.5km

Table 6 (Page 2 of 2). *Fibre Channel Media Capabilities*

Media variant	Fibre type	Transmitter Type	Wavelength	Data Rate (MBps)	Bit Rate (Mbaud)	Distance
12-M6-LE-I	MM 62.5 micron	LED	1300nm	12.5	132.8125	2m-1.5km

The range limits are designed for interconnection of equipment from several manufacturers subject to the fibre channel tolerance specifications. In some cases greater range may be achieved with specific knowledge of the components actually being used for a particular link.

8.3.3 Transmission Protocol

The transmission protocol in layer FC-1 is specified as an 8B/10B code. Each 8 data bits are encoded into a 10-bit transmission character.[102] The code is adaptive in the sense that it is designed to limit the run length of consecutive 1s or 0s and also maintain DC balance. See 7.2.12, "Character Coding" on page 394 for more discussion of these issues. The 10-bit transmission characters are divided into data characters which encode 8-bit bytes and 12 special characters. 10-bit transmission characters are further subdivided into a 6-bit sub-block and a 4-bit sub-block. The system maintains a *running disparity* which is either positive or negative according to whether the last transmitted (or received) sub-block had more 1s than 0s or vice-versa. The encoding of each data or special character is chosen according to the current value of the running disparity so that each data or special character has two valid forms for transmission. The remaining encodings are invalid.

Certain combinations of four special or data characters are called *Ordered Sets* and are used as frame delimiters for the different types of allowable frames, primitive signals (Idle and Receiver_Ready), and primitive sequences (Offline, Not_Operational, Link_Reset and Link_Reset_Response).

Frame types include:

SOFc1 Start of Frame Connect Class 1
SOFi1 Start of Frame Initiate Class 1
SOFn1 Start of Frame Normal Class 1
SOFi2 Start of Frame Initiate Class 2
SOFn2 Start of Frame Normal Class 2
SOFi3 Start of Frame Initiate Class 3

---

[102] The code used is the same code as used in the IBM ESCON (see 8.4, "ESCON and Inter-System Coupling (ISC)" on page 477) channels.

SOFn3 Start of Frame Normal Class 2
SOFf   Start of Frame Fabric
EOFt   End of Frame Terminate
EOFdt End of Frame Disconnect-Terminate
EOFa   End of Frame Abort
EOFn   End of Frame Normal
EOFdti End of Frame Disconnect-Terminate-Invalid
EOFni End of Frame Normal-Invalid

8.3.4 Signalling Protocol

Three classes of service are defined for fibre channel:

Class 1 - Dedicated Connection

Dedicated connections to connect two N_Ports are established and maintained by the fabric. Maximum bandwidth is guaranteed and frames are delivered in the order they are sent.

Class 2 - Multiplex

This is a connectionless service. The fabric may deliver frames out of order. In the event of link errors the source identifier of the frame may not be error free so such errors are not reported to the sender. Otherwise the fabric notifies whether delivery was successful or not.

Class 3 - Datagram

This too is a connectionless service with frames multiplexed by the fabric. However, in this case the fabric is only expected to make a best effort to deliver the frame and no acknowledgments are supported. Any recovery is the responsibility of the upper level protocol using the service. Again, frames may be delivered out of order.

In the absence of a fabric all classes of service become special cases of point-to-point.

The building blocks used from transmissions in FC-2 are:

Frame

The frame (mentioned in 8.3.3, "Transmission Protocol" on page 473) is the basic transmission unit of FC-2.

Sequence

A sequence is a unidirectional set of data frames sent from one N_Port to another N_Port together with the corresponding link control response frames.

The sequence has an sequence identifier (SEQ_ID) and each N_Port maintains the current sequence status in a Sequence Status Block (SSB).

Exchange

An exchange is a set of non-concurrent sequences sent between a pair of N_Ports. It is unidirectional if all the sequences are initiated by one N_Port; otherwise, it is bidirectional. The exchange has an exchange identifier (OX_ID) generated by the originating N_Port and another (RX_ID) generated by the responding N_Port. For class 1 and class 2 transmissions the RX_ID is communicated to the exchange initiator. Similar to the case for sequences, the progress of an exchange is maintained in an Exchange Status Block.

Protocol

FC-PH provides rules and data transfer protocols that are used by higher layers. These include:

Primitive Sequence Protocols

These use the primitive sequences to handle functions such as online/offline transition, and link initialization, failure or reset.

Fabric Login Protocol

This allows an N_Port to exchange parameters with a fabric. This may be an explicit login, or may be accomplished in an implicit fashion not defined by FC-PH.

N_Port Login Protocol

Before data transfer can occur the N_Ports exchange service parameters. Again, this may be an explicit login, or may be accomplished in an implicit fashion not defined by FC-PH.

Data Transfer Protocol

For class 1 service a connection request frame (SOFc1) is sent by the originator. After receiving R_RDY from the fabric and ACK from the destination N_Port the originator continues to stream frames and the destination responds with ACK for each one. The ACK for the last frame of the sequence is imbedded with EOFt (terminate) or EOFdt (disconnect-terminate) indicating the end of the sequence. Either end may send additional sequences within the exchange until a final frame indicates last sequence and last frame.

For class 2 service there is no connection request and the fabric returns R_RDY after each frame. Otherwise the protocol is similar to class 1.

The data transfer protocol for class 3 service is similar to class 2 except for the absence of ACKs.

N_Port Logout Protocol

An N_Port requests removal of its service parameters from the partner N_Port and frees up resources associated with the association using this protocol.

8.3.5 Open Fibre Control (OFC) Safety System

The OFC system is designed to shut down the optical power whenever there is a break (or disconnection) in the fibre. This is necessary for operation in the short wavelength band (780 nm) as the optical power level used in this band is relatively high. In some countries this power level is above the "Class-1" safety limit.

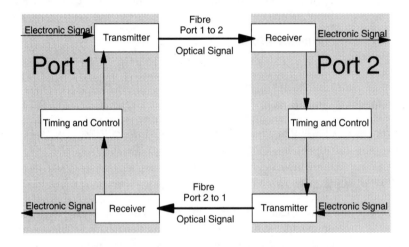

Figure 293. *Open Fibre Control System - Logic Structure*

The principle involved is extremely simple. An adapter is always both a transmitter and receiver. So an adapter's transmitter is shut down whenever its associated receiver is *not* detecting light. If there is a break in a fibre (say) from box 1 to box 2 then the transmitter in box 2 will be shut down. Box 1 then detects that its input light has been lost and shuts down its own transmitter. This process can be extremely fast (less than 1 millisecond) and will almost eliminate any danger of exposure to excessive optical power levels.

However, there is an obvious problem. How do you re-start communication (or start it in the first place)? The most common cause of an interruption to a link is just someone removing a connector plug and perhaps replacing it soon after. We have a situation of "deadly embrace" (deadlock) where each end waits for the other to start and therefore neither can start.

Both at startup and after a link break there is a protocol to establish the connection safely and reliably. When an adapter port is active but seeing the "loss-of-light"(LOL) condition it sends a pulse of light at regular (defined) intervals. While in this state if it then receives a similar pulse it determines that the other end adapter is there and turns its laser on. If the other adapter doesn't respond by turning its laser on within a specified interval the adapter goes back to the LOL state. When both lasers are turned on we have an active connection.

The protocol is actually quite a lot more complex than this. It is set up so that when adapters recognise that there is a connection, each adapter tests to see if its partner has the OFC system and if it is active. If this is not the case then the link will not function. Thus if a regular (non-OFC) adapter is connected to one with OFC capability the OFC capable adapter will refuse to function.

8.4 ESCON and Inter-System Coupling (ISC)

IBM Enterprise Systems Connection (ESCON) architecture was designed for interconnecting mainframe computers and their I/O controllers in a distributed system environment. It is optimised for this purpose and is not intended for general purpose communications in either the LAN or WAN environments. Nevertheless, it is a very advanced, high-speed, circuit-switched system and is useful as an example of what can be achieved with the circuit-switching technique.

With ESCON, users can construct distributed computer and peripheral configurations spanning quite large areas (a few kilometers). Optical connection is extremely beneficial in this environment for its high noise immunity, low error rates, high speed and, most important, electrical isolation. One of the major problems in computer cabling has been the potential for "ground loops".

The ESCON system is very well described in a special issue of the IBM Research and Development Journal (July 1992). The brief discussion here looks at ESCON as a local communications architecture. This is only a small aspect of the wider ESCON system.

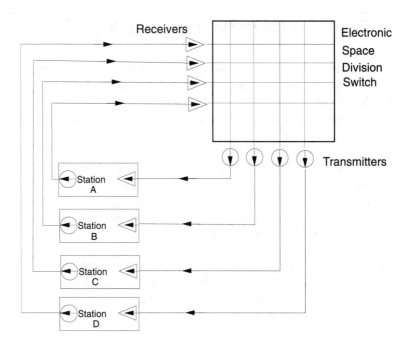

Figure 294. *Principle of the ESCON Director (Circuit Switch). Fibre optical links are used to connect stations to an electronic space division switch.*

The switching principle used in the IBM ESCON Director is illustrated in Figure 294. Conceptually, the Director is a conventional cross-point (space division) switching system. (Albeit its internal operation is far from conventional.) Copper wire connections from the stations (control units and processors) have been replaced with fibre but the switch itself is electronic.

Stations, whether controllers or processors (at the switching level the distinction has no meaning) connect to the ESCON Director on optical fibre. The Director is a (very) fast circuit switch. Above the physical connection structure known by the Director there is a logical "virtual link" (channel) structure unknown to the Director.

8.4.1.1 Method of Operation

Operation is very simple (in concept):

1. When a station is not connected to anything the Director is listening for any input.

2. When a station wants to communicate with another station it sends a connection request to the Director.

3. The Director receives the connection request and if the requested destination is not busy it makes the switched connection and passes the connection request on to the destination station.

4. From this point the Director is not involved in the communication. Data passes between connected stations freely (in synchronous mode) until either station sends a DISCONNECT request.

5. The director senses the DISCONNECT request and breaks the circuit (after the DISCONNECT has been sent on to the partner station).

The reason that ESCON works so well is the architecture of the Director itself. The Director pipelines connection and disconnection requests and can handle them at a maximum rate of one every 200 ns (that is 5 million per second). The time taken to make a switch depends on load (request rate) and number of active stations etc. but in most situations connections are made in between 2 and 3 μsec (plus any propagation delay). A stable operation at a rate of between one and two million connections (plus disconnections) per second can be sustained.

8.4.1.2 Performance

Looking at this system as a form of packet switch, to transfer a block of data we must:

1. Make a connection request.
2. Send the data.
3. Make a disconnection request.

Let us assume we want to transfer a 1,000-byte block. At a data rate of 160 Mbps a 1,000-byte block takes 50 μsec to transmit. If it takes 3 μsec to establish a connection and perhaps 2 μsec to clear it the total "overhead" is 5 μsec. This gives a total time of 55 μsec.

If the system was a real packet switch we wouldn't have the connection establishment and clearing overheads. But a real packet switch would have to receive the data block in full, perform processing to determine the routing, and then retransmit the data towards its destination. For the 1,000-byte block above that is 50 μsec times two for transmission time plus perhaps 2 μsec for route determination within the packet switch itself. A total time of 102 μsec. In this example the circuit switch clearly outperforms the packet switching technique.[103] (In the real environment of a computer channel I/O system performance will be even better than this example suggests because computers tend to transfer more than one block of data and control information per connection.)

8.4.1.3 Structure
Optical Links

The optical links use a wavelength of 1300 nm (dispersion minimum) over either multimode or single-mode fibre. (The single-mode option is a recently announced extension to allow for longer connection distances.) LED transmitters and PIN detectors are used at a link speed of 200 Mbaud.

Data on the link is coded using an 8/10 coding system. The data rate on the link is 160 Mbps (20 MBps). (This compares with the maximum speed of the electronic channel system of 4.5 MBps.) Conceptually this coding system is much the same as the 4/5 coding scheme used with FDDI (this is described in more detail in 8.1.5.2, "Data Encoding" on page 450). The reasons behind using a 10-bit code to transmit only 8 bits are:

1. Provide redundant codes to allow for data transparency (delimiters and control codes are not valid data combinations).

2. Provide a balancing of the number of ones and zeros within the transmitted data stream such that the number or ones and zeros is always equal[104] (DC balancing) and no string of like bits is ever longer than five. (This latter aids in timing recovery.)

---

[103] The example is a little simplistic because additional end-to-end protocol exchanges are needed in the real world. However, they have the same affect on both circuit and packet switching systems so they have been omitted.

[104] DC balancing is not really needed on optical fibre in current single-channel systems like this one. However, balancing enhances the operation of the electronics at either end of the circuit.

3. An additional level of error checking is obtained because errors most often cause a good data code to be changed into an invalid one.

4. Byte synchronisation is implicit in the code design such that the receiver can continually monitor byte alignment and if this is lost initiate action to re-establish byte synchronisation.

Data Blocks

Data blocks have a length which may vary from 7 bytes to 1035 bytes and contain two CRC check bytes. There is a header added to each block containing the origin and destination link identifiers and a control field. Whenever a station receives a block the CRC is checked and the block discarded if an error is found. Error recovery is done by retransmitting the affected block.

ESCON Director

The ESCON Director (IBM 9032 Model 1) is able to handle up to 60 connected stations at any one time and it allows for up to 30 simultaneous connections between stations (it is non-blocking). The total possible throughput of a Director is therefore 30 times 160 Mbps - 4.8 Gbps.

It should be noted however, that in a large system environment most of the traffic is between channels and control units. There will also be some channel-to-channel traffic but there will be little or no control unit to control unit traffic. Thus, actual throughput depends on how you use the system.

8.4.1.4 IBM ESCON Single-Mode Fibre Trunk Specifications

The following are the specifications of fibre needed for single-mode operation with IBM ESCON channel devices:

Operating Wavelength	1270-1340 nm
Mode Field Diameter	9±1 μm
Cable Attenuation @ 1310 nm	0.5 dB/km
Cutoff Wavelength	1280 nm
Zero Dispersion Wavelength	1310±10 nm
Dispersion Slope (max)	0.095 ps/(nm²-km)
Cladding Diameter	125±3 μm
Core Concentricity Error	1.0 μm
Cladding Non-Circularity (max)	2.0 %

8.4.2 Inter-System Coupling (ISC) Feature

The inter-system coupling feature is used to connect IBM mainframe computers together. This is *not* an input/output protocol. It is a protocol for connecting processor-to-processor for the purpose of coupled operation. Within the processors information transfer is initiated by processor instruction - not by an I/O operation.

Connection is always on dedicated point-to-point connections with a maximum distance of 20 km. The distance maximum is *not* the result of any optical consideration - rather is it caused by propagation delay issues.

Connections are on dual single-mode fibres (one in each direction). The fibre channel specification for 1,062.5 Mbaud is used with lasers on SM fibre at 1310 nm. ISC is however, not compatible with fibre channel. ISC uses the physical layer of FC and the OFC feature of FC. FC itself does not allow the OFC feature when operating at 1310 nm on SM fibre. Thus although everything in the ISC specification is derived from FC, it is an illegal combination of options as far as FC is concerned. Even though it is technically "unnecessary", IBM felt that the added safety of OFC was a benefit.

8.5 OptiConnect

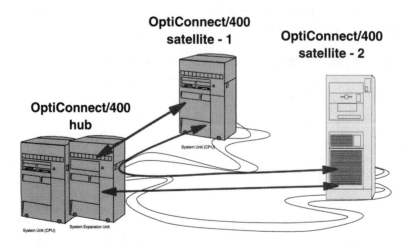

Figure 295. OptiConnect System

OptiConnect is an IBM proprietary technology used for interconnecting IBM AS/400 mid-range computers and for connecting these systems to peripheral devices. Based on the use of "CD-ROM" lasers at 780 nm on multimode fibre it is one of the first systems to make use of this short-wavelength laser technology.

OptiConnect operates among systems sharing the same bus (connected with fibre optic cables). Thus, it can achieve transport efficiencies that are not possible with a more general purpose, wide-area communications protocol.

OptiConnect is a combination of hardware and software that allows the distribution of work between multiple AS/400s thus increasing the processing capacity.

OptiConnect consists of the following:

1. Additions to OS/400 that provide fast path distributed data management (DDM) access across an optical bus

2. A connection manager that manages OptiConnect resources

3. An agent program that runs on the server on behalf of client requests

4. Additional AS/400 objects that support and control the connection manager and agent program

5. OptiConnect system adapters that are connected by fibre optic cables

OptiConnect allows AS/400 applications to perform inter-system database accesses much faster than previously possible. The ability to efficiently read data on nearby systems performs the following functions:

1. Multiple client systems can access databases on a serving system by splitting the processor load for an application across client and server systems.

2. The client system runs the non-database portion of an application, and the server system runs the database activity. By using multiple systems, you provide greater total processing capacity for database access than can be achieved by a single system.

3. Customer environments with multiple databases (or databases which can be partitioned into multiple databases) can extend the client/server database model to have multiple serving systems. Applications can access all the databases across OptiConnect systems without regard to the database location.

4. Ideally, applications and users can be assigned to the system that has the data they use most heavily. Less heavily used data can reside on any of the other systems. This allows you to spread applications to achieve the best balance and throughput.

5. Duplication of databases can be eliminated if the duplicates exist to decrease response time.

6. OptiConnect allows you to spread communications lines across several systems. Applications using the communications lines can run on any system and can access any database on any of the systems that are joined by OptiConnect.

8.5.1 OptiConnect Optical Specifications

OptiConnect uses 780 nm CD-ROM lasers on multimode fibre at either of two speeds:

1063 Mbps connections operate on 50 micron (core) MM GI fibre for a distance of between 4 metres and 500 metres. On 62.5 micron MM GI fibre the maximum distance is 170 metres. This is considered the normal OptiConnect configuration. Data encoding is 8/10 (as in ESCON and Fibre Channel) and therefore the instantaneous data rate is 800 Mbps or 100 MBps. At this distance the link loss budget is 6 dB.

266 Mbps connections operate at a distance of between 4 metres and 2 kilometres on 50 micron MM GI fibre. On 62.5 micron MM GI fibre the maximum distance is 700 metres at this speed. The reason for the lower speed is to allow for a greater amount of modal dispersion and hence go the added distance. The link loss budget at this distance is 12 dB.

All connections are point-to-point between system busses and are buffered at each end. This is to accommodate the difference in speed and synchronisation between the links and the system busses. The AS/400 system bus operates at a speed of 40 MBps (320 Mbps) so total end-to-end throughput can never exceed this regardless of the speed of the optical link.

8.6 Synchronous Optical Network (SONET) and SDH

Sonet (Synchronous Optical Network) is a US standard for the internal operation of telephone company optical networks. It is closely related to a system called SDH (Synchronous Digital Hierarchy) adopted by the CCITT (now the ITU-T) as a recommendation for the internal operation of carrier (PTT) optical networks worldwide.

Despite the name Sonet is *not* an optical networking system. It is an electronic networking system designed to use optical link connections. Nevertheless, Sonet and SDH are of immense importance for two reasons:

1. They offer vast cost savings in public communications networks by redefining the system of channel multiplexing. Public telephone oriented networks must provide a constant-bit-rate data transfer from one end of the network to the other. If the traffic is voice then this is typically 64 kbps but many faster speeds are also offered (such as T1/E1, T2, T3/E3 etc.). This is achieved through time division

multiplexing of user data channels throughout the network. Sonet/SDH offers a significantly better method of doing this.

2. Management of the cable plant. Within a typical telephone company there are many end-user service offerings. Each of these is a network in its own rite (including and especially the telephone network). Each of these networks needs link connections of various speeds connecting nodes (central offices) at arbitrary points around the country. However the company wants to manage and share its cable plant as a single entity.

   Sonet and SDH have extensive management and control facilities built into the protocols to facilitate the management and sharing of wide area cable plant.

Traditionally, public telephone company networks have been built by using a cascade of multiplexors at each end of a high-speed connection. In physical realization this resulted in the configuration illustrated in Figure 296.

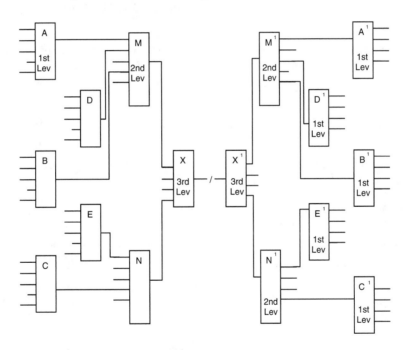

Figure 296. The Multiplexor Mountain. Each multiplexor illustrated exists as a separate physical device although many multiplexors may be mounted together on a single rack.

In order to use a high-speed interexchange link it was necessary to multiplex a very large number of slower-speed circuits onto it in stages. The faster the link, the more stages required.

There are a number of important points to remember here:

1. The internals of this structure are proprietary. Each pair of multiplexors in the system has to be manufactured by the same supplier. In the figure, the concept of multiplexor pairs is illustrated. A pair of multiplexors "see" a clear channel connection between them even though the connection might really go through several higher layer multiplexors. (In the figure multiplexors A and A', B and B' are multiplexor pairs.)

2. The multiplexing structure in the US is different from the structure used in Europe, and both are different from the structure used in Japan. This leads to compatibility problems when interconnecting systems between countries and also means that equipment designed and built in one country often cannot be used in another.

3. There is an enormous cost benefit to be gained by integrating the multiplexing function with the internal functioning of the telephone exchange and hence removing the multiplexors entirely. Modern telephone exchanges are digital time-division multiplexors in themselves.

4. If access is needed to a single tributary circuit (or small group of circuits) then it is necessary to demultiplex the whole structure and then remultiplex it.

Sonet and SDH eliminate these problems. A single multiplexing scheme is specified that allows:

1. A standardised method of internal operation and management so that equipment from many different manufacturers may be used productively together.

2. Multiple speeds of operation such that as higher and higher optical speeds are introduced the system can expand gracefully to operate at the higher speeds.

3. Worldwide compatibility. A single optical multiplexing hierarchy which applies throughout the world and accommodates the existing speeds used in both Europe and the US.

4. Many levels of multiplexing and demultiplexing to be accomplished in a single step. (You do not have to demultiplex the higher levels to gain access to the lower levels.)

5. Many different payloads (different-speed channels) to be carried through the system.

6. Access to low bandwidth (T-1, E-1 style) tributaries without the need to demultiplex the whole stream.

7. Considerably better efficiency than before. For example, the floating payload feature of Sonet eliminates the need for the customary 125 μsec buffers required at crosspoints in the existing ("plesiochronous") multiplexing schemes.

8.6.1 Sonet Protocol Structure

The basic structure in Sonet is a frame of 810 bytes which is sent every 125 μsec. This allows a single byte within a frame to be part of a 64 kbps digital voice channel. Since the minimum frame size is 810 bytes then the minimum speed at which Sonet will operate is 51.84 megabits per second.

```
810 bytes × 8000 frames/sec × 8 (bits) = 51.84 megabits/sec
```

This basic frame is called the Synchronous Transport Signal level 1 (STS-1). It is conceptualised as containing 9 rows of 90 columns each as shown in Figure 297 on page 488.

- The first three columns of every row are used for administration and control of the multiplexing system. They are called "overhead" in the standard but are very necessary for the system's operation.

- The frame is transmitted row by row, from the top left of the frame to the bottom right.

- Of course it is necessary to remember that the representation of the structure as a two-dimensional frame is just a conceptual way of representing a repeating structure. In reality it is just a string of bits with a defined repeating pattern.

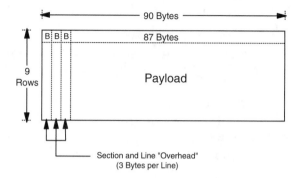

Figure 297. Sonet STS-1 Frame Structure. *The diagrammatic representation of the frame as a square is done for ease of understanding. The 810 bytes are transmitted row by row starting from the top left of the diagram. One frame is transmitted every 125 microseconds.*

The physical frame structure above is similar to every other TDM structure used in the telecommunications industry. The big difference is in how the "payload" is carried. The payload is a frame that "floats" within the physical frame structure. The payload envelope is illustrated in Figure 298. Notice that it fits exactly within a single Sonet frame.

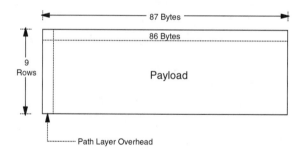

Figure 298. Sonet Synchronous Payload Envelope (SPE)

The payload envelope is allowed to start anywhere within the physical Sonet frame and in that case will span two consecutive physical frames. The start of the payload is pointed to by the H1 and H2 bytes within the line overhead sections (see Figure 299 on page 489).

Very small differences in the clock rates of the frame and the payload can be accommodated by temporarily incrementing or decrementing the pointer (an extra byte if needed is found by using one byte (H3) in the section header). Nevertheless, big differences in clock frequencies cannot be accommodated by this method.

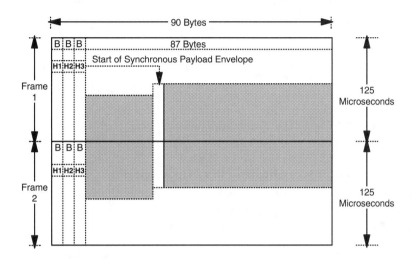

Figure 299. Synchronous Payload Envelope Floating in STS-1 Frame. The SPE is pointed to by the H1 and H2 bytes.

Multiple STS-1 frames can be byte-multiplexed together to form higher-speed signals. When this is done they are called STS-2, STS-3 etc. where the numeral suffix indicates the number of STS-1 frames that are present (and therefore the line speed). For example STS-3 is 3 times an STS-1 or 155.52 megabits per second. This multiplexing uses the method illustrated in Figure 300 on page 490.

An alternative method is to phase-align the multiple STS frames and their payloads. This means that a larger payload envelope has been created. This is called "concatenation" and is indicated in the name of the signal. For example, when three STS-1s are concatenated such that the frames are phase-aligned and there is a single large payload envelope it is called an STS-3c.

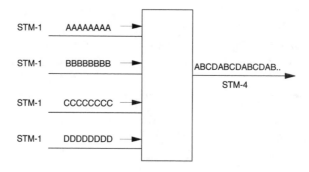

Figure 300. STM-1 to STM-4 Synchronous Multiplexing

8.6.2 Synchronous Digital Hierarchy (SDH)

In the rest of the world (outside of the USA), Sonet is not immediately useful because the "E-3" rate of 35 Mbps does not efficiently fit into the 50 Mbps Sonet signal. (The comparable US PDH signal, the T-3 is roughly 45 Mbps and fits nicely.)

The ITU-T has defined a worldwide standard called the Synchronous Digital Hierarchy, which accommodates both Sonet and the European line speeds.

This was done by defining a basic frame that is exactly equivalent to (Sonet) STS-3c. This has a new name. It is Synchronous Transport Module level one or STM-1 and has a basic rate (minimum speed) of 155.52 Mbps. This is shown in Figure 301.

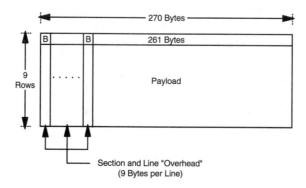

Figure 301. SDH Basic Frame Format

Faster line speeds are obtained in the same way as in Sonet - by byte interleaving of multiple STM-1 frames. For this to take place (as in Sonet) the STM-1 frames must be 125-µsec frame aligned. Four STM-1 frames may be multiplexed to form an STM-4 at 622.08 Mbps. This (again like Sonet) may carry four separate payloads byte multiplexed together (see Figure 300). Alternatively, the payloads may be concatenated (rather than interleaved) and the signal is then called STM-4c.

8.6.3 Tributaries

Within each payload, slower-speed channels (called tributaries) may be carried. Tributaries normally occupy a number of consecutive columns within a payload.

A US T-1 payload (1.544 Mbps) occupies three columns, a European E-1 payload (2.048 Mbps) occupies four columns. Notice that there is some wasted bandwidth here. A T-1 really only requires 24 slots and three columns gives it 27. An E-1 requires 32 slots and is given 36. This "wastage" is a very small price to pay for the enormous benefit to be achieved by being able to demultiplex a single tributary stream from within the multiplexed structure without having to demultiplex the whole stream.

The tributaries may be fixed within their virtual containers or they may float, similar to the way a virtual container floats within the physical frame. Pointers within the overhead are used to locate each virtual tributary stream.

8.6.4 Sonet/SDH Line Speeds and Signals

Table 7. Sonet Speed Hierarchy				
Signal Level	**Bit Rate**	**DS-0s**	**DS-1s**	**DS-3s**
STS-1 and OC-1	51.84 Mbps	672	28	1
STS-3 and OC-3 (STM-1)	155.52 Mbps	2,016	84	3
STS-9 and OC-9	466.56 Mbps	6,048	252	9
STS-12 and OC-12 (STM-4)	622.08 Mbps	8,064	336	12
STS-18 and OC-18	933.12 Mbps	12,096	504	18
STS-24 and OC-24	1244.16 Mbps	16,128	672	24
STS-36 and OC-36	1866.24 Mbps	24,192	1008	36
STS-48 and OC-48 (STM-16)	2488.32 Mbps	32,256	1344	48
STS-n and OC-n (STM-n/3)	n * 51.84 Mbps	n * 672	n * 28	n

8.6.5 Status

Sonet/SDH standards are now firm and equipment implementing them is beginning to become available. However, there are many desirable extensions that have not yet been standardised. For example, there is no standard for interfacing customer premises equipment to STS-3c (STM) available as yet. However, it is likely that this will happen in the future since the FDDI standard contains an interface to STS-3c for use as wide area operation of FDDI rings.

8.6.6 Conclusion

Successful specification of a system which integrates and accommodates all of the different line speeds and characteristics of US and European multiplexing hierarchies was a formidable challenge. Sonet/SDH is a complex system but it is also a very significant achievement. It is expected that equipment using SDH will become the dominant form of network multiplexing equipment within a very short time.

8.6.7 Sonet Rings

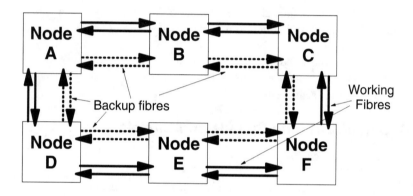

Figure 302. Sonet Ring Structure

In long distance wide area applications, Sonet networks may (and usually are) installed using a traditional nodal network structure. However, Sonet was designed to be operated using a "Ring" structure as illustrated in Figure 302. This structure allows for very fast and automatic service restoration in the case of a cable breakage. Commercially available Sonet equipment is usually able to restore service after a cable breakage in a time of between 20 ms and 40 ms.

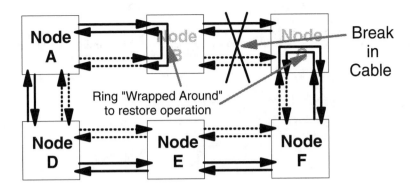

Break in Cable

Ring "Wrapped Around" to restore operation

Figure 303. Sonet Ring Restored after Cable Break

Rings are most appropriate in metropolitan area environments for two reasons:

1. Because users are distributed over an area of radius perhaps 50 km or more, cables are needed throughout the area anyway. The provision of cables and equipment locations is not an additional cost.

2. In some applications (although not in the critical telephone application) the additional propagation delay caused by routing in the opposite direction around the ring could impact the user application. For example, computer channel interconnections are highly sensitive to propagation delays. A connection by the shortest path on a ring may work fine but a connection in the opposite direction may not work at all or may work at a significantly reduced throughput.

8.6.8 Plesiochronous Digital Hierarchy

PDH is the digital networking hierarchy that was used before the advent of Sonet/SDH. The link speeds are included here for reference.

Table 8. PDH Speed Hierarchy - USA

Level	Speed in Mbps	Number of Channels
DS-0	64 kbps	1
T-1, DS-1	1.544	24
T-2, DS-2	6.312	96
T-3, DS-3	44.736	672
T-4, DS-4	274.176	4032

Table 9. PDH Speed Hierarchy - Europe		
Level	**Speed in Mbps**	**Number of Channels**
E-1	2.048	30
E-2	8.448	120
E-3	34.368	480
E-4	139.264	1920
E-5	564.992	7680

8.7 Asynchronous Transfer Mode (ATM)

Asynchronous Transfer Mode (ATM) is a new communications technology which is fundamentally and radically different from previous technologies. Designed to be a low cost way of building high speed communications networks ATM can handle any form of digital information (voice, data, video, image...) in an integrated way.

ATM is *not* an optical technology. It is an electronic one. However, like Sonet/SDH, ATM is designed to be run over optical communications links. Indeed ATM was developed to allow us to take advantage of the speed and error rate characteristics that optical communications brings. A number of important factors led to ATM development:

Technological Change

> Existing data networks were designed in the early 1970's for a technological environment quite different from the 1990's. In that time, communications lines were low in throughput, high in error rate and high in cost. In the 1990's (thanks to the advent of fibre and of better signal processing techniques) communications lines are very high in speed, low in error rate and low in cost. Existing network architectures (SNA, OSI, TCP/IP) were designed for the older environment and do not perform well in the new environment.

> The older communications don't scale up in speed very well. The reason for this is that while link speeds get faster and error rates dramatically reduce, we still haven't done anything to increase the speed of light! This is important. Propagation delays (5 microseconds per km) haven't changed. Most older protocols control data flow and error recovery by receiving detailed responses from the other end of the network. It takes time for these responses to travel through the network. Ultimately network throughput is limited by propagation

delays rather than link speeds. Thus a new communications architecture designed for the new environment became necessary.

New Requirements

Many new applications are made possible by high speed low cost communications and by the increased power of modern computing equipment (PCs and workstations). Many of these applications involve the integration of voice, video, image and traditional data. A vehicle was needed to allow these applications to be developed.

Cost of Switching Technology

Techniques for very fast switching of information are quite recent. Investigation of the economics of switching technology leads to the conclusion that very high speed switched networks are by far the most cost-effective way of constructing information networks.

Rationalisation of Divergent WAN and LAN Environments

Over the last 10 years or so LANs have developed in a very different way from wide area communications systems. The wide difference between LAN and WAN architectures means that integration of the two environments is difficult complex and expensive.

Because ATM can be used in both the local area network environment and in the wide area network environment it offers the prospect of easy, "seamless" integration between the two.

Around about 1988 the telecommunications (carrier) industry began to develop a concept called **Broadband Integrated Services Digital Network or B-ISDN**. This was conceived as a *carrier service* to provide high-speed communications to end users in an integrated way. The *technology* selected to deliver the B-ISDN service was/is called **Asynchronous Transfer Mode or ATM**.

Since then, ATM has expanded to cover much that is not strictly B-ISDN. B-ISDN is a carrier interface and carrier network service. ATM is a technology that may be used in many environments unrelated to carrier services. Discussion of the distinction between ATM and B-ISDN is pointless in the context of understanding the technology. For most practical purposes the terms ATM and B-ISDN are interchangeable.

8.7.1 High-Speed Technology

One of the driving forces behind ATM development was the need for a new technology that could take advantage of the changes in the technological environment. The current communications technology delivers a very different environment from that of the 1970's when most existing communications protocols were developed. It may be characterised as follows:

- Very high-speed communications links (10,000 times faster than what was available in the 1970's).

- Extremely low error rates. Traditional copper communications facilities deliver an error rate of about 1 in 10^6 bits transmitted. With optical fibre the rate is a million times better (1 in 10^{12}).

- The cost of digging up roads has not become any less. Thus it still costs about the same to install a given communications link but that link is many orders of magnitude faster. Thus the cost of sending x bits per second is significantly lower now.

- Propagation delay of electricity in a wire (or light in a fibre) is still the same - about 5 μsec per kilometre.

This changed environment means that existing communications protocols are no longer efficient:

- Existing switching node designs, especially when requiring switching decisions in software, just will not handle the data rates possible on current types of connection. New switch designs are needed.

- Error recovery by re-transmission at each stage of a connection is no longer an efficient thing to do. It takes too long and it requires too much logic to process in the available time.

- Existing flow and congestion controls take a very significant amount of processing in a switching node and cannot operate at the required throughput speeds. In any case, they are needed to optimise the usage of bandwidth. Although the cost of raw bandwidth is reducing, bandwidth is not, and will never be, available for free.

Existing networking systems (such as SNA and TCP/IP) *do* function in the new environment. The point is they just do not go much faster or give much higher throughput. A new communications network architecture is needed. This architecture is based on ATM.

- The system must be capable of switching data at the full speed of attached links.

- Flow and congestion controls *within* the network must be replaced with controls on entry of data to the network.

- Error recoveries must be done from end to end across the network (from end user to end user). The network does not have time to concern itself with error recovery.

- It is not a necessary consequence of high speed but the opportunity to have a single integrated network that handles many different types of traffic should be taken.

8.7.2 ATM Concepts

The key concepts of ATM are as follows:

Links and Switches (Nodes)

An ATM network is made up of many "switching nodes" connected together by point-to-point high speed links. The function of a switch is to receive data on one link and retransmit it onto another (outbound) link. End users are connected to ATM switches on point-to-point, bit-serial, link connections.

Links are conceived as being point-to-point bit serial connections. These may be direct fibre connections from one ATM switch to another or they may be connections formed through a Sonet/SDH network. Indeed, wide area ATM is designed to be run over Sonet/SDH. ATM wide area protocols are all Sonet/SDH interface protocols although you can use these without the intermediate Sonet network. The key is that ATM does not have the low level network management (and cable plant management) facilities necessary to operate a large WAN. In a practical case of a large national network ATM always needs to run over Sonet/SDH.

Cells

All information (voice, image, video, data...) is transported through the network in very short (48 data bytes plus a 5-byte header) blocks called "cells".

Virtual Channels

Information flow is along paths (called "virtual channels") set up as a series of pointers through the network. The cell header contains an identifier that links the cell to the correct path for it to take towards its destination.

Cells on a particular virtual channel always follow the same path through the network and are delivered to the destination in the same order in which they were received.

Hardware-Based Switching

ATM is designed so that simple hardware-based logic elements may be employed at each node to perform the switching. On a link of 1 Gbps a new cell arrives and a cell is transmitted every .43 µsec. There is not a lot of time to decide what to do with an arriving packet.

Adaptation

At the edges of the network user data frames are broken up into cells. Continuous data streams such as voice and video are assembled into cells. At the destination side of the network the user data frames are reconstructed from the received cells and returned to the end user in the form (data frames etc.) that they were delivered to the network. This adaptation function is considered part of the network but is a higher-layer function from the transport of cells.

Error Control

The ATM cell switching network only checks cell headers for errors and simply discards errored cells.

The adaptation function is external to the switching network and depends somewhat on the type of traffic but for data traffic it usually checks for errors in data frames received and if one is found then it discards the whole frame.

At no time does the ATM network attempt to recover from errors by the re-transmission of information. This function is up to the end-user devices and depends on the type of traffic being carried.

Flow Controls

In the original concept an ATM network was intended to have no internal flow controls of any kind. The required processing logic was thought to be too complex to be accommodated at the speeds involved. Instead ATM was envisaged as having a set of input rate controls that limit the rate of traffic delivered to the network.

This, in conjunction with a reliance on knowledge of the statistics of traffic would have worked fine for the types of traffic initially envisaged for ATM. That is, for voice and traditional data traffic. If you "add up" statistically many data or voice channels you get a very stable result indeed. However, when the extremely bursty characteristics of LAN (client/server) traffic was studied people realised that you couldn't have a stable network without some form of internal traffic management.

Today, wide area (telco style) ATM networks typically control the type of traffic they accept and still have no internal flow controls. Campus and local area ATM networks have extensive traffic management in order to avoid collapse due to congestion

Congestion Control

There is only one thing an ATM network can do when a link or node becomes congested. Cells are discarded until the problem has been relieved.

Some (lower-priority) cells can be marked such that they are the first to be discarded in the case of congestion.

Connection endpoints are *not notified* when cells are discarded. It is up to the adaptation function or higher-layer protocols to detect and recover from the loss of cells (if necessary and possible).

Thus traffic management (flow control) is used to avoid congestion situations arising.

8.7.3 The Structure of an ATM Network

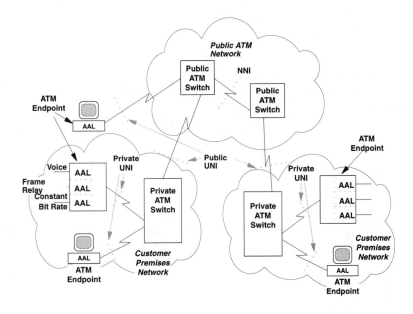

Figure 304. *ATM Network Structure Overview*

The conceptual structure of an ATM network is shown in Figure 304, above.

ATM Networks

In the referenced figure there are three quite separate ATM networks - two private and one public.

Private ATM networks are sometimes called "customer premises networks" and indeed they will very often be confined to a local area such as a building or a campus. However, a private ATM network can be distributed over a wide area by the use of carrier (non-ATM) links between ATM nodes. Such links could be copper-wire leased lines, "dark" fibres[105] or Sonet/SDH TDM connections.

ATM Switches

Four "ATM switches" are shown in the figure. These perform the backbone data transport within the ATM network. They are usually classified as either "Private ATM Switches" or "Public ATM Switches". The difference between private and public ATM equipment could be trivial in some cases but will often be quite major. Public and private switches will differ in the kinds of trunks (links) supported, in accounting and control procedures and in the addressing modes supported. There is also the obvious question of size. Public network equipment will usually need much higher throughput than will private equipment.

Public ATM switches are sometimes referred to as Network Nodes (NNs). This is incorrect as the term network node is not defined in ATM standards - even though there is a Network Node Interface (NNI).

Private ATM switches and networks are sometimes called Customer Premises Nodes (CPNs) or Customer Premises Networks. Again, this terminology while useful is not defined in the ATM standards.

ATM Endpoint

The ATM endpoint is a piece of end-user equipment that interfaces to an ATM network in a native way. An endpoint sends and receives ATM cells on link connections defined by ATM standards. An endpoint (and only an endpoint) contains an ATM Adaptation Layer (AAL) function.[106]

An ATM endpoint connects to the ATM network over the User Network Interface (UNI).

User Network Interface (UNI)

The UNI is specified exactly by the applicable standards.

There are two somewhat different UNIs called "public" and "private". The public UNI is for connection of end-user equipment to a public ATM network. The private UNI is for use within a single organisation's premises or for a private network using lines leased from the PTT.

---

[105] A dark fibre is a fibre connection provided by a carrier that is not restricted just like a copper wire "leased line". It is dark because there is no light in the fibre until the user puts it there.

[106] However, it must be noted that ATM switches will often contain ATM endpoint functions as well as switch functions.

The major differences between the two are:

1. Link types allowed.

   Some of the link types allowed at the private UNI use protocols that only work over very short distances (such as 100 metres). These would be obviously inapplicable to a public network interface.

2. Addressing formats.

   Public ATM networks will use E.164 addresses (similar to telephone numbers) while private networks will probably use addressing techniques derived from LANs or from OSI.

3. Another difference is which organisation specifies them.

   The public UNI is defined and controlled by the ITU-T. The private UNI is defined by the ATM Forum.

Network Node Interface (NNI)

As shown in the figure, this is the trunk connection between two Network Nodes (NNs). As the standard has evolved three distinct "flavors" of the NNI have emerged:

1. The **NNI-ISSI** will be used to connect ATM switches within a local area and belonging to the same telephone company.

2. The **NNI-ICI** is the "intercarrier" interface and will typically be used to interconnect ATM networks operated by different telephone companies. This could be the interface between the local carrier and the longline carrier (in the US) or an international connection.

3. The **Private NNI** allows connection of different ATM switches in a private network environment.

The differences between these interfaces is mainly one of emphasis. For example, the addressing formats used are likely to be different and you might not need accounting at a private NNI where you certainly do need it at the NNI-ICI.

Links

There may be one or many physical link connections between the nodes. These are shown as shaded areas in Figure 305 on page 503. Links between nodes may be carried as "clear channels" such as over a direct point-to-point connection but may also be carried over a Sonet/SDH connection or over a PDH connection.

Network Internals

In Figure 304 on page 499 the ATM public network is shown as a cloud. Representation of public networks as a cloud has become traditional since the first public data network standard, X.25. One of the reasons for the cloud representation was that the standard defined only the interface to the end user and the services to be provided by the network. The internals of X.25 networks are not covered by any standard. *Things are different in ATM.* The internals of the ATM network are in the process of rigorous standardisation and so while the end user may still see it as a cloud (because its internal detail will be masked from the end user) its internal protocols will be exactly understood.

Cells

As mentioned earlier, the ATM network transports data (including voice and video) as 53-byte "cells". The objective is to provide a very short, constant, transit time through the network. Within the network there are no error recoveries (there is error detection for cell header information). Flow and congestion control is done not by the detailed interactive protocols of traditional data networks but by control on the rate of admission of traffic to the network (and a strong reliance on the statistical characteristics of the traffic). When network congestion is experienced there is no alternative - cells must be discarded.

ATM Adaptation Layers (AAL)

End users of an ATM network will be of two kinds:

- Those that interface to the ATM network directly through either the public UNI or a private UNI

- Those that do not know anything about ATM and interface using a non-ATM protocol (such as Frame Relay)

In either case a significant amount of logic is required *over and above what is provided by ATM* in order to use the network productively.

For all types of users there are common tasks that must be performed in order to connect to the ATM network. In its definition ATM includes processing for these common tasks. This is called the **ATM Adaptation Layer (AAL)**. The AAL is the real end-user interface to ATM.

The AAL *never* interfaces to an external link or device. It is not like that. The AAL provides a programming interface and end users are connected to the ATM network by program functions external to ATM. The AAL only provides some common attachment functions - many protocol layers are usually required above the AAL for useful work to be performed.

Figure 304 on page 499 is perhaps a little misleading in the positioning of the AAL. End users using voice or Frame Relay or whatever must attach through an AAL *but a lot more than just the AAL code is needed.* AAL just provides a more convenient, standardised way of accessing the network from a program. The program then interfaces with other external links like voice or Frame Relay or higher layers of some other communication protocol.

8.7.3.1 Virtual Channels and Virtual Routes

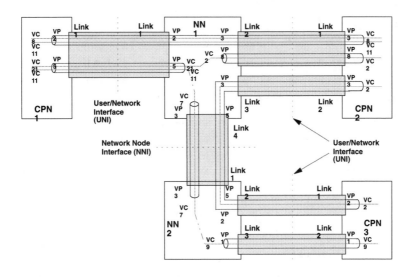

Figure 305. *Routing Concept in an ATM Network*

Perhaps the key concepts in ATM are those relating to how data is routed through the network. Figure 305 illustrates these concepts:

Virtual Path (VP)

A VP is a route through the network representing a group of virtual channels (VCs). VPs may exist:

1. Between ATM endpoints (as between endpoint 1 and endpoint 2 and between endpoint 2 and endpoint 3 in the figure)

2. Between ATM switches and ATM endpoints (as between ATM switch 1 and endpoint 1, ATM switch 1 and endpoint 2 and ATM switch 2 and endpoint 3 in the figure) and

3. Between ATM switches (as between ATM switch 1 and ATM switch 2 in the figure)

A VP may be routed through an ATM switch by reference only to the VP number or it may terminate in an ATM switch. A VP entering an endpoint always terminates in that endpoint.

Virtual Channel (VC)

The concept of a virtual channel is defined in ATM as a unidirectional connection between end users. However, the use of the acronym VC for many other purposes in communications (such as the virtual circuit in X.25), means that its use is often confused.

Virtual Channel Connection (VCC)

A virtual channel connection is the end-to-end connection along which a user sends data. The concept is very close to that of a virtual circuit in X.25. The major difference is that a virtual channel connection carries data in one direction only, whereas a virtual circuit is bidirectional.

Whilst a VCC is defined to be unidirectional, it must be noted that VCCs *always occur in pairs*. One VCC in each direction. Thus a bidirectional communication channel consists of a pair of VCCs (carried over the same route through the network).

The concepts of VC and VCC are likewise almost the same. The acronym VC is most often used in a generic context and VCC in much more specific ways.

Virtual Channel Link (VCL)

A virtual channel link is a separately identified data flow within a link or a virtual path. A virtual channel connection (VCC) through the network is a sequence of interconnected (concatenated) VCLs.

Links within Nodes

An ATM node may have many links attached. The maximum number of links and their addressing (numbering) within the node is *not* within the scope of the ATM standards.

VPs within Links

Within each link there are a number of VPs. The maximum number is defined by the number of bits allocated to Virtual Path Identifiers (VPIs) within the ATM cell header (8 or 12 bits).

VCs within VPs

Each VP has a number of VCs within it. The maximum number is restricted by the number of bits allocated to Virtual Channel Identifiers (VCIs) within the cell header (16 bits).

VPs and VCs are only numbers! They identify a virtual (logical) path along which data may flow. They have *no* inherent capacity restrictions in terms of data throughput.[107] That is, dividing the link into VPs and VCs has nothing whatever to do with division of link capacity. You could saturate any link no matter what the speed with data on just one VC - even if the link had all possible VPs and VCs defined!

A good analogy is the US road system where a single physical road can have many route numbers (sometimes up to 30 or more). The cars travelling on the road may consider themselves to be following any one of the numbered routes. But at any point in time all the cars on the road may consider themselves to be using the same route number.

8.7.4 Physical Link Types

One of the great advantages of ATM is that it can be used over many different kinds of physical media (fibre, copper, radio). There are many different standards and proposed standards to provide ATM connection in the different environments.

Wide Area Trunk Environment

This environment is primarily for interconnection of ATM switches within the carrier network. Since most carrier networks currently use SDH or Sonet networking for network management of the cable plant, ATM has been standardised to operate over SDH.[108]

Two link speeds are currently standardised:

- 155 megabits per second

- 622 megabits per second

Other (higher) speeds are planned.

---

[107] There are deliberate restrictions imposed on the rate of entry of data into the network but this is not relevant here.

[108] In principle SDH and Sonet are identical.

Wide Area Private Network Environment

While users of private ATM networks could use the link speeds standardised for carrier use it will be costly and impractical for this to happen in many countries. Also for interconnection to carrier networks from end-user premises a slower rate is perhaps appropriate in many situations. Rates proposed are:

- 1.544 megabits per second (US "T1")

- 2.048 megabits per second (European and Australian "E1")

- 34 megabits per second (European and Australian "E3")

- 45 megabits per second (American "T3")

These speeds have been standardised by either the American National Standards Institute (ANSII) or the European Standards Institute (ETSI).

Local Area Connection

Long distance communication typically requires different (and more expensive) physical attachments than shorter distances do. For example, on fibre, long distance (wide area) usually implies single-mode fibre and laser transmitters. Over shorter distances (such as 100 metres on copper wire or up to 3 km on fibre) we can use much simpler protocols and this results in a lower cost connection.

For LAN type connections the following link types are either standardised or proposed:

- 25 megabits per second.

  This protocol will operate over UTP class 3 (or UTP_5 or STP) and is very simple and therefore low in cost for workstation (PC) connection. At the electrical level it is derived from the token-ring signalling protocol and is therefore well established and well known.

- 51 megabits per second.

  This is a current standards proposal. Like the 25 megabit protocol it will operate over UTP or STP but it requires a more complex form of transmission protocol and therefore adapters using this are likely to be more costly than those at 25 megabits.

- 100 megabits per second.

  This is the physical layer of FDDI re-used for ATM. It will operate over copper STP cable or multimode fibre (at 1320 nm). Adapters operating at this speed are available now from a number of suppliers including IBM.

- 155 megabits per second.

Some suppliers are currently using the WAN 155 megabit interface for LAN application at 155 megabits. However, the WAN standard specifies the use of SDH, single-mode fibre and laser transmitters.

A simplified 155 megabit protocol designed for LAN application on multimode fibre is currently under discussion in standards bodies.

There are several proposals that would allow 155 megabit operation over UTP_3 copper cable but currently there is some doubt as to whether this will meet electromagnetic emission regulations. The protocols work - but radiate too much interference to meet laws at this time.

Table 10. ATM-UNI Interfaces

	Rate (Mbps)	Cell Throughput	System	Medium	WAN/LAN	Owner
DS-1 (T-1)	1.544	1.536	PDH	Cu	Both	ANSI
E-1	2.048	1.92	PDH	Cu	Both	ETSI
DS-3 (T-3)	44.736	40.704	PDH	Cu	WAN	ANSI
E-3	34.368	33.984	PDH	Cu	WAN	ETSI
E-4	139.264	138.24	PDH	Cu	WAN	ETSI
SDH STM-1, Sonet STS-3c	155.52	149.76	SDH	SM Fibre	WAN	ITU-T
SDH STM-4c, Sonet STS-12c	622.08	599.04	SDH	SM Fibre	WAN	ITU-T
FDDI-PMD	100	100	Block Coded	MM Fibre/STP	LAN	Forum
Fibre Channel	155.52	150.34	Block Coded	MM Fibre	LAN	Forum
DXI (RVX)	0-50	0-50	Clear Channel	Cu	LAN	Forum
Raw Cells	155.52	155.52	Clear Channel	SM Fibre	WAN	ITU-T
Raw Cells	622.08	622.08	Clear Channel	SM Fibre	WAN	ITU-T
Raw Cells	25.6	25.6	Clear Channel	Cu UTP-3	LAN	IBM
Raw Cells	51.84	49.536	Sonet Frame	Cu UTP-3	LAN	Forum
Raw Cells	100	100	Clear Channel	Cu UTP-3	LAN	Proposed
Raw Cells	155.52	155.52	Clear Channel	Cu UTP/STP	LAN	Proposed

8.7.5 Network Characteristics

Connection-Oriented Network

An ATM system is a connection-oriented system. There is no way to send data in an ATM network except on a pre-established connection (VCC). The system uses either call-by-call (switched circuit) setup or semi-permanent connections (set up by OA&M procedures).

At any particular moment in time the connection to which a particular cell belongs is identified by a unique number (the VPI/VCI) in the cell header. This number changes as the cell transits the network.

Guaranteed In-Sequence Delivery

Cells delivered to the network by an ATM endpoint over a virtual connection are transferred to the partner ATM endpoint in the same sequence as they were presented to the network. This is very important as it means that the end user (or the adaptation layer function) does not have to resequence cells that arrive out of order. But it also restricts the network to using a single path for any given virtual connection (at any particular point in time).

The payload (data) part of a cell may contain errors. Transmission errors within the data portion of the cell are *not* detected by the network (this is up to either the end-user equipment or the adaptation layer).

End-User Interface

The *only* way to interface to ATM is through a program of some kind. There are only two interfaces available for such a program to communicate with:

1. The ATM network layer interface. At this level the end-user sends and receives cells and processes them as desired. At this level the network does *no* checking for errors in the data portion of the cells.

2. At the ATM Adaptation Layer (AAL). The AAL is a layer which adapts the traffic to transport through the ATM cell network. Its major function is to take frames of data (or a continuous data stream) and break it up into a sequence of cells. At the other end of the network the mirror image of the sending AAL reconstitutes the original data. Note that in some options of this layer (AAL3/4 and AAL5) error detection is performed on the user data BUT *not* error recovery.

   At the user level this layer is identical in function to the "MAC" (Medium Access Control) layer of a LAN.

   - When a user program sends data that data is processed first by the adaptation layer, then by the ATM layer and then the physical layer takes over to send the data to the ATM network. The cells are transported by the network and then received on the other side first by the physical layer, then processed by the ATM layer and then by the receiving AAL. When all this is complete, the information (data) is passed to the receiving user program.

- The total function performed by the ATM network has been the *non-assured* transport (data can be lost) of user information from program to program.

- The user program mentioned here is quite obviously **not** end-user code in the normal sense of the term. In order to make the network useful a very significant amount of processing (protocols etc.) must be performed.

Looked at from a traditional data processing viewpoint all the ATM network has done is to replace a physical link connection with another kind of physical connection - all the "higher layer" network functions must still be performed.

8.7.6 Transporting Information in an ATM Network

Traditional Data and Image

The data transport service provided by ATM (through the adaptation layer) is logically identical to the service provided by a traditional LAN. That is, whole frames are delivered to the network (in this case the AAL) by the end user. At the destination a whole frame is delivered to the end user if there have been no errors. If there have been errors then nothing is delivered to the end user at all. (This is exactly the same as with Ethernet or token-ring.) the end user must have an end-to-end protocol capable of detecting the loss of a frame and requesting re-transmission etc. In the LAN environment the protocol commonly used is a standard called "LLC_2" or IEEE 802.2.

Within the ATM network data is of course broken up into cells and sent along connections. The principle is much the same as that of X.25 packet networks except that X.25 networks have error recoveries and flow controls within the network.

Constant-Bit-Rate (CBR) Traffic

The concept of constant bit rate traffic is that any stream of bits may be presented to the network on a standard interface (such as V.24 or X.21) and that the stream of bits will be carried transparently through the network and re-transmitted from the network on a destination link connection (also V.24 or X.21 etc.). This facility can be used to carry any kind of digital traffic at all. You get a transparent bit "pipe".

The problem here is that the network doesn't handle individual bits but rather carries information in cells. What has to happen is that as bits are received they are assembled into cells and when a cell is full that cell is sent across the network towards its destination. At the destination link, the cell is "played out" onto its destination link connection.

This is not simple. Cell and packet networks take time (albeit quite a short time) to transport cells across the network. In addition, the transit time can vary depending on instantaneous load on the network. This variation is called "delay jitter". Delay jitter is a much more significant problem than is transit time per se.

At any time there must be a cell being filled at the entry point to the network, a cell being played out at the destination and perhaps another cell in transit. This process adds to the transit delay (latency) experienced by the connection.

However, the real challenge in handling CBR traffic in ATM is timing (clock) synchronisation. If data sent to the network arrives even slightly faster than data is sent from the network then data queues will build up, transit time will increase and ultimately some data will need to be discarded. (This is called "overrun".) If data arrives into the network even slightly slower than it is sent from the network then the opposite happens and there comes a time when the sending interface will receive a clock pulse and there will be no data available to send. (This situation is called "underrun".)

This is a complex problem to solve. One possibility is to control the rate of sending from the network in such a way as to ensure that the amount of data waiting to be sent fits within predefined limits. This works reasonably well but implies the use of a significant amount of buffering and a relatively long latency. The other possibility (and the usual choice) is to ensure that data is transmitted from the network at exactly the rate at which it is received. This involves carrying information about the exact timing of the bit stream through the network and it also implies that the network itself has a common reference timing source - that the network is synchronised.

It is ironic that one of the biggest problems in constructing an Asynchronous Transfer Mode network should be synchronisation. Cell transfer is asynchronous but the network needs to be synchronised (but only if there is CBR traffic).

Processing Voice

Voice can be handled as just a special case of CBR transport as described above. This will be the common way of handling voice initially essentially because existing voice coding and compression schemes were designed for TDM networks and produce CBR bit streams.

When silence is suppressed voice becomes a lot more like data traffic in that cells are sent in bursts ("talk spurts").

In the voice application network latency causes echoes to become a problem. Even in an end-to-end digital circuit there is the possibility of echo from mechanical coupling between the earpiece and the microphone within the telephone handset. This causes a problem if the round-trip transit delay is more than about 60 milliseconds. In practical terms this means that echo cancellation is necessary on most ATM networks especially where voice compression is used (voice compression increases the network latency because it increases the time taken to fill or empty a cell).

Video

Like voice, video can be handled as a CBR service. However, video is inherently very variable in bandwidth usage and it is significantly more efficient to encode video in such a way that a variable rate stream of cells is produced.

This therefore has some of the challenges of CBR traffic (in the sense that the re-constructed video frames must have exactly the same frame rate as the sending station but in addition there is a challenge in planning how much network capacity should be allocated to the connection. If the peak rate is allocated then much capacity in the network is wasted. If a lower rate is allocated then there is significant danger in cell loss caused by congestion.

IBM Network BroadBand Services (NBBS) addresses this problem by carefully controlling the amount of bandwidth allocated to optimise as far as possible the use of the connection.

Multimedia Traffic

Multimedia traffic is of course just voice (or sound) data and video bundled together. There is considerable challenge in the synchronisation of the different information streams as network latency and jitter are quite different for the three types of traffic and there is not much latitude in the requirement for synchronisation of voice and lip movement for example.

8.8 Further Reading

S.A. Calta, J.A. deVeer, E. Loizides and R.N. Strangwayes (1992)

> *Enterprise Systems Connection (ESCON) Architecture - System Overview*: IBM Journal of Research and Development, Vol 36, No 4, July 1992. pp 535-576

Harry J. R. Dutton and Peter Lenhard (1995)

> *Asynchronous Transfer Mode (ATM) - Technical Overview*: Prentice Hall, 1995.

Harry J. R. Dutton and Peter Lenhard (1995)

> *High-Speed Networking Technology: An Introductory Survey*: Prentice Hall, 1995.

J.C. Elliott and M.W. Sachs (1992)

> *The IBM Enterprise Systems Connection (ESCON) Architecture*: IBM Journal of Research and Development, Vol 36, No 4, July 1992. pp 577-591

Chapter 9. Wavelength Division Multiplexing

Wavelength Division Multiplexing (WDM) is the basic technology of optical networking. It is a technique for using a fibre (or optical device) to carry many separate and independent optical channels. The principle is *identical* to that used when we tune our television receiver to one of many TV channels. Each channel is transmitted at a different radio frequency and we select between them using a "tuner" which is just a resonant circuit within the TV set. Of course wavelength in the optical world is just the way we choose to refer to frequency and optical WDM is quite *identical* to radio FDM.

Another way of envisaging WDM is to consider that each channel consists of light of a different colour. Thus a WDM system transmits a "rainbow". Actually at the wavelengths involved the light is invisible but it's a good way of describing the principle.

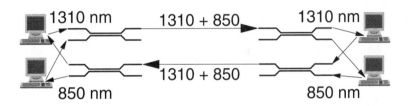

Figure 306. Simple (Sparse) WDM

There are many varieties of WDM. A simple form can be constructed using 1310 nm as one wavelength and 1550 as the other or 850 and 1310. This type of WDM can be built using relatively simple and inexpensive components and some applications have been in operation for a number of years using this principle.

Dense WDM however is another thing. Dense WDM refers to the close spacing of channels. Sadly, "dense" is a qualitative measure and just what dense means is largely in the mind of a particular individual. To some, a series of WDM channels spaced at 3.6 nm apart qualifies for the description. Others use the term to distinguish systems where the wavelength spacing is 1 nm per channel or less.

WDM is the basic technology for full optical networking.

9.1.1 Simple (Sparse) WDM

Figure 306 on page 513 shows an example of a very simple sparse WDM system using multimode fibres. Wavelength selective couplers are used both to mix (multiplex) and to separate (demultiplex) the signals. The distinguishing characteristic here is the very wide separation of wavelengths used (different bands rather than different wavelengths in the same band).

There are many variations around on this very simple theme. Some systems use a single fibre bidirectionally while others use separate fibres for each direction (as illustrated). Other systems use different wavelength bands from those illustrated in the figure (1310 and 1550 for example). The most common systems run at very low data rates (by today's standards). Common application areas are in video transport for security monitoring and in plant process control.

9.1.2 Dense WDM Links

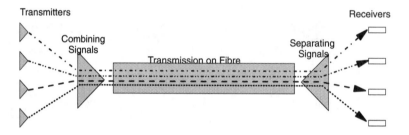

Figure 307. WDM Functions Schematic

Figure 307 shows the functions required to build a simple dense WDM shared optical link. Each optical channel is allocated its own wavelength - or rather range of wavelengths. A typical optical channel might be 1 nm wide. This channel is really a wavelength range within which the signal must stay. It is normally much wider than the signal itself. The width of a channel depends on many things such as the modulated linewidth of the transmitter, its stability and the tolerances of the other components in the system.

Transmitters

In practical terms the transmitter is always a laser. It must have a linewidth which (after modulation) fits easily within its allocated band. It must not go outside the allocated band so it should have chirp and drift characteristics that ensure this. Depending on the width of the allocated band, these characteristics don't need to be the most perfect obtainable. However they do have to be such that the signal stays where it is supposed to be.

Combining the Signals (Channels)

There are several ways of combining the signals. The most obvious is to use a number of 3-dB splitters or Y-junctions connected in cascade. The problem with this is that you lose 3 dB at each stage. With a large number (say 32) signals each one will be reduced to 1/32 nd of its initial strength. This is fine with a small number of channels but when you have a relatively large number then you will probably have to amplify the combined signal immediately after it is mixed.

Gratings and planar waveguide gratings have much lower loss and their loss is not dependent on the number of channels so these are most often used in systems with more than four channels.

Transmission and Amplification

In transmission on a fibre the main issue is controlling crosstalk effects. Channel spacings, widths and power levels are system variables that can be used to minimise crosstalk.

Amplification is a major issue. The ability to amplify the mixed signal is one of the things that makes WDM possible. However, when multiple amplifiers are used in a long link their non-linearities add up and cause significant difficulty. This is discussed in 5.2.1.2, "Gain Characteristics of EDFAs" on page 205.

Separating the Channels at the Receiver

This is more difficult than combining them. There are several possible techniques we can use:

- Reflective (Littrow) gratings
- Waveguide grating routers
- Circulators with in-fibre bragg gratings
- Splitters with individual Fabry-Perot filters

These are discussed later in this chapter.

Receiving the Signals

The receiver is relatively straightforward and is generally the same as a non-WDM receiver. This is because the signal has been de-multiplexed before it arrives at the detector.

It is obvious that each optical channel is independent from each other channel and provided the signals stay within their allocated bands there is no necessary relationship between them. For example, this means that one channel might run at 2 Gbps, another at 622 Mbps and a number of others at 200 Mbps.

9.1.3 Using Dense and Sparse WDM Together - An Example

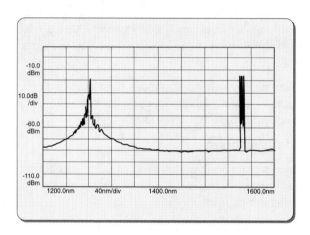

Figure 308. Spectrum of Dense WDM and Sparse WDM on the Same Fibre

Figure 308 shows a spectrum of a fibre being used for both dense WDM and sparse WDM at the same time. There is a single channel signal in the 1300 nm band and a 4-channel WDM group in the 1550 nm region. This was produced from a real operational system.

The 4-channel dense WDM group was produced with an IBM 9729. The single 1310 nm channel was an IBM ESCON channel connection. The signals were multiplexed and demultiplexed onto the fibre using a wavelength selective coupler.

Before the WDM system was installed the user had a single ESCON channel connection. By using the wavelength selective coupler they were able to add a pair of 4-channel WDM systems *without* installing any new fibre.

9.1.4 Building Photonic Networks - Technical Challenges

In constructing any photonic network from the simplest WDM system through to the most complex switched nodal network there are a number of significant technical challenges to be faced. These are summarised below:

Stabilising Wavelengths

Almost all wavelength specific optical devices are sensitive to changes in temperature. In addition, some devices such as lasers can shift in wavelength for other reasons (such as carrier density or material ageing). Within any optical networking system the stability of all wavelength sensitive devices is critical to system operation.

Wavelength Conversion

For large circuit-switched nodal optical networks it will be necessary to change the wavelength of individual channels as the signal is switched. Wavelength conversion technology is available but as yet not well developed.

Cascading Filters

In its transit through an optical network a signal passes through a number of devices which have filtering characteristics. The bandwidth, shape and alignment (of the centre wavelength) of these filters is critical to satisfactory system operation.

Wavelength Tunable Lasers

Tunable lasers are needed in many roles. In the switched nodal optical network the laser must switch wavelength when a channel is allocated for a particular connection. In many situations this switching may not need to be very fast (a few hundred microseconds would be more than adequate). In other situations such as shared medium LANs wavelength tuning needs to be very fast indeed if certain proposed network designs are to become feasible. Switching times of a few nanoseconds would be nice here.

Regardless of the switching time these lasers need to be very stable and select the desired wavelength very accurately in order for the signal to stay in-band.

EDFA Gain Flatness and Tilt

Throughout all but the simplest optical networks EDFAs will be extensively used. Equalising the gain between different amplified channels and making sure it doesn't vary with the power of any given channel is a significant challenge.

Equalising Signal Power

Perhaps the biggest engineering challenge in optical networks is in equalising the signal power between channels through a complex (and changing) series of components and processes. For example, in an add/drop multiplexor the added channel should exit the device with about the same level of power as the other channels passing through it.

Dispersion Compensation

As discussed in other sections of this book dispersion compensation is a significant issue for all WDM communication.

Optical Crossconnects and Switching Elements

First generation crossconnects and digital optical switches are now commercially available but there is a lot of room for improvement before this can be considered a stable "off-the-shelf" technology.

WDM Multiplexing and Demultiplexing

The mixing and separation of signals is an important issue in any WDM system. Devices with excellent characteristics are commercially available. However available devices are considered very high in cost and must reduce significantly if mass usage of the technology is to become a reality. Research in this area is focusing on cost reduction (especially in the area of WGRs). It is expected that the cost (of manufacture) of WGR devices will reduce by a factor of about 20 within the next few years.

9.2 Components for WDM Systems

In Chapter 5, "Optical Devices" on page 189 devices widely applicable to most optical communication systems were reviewed and described. However, devices specifically designed for WDM systems were omitted and are dealt with here.

9.2.1 Light Sources for WDM

Lasers needed for WDM systems are much the same as lasers for ordinary long distance communication. However, some requirements are more critical with WDM and a number of new requirements become apparent.

Spectral Width and Linewidth

In general in a dense WDM system we need a laser with only one line in its spectrum. This will mean either a DFB or a DBR laser. The required linewidth will depend on the number of channels in the proposed system and the tolerance of other components (such as grating demultiplexors). In general the narrower the linewidth the better but this will usually be a cost/benefit tradeoff.

Wavelength Stability

In most long-distance (single channel) systems we need very stable, narrow linewidth lasers to minimise the effects of dispersion and things like mode partition noise. However, in a WDM system we need to minimise the change in wavelength over time. A shift of a nm or two taking place over a few seconds might not bother a regular WAN single channel system but it would disrupt a WDM one.

The key problem here is "drift" of the laser's wavelength over time (perhaps a year or two). The high energy levels involved in the lasers cavity and on the end facets cause degradation of the materials over time and with this a wavelength shift. Some things can be done. For example, the presence of phosphorus as a component of the alloy semiconductor (such as in InGaAsP) can be a problem as the phosphorus tends to react with stray oxygen atoms forming an insulating compound. Much recent research has focused on replacing phosphorus in lasers in order to overcome this problem.

Tunable Lasers

Tunable lasers may be very important in future lightwave networks:

1. In "Broadcast and Select" LANs and MANs fast tuning of either the transmitter or the receiver is essential to the overall performance of the system.

2. In wavelength-routed networks (predominantly WANs) the sender will be told which channel to use (which wavelength) before a connection is established. It then needs to tune to that wavelength. In this case tuning need not be very fast but it should be very accurate.

3. In most current (early) WDM systems tuneability either at the transmitter or the receiver is not required. However, it is very difficult to manufacture lasers to an exact desired wavelength. What you do is make lots of them and choose the ones that happen to operate at the wavelength you want. Low cost tunability could help to overcome this problem and also the problem of laser drift.

There are various approaches to making lasers tunable and these were discussed earlier in 3.3.10, "Tunable DBR Lasers" on page 153 and 3.3.11, "External Cavity DBR Lasers" on page 156. Techniques break down into two basic types:

1. Varying the refractive index of the part of the DBR cavity adjacent to the grating.

2. Varying the wavelength reflected by an external grating in an external cavity laser design. This approach usually involves mechanical movement of the grating and is therefore relatively slow.

Multiwavelength Lasers

> One approach that allows very fast tuning is to build a number of lasers of different wavelengths together on the same substrate. Tuning can be accomplished very quickly by selecting which laser is to transmit. Alternatively, multiple signals may be sent simultaneously. This principle is discussed further in the next section.

9.2.1.1 Multiwavelength Lasers

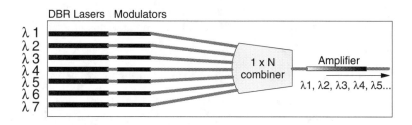

Figure 309. Multiwavelength Laser

Figure 309 shows the design of a multiwavelength array of lasers. Many similar designs have been reported in the literature. The aim is to produce a low cost WDM source for multiple channels at speeds of up to 2.4 Gbps. So far devices have not yet appeared on the commercial market and in fact appear to have a number of problems:

- It is very difficult to manufacture the DBR lasers to exactly the required wavelengths. The usual option of tuning through temperature control is not possible because they are all located on the same substrate.

- When the light is mixed (of course) a very large proportion of it is lost. This could potentially be overcome by using a waveguide grating structure and indeed these are being researched.

- Because of the loss of light you need the SOA[109] to amplify the combined signal. This introduces all the crosstalk and saturation problems of using an SOA with multiple wavelengths.

---

[109] Semiconductor Optical Amplifier

9.2.1.2 Multiline Lasers

A number of proposed WDM systems approaches require a "multiline" light source. The concept here is to produce many wavelengths in the same device. This has a number of significant potential advantages:

- You can save the cost of using multiple lasers.

- When multiple wavelengths are generated from a single source there is a fixed relationship between the wavelengths produced. Thus if we stabilise the device with reference to one wavelength we have stabilised it for all wavelengths.

The obvious disadvantage is that we can't modulate individual channels (wavelengths) by controlling the laser's injection current. Some form of external modulation of each channel is needed.

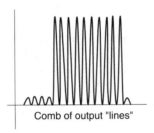

Comb of output "lines"

Figure 310. Idealised Output Spectrum of a Multiline Laser

Figure 310 shows the output spectrum that we would like to produce. This is quite different from the usual laser output. Figure 70 on page 133 shows the output spectrum of a typical unguided Fabry-Perot laser. In most laser designs we try to reduce the number of lines to only one and to minimise the width of that one. Here we want to modify the FP laser to produce lines of equal amplitude with the desired spacings.

9.2.1.3 Amplified Spontaneous Emission (ASE) Sources

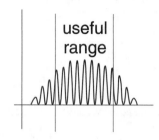

Figure 311. *FP Laser Output Spectrum Just Below Threshold*

It happens that an ordinary FP laser driven just below the lasing threshold produces a multiline spectrum very close to the spectrum we want. This is shown in Figure 311. This is called an "Amplified Spontaneous Emission" (ASE) source.[110] Because it is producing below the lasing threshold the total power is low *and* the power is distributed among many lines. Also, as shown in the diagram, the lines produced are different in amplitude. To be useful the signal needs to both be amplified and filtered or compensated in some way such that the lines produced are of equal amplitude.

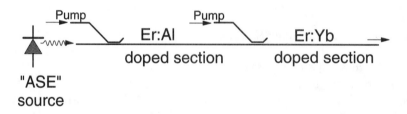

Figure 312. *Multiline Laser Design Based on ASE*

This suggests the idea of using the non-linearities in EDFAs to compensate for the non-linearities of the ASE source. This device is illustrated in Figure 312.

Power exiting from the back facet can be monitored and used to measure the wavelength of one of the lines. Wavelength stability would then be provided by controlling the temperature of the device so that a particular reference line matched a

---

[110] This name is problematic in the sense that lasing is happening in a very large number of very short duration bursts. This is shown by the fact that there are lines. A true ASE source wouldn't produce lines. However, the name used in the literature for this process is "Amplified Spontaneous Emission".

predetermined wavelength. (Of course, because of the fixed relationship between the lines all the other lines are stabilised by this process as well.)

The great benefit of this device is that each wavelength is related exactly to each other wavelength. If you stabilise one of them then you have stabilised all of them.

Of course you can't modulate an individual line by controlling the laser's injection current! In order to modulate each wavelength independently they would need to be separated into individual signals and separately modulated. This is not a big handicap as in the systems for which this device is proposed you have to separate the wavelengths anyway. There are ways of modulating individual wavelengths within a WDM stream without demultiplexing the whole stream. For example, an acoustic modulator can do this. In addition, an acoustic modulator can independently modulate multiple wavelengths within a WDM stream! See 5.9.5, "Acoustic Modulators" on page 314. In addition, some recent research has suggested the possibility of modulating individual wavelengths *within* the fibre while the signal is still a mixture of many wavelengths. If this is accomplished the possibilities for this kind of multiwavelength source would be expanded considerably.

A characteristic of using an ASE source is that the linewidths are relatively wide and the coherence length very short. This is a significant advantage in overcoming noise due to reflections in short distance systems for example. However, in long distance systems the wide linewidth creates a dispersion problem.

This type of device is still very much in the research stage. However, a number of very interesting systems possibilities exist for multiwavelength sources of this kind. See 10.3.6, "Metropolitan Area Add/Drop WDM with a Multiwavelength Source" on page 603.

9.2.2 Multiplexing (Combining) the Light

Superficially, combining a number of different light sources into a single stream should be easy. In the electronic world we could join many different signal sources together very simply and almost without loss of any signal. Unfortunately, in optics it just doesn't work this way.

Passive couplers such as those described in 5.4, "Splitters and Couplers" on page 234 combine light in exactly the way we want *but every time we join two fibres in a coupler we lose half the light!* If you combine eight signals on different fibres onto a single fibre using simple couplers then each individual channel in the combined output will be *one eighth* of the strength it started out at (a loss of 9 dB). If you combine 64 signals this way then each channel ends up at one-sixty-fourth of its original strength

(18 dB of loss). This applies no matter how the couplers are built (as a single fused fibre coupler or as a series of concatenated 3 dB couplers.)

However, there is another way. If we make use of the fact that these signals are all on different wavelengths then we can use Littrow gratings, Array Waveguide Gratings (AWGs) and similar devices to integrate the signal with a much lower loss. A typical commercial Littrow grating combining 32 channels has a loss (per channel) of around 6 dB (3/4 of each signal is lost). AWGs are quoted with total loss levels of around 5 dB for devices with up to 64 channels!

While even 5 dB still seems to be a lot, practical WDM systems to operate over metropolitan distances (up to 70 km or so) can be constructed without resort to amplifiers. While these devices are expensive (compared to fused couplers) it is possible to build a system that uses a single grating device for both multiplexing and demultiplexing so that the cost impact is minimised. This is discussed further in 9.2.4.5, "Waveguide Grating Routers (WGRs)" on page 528.

In systems with only a few channels (say four) then we can use simple couplers. If larger numbers of channels are involved then we might typically need a grating device or an amplifier after the multiplexor.

9.2.3 Transmission

In WDM systems we have all of the same system design issues that are present in the design of simple optical links. However there are a number of other issues that are unique to WDM systems (or at least have a much greater importance in the context of WDM).

Control of Dispersion

In general we have the same problems with dispersion that we have in a single wavelength situation and the same techniques for dispersion control can be used. But long links that are most subject to dispersion are also the ones that people want to use WDM for (such as undersea systems) so we see dispersion control as a critical element in systems design.

In WDM we want to use lasers with a minimal spectral width so that we can position channels accurately and allow for sufficient separation. This characteristic of course is also what we want to minimise dispersion.

One aspect of WDM is that in itself it is a dispersion control technique of sorts. Dispersion becomes more and more troublesome as the speed of the optical channel is increased. With WDM we can use multiple slower streams instead of a single much faster one! So a 4-channel WDM system at 2.4

Gbps per channel will have less of a problem with dispersion than a single-channel system at 9.6 Gbps.

Interference Effects

One of the issues in WDM is the mutual interference between the optical channels both within devices and during transmission. The two most important transmission effects are called "stimulated Raman scattering" and "4-wave mixing". Other effects occur in optical amplifiers when operating close to saturation. These are discussed in 9.4, "Systems Engineering in the WDM Environment" on page 547.

Amplifier (EDFA) Issues

Inequality of response between channels can be a serious issue in long distance WDM systems. This is discussed in 9.4, "Systems Engineering in the WDM Environment" on page 547.

Selecting Wavelengths

One possible way of limiting the crosstalk (noise) between channels is to space the WDM channels unevenly. That is, the spacings between the channels are calculated such that noise produced by 4-wave mixing and SRS falls between channels rather than within them. This is often suggested but the technique is seldom used in commercial systems.

9.2.4 Demultiplexing the Light

There are three generic approaches to demultiplexing:

1. Split the mixed light up into many mixed outputs (one per required output port) and then filter each port individually.

2. Split off a single channel at a time.

3. Demultiplex the whole bundle of optical channels in one operation.

The following are examples of each approach.

9.2.4.1 3 dB Splitter Array with Fabry-Perot Filters

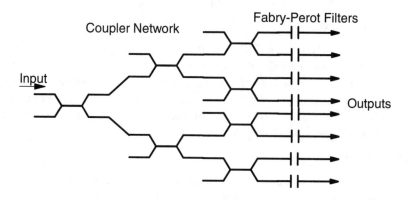

Figure 313. *Splitter Array with Fabry-Perot Filters*

In this configuration cascaded 3 dB splitters are used to divide the mixed signal up into as many equal outputs as necessary. Figure 313 shows an 8-port configuration. It is then necessary to separate each individual signal from the others. In this case the separation is achieved with separate Fabry-Perot filters. Of course it would be possible to replace the FP filters with FBGs and circulators (this would increase the precision of wavelength selection but also the cost). Equally the cascade of 3 dB splitters could be replaced with a single fused-fibre coupler.

This configuration has been used in research systems but it has a number of disadvantages:

- Loss of signal power in the system accumulates very quickly indeed. In the figure the total loss (if the splitters are perfect) is 9 dB per port *before* we incur an additional 3 dB for the FP filter. In a serious design for the WAN environment we would probably need an optical preamplifier to boost the signal before splitting.

- Built with fibre couplers this becomes messy and hard to manage. However, if built in planar technology this disadvantage is overcome.

- Cost tends to be linear with the number of ports. With a small number of ports this is an attractive approach. With a large number other approaches tend to be more cost-effective.

9.2.4.2 Circulators with FBGs

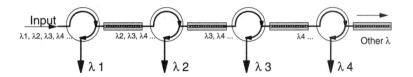

Figure 314. *Demultiplexor Using In-Fibre Bragg Gratings*

In this configuration each wavelength is separated from the multiplexed stream individually.

1. Input consisting of many mixed wavelengths arrives (from the left in the figure).

2. It enters the first circulator and is output into the first FBG

3. The FBG reflects the selected wavelength back to the circulator but allows all other wavelengths to pass. With many types of circulators this operation can involve an attenuation of 1 dB or less.

4. The selected wavelength travels around the circulator to Port 3 where it is output.

All other wavelengths continue through the FBG to the next circulator where the process is repeated for λ2. Individual wavelengths are demultiplexed as we proceed from one stage to another.

There are several considerations for this type of device:

- You can separate the circulators and FBGs so that each is located with its end device. The fibre is then connected in a ring configuration from device to device.

- It can be very selective and separate very narrow channels.

- Depending on the quality of the circulators you lose only about 1 to 1.5 dB per stage. This is quite good but still requires amplification if a large number of channels are involved.

- Cost is linear with the number of ports so it is a very competitive technology if the number of ports is small.

Some early commercial (4-channel) WDM systems use this principle.

9.2.4.3 In-Fibre Bragg Gratings with Couplers

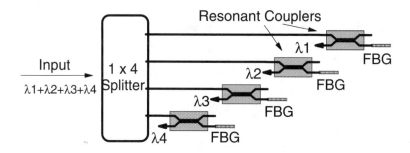

***Figure 315.** Demultiplexor Using In-Fibre Bragg Gratings with 3 dB Couplers*

Figure 315 shows another configuration using fibre Bragg gratings. Because of the use of 3 dB couplers it is significantly less costly than the configuration using circulators. In fact this configuration offers a narrowband filter with a "flat top" shape (ideal for WDM).

The big problem is the extremely high insertion loss which is 6+10log(n) dB per channel (where n=the number of channels). In practical applications the input would need to be amplified to a high level for the device to be considered practical.

9.2.4.4 Littrow Gratings

Littrow gratings were introduced earlier in 5.7.1.1, "Wavelength Selection" on page 263. They may be used for both multiplexing and demultiplexing. Commercially available in versions with up to 132 ports their main problem is cost. The mechanical problem of positioning many fibres very accurately means that these devices have a high cost. However if the number of ports required is large (20 or more) then Littrow gratings can be cost-competitive with other approaches.

The IBM 9729 WDM concentrator uses this type of grating because it can be bi-directional with input and output on the same fibre. You only need one grating at each end of the link. In addition they are proven and reliable in the field.

9.2.4.5 Waveguide Grating Routers (WGRs)

Waveguide grating routers are also known as Array Waveguide Gratings (AWGs).

The principles of operation of WGRs were discussed in 5.7.3, "Waveguide Grating Routers (WGRs)" on page 280. They are not gratings although they deliver the function of a grating. In fact they are a generalised form of the Mach-Zehnder interferometer.

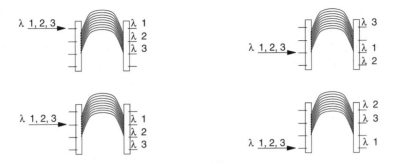

Figure 316. Array Waveguide Wavelength Router Schematic

Figure 316 shows the basic function. A multiplexed stream of wavelengths arriving on one input port is demultiplexed onto particular output ports as shown in the top left-hand part of the figure. The same multiplexed stream of wavelengths arriving on a different input port is demultiplexed onto *a different set of output ports*. This is shown in different sections of the figure.

It is possible to build a simple WGR device with only a single output port. In this case there is only one port on one side of the device but multiple ports on the other. In many cases this is the desired configuration for a WDM system and it saves significant cost in that you don't have to connect unused fibres to the device. This "pigtailing" cost dominates the device cost.

WGR devices are available commercially from several manufacturers. They are constructed in planar waveguide technology and have an insertion loss of around 5 dB.

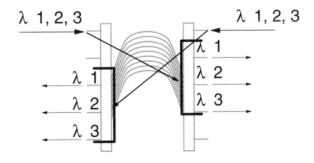

Figure 317. Bi-Directional Wavelength Multiplexor/Demultiplexor

A big advantage of the WGR is that it can be used in both directions simultaneously as shown in Figure 317. This means that a single device can be used for both multiplexing and demultiplexing while using dual fibres (one in each direction) for the multiplexed connection. This has significant implications in saving system cost as one device is needed rather than two.

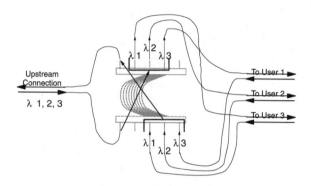

Figure 318. Wavelength Multiplexor/Demultiplexor

While the WGR will be used in conventional dense WDM configurations it has been suggested that it may make new applications of WDM economically attractive. For example this configuration might be used as a remote (passive) multiplexor in an FTTH (fibre to the home), PON (passive optical network) system. This is shown in Figure 318. A key aspect of this is that WGRs of up to 132 ports are available. A problem is that the device requires temperature control for stable operation and this is difficult if the devices are spread around suburban streets screwed to telegraph poles. Another problem is that the basic device is highly polarisation dependent. However, ways have been found to eliminate this as discussed in 5.7.3, "Waveguide Grating Routers (WGRs)" on page 280.

9.2.5 Add-Drop Multiplexors

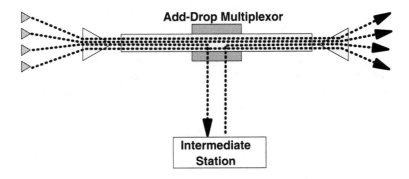

Figure 319. Add-Drop Multiplexor Function

An add-drop multiplexor adds and/or removes a single channel from a combined WDM signal *without* interfering with the other channels on the fibre. This function is illustrated in Figure 319. There are several devices which may perform this function such as:

1. Array waveguide gratings

2. Circulators with FBGs

3. A Cascade of MZIs

Operation of these devices as add/drop multiplexors is described in the following sections.

9.2.5.1 Array Waveguide Gratings

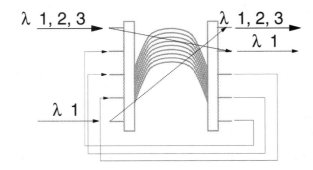

Figure 320. Array Waveguide Add-Drop Multiplexor

In this figure we see a WGR configured as an add-drop multiplexor. Wavelength λ1 is added to the multiplexed stream on the left of the picture and dropped (demultiplexed) from the input stream on the right of the figure.

This is a very versatile function. For example multiple channels can be added or dropped in the same operation. However, the signal loss is about 5 dB per pass through the device. So channels that aren't added or dropped experience an insertion loss of around 10 dB. In a system we need to equalise the signal power between channels (so that the newly added channels are about the same strength as the dropped ones) and probably to amplify the whole stream as well.

For adding and dropping a single channel there is a much better configuration available as shown in Figure 321.

9.2.5.2 Circulators with In-Fibre Bragg Gratings

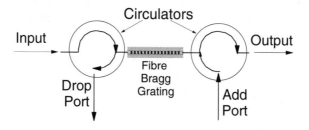

Figure 321. Add-Drop Multiplexor Using FBG and Circulators

Here we are using an FBG with a pair of circulators to add and drop a single channel. Operation is as follows:

- The signal enters at the left of the figure and is routed through the circulator to the FBG.

- The non-selected wavelengths pass through the FBG to the next circulator.

- The selected wavelength is reflected by the FBG and then directed out of the next circulator port.

- The wavelength to be added (which must be the same as the one just dropped) enters through the "add-port" of the rightmost circulator.

- It travels around to the FBG and is reflected back to the circulator. This process mixes the added channel with the multiplexed stream.

This configuration has a relatively low loss of 3 dB for the multiplexed stream. It could be very suitable for operation in a looped metropolitan area network (MAN) where a single fibre loop interconnects many locations within a city area.

9.2.5.3 Cascaded Mach-Zehnder Interferometric Filters

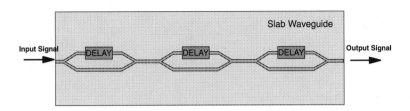

Figure 322. *Filter Using Cascaded Mach-Zehnder Interferometers*

The simple Mach-Zehnder interferometer described in 5.9.8, "Modulation Using a Mach-Zehnder Interferometer" on page 323 can be used as a wavelength selective filter. The *amount* of delay difference between the arms of the device translates into a phase difference which translates into an amount of attenuation. A given *amount* of delay (measured in time) results in a *different amount* of phase delay depending on the wavelength. Thus if the two arms are different in length or if there is something that changes the propagation time in one of the arms then the effect will be different depending on the wavelength.

The problem with the simple (single stage) MZI is that it does not exhibit a very sharp filter cut-off. Instead of passing a single well defined band of wavelengths it passes a wide band of wavelengths all of which are attenuated by varying amounts. This is exactly the same situation which was illustrated for Fabry-Perot filters in Figure 192 on page 291. A single stage MZI corresponds to an FP filter with mirrors of very low reflectivity. A multi-stage one has characteristics similar to an FP filter with high reflectivity mirrors.

To build an MZI with good usable filter characteristics we need to use multiple stages connected in series (or cascade). This is illustrated in Figure 323 on page 534.

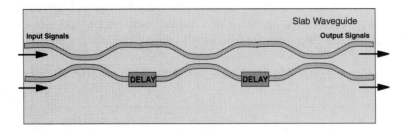

Figure 323. ADM Using Cascaded Mach-Zehnder Interferometers - Principle

Figure 323 shows an interesting device which is being researched in a number of projects. It is a series of resonant couplers built on a planar substrate to form a series of "Mach-Zehnder Interferometers" (MZIs). A single wavelength can be added and/or removed from a multiplexed stream without disturbing the other wavelengths.

The device is similar to the series of MZIs described above except that instead of using Y-couplers it uses resonant couplers. This gives the designer another parameter (coupling length) which can be used to control the device's operation.

A WDM multiplexed stream can be passed through one waveguide and a selected wavelength added and dropped from the other waveguide. Tuning is accomplished by arranging a variable delay in one waveguide through heating the material with resistance heaters.

The major problem with this device is its size. To get effective operation you need around 15 couplers in cascade. Given that the minimum bend radius of curves in most planar technology is 15-20 mm or so the device ends up being very long (perhaps 30-40 cm). Current planar fabrication technology cannot handle devices of this size and even if it could the cost would be very high.

The solution to this is to use waveguide material with a "high" RI contrast between the waveguide and the substrate. (Here the word "high" means an RI difference of around .02.) With the high RI contrast we can have much tighter radius bends in the waveguide and hence make the device significantly smaller. The smaller device can be made with existing chip manufacturing technology.

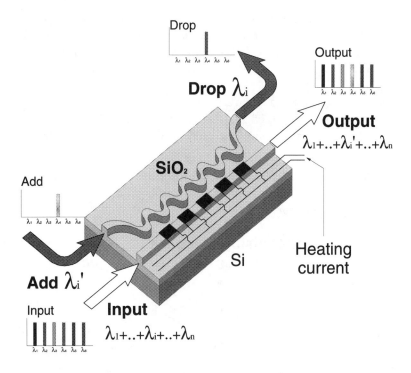

Figure 324. Add-Drop Multiplexor Using Cascaded Mach-Zehnder Interferometers

Figure 324 illustrates an experimental device being developed by IBM Research. It is built in silica technology on a silicon substrate. The waveguides are formed by doping the silica with a high (7%) concentration of SiON (silicon oxynitride) giving an RI of 1.48. This allows bends in the waveguide to be 1-2 mm in radius. The overall device is 7 cm long with 15 cascaded couplers. The device illustrated is tunable through the controlled heating of localised areas on the waveguide. These heaters are build from Cr electrodes with Au wires connecting to them.

There are three potential problems in using high RI materials in this way;

1. The high RI means that the waveguide must be very narrow (of the order of 3 microns) wide in order to remain single-moded. This is not so much of a problem in itself but it means that coupling to a fibre becomes very difficult.

2. The high RI material has a higher attenuation than standard silica waveguides. This is not a significant problem because the dimensions are very much smaller and so the signal has a lot less distance to travel in the high attenuation material.

3. The very narrow waveguide is not smooth on its edges. Production technology for integrated circuits uses a raster scanning technique to build the masks for integrated circuit production. This raster scan produces a matrix of dots. The waveguides are thus constructed of many small dots. Thus waveguides that are straight and have 90° bends (in line with the axes of the chip) are smooth sided. But optical waveguides can't have 90° corners! Curved or diagonal lines have a step like roughness on the edges. These regular corrugations on the edge of the waveguides can act as gratings and cause many unwanted effects if not properly controlled.

In fact this applies to all planar waveguide devices made by the process of silicon chip manufacture. While it is a potential problem, in the real world it does not create a serious limitation.

9.2.6 Optical Space-Division Switches

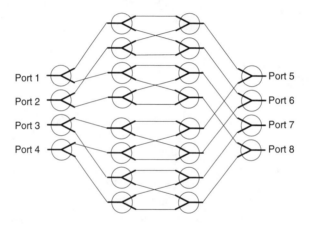

Figure 325. *4 x 4 Optical Space-Division Switch*

An optical space-division switch is designed to connect any input port to any output port as desired by the user. Typical switches are built up from an assembly of simple digital optical switches such as those described in 5.9.2, "Optical Switching Elements" on page 302. This would normally be built on a planar substrate as a single planar device.

Only one wavelength is present on any input waveguide (input is single channel per waveguide). Any input may be switched to any output but two inputs may *not* go to the same output at the same time. The device is bi-directional and when a connection has been established between an input port and an output port that particular connection may be used in either (or both) directions.

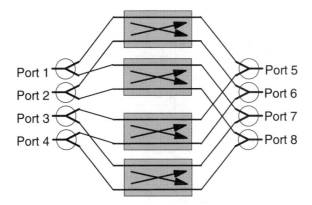

Figure 326. *Optical Switch Using Crossconnect Switch Elements*

Figure 326 shows the same switch as in Figure 325 on page 536 with the main part of the switching fabric implemented as crossconnects rather than as simple digital optical switches. There is a significant saving here in complexity and number of required elements. Optical crossconnects are discussed in 5.9.2.1, "Optical Crossconnects (OXCs)" on page 303.

9.2.7 Optical Switching Nodes

The optical space division switch discussed in 9.2.6, "Optical Space-Division Switches" on page 536 above establishes bi-directional optical connections between input and output ports. However, it is not wavelength sensitive and it will switch from one port to another regardless of which wavelength is in use. In fact, it can connect optical WDM streams consisting of many wavelengths from one port to another.

Crossconnects and Switching Nodes

In the context of switching *elements* a crossconnect is a switch element with two input and two output ports. See 5.9.2.1, "Optical Crossconnects (OXCs)" on page 303.

In the context of networks a crossconnect is a switching node whose state is changed by the network management system rather than by signalling within the network. This means that change of the state of a crossconnect is something that takes place on a timescale of seconds rather than of micro-seconds.

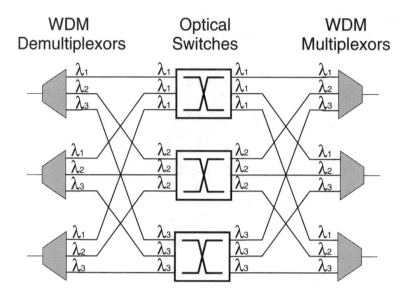

Figure 327. *Structure of an Optical Switching Node*

To make a useful optical "crossconnect" or switching node we want to switch individual wavelengths. This means that before we switch channels we need to demultiplex the incoming WDM stream so that one wavelength only appears at each input port of the switch fabric. At the output we need to re-multiplex the separate wavelengths onto their intended output fibres.

A schematic of a useful optical switching node is shown in Figure 327. Each "optical switch" in the figure is similar to the switch described in 9.2.6, "Optical Space-Division Switches" on page 536. We are assuming that the same three wavelengths are present on each of three input ports. The task is to switch any input channel (3 ports x 3 wavelengths each equals 9 channels) to any output port. That said, we can't switch the same wavelength from multiple inputs to the same output port. First, it is not a logical thing to do because the signals will mix and the result will be garbage! Second, if we were to try to do that there would be somewhere in the switch fabric (in the WDM multiplexors) where it was not possible - or at least not possible without very high additional attenuation. This is the reason for the fact that in the switch in the figure each switch element is configured to handle only one wavelength!

Because you can't have the same wavelength coming from different input ports going to the same output, this switch is restricted in the connectivity options it can offer. In order to offer fully any-to-any connections it would need to be able to change wavelengths during the switching process. Switches with this capability are discussed next.

Of course all such switches are electronically controlled! If this is a crossconnect then the computer controlling the switching element will be operated from a "network management console". That is, a third party operator (not one of the parties to the connection) will enter commands to change the state of the switch.

If this is considered a real communications "switch" then end-user devices request a connection to be made through a system known as the signalling system. There would need to be some process in the node to effect bi-directional communication between the switch and the end-user devices in order to pass information necessary to establish the connections.

9.2.7.1 Optical Switching Node with Wavelength Conversion

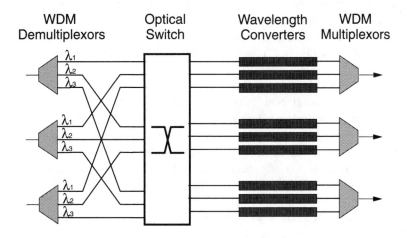

Figure 328. *Optical Switching Node with Wavelength Conversion*

In small networks consisting of only a few nodes, the limitation of having to retain the same wavelength from end-to-end through the network is not too serious. However, as discussed in 10.1.5.3, "Nodal Networks" on page 581 as the network gets larger so the inability to change wavelengths becomes more and more limiting.

A node architecture such as the one shown in Figure 328 allows for full connectivity between input optical channels and output ones. This is done by changing the wavelengths as needed within the switch.

Notice the differences between this figure and Figure 327 on page 538. First we have added devices to change the wavelength. Second the switch element has become significantly larger. In the case without wavelength changing we only needed three switches each of three ports in and three ports out. In the wavelength changing case we need a switch of nine ports by nine ports! This is because in the first example we didn't provide switch paths for traffic combinations that were impossible. In the second case we need to provide for universal connectivity.

The major problem with this type of switch is cost. Several devices which can change wavelengths are available but all of them are quite expensive. With careful design you can reduce the number of wavelength changers without limiting function and thus save some cost.

9.2.8 Wavelength Converters

A fully functional wide area optical network may be conceived of as a set of distributed routing (or switching) nodes. End user equipment may be connected to some or all of these nodes. Interconnections between nodes would be by fibres each of which might carry a number (say 64 or so) of optical channels. Networks of this type are discussed further in Chapter 10, "Lightwave Networks" on page 569.

In very small networks of the above type we can dynamically allocate particular wavelengths to individual connections and perhaps route the signal from end-to-end across the network without needing to change the wavelength. However when such a network is scaled up to reasonably large size then allocation of unique end-to-end wavelengths becomes very difficult if not impossible. The network could have many vacant optical channels (wavelengths) on all of its links but a single unique wavelength may not be available on any possible path between two end users!

To overcome this problem it will be necessary to change the wavelength of some signals as they traverse the network.

Wavelength conversion is still very much a laboratory technology. The author knows of no commercially available products that perform this function. However, in the future it may become a very important one so some of the principles are discussed here.

There are several principles that fully optical wavelength converters may use:[111]

---

[111] We ignore here the obvious conversion of receiving the signal, converting it to electronic form and then re-transmitting.

Amplitude Gain Crosstalk in SOAs

Semiconductor Optical Amplifiers (SOAs) have severe crosstalk when operated close to saturation. We can make intentional use of this crosstalk to transfer the information from a signal at one wavelength to another. This is further discussed in 9.2.8.1, "Cross Gain Modulation (XGM) in SOAs" on page 542.

Cross-Phase Modulation in SOAs

Operated at saturation intensity modulation in one signal stream can affect the refractive index of the active region in an SOA. This changes the phase of all signals passing through it. The phase difference can be converted to an amplitude modulation later in a Mach-Zehnder Interferometer.

Four-Wave Mixing (FWM) in SOAs

The phenomena of four-wave mixing was discussed earlier in 2.4.5.1, "Four-Wave Mixing (FWM)" on page 88. In this case you take an unmodulated "probe" signal and mix it with the original signal. The wavelength of the probe is chosen so that one of the sideband signals produced will have the desired wavelength. Of course then there is the problem of separating the desired signal from the input signal and the probe but this can be done in various ways such as with a circulator and an in-fibre Bragg grating. FWM will work at very high bit rates and is modulation independent.

Difference Frequency Generation (DFG)

The principle here is very similar to four-wave mixing. However, it is a non-linear effect experienced within waveguides at relatively high power levels. Its attractions are that it offers the prospect of very low noise operation and it can shift multiple wavelengths at the same time. In addition, it's fast and bidirectional. However, it is low in efficiency and very polarisation sensitive.

Frequency Shifting with Acousto-Optic Modulators

As discussed previously in 5.9.5, "Acoustic Modulators" on page 314 acoustic filters and modulators shift the optical frequency by the amount of the acoustic frequency.

To get any really significant shift in wavelength (say 1 nm) you need a very high acoustic frequency indeed (130 GHz). This acoustic frequency is not possible at this time but for smaller wavelength shifts of around 1 GHz or so this is an excellent technique.

9.2.8.1 Cross Gain Modulation (XGM) in SOAs

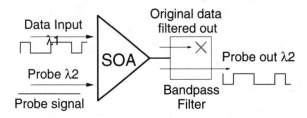

Figure 329. *Wavelength Converter with Cross-Gain Modulated SOA*

The principle here is quite simple. When you feed a relatively high level signal to an SOA it saturates. That is, the gain medium gives up all (or nearly all) of its excited state electrons and for a short time (until more energy is supplied by the pump) it cannot amplify any more. If you feed two WDM signals to an SOA at saturation you get very severe crosstalk between them for the above reason.

The principle makes use of this crosstalk effect. You feed a (modulated) signal at a relatively high level to the SOA. Mixed with this you have another (lower level) unmodulated signal at a different wavelength (called the probe). On exit from the SOA the probe signal will now carry the modulations from the original data signal. However, the modulations are the inverse of the modulated input signal!

The original signal is then filtered out and we have changed the wavelength - albeit we now have a signal which is the inverse of the one we started with. (This is not always the problem it might seem!)

Signal levels are a problem. To make this work you need a relatively high level data signal and a low level probe signal. This means that you probably need to preamplify the data signal before entering the SOA and post-amplify the probe (the new data signal) at the output.

9.2.8.2 Cross Phase Modulation (XPM) in SOAs

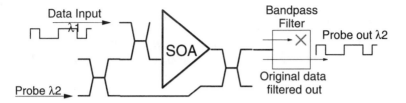

Figure 330. *Wavelength Converter with Cross-Phase Modulated SOA. The device is a Mach-Zehnder interferometer with an SOA in one arm. The phase modulation of the probe signal in the SOA is converted to amplitude modulation by interference in recombination.*

When an SOA saturates the gain characteristics change (as we have seen above). However, gain saturation is accompanied by a change in carrier density in the active region (the cavity). A change in the carrier density implies a change in the refractive index.

In this device we make use of the changed refractive index to change the *phase* of the probe signal rather than its amplitude. The changes in phase are converted to changes in amplitude by virtue of the fact that the SOA is situated in one arm of a Mach-Zehnder interferometer. (See 5.9.8, "Modulation Using a Mach-Zehnder Interferometer" on page 323.)

A great advantage of this approach is that the output from the wavelength converter is *not* inverted.

9.2.8.3 FWM and DFG

Four-Wave Mixing (FWM) and Difference Frequency Generation (DFG) are closely similar processes.

- In FWM two signals mix to produce two new signals:[112]

$$f_3 = 2f_1 - f_2$$
$$f_4 = 2f_2 - f_1$$

- In DFG two signals mix again to form two new frequencies:

---

[112] It is much easier to understand the effects here if frequency is used instead of wavelength for the description.

$$f_3 = f_1 - f_2$$
$$f_4 = f_2 - f_1$$

The difference in these processes is due to the medium within which the process takes place. FWM takes place in a so-called third-order medium such as standard fibre or an SOA. DFG takes place in a second-order medium such as a lithium niobate waveguide.

The process is illustrated in Figure 331.

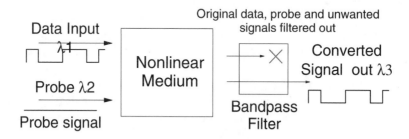

Figure 331. *Wavelength Converter Using FWM or DFG*

Both processes can operate at high bit rates and are modulation format independent. DFG produces only one output signal whereas FWM produces two one of which must be filtered out. Notice that the probe signal in FWM is close to the wavelength of the input (and output) signals. In DFG the pump wavelength is around half (twice the frequency) of the signal wavelength. One problem is that the wavelength of the output signal is a function of the wavelength of the input signal. So unwanted variations in the input signal create similar wavelength variations in the output.

Both techniques have a potentially major advantage in a system. The output is the spectral inverse (phase conjugate) of the input signal. Thus a dispersed pulse is inverted and may be "undispersed" in its transit through the next stage of transmission on a fibre. This is discussed further in 7.5.5, "Mid-Span Spectral Inversion" on page 418.

9.2.8.4 Opto-Electronic Conversion
In the context of the pure optical conversion methods discussed above converting the signal to an intermediate electronic form almost seems like cheating. However, this is perhaps the major current technique and is used in many current WDM systems for the connection of end user equipment.

In truth there are two quite distinct environments here:

1. Within an all-optical WDM network where a channel (wavelength) arriving at an intermediate node must be changed to a different wavelength in order to route it onwards to the next optical node.

2. At the end-user interface of either an optical network or one of today's typical WDM systems. In this case attachment to the end user is often in the 1310 nm band and may even use LEDs on MM fibre! In this environment most optical conversion techniques wouldn't work anyway.

In opto-electronic conversion the signal is received using a regular pin diode or APD and converted to electronic form. In practice it is usually "cleaned up" here. That is, the signal is converted into a digital pulse with clean sharp edges. However, in order to retain bit-rate and digital code independence the signal is usually *not* re-timed. This "cleaned up" signal is used to drive a laser transmitter at a specified wavelength.

While this is not aesthetic it is pragmatically a very useful thing to do. The "cleaning up" of the signal actually removes much (but by no means all) of the effects of dispersion! When the pulse is cleaned up you have to choose a signal level at which you make the decision between a "0" and a "1" bit. This process inevitably cuts some of the received dispersion off from the edges of the pulse. It cannot remove all dispersion and therefore is not as good as full regeneration in this regard but it does remove a lot of it whilst retaining code and speed independence (so long as the signal is digital).

The disadvantages of electronics are that it consumes a lot of power, adds significant noise to the signal and it is hard (read expensive) to design for very high bit rates because of the problem of crosstalk.

In experiments with the IBM 9729 it has been found that good quality communication was possible at a distance of 350 km (using intermediate 9729s to regenerate the signal). Had amplifiers been used instead the signal would have reached its limit due to dispersion in about 150 km. This is discussed further in 10.5.7.2, "Control of Dispersion" on page 620.

As a technology for intermediate switching nodes electronics should be regarded as an interim technology which is useful in the short term.

As a technology for interfacing an optical network to end-user equipment there is really no viable alternative to electronics where:

1. The end-user connection uses the 1310 nm band.

2. The end-user connection is on MM fibre.

3. The quality of the end-user's laser is problematic (low) or uncontrolled.

9.3 Standards for WDM

The International Telecommunications Union (ITU) is working on a number of *draft* standards for the operation of WDM links and of optical networks. None of these are yet firm as there are significant disagreements. However, the industry has begun to adopt aspects the draft standards (principally the wavelength grid) in product implementations.

Standards in this area are critical for several reasons:

1. In the early phase of a new technology you need the suppliers of components to supply devices as regular commercial (reasonably priced) components rather than as very expensive make-to-order devices. Standards are required for this to happen.

2. The longer term goal is to allow the building of systems which use different equipment from many different suppliers. Such equipment needs standards to allow interoperation. In the early days of a new technology it is unrealistic to expect that such standards will appear by magic. Many people involved have different opinions and points of view and few systems are in operation in the field yet - so there is very little practical experience. However, the earlier that such standards can be developed the better it will be for the whole industry.

9.3.1.1 G.692 (Point-to-Point WDM)

The ITU draft standard G.692 is entitled "Optical Interfaces for multichannel systems with optical amplifiers". This is intended to cover long distance point-to-point WDM systems using STM-4, STM-16 and/or STM-64 on 4, 8, 16 or 32 channels. The maximum link distance for a system without amplifiers is 160 km or up to 640 km with optical amplification.

The draft standard specifies a wavelength reference grid based on 100 GHz spacings and a reference (centre) frequency of 193.1 THz. This (193.1 THz) approximately equals 1,553.5 nm. (Interesting that they specify these wavelengths in Hz and not nm.) Users are free to use any wavelength on the grid in an arbitrary way! Users are also free to select which part of the spectrum they use. Unequally spaced channels are allowed provided the channel wavelengths are situated on the grid.

Early system implementations tend to use:

- 4 channels with 400 GHz (3.2 nm) spacing

- 8 channels with 200 GHz (1.6 nm) spacing

- 16 channels with 200 GHz (1.6 nm) spacing

- 32 channels with 100 GHz (.8 nm) spacing

For supervisory information an extra channel is needed. There is no standard for the format, bit rate or modulation protocol for this channel. Users are allowed to select any one of the nominated supervisory wavelengths (1310, 1480, 1510 and 1532 nm).

There is another recommendation (G.681) which specifies how optical equipment and systems may be constructed using a number of logical function blocks.

9.3.1.2 An Optical Network Standard

G.692 described above covers only point-to-point WDM links. There is a need for a standard covering more extensive optical networks. In April 1997 the ITU-T (Study Group 15) specified a framework for the development of a series of standards to cover optical networks. Note they have alphabetic identifiers rather than numbers at this stage of standards development.

G.onf Framework for an optical network

G.otn Network architecture

G.oef Equipment functions

G.oni Information model

G.onm Management aspects

G.ons Frame formats

G.onp Physical layer

G.onc Components

At the time of writing the committee had not agreed on the definition and scope of just what constitutes an optical network. In fact this is a serious issue and there are many conflicting opinions.

9.4 Systems Engineering in the WDM Environment

In the communications world systems engineering is the art of taking many devices and integrating them into a system that does something useful for somebody. This is a non-trivial exercise as interactions between different types of equipment and their operation in a field environment must be well understood.

There are many issues to be considered:

1. Determining the width and spacing of wavebands

2. Stabilising the wavelength of wavelength-sensitive components

3. Filter alignment in cascades of filters

4. Control of non-linear effects

5. Control of dispersion

6. Control of cross-talk

7. Dynamics of optical amplifiers

8. Control of system noise (especially ASE)

9.4.1 Fitting the Signal into Its Allocated Waveband

The principle of WDM is just the same principle we use in radio or television broadcasting. Different "channels" are sent on different wavelengths (or frequencies) on a shared medium. It would seem reasonable that we could send as many different channels as we like on wavelengths spaced arbitrarily close to one another. Unfortunately this is not true.

1. The signal has a finite "width" (occupies a finite band of wavelengths) regardless of what we do. Modulations (the information part of the signal) cause a broadening of the signal by at least twice the frequency of the modulation.

2. While it is possible to build lasers with a very narrow linewidth (10 kHz in the lab), most practical lasers have a linewidth of a few hundred GHz.

3. Lasers chirp and drift in wavelength.

4. Filters (such as Littrow gratings or AWGs) used in both transmission and reception cannot be made with absolute accuracy (of their centre wavelength).

5. Filters are *never* square (ideal). They pass different wavelengths with different degrees of attenuation.

Thus to build a WDM system we allocate bands of wavelengths (one per channel) which are significantly wider than the signal. This is illustrated in Figure 332 on page 549.

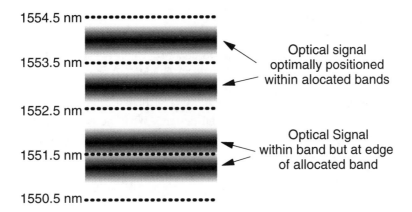

Figure 332. Fitting Optical Channels into Their Allocated Wavebands. Optical power intensity is represented by the intensity of grey level in the picture.

In this figure the signals in the upper (in the picture) two bands are almost centred but in the lower two bands they are very close to the edges of the band. While allowing the signal to reside anywhere within the waveband would be fine in concept, we can't filter (separate channels) with any great degree of precision. Therefore we need two bands as illustrated in Figure 333.

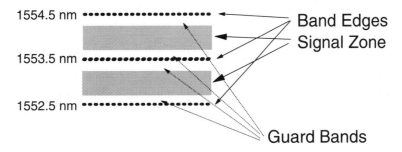

Figure 333. A More Practical Waveband Allocation

This is the practical case. There is a (reasonably narrow) band within which the optical signal must stay defined by the filters (the gratings or whatever is used to multiplex and demultiplex the signals). Outside this centre band there is another "guard band" where channels overlap and we should not have any signal.

9.4.1.1 Cascading Filters

As discussed earlier in 5.8.1.1, "Filter Characteristics" on page 287, most of the devices we want to use in WDM networks are wavelength selective filters of one kind or another. This is particularly true of switches, gratings, AWGs etc. and even EDFAs act as filters if their response is non-linear. In optical networking we will often need to pass a signal (usually a pulse) through a series of these types of optical devices. This process requires careful planning and design. What we are dealing with here is essentially *analogue* processing. The principles involved are just the same as those of the analogue electronics of the past but in today's digital world much of this has been forgotten.

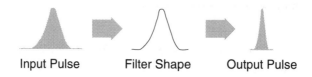

Input Pulse   Filter Shape   Output Pulse

Figure 334. Effect of Non-Square Filter on Signal Pulse. The x-axis represents the wavelength and the y-axis the pulse power or filter attenuation.

In an ideal world all filters would have a "square" profile with nice sharp edges. Arriving pulses would either pass or be blocked depending on their wavelength. However the world is not ideal and no filter is really ideal. Indeed most filters we meet in the optical world have a bell shape of one kind or another. Figure 334 shows the effect of a typical filter on a typical input pulse. One might expect if the pulse and the filter were the same shape and "aligned" properly then the filter would pass the pulse unchanged! Of course a moments thought will show that this isn't true and the effect shown in the figure will occur. The input pulse will be significantly narrowed!

Input Pulse   Filter 1   Filter 2   Output Pulse

Figure 335. Effect of Multiple Filters on Signal Pulse

Figure 335 shows the effect of multiple filters in succession. This happens a lot. For example, in a WDM system (using gratings for both multiplexing and demultiplexing) every pulse passes through two gratings in succession. The effect is that the input pulse is narrowed even further.

Another (perhaps better) way of looking at this is to say that a succession of filters can be summed to have the characteristics of a single (much narrower) filter.

There are a number of interesting points here:

1. Narrowing a pulse is *not* necessarily bad. For one thing it will reduce the effects of chromatic dispersion (by reducing the breadth of wavelength in the pulse).

2. When filters are not *exactly* aligned with one another (when the centre wavelengths are not exactly the same) the narrowing effect is even greater. This means that filter alignment is a critical issue in the building of optical networks.

3. Narrowing the filter bandwidth reduces the possible allowed signal linewidth *and* takes away the margin for misalignment of the transmit laser with the filter(s). Even though the allocated band of wavelengths may be quite large (say 1 nm) the window allowed by the filters may be as narrow as perhaps .2 nm. This would require extreme precision and stability on the part of the transmitting laser. The narrowed passband can also be a source of noise if the laser has any chirp or drift.

4. The attenuation of a series of concatenated filters is *not* the sum of the attenuations of all the filters. Or rather, if you look at a particular input signal and say that a particular filter attenuates the signal by 6 dB then a series connection of two filters will *not* attenuate by 12 dB but perhaps by as little as 8 or 9. The reason for this is that the signal has been narrowed and shaped in its transit through the first filter and when it enters the second filter it no longer has the same profile as the original signal.

   Thus when the centre wavelengths are closely aligned the attenuation of a pair of filters can be significantly less than the sum of the attenuations of each of them. However, when the centre wavelengths are not aligned attenuation can increase very rapidly to the point where essentially nothing gets through!

9.4.1.2 Crosstalk

Crosstalk occurs in devices that filter and separate wavelengths. A small proportion of the optical power that should have ended up in a particular channel (on a particular filter output) actually ends up in an adjacent (or another) channel.

Crosstalk is critically important in WDM systems. When signals from one channel arrive in another they become noise in the other channel. This can have serious effects on the signal-to-noise ratio and hence on the error rate of the system.

Crosstalk is usually quoted as the "worst case" condition. This is where the signal in one channel is right at the edge of its allowed band. Crosstalk is quoted as the loss in dB between the input level of the signal and its (unwanted) signal strength in the adjacent channel. A figure of 30 dB is widely considered to be an acceptable level for most systems.

9.4.2 Stabilising Wavelengths

Perhaps the biggest single problem in using WDM technology is making sure that a particular channel in the system (a wavelength) is *the same* throughout the system. When we transmit on a particular channel we must be sure that the transmission is on the intended wavelength within some designed system tolerance. When a wavelength is demultiplexed we need to be sure we have detected the correct one. When a number of channels are put onto the same fibre we must be sure they don't interfere with one another. Thus stable wavelengths are critical to system operation.

Temperature Control

In stabilising wavelengths the critical issue for almost every component in the system is *temperature control*. Every wavelength-sensitive component in the system changes its wavelength with change in ambient temperature. The problem is much more significant in devices that themselves consume power and therefore heat up (such as lasers) but applies also to gratings and to devices that require precise positioning of fibres (such as circulators).

That said, some components are significantly more sensitive to temperature than others. With most lasers we need to cool them individually with solid state (Peltier effect) coolers. Other components (such as Littrow gratings) need individual cooling (or even heating). However, since these do not produce heat of their own we can do a lot to minimise the problem with insulation.

Another obvious approach is to make optical devices (especially planar ones) from materials with very low coefficients of expansion. This minimises the problem. However while such materials are available they are not always suitable for desired application.

Fibre Bragg gratings can be compensated very well indeed by mounting them on a carefully designed stage tensioned with a bi-metal strip. This strip is arranged to apply a varying tension onto the fibre depending on the temperature. The applied tension in the fibre changes the wavelength of the grating in the direction opposite to the wavelength change caused by heat in the fibre. The two effects can be made to balance and we then have a temperature stable FBG! (These are commercially available.)

Laser Chirp and Relaxation Oscillation

Chirp and relaxation oscillation were discussed earlier in Chirp on page 136 and Relaxation Oscillations on page 137. Both cause rapid shifts in the wavelength of a laser pulse immediately after its beginning.

In a WDM system these both cause a broadening of the laser linewidth. Interaction of the wavelength shifts with filters in the system can be a prime source of noise.

Both of these can be minimised by choosing lasers designed for minimal chirp. Also, if you drive the laser to somewhat less than its maximum power the effects are lessened as carrier depletion in the cavity is minimised.

The best way to avoid these problems is to use an external modulator. This way the laser produces a constant stable light level and the external modulator adds the information to it. Hence there is no chirp or relaxation. The main issue here is the high insertion loss of many external modulators. From 6 dB to 12 dB might be expected depending on the type. But most of this insertion loss is due to pigtailing losses. If you integrate a modulator on the same chip as the laser then losses can be minimal. See 3.3.5, "Integrated Absorption Modulators" on page 147. Lasers with integrated "external" (mainly absorption) modulators are available commercially.

Laser Drift

Over time in operation, lasers tend to drift in wavelength. This is due to degradation of the materials. Drift is a major problem for WDM systems and some form of compensation needs to be applied.

Frequency Referencing

Perhaps the best way of ensuring that the lasers don't drift is to continuously monitor the wavelength produced and adjust the laser accordingly. Many lasers can be tuned over a small range of wavelengths (such as half a nanometer) by varying the operating temperature.

The problem is in constructing an accurate way of measuring the wavelength. The two leading ways of achieving this are:

1. The use of fibre Bragg gratings. FBGs can be very narrow and accurate filters and they are (or can be made) very temperature stable. However, they have the significant problem that they operate in reflection. This means that you need a circulator to separate out the reflected light.

2. Fabry-Perot filters (or Etalons) can be made very easily by depositing a controlled thickness of a dielectric material. These transmit light at the selected wavelength.

The technique here is to construct a feedback loop by passing light from the laser's back facet through the appropriate filter and then to a detector. The device can then be automatically adjusted (by varying the temperature) to provide the maximum output through the filter. This ensures that the laser stays at the desired wavelength.

A better way might be to use a laser with an external fibre cavity and an FBG as its exit mirror. This ensures that the laser produces a very stable wavelength in the first place. However, this tends to cost a fair bit more.

9.4.3 Controlling Non-linear Effects

Various non-linear effects prevalent in fibre transmission were discussed in 2.4.5, "Non-Linear High-Power Effects" on page 87. In the WDM world all of these need consideration and control for the system to operate successfully.

Four-Wave Mixing (FWM)

FWM was described in 2.4.5.1, "Four-Wave Mixing (FWM)" on page 88. Potentially FWM (also called FPM - Four Photon Mixing) is a most serious issue for WDM systems. It is influenced very strongly by two factors:

1. Channel spacing

2. Fibre dispersion

FWM increases rapidly as channels are spaced closer and closer together. While FWM could affect multiple channels in practice it occurs only between adjacent channels.

For FWM to take effect each channel must stay in-phase with its adjacent channel for some considerable distance. Thus if fibre dispersion is high (as when using standard fibre in the 1550 nm band) then the effects of FWM are minimised. With DSF fibre (dispersion less than 1 ps.nm.km) the FWM effect is maximised.

Using DSF fibre (with a zero dispersion in the 1550 nm band), FWM causes some degradation at channel spacings of less than 80 GHz. At a channel separation of 25 GHz around 80% of the energy in the two signals will be transferred into sum or difference frequencies!

Using standard fibre in the 1550 nm band (dispersion = 17 ps/nm/km), FWM effects disappear when channel separation is greater than 25 GHz. However at a separation of less than 15 GHz the effect (even on standard fibre) becomes severe.

So called Dispersion Optimised Fibre (see 2.4.2.3, "Non-Zero Dispersion-Shifted (WDM-Optimised) Fibre" on page 80) has almost the same effects on FWM as standard fibre does but with a lot less dispersion.

One way of minimising the impact of FWM is to place WDM channels such that the generated signals do not fall within other WDM channels. Thus they don't interfere with other channels too much. This does help but it cannot overcome the problem of noise generated in the source WDM channels by power being transferred out of them. In addition, some WDM devices are difficult to construct if wavelength spacing is uneven (reflective gratings for example).

Stimulated Brillouin Scattering (SBS)

SBS is really a single channel phenomena but nevertheless it must be taken into account in WDM situations. SBS depends on a number of things:

1. Signal linewidth

   The narrower the linewidth the more of a problem SBS becomes. SBS is generally not a problem with channel bandwidth greater than 100 MHz.

2. Signal power

   There is a threshold value below which SBS will not cause a problem.

3. Fibre core size

   The narrower the core, the higher the power concentration and thus the greater effect from SBS.

4. Wavelength

   SBS has a bigger effect in the 1550 nm band than in the 1310 nm band.

These dependencies were summarised in Figure 48 on page 90. As a rule of thumb you don't need to worry about SBS until the signal power per channel required gets above about 5 mW.

Stimulated Raman Scattering

SRS occurs between signal channels and between groups of channels. There is a good "rule of thumb" which can tell us when SRS is likely to become a problem.

"To keep degradation due to SRS down to acceptable levels the product of total power and total optical bandwidth must be less than 500 GHz/W."[113] This is quite a lot. The bandwidth quoted is the spread of the WDM channels. Thus two channels separated by 20 nm have the same "bandwidth" (for this purpose) as 20 channels spaced 1 nm apart. For example if we have (say) 10 channels with a spacing of 200 GHz (roughly 1.6 nm) the bandwidth in the formula would be 200 x 10 = 2000 GHz. So the total power of all 10 channels would be limited to 250 mW in this example. If we had 20 channels spaced over the same range (using 100 GHz spacings) then the total power available to all channels would be the same as in the previous example (250 mW). A watt is a very large amount of power. In most WDM systems each channel will be well below 10 mW for other reasons.

In addition, SRS is influenced by fibre dispersion. Standard fibre reduces the effect of SRS by half (3 dB) compared with DSF fibre.

Carrier-Induced Phase Modulation (CIP)

CIP includes both Self Phase Modulation (SPM) and Cross Phase Modulation (XPM) as described in 2.4.5.4, "Carrier-Induced Phase Modulation (CIP)" on page 92.

For systems employing any form of On-Off Keying (OOK) modulation CIP is not a significant issue.

For systems employing any modulation technique where the phase of the signal is significant these effects are critical. Such techniques include:

- Analogue modulation

- Phase-Shift Keying (PSK)

- Coherent reception

To avoid degradation by CIP effects the *total power of all channels taken together should be less than 20 mW*. This is the most restrictive limitation in WDM systems. Thankfully it does not affect digital OOK systems.

---

[113] It is painful to have to quote bandwidths in both nanometers and gigahertz. Nanometers is the convenient measure used throughout this book. But 1 GHz in one particular part of the spectrum represents a *different* amount of nm than 1 GHz in another part of the spectrum. The effects being discussed are best described in GHz. Hence the use of both measures.

9.4.4 Control of Dispersion in WDM Systems

Dispersion control in WDM systems is much the same as in single-channel systems described in 7.5, "Control of Dispersion in Single-Mode Fibre Links" on page 411. However, there are some differences:

1. The use of dispersion-shifted fibre is not practical because of concerns with four-wave mixing effects.

2. Compensation using DCF fibre has to be very carefully done to balance the dispersion characteristics of the cascaded fibres such that dispersion is zero over the whole range of amplified wavelengths. This is difficult.

3. When using FBGs you need a very long chirp indeed to compensate over the whole wavelength range. Very long chirped gratings are very hard to make. Sampled FBGs offer a solution to this problem. Also you can have a separate chirped FBG for compensation of each channel individually. However, in this last case you have to keep the channels far enough apart so that the edges of one filter do not interfere with the signal in an adjacent band.

9.4.5 Amplifier Issues

The most important characteristics of an amplifier are its gain, its power output and (for WDM systems) its range of amplified wavelengths. It is important to choose an amplifier with the right characteristics for the application.

The "natural" amplified range of a simple EDFA is about 1535-1560 nm. This can be expanded by the use of co-dopants and amplifiers with an amplified range of around 40 nm are currently available.

In general there are three types of EDFAs:

1. Power amplifiers are placed immediately after the mixing stage at the transmitter end of the system. The input power level will be relatively high. The limitation here is likely to be total output power of the amplifier.

   For example if we want to amplify a mixed WDM stream of 10 channels from -5 dBm by 8 dB the total output power of the amplifier will be 10 channels at 3 dBm (that is, 2 mW). Total amplifier power needed in this case is 20 mW.

2. Line amplifiers receive a relatively low level signal and must amplify it by as many dB as possible (30 is a good number). The limitations here are gain, noise and total output power.

3. Preamplifiers need to be quite sensitive, have a low level of noise and reasonably high gain *but* typically they don't need a high level of signal power at the output.

Depending on the system a figure of (say) -20 dBm per channel may be sufficient output power.

When a number of EDFAs are operated in cascade over a long distance there are four issues that must be considered:

1. Dynamic non-linearity of the amplifier gain profile

2. Generation of rapid transient power fluctuations

3. Noise introduced by the amplifiers

4. Polarisation dependent effects

Of these the first three are significant effects but the fourth is minor except in the case of systems with very large numbers of amplifiers.

9.4.5.1 Dynamic Non-Linearity of the Amplifier Gain Profile

This means that the gain at some wavelengths is significantly greater than the gain at other wavelengths over the amplifier's bandwidth. The problem is dynamic in that an amplifier may give a good linear response when all channels have signal power and a drastically skewed response when one channel ceases to have a signal. Over a cascade of many amplifiers this leads to some channels being amplified too much and others being lost. This is a serious problem when many amplifier stages are involved. Four approaches may be used (individually or in combination) to counter this problem:

1. Careful amplifier design (especially in the use of co-dopants) can produce amplifiers with minimal non-linearity. Amplifiers using ZBLAN as host glass are significantly more linear in response than ones using silica; however ZBLAN-based amplifiers have other problems. Co-dopants (used in silica glass) can significantly affect the amplifier gain curve and this is the common approach. In addition, the use of dual cores within the fibre of an amplifier is shown to flatten the gain.

2. In a link with many amplifiers in series (or cascade) amplifiers with different characteristics can be used such that the non-linearities introduced by one amplifier are balanced (compensated for) in the next.

3. Filters can be used to attenuate some channels selectively. Amplifiers with an almost flat response are commercially available. This is achieved using blazed fibre Bragg gratings to selectively attenuate the high gain regions. This approach works but a lot of power is wasted (reflected out of the system) by the FBGs. Thus amplifiers of this kind don't have as much gain as others. Also, this doesn't address the dynamism in the process - you can arrange a perfectly flat gain with all channels at full power but when one drops out the gain becomes non-linear.

4. Channels may be pre-emphasised at the transmitter such that the channels that will receive least amplification are transmitted at higher power levels than those that will not. The opportunity to do this is limited by many factors but real systems have been reported using a power level difference of up to 7 dB.

The topic of gain flattening EDFAs was discussed in 5.2.1.2, "Gain Characteristics of EDFAs" on page 205.

9.4.5.2 Generation of Rapid Transient Power Fluctuations

When a number of EDFAs are operated in cascade the effect of an abrupt change in the system load can produce a rapid transient in the power produced by the system. This is again counter to intuition as the long upper-state lifetime of erbium suggests that any power effects will be slow and should stabilise quickly. But this is not the case.

An abrupt change in system load can be caused by the sudden loss of one channel from a WDM stream. The amplifiers are usually operated well into saturation. This means that there is only sufficient energy storage in the upper state erbium for a short duration of operation. Should the pump stop there is sufficient input signal power to deplete the inversion quite quickly (100 microseconds or so). Thus the amount of energy storage in the device is quite small in comparison to the rate at which energy is passing through it. This means that the gain of the amplifier can change quite quickly when system conditions change. It all happens this way:

- When one channel stops, instantaneously there will be no change to the gain and no effect on the other channels. However the pump will continue at its original level and the gain for the remaining signal channels will increase quite quickly.

- Propagation time between amplifiers is quite long. At 5 microseconds per kilometer it will take 250 microseconds for the signal to reach the next amplifier (if the spacing is 50 km).

- So *before the gain on the first amplifier has built up the second amplifier sees the loss of a channel and its gain (for the remaining channels) starts to build up too.*

- So the gain (for the remaining channels) of each amplifier in the chain rapidly builds up.

- A few microseconds later the first amplifier is applying a higher gain to all its remaining channels. In turn each amplifier will apply a higher and higher gain to a stronger and stronger signal!

- Before the amplifiers down the chain have time to respond a power surge is built up. This power surge can saturate the receivers and cause a period of errors lasting a few milliseconds on the remaining channels.

A number of techniques for controlling this type of surge are being investigated.

9.4.5.3 Noise Introduced by the EDFAs

The predominant source of noise in a chain of EDFAs is caused by Amplified Spontaneous Emission (ASE). While the effect is trivial in systems with only a few amplifier stages it can become significant over a large number of stages. ASE was discussed in 5.2.1.13, "Noise in EDFAs" on page 215. One method of control is to filter out all unwanted wavelengths at regular intervals along the link. This can be done using "blazed" FBG filters. Of course in a WDM system the demultiplexing operation at the receiver end also gets rid of most accumulated noise at non-signal wavelengths.

The main control here is link design. It you let the signal decay to a low level and then have to apply a very large gain you will get a lot of noise added with the large gain. To minimise noise you should keep the signal level reasonably high and amplify relatively often. For example on a given (hypothetical) link with a given SNR as the objective then:

- Two amplifiers spaced at 150 km apart could cause so much added noise that the maximum SNR would be reached after only 300 km.

- With an amplifier spacing of 100 km it takes 29 amplifiers to get to the same SNR - a distance of 2,900 km.

- By amplifying every 50 km you might have in excess of 300 amplifiers for a distance exceeding 15,000 km!

- Indeed the optimal amplification scheme would be to dope the SMF core with a little erbium and inject pump at regular intervals so that the entire long distance link becomes an amplifier! This scheme seems a bit impractical for a number of reasons but it has been quite seriously suggested. For now this is just a dream.

Of course, nobody wants to amplify too frequently. Amplifiers have to be housed and powered and regardless of the cost of the amplifier itself the associated costs are very high. So the trick is to design the link such that the signal quality is maintained but also that the number of amplifier stages is kept to a minimum.

9.4.5.4 Polarisation Effects in EDFAs

Polarisation effects are very small in EDFAs and can be ignored in most short distance systems. However, it can accumulate and cause problems in long distance systems with large numbers of amplifiers.

There are three separate polarisation effects which need to be considered:

1. Polarisation Dependent Gain (PDG)

2. Polarisation Dependent Loss (PDL)

3. Polarisation Mode Dispersion (PMD)

The last here is of course caused by the fibre link rather than the amplifiers.

Polarisation Dependent Gain (PDG)

PDG is a characteristic of the EDFA itself. When the amplifier is operated in saturation and the signal is polarised the amplifier exhibits a higher gain in the polarisation state *orthogonal* to that of the signal itself. This is caused by individual atoms of erbium having slightly greater propensity to lase in one polarisation than the other depending on their orientation within the glass material. If erbium atoms when they are originally excited have random orientations then a saturated signal level in one polarisation can leave a higher gain state in the orthogonal polarisation.

Lasers produce a highly polarised output and although the polarisation state changes as the signal travels down the fibre, the signal is always polarised to some degree. Amplifiers are almost always operated in saturation. Thus you get slightly (.1 dB) higher gain for the ASE noise in the orthogonal polarisation than you get for the signal itself. This worsens the signal-to-noise ratio. Since this is a dynamic effect, as the signal polarisation changes (minute by minute) PDG continues to offer higher gain in the state orthogonal to the signal. That is, PDG "tracks" the signal.

With only a few amplifiers the effect is trivial. With a long chain of concatenated EDFAs the SNR can be worsened by as much as 5 dB.

PDG is a saturation effect. If you change the polarisation state of the signal faster than the gain recovery time of the erbium you can make PDG effectively disappear. This can be done by randomly scrambling the polarisation state of the transmitted signal. This polarisation scrambling can be quite slow (around 10 kHz) as the gain recovery time of the erbium is relatively long. This is not really scrambling in the sense that scrambling usually implies randomisation. Polarisation is changed regularly from one state to its orthogonal one using a device such as the one described in 5.9.7, "Phase Modulators" on page 322.

Polarisation scrambling is reported to give a typical 4 dB improvement in the SNR on very long amplified links. It is currently used in some long distance undersea systems.

Alternatively, the effect of PDG can be removed if you use an EDFA which is designed deliberately to have no polarisation dependence. Amplifiers of this kind were described in 5.2.1.12, "Control of Polarisation Mode Dependence (PMD)" on page 214.

In a WDM system the effects of PDG are significantly lessened by the presence of multiple channels. Statistically there is very little chance that all channels will be in the same polarisation state at the same time. The probability exists but it is very small. Thus the chances are that both polarisation states will experience much the same level of signal power at all times.

Polarisation Dependent Loss (PDL)

Most EDFAs exhibit a slightly higher gain to a signal in one polarisation state than they do to a signal in the orthogonal polarisation. This is caused by slight polarisation dependence in the optical components of which the amplifier is made and by the polarisation orientation of the pump.

The arriving optical signal is polarised in some direction and this keeps changing over time (a timescale of minutes). Thus the gain of the signal varies over time. But the ASE noise in the system arrives in all polarisations (it is unpolarised) and experiences a fixed gain. Thus we see a variation in the SNR with time.

The effect is not as bad as might be expected as in a long chain of amplifiers, at a particular instant in time, each amplifier will have a different amount of SNR degradation on the signal. Thus the PDL of the system is not the sum of the PDL of all the amplifiers but rather the root mean square. Taga (1995) reports that a chain of 100 EDFAs with a PDL of .3 dB each worsens the system PDL (expressed as SNR) by a total of 3 dB.

PDL (like PDG) can be countered by polarisation scrambling of the input signal. However, PDL is not dependent on the saturation state of the erbium. The axes of polarisation along which PDL has effect do not change with the polarisation of the input signal. To counter PDL you have to scramble the polarisation state of the signal at a frequency of a few times more than the bit rate.

Polarisation Mode Dispersion (PMD)

PMD is an effect predominantly due to the fibre in the link rather than the amplifiers. Like other forms of dispersion it needs to be controlled and the total kept generally below .2 of a bit time over the whole link.

PMD acts on a channel-by-channel basis and there are no special differences between the single channel environment and the WDM environment. Again, this effect is quite small in most systems.

9.4.6 Noise in WDM Systems

Noise is a significant issue in *every* communication system. In the optical world (and especially in WDM) there are many sources of noise. The good news is that most of the noise sources are so small that we can ignore them. In other cases the action we take to mitigate one form of noise also mitigates many others. The dominant noise sources in WDM systems are amplifier ASE and thermal noise in the receivers. However, in the design of any system it is very important to be aware of all the potential sources of noise so that they can be avoided or mitigated.

Laser Noise

The most important sources of noise from the lasers are:

1. Chirp and relaxation oscillation

2. Relative intensity noise (RIN)

3. Phase noise

4. Pulse shape distortion

In intensity modulated systems RIN and phase noise are not serious problems. (See Relative Intensity Noise (RIN) on page 137.) Chirp and pulse shape distortion are however significant potential sources of noise.

The nature of chirp was discussed in Chirp on page 136. Chirp broadens the signal linewidth such that dispersion has an enhanced effect. In addition a chirped source interacts with the filters in the system such that different amounts of attenuation occur at different points in the (wavelength varying) pulse. Thus chirp can be a major source of noise in high speed systems.

Chirp can be almost eliminated by the use of external modulators. The laser produces a constant, unmodulated signal and an external device adds the modulations. External modulators are almost always used in systems faster that about 1 Gbps. These were discussed in 5.9, "Modulators and Switches" on page 300.

Lasers by there nature do not produce an exactly square pulse. There is always some distortion. Of course chirp also causes distortion of the pulse shape. Distortion of the pulse shape makes it more difficult for the receiver to determine exactly when a pulse begins and when it ends. Thus a jitter effect is created where the timing relationship of received bits is not the same as what was transmitted. In some systems this can be a significant problem. However, this is also a source of uncertainty in detection and thus can be regarded as a worsening of the SNR and as such, a source of noise.

Multiplexor Noise

The multiplexing function in most cases is not a source of noise in the system. However, often the multiplexors have the characteristics of filters. In this case if either the filter bandwidth is too narrow or if the centre wavelength is not aligned correctly, interaction of the signal with the filter will produce distortion and noise.

Transmission on the Fibre

Unlike electric wire fibre does not pick up noise from outside the system. Neither is it subject to thermal noise. Dispersion of the pulse due to the fibre characteristics is a very significant source of signal degradation. In addition, the non-linear effects described earlier in 9.4.3, "Controlling Non-linear Effects" on page 554 can be significant and must be taken into consideration in every system design.

System Interactions

One important source of signal degradation is caused by the interactions between a chirped laser source and reflections from connectors within the system. This is called "return loss variation" and was discussed in 7.4.4, "Reflections" on page 408. Much of the problem can be mitigated by placing an isolator immediately after the transmit laser.

Amplifier Noise (ASE)

ASE from the amplifiers is perhaps the most significant source of noise in long distance WDM systems. This was discussed in 9.4.5, "Amplifier Issues" on page 557.

Demultiplexor Noise

The demultiplexing function is a filtering function which can be an important source of noise:

- No filter is perfect and there will be some crosstalk introduced between channels. This is just signal power that should be directed to one particular output arriving on a different output. The amount of crosstalk that the system can tolerate is an individual thing and varies with the system involved. However a good rule-of-thumb is that introduced crosstalk should be more than 30 dB *below* the signal power level.

- Just as with the filtering aspect of the multiplexor alignment, filter shape and filter bandwidth must be carefully selected so that they won't introduce distortions to the signal. Most important is that the filter should have a flat passband. Of course good alignment of the centre wavelength is critical.

Receiver Noise

Electronic receivers always add noise to the system:

- The most often mentioned source of noise is "shot noise". Shot noise is the random variation in arriving photons (or electrons) in very low level signals. An optical signal of a given intensity is in fact a randomly varying thing. This is a law of physics not an engineering rule. Thus shot noise represents the ultimate noise limit of any system. However, the noise level represented is so low that it is not a practical concern.

- The big noise source in PIN-diode receivers is "thermal noise". This is generated in all electronic components such as resistors, diodes and amplifiers. In addition APDs produce extra noise as a result of their basic amplifying design.

- In practical receivers there is also distortion due to radiations from wires in the receiver and effects due to the build up of a direct current component (if the signal is not DC-balanced).

9.4.7 Summary

The engineering of a WDM system is a very complex matter of balancing many competing effects. Some of these effects are the same as we know from single-channel systems. Others are new with WDM.

Channel Separation and Signal Bandwidth

To minimise the effects of SRS and to get optimal gain flatness from amplifiers we would like to space channels as closely together as possible. Of course this enables us to have more channels (if needed) and thus more capacity.

However, the effects of FWM prevent channels being spaced too closely together.

Component Precision and Cost

In general the more precise and stable optical components become the more they cost. The narrower a laser's linewidth and the more stable its signal the more it costs. Similar considerations apply to gratings, filters and most other components. This is a big factor in deciding channel bandwidths and spacings.

Control of Dispersion

The principle means of controlling dispersion are the minimisation of signal bandwidth and the use of some dispersion compensation scheme. The use of

DSF fibre at its zero-dispersion wavelength is not possible because of the FWM problem.

To a point you can minimise the signal bandwidth but bandwidth is broadened by the modulations themselves and if you make the signal bandwidth less than about 80 MHz limitations due to the effects of SBS start to take effect.

In systems with distances beyond about 100 km at speeds of 2.4 Gbps and above some form of dispersion management or compensation will be necessary.

Signal Power (per channel)

One of the critical aspects of system cost is the need to maximise the distance (span) between amplifiers. The cost of the amplifiers is not the main item. The cost of housing them and maintaining them at way-stations along the cable is significantly higher than the cost of the amplifiers themselves. But every time we double the signal speed the receiver becomes (at least) 3 dB less sensitive! Thus we want to maximise the power sent per channel.

However there are many effects that limit the amount of power that we can use:

- The maximum power of available transmitters. This is really the maximum output power of an EDFA placed at the transmitter. Until recently this was about 200 mW but with the advent of multi-stripe, cladding-pumped EDFAs the limit is today around 10 watts. (Thus this is no longer a practical limitation.)

- The non-linear effects (SBS, SRS, CIP) impose severe restrictions on the amount of power that can be used per channel depending on many factors.

- Safety issues are also very important. Almost all WDM systems will be (justifiably) classified as dangerous and need safety systems and should be sited in a special location where access is available only to qualified service personnel.

Noise

As discussed above, the effect of ASE accumulation is perhaps the major determinant of amplifier spacing.

Fibre Type

To minimise dispersion we would like to use DSF. However, DSF significantly increases problems with FWM and SRS. Either standard fibre or dispersion optimised fibre (DOF) should be used.

9.5 Further Reading

Neal S. Bergano (1996)

Wavelength Division Multiplexing in Long-Haul Transmission Systems: IEEE Journal of Lightwave Technology, Vol 14, No 6, June 1996. pp 1299-1308

Michael S. Borella, et al. (1997)

Optical Components for WDM Lightwave Networks: Proceedings of the IEEE, Vol 85, No 8, August 1997. pp 1274-1307

T. Durhuus, et al. (1996)

All-Optical Wavelength Conversion by Semiconductor Optical Amplifiers: IEEE J. of Lightwave Technology Vol 14, No 6, June 1996. p 942

Fabrizio Forghieri, R.W. Tkach, A.R. Chraplyvy and D. Marcuse (1994)

Reduction of Four-Wave Mixing Crosstalk in WDM Systems Using Unequally Spaced Channels: IEEE Photonics Technology Letters, Vol 6, No 6, June 1994. pp 754-756

F. Heismann, D.A. Gray, B.H. Lee and R.W. Smith (1994)

Electrooptic Polarisation Scramblers for Optically Amplified Long-Haul Transmission Systems: IEEE Photonics Technology Letters, Vol 6, No 9, September 1994. pp 1156-1158

Scott Hinton (1995)

Photonic Switching Fabrics: IEEE Communications Magazine, April 1990. pp 71-89

Hidenori Taga, Noboru Edagawa, Shu Yamamoto and S. Akiba (1995)

Recent Progress in Amplified Undersea Systems: IEEE J. of Lightwave Technology, Vol 13, No 5, May 1995. pp 829-840.

Hidenori Taga (1996)

Long Distance Transmission Experiments Using the WDM Technology: IEEE J. of Lightwave Technology Vol 14, No 6, June 1996. p 1287

M.G. Taylor (1993)

Observation of New Polarisation Dependence Effect in Long Haul Optically Amplified System: IEEE Photonics Technology Letters, Vol 5, No 10, October 1993. pp 1244-1246

R.W. Tkach, A.R. Chraplyvy, Fabrizio Forghieri, A.H. Gnauck and R.M. Derosier (1995)

Four-Photon Mixing and High-Speed WDM Systems: IEEE J. of Lightwave Technology, Vol 13, No 5, May 1995. pp 841-849

Jay M. Wiesenfeld, Bernard Glance, J.S. Perino and A.H. Gnauck (1993)

Wavelength Conversion at 10 Gb/s Using a Semiconductor Optical Amplifier: IEEE Photonics Technology Letters, Vol 5, No 11, November 1993. pp 1300-1303

S.J.B. Yoo (1996)

Wavelength Conversion Technologies for WDM Network Applications: IEEE J. of Lightwave Technology Vol 14, No 6, June 1996. p 955

Chapter 10. Lightwave Networks

The vast majority of optical communications systems in use today all share a common feature. Logically they could be implemented just as easily on copper wire. In other words, fibre has been used as a substitute for copper wire (although with many advantages, including speed). A number of the more significant system architectures of this type were described in Chapter 8, "Optical Link Connections in Electronic Networks" on page 439.

Around the world there is a significant amount of research going on aimed at producing a generation of "lightwave networks" which would operate quite differently from the systems we have today. This is because it is widely believed that in the five-year future there will be a demand for networks with large numbers of workstations (thousands) each of which could generate a sustained data rate of perhaps 1 Gbps. Basic technologies required to build truly optical WDM networks exist and were discussed in Chapter 9, "Wavelength Division Multiplexing" on page 513.

It was mentioned earlier (2.2.2, "Transmission Capacity" on page 41) that the potential data carrying capacity of fibre is enormous - at least a thousand times today's 10 Gbps practical limit of a single channel. The aim is to make use of this to build networks with capacities of two or three orders of magnitude greater than we have today.

This is not as easy to do as it sounds.

1. We can't increase the transmission rate because the electronics needed just won't go that fast. Today's practical maximum speed is around 10 Gbps (up to 40 in the lab) for a single channel. In addition, as transmission speeds get faster, the cost of the necessary electronics increases exponentially.

2. Fibre cabling is quite restrictive when it comes to constructing a multi-user LAN or MAN of the traditional "shared medium" type that we know in the electronic world:

   - If the fibre is to be used as a bus then taps need to be made in order for a station to receive or transmit. On the receive side, a splitter is inserted in the fibre and a proportion of the light directed to the station with the rest going on to the next station. This means the bus loses a fixed proportion of its light (perhaps .5 dB) at every receive station. However, since the amount of light on the bus keeps getting less the proportion of light removed at each tap needs to increase as you go down the bus. This means that the bus has to be carefully planned with power levels in mind and proportional couplers configured accordingly.

This is quite different from electrical transmission where a tap can be inserted for a single station with only trivial loss of signal.

- Fibre is basically a unidirectional medium so we can't have a true (bi-directional) bus structure.

- When data is to be sent from a station onto the fibre, a coupler must be inserted to combine the signal already on the fibre with the incoming signal from the station. This is a more serious problem. If a simple resonant coupler (or Y-coupler) is used then a significant proportion of the signal already on the cable will be lost. This cannot be avoided if the light being added is at the same wavelength as the signal on the cable. Only by using devices that exploit wavelength dependencies can you avoid very serious losses here.

These problems don't so much represent "limitations" but rather are characteristics of the fibre medium. Some characteristics of the fibre medium mean that we can't use fibre in exactly the same way as we did an electrical signal. But other characteristics suggest that we can do many things with light that would be difficult or impossible with electricity.

10.1.1 Objectives

The way in which we approach building a lightwave network is critically dependent on the job the network has to perform and the environment in which it must operate. There are a number of different environments for which lightwave networks look promising but the technical design for one environment can be very different from the technical design of a lightwave network in a different environment. These environments can be roughly classified as follows:

Local Communications

This is the interconnection of computers and computer devices in close proximity to one another. It also includes the interconnection of the "internals" of the computer itself. This means the connection of the processor to its memory for example. Or more likely, the interconnection of multiple processing elements with multiple memories.

A current example of the use of fibre to replace a computer I/O channel is the IBM "ESCON" channel. This device is an enormous advance of its electronic predecessor but it only uses fibre as a transmission medium - all of the switching is electronic. This was discussed earlier in 8.4, "ESCON and Inter-System Coupling (ISC)" on page 477.

Local Area Networks and Metropolitan Area Networks

Early research in lightwave networks was concentrated in the LAN area but recently the research focus has shifted to the MAN.

- In the late 1980's it was felt that very high throughput LANs were needed and that optical LANs would be attractive in that role. It was widely believed that the requirement for gigabit speeds at the workstation would be primarily for communication within a single workgroup.

  Also, in the late 1980s corporate users were uniformly unable to obtain (lease) "dark" fibre over distances of more than a few hundred metres. ("Dark fibre" is so-called because you lease only the fibre from the carrier and put your own light into it.) This was partly because of worldwide legal and administrative restrictions surrounding the construction of private wide area networks. Even today, in many countries you can't get private dedicated optical fibres for any money. In other countries it is very expensive.

- While optical LANs proved possible and technically attractive the demand for shared medium extremely high speed LANs was satisfied by slower speed (lower device speeds but significantly greater network throughput) electronic switches.

- In the late 1990s worldwide "deregulation" of carrier monopolies has meant that fibre can be obtained at fair prices in many countries. Thus there is now an opportunity for corporate users to build private corporate optical networks - at least in the metropolitan area.

Wide Area Networks

This is a completely different type of environment to the local one. There is an enormous amount of work going on in applying fibre optics to wide area communication. Indeed, in most countries optical fibre is now the primary means of wide area communication. Most of the work has been centered on using fibre for transmission only - replacing traditional wire but not changing the basic design of systems. This is changing rapidly with the advent of WDM systems in the WAN.

Undersea Systems

Probably the most advanced optical communications networks are those used for undersea communication.

In a land-based network the most significant cost is the cost of digging a trench in which to bury the fibre. Thus once you have dug your trench you might as well put a lot of fibres into it because additional fibres don't cost much and it is good to have extra capacity for the future.

In the undersea situation things are quite different. You need amplifiers (or repeaters) at certain intervals and these cost a significant amount of money to install and *much more* to maintain. Thus in the undersea environment there is a very large financial incentive to minimise the number of fibres in the cable. When you put down your cable one or two spare fibres might be useful but a large number of additional fibres would be no use unless you put in the (unneeded) amplifiers etc. to operate them. (You can't go back and add equipment later.)

In 1997, the first production WDM wide area connections are coming into use in the undersea environment. A number of very advanced new networks have been reported as being in the advanced stages of planning. These are well in advance of any current land based networks.

Local Distribution Networks

This is the "fibre to the home" environment. The objective is to replace existing cable television and telephone distribution systems with a wideband system capable of carrying the above traffic but also able to carry new services. These services could be things like interactive video entertainment or just the ability to "dial a movie," that is, to see any movie on demand at any time *without* needing to rent a tape. The key issue here is cost. Any system that aims to replace the existing copper telephone connection to every home must be cost-effective. This is discussed further in Chapter 11, "Fibre In The (Local) Loop - FITL" on page 633.

Of course there are issues in design of a network which reach well beyond the technical parameters. For example, one of the first lessons learned by the early implementers of MAN networks has been that users are not willing to allow their data to transit any other company's premises. So a public MAN network using WDM would be commercially unacceptable if the multiplexed WDM stream was delivered to every end user. This means that an add/drop multiplexed WDM MAN would need to site the add/drop multiplexors (ADMs) on the service provider's premises.

10.1.2 Optical Network Technologies

We can consider the development of optical systems as having a number of stages:

Single Channel Systems

This is the simplest possible system. Each physical link carries a single channel and each end of the link is terminated and processed electronically.

Wavelength Division Multiplexing (WDM) Systems

In simple WDM we advance from one channel per link to many channels but we still use electronics at each end of the optical link to route the signals and build a network. WDM technology came out of the laboratory in 1996 and several long undersea WDM links were installed in full production. A number of companies also introduced commercial products for WDM networks.

Even simple WDM links include amplifiers and perhaps devices to flatten the gain curve of the amplifier. But this is still to be considered "simple" from the network point of view.

Simple Optical Networks

A simple optical network is where there is some optical processing or switching of the signal performed. A series of WDM connections with optical add/drop multiplexors at the nodal points qualifies for this description. Another example might be a broadcast and select LAN or MAN optical network. Early commercial networks of this kind are scheduled for installation in 1997.

Simple here means the use of very elementary levels of logic (such as optical add/drop multiplexors) it *does not mean small*. There are a number of very large networks of this kind being planned.

Wavelength Routed Optical Networks

The concept here is that we have a true network consisting of optical fibre links with optical "routing" nodes at the intersections. Individual signals are routed through the network based on their wavelength. Individual wavelengths are not changed in the routing nodes and paths through the network (while changeable) are at least semi-permanent. The network is relatively static. This is further discussed in 10.1.5.3, "Nodal Networks" on page 581.

Optically Switched Networks

Optically switched networks are something of an ideal. The network topology is essentially the same as for a wavelength routed network. However, there are two big differences:

1. Wavelengths are changed at the nodes.

2. New paths can be set up and torn down relatively quickly.

This therefore becomes an optical circuit switched network.

Optical Time Division Multiplexing (OTDM)

An OTDM network offers end-to-end synchronous digital connections using the principles of TDM as discussed earlier in 8.6, "Synchronous Optical Network (SONET) and SDH" on page 484. Although OTDM appears to be near realisation in practical networks as yet there are no operational OTDM networks. The principles of TDM applied in optical networks are discussed in 12.5, "Optical Time Division Multiplexing (OTDM)" on page 663.

Optical Packet Switching

These (if they existed) would be true meshed networks where data was transported in short blocks (called packets or cells). This is how most modern electronic networks (ATM, TCP/IP) work. To achieve this we would need optical logic processing as well as optically activated switches etc. In 1997 there are many reports of research related to the components needed to construct such networks but no reports of working prototypes. Unless there is a major scientific breakthrough sometime soon this form of network is at least 10 years off.

10.1.3 Sharing the Fibre

There are four principal ways in which the fibre can be shared among multiple users. These are the same ways that we are used to in the electrical world.

Block Multiplexing

This is the technique of existing electronic LANs. Frames of data from many users are intermixed on the same data channel. It's not a very good idea here because it doesn't satisfy our objective of gaining a few orders of magnitude increase in capacity. The medium is used as a single channel which, of course, is limited to electronic speeds.

However, within another multiplex structure (such as WDM) this technique can be used very effectively to sub-multiplex single channels. The CSMA technique has been used in a number of experimental networks to enable sharing of a control channel.

Code Division Multiple Access (CDMA)

This technique allows multiple users to share the same channel by transmitting different types of signal encoding *at the same wavelength*. The principles are described in 12.4.2, "Code Division Multiple Access (CDMA)" on page 661. However, if transmitters and receivers are limited to electronic speeds the chip rate would have a maximum of about 10 Gbps. The data rate available for individual channels would be significantly lower than this. However, with optical correlation filters at the receiver the need for extremely high-speed electronics is lessened and CDMA may indeed become a practical technique. In addition, in the context of purely optical networks it seems that CDMA may be useful as a sub-multiplexing technique.

At lower speeds it may be that CDMA is a good low-cost way of sharing the bandwidth in a passive optical network (PON) access network. (See Chapter 11, "Fibre In The (Local) Loop - FITL" on page 633.)

Time Division Multiplexing

TDM techniques do work nicely on a fibre. TDM uses a single channel which is accessed (although at different times) by many devices. This means that each device must be able to transmit and receive at the full speed of the channel. This brings us back to the same problem of the speed of the electronics. If the TDM function is performed electronically you could have one channel only and that would be limited by electronic speeds. TDM does, however, reduce the electronics cost a bit by enabling the device to use less high-speed electronics than it otherwise would.

It is possible to perform TDM totally optically. This is important and looks to be highly practical. With single-channel soliton systems operating in the 100-200 Gbps range OTDM may be the only way of processing the information. For a discussion of optical TDM technology see 12.5, "Optical Time Division Multiplexing (OTDM)" on page 663.

TDM techniques can be used on individual channels within a group which is multiplexed by WDM. In this case TDM becomes a sub-multiplexing technique within a WDM system.

Wavelength Division Multiplexing (WDM)

Wavelength Division Multiplexing is just another way of saying Frequency Division Multiplexing.[114] When dealing with the very high frequencies of light it is much more convenient to talk about wavelength rather than frequency. Of course, these are the same thing expressed differently:

$$Wavelength = \frac{speed\ of\ light}{frequency}$$

Many independent "channels" are derived on the medium by sending separate signals at different wavelengths. Provided they are kept somewhat apart they

---

[114] In the world of optical communications, it has been usual to talk about the wavelength of a signal or a device without reference to frequency. However, when you get to very narrow linewidth lasers and coherent detection systems, these are normally expressed in MHz or GHz.

do not interfere with one another (or rather there isn't enough interference to bother us too much). Device A can send to device B using wavelength λ_1 at the same time as device C is sending to device D using wavelength λ_2. The beauty here is that each communication can take place at full electronic speed quite independently of the other.

This means that the data rate being operated on the fibre is (number of channels) × (data rate of each individual channel). In this way we can get much greater data rates on the fibre than electronic circuits will allow.

In this discussion we are considering the building of a single logical network. This means that all stations use the same modulation techniques, speeds, etc. Each channel is operated in the same way.

However, it should be pointed out that a major advantage of WDM is the insensitivity to modulation technique and speed between different channels. Different channels can operate at different speeds with different (even analogue) modulation techniques. A network that allows many different kinds of users (using different modulation techniques and transmission speeds) using an overall "virtual circuit" approach may well find practical application in MAN networks of the future.

So it should not be surprising that the bulk of research on lightwave networks is being done on WDM systems.

10.1.4 Modes of Data Transfer

Broadly there are two types of network:

1. Circuit switched networks

2. Packet (or cell) switched networks

A circuit-switched network provide an end-to-end "transparent" connection between two end users. This might be a stream of bits in a digital network or an analogue frequency (electronic) or analogue wavelength (optical). The characteristic here is that whatever is sent by one end user is transferred to the other end user in a continuous stream across some form of dedicated connection. In the digital world this means that the connection runs through the network at exactly the same speed and is synchronised to itself and the system clock. A good example of such a network is the telephone network.

In packet switched networks end users send data to the network in short units called blocks, frames, cells or packets. These packets of data share intermediate resources with one another within the network on a demand or priority basis.

Within the packet-switched network environment there is another very important distinction:

- Connection-oriented networks
- Connectionless networks

In a connection-oriented network there is a marked path through the network for each "connection" between pairs of end users. This marked path must be set up in some way before data transfer can take place. However, once the connection has been set up data packets follow a fixed, predetermined path between end-users. The presence of a connection does *not necessarily* mean that network resources along the path are reserved for that connection. Indeed all resources (nodes, links, buffers etc.) are normally shared.

Connections are either set up dynamically at the request of one or other of the end-users (call setup by "signalling") or by a network management process. Networks where connections are only set up by network management are called "crossconnect" networks.

In a connectionless network the switching node makes a decision where to send each packet individually based on an address placed in the beginning of the data. This means that there is no need to pre-setup or predefine a connection. But it also means that each node must do significant processing for each packet in order to determine its ongoing path. It also means that the network doesn't know about connections between end-users so it is very difficult to perform flow and congestion control etc.

ATM, X.25 and SNA are examples of connection-oriented networks. IP (Internet) and LAN switched networks are examples of connectionless networks.

10.1.5 Network Topologies for the MAN or WAN

10.1.5.1 Broadcast and Select Networks

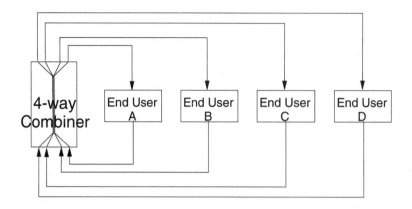

Figure 336. Broadcast and Select Network - Principle

The Broadcast and Select network is perhaps the simplest form of optical network. Proposed mainly for LAN applications early prototypes were built and trialled in the early 1990's. A description of one such trial is given in 10.3.5.2, "IBM "Rainbow-1"" on page 600.

The concept here is very simple. Each end user device is allocated a unique wavelength on which it is allowed to transmit. A fibre from each end user device is connected to a "hub" where the signals from all the end users are mixed. Another set of fibres travels from the hub - one to each end user. Each end user then receives the signals from every other user. It is up to the individual end-user to select the correct wavelength of the user it wants to listen to. This can be done by static definition or dynamically (the users could have tunable receivers).

This principle can be used to build very limited and static networks or (using tunable transmitters and receivers) quite complex and dynamic ones. Propagation delays prevent this kind of network topology being of much interest in the wide area or even in large metropolitan area situations. However, it seems eminently practical in large campuses and the (geographically) small MAN environment.

10.1.5.2 Add-Drop Multiplexed (ADM) Networks

Perhaps the simplest form of true optical network is the "Add-Drop Multiplexed Network". The concept is illustrated in Figure 337 on page 579.

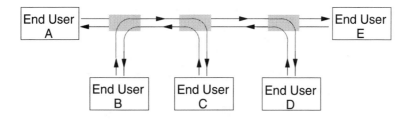

Figure 337. *Add-Drop Multiplexing Concept*

An optical WDM link passes through many locations. At each intermediate location one or more individual optical channels are removed (dropped) from the WDM stream and terminated in a local device.

In the figure:

- There is an optical WDM link between locations A and E.

- This link consists of two fibres (one in each direction).

- There may be many independent optical channels going from A to E.

- Locations B and C have a bi-directional connection on the WDM link using a wavelength that is *not* otherwise used by the channels from A to E.

- In this illustration the wavelength that is used for communication between B and C is not used for the rest of the link. Of course it could be re-used for example for a connection between D and E (but such a connection is not shown).

- There is a connection between A and D using a separate wavelength.

- Because these are WDM connections each channel is completely independent of each other channel and may use different speeds and codes etc.

The concept here is clear. The cable is "tapped" at intermediate points and individual channels removed or added. Note that this is directional so that for example the wavelength used for the channel from B to C could be re-used for a channel from A to B and another from C to D or E. At a particular "drop" a single wavelength implies two possible (full-duplex) connections - one downstream and one upstream. Devices used for the add/drop function are wavelength selective and don't have the loss problems of passive taps. See 9.2.5, "Add-Drop Multiplexors" on page 531.

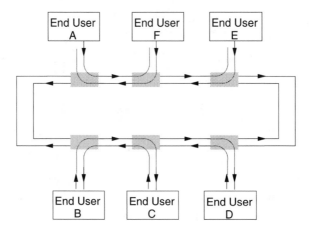

Figure 338. *Add-Drop Multiplexed Ring Network*

Figure 338 shows a more complex "ring" type of ADM network.

- Each end user can (or rather could) communicate with any other end user in either direction around the ring.

- In this case we have connections between A and F, B and C and D and E.

- Wavelengths can be re-used either by the same user (having an upstream channel and a downstream channel to different end-points) or by different end users.

- One interesting possibility might be for two users to have two (bi-directional) channels connecting them. In other words they would have one channel in each *different* direction around the ring. This system would allow for full continued operation in the case of a break in the ring. However, it would use a single wavelength around the entire ring. This would prevent the wavelength from being re-used by any other user. Since at the present time the maximum number of WDM channels on a structure like this is around 32 then this would take a significant amount of the system's resource.

There are many ways to add and drop an optical channel into a WDM stream. A number of these are discussed in 9.2.5, "Add-Drop Multiplexors" on page 531.

The major technical issues are just those of point-to-point WDM systems however there is one more. Each add/drop device attenuates the WDM signal stream by between 2 and 6 dB (depending on the type of device). In addition the add/drop devices introduce some crosstalk. The ADDed WDM channel is not attenuated compared to the rest of the channels in the stream. In a campus or MAN environment this may not cause a problem since it may be possible to design the system in such a way as to minimise its impact. However in large WAN ADM networks (several are planned) the signal needs to be equalised and (perhaps) amplified at each drop location.

Early planned add/drop networks are fixed in their nature. That is, optical channels are planned and installed using fixed wavelengths and non-tunable devices. In time, however, a dynamic circuit-switched style of operation will be possible where end users can request channels dynamically from the system. When a channel was allocated the end user would need to tune to the correct wavelength and the ADM device would need to adjust its wavelengths also. To achieve this we would need a control system capable of communication with all the network end users and capable of dynamically re-configuring the network. Logically such control systems are very well known and established in electronic networks. However, building tunable optical devices to the precision required has not yet been achieved.

10.1.5.3 Nodal Networks

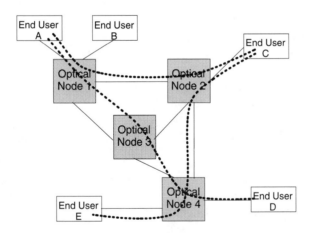

Figure 339. Network Using Optical Switching Nodes

Figure 339 shows a topology which can be regarded as the traditional "network". Each end user is connected on a physical link connection to one or more routing "nodes" of the network. Each node is itself connected to other nodes in the network and (optionally) to some end users. Information flows from one end user to another over a series of links and nodes.

There are many different types of network using quite different operational principles which have this basic structure. In general they can be classified into three types:

"Wavelength Routed" Networks

This is probably the simplest kind of nodal network. The basic concept is illustrated in Figure 340 on page 583. Each wavelength is part of a (unidirectional) circuit between end user devices. In the illustration the node-to-node trunks are WDM links but the links to each end user are not. This is simply for the purposes of illustration. In a network of this kind the links to end users would normally be (at least capable of) WDM.

A circuit connecting end-users consists of one wavelength path in one direction and another wavelength path in the opposite direction. In principle the two directions of traffic don't have to follow the same path through the network but in practice they almost always will. (Using the same path for both directions significantly simplifies fault location and network management.)

On any particular link wavelengths must (obviously) be unique. You can only have one signal at a particular wavelength. However, wavelengths may be reused in different parts of the network. This is an important feature. The same wavelength may be used for different purposes on different interconnecting fibres. Thus if wavelength "3" is used for the connection from Workstation 1 to Workstation 3 (in the figure) then it would be possible for the same wavelength to be used for the connection from Workstation 2 to Workstation 4. All this depends on the internal design of the switching nodes - different designs may impose restrictions but in principle there is very little limitation in the reuse of wavelengths in different parts of the network. This is an advantage over reflective star-based networks where all wavelengths must be unique.

In very simple networks of this kind it would be possible to use fixed wavelength transmitters and receivers in the end user nodes. If this were done, each circuit would need to be carefully planned and each end user allocated exact wavelengths. However, this would not be practical in any network larger than two or three nodes.

A practical design for a "wavelength routed" network must allow for network re-configuration on command from the network management system. Thus end-to-end channels are fixed for a period of time and can be changed on command by network management. Networks of this type are often called "Crossconnect Networks".

In order to build such a network we need some method of specifying the wavelength to be used by each end user. This means that either:

1. Tunable transmitters are needed in the end-user nodes, or

2. The entry switching node must have some means of changing the wavelength of inbound channels.

Depending on how the switching nodes are organised we may need tunable receivers as well. The need for tunable receivers depends on whether the network switch node at the exit point from the network selects an individual wavelength and sends it to the end user or whether it sends a mixed WDM stream to the end user device.

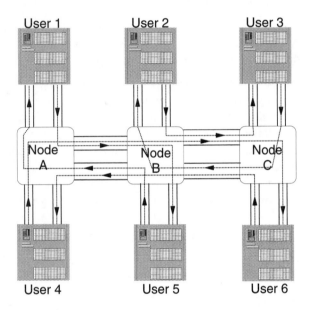

Figure 340. Wavelength Selective Network - Concept. Connections through the network are formed by routing individual wavelengths.

Wavelength Switched Networks

An advance on the "wavelength routed" network case described above would be the fully switched optical network. The difference between the two being that a switched network is able to establish new connections dynamically, on demand from the end-user equipment. The protocols used between the end user and the network to request the setting up of new connections or the termination of old ones is called "signalling". In addition the protocols used between switches to coordinate the setting up of connections are also called signalling protocols.

The first requirement here is to have a data path between the end-user equipment and the switch to which it is attached. In the optical domain perhaps that could be an additional channel operated in the 1310 nm band.

Of course each optical switch is controlled by an electronic control point (a computer) which controls the internal switching fabric. This control point also communicates with the end-user devices and other switches to set up and tear down connections. It also monitors the operation of the switch and connects to the network management system.

The switching principles involved here look superficially like the ones we know well from electronic networking systems such as ATM. However, the optical case is significantly more difficult than the electronic one.

The problem is that it is difficult to change the wavelength of a single channel (by passive optical means) within the network. The transmitting and receiving stations must use the same wavelength. This is not a problem for the workstations themselves but is a very significant problem for the network. If you can't change the wavelength of the signal as it traverses a switching node then as the network gets larger there will be an increasing number of situations where there are plenty of vacant channels between two end users but no way of allocating a unique wavelength to the connection!

In traditional networks (such as ATM) the subchannel (in ATM the VPI/VCI) changes at every switching node. Without this function the problem of allocation of wavelengths becomes very difficult in any kind of complex network.

This means that a fully switched nodal optical network of any size needs to have a means of changing wavelengths at each switch. Switching nodes with this ability were discussed in 9.2.7.1, "Optical Switching Node with Wavelength Conversion" on page 539.

Optical Time Division Multiplexed (OTDM) Networks

OTDM networks have been extensively researched and are close to early commercial reality. In the future this principle will be particularly useful in soliton-based networks. Since these networks are still in the research stage they are discussed in 12.5, "Optical Time Division Multiplexing (OTDM)" on page 663.

Optical Packet Switched Networks

Fully optical packet switched networks are a very long way from any form of reality. There are not even research prototypes yet available. The principles involved are discussed in 12.6, "Optical Packet Switched Networks" on page 670.

10.2 WDM for LANs (and Small MANs)

10.2.1 Network Topology

The objective of the network topology design is to provide a path from the transmitter of any station to the receiver of any other (any-to-any connectivity). This would seem to be simple but the unique characteristics of fibre and the use of the WDM technique combine to place a number of restrictions on the kinds of network topologies which are possible.

Ring Topologies

Ring topologies are receiving increasing attention as topologies for MANs and even for large scale wide area applications. Rings are attractive because they can be constructed such that they are "self healing". That is, a break in the ring can be automatically bypassed by routing a backup path in the opposite direction around the ring.

The predominant method of using an optical ring is called "Add/Drop Multiplexing" and is described in 10.1.5.2, "Add-Drop Multiplexed (ADM) Networks" on page 578.

Hub-Based Rings

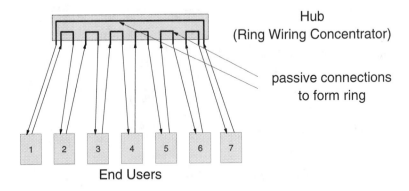

Figure 341. Ring Wiring Concentrator

In the WAN and MAN environments you can economically construct dual-ring structures which allow for self-healing in the case of ring breakages. In the LAN this is a lot more difficult.

- LANs tend to have many more stations than we need in the WAN or MAN.

- The cost of a self-healing dual ring structure tends to get higher than we would like.

- In LANs we need to do many more changes (adds and deletions to the ring) than we need in wider area applications.

Rings are still attractive for many reasons so "hubs" such as the one illustrated in Figure 341 on page 585 are often used. This provides a logical ring (the signal passes around the ring) but a star wiring structure. The advantages are as follows:

- Breaks in the ring can be quickly bypassed by jumpering at the hub. In electronic rings this can be done automatically.

- The ring can be re-configured with new users being added and old ones removed very easily - again by jumpering at the hub.

- The hub (while in principle passive) can be used to monitor and control access security etc.

- In an optical ring we could envisage perhaps amplifying the signal and/or re-shaping it at the hub.

Folded Buses

A folded bus system is shown in Figure 342.

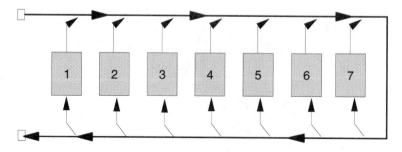

Figure 342. Folded Bus Configuration. Stations (1 to 7) transmit on different wavelengths each onto the top part of the bus where the signals mix. Taps on the return section deliver the mixed signal (although with varying strength) to each node.

These will work but in all but the smallest networks will require amplifiers to boost the signal at frequent intervals down the bus.

The problem is that as the fibre is tapped at each station a fixed proportion of the signal power is removed and sent to the station. This can be from 50% to perhaps 5%.

In the extreme case where 3 dB couplers might be used the signal is split by half at each station - half carries on along the bus and half goes to the attached station. In Figure 342 on page 586, station 7 will get half the signal and then station 6 will get half of that (1/4 of the original signal). Station 5 will get half of that (1/8) of the original signal until station 1 will get 1/128th of the original signal. If there are n stations on the bus the signal degrades to $\frac{1}{2^n}$ of what it was originally (where n = the number of stations).

When splitters that direct a smaller proportion (say 5%) of the signal to the attached station are used the problems are essentially the same but are lessened somewhat. You have to amplify less often but you still have to plan carefully to distribute the signal power as needed.

Another problem is the combining of the signal at the output of the workstations. If the signal is placed on the bus using a simple Y-coupler or resonant coupler there is *no way* of inserting a *same wavelength* signal without very significant loss of the combined signal. Because the wavelengths are different we *can* combine them with low loss but we need to use a relatively complex device such as that described in 9.2.5, "Add-Drop Multiplexors" on page 531 to do it. In addition the insertion loss of this device will be between 4 dB and 6 dB.

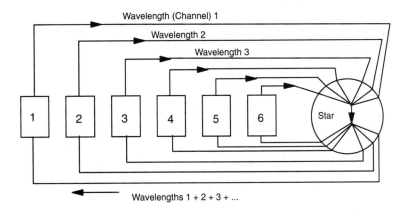

Figure 343. Reflective Star Configuration. On the transmit side, a separate fibre connects each station to the input side of the star. The signals are mixed and then split. Separate fibres deliver the mixed signal (all channels) to each station.

Passive (Reflective) Stars

This configuration is illustrated in Figure 343. These have been used in several experimental systems because they can support many more stations without amplification than can bus networks.

As shown in the figure, separate fibres are connected from each station to the star. This device is really a combiner followed by a splitter. All incoming signals are combined onto a single fibre and then this is split to direct 1/n part of the combined signal back to each station. That is, the output signal is reduced by $10\log_{10}N$ - where N equals the number of stations. Of course, a topology like this can handle significantly more stations than can the bus topology described above.

A feature of the topology is that the star is a passive (non-powered) device - a characteristic considered very important for reliability.

Nevertheless, any fibre LAN or MAN topology will require amplifiers if a meaningful number of devices is to be handled.

Tree Structures

Tree structures such as that shown in Figure 344 are also possible.

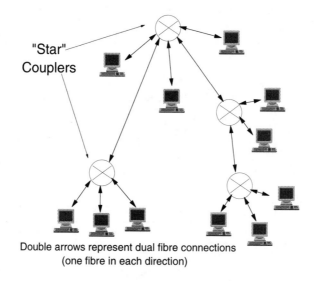

"Star" Couplers

Double arrows represent dual fibre connections
(one fibre in each direction)

Figure 344. Tree Configuration. Stations transmit on different wavelengths to a small local reflective star or coupler. Loops in the structure are not allowed.

In general a number of couplers or stars can be interconnected such that anything sent by one station will be received by all stations. This can be very effective in a distributed topology where a number of "hubs" interconnect a few stations each and are connected together to form a larger LAN structure.

As always there are a few problems:

- The relative signal strength of different transmitting stations will be very different (perhaps 20 dB or so) at the receiver. Some proposed access protocols rely on a transmitting station being able to receive its own signal in order to detect collisions. Of course a tree topology allows this. But collisions could be quite hard to detect if the colliding station is a long way away in the network.

- There can't be any loops in the structure. If multiple paths exist between stations in the network, the signal will go on all paths. When such a signal is received it will collide with itself and become garbage at the receiver.

It can be seen that the topology design is quite complex and is critical to the success of any optical networking scheme.

10.2.2 Transmission System Design

Building tunable transmitters and receivers is quite difficult to do. This is mentioned in 3.3.10, "Tunable DBR Lasers" on page 153. The important parameters are:

- The speed at which transmitters and receivers are able to tune to the required frequency.

- The stability with which a frequency is maintained.

- The tunable range.

- The linewidth of the transmitter and the selectivity of the receiver.

- Of course the above all interact to determine how close channels may be packed together. The closer together they are, the more you can have within a given tuning range and the faster the tuning will be.

10.2.2.1 Stabilising Wavelengths

The biggest problem in WDM system design is stabilizing the wavelengths. This was discussed in 9.4.2, "Stabilising Wavelengths" on page 552 in relation to individual components.

At the systems level there are a number of things that we can do to help stabilise the wavelengths:

1. In a system using direct modulation of the laser drive current the data encoding scheme is important. Lasers have a problem very similar to "baseline wander" in electronic systems. If you send a lot of pulses one after another then the temperature in the laser cavity increases and causes a wavelength shift. This is a bit different from the chirp and relaxation oscillation issue. So what you need to do is use data encodings that have a roughly equal number of 1 bits and 0 bits. A single 1 bit doesn't have a great effect on the wavelength but a long sequence does.

2. Create a "comb" of reference frequencies:

   • Construct a special Fabry-Perot laser with a large number of modes.

   • Stabilise one of these with an FBG and a feedback loop.

   • Distribute this reference comb around the network where it may be used either to stabilise other lasers or (after amplification) become the network wavelength source.

   Of course this means that you have to have additional fibres to act as distribution medium - and this is an extra cost. A network using this principle is described in 10.3.6, "Metropolitan Area Add/Drop WDM with a Multiwavelength Source" on page 603.

3. Build a network with all of the tunable components in a central location (hub) along with the reflective star. In this configuration a single multimode laser could be used to produce a comb for all variable transmitters, receivers and filters in the system. Individual workstations would have fixed transmitters and receivers.

4. Transmit a frequency reference somewhere a bit separate from the comb of channels. Each station would then have a special receiver for this channel and this could be used to stabilise all other devices in the system.

All of these alternatives are costly - but some more than others.

10.2.3 Access Protocols for the Shared Medium

If there are a number of stations connected to a common medium and two of them want to communicate, all we have to do is select a mutually agreed wavelength/s (channel/s) for them to use and communication is immediately possible (provided no other station is using the selected channel/s).

Note: In any communication between two stations (A and B) there are almost always two channels involved - one for each direction (A-to-B and B-to-A).

In the simple case, we could allocate a channel to a group of devices with a pencil and paper - by system definition. This would mean that these devices were able to use the nominated channel/s all of the time but they would be unable to communicate with other devices on the network. This might sound silly but it is not at all! A carrier organization (PTT) might well connect a MAN type structure around a city area and allocate channels to various customers on a fixed basis. This is a very practical structure but avoids the issue.

Our objective in creating a "lightwave network" is to provide any-to-any connectivity for all attached stations. But then there is the question of how do we want it to operate:

1. Do we want it to operate like a traditional LAN with single blocks of data individually addressed on a block-by-block basis?

2. Or are we happy with a "virtual circuit" approach where pairs of stations are given a channel for a period of time, perhaps a few seconds (or milliseconds)?

Most WDM access protocols require either transmitters or receivers (or both) to tune to a particular channel before data transfer can take place. This can take a significant length of time (compared with the transmit time for a single block). A virtual circuit approach can tolerate a relatively long delay in circuit establishment but offers instant access for data blocks after the first.

A connectionless (traditional LAN) approach means that you have the same delay for every block transmitted. Of course, a virtual circuit approach is very inefficient if a channel is occupied for a long period of time with only occasional data transfer. In this case, it would be better to use a connectionless system and share the channel capacity.

When station A wants to send data to station B then they have to find a vacant channel and both tune to it before station A can commence sending. The central problem for the access protocol is: "How do we arrange for stations wanting to communicate to use the same channel (wavelength)?" This is not a trivial problem! First, the stations must have some ability to vary their operating wavelength (switch from channel to channel). We could have:

- Each station allocated to a fixed transmitting channel and all stations able to tune their receivers to any channel at will.

- Each station could be allocated a fixed receiving frequency and a tunable transmitter.

- Both transmitter and receiver could be tunable.

- Stations could have multiple (say two or three) receivers and/or transmitters.

Fixed Receivers - Tunable Transmitters

An obvious method of operation would be to have receivers fixed to a dedicated channel (one station per channel) and each station would have a tunable transmitter. In operation, all a station would have to do to send to another station would be to tune to its channel and transmit.

But there is then the possibility of two or more stations trying to transmit to the same destination at the same time and collisions occurring.

Fixed Transmitters - Tunable Receivers

In this system each station transmits on its own fixed channel and receivers must tune to this channel in order to receive the data. This is often called the "broadcast and select" principle. There are two problems here:

- How does a station know to which channel to tune its receiver? It has to know (somehow) that a particular station wants to send it data.

- If station A wants to send to station B, there would always be a free channel (because station A has a dedicated transmit channel) but station B's receiver could be busy receiving something from station C somewhere else in the network. This is sometimes called "receiver collision".

This is, in fact, a very promising principle. There are several proposed access protocols that aim to solve the above problems. See 10.3.5.2, "IBM "Rainbow-1"" on page 600.

There is another benefit here. All receivers (or a subset) could tune to the same channel. This allows for a broadcast ability. But this may not be practical because of the need to get all receivers listening to the same channel at the same time - some may already be busy receiving something different.

Both Transmitter and Receiver Tunable

Of course, this is by far the ideal system if only you could make it work. In systems where either a receiver or transmitter is dedicated to a particular channel you are limited to a maximum number of stations equal to the number of channels in the system. (Of course, it is possible to put multiple stations on the same channel but then there are new problems of conflict.)

From a usage efficiency point of view, tuning both the transmitter and receiver is by far the best. This is because we can potentially have many more stations than channels and all stations contend for the same pool of capacity. (Of course, we may not always care about usage efficiency in an environment where capacity is almost endless!)

This is not a silly idea at all. A network of perhaps 1000 stations might be easily supported on a system offering only (say) 100 channels. Twenty channels packed closely together would allow the use of a very narrow tuning range and hence very fast tuning.

But in this configuration, now both stations must have a mechanism for deciding which channel they will use. Another point is that if there are more stations than channels then there is the possibility of "blocking" (a station wanting to transmit when there is no free channel) - and this possibility must be provided for - the problem is not so much the possibility of blocking but the additional complexity in system protocols needed to handle the situation.

An access protocol is the mechanism used to determine just which channel should be used by each new communication.

The biggest problem for the access protocol is exactly the same for all high-speed LAN/MAN protocols. *Although the speed of data transmission has increased by many orders of magnitude, the speed of light in a fibre and of electricity in a wire (at about 5 μsec per km) hasn't changed.* Propagation delays are exactly the same as they are for traditional LANs, so propagation delays become much longer than block transmission times and therefore very significant in terms of efficiency. Of course the problem increases significantly with distance. It has the most effect on systems:

1. Which have any protocol exchange for pretransmission coordination (because each round-trip between sender and receiver incurs two propagation delays)

2. Which use CSMA/CD protocols (because the probability of collision increases with propagation delay)

In general terms there are a number of options:

Controlling Station

The simplest method available is to have a station somewhere on the LAN responsible for allocating channels to stations on a demand basis.

A typical system of this kind would have two control channels (one for each direction - to or from the controlling station). When a station wants to send some data it asks the control station for a channel and the control station allocates one from its knowledge of the pool of free channels - it also knows if the intended receiver is currently busy with some other communication. It then sends a control packet to the requester and to the intended destination allocating the channel. When communication is complete one of the stations needs to notify the control station that the channel is free.

This kind of system is simple and easy to implement but it has a number of problems:

1. While the allocation of channels can be near to optimal, it takes a long time to complete. A few hundred μsec as a minimum. At a speed of one Gbps a frame of 1000 bits takes only one μsec to transmit. Thus it would be a very inefficient protocol for traditional LAN (connectionless, packet) type of operation (but quite good for a virtual circuit environment).

2. The control station represents a single point of failure and therefore would need to be duplicated and even then would detract from the reliability of the system.

3. The cost of the control station adds a significant "entry cost" to the system. (Users who want to start with only a few stations are forced to buy a control station.)

4. If the control function is decentralised (for example, put into every adapter) it adds cost to each adapter.

Control Channel

Many proposed systems coordinate their transmissions by using a dedicated control channel which is shared among all attached stations. The protocols used on this control channel are not difficult because the load will be very low. CSMA/CD has been suggested as have Aloha and Slotted Aloha mechanisms.

This can be used to distribute the control function among the stations. The main problem is that any coordination before transmission takes time. This time, added to the transmit time of every block can severely degrade the efficiency of the system.

An interesting proposed protocol using a control channel is described in 10.3.3, "Coordination on a Control Channel" on page 597.

Dynamic Allocation

This class of systems uses neither a control channel nor a centralised station to coordinate transmissions. Most of the proposed and experimental systems described below use this approach.

10.3 Some Possible Systems Approaches

10.3.1 Centralised WDM Circuit Switch

A WDM circuit-switching system is illustrated in Figure 345. This performs the same logical switching function as an electronic circuit-switching system but the switching function is performed optically. All the tunable equipment (lasers) is kept in a centrally managed location.

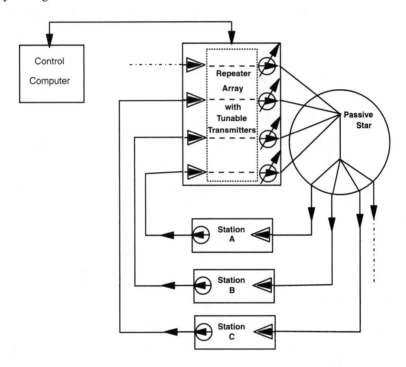

Figure 345. Wavelength Switching System

Each station transmits on a dedicated fibre (on a fixed wavelength) to the switch. Each station receives on a different wavelength. (So the maximum number of stations is determined by the number of available channels.) The switch receives the optical signal and re-transmits it on the wavelength of the intended receiver. The "star" mixes the signals from the switch so that each receiver sees all the signals.

The logical connection of a transmitter in a station to a receiver in another station is performed by wavelength tuning. The system is constructed as follows:

- Each station has a fixed wavelength transmitter and a fixed wavelength receiver. Wavelength used in this section of the system is irrelevant. All stations could use the same wavelength to transmit.

- The signal is received by an array of electronic repeaters where the transmitter at each repeater is tunable.

- Each station receives on a unique wavelength (also fixed).

- When Station C is to send to Station A then the transmitter in the switch (corresponding to Station A) is tuned to the wavelength of the receiver in Station C.

This is a circuit-switched system.

- When a station is not communicating with another station its transmissions are received by the control computer.

- To make a connection a station places a "call request" with the control computer.

- If the destination station is available the control station will exchange a message with it to confirm that it will accept this connection.

- If all is OK then the control computer will tell the requesting station that a connection will be made.

- The control computer will then connect the two stations by tuning the wavelengths of both stations to point to each other.

The major disadvantage with this approach is the relatively long circuit establishment time (it requires program intervention in a controlling computer) but the electronic switch it replaces has exactly the same problem.

It is obvious that placing a tunable transmitter within each station would eliminate the need for the tunable repeater array. But the centralised switch approach has some significant advantages:

1. Very simple centralised control. There is no problem with "collisions".

2. All the transmitters can be controlled from the same frequency reference. This means that potentially the channels could be more densely packed. However, receivers would still require stabilization in some way.

3. A major advantage of this configuration is that (at very high speeds) it should be significantly lower in cost than a fully electronic crosspoint switch.

10.3.2 Multichannel CSMA/CD

In this proposal the network would be configured exactly as in Figure 343 on page 587.

- In this proposal each station is equipped with:

  - One tunable transmitter

  - One tunable receiver

  - One fixed receiver

- Each station receives data *only* on its *fixed* receiver.

- The tunable receiver is used for collision detection on the station's transmit channel. (This helps significantly in cost since both tunable elements are always tuned to the same wavelength.)

- When a station wants to transmit it tunes both its transmitter and its tunable receiver to the channel on which the other station receives.

  It then operates a (more or less standard) CSMA/CD protocol.

  It listens to see if there is any data on its intended transmit channel. If there is none, it will transmit. While it is transmitting it monitors the receive channel to detect possible collisions. If there was a collision, the transmitter backs off for a random amount of time before retry.

- This system will work over the star or bus topologies but may have problems with the tree structure. In order to detect collisions the signal received from its own transmitter must not be too strong so as to swamp the colliding station's signal.

The system is simple and offers very fast packet switching access time. It also has the advantage of being able to have multiple stations on each channel. Statistically this is not as good as having a fully tunable transmitter and receiver system because two devices on the same channel may conflict when there are plenty of other channels which are not currently busy. But it offers other advantages in access speed and the absence of any need for pretransmission coordination.

10.3.3 Coordination on a Control Channel

There are many proposals for using a control channel to coordinate transmissions presented in the literature. Most of these have proposed either a TDM (slotted) or a CSMA approach to administration of the control channel itself.

An extreme solution might be for each station to have a fixed transmitter and receiver (tuned to the control channel) and tunable ones for the data. Every station would keep track of the channels in use and when a station wanted to send, it would tell the receiver (and all other stations) that it was about to use channel x. It would then notify other stations when the channel was free. Although the chance of collision could be minimised by having each transmitter select the next channel to use based on a (different) random number there is still some chance of collision and such a system would be quite costly.

An example of such a system is given below:

- The network topology could be any of the three possibilities (star, bus, or tree) described above.

- Each station would have both receiver and transmitter tunable.

- When a station wants to send to another, it does the following:

  1. Selects a channel with no signal on it (by using its receiver to scan).

  2. Tunes its transmitter to the control channel and sends a control packet to tell the receiver that a packet will be following on the (nominated) channel. The transmission channel number is included in the control packet.

  3. Tunes its transmitter to the nominated channel.

  4. Waits until the receiver can be assumed to have tuned and stabilised.

  5. Sends the packet.

- Of course, this is not a particularly good protocol:

  – There is a lot of time taken up in receiver and transmitter tuning.

  – There is the possibility of collision on the control channel and the intended receiver never receiving the control packet.

  – There is a significant probability of collision on the data channel.

  – The receiver might not be listening to the control channel at all - it might be busy receiving something else.

Even though there are significant problems, there are many proposed improvements to the above and these improved protocols are serious contenders for systems in the future.

10.3.4 Code Division Multiple Access (CDMA)

Optical CDMA is a good candidate for a medium access control protocol in a shared medium LAN. In this case every device uses the same wavelength and therefore bus-based solutions would be unattractive as they involve too much loss. However, CDMA would be a very attractive way of operating a reflective star network.

Optical CDMA is discussed in 12.4, "Optical Code Division Multiple Access (CDMA)" on page 656.

10.3.5 Experimental Systems

10.3.5.1 Lambdanet

Lambdanet was an experimental WDM system designed to explore a number of different possible uses.

The network topology is a broadcast star as shown in Figure 343 on page 587 and discussed above.

- The experimental configuration used 18 stations.

- A 16x16 star coupler was used and extended to 18 connections by attachment of two smaller coupling devices.

- The network itself is totally passive except for the attached stations.

- Each station transmits on a fixed unique frequency.

- The thing that makes Lambdanet different from other proposed architectures is that *nothing is tunable*. Each station separates the received signal (all 18 wavelengths) using a diffraction grating and then feeds each separate signal to a separate receiver! Thus a Lambdanet station receives all transmissions and decides which ones to process electronically.

The technical characteristics of the system were as follows:

- Lasers were the Distributed Feedback (DFB) type.

- Wavelengths were from 1527 to 1561 nm with a 2 nm channel separation.

- Receivers were commercial (InGaAs) APD receivers.

- "Regular" (non-dispersion shifted) single-mode fibre was used.

- Two data rates were experimented with - 1.5 Gbps and 2 Gbps.

Applications thought suitable for this technology include:

- Providing Exchange (Central Office) to Exchange multiplexed bearers for:

  1. Traditional PTT services such as telephone and synchronous data (such as "T1 links"). This could be done by traditional TDM techniques applied to the WDM channels.

  2. Constructing private "virtual" data networks for individual organizations. This could be done also by TDM sharing of the WDM links.

- One-way video distribution. This would become particularly important in a "fibre to the home environment".

10.3.5.2 IBM "Rainbow-1"

Rainbow-1 is a prototype WDM LAN system developed by IBM Research.[115] It was publicly demonstrated at the TELECOM-91 exhibition in Geneva in October 1991.

The system consists of a passive "reflective star" connected to 32 IBM PS/2 computers. The electronic and optical components are built on two standard MicroChannel cards - this gives them the ability to be used in other products that use the MicroChannel such as the IBM 3172, the IBM RS/6000 and some models of the IBM 4300 processor series). As many as 32 simultaneous 200 Mbps data channels can operate simultaneously. The system design is illustrated in Figure 346.

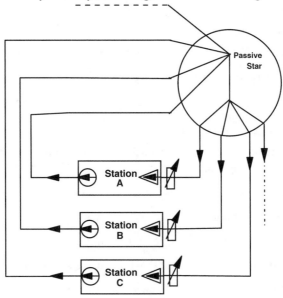

Figure 346. *Rainbow-1 System Design. The design features a passive network with fixed transmitters and tunable receivers. The receivers are actually fixed incoherent detectors preceded by tunable Fabry-Perot filters.*

---

[115] Rainbow is a research project, *not* a product. IBM cannot make any comment on what uses, if any, may be made of the Rainbow technology in future IBM products.

Overview

- Each station is equipped with a fixed frequency transmitter and a tunable receiver.

- Each station is allocated a unique wavelength from a band of wavelengths from 1505 to 1545 nm.

- The tunable receivers are actually fixed frequency incoherent detectors each of which is preceded by a Fabry-Perot tunable filter with a tuning range of 50 nm. The tuning rate is about 10 μsec per nm which gives an average time to locate a channel as 250 μsec.

- Simple OOK[116] modulation is used. It is noted, however, that the system needs some form of coding that provides sufficient transitions in the data for the receiver PLL to synchronise.

- Data rate is 200 Mbps over standard 8-micron single-mode fibre.

The system operates as follows:

- When station A wants to establish a connection with station B, it does the following:

  1. Begins sending a setup request to station B. Note this is sent on its own (station A's) dedicated transmit wavelength. This is a continuous repetition of the same (very short) message and synchronization.

  2. Tunes its receiver to the wavelength of station B's transmitter.

- If station B is busy doing something else (such as receiving data from another station), station A will continue sending the setup request.

- When station B is not communicating with another station it continuously scans across the range of all wavelengths looking for a setup request addressed to itself.

- When station B receives a setup request addressed to itself it locks its receiver on to the signal from station A and immediately sends a confirmation to the other station. It is able to do this since its transmitter is not tunable and station A must already be waiting for a response.

- Both stations are then able to exchange data freely until they agree to disconnect. At this point both stations begin scanning all channels again looking for the next setup request.

---

[116] On-off keying

Due to the timings involved (up to one millisecond to make a connection) it will be seen that this is a "short hold mode" circuit-switching system rather than a packet switch.

Details

- The system was built with commercially available optical and electronic components.

- The transmitter lasers had an unmodulated linewidth of less than 350 MHz. These were modulated in such a way as to reduce the chirp problem but the major factor in the control of chirp was the relatively wide channel spacings.

Conclusion: The system works well. A summary of the lessons learned may be found in the paper by Paul E. Green (1992). Rainbow is a research prototype and it is expected that the project will continue. The ultimate aim is to prove the feasibility of a 1000 station WDM LAN/MAN operating at 1 Gbps.

10.3.5.3 IBM "Rainbow-2"

Rainbow-2 is the next generation of experimental LAN system from Rainbow-1. It was developed during 1993 and 1994 and is currently working in the laboratory. In principle, it is the same as Rainbow-1; however, in practice it is quite different:

- Rainbow-1 was a LAN system oriented to interconnecting user workstations. Rainbow-2 is intended to provide supercomputer interconnection and access.

- Rainbow-1 was implemented on a PS/2 adapter card where Rainbow-2 is an external box. This external box implements many functions for offloading processing from the host computer.

- The optical principles and protocols of the two projects are very similar but Rainbow-2 begins to explore systems aspects of how to take advantage of the enormous bandwidth now available.

- The Rainbow-2 project connects 32 stations at a speed of 1 Gbps per station over metropolitan area distances (max 15 km).

More information can be found in Green (1994).

10.3.6 Metropolitan Area Add/Drop WDM with a Multiwavelength Source

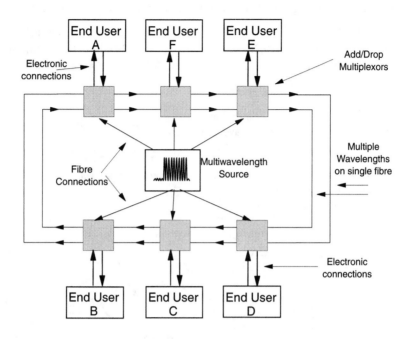

Figure 347. *Add/Drop WDM Network with Multiwavelength Source*

One suggested approach to reducing the cost of WDM systems is to have only one source of light producing multiple wavelengths. This source can be stabilised and its cost is not so critical as it is shared by the whole network.

The concept is illustrated in Figure 347:

- A single stabilised laser source produces multiple wavelengths (lines). A multiwavelength source suitable for this type of network was described in 9.2.1.2, "Multiline Lasers" on page 521.

- This source is amplified and then split so that there is one output for each end user.

- A dedicated fibre connection is used to distribute the whole spectrum of produced wavelengths to each end user.

- As shown in Figure 348 on page 604 each end-user workstation selects its operational wavelength from among the mixture of wavelengths received by using a tunable FP filter.

- The end-user station then must modulate its selected wavelength. This is done with a separate modulator.

- The selected wavelength is then added to the ring as shown in the figure.

- The add-drop operation of the end-user station using circulators and a fibre Bragg grating was discussed in 9.2.5.2, "Circulators with In-Fibre Bragg Gratings" on page 532. Of course there are other ways of achieving the optical add/drop function.

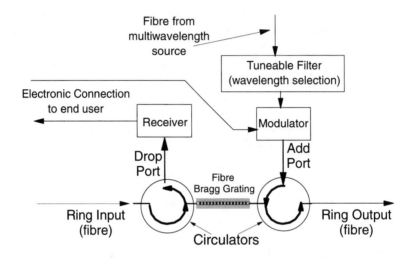

Figure 348. Add/Drop WDM Station with Multiwavelength Source

There are a number of major problems with this type of network in practical application:

1. The cost of providing the extra fibre to distribute the multiwavelength signal is quite high and may exceed the cost of stabilised individual lasers.

2. The additional fibre used to distribute the signal is subject to being broken or cut and is therefore an exposure for the reliability of the system.

3. Signal levels may require amplification at certain points and if this is the case the cost of the amplifiers will certainly make the total cost prohibitive.

10.4 WDM Research Demonstrators

There is a high level of friendly competition between various research groups working on WDM systems. At the systems level research groups produce "demonstrators". These systems are working prototypes but don't carry any real data and are not installed "in the field". They are usually three to five years ahead of what is actually being used in the field but they illustrate the potentials and show up the problems.

At the time of writing many research groups are working on extending the bits-per-second capability of fibre links using WDM. Here are some current results from the professional literature:

80 Gbps (Hitachi)

> This system used 8 channels of 10 Gbps for a distance of 1171 km. This was constructed using multiple passes through a 90.1 km loop using standard fibre balanced with dispersion compensating fibre. EDFAs were equalised using filters. A BER of better than 10^{-9} was achieved.
>
> See Sekine et al. Electronics Letters, June 22, 1995.

100 Gbps WDM (AT&T)

> This system used 20 channels at 5 Gbps for a distance of 6300 km. The important system characteristics were:
>
> - Channel spacing of 0.6 nm.
>
> - Standard NRZI data encoding.
>
> - The experiment used multiple (5) passes through a 1260 km fibre loop.
>
> - A "dispersion-managed" link design was used with 25 sections of "negative dispersion" (-2 ps.nm.km) fibre each of 46 km and 2 sections of positive dispersion (24 ps.nm.km) fibre each of 50 km. Combined with a design intent of using low power for each channel (-8 dBm) this minimised the potential problem with four wave mixing.
>
> - Twenty-seven EDFAs were used and pre-emphasis of up to 7 dB was used to compensate for amplifier nonlinearities.
>
> - The achieved BER was better than 6×10^{-10} for all channels.
>
> - See Bergano et al., Postdeadline paper at ECOC'95, (1995).

2.64 Tbps WDM Experiment (NEC)

> This is the highest capacity reported thus far. The system characteristics were:

- 132 channels at 20 Gbps.

- Coding used was duobinary.

- Channel spacing was quoted as 33.3 GHz (.25 nm) in the band 1529-1564 nm.

- 120 km spans between gain-compensated EDFAs.

- This system is described in a postdeadline paper from the ECOC'96 conference.

320 Gbps (Bell Labs, Lucent)

Sixty-four 5 Gbps WDM channels were transmitted over a distance of 7200 km. in this experiment a very narrow optical bandwidth (19 nm in total) was used. Interactions between optical channels caused by the fibre nonlinearity were minimised by using a large mode field dispersion shifted fibre.

See Neal S. Bergano et al. (1997).

1 Tbps (Bell Labs, Lucent)

This demonstration used 100 channels each at 10 Gbps with 50 or 100 GHz channel spacings. A 400 km link was constructed using TrueWave fibre. Gain-flattened ultra-wideband EDFAs were used.

See A.K. Srivastava et al. (1997).

1 Tbps (NTT)

This system is the first to use two wavelength bands simultaneously. Fifty channels, twenty in the 1550 nm band and thirty in the 1580 nm band were used. All channels carried a data rate of 20 Gbps over a distance of 600 km.

See S. Aisawa et al. (1997).

10.5 The IBM 9729 - A WDM System for the Metropolitan Area Network

The IBM 9729 is the first "standard product" implementation of WDM principles designed for the short distance metropolitan area environment. It originated in 1994 as a field research experiment. The IBM 9729 is a point-to-point multiplexor that enables the user to carry up to 10 full-duplex information streams over a single fibre (NOT a pair) for distances of up to 50 km. The fibre carries 20 channels (of up to 1 Gbps each) - 10 in one direction and 10 in the other.

Figure 349. The IBM 9729

The original research project was motivated by the desire to explore the technical possibilities of WDM technology in a production environment. An experimental IBM 9729 system was installed at a customer site in the U.S. in 1994. This is believed to have been the very first production use of dense WDM optical multiplexing in the world. At the time it was felt that WDM technology would emerge one day as an important networking technique for the corporate MAN *but* it was considered that this time was still a long way off. However, due to very high (unexpected) customer demand, the 9729 became a standard product in October 1996.

10.5.1 9729 Applications

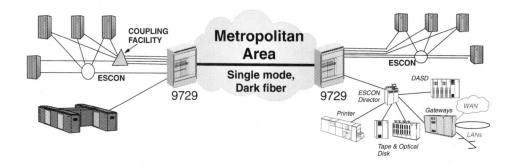

Figure 350. The IBM 9729 System Configuration

The primary application of the IBM 9729 is for interconnecting two or more large mainframe computer sites in the same city. For example, this might be a large mainframe complex and a backup site. This interconnection typically requires several parallel high bandwidth connections. In addition these large sites (buildings or campuses) often have many other communications requirements such as LAN interconnections and voice channels.

An important consideration is that while "dark fibre" is available in the U.S. (and to a limited extent in other countries) it is expensive. (The typical cost is around US $150 per month per mile per strand.) The use of WDM between major sites can bring a big saving in the cost of fibre.

Computer channel connections are *very* different from traditional communications ones. They are designed to operate in a machine room between computers and I/O devices with very fast response times at very high speeds. They were not designed to operate over a wide area.

The IBM processor-to-processor channel protocol (ESCON) is a circuit-switched protocol. The reason for this is the very fast response times required at the computer channel level. Thus in ESCON protocol you make a connection (just like making a telephone call) between the processor and an I/O device before you can start to transfer data. In practice the time you need to hold this call is very long in relation to the data transfer time. The result is that when interconnecting computer centres you often need a large number of ESCON channel connections (sometimes up to 50 or 60).

Mainframe interconnection is *not* the only application. Other communications applications are also very important. LAN (client/server) traffic can require very fast response time and the load on most corporate LANs has recently been increasing very quickly. Some of this is caused by the innovation of corporate "intranets". Most organisations choose not to bridge LANs directly or to extend the LAN protocols off the campus. LAN segments are usually interconnected through either an infrastructure based on interconnected LAN switches or one based on ATM. (The older technique of interconnection based on multiprotocol routers is important but this is now considered obsolescent.) Currently ATM is by far the most popular technique for interconnecting LANs or LAN segments. Thus interconnection of sites using ATM and/or FDDI is an increasing requirement. In addition most users who have a large amount of data traffic have some measure of voice traffic and there is often a need to interconnect the PBX equipment.

The use of WDM offers a number of significant advantages:

1. Cost Saving

   In the case of the IBM 9729 a single strand of fibre replaces up to 20 separate fibres. This can mean a very large cost saving in rental of fibre.

2. "Protection Switching"

   If you have a large number of fibres connecting the same two end-points usually they will be in the same cable. If you want to provide a backup path between the two systems you need more fibres on the other route. Switching perhaps 100 fibres from one path to another in a failure situation is a major problem! If many channels are carried on the same fibre then it is only necessary to switch a single fibre (or rather, a small number of fibres) from the primary to the backup path. This makes automatic switchover and protection switching very much easier and a lot lower in cost.

3. Protocol independence

   A major attraction of using WDM to share the fibre rather than other available techniques such as TDM is that each channel can be completely independent of each other channel. That is the protocols can be totally different. You might have a few channels of ESCON, some ATM, an FDDI connection as well as a few fast Ethernet connections - all sharing the same strand of fibre. Other multiplexing techniques (such as SDH/Sonet) are TDM based and require that all users conform to the same protocol AND that all connections be synchronised to the same clock! The requirement for clock synchronisation is difficult and expensive to meet. With WDM you have no such requirement.

10.5.2 Characteristics

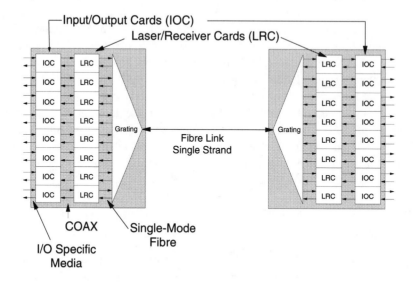

Figure 351. *IBM 9729 System Structure. Multiple optical wavelengths are carried on a single fibre point-to-point between two locations.*

The important features of the IBM 9729 are as follows:

Twenty Optical Channels

Twenty different wavelengths are used providing twenty optical channels each of which may operate at speeds up to 1 Gbps.

Single Strand of Fibre

Bi-directional traffic is handled on a *single strand* of fibre. This is possible because at the distances involved we do not need to amplify the signal. Of course, the use of a single strand saves fibre cost as providers usually charge per strand of fibre.

Distance

The nominal maximum distance between IBM 9729s is 50 km. This was a design point since it covers most metropolitan area requirements and at this distance we do not need to amplify the signal. If only the slower speed protocols such as FDDI (and ATM-100 and Ethernet-100) are used this distance can be increased to 70 km. For longer distances a pre-amplifier at the receiver end could allow a distance of perhaps 150 km whilst preserving both the ability to use a single fibre *and* the characteristic of low power transmission. It is considered important in the corporate network environment to keep the power low enough for the box to be rated as "Class 1" (that is, inherently safe).

For distances above 100 km we would need to use dual fibres (one in each direction) so that standard EDFAs could be used to boost the signal at intermediate points along the cable. (In fact, EDFAs can be bi-directional but this is extremely difficult to do in practice and commercial bi-directional EDFAs are not yet available.)

Standard Fibre Recommended

"Standard" (non-dispersion shifted) fibre is recommended. This is partly in recognition that the majority of installed fibre is of this kind and partly because the use of this fibre minimises crosstalk problems.

Protocols Supported

The following protocols are supported and may be used in any desired mixture (each channel is completely independent from each other channel):

- ESCON (160 Mbps/200 Mbaud)
- FDDI (100 Mbps/125 Mbaud)
- ATM-100 (100 Mbps/125 Mbaud)
- Ethernet-100 (100 Mbps)
- ATM-155 (155 Mbps)
- OC-3 (155 Mbps)
- Sysplex Timer (16 Mbps)
- ISC (800 Mbps/1.0625 Gbaud)

Dual Fibre Switching Feature

As an option the user may have two independent fibre trunks between IBM 9729s. Ideally these trunks would have different physical routings. If the active trunk fails for any reason (for example the cable is cut) then both 9729s (at each end) automatically switch to the backup path. This switching can be completed in less than two seconds and hence the "higher layer" protocols can recover from the failure transparently.

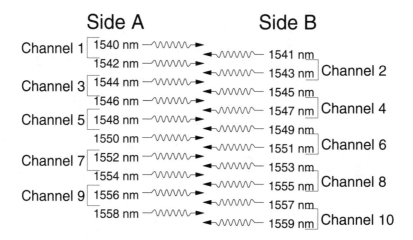

Figure 352. IBM 9729 Wavelength Allocation

Channel Wavelength Allocation

As shown in Figure 352, channels are spaced 1 nm apart. However the signal direction is alternated so that signals travelling in the same direction are separated by 2 nm. The wavelength range of between 1540 nm and 1560 nm was chosen as it is in the optimum range for amplification with an Erbium Doped Fibre Amplifier (EDFA). This may become important for distance extension in the future.

Reliability and Availability

Power supplies and cooling are duplexed and the system will operate normally in the presence of power supply and/or cooling fan failure. All cards such as the adapter cards (IOC and LRC), diagnostic card and grating controller etc. are "hot pluggable" and hence may be inserted and removed while the 9729 is operating.

System and Network Management

Each IBM 9729 is managed by a locally connected PC or workstation running SNMP management software. In turn these may be managed by a system-wide or an organisation-wide central management workstation.

Class 1 Operation

The IBM 9729 is designed for Class-1 operation. No special provisions need to be made for the fact that lasers are used as the power levels are designated as "inherently safe" by the relevant regulations.

This is important as the product is designed to be operated by people without special training in fibre optics. In contrast to equipment operated by telephone companies (which is operated and installed by engineers and trained technicians), this equipment must work in a computer room or office environment.

10.5.2.1 Overview of Operation

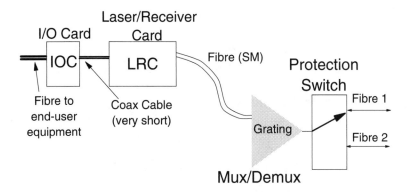

Figure 353. IBM 9729 Major Components and Data Flow

The major components of the IBM 9729 are shown in Figure 353. Overall operation is as follows:

- An optical signal from the end-user equipment is received and converted to electronic form on an adapter card called an IOC (I/O Card).

  There are a number of different IOCs which apply to different end user protocols.

- The signal is sent from the IOC over a pair of very short coaxial cables to the LRC (Laser/Receiver Card). Each LRC card in a system operates at a different wavelength. The laser has been selected and tuned to operate on one and only one specific channel. The received (square wave) electronic signal is used directly to modulate the drive current of the transmitting laser.

  Each laser is tuned to a different wavelength, so the system uses 20 different optical wavelengths (10 in each direction). This provides up to 10 full-duplex channels each of which is quite independent and runs at data rates of up to 1 Gbaud.

- The output from the transmit laser is connected on a short single-mode fibre to a specific port on the grating multiplexor.

- The grating is the heart of the system. It is used bidirectionally both to mix the output of the transmit lasers before sending on the single fibre and to split the wavelengths up and direct them to different receivers when receiving.

- When the signal is received by the partner 9729 the grating assembly receives the mixed signal and directs each channel to a different incoming fibre depending on the signal wavelength.

- The signal is then received on the LRC card and made electronic. This electronic signal is re-shaped (made into a square wave) just as happened in the transmit direction.

The signal is then passed from the LRC card to the IOC card and it is used to control the transmitter (laser or LED) for forwarding on to the end-user.

10.5.3 Grating Assembly (9729)

The grating assembly is the heart of the IBM 9729 system. It performs multiplexing of outgoing signals and demultiplexing of incoming ones as shown in Figure 354.

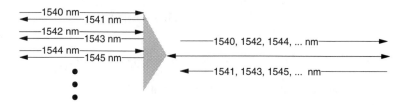

Figure 354. Grating Function

In physical construction it is a Littrow (reflective) grating combined with a concave mirror as discussed in 5.7.1, "Planar Diffraction Gratings" on page 260. This is illustrated in Figure 355 on page 615. While in the 9729 it is used in bi-directional mode there is nothing at all that restricts the directionality at the grating level. What it does is direct 20 wavelengths either to or from a common fibre from 20 individual fibres - as shown in the figure. There would be nothing to prevent the grating being used to transmit 20 channels simultaneously or to receive 20. Provided it's at the correct wavelength (different for each fibre) a signal arriving on the fibre will be merged onto the common input/output fibre. A signal arriving on the common fibre will be routed to one of the 20 channels depending on its wavelength. In the 9729 it happens to be used in both directions. Some fibres are used in one direction and some in the other.

The grating is able to select an individual channel from among all other received channels with crosstalk and noise (picked up from the other channels) of less than -55 dB.

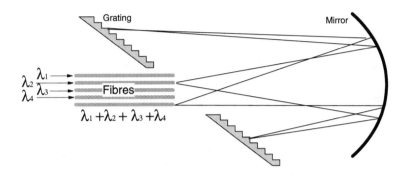

Figure 355. *Grating Assembly Schematic*

The reason a grating is used to mix the outgoing laser signals is that this is the only way you can mix optical signals with a tolerable amount of loss. If you used a fused fibre coupler or a star coupler you would lose so much light an amplifier would be needed to boost the signal again before transmission.

The nominal insertion loss of the grating (including its connectors) is 6 dB in each direction. (The measured figure is somewhat better than this but 6 dB is the design assumption based on worst case conditions.) Thus a signal originating on one LRC in one 9729 and received in another 9729 will suffer a maximum of 12 dB of attenuation due to the gratings.

A very important part of the grating assembly is the temperature control system. The grating (of course) expands and contracts with variations in ambient temperature and while it doesn't produce any heat itself it is affected by the heat of the environment around it. The centre wavelength of each channel changes by .01 nm per degree C of change in the grating temperature.

In early versions of the IBM 9729 the grating was operated at a temperature of 22° C using a relatively simple temperature control mechanism. Later versions now operate at 29° C and use a much more sophisticated temperature controller. When the system is operated at 29° C the centre wavelengths are all shifted (increased) by .07 nm. Thus communicating pairs of IBM 9729s at opposite ends of a link *must* use the same grating temperature (because if the temperatures were different then the wavelengths would be different).

10.5.4 Laser/Receiver Cards (LRC)

The LRC cards are the tranceivers that send and receive optical signals on the common trunk. While there is no protocol sensitivity at all about the LRC card and all cards are "the same" they differ because each wavelength requires a different laser. The lasers must be manufactured for the particular wavelength they are to use.

On the transmit side a very high precision DFB laser is used. These lasers have their own feedback control of power level and individual temperature control. A limited amount of tuning (over a range of about 1 nm) is possible and this is used to fine-tune the lasers to the exact channel wavelength. Also, over time the lasers drift a bit and should be re-aligned about once per year. A square wave signal arriving from the IOC card is used to modulate the drive current of the laser directly.

The lasers are operated so that a "0" logic level is still *above* the lasing threshold. Thus the laser is transmitting a low level signal even in the zero state. This is done to reduce (almost eliminate) laser "chirp". It has the additional benefit of reducing the linewidth and thus reducing dispersion.

On the receive side the LRC card has an indium phosphide Avalanche PhotoDiode (APD). The receivers are sensitive to signals at any (and all) wavelengths used by the system. They have no way of distinguishing between signals by wavelength. Thus it is up to the grating to discriminate and select an individual signal and route it to the correct receiver. The received signal is re-shaped before sending to the IOC card but it is not re-clocked.

There is only one type of LRC card and this is used for all protocols. However, since each laser is manufactured to an exact centre wavelength LRC cards are specific to that particular wavelength. Thus there are 20 "different" LRC cards representing the 20 possible wavelengths.

The LRC cards are controlled from a central diagnostic and control processor card. At one second intervals each LRC card is checked to determine if light is being received. If there is no light at the receiver then the LRC card's laser is turned off. Intermittently, when light is not being received, the LRC card laser sends a pulse of light. At the receiver this is a signal to turn on its laser. Thus a version of the "Open Fibre Control" system is used so that no laser is allowed to transmit for very long unless a signal is being received in the other direction. This is done to increase the level of safety. (Under the current regulations this is unnecessary as the total power of all lasers in the box is less than the "Class-1" safety limit. However, it is felt that additional safety beyond that required by the regulations is worthwhile.)

10.5.5 I/O Cards (IOC)

At the present time there are three different IOC cards.

- FDDI card

  This uses an LED transmitter in the 1280-1320 nm wavelength band on MM fibre. It may also be used for 100 Mbps ATM and 100 Mbps Ethernet as these use the same optical specification as FDDI.

- ESCON card

  This also uses an LED tranceiver in the 1300 nm band on MM fibre. It may be used also for 155 Mbps OC-3 signals such as Sonet/SDH and 155 Mbps ATM.

- Inter-System Coupling (ISC) card

  This uses the IBM ISC 1.0625 Gbps protocol. Using a laser transmitter at 1310 nm this protocol uses SM fibre for attachment to the end-user system or device.

  This card recovers and regenerates the timing (clocking) of the data stream. In addition it has the OFC (Open Fibre Control) safety interlock. It may only be used for ISC protocol links.

The detailed function of the IOC depends on the particular IOC card and protocol in use.

- FDDI IOC

  Processing performed by the FDDI card is very simple indeed. The received optical signal is "cleaned up" (made into a square pulse again) and However, there is *no* clock recovery or retiming of the signal. This is an important feature as it allows the system to handle any protocol provided it uses compatible wavelengths and power levels and does not exceed the speed handling capabilities of the IOC's electronics.

- ESCON IOC

  In principle this card is the same as the FDDI card. However, it is *code sensitive*. It will handle ESCON, ESCON Timer (ETR) and OC-3 signals. The problem is that these need to be handled differently because of end-system behaviour and product requirements. For example, loss of light on an ETR timer link can have a catastrophic effect on the end system unless properly handled. In addition, some service providers wish to use the IBM 9729 to offer an ESCON interconnection service but wish to prevent the connection being used for OC-3 traffic. There is a feature present to detect the presence of OC-3 traffic and prevent it if required.

- ISC

On the Inter-System Coupling Channel (ISC), 1.0625 Gbaud protocol timing is recovered and the signal re-generated. However, the frame structure is not inspected and the code structure is not decoded. The optical signal is unchanged except for re-timing to remove the jitter. In addition this card has an "open fibre control" (OFC) system which conforms to the ISC requirements.

In the future should copper based protocols require attachment the IOC would need to decode and recode the protocol. At the present time the IBM 9729 does *not* handle this kind of protocol.

10.5.6 Dual Fibre Switching Feature

The dual fibre switching feature is a physical switch on the trunk side of the grating. It is electronically activated to switch from one trunk fibre to another when the operational trunk fails.

At one-second intervals the control module monitors the LRC cards to determine if any are receiving light. If none of the LRCs is detecting light then a switch will be made to the backup fibre. Once switched to the backup fibre the lasers are switched ON in sequence over a period of about 1 second (for safety control reasons). Thus the switchover should occur in less than 2 seconds from the active fibre being broken.

If light is not detected on the backup fibre then a switch is made back to the primary fibre. It would be possible for the 9729s at each end of a link to keep switching from one fibre to another even if both were operational. There is a protocol in place which ensures that should this happen the 9729s will synchronise with each other and make connection quickly.

10.5.7 System Engineering Considerations

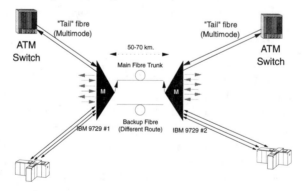

Figure 356. End-to-End Configuration

The important engineering considerations with this type of WDM system are:

1. Control of crosstalk and noise

2. Control of dispersion

3. Signal jitter

These all contribute to the signal quality available at the receiver and hence to the maximum possible distance.

10.5.7.1 Control of Crosstalk and Noise

There are many effects that can contribute to the generation of crosstalk and noise in a WDM system. These were introduced in 2.4.5, "Non-Linear High-Power Effects" on page 87. In order for a WDM system to operate correctly these effects need to be considered in the basic system design.

In the 9729 the following design characteristics contribute to minimisation of these problems:

Maximum Power Level

> The maximum power level employed both for individual optical channels and for the total is much lower than required to produce most of the non-linear effects. Each channel is transmitted at a maximum power level of -9 dBm and the total of 10 channels can never exceed 0 dBm. SBS and SRS effects require much higher power levels to become a problem.

Wavelength Selection

> Wavelengths are chosen at intervals of 1 nm (2 nm for channels travelling in the same direction). Four-wave mixing occurs at the sum and difference frequencies of the channels involved. When you use channel spacings expressed as a constant in nanometers the generated harmonics (if any) fall outside the centre wavelengths of the other channels. This is because a constant spacing in nanometres implies a *different* spacing in frequency terms.

> For example the 1 nm "gap" between the wavelengths of 1550 nm and 1551 nm represents a frequency bandwidth of 124.789 GHz. The same 1 nm gap between the wavelengths 1560 nm and 1561 nm equals 123.195 GHz.

Use of "Standard" (Non-Dispersion-Shifted) Fibre

> This is recommended even though the user is free to decide. Because of the quite large dispersion in the 1550 band when using unshifted fibre there is not a lot of time for FWM effects to build up. Of course the use of unshifted fibre brings with it an increased concern about dispersion but in practical

terms most installed fibre is unshifted (standard) and cannot be economically changed. So we need to use unshifted fibre for practical reasons anyhow.

Use of the Grating Demultiplexor

The particular type of Littrow grating demultiplexor used is extremely high in cost but offers a very high selectivity between channels. Crosstalk (introduced by the grating) is less than 55 dB.

10.5.7.2 Control of Dispersion

There are no dispersion compensating techniques as such used in the IBM 9729. The use of these techniques (such as chirped fibre Bragg gratings or dispersion compensating fibre) may be necessary when using the IBM 9729 over distances longer than about 50 km. Of course this strongly depends on the speed of the connection.

There are two principal factors:

Laser Linewidth

The "nominal" linewidth of the lasers used in the 9729 is .3 nm at 20 dB below the peak of the pulse. This is narrowed some by operating the laser just above threshold and therefore minimising the effect of chirp. Further the gratings function as wavelength selective filters and tend to narrow the linewidth.

At 1 Gbaud we can afford a maximum dispersion of 200 ps (this is 20% of a 1 ns pulse). Standard fibre has a dispersion of 17 ps/nm/km and therefore we can get to around 50 km before dispersion becomes too much of a problem.

At 200 Mbaud we can go approximately 5 times this, or about 250 km. Of course these figures are very rough guidelines and point up the need to test each proposed configuration if it in any way approaches the limits.

Dispersion can be significantly lessened and distance improved by using lasers with a narrower linewidth and external modulators. Also, special fibre with low dispersion (about 4 ps/nm/km) would allow the signal to go much farther (about 4 times) whilst avoiding interference effects. Zero dispersion fibre is not recommended because of the possibility of interference (due to FWM) between optical channels. In fact, there is very little likelihood of FWM causing a problem and the system will probably work fine on DSF but this has not been tested and so is officially not supported.

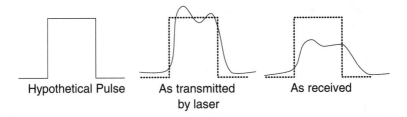

Hypothetical Pulse   As transmitted   As received
                        by laser

Figure 357. Evolution of an Optical Pulse

Pulse Re-Shaping and Re-Clocking

Signal distortion and dispersion during transmission over an optical communication system were discussed in 7.2.1.2, "Receiving the Data" on page 379. As shown in Figure 357, a "square wave" used to modulate the transmit laser will be changed quite a lot at the output of the receiver.

The overall system design of the IBM 9729 allows for user-attached equipment to be some distance from the 9729 itself. For example an FDDI device may be up to 2 km (on the downstream side) away from the 9729. Connected by MM fibre an FDDI pulse arriving at the 9729 after 2 km of travel will be significantly dispersed. If this was simply amplified and then used to modulate the laser on the LRC card the best we could hope for would be the accurate transmission of a very dispersed signal. In fact the transmit laser will add its own distortions to the signal and there will be more dispersion as the signal travels over the trunk. When received at a destination 9729 the problem would occur again and received dispersion would be propagated and compounded as the signal was re-sent out to the destination end-user.

To combat this effect the 9729 re-shapes each received signal into an electronic "square" (the corners are square) pulse. This is done through a/c (transformer) coupling of the APD output and through filtering of the signal. Thus there is jitter and some dispersion in the "cleaned up " square wave pulse as it transits the 9729.

Thus the 9729 removes much of the effect of dispersion and distortion from the pulse during its travel. However, without re-clocking the signal it cannot remove all the jitter or all of the dispersion. Therefore before using the 9729 system with end users located at significant distance (more than 100 metres) away the user should evaluate whether the introduced jitter (and dispersion) will be within acceptable limits.

10.5.7.3 *Distance Limitations*

The maximum link distance supported is 70 km for FDDI (and 100 Mbps ATM) protocols. However, this depends on the fastest single channel rate in use. A channel speed of 200 Mbps (ESCON) requires that the maximum link distance be reduced to 50 km.

In reality distance is limited by four things:

1. Fibre attenuation

   In so far as distance is primarily power limited attenuation of the fibre is a critical issue. Modern fibre has a nominal attenuation of .24 dB/km in the 1550 nm band. Installed, a good rule of thumb is .26 dB/km. However it is possible to buy very special fibre with an attenuation of only .18 dB/km. For a transmission speed of 200 Mbps the IBM 9729 has a link budget of 15 dB. The maximum distance is really the length of fibre you can get to with 15 dB attenuation.

2. Transmitter power and receiver sensitivity (link budget)

   The link budget (the amount of power you have to play with on the link) is just the difference between transmitter power and receiver sensitivity adjusted to allow for other components (such as the gratings and the connectors) and for component aging. However, you also have to consider that receiver sensitivity reduces by about 3 dB whenever you double the line speed. (See 7.4.1, "System Power Budgeting" on page 398.)

   The specifications of the IBM 9729 are as follows:

   - Transmitter power:

     - Laser diode output to pigtail: = -0.5 dBm

   - Grating loss (each grating): 6 dB (worst case)

   - Loss allowance in splices and connectors: 3 dB (each end)

   - Margin: 3 dB.

   - Receiver sensitivity:

     - -39 dBm at 200 Mbps with a BER of 10^{-12}.

     - -31 dBm at 1.06 Gbps with a BER of 10^{-12}.

3. Dispersion

   Dispersion of the pulse limits the distance because the receiver must recover a usable signal. The ability of the receiver to do this varies quite a lot with the design of the receiver itself and with the communication protocol. Dispersion is a major source of jitter.

4. Jitter

Many protocols have strict jitter requirements. The amount of jitter increases with distance due primarily to the effects of dispersion. For example Sonet/SDH protocol has very strict jitter requirements which are hard to meet. Other protocols (such as 100 Mbps ATM) have much less stringent jitter requirements.

The above are the factors involved in limiting the usable distance of the optical signal. **There are many other factors introduced by "higher layer" protocols which also limit the distance.** These limitations are a reflection of the necessary time delay involved in signal propagation. The signal travels at about 2/3rds of the speed of light (that is about 5 microseconds per kilometer of travel) in each direction. While this seems very fast it can provide a significant limitation for some devices and systems. For example:

- Device timing constraints limit the distance on some ESCON devices to distances significantly less than the capability of the IBM 9729.

- Ethernet-100 can be used as a point-to-point protocol connecting LAN switches or routers. In this application use of Ethernet-100 over a long link with WDM can be highly practical and cost-effective. However, if an Ethernet-100 connection is used as a part of an Ethernet "collision domain" (that is, if you operate the connection as part of a regular Ethernet LAN) then the maximum distance between any two devices in that domain is 200 metres!

The important fact here is that the maximum distance for any particular proposed application *could* be significantly less than the distance allowed by the IBM 9729.

10.5.8 Network Management

A system overview of IBM 9729 network management is shown in Figure 358 on page 624. Within each 9729 there is a "Diagnostic Card". This is a microprocessor which is able to monitor many aspects of the internal functioning of the 9729. This processor maintains information about status and accepts some control commands from the management system.

Each 9729 is managed by a PC or workstation directly connected to the diagnostic card using an RS-232 interface. This PC runs the Simple Network Management Protocol (SNMP) agent and subagent software. The subagent software interacts with the diagnostic card to gather status information (in the form of MIBs - Management Information Blocks) and to relay control commands.

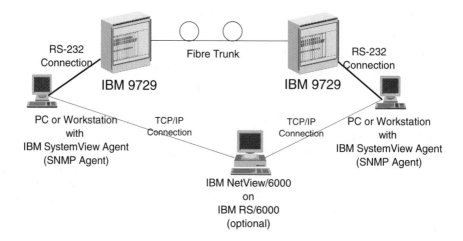

Figure 358. IBM 9729 Network Management Configuration

The SNMP agent software is a TCP/IP end user which interrogates the sub-agent and interfaces with the end user via a screen and keyboard and with an (optional) organisation wide network management system.

All the IBM 9729s in an organisation may be managed (together with the rest of the organisation's network equipment) through a centrally located workstation (IBM RS/6000) running IBM NetView/6000 software. This central management system is optional.

10.5.9 Systems Potential

The first implementations of the IBM 9729 are simple point-to-point multiplexing which are aimed at saving the cost of having multiple fibres. But there is an interesting possibility of interconnecting many of them into a network such as is shown in Figure 359 on page 625.

This suggests the possibility of a type of network midway between today's electronic networks and tomorrow's all optical ones.

- In today's world, optical fibres are just used as "optical wire" where an optical fibre replaces an electric wire for long-distance interconnection and nothing much else changes. ATM and SDH networks fall into this category.

- In the future we expect to have wide area networks with fully optical routing from end-to-end but this seems some years away. This was discussed earlier in 10.1.5.3, "Nodal Networks" on page 581.

- Connecting IBM 9729s into a network configuration gives a compromise solution which could be implemented today. That is, we construct a multiple-wavelength optical network *but use electronic switching at the nodes*. This gives many of the advantages (especially the increased bandwidth) of the fully optical approach in a technique that can be implemented today.

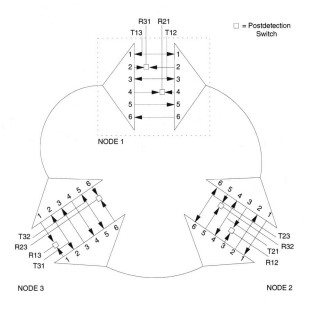

Figure 359. IBM 9729 Ring Network

This compromise solution could in fact be quite attractive if specially designed opto-electronic components were used for the crosspoints. IBM research is exploring this kind of architecture (see Green 1994). The figure shows a simple ring configuration. Other configurations (of arbitrary complexity) are possible but then there is a significant problem in network control and path allocation, etc.

10.6 Architecture of a First-Generation WDM for the WAN

In 1996 and 1997 many of the world's long distance telephone companies installed experimental WDM equipment in operational trials. What follows is a description of one trial system. It is interesting and instructive as it illustrates a very simple but not always obvious approach.

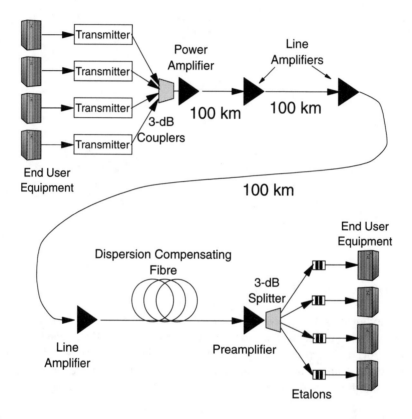

Figure 360. *First Generation WAN WDM System - Architecture. One direction only is shown. An identical equipment configuration is used in the opposite direction.*

Objectives

The primary objective of using WDM in the terrestrial WAN environment is to gain higher bandwidth on the fibre. Although it is possible to operate a single-channel optical system at 10 Gbps this is quite costly. Firstly, the cost of equipment involved is very high and second amplifier spacings have to be much closer together (than for operation at lower speeds) and hence many more amplifiers are needed on a link. Housing and maintaining amplifiers at intermediate points on a WAN link is very costly indeed.

It is economically attractive to use a WDM approach with multiple 2.4 Gbps channels. However, the objective is not the independence of channels, it is increased capacity. All end-user equipment will be Sonet/SDH.

Design Overview

The overall characteristics of the system are as follows:

1. Four channels at 2.4 Gbps.

   As a first generation "trial" system only four channels are needed.

2. WDM link distance is 310 km.

3. Channel spacings are 3.6 nm in the 1550 nm band to conform to the ITU standard wavelengths.

4. Dual fibres are used (one in each direction) and as the system has to operate on installed fibre it is designed for use with standard fibre.

5. To get to the required distance of 300 km amplifiers are needed at spacings of around 100-120 km.

6. The technical design uses amplifiers rather than sophisticated and complex optical devices such as gratings or WGRs. This is what makes the system interesting.

7. Because of the fact that most of the equipment will be sited in locations where human access is either limited or difficult, network management must be excellent.

The Transmitters

The transmitters receive their input from the end-user equipment on single-mode fibre in the 1310 band. This is the operating wavelength of the Sonet/SDH equipment. The signal is received (with a PIN diode receiver) and converted to an electrical signal.

Trunk lasers are DFB type with a linewidth of around .1 nm. These are stabilised in wavelength by the use of Peltier coolers. The lasers transmit all the time and the modulation is introduced externally by using modulators of the Mach-Zehnder type on lithium niobate. Modulators of this kind were described in 5.9.8, "Modulation Using a Mach-Zehnder Interferometer" on page 323.

External modulation is used here to minimise the effects of laser chirp. This is not too much of a problem for the WDM characteristics of the system but chirp broadens the linewidth of the signal and thus increases dispersion. Dispersion is a problem in this system (2.4 Gbps for 300 km on standard fibre).

Mixing the Signals

Signal mixing is accomplished by the use of simple 3 dB couplers as discussed in 5.4.1.3, "3 dB Couplers" on page 240. This will have an insertion loss of about 8 dB (excess loss of 2 dB).

Transmission Issues

After the signal is mixed it is amplified by a power amplifier such that each channel has a power level of about 3 mw (4 dBm).

Potential problems with FWM and SRS are minimised by keeping the signal power (per channel) to a maximum of 3 mw, using a wide (3.6 nm) channel spacing and by using standard fibre for the link.

Line Amplifiers

Amplifiers are used to boost the signal at approximately 100 km intervals. Thus a gain of about 30 dB is needed. In this system of only 4 cascaded amplifiers gain flatness is important but not absolutely critical. Flattened response amplifiers are used.

Dispersion Compensation

Since the distance is over 300 km on standard fibre some form of dispersion compensation is necessary. In this case a reel of dispersion compensating fibre is used at one end of the link. Because of the attenuation in the DCF an additional line amplifier is needed to boost the signal through the additional fibre.

Demultiplexing the Signal

At the receiver end the signal is split into four identical mixed (WDM) signals by the use of 3 dB couplers. This reduces the signal level by about 8 dB. As the signal was already very low it was pre-amplified before being split up.

Each of the four WDM streams are then sent to individual Fabry-Perot Etalons (filters) which pass only the desired wavelength for the specific channel.

Connection to the End-User Equipment

The demultiplexed signal is then sent on SM fibre directly to the end-user equipment. This is a very surprising thing BUT it works well and has some key advantages.

The end-user equipment is Sonet/SDH and was designed for operation in the 1310 nm band. The signal being sent to it from the WDM demultiplexor is in the 1550 nm band! The fact is that this works. However, it is perfectly possible to build a receiver that works well in the 1310 band and will not "see" a 1550 signal at all! It seems however that manufacturers of Sonet/SDH equipment have chosen receivers that are sensitive to light at 1550 nm.

In principle this appears to be simply a cost-cutting measure. However, there is a major advantage. To convert the signal (unnecessarily) back to the 1550 nm band before sending to the end-user involves receiving it, converting to an electronic signal and then re-transmitting. This process adds noise and (more importantly) jitter to the signal. The jitter tolerance of a 2.4 Gbps Sonet/SDH signal is very tight and any increase in jitter would add to the error rate of the system.

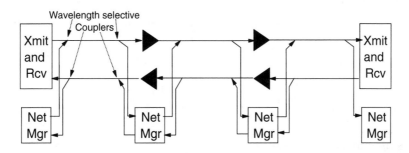

Figure 361. *Network Management Channel*

Network Management Out-of-Band Channel

An additional WDM channel is carried (in the 1310 nm band) to provide an independent connection for network monitoring and management. The principle is illustrated in Figure 361.

Wavelength selective resonant couplers are used to multiplex the 1310 nm signal onto the WDM trunk. This is done with very little loss.

Superficially, with fibre attenuation at 1310 (.4 dB/km) much higher than attenuation in the 1550 band we would have a problem with operational distance. (The 1310 signal couldn't go as far as the 1550 ones and hence this would limit our amplifier spacings.) This problem is mitigated in a number of ways:

1. The NM channel doesn't need to be very fast, 16 Mbps in this example. This means that the receivers can be much more sensitive than ones used at the higher rates of the WDM signals.

2. The NM channel doesn't transit the entire distance of the WDM link. It is "dropped off" and regenerated at every amplifier site. (This is necessary so we can manage the amplifier.)

3. Signal power used here can be quite high and we can use a much wider linewidth signal. This is because we don't have the potential crosstalk issues that exist between the WDM channels. The wide linewidth significantly reduces the possibility of any crosstalk with the WDM stream and is fine since the fibre in use has its dispersion zero at 1310 nm.

10.7 Further Reading

Anthony S. Acampora (1994)

The Scalable Lightwave Network: IEEE Communications Magazine, December 1994. pp 36-42

S. Aisawa et al. (1997)

Ultra-Wide Band, Long Distance WDM Transmission Demonstration: 1 Tb/s (50 x 20 Gb/s), 600 km Transmission Using 1550 and 1580 nm Wavelength Bands: OFC'97 Postdeadline paper.

Neal S. Bergano et al. (1997)

320 Gb/s WDM Transmission (64x5 Gb/s) over 7,200 km using Large Mode Fibre Spans and Chirped Return-to-Zero Signals: OFC'97 Postdeadline paper.

Charles A. Brackett (1990)

Dense Wavelength Division Multiplexing Networks: Principles and Applications: IEEE Journal on Selected Areas in Communications, Vol 8, No 6, August 1990. pp 948-964

Peter J. Chidgey (1994)

Multi-Wavelength Transport Networks: IEEE Communications Magazine, December 1994. pp 28-35

Nicholas R. Dono, Paul E. Green, Karen Liu, Rajiv Ramaswami and Franklin Fuk-Kay Tong (1990)

A Wavelength Division Multiple Access Network for Computer Communication: IEEE J. of Selected Topics on Selected Areas in Communications, Vol 8, No 6, August 1990. pp 983-993

Kai Y. Eng, Mario A. Santoro, Thomas L. Koch, J. Stone and W.W. Snell (1990)

Star-Coupler-Based Optical Cross-Connect Switch Experiments with Tunable Receivers: IEEE Journal on Selected Areas in Communication, Vol 8, No 6, August 1990. pp 1026-1030

Steven G. Finn and Richard A. Barry (1996)

Optical Services in Future Broadband Networks: IEEE Network, November/December 1996. pp 7-13

Ori Gerstel (1996)

On the Future of Wavelength Routing Networks: IEEE Network, November/December 1996. pp 15-20

Matthew S. Goodman (1989)

Multiwavelength Networks and New Approaches to Packet Switching: IEEE Communications Magazine, October 1989. pp 27-35

Matthew S. Goodman et al. (1990)

The LAMBDANET Multiwavelength Network: Architecture, Applications and Demonstrations: IEEE Journal on Selected Areas in Communications, Vol 8, No 6, August 1990. pp 995-1003

P. E. Green (1992)

An All-Optical Computer Network: Lessons Learned: IEEE Network, March 1992. pp 56-60

Paul S. Henry (1989)

High-Capacity Lightwave Local Area Networks: IEEE Communications Magazine, October 1989. pp 20-26

Godfrey R. Hill (1989)

Wavelength Domain Optical Network Techniques: Proceedings of the IEEE, Vol 7, No 1, January 1989. pp 121-132

Leonid G. Kazovsky, Thomas Fong and Tad Hofmeister (1994)

Optical Local Area Network Technologies: IEEE Communications Magazine, December 1994. pp 50-54

A.K. Srivastava et al. (1997)

1 Tb/s Transmission of 100 WDM 10 Gb/s Channels over 400 km of TrueWave Fiber: OFC'97 Postdeadline paper.

Chapter 11. Fibre In The (Local) Loop - FITL

The connection between the local telephone exchange and the end user is called the "local loop". This is by far the largest and most pervasive communications environment in the world. There are in the world a few hundred million local loop connections.

Until quite recently there have been only two forms of local loop:

1. Telephone network connections

2. Cable television connections

These have formed separate and distinct local loop networks. However, times are changing. New services such as "video-on-demand" and high-speed Internet access require vast increases in local loop capacity. A new competitive commercial environment has brought the desire to provide all of these services from a single multi-function network.

The existing local loop plant around the world when looked at as a single investment is the world's most valuable artifact. Replacing it with a better technology will not be easy or low in cost. However, change is beginning and many people believe that fibre optical technology can play a major role in the new local loop network.

11.1.1 System Requirements

The new local loop networks need to handle a wide variety of new applications and types of traffic. Some of these are summarised below:

Analogue Television Distribution

> This is perhaps the most basic requirement. Required bandwidth is 500 MHz. The television signals are subcarrier multiplexed into a single 500 Mhz wide signal. Traffic is one-way only (from distribution hub to end-user). All the signal streams sent out to every end user are the same!

Video "On-Demand"

> This application is where the end user orders a movie and it is played immediately to the individual end user. Again this is one-way for the movie but a channel in the user-to-network direction is needed to communicate commands such as movie selection, pause and rewind etc.

> Bandwidth required could be analogue as part of a subcarrier multiplexed broadcast signal (for example channel allocations above 500 MHz could be used). Indeed this is what is done in some HFC systems.

The video program originates on a server disk somewhere and is stored in compressed form to save disk storage space. This will typically be in the MPEG-2 format with a maximum data rate of around 6 Mbps. This could be delivered as a 6 Mbps (maximum) variable rate digital data stream all the way to the end user.

Interactive "Personal" Video Telephone

Some people consider this the "killer" application because it makes living away from a major city environment significantly easier. Apart from the obvious social advantages it makes working from home significantly more effective. Also, it makes possible things like remote medical diagnosis etc.

This application requires a different amount of bandwidth depending on the desired quality. Some people consider that 128 kbps can deliver an adequate quality. Many (arguably adequate) video-conference systems use only 384 kbps. However, for really good quality this application needs a bi-directional 2 Mbps of bandwidth. In addition end-to-end transit delays must be kept to a minimum as interactive discourse is difficult if the delay exceeds a few hundred milliseconds.

Video Conferencing

Video conferencing has the same basic requirements as personal video conferencing described above. However, the quality needs to be good and you also need a hub somewhere where the signals can be combined to produce a single image for the end user.

Home Shopping

The concept here is for highly graphic images of goods to be displayed on demand with a very fast response time. In many cases this will be a moving image. In this case the system demand can be up to a few megabits per second. However there is no problem with system jitter or end-to-end delays as the user is able to wait a few seconds before a movie sequence is displayed for example. Of course, a channel from the user to the system (in the upstream direction) is necessary both so that the user can search for goods and (very important) so they can place orders.

Plain Old Telephone Service (POTS)

If we have a high bandwidth system we would like to use it for regular telephone (and regular modem) traffic as well. This is a very low bandwidth application (64 kbps digital will do it nicely) but has critical end-to-end delay restrictions. In addition, we are all used to powering the telephone from the network. Telephones are used in emergencies and they need to be available when local power is lost. This is a significant challenge.

High-Speed Internet Access

Currently Internet access is regarded as perhaps the major short-term application. WWW in many peoples minds stands for "wait wait wait" rather than world wide web! Two megabits full duplex is regarded as a benchmark (provided the network infrastructure and the application servers can support this speed.) There is little requirement here to minimise jitter. Most traffic is client/server and jitter can be buffered out. (Of course this will change if Internet telephones or interactive video over Internet become in any way serious!)

Future Digital Television (or HDTV)

Some time in the future television broadcasting (and cable systems) will change to a digital standard. This will require significantly more bandwidth per channel than the analogue system. There are many systems alternatives here but the good news is that transmission may be digital and therefore it will be easier to integrate with other traffic.

11.1.2 The Existing Telephone Network

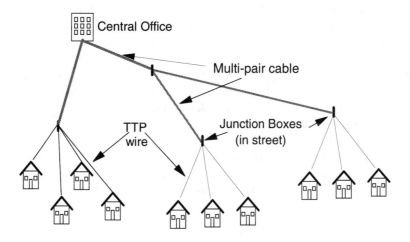

Figure 362. Traditional Telephone Local-Loop Cabling

The telephone network "local loop" consists of point-to-point connections between end users (typically householders) and a "central office" (telephone exchange). These connections take the form of thin copper wire (24 or 26 gauge) twisted pairs. Their maximum length is typically between 4 km and 7 km depending on the wire thickness although the average length is significantly shorter than this (1-2 km).

At the entry point to the Central Office (CO) wires are typically contained in cables of up to 600 pairs. These cables terminate in junction boxes in the street where other (smaller) cables take the connection to other junction boxes and ultimately to the end user's location (home).

This topology is fine for analogue voice communication. Because the analogue voice signal is very narrowband, over the years installed systems have developed many undesirable characteristics. These characteristics don't affect the voice signal too much but provide a very significant limitation for use as a high speed distribution system.

In the late 1980's a digital system was developed using this wire called "Narrowband Integrated Services Digital Network" (n-ISDN). This gives a bi-directional digital connection of 144 kbps.

Today using very sophisticated signal processing techniques (DMT and CAP)[117] a system called variously HDSL, ADSL, VDSL or xDSL has been developed. Hi-speed Digital Subscriber Line (HDSL) provides a full-duplex (bi-directional) data channel at 2 Mbps on an existing subscriber loop connection. Asymmetric Digital Subscriber Line (ADSL) allows 6 Mbps in one direction (from the central office to the user) and 384 kbps in the other. Very High Speed DSL (VDSL) allows up to 20 Mbps in the downstream direction but requires much shorter cable distances (such as 200 metres). xDSL is just a generic way of talking about all of the others.

In proposed systems (prototype HDSL modems are available today) the digital signal is sent over the existing telephone line *without affecting the existing telephone itself*! That is, you can still use an analogue telephone in the traditional way at the same time as the wire is being used for xDSL transmissions.

The xDSL protocols are however about the limit of copper twisted pair local loop technology. This is adequate today for high-speed home Internet access and for single-channel video-on-demand but may not be adequate for much else.

---

[117] DMT is described further in Dutton and Lenhard (1996).

11.1.3 Cable Television Networks

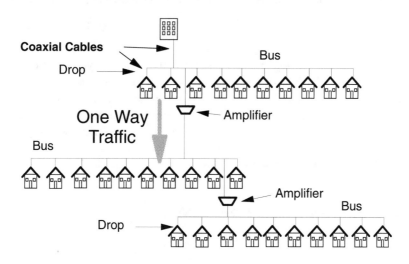

Figure 363. *Traditional Cable TV System Cabling*

The Cable Television industry was born out of the desire of groups of people for good quality television reception. In the early days of television people got together and set up "Community Antenna TV" (CATV). This was just a number of households setting up a common antenna to improve TV reception for themselves. After a while people realised that you could put other (non-broadcast) program sources onto the cable and the cable TV industry was born.

Figure 363 shows the typical cabling structure of a traditional cable network. A coaxial cable passes along a street and houses are "dropped" from it. Amplifiers are used to boost the signal from one street to another.

This system is a one-way distribution system. No communication (on the cable) is possible upstream from the house to the central office (distribution centre). At its peak systems like this extended for many kilometres from the distribution centre and the signal was amplified up to 7 times along its path. Some cable systems got to a size where a single cable from the distribution centre supported up to 200,000 homes! Of course, this meant that if the cable was broken close to the distribution centre all of the connected homes lost their service!

This raises the general question of service quality. CATV networks are traditionally not designed for high levels of system availability. The signal is *only* television - entertainment. We don't tend to mind too much if the service is lost for a day or two occasionally. So CATV networks in the field are usually installed to much lower levels of quality than the telephone service. But what if we want to put telephone onto the cable? Clearly the cable system will have to be upgraded to significantly higher levels of reliability.

In principle, the signal on the cable is just the same signal as you get from a regular TV antenna - just the broadcast signal. This signal contains frequencies up to 500 MHz. In recent years simple encryption has been used to provide the ability to charge different rates for different levels of service (additional channels etc.) and the set-top box appeared as the interface between the TV set itself and the cable.

Today most traditional cable systems have been upgraded to "Hybrid Fibre-Coax" systems which are discussed next.

11.1.4 Hybrid Fibre-Coax (HFC) Networks

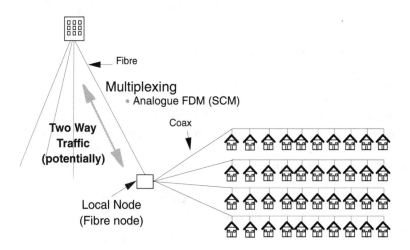

Figure 364. Hybrid Fibre-Coax (HFC) Network Cabling

An HFC system is a development of the traditional cable system. Users are connected to a coaxial (copper) cable "bus" in the street just as in a regular cable system. The difference is that the signal is now sent from the distribution centre to "the end of the street" on single-mode fibre! This gives a number of very significant improvements:

1. The area served can be a long way (up to 100 km) from the central office.

2. Signal quality is significantly improved since there is no longer a cascade of electronic amplifiers involved.

3. Reliability is significantly improved since there can be fewer end users on a single connection to the central office. (Usually this is only around 2000 but can still go as high as 20,000 in areas of high density population such as in a major city.)

The characteristics of this connection are unique. It is the *only* widespread use of analogue modulation of communications lasers! The technique is called "subcarrier multiplexing" (SCM). The signal is prepared in the distribution centre *exactly* as though it was to be put directly onto the cable. That is, many RF subcarriers are mixed and a single composite stream with a bandwidth of 500 MHz is produced. This stream is then used to modulate a laser transmitter using analogue modulation! As described elsewhere in this book analogue modulation of a laser's injection current is very difficult because of non-linearities in the laser's response. Practical systems do modulate the laser's injection current although in recent times external modulators have begun to be used. The lasers involved are specially designed for this application. This is the major common use of analogue modulation of an optical signal (in communications systems). A second use exists for mobile telephone base stations as described in 11.2, "Mobile Telephone Base Station" on page 647.

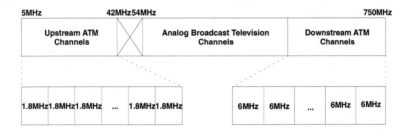

Figure 365. *Proposed Spectrum Allocation for Bi-Directional HFC*

HFC is increasingly used for communication with individual end users. This communication can be fully bi-directional as in the case of Internet access or primarily only one way with a backward control channel as in the video-on-demand application. In order to achieve this HFC is enhanced in the following ways:

- The bandwidth of the communications system is increased to 750 MHz (in some systems 1 GHz). This requires a significantly higher standard of cable installation practice than has been traditional in the industry.

- Bandwidth above the 500 MHz line is allocated for additional upstream and downstream channels. Figure 365 shows one scheme for allocating bandwidth on the cable.[118]

- A new protocol is introduced to allow the sharing of the common bus medium (in the upstream direction) by multiple sources. (This is the hard part.)

- Additional fibres are needed to carry traffic in the upstream direction. (It is possible to carry the upstream signal on the same fibre as the downstream one but in general this is not done.)

- To access the system each end user (house) needs a "cable modem" which is an RF device which places the upstream traffic onto the cable according to the rules of the MAC (medium access control) protocol.

HFC is attractive because it is an extension of an existing system and costs are relatively low. However, the shared nature of the end-user connection provides a significant limitation for future increases in speed or function.

This shared nature of the cable combined with the need for individual point-to-point communication with end users means that far fewer houses can be accommodated on one connection. What happens here therefore is that the service area of the HFC connection is broken up into many smaller service areas. Each of these smaller areas now requires its own dedicated upstream fibre to the distribution centre (central office). However, each fibre node is probably housed in the same physical location. This leads to the need for parallel point-to-point connections between the fibre node location and the distribution centre. WDM multiplexing is an obvious advantage here as it saves having large numbers of parallel fibres.

11.1.5 Fibre-to-the-Curb/Street/Neighbourhood (FTTC/FTTS/FTTN)

As mentioned above, HFC has a severe inherent limitation in the fact that it uses a shared medium (a bus cable) for end user access. Many people believe that this is not adequate for the long term. The suggestion is to use radial cabling in the street such that there is a dedicated connection for each end user. This gives extremely high capacity to each user and improves reliability and manageability but at increased cost. This has been called "Fibre-To-The-Curb" but the last word is often replaced to indicate a larger or smaller service area.

---

118 At the time of writing there is no approved standard for this allocation.

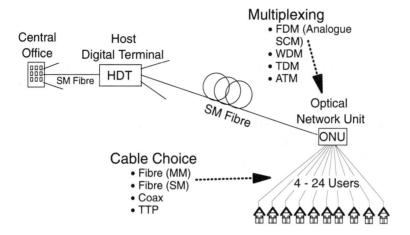

Figure 366. Fibre-to-the-Curb Cabling Alternatives

Figure 366 shows the general architecture and various alternative protocols that might be used for parts of the system. *So far while there are trial FTTC systems in operation in various parts of the world there is no generally deployed system anywhere.*

Three things seem generally agreed about FTTC systems:

1. The need for a large bandwidth from the distribution centre to the end user for carrying traditional broadcast TV services.   Many people feel that the most cost-effective way of handling this is as a traditional analogue signal.

2. The use of SM fibre from the distribution centre to the curb.

3. The need for primarily radial connections between the end users and the distribution centre (central office).

Most of the other system parameters are certainly not agreed. Probably the first is the choice of cable to be used from the local fibre node to the end user:

Coaxial Cable

> Coax has been used in trials (see the next section on the Cambridge Trial). It is low cost and a well known technology. It has a bandwidth over short distances of in excess of 1 GHz and simple modulation techniques may be used. Most of the end-user equipment can be very close to or the same as for HFC. However, coax is bulky and heavy. This makes it difficult to use for star type cabling in the suburban environment.

Telephone Twisted Pair (TTP)

TTP (traditional telephone wire) has been used in FTTC trials in a number of places. For very short distances (such as 50 metres) you can get quite high speeds (around 50 MHz) without special signal processing or coding. If techniques like VDSL are used much higher speeds (up to 20 Mbps) may be obtained over longer distances (200 to 500 metres).

If cable is to be installed new, UTP class 5 may be used which roughly triples the bandwidth potential over existing TTP. However, the big attraction of using TTP is in very densely populated areas where existing wire may be re-used for the new system. In high-rise urban living situations this can be very important as the bulk of coax may make it unusable.

Multimode Fibre

Fibre is of course the best technical solution. In this case where distances are almost always less than 500 metres multimode (even step-index) would be perfectly adequate. However, GI multimode fibre is relatively expensive compared to single mode.

Plastic Fibre and HPCS

This is lower in bandwidth than standard MM glass fibre but the cost of joining it in the field and of pigtailing devices is significantly lower than for standard MM.

Single-Mode Fibre

This is of course the best technical environment but it is also the most costly. Single-mode fibre itself is very low in cost. The major cost is in attaching devices to it (pigtailing). In a truly passive optical network SM fibre is almost a requirement here. This is discussed further in 11.1.6, "Passive Optical Networks (PONs)" on page 645.

Then there is the question of how to share the upstream connection between local node and distribution centre. In this case probably WDM is the technology of choice since the reason we are using FTTC is to give a very large capacity to each end user and at the present time it is difficult to get much more than 2.5 Gbps on a single channel otherwise.

However, within each WDM channel we need to further sub-multiplex. For this there are many possible techniques. However, for standard TV distribution subcarrier (analogue) multiplexing seems to be the technology of choice where packet (or cell) multiplexing using ATM seems to be the choice for digital communication.

11.1.5.1 The Cambridge Trial

In 1996 an interesting FTTC distribution system was trialed in Cambridge in the UK. While the connection to the end-user (houses) was through standard TV coaxial cable, the network structure is innovative and interesting. It is a good pointer to what may happen in the future with optical networks.

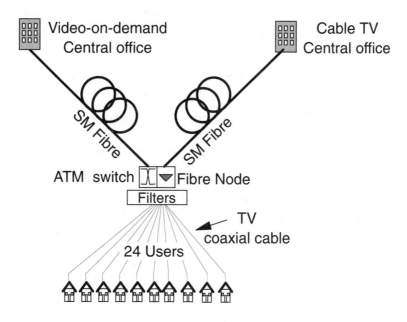

Figure 367. *Cambridge Trial Network - Structure*

The important characteristics of the network are as follows:

Connection to the End-User

> As shown in Figure 367 connection to the end user is radial (point-to-point) from a distribution hub in an equipment cabinet located in a restricted local area. Thus it is an FTTC system.

> Each end-user is connected to the hub by a point-to-point TV coaxial cable. This is the expensive part since to cable a street you have to have many cables travelling together from the distribution hub to each house. However, TV coax at the distances involved is a very high bandwidth medium (competitive in bandwidth capability with MM fibre).

Distribution Hub Equipment

Each hub has two separate pieces of equipment:

1. A "fibre node" exactly as in an HFC system

   This node receives a one-way optical signal from a cable distribution centre using SCM. The signal is received, made electronic, amplified and placed onto every end-user cable connection.

2. An ATM switch

   This switch is connected upstream to a distribution point of its own (which could be a different point from the cable TV distribution point).

There is an ATM point-to-point connection from this switch to each end-user. Each end-user has a dedicated connection. However, the ATM connection and the CATV connection share the same coaxial cable to the end-user.

Sharing the End-User Connection

The cable to the end-user is shared by electronic frequency division multiplexing (FDM). Of course all of the TV channels are FDM anyway but the ATM connection is added as a "baseband" onto the cable. This ATM connection is allocated the frequency space from 0-30 MHz on the cable and it is used in *both directions*.

To implement this passive electronic filtering is used.

At a technical level the system works very well.

- The 25 Mbps ATM connection to every home is plenty of bandwidth for all of the network services listed earlier in this chapter.

- Upstream connection of the ATM switch is through a 155 Mbps SM fibre connection.

- Video-on-demand is delivered in compressed form (using MPEG compression) at a variable rate up to 4 Mbps.

- Standard TV distribution is exactly the same as always.

- There is no telephone on the system although it would be very easy to add.

This system could be a real pointer to the future. Although it uses a significant amount of electronics in the distribution hubs (an ATM switch!), the switches are low in capacity, restricted in function and in consequence very low in cost. If the coaxial cable to the end-user was replaced with a MM fibre using CD lasers we would have a very interesting system indeed.

11.1.6 Passive Optical Networks (PONs)

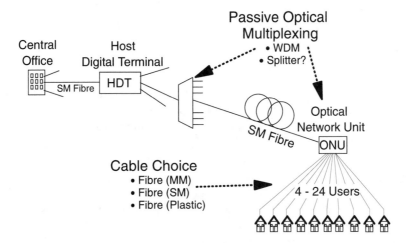

Figure 368. *Passive Optical Network - Potential Solutions*

It seems generally agreed that if a cost-effective way can be found to build one then a totally passive optical network would be the best long-term solution for the access network. The reasons for this assessment are as follows:

1. Such a network is assumed to have a very high bandwidth (at least potentially) for each end user. This would allow for future (unforeseen) high-bandwidth applications.

2. A network with no active components in it is likely to have a very much reduced need for maintenance. (Passive components go wrong less often than active ones.) Thus it is likely to be very reliable.

3. Passive network equipment requires a lot less maintenance than does active equipment. Therefore it does not need to be easily accessible for maintenance. This makes it possible to site equipment so that it is less accessible to vandals etc. Of course you still need access sometimes - but it doesn't have to be quite so convenient.

4. In any real PON you will probably need amplifiers within the network. The presence of these would mean that the network was no longer very passive. However, remote pumping might be a possible solution to the desire to remove all the electronics.

One characteristic that is key to local loop networks is that they change a lot. New users are added and old ones removed very frequently. Cables (even buried ones) are cut or broken relatively often for reasons unrelated to the system. For example the cable might be cut or damaged by someone digging a trench to install a water pipe or by someone constructing a new driveway or by a motor accident knocking down a telephone pole. So it is very important that any new local loop technology be very easy to install and maintain. In this respect fibre is significantly more difficult (and more expensive) than copper cable.

So far, there have been many proposed PON designs reported in the scientific literature but few (if any) field trials and there have been no PON systems deployed. The major reason for this has been the very high capital cost of fibre equipment and devices. It would be easily possible today to build a PON using WDM technology and SM fibre that satisfied all of the requirements. However, it would probably cost in excess of thirty or forty thousand US dollars per user! We need a system that costs a few hundred dollars per user (for capital equipment). We are assuming that the installation cost will be similar no matter which detailed system design is used.

11.1.6.1 Alternative Architectures

When a PON is first suggested many people conclude that the network would provide a "clear channel" bi-directional connection from the CO to the end-user using some form of WDM. While this is an ideal, there are many alternatives.

If for example, the ONU[119] was a simple optical splitter, then both downstream and upstream connections would be shared. This would be logically similar to the HFC system described earlier in 11.1.4, "Hybrid Fibre-Coax (HFC) Networks" on page 638. In this design, although users are not strung from a "bus" cable running down the street, they are logically connected to a bus at the ONU (which becomes a hub). Access protocol schemes similar to those used in HFC would need to be used here. A TDM scheme may be used in the upstream direction to give users shared access to the system.

Such a scheme might send downstream TV channels as a single SCM channel in the 1300 nm band. It may then use a single SCM channel to contain many (digitally modulated) downstream end-user connections in the 1550 nm band. Upstream could be handled in the 1500 nm band by TDM.

---

[119] Optical network unit

11.2 Mobile Telephone Base Station

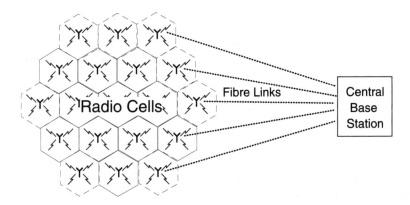

Figure 369. *Mobile Cellular Telephone System with Remote Central Base Station*

The burgeoning growth of Personal Communications Systems (PCS) such as mobile telephone and mobile data services is presenting a significant problem to network operators.

PCS systems are made up of small geographic areas called "cells". Each cell can be from a few kilometers in diameter (in areas of low demand) to only a few hundred metres in diameter (in areas of high demand). Each cell has its own radio base station. Frequencies (wavelengths) used in each cell are different from those used by adjacent cells but the same frequencies are re-used many times throughout the system. This is the way we get a large number of channels from a small available frequency spectrum.

As the system acquires more and more users cells are made smaller and smaller to accommodate the traffic. This brings a major problem. The base station equipment must be placed in a secure, well maintained location where access is easy for service personnel. Siting of base station equipment is costly and difficult.

A very attractive alternative is to use the configuration illustrated in Figure 369. The base station is placed in a central location (the Central Base Station) and the antenna is placed in the field. This allows for the siting of many (perhaps all the stations for a city area) stations in a central location where full-time staff can be available for maintenance and where spare parts etc. can be stored.

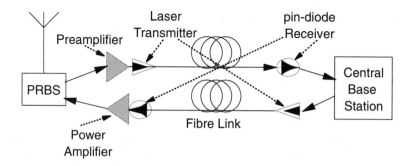

Figure 370. Communication System - Logical View

In order to make the antenna system remote a fibre connection using subcarrier multiplexing (SCM) is used between the CBS and the PRBS (Passive Radio Base Station) in the field. This is shown in Figure 370. This is the same type of communication as was described earlier for HFC.

- The base station operates quite normally as it would if it were sited within its cell.

- The signal *exactly* constructed as if it were to be placed directly on the antenna (but of course *not* at full power) is used to modulate an optical carrier. This is analogue modulation and requires either a very special laser or a carefully designed external modulator for communication to be satisfactory (you need a linear response).

- At the remote antenna (the PRBS) the signal is received on a simple pin diode receiver, fed to a power amplifier and thence directly to the antenna.

- In the reverse direction the same process occurs.

- The signal received on the antenna is filtered to make sure that only signals within the band of interest are present, amplified, and used to modulate an optical signal.

- Back at the base station the signal is received on a pin diode and fed back to a standard (unmodified) base station receiver.

This allows for the minimum equipment to be kept at the antenna site and therefore provides high reliability and low cost.

As the density of connections builds up it is expected that WDM will be used to share fibre links out in the network.

11.2.1.1 Non-Mobile Radio

It is obvious that the structure described above supporting mobile telephones could equally well be used to support fixed telephones. Around the world there is considerable interest in doing this as there is a big cost saving in removing the need for the dedicated wired (or fibred) connection to the end-user. It has been canvased as a competitor for wired connections.

Logically it is the same structure as described earlier in 11.1.5, "Fibre-to-the-Curb/Street/Neighbourhood (FTTC/FTTS/FTTN)" on page 640 with the cable connection between the ONU and the user replaced by a radio link. However a system like this would not be a very high-bandwidth technology. It would be a good technology for telephone and very low speed data connection and may well offer a lower cost than fixed installations.[120]

11.3 Further Reading

Yih-Kang Maurice Lin, Dan R. Spears and Mih Lin (1989)

> *Fibre-Based Local Access Network Architectures*: IEEE Communications Magazine, October 1989. pp 64-73

Nicholas J. Frigo (1996)

> *Local Access Optical Networks*: IEEE Network, November/December 1996. pp 32-36

---

[120] The cost of the mobile application is significantly increased by the need to support user mobility. If the users are not mobile the system cost is significantly lower.

Chapter 12. Research Directions

12.1 Solitons

Some researchers (Mollenauer, 1991) are working on a novel method of propagating pulses in a fibre without dispersion. The word "soliton" is a contraction of the phrase "solitary solution" because the phenomenon represents a single solution to the propagation equation. Also, in physics, particles tend to be named with the suffix -on (electron, proton, neutron, photon...) and the word soliton therefore suggests particle-like behavior.

In the optical communications world there is immense interest in solitons. This is due to the fact that solitons travel without dispersion of any kind on standard (highly dispersive) fibre. There is no need for dispersion compensation no matter how great the distance travelled. One of the consequences of this is that it becomes possible to have single-channel data streams of between 100 and 200 Gbps! In addition, in a WDM system there is little (some but small) interaction between channels using solitons.

The effect works as follows:

- Chromatic dispersion in standard fibre at wavelengths longer than 1310 nm causes shorter wavelengths to travel faster than longer ones. Thus a pulse composed of many wavelengths tends to disperse such that the shorter wavelengths tend to move towards the beginning of the pulse. This is called the "anomalous dispersion regime".

- The presence of light in a fibre at a sufficiently high intensity causes a very slight transient *change* (decrease) to the refractive index of glass.

- Light travels faster in glass of a lower refractive index.

- Thus if a pulse is intense enough to modify the RI the phase and frequency of light within the pulse are changed. This is called self-phase modulation (SPM) and is caused by the "non-linear Kerr effect". This is discussed in 2.4.5.4, "Carrier-Induced Phase Modulation (CIP)" on page 92. SPM causes a chirp effect where longer wavelengths tend to move to the beginning of a pulse and the shorter ones to the end. This is the opposite direction to the direction of chromatic dispersion (at wavelengths longer than 1310 nm in standard fibre).

- So, if you have a pulse of sufficiently high intensity and short-enough duration[121] the faster (high-frequency components) at the beginning of the pulse are slowed down a bit and the slower (low-frequency components) in the back are speeded up.

- Thus, if the pulse length and the intensity are right, the two effects (chromatic dispersion and SPM) strike a balance and the pulse will stay together without dispersion over quite a long distance.[122]

  Note, as they travel solitons still suffer attenuation and therefore require amplification to retain their peculiar non-dispersive characteristics.

What is happening is the balancing of two dispersive effects in the fibre - the effects of chromatic dispersion and the effect of self-phase modulation (SPM). It is interesting that you need a dispersive medium (such as standard fibre) to make this work. This is because soliton formation is a balance between two non-linear effects. The dispersion created by the two effects *must be in opposite directions* otherwise all you would get is increased dispersion. In standard fibre this means you need to operate in the "anomalous dispersion regime" (wavelengths longer than 1310 nm) because it is only in this wavelength range that GVD operated to put the short wavelengths first. Thus a soliton can travel without dispersion in a dispersive medium for as long as its power is maintained. If the pulse disperses slightly the compression process is enhanced and the pulse returns to its stable shape. If the pulse narrows for any reason then the compression process is reduced and it spreads out to its natural shape again.

If you launch a pulse of around the right energy and of about the right duration into a fibre medium then after a quite short travel on the fibre it will evolve into the characteristic sech (hyperbolic secant) shape of a soliton.

Making soliton transmission work involves using amplifiers at regular intervals and working with a signal which is significantly more intense than typical existing systems. This is the big practical problem of soliton transmission. As discussed elsewhere in this book there are very real and quite low maximum power limits on the signal imposed by effects like SBS and SRS. Thus to retain the soliton shape and characteristics you have to amplify at intervals of between 10 and 50 km!

---

[121] 30 to 50 picoseconds - or about a centimeter.

[122] Solitons can happen in other media where waves propagate such as waves in water. The *Scientific American* magazine of December 1994 has an excellent article on this subject.

Nevertheless, solitons offer a prospect of virtually error-free transmission over very long distances (although amplified along the way) at speeds of over 100 Gbps. To make use of soliton systems we will also need to use optical TDM as the electronic systems to which the link must be interfaced cannot operate at these very high speeds.

Soliton technology is in the laboratory prototype stage right now but it looks very attractive for long-distance links in the future.

12.1.1 Dark Solitons

If you have a small gap within an unbroken high power optical beam or a very long pulse, the gap in the beam can behave exactly like a regular soliton! Such gaps are called "dark" solitons.

12.1.2 Light Guiding Light (Spatial Solitons)

In the earlier mention of Solitons the effect was used to compress and hold together (in time) optical pulses within a waveguide structure (a fibre). If you send a very intense beam of light into a block of dispersive substance (such as silica) it forms a beam which holds together in the transverse direction without spatial (lateral) dispersion. Thus it travels in the material as though it was in a waveguide although it is not!

What happens is that the beam constructs its own waveguide due to the RI modification aspect of very high optical power. This is caused by the creation of a balance between diffraction effects and SPM. Diffraction is a very similar mechanism to dispersion. The process is the same as for temporal solitons as described in 12.1, "Solitons" on page 651 except that the effect is spatial rather than temporal.

A waveguide constructed this way with a beam of intense light could potentially be used as a guide for light at other wavelengths! Thus we could build very fast optical switches and perhaps even logic devices by carrying light literally along beams of (different wavelength) light.

Research in this area is still in its infancy but the prospects are fascinating.

12.2 Advanced Fibres

Since the mid-1970's there has been great enthusiasm and a lot of research into fibres made from heavy metal halides. The most attractive of these is zirconium fluoride.

In theory these glasses could have attenuation as low as .01 or .001 dB per kilometer. This suggests the prospect of cable spans as long as perhaps 5000 km without the need for repeaters or amplifiers! You could cross the Atlantic Ocean without having any active component in the path. The implications for cost saving here are enormous.

The most researched glass here is called ZBLAN glass. ZBLAN stands for zirconium, barium, lanthanum, aluminium and sodium (Na). These are used in combination as their fluorides. However the dominant glass-forming component is zirconium fluoride. To get a glass with a lower refractive index to use as the cladding some of the zirconium is replaced by hafnium (now called ZHBLAN glass).

The optimal (lowest attenuation) wavelength window for ZBLAN glass is around 2.55 nm. This means that to use it new lasers and detectors would need to be developed at this (quite long) wavelength. Fibres, however could have significantly thicker cores (say 15 microns) and remain single moded. This would mean that we could transmit at much higher powers than we use on regular glass because the field intensity (electric and magnetic) is lower in the larger core. Indeed this would form a totally new optical transmission technology.

However, in the mid 1990's most of this research has ceased. There were significant problems with crystalline structures forming in the glass and creating very high scattering losses. Researchers have been generally unable to realise the very low attenuation figures that were promised. However, there is still use of fluoride glass in some optical devices. For example, it is used as a host glass for Pr doped fibre amplifiers.

12.3 Plastic Technology

Plastic fibre (see 2.5, "Plastic Optical Fibre (POF)" on page 94) has been available for many years and is used in many niche (short distance) applications. It has been slow to be adopted for telecommunications but nevertheless much research is continuing aimed at improving it. Plastic amplifiers (see 5.2.4, "Plastic Fibre Amplifiers" on page 224) have also recently been demonstrated. The word "plastic" is a bit misleading and it is generally better to talk about "organic" materials as many of the materials used are not strictly plastics. However the term plastic is widely used.

At the present time there is a significant amount of research into two additional areas:

1. The use of plastic semiconductors to make lasers, and

2. The development of plastic technology for use in planar waveguide devices.

Both of these research directions are aimed at reducing the cost of optical components - perhaps arriving at a technology "system" including plastic lasers, fibres and devices.

At the present time a Waveguide Grating Router (WGR) such as the one described in 5.7.3, "Waveguide Grating Routers (WGRs)" on page 280 costs about US $4,000 to manufacture in commercial quantities using SOI (Silica on Insulator - in this case Silicon) technology.[123] In the industry it is expected that this cost will be reduced to about US $250 within two years (by 1999). A plastic WGR might well cost around only US $20 to produce. The incentive behind this research is obvious.

12.3.1 Plastic Planar Waveguide Devices

Currently many researchers are investigating the feasibility of using plastic to build planar waveguide devices. The motivation here is primarily to reduce the cost of devices such as WGRs but there are other potential benefits as well.

The paper by Y. Shi et al. (1996) describes the construction of MZI type modulators using thin layers of polyurethane on a silica substrate. In this case the polymer is both a lower cost technology than crystalline materials but has a much higher electrooptic coefficient and so produces a better device. These devices were produced by "spin coating" the polymer onto a flat silica substrate. These modulators produce performance adequate to many commercial applications at a reportedly lower cost than competitive devices. In this case it is reasonable to expect that they will be available commercially quite soon.

It may be possible to do even better than polymer coating on silica or silicon. For example it may be possible to build devices using similar technology to that used in the CD-ROM disk. CD-ROM disks are manufactured using plastic injection moulding techniques. These techniques have turned out to provide very high precision at extremely low cost!

12.3.2 Plastic Semiconductor Lasers

The obvious problem in making plastic lasers is that you need to pump energy into them (as you do with all lasers)! But plastic is generally an insulator and so pumping has until recently had to be by light produced in another laser. Lasing was demonstrated in organic materials as early as 1966 with a ruby laser as the energy source. The cost of a pump laser *and* an external modulator makes the overall cost of an optically pumped device unattractive.

However, recently a new class of optical materials has been invented which *semiconducts* just like crystalline materials. There are two different classes of these organic semiconducting materials:

---

[123] Cost not price.

1. Polymer based materials

2. Low molecular weight (non-polymer) organic materials

To date, people have produced organic LEDs (OLEDs) intended for display applications using semiconducting organic materials. See the paper by Z. Shen et al. (1997).

At the present time the author knows of no reports of successful organic semiconductor lasers (OSLs), but many of the necessary prerequisites have been studied.

The paper by V. Bulovic et al. (1997) describes the construction of a laser made from organic semiconducting materials. Although the laser was pumped optically, this project enabled the study of many of the issues surrounding device design for an electrically pumped OSL. This laser was made from a thin film of an organic semiconductor called Alq3[124] doped (between 1% and 10%) with a laser dye called DCM.[125] The principle of operation is similar to that described in 5.2.1.6, "Co-Dopants" on page 209. DCM is the lasing medium but it is the Alq3 that is pumped. Pumping was done optically at 337 nm and the lasing wavelength was 645 nm. The organic materials were spin-coated onto a silica substrate. It was found that the lasing wavelength could be tuned between 620 nm and 650 nm by adjusting the dopant (DCM) concentration. In addition the device proved to have very little wavelength variation with temperature change.

The above study is still a long way from achieving an electrically pumped device but the prospects look very exciting. The manufacturing process is simpler than that for crystalline materials and should therefore yield a lower cost device.

Of course the question of the long term stability of such devices is still to be evaluated. Some people feel that polymers may degrade over time but others point out that similar problems have been solved with other plastics.

12.4 Optical Code Division Multiple Access (CDMA)

Code Division Multiple Access (CDMA) is one of a family of transmission techniques generically called "Spread Spectrum". These techniques are well developed in the

---

[124] Alq3 is an abbreviation for tris-(8-hydroxyquinoline) aluminium.

[125] DCM is an abbreviation for 4-(dicyanomethylene)-2-methyl-6- (4-dimethylaminostyryl)-4H-pyran.

world of radio communications systems. In the optical world CDMA has been suggested as a possible technology in two roles:

1. Optical shared medium LANs

2. Local access networks

The concepts of spread spectrum and of CDMA seem to contradict normal intuition. In most communications systems we try to maximize the amount of useful signal we can fit into a minimal bandwidth. In spread spectrum we try to artificially spread a signal over a bandwidth much wider than necessary. In CDMA we transmit multiple signals over the same frequency band, using the same modulation techniques at the same time! Traditional thinking would suggest that communication would not be possible in this environment. There are of course very good reasons for doing this. In a spread spectrum system we use some artificial technique to broaden the amount of bandwidth used. This has the following effects:

Capacity Gain

Using the Shannon-Hartly law for the capacity of a bandlimited channel it is easy to see that for a given signal power the wider the bandwidth used, the greater the channel capacity. So if we broaden the spectrum of a given signal we get an increase in channel capacity and/or an improvement in the signal-to-noise ratio.

This is true and easy to demonstrate for some systems but not for others. "Ordinary" frequency modulation (FM) systems spread the signal above the minimum theoretically needed and they get a demonstrable increase in capacity. Some techniques for spreading the spectrum achieve a significant capacity gain but others do not.

The Shannon-Hartly law gives the capacity of a bandlimited communications channel in the presence of "Gaussian" noise. (Every communications channel has Gaussian noise.)

$$Capacity = B \ \log_2 (1 + \frac{P_S}{2 \, N_0 \, B})$$

Where P represents signal power, N noise power and B available bandwidth.

It is easy to see that with P and N held constant, capacity increases as bandwidth increases (though not quite as fast). So, for a given channel capacity, the required power decreases as utilized bandwidth increases. The wider the bandwidth the lower the power we need to use for a given capacity.

Security

Spread spectrum was invented by military communications people for the purpose of battlefield communications. Spread spectrum signals have an excellent rejection of intentional jamming (jammer power must be very great to be successful). In addition, the Direct Sequence (DS) technique results in a signal which is very hard to distinguish from background noise unless you know the peculiar random code sequence used to generate the signal. Thus, not only are DS signals hard to jam, they are extremely difficult to decode (unless you have the key) and quite hard to detect anyway even if all you want to know is when something is being transmitted.

Immunity to Multipath Distortion

Some spectrum spreading techniques have a significantly better performance in the presence of multipath spreading than any available narrowband technique. This will be discussed later.

Interference Rejection

Spread spectrum signals can be received even in the presence of very strong narrowband interfering signals (up to perhaps 30 dB above the wanted signal).

Multiplexing Technique (CDMA)

Some techniques of frequency spreading enable the transmission of many completely separate and unrelated channels *on the same frequency and at the same time as other, similar signals.*

12.4.1 Direct Sequence Spread Spectrum (DSSS)

Also called "Pseudo Noise" (PN), DSSS is a popular technique for spreading the spectrum. Figure 371 shows how the signal is generated.

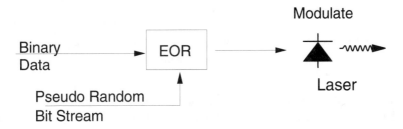

Figure 371. Direct Sequence Spread Spectrum Modulation - Transmitter

1. The binary data stream (user data) is used to "modulate" a pseudo-random bit stream. The rate of this pseudo-random bit stream is much faster (from 9 to 100 times) than the user data rate. The bits of the pseudo-random stream are called *chips*. The ratio between the speed of the chip stream and the data stream is called the *spread ratio*.

2. The form of "modulation" used is typically just an EOR operation performed between the two bit streams.

3. The output of the faster bit stream is used to modulate a radio frequency (RF) or optical carrier.

4. Any suitable modulation technique could be used but in practical radio systems a very simple bi-polar phase shift keying (BPSK) approach is usually adopted. In optical systems NRZ coding is typically used.

Whenever a carrier is modulated the result is a spread signal with two "sidebands" above and below the carrier frequency. These sidebands are spread over a range plus or minus the modulating frequency. The sidebands carry the information and it is common to suppress the transmission of the carrier (and sometimes one of the sidebands). It can be easily seen that the width (spread) of each sideband has been multiplied by the spread ratio.

At first sight this can be quite difficult to understand. We have spread the spectrum *but in order to do it we have increased the bit rate by exactly the signal spread ratio.* Surely the benefits of spreading the spectrum (such as the capacity gain hypothesized above) are negated by the higher bit rate?

The secret of DSSS is in the way the signal is received. The receiver knows the pseudo-random bit stream (because it has the same random number generator). Incoming signals in the analogue processing stage are correlated with the known pseudo-random stream. Thus the chip stream performs the function of a known waveform against which we correlate the input.

Correlational receivers can be constructed in several ways but they almost always take the form of a tapped delay line. There are many ways to do this. Two examples are as follows:

1. In an optical device we might detect the optical signal first, then use it to drive an electronic Surface Acoustic Wave (SAW) Filter. This works but requires a receiver with a very high frequency response since it must respond to the chip rate rather than the bit rate.

2. All-optical correlational filters are possible and have the great advantage that the electronics associated with them don't need to be very fast.

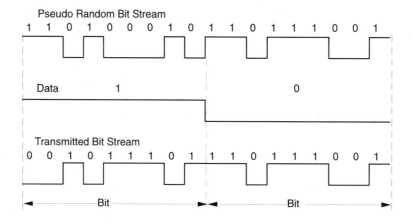

Figure 372. Direct Sequence Spread Spectrum Modulation. A pseudo-random bit stream much faster (here 9 times the speed) than the data rate is EORed with the data. The resulting bit stream is then used to modulate a carrier signal. This results in a much broader signal.

12.4.2 Code Division Multiple Access (CDMA)

The DSSS technique gives rise to a novel way of sharing the bandwidth. Multiple transmitters and receivers are able to use the same frequencies at the same time *without* interfering with each other! This is a by-product of the DSSS technique. The receiver correlates its received signal with a known (only to it) random sequence - all other signals are filtered out.

This is interesting because it is really the same process as FDM. When we receive an ordinary radio station (channels are separated by FDM), we tune to that station. The tuning process involves adjusting a resonant circuit to the frequency we want to receive. That circuit allows the selected frequency to pass and rejects all other frequencies. What we are actually doing is selecting a sinusoidal wave from among many other sinusoidal waves by selective filtering. If we consider a DSSS signal as a modulated waveform, when there are many overlapping DSSS signals then the filtering process needed to select one of them from among many is exactly the same thing as FDM frequency selection except that we have waveforms that are not sinusoidal in shape. However, the DSSS "chipping sequences" (pseudo-random number sequences) *must be orthogonal (unrelated)*. Fortunately there are several good simple ways of generating orthogonal pseudo-random sequences.

For this to work, a receiving filter is needed which can select a single DSSS signal from among all the intermixed ones. In principle, you need a filter that can correlate the complex signal with a known chipping sequence (and reject all others). There are several available filtering techniques which will do just this. The usual device used for this filtering process is called a Surface Acoustic Wave (SAW) filter.

CDMA has a number of very important characteristics:

"Statistical" Allocation of Capacity

> Any particular DSSS receiver experiences other DSSS signals as noise. This means that you can continue adding channels until the signal-to-noise ratio gets too great and you start getting bit errors. The effect is like multiplexing packets on a link. You can have many active connections and so long as the total (data traffic) stays below the channel capacity all will work well. For example, in a mobile telephone system, (using DSSS over radio) only about 35% of the time on a channel actually has sound (the rest of the time is gaps and listening to speech in the other direction). If you have a few hundred channels of voice over CDMA what happens is the average power is the channel limit - so you can handle many more voice connections than are possible by FDM or TDM methods.

This also applies to data traffic on a LAN or access network where the traffic is inherently bursty in nature. However, it has particular application in voice transmission because, when the system is overcommitted there is no loss in service but only a degradation in voice quality. Degradation in quality (dropping a few bits) is a serious problem for data but not for voice.

No Guard Time or Guard Bands

In a TDM system when multiple users share the same channel there must be a way to ensure that they don't transmit at the same time and destroy each other's signal. Since there is no really accurate way of synchronizing clocks (in the light of propagation delay) a length of time must be allowed between the end of one user's transmission and the beginning of the next. This is called "guard time". At slow data rates it is not too important but as speed gets higher it comes to dominate the system throughput. CDMA of course does not require a guard time - stations simply transmit whenever they are ready.

In FDM (and WDM) systems, unused frequency space is allocated between bands because it is impossible to ensure precise control of frequency. These guard bands represent wasted frequency space. Again, in CDMA they are not needed at all.

Requirement for Power Control

DSSS receivers can't distinguish a signal if its strength is more than about 20 dB below other similar signals. Thus if many transmitters are simultaneously active a transmitter close to the receiver (near) will blanket out a signal from a transmitter which is farther away.

The answer to this is controlling the transmit power of all the stations so that they have roughly equal signal strength at the receiver. In a reflective-star type optical LAN topology this is not a problem since there will be very little variation in signal levels. But in some possible access network configurations it could be a limitation.

Easier System Management

With FDM and TDM systems users must have frequencies and/or time slots assigned to them through some central administration process. All you need with CDMA is for communicating stations to have the same key.

12.4.3 Practical Optical CDMA

Optical CDMA is still very much a research technology. In the early 1990's it was proposed as a technology for shared medium LANs but since then the shared medium

LAN itself has proven more costly than switch based star networks. Thus there isn't a lot of interest in shared medium LANs in either the optical or electronic world.

Today however finding a low cost technology for the upstream transport in a passive optical network is a significant and important challenge. CDMA might well be a good choice here.

Practical optical CDMA systems have some differences from RF ones:

1. Instead of using a random number generator to generate the chipping sequence a fixed sequence only as long as one data bit is likely to be used. For example you might have 31 chips per bit and the chipping sequence would be the same for every bit transmitted.

2. Zero data bits are not transmitted at all. This nets out to saying that a 1 bit (for a particular end-user) is transmitted as an invariant 31-chip sequence.

3. The codings used in an optical system need to be different from those used in an RF system as we don't have a negative signal state in optical communications. We only have positive (or zero) states.

12.5 Optical Time Division Multiplexing (OTDM)

Time Division Multiplexing (TDM) is a time-honoured technique in electronic communications. It provides a very simple and effective way of sub-dividing a high-speed digital data stream into many slower speed data streams. Indeed most optical communications links are really TDM data streams but the TDM is done electronically rather than optically and the optical transmission system processes a single high-speed stream. SDH and SONET are standards for electronic TDM over an optical carrier.

There is much interest in TDM for optical communications *but* this interest is for completely different reasons than the reasons we use TDM in the electronic world. Basically the problem is that we can make optical signals go many times faster than the associated electronics. We can demonstrate soliton transmission at perhaps 200 Gbps but the fastest modulators will only go at perhaps 30 Gbps. Thirty Gbps is very fast indeed for electronic circuitry.

As with all "technological limits" this limit changes (improves) with the on-going development of technology. However, it seems that the maximum speed of an optical link is likely to remain significantly faster than the maximum speed of the driving electronics. The electronics will get faster in time - but then, so will the optics.

OTDM is aimed at allowing the optical signal stream to run at speeds significantly in excess of the maximum speed of the electronics.

12.5.1 TDM Concept

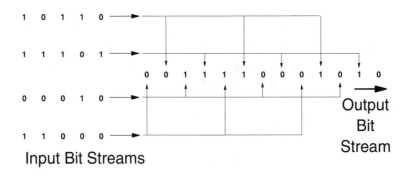

Figure 373. *Time Division Multiplexing (TDM) - Concept*

Figure 373 illustrates the principle of time division multiplexing. In the illustration there are four slow-speed bit streams merged into a single high speed stream at four times the speed of any one of the component signals. Each input stream is assigned one bit in every four in turn. There are a number of points to note:

- In the illustration we are allocating places (time slots) in the high-speed data stream at the individual bit level. This is not necessary. In the electronic communications world time "slots" in a TDM system are often allocated on the basis of 8-bit groups or even in larger groupings such as 53-byte "cells" etc. However, in optical TDM proposed systems use the "bit-interleaving" technique almost exclusively.

- The data stream is arranged in repeating patterns of time slots usually called "frames". In the example a frame would be just four bits. Thus input channel x might be allocated bit number 3 in every frame.

- It is not necessary for each of the slow-speed streams to be the same. For example, we could TDM three signals at different rates by allocating a different number of bits in each time frame to each stream. Thus input stream 1 might be allocated bit numbers 1, 3, 5, 7..., stream 2 might be allocated bits 2, 6, 10... and stream 3 bits 4, 8, 12... In this example stream 1 would be twice the rate of either stream 2 or stream 3.

- There is very little delay experienced by the slow speed streams due to their travel over the higher speed "trunk". There will be a need for some speed-matching buffering at the points of multiplexing and demultiplexing but this can usually be limited to a single bit.

- Once the time slots are allocated each subordinate signal stream has a fixed and invariant data rate. This can be changed by reallocating the bits but this is difficult to do dynamically, takes time and wastes resources.

- Each signal stream *must* be synchronised to the higher speed stream! This is the most significant problem in TDM. Each slow speed stream *must* deliver its bits at *exactly* the correct rate or there will be times when a bit needs to be transmitted and it has not yet arrived or times where too many bits arrive and some must be discarded. Neither of these situations is compatible with error-free transmission. Of course at the destination each slow speed stream must be received at exactly the rate that the bits are delivered from the high speed one. TDM takes no prisoners!

12.5.2 TDM Network Principles

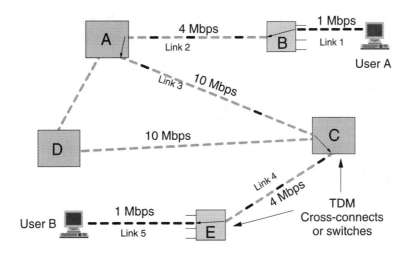

Figure 374. Principle of a TDM Network

Figure 374 illustrates the general principle of a TDM network. For the sake of illustration we will assume that data is multiplexed in units of a single byte. In the figure we have illustrated a 1 Mbps synchronous connection between the two end users (User A and User B). The network is configured as follows:

- User A is connected on a dedicated link to Node B at a speed of 1 Mbps (125,000 bytes/sec). Note that the timing for the link is provided by Node B not by the end user. This means that Node B sends a clock signal to User A each time that a bit is to be sent.

- Node B has been set up with a rule that says "whenever a byte is received on Link 1 place it into time-slot x of Link 2".

- Node B has a connection with Node A at a speed of 4 Mbps. Our connection between end users is allocated to this link and so gets every fourth byte on Link 2.

- Node A has a rule that says "whenever time-slot x of Link 2 arrives take the data in it and place it into time-slot y of Link 3".

- Node A to Node C is a 10 Mbps link which will also carry our end-user connection. Thus only 1 byte in 10 on the link will belong to this particular end-user connection.

- Node C to Node E is at 4 Mbps (same as B to A) and again we get every fourth byte.

- Node E is connected directly to User B at a dedicated speed of 1 Mbps. Clocking for this link is again provided by the network not the end user.

- Note that each connection is bi-directional (although strictly it doesn't need to be).

Thus we have an end-to-end connection where data is passed on from link-to-link one byte at a time in a strictly controlled way. Of course, the 10 Mbps connection and the 4 Mbps connection must have a *strictly* identical timing source. If the timing relationship between the two links was to vary even slightly loss or corruption of data would result.

Connections can be set up in two ways:

1. By network management

   In this case the node is called a "cross-connect". Connection setup or tear-down may take from a few minutes to a few days.

2. By signalling

   Signalling means by request in real-time by the end user. Connection setup may take from about 10 ms up to about a second depending on the type of network and it's size. In this case the nodes are called "switches".

The best known switched TDM network is the telephone network. In the optical world, operating at much higher speeds, it is likely the early networks will be cross-connects only.

12.5.3 Optical TDM Principles

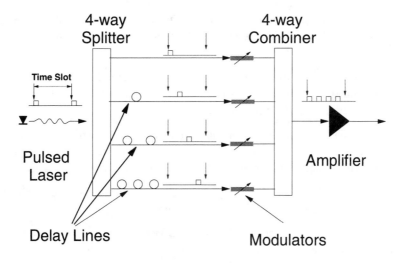

Figure 375. *Optical TDM Configuration*

Figure 375 illustrates one particular proposed method for building an optical TDM system. The system illustrated shows four streams merged into one. The modulation technique used is RZ coding as discussed in 7.2.1.4, "RZ Coding" on page 383. RZ coding is used because it alleviates the extremely difficult problem of synchronising different bit streams into adjacent time slots. (In RZ coding a 1-bit is represented by the laser ON state for only the first half of the bit-time.) There will always be some jitter in the slow stream bit stream as it is mixed into the faster stream. In addition any optical pulse will be bell shaped rather than square. Thus no matter what we do there will be gaps between the bits. The system operates in the following way:

1. Each time slot (illustrated by the downward pointing arrows) is sub-divided into 4 bit times.

2. Each bit-time (in conformity to the RZ code in use) is further divided into two halves. For a "1" bit the first half of the bit time will be occupied by an optical pulse (and the second half will be dark). For a "0" bit the whole bit time will be dark.

3. A laser produces a short pulse (for half a bit time) at the beginning of each time slot. In this example the laser is ON for one-eighth of the time slot.

   This can be done in many ways. Self-pulsating laser diodes have been suggested (See 3.3.7, "Mode-Locking and Self-Pulsating Lasers" on page 148.). However a standard laser with an external modulator or an integrated modulator may be more appropriate because we want to avoid laser chirp.

4. The laser signal is split 4-ways. (There are many ways to do this - concatenated 3 dB couplers being the most obvious.) A planar free-space coupler will also do this and would be used if the whole TDM device were built on a single planar substrate.

5. Each signal (except one) is then delayed by a fixed amount. This delay is easily and conveniently provided by using a loop of standard fibre. Of course each signal is delayed by a *different* amount.

6. Then each signal is separately modulated to carry it's own unique information stream. The trick here is to synchronise the modulators accurately given that their response will be much slower than a single bit time (at the full link speed).

7. The signals are then re-combined (perhaps using concatenated 3 dB splitters or a free space coupler) to form a single data stream.

8. During all this the original signal has lost a very large amount of power. Each pulse will lose a minimum of 6 dB in each of the 4-way splitter and the combiner. In addition there will be loss in the modulator. It would be a very good modulator if the insertion loss was only about 6 dB. So in total each output bit pulse will be at least 18 dB (and maybe as much as 25 dB) less than the original pulse amplitude as it left the transmit laser.

The whole stream then must be amplified to reach a strength suitable for transmission on the link. Indeed, if soliton transmission is to be used (and we can't go at 100 Gbps rates any other way), there will need to be a very high level of amplification. The power level needs to be around 3 mw or above for a soliton to form. Hence we will probably be looking for around 40 dB or more of gain from the amplifier! (This is no problem for a multi-stage EDFA but there is an interesting challenge here in amplifier design to manage the amplified spontaneous emission.)

12.5.4 Demultiplexing the TDM Signal

The interesting challenge in OTDM comes in receiving and demultiplexing the signal. In principle this is relatively easy to do electronically but the electronics won't go that fast! This is the reason we are using OTDM in the first place. We want OTDM to operate at 100 Gbps and above and currently the maximum speed you could do this with electronics is about 30 or 40 Gbps. So we need to do this optically.

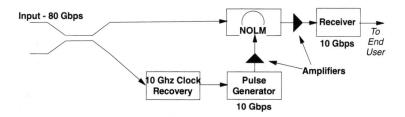

Figure 376. Demultiplexing the OTDM Stream

To demultiplex the OTDM data stream we must extract each slow(er) speed data stream based on timing. There are two processes here:

Extracting the Data

> Data for a single channel may be extracted as shown in Figure 376. A Non-linear Optical Loop Mirror (NOLM) is used as an AND gate to select every nth pulse (in the figure n=8) from the TDM stream. The principles of a NOLM suitable for this purpose are discussed in 5.9.3.3, "The NOLM as a Logic Gate" on page 309.

Add/Drop Multiplexing

> A device capable of being either an add/drop multiplexor or a simple demultiplexor is discussed in 5.9.3.4, "Optical ADM for OTDM using Mach-Zehnder Interferometer" on page 311.

Extracting the Timing

> Each bit in the higher speed signal is identified by its arrival time. Thus the first problem is to derive an electronic clock signal (at the slower rate of one of the component streams) and ensure that it is accurately synchronised to the incoming bit stream. This is the most difficult aspect of OTDM.

12.6 Optical Packet Switched Networks

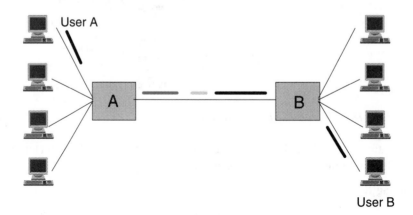

Figure 377. *Packet Switching - Principle*

Packet switched networks are far and away the most common form of data network. Here we use the word data to mean any information that is not real-time voice or video. IP (the Internet), SNA, X.25 and ATM are examples of packet switched networks.

In a packet switched network data is transferred from one user to the other in groups of bytes variously called packets, cells, frames or blocks. While there are technical differences between these terms (usually depending on the context within which they are used) the principle involved is the same:

- A packet of data is sent from a user to the network. This may be variable in length and delimited by some control sequence or it may be fixed in length.

- The packet contains a header prepended to the front which contains information that allows the network to determine the destination to which the data must be routed. This header may consist of either the network address of the desired destination or an identifier that allows the network to choose which of a selection of predefined routes (called circuits) is to be used for the data.

- The network node (also called a switch) receives the packet and places it on an outbound link connection towards the destination.

- This happens through many stages until the packet reaches its destination end user.

There are a number of important characteristics here:

1. Many end users may send to the same destination end user at the same time.

2. Each node-to-node link within the network is shared on a (usually) first-come first-served basis among all end users. This is a form of block-multiplexing as mentioned in 10.1.3, "Sharing the Fibre" on page 574.

3. Data transfer *within* the network is asynchronous. There is no timing relationship between data arriving within a node and its onward transfer.

There are a number of functions needed in the network equipment to implement a packet switching structure:

Logic

> In an electronic packet switched network, when a packet arrives at a node it is received in its entirety first. Logic is then needed within the node to determine which outbound link is the correct one for this packet. This function varies in complexity and is performed using information from the header of the packet.

> In an optical system we can avoid the need to receive and store the packet. We could have a very simple decision scheme that based its logic on the first few bits in the packet (in the header). It would be possible to perform the switching operation as the packet is being received without the need to store it provided the outbound path (link) is free. Nevertheless, we need to perform logic on parts of the header in order to determine the destination of the packet.

Storage

> Because you can never guarantee that the appropriate outbound link is available when it is needed you need to be able to store the packet until the link is free.

Flow and Congestion Control

> Because there is always a possibility of too much data being sent to the same destination or same intermediate link causing network congestion there must be some mechanism to control the flow of data within the network. If necessary we need a mechanism to tell end users to stop transmitting or to slow down when needed.

At the present time each one of the above functions is exceedingly difficult to perform completely optically:

- You can store data in an optical delay line but this is extremely limited and it introduces timing synchronisation issues.

- You can perform limited logic and routing functions optically provided that the decision logic required is extremely simple.

It would be fine to perform the logic in electronics provided the information was able to stay optical.

- Flow and congestion control also requires significant logic which we can't do today in the optical domain.

But whilst there is a beginning, the need to combine all these things within a working device makes optical packet switching (at least in nodal networks) a dream for the (far) future.

12.7 Optical Interconnects

Within large electronic devices such as computers and communications switches components and sub-assemblies are connected together using electric wires. As circuit and device speeds increase the problems in using electric wire connections increases significantly.

There are many kinds of interconnections. Between components on a chip, between chips on a circuit card, between cards on a backplane and between frames. A general rule is that as the length of interconnections becomes longer then the number of required connecting wires becomes less. Chip-to-chip connections often involve hundreds of wires. Frame-to-frame connections are usually between 20 and 50 parallel wires.

As electronic speeds have increased there has been increasing need to process the signal before and after transmission on an interconnect. In addition as speed increases there is an increasing need to shield individual wire pairs etc. This means large and expensive cables.

In principle an optical interconnect offers significant advantages over an electronic one:

Insensitivity to EMI

> Optical links are in themselves immune to EMI problems. They don't pick up interference from surrounding electromagnetic fields and they don't create any.

> Unfortunately this is not quite true because optical receivers often require a lot of gain and a high gain device (the receiver) in close proximity to other electronic circuitry can often cause a problem. One suggestion for minimising the EMI is to use the highest possible transmitter power so that you can use minimal amplification at the receiver.

No Problem with Ground Loops

For connections between frames (as distinct from within them) ground loops can be a problem with electronic connections if you are not very careful in the design of the connection. Of course optical connections have no problems with ground loops.

Improved Skew Characteristics

Multi-strand cables all have a problem with skew - that is a signal on one wire arriving before its companion signal on another wire. This problem is much more severe in electrical cables than in optical ones.

Less Complex (and Costly) Signal Processing Required

As speeds increase electronic processing needs to get much more complex just to drive the link. In other words, even if the cable is only a few metres in length it still may require complex analogue signal processing. Optical tranceivers are going to cost more than electronic ones but this cost will be at least partly offset by a saving in the cost of analogue electronics to drive a copper connection.

Today, there is significant interest in using optical interconnects for connections between equipment frames. That is, for distances of 1 to perhaps 100 metres at speeds of up to 1 GB (gigabyte) per second.

There are many people developing prototype optical interconnect systems for this environment. The big challenge is cost. Electronic hardware is very cost competitive and any optical interconnect would need to be very low in cost to compete with copper. Proposed systems typically have the following characteristics:

1. They use MM fibre.

   As the dominant cost involved is in building accurate connectors and fitting them to cables it is extremely important to allow for large tolerances. This is done by using MM fibre.

2. Multiple (20 to 50) parallel fibres are used in a flat cable.

At the present time some optical interconnects are in use in specialised equipment but as yet they are not generally used. Early high performance (1 Gbps) systems are becoming available at competitive prices and it is expected that they will gain relatively fast acceptance in high end equipment.

12.8 Coherent Detection

It almost goes without saying that the output of the detectors discussed in Chapter 4, "Optical Detectors" on page 169 is *not* at the frequency (wavelength) of light (the electronics would not go that fast). What you get is electrical pulses (hopefully) similar to the modulations in the original signal.

> This is just like the operation of a "crystal set". A crystal set uses a tunable resonant circuit to select the frequency and then the output is fed to a simple half wave rectifier (the crystal). The output is just the original signal rectified.

This, very simple, method of detection is called "incoherent detection".

Most electronic radio receivers use a quite different method called "heterodyne detection". In the optical world heterodyne detection is called "coherent detection". (In electronics the word coherent is used in a much narrower sense. It is reserved for systems where the detector "locks on" to the phase of the received signal.)

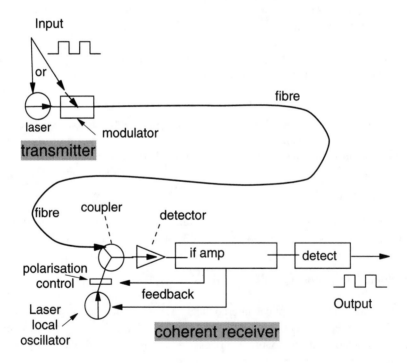

Figure 378. An Optical Transmission System Using Coherent Detection

Optical coherent detection (as illustrated in Figure 378) has two major advantages over incoherent detection:

1. Receivers can be significantly more sensitive than incoherent ones (by 15 to 20 dB). In general this is true of systems reported in the research literature.

   However, some researchers (Green 1992) claim that incoherent detectors built with an optical preamplifier can be just as sensitive and are a lot less complex.

2. In WDM systems, where there are many channels packed closely together, coherent detection allows a much better rejection of interference from adjacent channels. (This allows channels to be packed more closely together.)

In addition, there are some other advantages, such as better noise rejection.

Optical coherent detection systems can be used for all the possible types of modulation (ASK, FSK, PSK, PolSK); however, they require a linewidth significantly less than the bandwidth of the modulating signal. This means that you can't use coherent detectors with LED transmitters (or with unmodified Fabry-Perot lasers). Also, they will not work in the presence of any significant level of frequency chirp. Thus, if ASK (OOK) is used, you either have to do something to the transmitter to minimize chirp or you should use a fixed laser with an external modulator.

The principle of coherent detection is relatively simple: When two signals (electrical, optical, sound, etc.) of nearly the same frequency are mixed, then additional frequencies representing the sum and difference of the two original signals are generated.

> *We use this principle when tuning musical instruments. When two instruments play the same note slightly out of tune with one another, you can hear a rapid variation in loudness of the combined sound. This variation is the "difference frequency." (Sometimes, unkindly, said to sound "like a nanny goat".) As the instruments are adjusted towards one another and the difference is only a few Hz then you can count the cycles.*

An optical coherent receiver does exactly this.

- A local light source (called the local oscillator - LO) is used to generate a frequency very close to the frequency of the signal carrier.

- The two signals are mixed together.

- They are then fed to a detector.

  If detectors were infinitely fast, and if electronic signals could approach the frequency of light then you would need to put a low pass filter in front of the detector. In this case you don't. The detector will pass only the "difference frequency" because it isn't fast enough to detect anything else!

- What you have now is a difference frequency in electronic form which contains all the modulations of the original signal.

- The signal is now amplified through a number of stages.

- The amplified signal can now be processed (filtered, detected) by any of the established techniques of electronics.

You can "tune" the receiver to almost any frequency by varying the LO frequency. Of course, feedback in various forms is necessary to make a system like this stable. The system is illustrated in Figure 378 on page 674.

There are two significant problems with coherent reception, both of which can be solved, but at a cost:

1. Optical coherent receivers are highly polarization sensitive *and* standard single-mode optical fibre does not respect polarization. However, polarization changes slowly and in single-channel systems it can be compensated for. In multichannel WDM systems, acquiring the polarization of a channel quickly after tuning is quite a challenge. (However in a WDM system, if we used fibre that retained polarization, we could put alternate channels at orthogonal polarizations and pack the channels even more closely together.)

   Various solutions (including using two detectors with orthogonal polarization) have been suggested - but this would significantly increase the cost of such a device.

2. Stabilisation of the frequencies of both transmitter and receiver within close tolerances is very difficult.

Prototype coherent receivers have been available in laboratories since the middle of the 1980s and have been used in many experiments. However, to the knowledge of the author, coherent receivers are not yet available in any commercial system.

12.9 Further Reading

Daniel J. Blumenthal, Paul R. Prucnal and Jon R. Sauer (1994)

> *Photonic Packet Switches: Architectures and Experimental Implementations*: Proceedings of the IEEE, Vol 82, No 11, November 1994. pp 1650-1667

V. Bulovic, V.G. Kozlov, P.E. Burrows and S.R. Forrest (1997)

Organic Semiconductor Lasers: From Infra-Red to Blue on a "Plastic Chip": IEEE Lasers and Electrooptics Society Newsletter, Vol 11, No 5, October 1997. pp 3-5

A. D. Ellis et al. (1995)

Ultra-High-Speed OTDM Networks Using Semiconductor Amplifier-Based Processing Nodes: IEEE J. of Lightwave Technology, Vol 13, No 5, May 1995. pp 761-770

Fumitomo Hide, et al. (1996)

Semiconducting Polymers: A New Class of Solid-State Laser Materials: Science, Vol 273, 27 September 1996. pp 1833-1836

Kenneth P. Jackson, et al. (1985)

Optical Fibre Delay-Line Signal Processing: IEEE Transactions on Microwave Theory and Techniques, Vol MTT-33, No 3, March 1985. pp 193-210

Richard A. Linke (1989)

Optical Heterodyne Communications Systems: IEEE Communications Magazine, October 1989. pp 36-41

Linn F. Mollenauer, James P. Gordon and Stephen G. Evangelides (1991)

Multigigabit soliton transmissions traverse ultralong distances: Laser Focus World, November 1991. pp 159-170

Paul R. Prucnal, Mario A. Santoro and Ting Rui Fan (1986)

Spread Spectrum Fiber-Optic Local Area Network Using Optical Processing: IEEE J. of Lightwave Technology, Vol LT-4, No5, May 1986. pp 547-554

Jawad A. Salehi (1989)

Code Division Multiple-Access Techniques in Optical Fiber Networks - Part 1: Fundamental Principles: IEEE Transactions on Communications, Vol 37, No 8, August 1989. pp 824-833

Z. Shen, P. E. Burrows, V. Bulovic, S. R. Forrest and M. E. Thompson (1997)

Three-Color, Tunable, Organic Light-Emitting Devices: Science, Vol 276, 27 June 1997. pp 2009-2011

Yongqiang Shi, et al. (1996)

Fabrication and Characterisation of High-Speed Polyurethane-Disperse Red 19 Integrated Electrooptic Modulators for Analog System Applications: IEEE J.

of Selected Topics in Quantum Electronics, Vol 2, No 2, June 1996. pp 289-299

Dave M. Spirit, Andrew D. Ellis and Pete E. Barnsley (1994)

Optical Time Division Multiplexing: Systems and Networks: IEEE Communications Magazine, December 1994. pp 56-62

Appendix A. An Introduction to Semiconductors

A basic understanding of semiconductors is fundamental to comprehension of much of the material in this book, in particular the chapters on lasers and detectors. This short chapter is intended more to refresh the reader's memory than to explain new ideas.

Any discussion of solid state electronics must begin with at least a basic understanding of "semiconductors".

A.1.1 Chemistry 101 Revisited

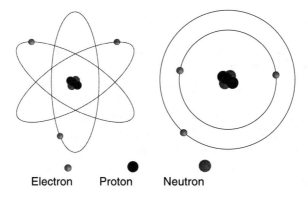

Electron   Proton   Neutron

Figure 379. Bohr Model of the Atom

All matter is composed of atoms linked or bonded to other atoms in various ways. An atom is itself composed of three basic particles - protons, neutrons and electrons as shown in Figure 379. It can be thought of as a central very dense nucleus containing the protons and neutrons at the centre of a "cloud" of electrons. The electrons move very quickly in orbits around the nucleus.

Protons carry a positive electrostatic charge and electrons carry a negative charge. Each atom contains the same number of protons as electrons and therefore the total electrostatic charge is zero.

Each atom which contains a given number of protons in its nucleus (regardless of the number of neutrons, which varies) has identical chemical properties with all other atoms having the same number of protons. Each atom is considered a unique "Element" identified by the number of protons in its nucleus.

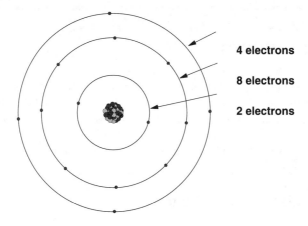

4 electrons

8 electrons

2 electrons

Figure 380. Electron Orbits (Shells) in the Silicon Atom

As can be seen from Figure 380 electrons orbiting a nucleus are arranged in "shells". The most important characteristic in the chemical behavior of any element is the number of electrons in its outermost shell. The maximum number of electrons an atom can have in its outer shell is eight. For this limited discussion we can consider that this outer shell needs to be "filled" (have eight electrons in its outermost shell) to enter a chemically stable state. A filled outermost shell is a more stable state than the "natural" state of a single isolated atom. However, most atoms don't have sufficient electrons to fill their outermost shells. Chemical bonding takes place when atoms either "lend" electrons to one another or "share" electrons with each other in order to reach lower energy (and therefore more stable) states.

You can get to a stable (filled) outer shell by two paths:

1. By stealing an electron from somewhere else. If the element has (say) 7 electrons in its outer shell it can reach the magic 8 by gaining an electron from somewhere.

2. If the element has 1, 2 or 3 electrons in its outer shell then it can (often) reach a more stable configuration by giving these up. In this case the shell below (usually already filled) becomes the outer shell.

Atoms bond together essentially for the purpose of filling this outermost shell. There are three generic types of chemical bond.

1. The Metallic Bond. Metals (in general) have between one and three electrons in their outer shells. (Most have two.) They consist of atoms grouped together with the outer (valence band) electrons held only very loosely. These electrons are free to wander through the metal at random and are held in place only by the generic

electrostatic charge of all the atoms in the material. Thus electrons in a metal are often referred to as an "electron sea".

This ease of movement of electrons within the material is responsible for the electrical conductivity characteristic of metals.

2. The Ionic Bond. This is where an atom "steals" some electrons from another atom in order to fill its outer shell and thus reach a relatively stable state. An atom which has gained electrons in this way is called a negative ion. Simultaneously with this another atom gives up electrons from its outer shell so that it may reach the (relatively) stable state of the filled (8 electrons) shell below. An atom which has lost electrons in this way is called a positive ion. The atom which received the electrons is then attracted (electrostatic attraction) to the atom that lost the electrons and a material (normally composed of two or more different elements) is formed.

A good example here is sodium chloride (common salt). A sodium atom gives up one electron (it only has one in its outer shell) and becomes a sodium ion. A chlorine atom (which has 7 electrons in its outer shell and needs another one for stability) gains the free electron to become a chlorine ion.

Ionic bonds are not too interesting in the current context.

3. The Covalent Bond. This is the important type of bond for the building of semiconductors. Covalent bonding occurs when two atoms "share" some of their outer electrons such that each has a share of eight electrons.

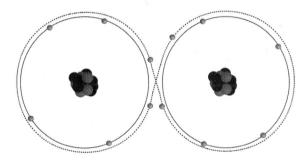

Figure 381. Oxygen Atom Example

A.1.1.1 Molecules and Covalent Bonding

A group of atoms bonded together with covalent bonds is called a "molecule". A good example of a covalent bond can be found in Figure 381. This is an oxygen molecule. It consists of two oxygen atoms joined together with a covalent bond.

Oxygen has an outer shell with six electrons. When two oxygen atoms bond to form O_2 each oxygen atom gives up a "share" of two of its electrons in return for a share of two of the other atom's electrons. All four electrons commence to orbit *both* atoms as suggested in the figure. Thus each atom has a complete outer shell of eight electrons - if only for part of the time.

Molecules are held together by a number of forces (the main ones being electrostatic, magnetic and gravitational). The complex interaction of these forces is the ultimate source of the characteristics of all matter and in particular, here, of the behavior of semiconductors.

In general, covalent bonds are quite strong and the electrons that participate in them are *not* free to wander through the material. This is the reason that most materials comprised of covalent bonds are very poor conductors of electricity.

Within a molecule an atom can bond to one or more (up to 8) other atoms. Thus very large molecules which consist of millions of atoms are not just possible but indeed very common. A DNA molecule can consist of a few million atoms, a diamond (depending on size) up to perhaps 10^{18} atoms, a silicon "wafer" as used in the semiconductor industry is a single molecule and may be as large as 10^{24} atoms.

It is obvious that molecular structures are determined by the possibilities of geometry and by the forces present. It is important to remember that all structures are three dimensional but of course we must illustrate them in two dimensions. Atoms vary vastly in size. They can have any number from 1 to 8 electrons in their outer shells. An element with eight electrons in its outer shell is very stable (unreactive). Indeed for a long time such materials were thought to be inert (the "inert gases") but in fact you can make compounds from them. (Teflon - used in non-stick cookware is one such compound.)

A critical point for the understanding of semiconductors is that the bonding (or valence) electrons within a molecule are *not* restricted to taking part in a single bond. Within a single molecule the bonding electrons take complex paths (or orbits) which may traverse many different atoms. These paths may change over time.

A.1.2 Why Does a Conductor Conduct?

For that matter, why does an insulator insulate? While these questions are fundamental to understanding the operation of semiconducting devices the answers are not easy. A good intellectually satisfying answer requires an understanding of quantum mechanics which is a little[126] outside the scope of this book. However we may attempt a very general explanation.

- In most solids and especially in crystalline structures atoms are packed very closely together.

- If we impose an electrical potential across a solid, electrons travelling through it are controlled by the rules of physics that apply to the atoms of which the structure is made. This means that electrons cannot just randomly move through matter. They are controlled by the characteristics of the structure they are passing through.

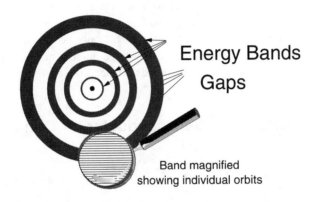

Band magnified
showing individual orbits

Figure 382. Energy Bands

- If we consider an unbound atom for a moment we see that electrons orbit the nucleus at specific distances (radii). The further away from the nucleus that a particular electron happens to be, the higher the energy of that electron.

However, electrons may *not* just use any old orbit. For each atom there is a particular set of orbital positions that an electron may take. An electron may *not* take a position between two orbits. Thus electrons may gain and lose energy in a series of "quantum" steps and may not hold energy levels in between. This is key to the whole subject.

Thus when an electron gains energy it must do it by gaining a discrete quantum of energy. When it does so it moves to a new orbital position farther away from the nucleus. When an electron loses energy it gives up that energy in a discrete quantum (sometimes in the form of a photon).

---

126 light years

Only one electron may occupy one orbital position at any one time.

- In a molecule consisting of a number of covalently bonded atoms, the bonding electrons occupy complex orbits that include many of the atoms in the molecule.

Electrons in the inner shells of each atom stay orbiting their individual atoms and do not participate in the bonding process. Nor are they available to conduct electricity. They exist in relatively low energy states tightly bound within their particular atoms. Only electrons from the valence band (or shell) take part in covalent bonding.

When a number of atoms are covalently bonded together the valence electrons orbit more than one nucleus. (This is the nature of covalent bonding.) When this happens you have the same rules as above but modified to account for the fact that we now have much more complex orbits. Electrons can still only occupy a fixed set of orbits but since there are many nuclei there are a very large number of potential orbits. Thus when we discuss molecules we discuss "bands" rather than shells to describe electron orbits.

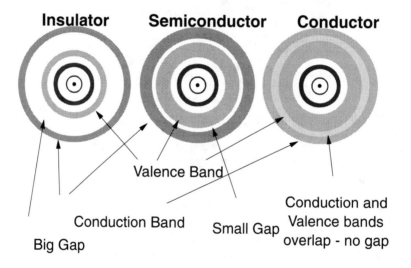

Figure 383. Energy Bands and Electrical Conduction

In each material you have two bands as illustrated in Figure 383.

1. The valence band - representing the energies that bonding electrons may take

2. The conduction band - representing the energies that electrons must have to conduct electricity in that material. Electrons in the conduction band have a higher energy state than electrons in the valence band.

It must be noted that energy states between the two bands are *not possible*. So the three types of material may be represented as in the figure.

Conductors result where the valence band and the conduction band overlap.

Insulators result where the conduction band is at a much higher energy than the valence band. To move from the conduction band to the valence band an electron has to gain a specific quantum of energy. Potentially it could do that from ambient heat or from the energy present in an externally applied electric field but if the gap is very large this may not be easy.

Semiconductors result when the valence and conduction bands are close enough to each other for electrons to be promoted from the valence band to the conduction band by ambient heat.

So, if we take a piece of insulator (such as diamond) and apply an external voltage, why don't electrons just leave the negative contact and migrate through the structure until they reach the positive contact? Well, they could if the electric field was strong enough for an electron to launch directly into the conduction band. In diamond this is a lot of energy and you would have to apply a few thousand volts to get there. In silicon we make use of this effect in some devices (such as Zener diodes).

In practical situations we need electrons to be present in the conduction band within a material for that material to conduct electricity. Alternatively we need an external energy source (such as heat or a strong electric field) to give energy to electrons in the valence band and thereby promote them to the conduction band. (In a semiconductor we also have "holes" but that explanation belongs later.)

A.1.3 Conductors

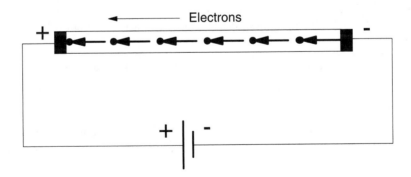

Figure 384. *Electricity Flow*

Electricity travels very quickly through a wire (about 2/3 of the speed of light). However electrons themselves move very slowly! In a metal you have a lot of atoms surrounded by a very mobile "sea" of electrons. When you apply a negative potential to one end (a surplus of electrons) the electrons nearby are repelled away from that end. As these electrons move away they repel others further down the wire which repel others and so on until the force reaches the other end of the wire. Thus electrical force in a metal (wire) moves very quickly (around .7 of the speed of light). However the electrons themselves only move (called drift) quite slowly.

In fact at the sub-atomic level electrons do move very quickly indeed. However, free electrons do not go very far (a few atomic diameters) before they collide with some atom or other in their way. When they collide they bounce off (with "no" loss of energy) in various directions. This direction can often be the exact direction in which it came! Figure 389 on page 693 shows a hypothetical path of an electron in a solid. Thus, the net speed of migration of electrons in a wire carrying electricity is only a few millimetres per second!

A.1.4 Semiconductors

Semiconductors are materials that exhibit properties that are between a metal and a non-metal. Their electrical properties are part way between a conductor and an insulator - thus they are called "semi-conductors". (Actually they are much closer to insulators than conductors.) A number of materials have these properties:

1. The crystalline forms of most elements of Group IV (valency 4). (silicon, germanium, tin)

2. Some forms of specific elements - boron (Group III), arsenic and antimony (Group V), selenium and tellurium (Group VI).

3. Crystalline alloys of elements in Group III (valency 3) with elements of group 5 (valency 5). Gallium arsenide (a compound or alloy of gallium and arsenic) is a good example here.

4. Some compounds of elements of Group VI with elements of Group II.

Probably the most versatile elements are those with four electrons in their outer shell (Group IV - carbon, silicon, germanium, tin, lead). The lighter three of these don't easily form Ionic bonds because a total loss or gain of four electrons creates too much imbalance in electrostatic charge. Because of the fact that they can have four bonds to four other elements, covalent compounds of endless complexity can be formed. (Indeed DNA is a single carbon-based molecule.)

All of these elements can exist in multiple physical forms. Carbon can take many forms such as graphite (a form a bit like a classical metal) which conducts electricity very well or diamond (a crystalline form) which is an insulator.

Almost anyone who has ever soldered an electrical connection knows the difference between a good soldered joint (where the metal solidifies in a polymorphic form) and a "dry joint" where the solder crystallises. Polymorphic solder is a very good electrical conductor. Solder (an alloy of Lead and Tin) in its crystalline form *is a semiconductor!*.

In fact carbon is not classified by chemists as a semiconductor even though diamond does semiconduct at relatively high temperatures (well above room temperature). The technical reason is that carbon has very strong molecular bonds which do not break down very easily (the energy "gap" between the valence band and the conduction band is greater than that provided by ambient heat at room temperature.) It would be somewhat difficult in practice to use carbon as a basis for semiconductor electronics since it is hard to grow large, extremely pure diamonds to cut up and use as chips!

A major difference between semiconductors and conductors is their electrical behavior at different temperatures. In general, when you heat up a semiconductor its resistance to the flow of electricity decreases (or its conductance increases). In metals the opposite happens. As the temperature of a metal increases then its resistance also increases (or conductance decreases).

Today silicon is the most commonly used semiconductor although germanium was used almost exclusively in early (1950's) solid state devices. Silicon (like most elements) can take a number of physical forms. So-called "poly-silicon" is not unlike graphite. It resembles a metal in its electrical conductivity properties. Crystalline silicon is the base for almost all semiconductors today.

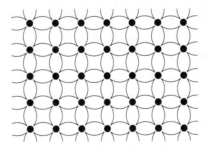

Figure 385. Silicon Crystal Lattice

A silicon crystal lattice is illustrated in Figure 385. Each silicon atom is bonded to four other silicon atoms with covalent bonds. Note that although the picture is two-dimensional the crystal structure is (of course) three dimensional. A perfect silicon crystal (at a temperature near absolute zero) has no free electrons and thus cannot conduct electricity. A pure silicon crystal at any temperature above absolute zero will have some bonds broken by the random action of heat and so there will be some free electrons in the structure and you will get some conduction.

In addition to using pure silicon or germanium you can also use crystals made of almost any alloy of elements in Group III (with three electrons in their outer shell) with elements in Group V (with five electrons in their outer shell). The best known material used in this way is gallium arsenide although there are many others.

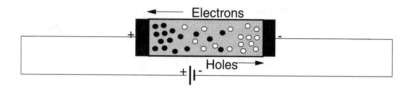

Figure 386. Conduction in an Intrinsic Semiconductor

A.1.4.1 Electrical Conduction in an Intrinsic Semiconductor

An "intrinsic" semiconductor is a uniform material that can act as a semiconductor without the need to introduce anomalies in the structure by doping. Pure crystals of silicon, germanium and gallium arsenide are intrinsic semiconductors at room temperature.

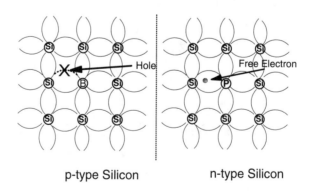

Figure 387. Doped Silicon

A.1.4.2 Dopants

Semiconductors don't get very interesting (or useful) until you introduce dopants. A dopant is a very small (indeed minuscule) amount of a controlled impurity introduced into the crystalline structure.[127] The presence of the dopant is responsible for the properties of the semiconductor.

Figure 387 on page 688 (left) shows a silicon crystal lattice doped with boron. Boron has three electrons in its outer shell. The regular crystalline structure remains but now there is a "hole" in it. A boron atom takes the place of a silicon atom in the structure. The structure is too strong to be changed by the single impurity atom and thus we have a missing bond in the structure.

Figure 387 on page 688 (right) shows a silicon crystal doped with phosphorus. Phosphorus has five electrons in its outer shell. Here the same thing happens as with boron except that we now have an electron too many rather than an electron too few as far as the lattice is concerned. The crystal structure is too strong to be deformed by the impurity but there is an electron "left over" after all the bonds are formed.

Thus we have two different kinds of semiconducting silicon. A type with excess holes in the lattice (called p-type silicon) and a type with excess electrons (called n-type silicon).

A.1.4.3 Properties of Semiconductors

There are a number of critical points here which are not all obvious:

1. n-type silicon can conduct electricity because it contains free and mobile electrons. But the concentration of dopant is kept so very low that the material no longer acts as a conductor but "semiconducts" instead. If you increase the concentration of dopant too much you get a conductor as a result and since the devices we plan to make rely on semiconductor effects, the material would no longer work.

2. p-type silicon can also conduct electricity. Although there are no free electrons the holes can act as though they are positively charged particles. In reality the bound electrons migrate in the opposite direction to hole movement but it is a very good conceptualisation to consider the holes as moving.

3. Electricity travels considerably faster in n-type silicon than it does in p-type silicon. Free electrons move faster than holes.

---

[127] In typical semiconductor VLSI the level of dopant is 1 part in 10^8. This is 1 gram of dopant material to 100 metric tons of silicon!

4. Electrons in the valence band take complex paths orbiting many atoms rather than staying in orbits linking pairs of atoms. This leads to a concept where the lattice is bound together not so much by individual bonds between atoms but rather by a "cloud" of electrons which act together to bind the whole structure. Electrons involved in bonding (within the valence band) are bound within the lattice and cannot easily escape. They move around the structure on specific (but indeterminate) paths at high speed.

As mentioned before, holes can move around. At first sight, this is not sensible. A hole is the absence of an electron at a particular point in the lattice. Holes are an absence of something rather than a presence and quite obviously can't move in themselves. However, they appear to move because electrons in the lattice, while confined to the bonding structure (to orbits around atoms), can jump from one path (around one nucleus) to other paths. If there is a vacant path (such as created by a hole) it is relatively easy for an electron to jump from a nearby orbital path to take the vacant one. Holes don't need to stay anywhere near the anomaly in the basic atomic structure which created them but do tend to stay nearby because of electrostatic attraction. A hole is there because a nucleus in the structure has a valence of 3 rather than 4 and the atom is held inside a structure where it "should" have four. If the hole moves away from the anomaly then the electron structure near the anomalous atom has one electron too many. Thus there is a net negative charge in this region and electrons will tend to be repelled (or holes attracted).

Free electrons are in the "conduction" band (a high energy state) and move through the lattice via diffusion. Electrons bound within the lattice also move but these are travelling in a finite number of fixed possible orbits. As these shift from orbit to orbit the holes in the lattice appear to move as though they were positive charges. Hole movement therefore is really the movement of electrons in the valence band (in the opposite direction to the notional movement of the hole.

5. It is easily possible for a lattice with holes in it to coexist with mobile free electrons *in very close proximity* without much interaction between the two. This is an important issue. The whole operation of semiconductor devices depends on electrons "recombining" with holes in many situations. The very important point is that the electrons which hold the lattice structure together are not "free". There can be *both* free electrons and holes present in close proximity at the same time because they represent different energy states.

When an electron in the conduction band occupies a hole in the valence band there is a release of energy. This release of energy is the basis for the operation of LEDs and lasers.

6. When a dopant is used the quantity is extremely low. A level of 1 atom in 10^8 is a typical level.

To get an idea of what this means, consider a room 4 metres square and 3 metres high (about 12 feet square and 9 feet high). If this room was filled with marbles of 1 cm diameter then it would contain 144×10^6 marbles. If each one of these represented a single atom, then a typical dopant level would be represented by a *single* marble. Thus one marble (atom of dopant) in a large room full of marbles (representing atoms of silicon) illustrates about the right proportion of dopant. A very small quantity indeed.

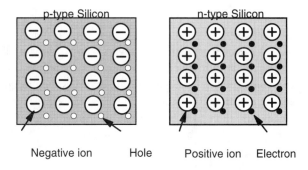

Negative ion   Hole   Positive ion   Electron

Figure 388. *Doped Silicon. p-type has an excess of holes (mobile positive charges) and n-type has an excess of electrons (mobile negative charges).*

A.1.4.4 n-type Silicon

Consider n-type silicon as illustrated on the right in Figure 387 on page 688. We have an atom of phosphorus[128] locked into a silicon lattice. When the lattice structure of bonds is formed there is an electron "left over". Of course this electron is necessary to balance the charge between the nucleus of the phosphorus atom and the electrons around it but there is no place for it in the bonding structure. It becomes free and will wander (very slowly and quite randomly) throughout the crystal influenced mainly by the movement due to heat. Albeit that it will tend to stay near the bound phosphorus atom (or another one) because of electrostatic attraction to the net positive charge. However, this is a relatively weak force and is overcome just by energy imparted by heat.

---

[128] Or any other element of Group III - such as arsenic or antimony.

When the electron moves away from its previous owner (the phosphorus atom) then we are left with an atomic structure with a positive charge (it is no longer balanced by the electron that just wandered away). This positively charged atom in the lattice is called a "positive ion". When the lattice is first formed the positive ion is paired with a free electron. The positive ions consist of atoms locked into the structure in such a way that they cannot move in any way.

There are also some holes present in n-type silicon. These are created by the action of heat on the undoped silicon lattice. Many of them will be filled (and will thus disappear) by recombination with the excess electrons in the structure. Nevertheless there will be some holes.

A.1.4.5 p-type Silicon

P-type silicon is just the same principle as n-type. Some dopant (this time with 3 electrons in its outer shell) is introduced into the silicon. Boron is often used for this purpose. The boron atom becomes locked into the crystal structure and is immovable. However, boron cannot contribute 4 electrons to the bonding process - because it only has three. This means that there is a hole left in the lattice where an electron should be but where it is absent. At least that is how it starts out.

As emphasised before, the electrons that hold the lattice in place move around the lattice very quickly. They take paths orbiting many of the atoms in the structure. So what happens is that the hole in the lattice structure is able to move through the crystal. (In reality only the electrons move BUT...)

This results in the hole being able to move away from the boron atom which was responsible for creating it. Thus we are left with a place in the structure (around the boron atom) where there are too many electrons (we have the right number for completing the lattice but too many to balance the numbers of protons in the nuclei of nearby atoms). Thus we have a fixed "negative ion" within the lattice.

So when it is first formed we start with a hole in the lattice around the impurity boron atom but as soon as the hole migrates away we are left with a negative ion where the hole should be and a hole (positive charge) somewhere else.

In p-type silicon there are some free electrons available in the structure (ones that were created by the action of ambient heat but haven't yet recombined with holes).

A.1.4.6 Majority and Minority Carriers

In n-type silicon electrons are called the "majority carriers" because there are far more electrons available than holes. In n-type silicon holes are referred to as the "minority carriers". In p-type silicon it is the other way around. Holes become the "majority carriers" and electrons the "minority carriers". In further discussion most effects apply to either p-type or n-type silicon but to either electrons or to holes depending on which one is in the majority. Thus electron behavior in n-type and hole behavior in p-type is generically referred to as majority carrier behavior.

A.1.4.7 Electrical Conduction in Semiconductor Devices

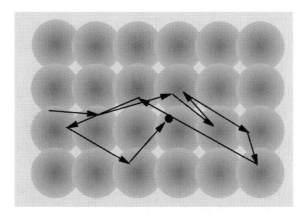

Figure 389. *Free Electron Movement within a Crystal Lattice*

Diffusion

The term diffusion describes the behavior of free (conduction band) electrons and holes within a solid **when there is no external electric field applied**. What happens is that the electrons move at random throughout the solid (say a piece of metal) in the same way as the molecules of a gas move within a confined space such as a jar. Each electron takes a random path but on average the density of electrons throughout the solid is the same in all places. This is because electrons carry the same charge and hence repel each other. Where they can move freely through a solid they fill the whole available space relatively evenly.

Gas in a jar behaves in exactly the same way. If you have gas under pressure in a jar and then open it, the gas will propel itself out into the surrounding air very quickly. The mechanism here is just diffusion at work. Pressure will tend to even up over the whole space occupied very quickly.

Drift

Drift is the term used to describe the movement of electrons in a semiconductor under the influence of an electric field. The electric field causes the electrons to be accelerated in the direction of the positive contact (positive end of the wire) away from the negative contact. But they don't get very far. They very soon find an atom in the way and they bounce off (just at they do in regular diffusion). However the external force of the electric field causes a net movement of electrons (called current).

A good way of thinking about drift is as diffusion in a particular direction under the influence of an external electrostatic or magnetic field.

A.1.5 p-n Junctions

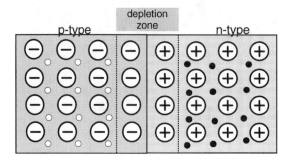

Figure 390. *p-n Junction*

Figure 390 shows a semiconductor junction diode. At one side of the junction we have p-type silicon and at the other n-type. The most important thing to understand about such a junction is that it is a molecular junction. You *cannot* take two pieces of doped silicon, polish them highly and clamp them together to form this kind of junction. The p-type and n-type regions must be part of the same contiguous silicon crystal.

In the early days (1950's) junction diodes and transistors were made by spot welding wires coated with dopant onto the opposite faces of a germanium crystal. In silicon VLSI, dopants are diffused into the crystal after it is formed by using gaseous compounds at temperatures of around 1100° C.

Immediately after the junction is formed holes will *diffuse* across the junction from the p-type to the n-type. At the same time electrons will diffuse from the n-type to the p-type. Since holes and electrons are of opposite charge and move into close proximity, many of them will re-combine with electrons filling available holes. This leaves negatively charged ions within the p-type and positively charges ions within the n-type. Thus at the junction we have a net negative charge in the p-type silicon and a net positive charge in the n-type. The region around is called the "depletion zone" because charge carriers (electrons and holes) have been eliminated. Thus the zone is depleted of charge carriers (as illustrated in the figure).

As the charge builds up new carriers find it difficult to cross the junction because they are repelled by the charge on the other side. Thus, more electrons can't cross the junction from the n-type side because of the negative charge on the p side. Likewise holes from the p-type side are repelled from the junction by the positive charge on the n-type side.

A.1.6 Semiconductor Junction Diodes

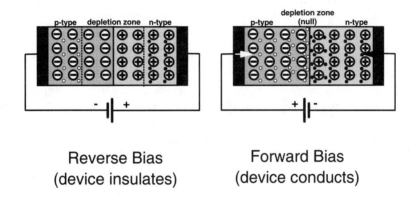

Reverse Bias
(device insulates)

Forward Bias
(device conducts)

Figure 391. Electrical Potentials across a p-n Junction

Figure 391 shows a p-n junction with an electrical potential applied across it. When the field is applied in one direction the device conducts electricity (called the forward direction). When the field is applied in the opposite direction (the reverse direction) no current can flow.

Forward Bias

> When we connect an electrical potential across the junction with the negative pole connected to the n-type material and the positive pole connected to the p-type material then the junction conducts.

> On the n-type side free electrons are repelled from the contact and pushed towards the junction. On the p-type side holes are repelled from the positively charged contact towards the junction. At the junction electrons will cross from the n-type side to the p-type side and holes will cross from the p-type side to the n-type side.

As soon as they cross (or perhaps a bit before) most holes and electrons will re-combine and eliminate each other.

> When this happens the free electrons must lose a quantum of energy to fill the available hole. This quantum of energy is radiated as electromagnetic energy with the wavelength depending on the size of the energy "gap" that the free electron crosses when it fills the hole. This phenomenon is called **Injection Luminescence**.

> If you choose your materials correctly this emits visible light and you have built an LED.

Some electrons and holes (by chance) don't recombine and continue through the material until they reach the other contact - but this is a very small number. In this context they are called "minority carriers".

The key to operation however is that electrons and holes must be able to leave the contacts and enter the silicon. This is possible because of the ions present in the material. On the n-type side, near the contact, the positively charged ion provides a place for an electron emitted from the contact to enter the silicon lattice. On the p-type side, the negatively charged ions have an electron that is only very weakly held in the lattice. This electron is easily attracted out of the lattice on to the positive contact and thus a new hole in the lattice is born.

Thus electrons enter the n-type material at the contact and flow to the junction. Holes are created at the contact in the p-type material (by loss of electrons to the positive contact) and flow to the junction. Holes and electrons combine and are annihilated at the junction.

Thus electricity flows through the device.

Reverse Bias

When a voltage is applied in the "reverse" direction no current flows at all.

A negative charge is applied to the contact on the p-type side and a positive charge is applied to the contact on the n-type side. In this case the contacts both attract the mobile charges. On the n-type side the mobile electrons are attracted to the positive contact and on the p-type side holes are attracted to the negative charge on the contact. Thus the depletion zone enlarges and there is no conduction.

There is however a small current caused by the random ionisation of covalent bonds within the depletion zone. Heat causes the random breaking of a bond creating both a hole and a free electron. The free electron is attracted by by the electric field towards the positive contact and the hole is attracted towards the negative contact. The free carriers can cross the junction if necessary. This process is continuous at room temperature thus there is a small current. This current is independent of the applied voltage but varies with temperature.

A.1.7 The Bipolar Junction Transistor (BJT)

In the beginning there was the "transistor". Although there were many different types they all used the same basic principle. Later, a new type of transistor operating by a different principle was invented. In order to distinguish between the two types the term "Bi-Polar Junction Transistor" (BJT) was coined to refer to the earlier type. The new family of transistor devices is generically called the "Field Effect Transistor" (FET).

The BJT is basically an amplifier of electrical *current*. That is, variations of current in one circuit are repeated as larger current variations in a different circuit. Of course depending on the way it is connected into an electrical circuit, the BJT can be used as a voltage amplifier. However, the basic process involved is one of current amplification.[129]

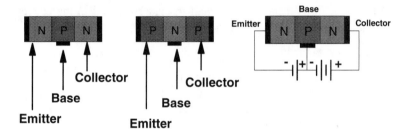

Figure 392. Basic BJT Configurations

A BJT consists of two semiconductor p-n junctions connected back-to-back. Figure 392 shows schematics of the two types of BJT. These are referred to as n-p-n and p-n-p configurations depending on the type of doped silicon used. As will be seen pnp and npn transistors have similar characteristics but the polarity of the currents must be reversed (because the material types used are reversed).

---

[129] FETs are voltage amplifiers.

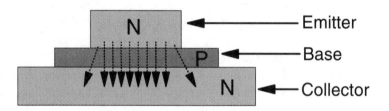

Figure 393. Practical Construction of a BJT

It is easy to be misled here by the way in which the schematics are usually drawn. The whole operation of the BJT relies on the fact that the "base" region is very thin. There are three doped regions which have different functions. These are called the "emitter", "base" and the "collector". From the diagram it seems that the emitter and the collector are interchangeable. To a point this is true. Many commodity discrete component transistors can be used in just this way but there are differences in practice as shown in Figure 393:

1. The emitter region is usually quite small in area compared to the collector. Also it is usually heavily doped to provide a good supply of charge carriers.

2. The base, as mentioned before is very thin.

3. The collector is often quite large in order to dissipate the heat.

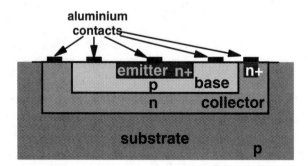

Figure 394. Bipolar Junction Transistor (BJT) in VLSI Implementation

When implemented in VLSI technology a BJT looks a lot different from its realisation as a free-standing device. This is because large numbers of them have to be built on a single substrate by lithographic techniques. However, as can be seen from Figure 394 the basic form is unchanged.

A.1.7.1 BJT Operation

In operation a small current in the emitter-base circuit controls a much larger current in the emitter-collector circuit.

There are three important things to understand about BJT operation:

1. The very thin base region. The phenomena of "transistor operation" is caused by charge carrier interactions in the base.

2. The fact that the material used is a semiconductor. Charges (both electrons and holes) travel quite slowly in a semiconductor.

3. There is almost *no* charge gradient over the majority of both the emitter and collector regions. This means that charge carrier movement in the device is almost always due to diffusion (see A.1.4.7, "Electrical Conduction in Semiconductor Devices" on page 693). Only in the depletion zones is there a sufficient charge gradient for carriers to move due to drift.

There are a number of ways to connect the device into a circuit and the "common base" configuration is used for the following example.

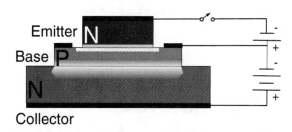

Figure 395. *Operation of a BJT Stage 1*

Figure 395 shows the device with the B-C junction reverse-biased and the emitter left floating (unconnected). In this case there is no current flow in the device. There is a large depletion zone at the B-C junction and a smaller depletion zone at the E-B junction (caused by the "natural" interaction of charges at every unbiased PN junction).

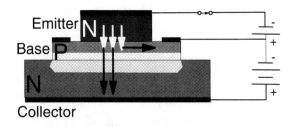

Figure 396. *Operation of a BJT Stage 2*

In Figure 396 the E-B junction is forward-biased and thus allows a current to flow. The B-C junction is still strongly reverse-biased and there should be *no* current flow across it. However, this is not what happens. There is a significant current from emitter to collector through the base!

When the E-B junction is forward-biased a number of things happen:

1. Electrons are allowed to travel from the emitter into the base region (this is the action of forward-biasing). Thus there is a current flow from emitter to base.

2. Having entered the base, the electrons still have to travel to the electronic contacts on the base to complete the circuit.

3. The base is very thin compared to the distance these electrons have to travel and the travel is slow.

4. In the meantime these same electrons diffuse throughout the base under the influence of local charges and of ambient heat.

5. Some (most) of these electrons enter the depletion zone between the base and the collector.

6. When they enter the B-C depletion zone they are caught by the influence of the B-C charge (the attractive charge due to the positive bias on the collector) and *drift* onward towards the collector.

7. Thus there is a current flow from emitter to collector.

8. The E-C current flow is mediated by the current flow from emitter to base. Due to the geometry of the device the E-C current flow can be quite large where the E-B flow is many times smaller.

Thus a small current flow in the E-B circuit controls a much larger current flow in the E-C circuit. Thus the device will amplify currents.

A.1.8 Field Effect Transistors (FET)

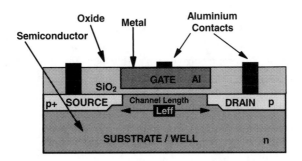

Figure 397. Insulated Gate Field Effect Transistor (IGFET)

The Field Effect Transistor uses a completely different principle to that used by the BJT. It is much more like the operation of a traditional thermionic valve. It is very popular (indeed it is the basis of the vast majority of current integrated circuit devices). This is partly because it is easier to fabricate in integrated circuit form but predominantly because it is a voltage controlled device. That is the flow of current through the device is controlled by the presence of an electrical charge rather than by a current flow. In the particular configuration of FETs called CMOS (Complementary Metal-Oxide Semiconductor) digital circuits consume *no* current at all in the steady state and only a very small amount during switching. This means that they don't consume much current or produce much heat. Thus you can make very large numbers of them in a very small area - a characteristic which both decreases their cost and increases their speed.

Figure 397 shows the basic configuration of a FET. Two electrical (metallic) contacts (called the Source and the Drain) are connected by a semiconducting region called the Channel. There is no p-n junction separating the source and the drain. The channel may be either p-type or n-type silicon.

When a potential difference is applied between the source and the drain a current flows through the semiconducting channel.

The gate electrode is either a metallic contact electrically isolated from the channel by a layer of insulating material or a region of doped silicon of opposite type to that of the channel. The figure illustrates the first mentioned type (the insulated gate FET). Thus the channel-to-gate region can be a p-n junction and indeed even when it isn't it acts like one.

When there is no charge on the gate area a current can flow from source to drain. When a charge (of the right sign) is present on the Gate it acts to attract or repel charge carriers in the channel.

In operation there is always a reverse-bias between the source and the gate electrodes. When there is a high reverse bias, charge carriers are attracted away from the channel. With no charge carriers present current can't flow between the source and the drain - because there is nothing to carry it. With only a very low reverse bias between the source and the gate the area of depleted carriers around the gate electrode is minimal. Thus carriers are present in the channel and current can flow.

Note that there is *never* a current flow between the source and the gate! There is always some reverse-bias present. This results in a very high resistance in the source-gate path. Thus the current flow in the source-drain circuit is controlled by *voltage* changes on the gate. This contrasts with the bipolar transistor where changes in current flow control the device.

A.1.9 Further Reading

An excellent text on the above subject is the book by Millman and Grabel (1987). See the list of texts at the end of Chapter 1.

Appendix B. An Introduction to Communications Networks

> **Definition of a Network**
>
> A means of delivering information from one place to another over a shared infrastructure.

B.1 Function Layering and the ISO Model

In the late 1970's the International Organisation for Standardisation (ISO) proposed a theoretical model (called the "ISO Model") for describing the process of communication between pairs of devices across a network. This model proposes a "layered" structure and has proven of immense value to people wishing to analyse and describe communication networks and devices.

Through the late 1970's into the 1990's the International Organisation for Standardisation also developed an extensive and detailed standard for communications called "OSI" for "Open Systems Interconnection". OSI failed in the marketplace for many reasons but prime among them was that it took so long to develop that when it was finished it was a standard for 1970's technology in the era of the 1990's. Perhaps more important was that it was eclipsed by the growth of the TCP/IP protocol on which the Internet is based. *However, the ISO model is still very useful as a reference in describing data communications processes.*

B.1.1 Layered Communication Architectures

Let us assume that we wish to communicate between two devices (A and B) connected together by a simple communications link. Further let us assume that the information we wish to send consists of "frames" or "blocks" of computer data variable in length on average 100 bytes long. In this simple case the link will be bi-directional and will consist either of four copper wires (one pair in each direction) or two fibres. When there is some information to send a device only needs to place the information serially onto the communications link.

Before there can be any communication the characteristics of the signal need to be agreed between the two devices. That is:

- We need to agree (in electrical or optical terms) just what constitutes a "ONE" bit and what constitutes a "ZERO" bit. In the simplest case a ONE might be signalled by the presence of a voltage (or the presence of light in a fibre) and a

ZERO by its absence. In more complex cases the ONE might consist of a "tone" of (say) 700 Hz and a zero of a different tone of (say) 1100 Hz.

- The receiver has to know what level of signal should be interpreted as meaning that there is a signal present or not. For example if a ONE is signalled by the presence of a voltage of nominally 3 volts how is the receiver to interpret a voltage of one volt?

- Both sender and receiver need to have agreed to the speed of data transmission. If there is no agreement then a string of bits such as '0101' could just as easily be interpreted as '00110011' for example. This is not always strictly true. In some protocols there is a "training sequence" sent at initialisation that allows the receiver to determine the speed in use. Of course agreement on speed is always relatively imprecise. The exact timing (at the receiver) is always derived from the data stream.

Thus in order to send a stream of bits between one device and another each device must agree on the electronic (or optical) characteristics of the signal and how it is coded.

But the computer data we are sending consists of bytes (8-bit characters) of data. We have to agree on how these characters are serialised and deserialised (which end of the byte is - high-order or low-order - sent first). Also we must have a method of detecting the boundary between bytes. The receiver needs to be able to work out where the boundaries between bytes are.

Now that we are able to send and receive streams of bytes we need to be able to determine where the boundary between frames (or blocks) of data are.

There are many ways to achieve the above objectives.

1. In very basic communications systems each byte is delimited by a START bit at the beginning and a STOP bit at the end. In this case bits within each character will bear a strict time relationship to one another but individual characters will have indeterminate "gaps" in time between them.

   In systems like this we normally use special characters (unique bit combinations) to signal the logical beginning and end of each data frame. However, when this is done we lose the ability to send "transparent data". If some combinations of characters are used for special purposes such as signalling the beginning and end of data frames then we quite obviously can't use these to represent data. (In most modern protocols there are algorithms which have the ability to exchange data transparently by doing something to render control characters unique.)

2. In more complex systems when a data frame begins the bits within that frame bear a fixed timing relationship with one another and thus if we can establish where the very first bit of the frame is then we can simply choose every 8-bit group from then on as a single byte. Of course this means that we must have some unique way of signalling the beginning of a data frame.

Thus in this most basic aspect of communication we have two operations we must perform in sequence:

1. Send a stream of bits from one end of the link to the other. In the most basic case this stream of bits may have highly erratic timing.

2. Use a set of agreed rules to take frames of data and convert them into a serial stream of bits at the transmitter end and to reconstruct them at the receiver.

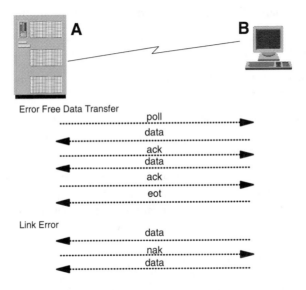

Figure 398. *Communications Protocol - Principle*

In traditional data communications (between computers and their devices) it is extremely difficult to ensure that when one end of the link wants to send information that the other end is ready to receive it. So it is commonly agreed that one end of the link should be a "primary" and the other end the "secondary". By the sending of special frames of control information the primary and secondary ends of the link are able to arrange that information is sent only when the other end is able to receive it. Now we have added the need to have a short prefix at the beginning of data frames in order to identify whether the frame contains real data or control information.

Controlling the flow of data on a link is the job of a "communications protocol" as shown in Figure 398. Such a protocol is simply an agreed set of rules which govern a particular communication. The procedure in the example proceeds as follows:

1. The primary end sends a POLL command to the secondary device. POLL says roughly "do you have any data for me".

2. The secondary device sees the POLL and in fact does have data so the data is sent.

3. When the primary has received the data it sends an ACK(nowledgment) to say the data has arrived.

4. The secondary may now send another frame of data if there is one to send.

5. In the example more data is available and so it is sent.

6. The primary sends ACK to confirm the receipt of the second frame of data.

7. At this point the secondary has no more data to send so it sends EOT (end of transmission).

8. In the common case the primary would next wait for a short time delay (around .2 of a second) and send a POLL again.

9. If an error is detected in a data frame when it is received (or if nothing is received in a given time) then the primary will send NAK (negative acknowledgment) causing the secondary to re-send its data.

10. In the case where the primary has data to send to the secondary it will start by sending a SELECT command (roughly meaning "are you ready to receive?") to the secondary. If the secondary is ready to receive it will send an ACK and the primary will then send some data.

The above is a very rough description of a protocol called BSC (Binary Synchronous Communication) widely used in the late 1960's and 1970's. One of the many things omitted from the description is the fact that every data frame carries a 2-byte trailer which is mathematically derived from the bits within the frame. At the receiver the mathematics is repeated as the frame is received and if the calculated trailer is different from the received trailer we know there has been some communication error and so NAK would be sent in response.

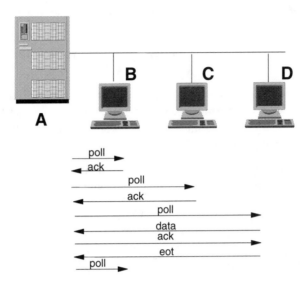

Figure 399. *Communications Protocol - Principle*

In the preceding description the reason for having one of the end devices on the link control when data is sent was simply because computers and data terminals of the 1960's were very limited in capability and just couldn't accept data at any old time.

An extension of the principle is shown in Figure 399. Here we have multiple devices attached to the same communications line (this is a "multidrop link"). In this example there is one primary and many secondaries. Data transfer is possible *only between the primary and one secondary* at any moment in time. The protocol proceeds as follows:

1. The primary asks device B if it has any data (POLL).

2. Device B responds with a NAK to say it has nothing.

3. The primary asks device C if it has any data.

4. Device C responds that it has nothing also.

5. When the primary POLLs device D it does have data and sends it immediately. From here the protocol will proceed as described in the previous example.

6. When communication is complete the primary will POLL device B again.

7. At any time the primary could interrupt the POLLing, send a SELECT command and send data to one of the secondaries.

The details of the protocol are not interesting. However, we notice that we are now performing two additional logical functions:

1. Controlling the flow of data on the link to suit the characteristics of the attached devices.

2. Controlling access to the link so that only one device (at least only one *secondary* device) is allowed to transmit at any one time. This is needed because if more than one device was to transmit the signals would interfere with one another and the receiver would get garbage.

   In today's world this function is called "Medium Access Control" (MAC) because it controls which device has access to the communications medium at any time.

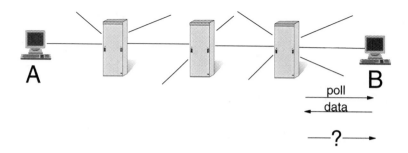

Figure 400. Communications Protocol - Network Problem

Now let us take the above example and place a network between the computer and its terminals. This is shown in Figure 400. In principle the network consists of a number of computers each of which receives data and re-transmits it onward towards its ultimate destination. These computers in today's terminology are called "routers".

Look what happens when the right-hand most router requests data from device B. Its sends a POLL and receives some data. **Now what?** We have a difficult logical problem! The only things the router can now do is to send ACK or NAK (or perhaps withhold a response). *But the ACK means (at least) three different and logically competing things!* It means:

1. I have received that data OK (without errors). Potentially now the link is free to do other things.

2. I am now responsible for the integrity of the data. Meaning you (the secondary) can discard your copy because I have it.

3. Please send the next block!

But:

- If I send ACK to free up the link and then the router fails (goes down) then data is lost. This is not good. In some types of early network the router logged each data frame to a local disk before sending ACK to mitigate this problem.

- If I send ACK I am asking the attached device to send more data. But what if there are not enough buffers are available in the router to receive that data? This would cause congestion problems in the router.

- But I must send something quickly or the terminal device will think it has an error and commence an error recovery protocol. (There are many possible variations here and early networks used lots of different approaches.)

The heart of the problem is that the simple ACK is being used for multiple (logically independent) functions:

- To control (network) end-to-end data integrity

- To control data flow in the network

- To be part of the mechanism that controls access to the link

It is clear that if we are to be successful in building computer networks individual logical functions need to be implemented by separate mechanisms. In the above discussion we have identified many functions:

1. The transmission and reception of a stream of bits

2. The translation of frames of user data to and from that stream of bits

3. Control of access to a shared communications medium (MAC)

4. Local (device to adjacent device) error detection

5. Local error correction (by retransmission)

6. End-to-end (across the network) verification of data integrity

7. Control of data flow on the link between the user device and the network

8. Control of data flow between end user devices through the network

9. Destination determination

   Implied, though it wasn't discussed was the presence of a means of determining where each block of data was destined. That is, we implied that each block of data had some kind of header that allowed the network to determine the next hop on which the data should be sent

It is clear (or it should be) that the above functions are built one upon another. You can't assemble bits into characters and characters into frames until you have a stable stream of bits with which to work. You can't have a medium access control procedure until you have a way of sending and receiving data frames.

The ISO Model then is simply a definition of the necessary network functions and a structuring of them into a "natural" hierarchy.

B.1.2 The ISO Model

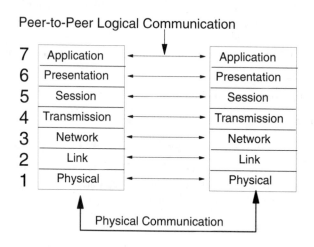

Figure 401. *Layering of Functions in the ISO Model*

Figure 401 shows the basic structure of the ISO model.

1. Each layer communicates with the layer above and the layer below by processes internal to whichever device is implementing the protocol.

2. In theoretical jargon the "n"th layer receives services from the "n-1"th layer and provides services to the "n+1"th layer. For example, the link layer receives a stream of bits from the physical layer, performs its functions and then passes frames to the network layer. (This works in both directions.)

   Another way of expressing this is to say that the layers have a client/server relationship with their adjacent layers. Layer 2 (the link) layer obtains services from layer 1 (the physical layer). In this case the link layer is the client of the physical layer. The physical layer is the server for the link layer.

3. Physical communication across a link takes place between layer 1 (physical layer) entities.

4. There is also communication *between* peer layers. The model only applies to pairs of peer entities. The link layer communicates with its peer link layer, the transmission layer communicates with its peer. This is necessary for each layer to perform its function. For example, the link layer checks for errors and may perform error recovery. To do this information must be communicated between pairs of link layers without the intervention of the rest of the system.

| phy | link | network | transmission | session | presentation | data |

Figure 402. OSI Data Frame Format. OSI is one possible implementation of the ISO Model. In OSI communication between peer layers is usually performed using special headers on each data frame.

This communication takes place either by the use of special headers on each message or by the use of unique control messages.

The logical functions of the various layers are as follows:

Physical Layer (Layer 1)

As discussed above the primary function of the physical layer is to take a stream of bits presented to it by a link layer and to deliver that stream of bits *unchanged* to the partner link layer at the other end of a physical link. Thus the scope of the physical layer is across a physical link.

Link Layer (Layer 2)

The link layer accepts frames (or "blocks") of data from a network layer and delivers them to the partner network layer at the other end of a single physical link connection (*not across the network*).

Network Layer (Layer 3)

The network layer routes data frames from one network port to another. In addition it provides a multiplexing function on the link layer such that a single link layer may support many logical link connections. That is, a single network port can support data transfer with multiple network ports at other places within the network. There are a number of other necessary functions here such as control of the flow of data from the user to the network.

For the network layer to function there must be a header appended to the front of the data containing information that the network can use to route the data towards its destination. For this to happen we have assumed the presence of a network-wide addressing structure such that network ports can be specified uniquely.

Transmission Layer (Layer 4)

The network layer has provided a connection between end users across the network. Depending on the type of network, this connection may not be very reliable. The primary function of the transmission layer is to provide end-to-end error detection and recovery (data integrity). This function provides the same function as the error recovery function at the link layer (layer 2) except that it operates across the network rather than a single link. Albeit that there are many errors that can apply in the network context that cannot occur across a link such as the delivery of frames in a different sequence from that in which they were delivered to the network.

Session Layer (Layer 5)

This layer provides a mechanism to multiplex many logically independent connections onto the same network connection.

Presentation Layer (Layer 6)

The presentation layer transforms the data into a form expected by the user application. For example this function may include code translation.

Application Layer (Layer 7)

After all this network processing it is sobering to realise that somewhere there is a user and they may want to process some data. The application layer is where they do it.

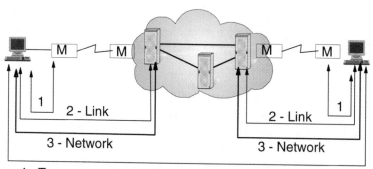

Figure 403. Scope of Layers - 1

Figure 403 summarises the scope of the various layers. In the diagram layer 1 exists between the user and a local modem but (of course) there is another layer 1 between the two modems. Layers 2 and 3 communicate between the end user device and the network where all the higher layers pass end-to-end over the network and apply only to the user devices.

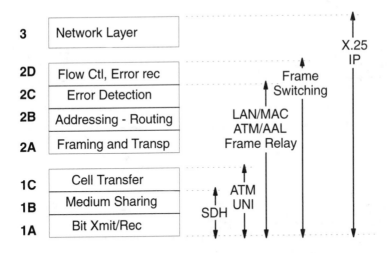

Figure 404. *Sub-Layers and Networks*

It is important to note that each layer may be broken down into many sub-layers (these are not specified in the model but are allowed). One such conceptual layering is shown in Figure 404.

The various functions performed by sub-layers are optional and therefore the sub-layers themselves are optional. For example error recovery at the link layer is optional and thus the sub-layer for recovery may be present or not.

Indeed whole layers are optional in the sense that they can be left out if their function is not needed. The session layer (layer 5) was often omitted from early implementations of OSI in real products.

Figure 404 illustrates different communication network architectures and the extent of their functions within the ISO Model. This is contentious. Each of the network architectures provides a "networking" function. The ISO Model specifies that "networking" takes place at layer 3 (the network layer). Although the functions provided by each of the network architectures (minus the networking function) line up with the layers of the model as shown, an alternative view is to say that networking takes place at layer 3 and map the other functions accordingly. For example ATM and X.25 are almost identical in concept and function. Basically ATM is X.25 *without the error recovery protocols! Yet ATM is accepted as being "layer 1" and X.25 as "layer 3".*

B.2 Networks of Networks

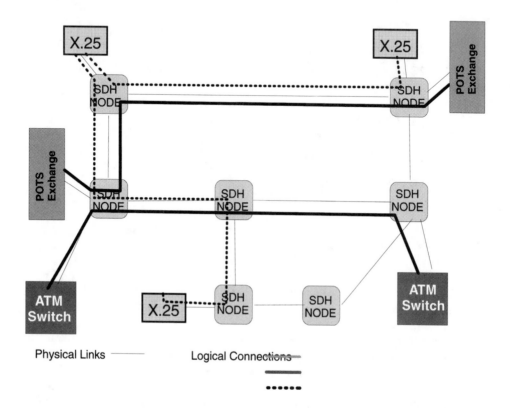

Figure 405. *ATM, POTS and X.25 over an SDH/Sonet Backbone*

In today's practical networks we *almost never* use a single network architecture. Practical networks are built as a hierarchy of many network architectures.

Figure 405 illustrates the principle. Here we have a shared network infrastructure based on SDH/Sonet protocols. Three other networks are built "over the top" of it. In the example we have a POTS (Plain Old Telephone System) network, an ATM network and an X.25 network all sharing the same link infrastructure based on SDH/Sonet. This structure is considered ideal by many large carrier organisations.

Many practical networks have significantly more layers of networks than the above suggests. For example we could have IP built over frame relay built over ATM built over SDH/Sonet. While this might look wasteful, in fact it is the predominant way of delivering network services in the real world. Most major telecommunications carriers have many examples of networks structured in just this way.

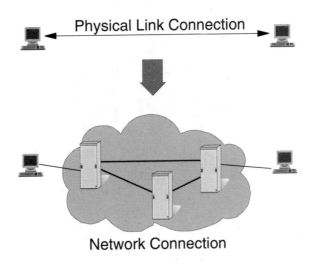

Figure 406. *Network Replaces a Point-to-Point Physical Link*

Another way of looking at network hierarchies is to consider Figure 406. Here a network replaces a direct physical link connection between two communicating devices. This is not always as simple as it looks. Many networks require complex interfacing and signalling protocols (such as a signalling protocol to set up a connection) and these protocols need to be understood by the attaching device in order to connect to the network. So, while is it sometimes possible to replace a physical link with a network in a *transparent* way - usually this is not possible and the attaching device needs to understand the network protocols.

Figure 407 on page 716 shows the next stage. Here a point-to-point link within a network is replaced by *another network.* As mentioned above this is a very common practical situation.

It appears that by having layers of networks we are building up layers of redundant function. In some cases this is true - although there is almost always a good reason for doing it. In other cases, where the networks are designed to operate together they can be installed in complementary ways.

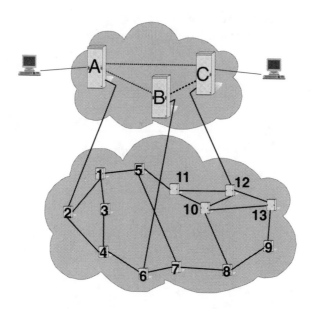

Figure 407. A Network Replaces a Link within Another Network.

A good example here might be where an ATM network is installed "over the top" of a Sonet network. You could use the networking abilities of both Sonet and ATM and in this case there would be redundant function. However, if the Sonet equipment merely provided point-to-point connections between ATM switches and ATM was allowed to do all the networking there is little or no redundancy. Here Sonet would be used to manage the fibre optical cable plant and to provide redundant paths (through Sonet rings). ATM would do all of the data switching (networking). This is in fact the "vision" held in mind by the people who devised the ATM standards.

B.2.1 The Role of Optical Networks

The reason for the above discussion was to show that different forms of networking can (and should) be built "on top" of one another. In the case of practical optical networks today we have four different possible structures:

1. Point-to-Point WDM

2. Add-Drop Optical WDM Networks

3. Optical TDM Networks (with an add/drop function).

4. Wavelength Routed Networks

At the present time we can define three optical networking layers:

Optical Link Layer

This is the lowest layer in an optical network and includes the protocols necessary to manage a point-to-point optical link. However, it does not contain the transmission protocols or the coding structures as this is done at the next layer.

WDM Networking Layer

This layer provides end-to-end transparent optical transport through the network. It applies to both add-drop and nodal networks.

OTDM Layer

An OTDM networking system can be (optionally) built above a WDM structure.

B.3 Further Reading

John D. Day and Hubert Zimmerman (1983)

The OSI Reference Model: Proceedings of the IEEE, Vol 71, No 12, December 1983. pp 1334-1340

Appendix C. Laser Safety

Figure 408. Hazard Warning Symbol Designating Laser in Operation

It is widely believed that because of their very low power, communication lasers cannot ever be a safety hazard. *This is not true.* Because lasers deliver light in a concentrated (parallel, narrow-beam, in-phase) form the light produced *can* be a hazard even at the very low power used in communications.

A good illustration of this is found in long distance fibre communications systems where optical power levels of up to .5 of a watt are often used. (Half a watt doesn't seem very much to someone with a background in electronics.) The connectors on these systems often develop pitting and damage caused by technicians unplugging the connectors with the power turned on. The very short duration of high intensity signal light as the connector is removed can burn the aluminium ferrule of the connector! At a power level of only half a watt!

Many factors influence the degree of hazard. Light intensity, wavelength, and exposure duration are the most obvious. The intensity of ambient light is also important. Because the pupil in the eye closes in the presence of bright sunlight, laser emissions (say from surveying instruments) viewed in bright sunlight are much less of a hazard than when the same emissions are viewed in a darkened room.

Standards organizations around the world have developed a set of safety standards and a classification mechanism for lasers so that the hazard can be controlled.

A "Class 1" laser is defined as one that "is inherently safe (so that the maximum permissible exposure level cannot be exceeded under any condition), or are safe by virtue of their engineering design". Most (but not all) communication lasers fall into this category. It is common, however, for a communication laser to have a Class 1 emission level at the point of entry to the fibre *but a much higher level once the covers are removed from the device.*

The *only* good reference is the appropriate standard, (IEC 825-1), itself (these have minor differences country by country). However, as a rough guide, the following are the Class 1 limits for exposure durations of up to 100 seconds:[130]

Wavelength 700 to 1050 nm

> 0.7 mW x C

> Where C represents a number of correction factors depending on wavelength and exposure duration. For a communications laser operating at 800 nm the adjusted figure is .35 mW.

Wavelength 1050 to 1400 nm

> 3.5 mW x C

> Again C here represents a number of correction factors depending on wavelength and exposure duration. For a communications laser operating in the 1310 nm band with 100 seconds exposure duration the adjusted figure is 8.8 mW.

Wavelength longer than 1400 nm

> 10 mW

Notice the large variation in allowable levels with wavelength.

The maximum allowable launch power for FDDI is -6 dBm at 1300 nm. This corresponds to .25 mW of power. Since the Class 1 limit at 1300 nm is 8.8 mW we can conclude that any FDDI transmitter that meets the FDDI specification for maximum power output also meets the Class 1 standard at launch into the fibre. (Under the covers it may not.) Another thing that should be kept in mind is that the limit at 1550 nm is significantly higher than the limit at 1300 nm. This is another advantage for longer-wavelength systems.

---

[130] These figures are intended to give the reader a "feel" for the magnitude of the numbers. They *must not be relied upon for any use except conceptual understanding.* When designing products the reader should consult the standard itself.

A careful analysis must be made of any optical fibre communication with laser power emission levels approaching 1 milliwatt or more. This is particularly true for short-wavelength diode systems, which have a lower allowable power level.

In the US, the Federal Food and Drug Administration (FDA) regulates and enforces a laser product performance standard through the Center for Devices and Radiological Health (CDRH). The standard is Part 1040.10 of Title 21, Subchapter J of the US Code of Federal Regulations. The standard applies to laser communication products as well as all other laser products. All laser products sold in the US must be certified by the manufacturer with CDRH.

Throughout the rest of the world, IEC 825 is the primary standard, and is the base document for the European Norm 60825, which is a mandatory standard for laser products in Europe. All IBM laser products are certified to IEC 825. This is the most restrictive of the current standards.

A voluntary standard in the US, ANSI/Z136.2, addresses the specific topic of the safe use of optical fibre communication systems utilizing laser diode and LED sources. It contains all the basic mathematical relations to describe what are safe levels as a function of laser (LED) wavelength, NA of multimode fibres or mode field diameters of single-mode fibres, use of optical aids or not, viewing distance, etc. The criteria document for the development of this standard is a technical paper entitled "Toward the development of laser safety standards for fibre-optic communication systems" by R.C. Petersen and D.H. Sliney (see bibliography).

As our knowledge of the safety aspects increases, it is to be expected that relevant standards committees will modify the standards in line with better knowledge. In this light, these standards were revised in 1992 and the maximum allowable power levels were significantly *increased*. It is felt that it is now unlikely that further increases will take place for some time.

Always treat connected optical fibre as a potential hazard. Never look directly at the end of it. In any case all of the wavelengths used for communication are invisible - there is nothing to see.

C.1.1 Handling Fibre

Glass fibre is very thin. It is also quite rigid and it can be sharp. If you touch the end of an unclad glass fibre to your skin it is quite possible for the glass to penetrate and then break off! A tiny sliver of glass is left inside. This can be extremely painful and and in some circumstances could be life threatening.

The need for great care applies at all times but especially when making fibre joins or fitting connectors. Typically these operations produce left over short lengths (around 1 cm or less) of fibre which are hard to see and very dangerous. Whenever you produce such a piece of fibre dispose of it immediately into a properly designed container. Imagine what could happen if a very small piece of fibre was sticking to one of your fingers when you rubbed your eyes! **Take extreme care when handling fibre.**

Appendix D. Acronyms

ABF   Air Blown Fibre

ACK   Acknowledgment

ADM   Add-Drop Multiplexor

ADSL   Asymmetric Digital Subscriber Line

AEL   Accessible Emission Limit

AON   All-Optical Network

AOTF   Acousto-Optical Tunable Filter

APD   Avalanche PhotoDiode

ASE   Amplified Spontaneous Emission

ATM   Asynchronous Transfer Mode

AWG   Array Waveguide Grating

BER   Bit Error Rate

BEDSFA   Broadband Erbium Doped Silicon Fibre Amplifier

BISDN   Broadband Integrated Services Digital Network

CATV   Community Antenna Television

CBS   Central Base Station

CCITT   Comite Consultatif International Telegraphique et Telephonique (a.k.a. ITU-TS)

CD   Compact Disk

CDMA   Code Division Multiple Access

CFR   Cross-coupling Fibre Ring resonator

CIP   Carrier-Induced Phase Modulation

CNR   Carrier to Noise Ratio

CMOS   Complementary Metal Oxide Semiconductor

CW   Continuous Wave

dB   Decibel

dBm   Decibels above/below one milliwatt

DBR	Distributed Bragg Reflector (laser)
DCF	Dispersion Compensating Fibre
DCM	4-(dicyanomethylene)-2-methyl-6- (4-dimethylaminostyryl)-4H-pyran
DFB	Distributed FeedBack (laser)
DFG	Difference Frequency Generation
DFR	Direct-coupling Fibre Ring resonator
DH	Double Heterostructure
DMD	Differential Mode Delay
DSF	Dispersion Shifted Fibre
DSHI	Delayed Self-Heterodyne Interferometer
DUT	Device Under Test
DWDM	Dense Wavelength Division Multiplexing
EA	Electro-Absorption
ECL	Emitter Coupled Logic
EDFA	Erbium Doped Fibre Amplifier
EDFFA	Erbium Doped Fluoride Fibre Amplifier
EDSFA	Erbium Doped Silicon Fibre Amplifier
EH	Electric Magnetic (H = magnetic)
EIA	Electronic Industries Association
EMC	ElectroMagnetic Compatibility
EMD	Equilibrium Mode Distribution
EMI	ElectroMagnetic Interference
EMV	Effective Mode Volume
FBT	Fused Biconical Taper
FC	Fibre Channel
FDDI	Fibre Distributed Data Interface
FDHM	Full Duration at Half Maximum
FDM	Frequency Division Multiplexing

FEC	Forward Error Correction
FEL	Free Electron Laser
FET	Field Effect Transistor
FFP	Fibre Fabry-Perot filter
FITL	Fibre In The Loop
FOTP	Fibre Optic Test Procedure
FP	Fabry-Perot
FPI	Fabry-Perot Interferometer
FPM	Four Photon Mixing
FSC	Free Space Coupler
FSK	Frequency Shift Keying
FSR	Free Spectral Range
FTTC	Fibre To The Curb
FTTH	Fibre To The Home
FTTN	Fibre To The Neighbourhood
FWHM	Full Width Half Maximum
FWM	Four Wave Mixing
GbE	Gigabit Ethernet
GI	Graded-Index
GRIN	GRaded-INdex
GVD	Group Velocity Dispersion
HDSL	High-Speed Digital Subscriber Line
HE	Magnetic Electric (H = magnetic)
HPCF	Hard Plastic Coated silica Fibre or Hard Polymer Clad silica Fibre
HPCS	Hard Plastic Coated Silica or Hard Polymer Clad Silica
HWHM	Half-Width Half-Maximum
Hz	Hertz
IC	Integrated Circuit

IEEE	Institute of Electrical and Electronic Engineers
IP	Internet Protocol
IR	Infra-Red
ISDN	Integrated Services Digital Network
IVPO	Inside Vapour Phase Oxidation
LAN	Local Area Network
LASER	Light Amplification by the Stimulated Emission of Radiation
LEOS	(IEEE) Lasers and Electro-Optics Society
LD	Laser Diode
LED	Light Emitting diode
LOL	Loss Of Light
LP	Linearly Polarised
LW	Long Wavelength
MAN	Metropolitan Area Network
Mb	Mega bit
MB	Mega Byte
MBd	Mega Baud
MBE	Molecular Beam Epitaxy
MCVD	Modified Chemical Vapour Deposition
MESFET	Metal Schottky Field Effect Transistor
MFD	Mode Field Diameter
MISFET	Metal Integrated Semiconductor Field Effect Transistor
MM	MultiMode
MOS	Metal Oxide Semiconductor
MOSFET	Metal Oxide Semiconductor Field Effect Transistor
MQW	MultiQuantum-Well
MTBF	Mean Time Between Failures (or Before Failure)
MZ	Mach-Zehnder

MZI	Mach-Zehnder Interferometer
n-ISDN	Narrowband Integrated Services Digital Network
NA	Numerical Aperture
NOLM	Non-Linear Optical Loop Mirror
ns	nanosecond
NTSC	National Television Standards Committee
OADM	Optical Add-Drop Multiplexor
OEIC	Opto-Electronic Integrated Circuit
OFC	Open Fibre Control
OFDM	Optical Frequency Division Multiplexing
OFL	Over-Filled Launch
OLED	Organic Light-Emitting Diodes
OOK	On-Off Keying
OSL	Organic Semiconductor Laser
OTDM	Optical Time Division Multiplexing
OTDR	Optical Time-Domain Reflectometer
OVD	Outside Vapour Deposition
OVPO	Outside Vapour-Phase Oxidation
OXC	Optical Cross-Connect
PAL	Phase Alternating Line
PANDA	Polarisation maintaining AND Absorption reducing
PCN	Personal Communication Network
PCOF	Primary Coated Optical Fibre
PCS	Personal Communication System
PCVD	Plasma-activated Chemical Vapour Deposition
PDG	Polarisation Dependent Gain
PDL	Polarisation Dependent Loss
PIC	Photonic Integrated Circuit

PIN	P-doped silicon, Intrinsic silicon, N-doped silicon junction
PMD	Polarisation Mode Dispersion
PMF	Polarisation Maintaining Fibre
PMMA	Poly-Methyl MethylAcrylate
POF	Plastic Optical Fibre
PON	Passive Optical Network
POTS	Plain Old Telephone System
PRBS	Passive Radio Base Station
PrDFA	Praseodymium Doped Fibre Amplifier
QCSE	Quantum Confined Stark Effect
RAPD	Reach-through Avalanche PhotoDiode
RECAP	REsonant CAvity Photodetector
REDFA	Rare-Earth Doped Fibre Amplifier
RFI	Radio Frequency Interference
RI	Refractive Index
RIN	Relative Intensity Noise
RMS	Root Mean Square
RO	Relaxation Oscillation
ROFL	Radial Over-Filled Launch
Rx	Receiver
SAW	Surface Acoustic Wave
SBS	Stimulated Brillouin Scattering
SCM	SubCarrier Multiplexing
SCMOL	SubCarrier Multiplexed Optical Link
SCOF	Secondary Coated Optical Fibre
SDH	Synchronous Digital Hierarchy
SHG	Second Harmonic Generation
SHIP	Silicon Hetero-Interface Photodetector

SI	Step-Index
SLA	Semiconductor Laser Amplifier
SLD	SuperLuminescent Diode
SM	Single Mode
SNR	Signal-to-Noise Ratio
SOA	Semiconductor Optical Amplifier
SOI	Silicon On Insulator or Silica On Insulator
SONET	Synchronous Optical Network
SQW	Single Quantum Well
SRS	Stimulated Raman Scattering
STP	Shielded Twisted Pair
SW	Short Wavelength
TDM	Time Division Multiplexing
TE	Transverse Electric
TEM	Transverse Electro-Magnetic
TM	Transverse Magnetic
TP	Twisted Pair
TR	Token-Ring
TWA	Travelling Wave Amplifier
TWSLA	Travelling Wave Semiconductor Laser Amplifier
Tx	Transmitter
UV	Ultra-Violet
VAD	Vapour-phase Axial Deposition
VCSEL	Vertical-Cavity Surface-Emitting Laser
VDSL	Very high speed Digital Subscriber Line
WDM	Wavelength Division Multiplexing
WGR	Waveguide Grating Router
XGM	Cross Gain Modulation

XPM   Cross Phase Modulation

YLF   Yttrium Lithium Fluoride

ZBGA   Zirconium Barium Gadolinium Aluminium (Fluoride)

ZBLA   Zirconium Barium Lanthium Aluminium (Fluoride)

ZBLAN Zirconium Barium Lanthium Aluminium Sodium (Fluoride)

ZMD   Zero Material Dispersion

Appendix E. Some Useful Facts

E.1.1 The Visible Spectrum

In optical communications we almost never use visible light. However, it is useful to know the wavelengths of the colours in the visible spectrum.

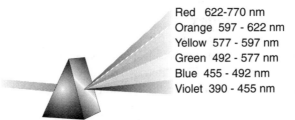

Red   622-770 nm
Orange 597 - 622 nm
Yellow 577 - 597 nm
Green 492 - 577 nm
Blue 455 - 492 nm
Violet 390 - 455 nm

Figure 409. *The Visible Spectrum*

It's an interesting aside that people often talk about the "blue end" or the "red end" of a spectral range *even when they are not talking about visible light*. For example someone might refer to the "blue end" of an optical amplifier's range when they mean a wavelength of around 1535 nm. 1535 nm is in the infrared but it is at the short-wave end (the blue end) of the amplifier's spectrum. Thus the word "blue" sometimes means "short-wave" and "red" sometimes means "long-wave" regardless of any relationship with the visible spectrum.

E.2 Units of Measure

E.2.1 Fractions and Multiples

Prefix	Symbol	Value	Prefix	Symbol	Value
deci	d	10^{-1}	deca	da	10
centi	c	10^{-2}	hecto	h	10^2
milli	m	10^{-3}	kilo	k	10^3
micro	μ	10^{-6}	mega	M	10^6
nano	n	10^{-9}	giga	G	10^9
pico	p	10^{-12}	tera	T	10^{12}
femto	f	10^{-15}	peta	P	10^{15}
atto	a	10^{-18}	exa	E	10^{18}

1024	K	2^{10}
Byte	B	
Bit	b	
Angstrom	Å	10^{-10} metres

E.3 Some Basic Concepts

E.3.1.1 Refractive Index

The speed of light in a vacuum (in free space) is 2.998 x 10^8 metres per second. Whenever a material is present the speed of light is reduced by an amount depending on the material characteristics. The "Refractive Index" (RI) of a material is the ratio of the speed of light in a vacuum over the speed of light in the material in question.

$$RI = \frac{C_{material}}{C_{freespace}}$$

E.3.1.2 Extinction Ratio

Extinction ratio is a concept related to digital signals where a digital 1 and a digital 0 are represented by different signal levels. The ER is simply the ratio of the power level representing a 1 bit to the power level representing a 0 bit.

$$ExtinctionRatio\ (ER) = \frac{Power_{1\ bit}}{Power_{0\ bit}}$$

This is a very useful concept because ones and zeros are usually not represented by absolute power levels but rather in relation to one another. Thus a change in line state by -15 dB might represent a transition from the 1-state to the 0-state. This would be true at the transmitter where the signal level representing a 1-bit might be as high as 10 milliwatts or after transmission over 100 km of fibre where the signal level of the 1-bit may be perhaps only .001 of a milliwatt.

It is important to note that a 0-state is usually not a complete absence of power. The extinction ratio is *never* infinite. In many systems the laser is run (slightly) above threshold in the 0-state and thus some power is always transmitted. At the receiver there is always some current in the zero state caused by thermal noise in the detector and in the receiver circuit.

E.3.1.3 Optical Decibels

Throughout almost every activity in the planning and design of communications systems and devices we are constantly faced with calculating losses and gains of signal power. This is fundamental to everything we do. The decibel is a very convenient way of expressing an amount of loss or gain within a system or the amount of loss or gain caused by some component of a system.

When power is lost such as during the transit of a signal along a transmission line you *never* lose a fixed amount of power - you always lose a proportion. For example if an electrical signal is attenuated from 1 milliwatt to 1/2 of a milliwatt in its transport on a transmission line then the transmission line has an attenuation of .5. If we sent a signal of 1/4 of a milliwatt on the same transmission line then it will be attenuated to 1/8 of a milliwatt. In each case a fixed proportion (1/2) of the power is lost but the absolute amount of the loss is quite different. The same applies for example in amplifiers where power is gained.

When you have to calculate the total losses and gains in a system you have to *multiply* the loss and gain proportions for each element of the system. This is hard to do mentally - especially when many stages are involved.

Decibels are logarithms. This allows us to easily and conveniently calculate the total loss/gain characteristics of a system by just adding them up! This is very convenient and once you get used to it, natural.

The Decibel originated as the "Bell" and was first defined by Alexander Graham Bell. A Bell is the logarithm of the ratio of a signal's *power* with some reference power level. A deci-bel is just one tenth of a Bell and was invented because the Bell unit was too large for convenient manipulation.

Usually a dB is the amount of loss or gain of signal *power*. In the case of a component that attenuates a signal, the attenuation in dB is 10 times the log (base 10) of the ratio of output power to input power.

$$Attenuation \ = \ 10 \log_{base10} (\frac{Power_{output}}{Power_{input}})$$

A very misleading situation can arise when optical power ratios (quoted in dB) are quoted in conjunction with electrical power ratios (also quoted in dB). This can be illustrated very easily. If you take an optical signal of a particular power level and feed it to an electronic detector you get a certain amount of photocurrent. If you double the amount of optical power and feed it to the same detector then you get (or we hope we get) twice the photocurrent output. So the optical signal level has doubled (increased by approx 3 dB).

But now if we look at electrical power we get something different. Electrical power is proportional to *the square of the current not current itself.* Thus:

$$Attenuation_{electrical} = 10 \log(\frac{Output\ power_{electrical}}{Input\ power_{electrical}})$$

Expressed as current this is:

$$Attenuation_{electrical} = 20 \log(\frac{Output\ current}{Input\ current})$$

Thus if you measure (say) the loss on a transmission link by taking the ratio of the optical powers involved you will get *half* of the figure you would have obtained if you measured the current received at a detector. The ratio dB$_{optical}$ is half as large as the ratio dB$_{electrical}$. This can be confusing in a number of situations. For example a loss of 20 dB on an electrical cable is equivalent to the loss of 10 dB in an optical one.

When losses/gains are quoted in dB you should always be sure of the context in which the measurement has been made. Never mix optical and electrical dB.

E.3.1.4 dBm

As noted above, a dB is a ratio of signal powers. Sometimes it is convenient to quote a power level in dB but if you do that it must be in relation to some fixed power level. A dBm is the signal power level in relation to one milliwatt. Thus:

$$Powerlevel\ (dBm) = 10 \log_{base10} (\frac{Signal\ power}{1\ milliwatt})$$

This can apply to either optical power or electrical power but you have to be consistent in usage. In most optical usage dBm relates to an *average* power level rather than a peak or instantaneous one.

Therefore a signal level of 3 dBm is 2 milliwatts. A signal power of .5 of a milliwatt is -3 dBm. A signal power of 20 dBm is 100 milliwatts. One milliwatt is 0 dBm.

E.4 Wavelength Hall of Fame

When you first become involved in fibre optics it is easy to become confused at the significance of certain wavelengths. Wavelengths are often quoted assuming that the reader understands that this wavelength has certain characteristics. Following is an overview of some important wavelengths used for optical communications:

244 nm   Resonant wavelength of the Si-Ge "wrong-bond". Exposure of Ge doped silica glass to this wavelength causes a permanent increase in the RI of the exposed material.

400 nm   Short wavelength limit of the visible spectrum (violet).

488 nm   Wavelength of the Ar^{++} laser. Can be frequency doubled to produce 244 nm.

560 nm   Centre wavelength of sunlight.

570 nm   First transmission wavelength for plastic optical fibre.

650 nm   Second transmission wavelength for plastic optical fibre.

700 nm   Long wavelength limit of visible spectrum (red).

780 nm   Wavelength of CD-ROM lasers increasingly used for short distance data communication.

800-950 nm   First communications "window" for fibre transmission.

980 nm   Pump wavelength for erbium.

1017 nm   Pump wavelength for praseodymium.

1064 nm   Pump wavelength for ytterbium.

1280-1350 nm Second communications "window" for fibre transmission.

1310 nm   Zero dispersion wavelength of standard fibre.

1385 nm   OH bond resonance absorption peak in fibre.

1480 nm   Pump wavelength for erbium.

1510-1600 nm Third communications "window" for fibre transmission.

1535-1560 nm Amplification range of basic (first generation) EDFA.

10,400 nm   Characteristic wavelength of CO_2 laser.

Appendix F. Special Notices

This publication is intended to help IBM and customer I/T professionals understand the technology of optical communications. While IBM products are mentioned in the text they are mentioned by way of example only. The information in this publication is not intended as the specification of any programming interfaces that are provided by IBM. For information about specific IBM products please see the official product manuals.

References in this publication to IBM products, programs or services do not imply that IBM intends to make these available in all countries in which IBM operates. Any reference to an IBM product, program, or service is not intended to state or imply that only IBM's product, program, or service may be used. Any functionally equivalent program that does not infringe any of IBM's intellectual property rights may be used instead of the IBM product, program or service.

Information in this book was developed in conjunction with use of the equipment specified, and is limited in application to those specific hardware and software products and levels.

IBM may have patents or pending patent applications covering subject matter in this document. The furnishing of this document does not give you any license to these patents. You can send license inquiries, in writing, to the IBM Director of Licensing, IBM Corporation, 500 Columbus Avenue, Thornwood, NY 10594 USA.

Licensees of this program who wish to have information about it for the purpose of enabling: (i) the exchange of information between independently created programs and other programs (including this one) and (ii) the mutual use of the information which has been exchanged, should contact IBM Corporation, Dept. 600A, Mail Drop 1329, Somers, NY 10589 USA.

Such information may be available, subject to appropriate terms and conditions, including in some cases, payment of a fee.

The information contained in this document has not been submitted to any formal IBM test and is distributed AS IS. The use of this information or the implementation of any of these techniques is a customer responsibility and depends on the customer's ability to evaluate and integrate them into the customer's operational environment. While each item may have been reviewed by IBM for accuracy in a specific situation, there is no guarantee that the same or similar results will be obtained elsewhere.

Customers attempting to adapt these techniques to their own environments do so at their own risk.

Any pointers in this publication to external Web sites are provided for convenience only and do not in any manner serve as an endorsement of these Web sites.

The following document contains examples of data and reports used in daily business operations. To illustrate them as completely as possible, the examples contain the names of individuals, companies, brands, and products. All of these names are fictitious and any similarity to the names and addresses used by an actual business enterprise is entirely coincidental.

The following terms are trademarks of the International Business Machines Corporation in the United States and/or other countries:

AIX®	AIX/6000®
AS/400®	Enterprise System/9000®
Enterprise Systems Architecture/390®	Enterprise Systems Connection Architecture®
ES/9000®	ESA/390 *.
ESCON XDF	ESCON®
IBM®	NetView®
OS/2®	OS/390
Parallel Sysplex	RISC System/6000®
RS/6000	S/370
S/390®	S/390 Parallel Enterprise Server
Sysplex Timer®	System/370
S/390 Parallel Enterprise Server	

The following terms are trademarks of other companies:

Tru-Wave is a Trademark of AT&T.
SMF-LS is a Trademark of Corning Inc.
LEAF is a Trademark of Corning Inc.
Selfoc® is a registered Trademark of the Nippon Sheet Glass Company.

C-bus is a trademark of Corollary, Inc.

Java and all Java-based trademarks and logos are trademarks or registered trademarks of Sun Microsystems, Inc. in the United States and other countries.

Microsoft, Windows, Windows NT, and the Windows 95 logo are trademarks or registered trademarks of Microsoft Corporation.

PC Direct is a trademark of Ziff Communications Company and is used by IBM Corporation under license.

Pentium, MMX, ProShare, LANDesk, and ActionMedia are trademarks or registered trademarks of Intel Corporation in the U.S. and other countries.

UNIX is a registered trademark in the United States and other countries licensed exclusively through X/Open Company Limited.

Other company, product, and service names may be trademarks or service marks of others.

Index

Numerics

A

Arsenic   686
ASE   68, 206, 215, 404, 414, 522, 560, 564
ASK   379
Asymmetric couplers and taps   241
Asymmetric digital subscriber line   398
Asymmetric three-port circulator   254
Asynchronous transfer mode   494
ATM   425, 494, 577, 714
   Concept   497
   Forum   501
   Layer   508
   Network   499
   Private network   499
   Switch   500, 503
ATM adaptation layers   502
ATM cell   497
ATM endpoint   500
ATM-100   610
ATM-155   611
Atom   679
Attenuation (fibre)   32, 398
Automatic fusion splicer   348
Availability   612
Avalanche photo-detector   388
Avalanche photodiodes   177
AWG   280, 287, 528
AWG as ADM   531
Axes of polarisation   83

B

B-ISDN   495
Bad connector   409
Balancing dispersion   417
Ball lens   114
Bandgap   107
Bandgap energy   106, 107
Bandwidth   407
Bandwidth (amplifier)   204
Bandwidth (FBG)   268
Bandwidth (filter)   289

Bandwidth occupancy   392
Bandwidth requirements (signal)   423
Bandwidth.distance product   47
Beamsplitter prism   247
Bend loss   74
Bending cables   8
Bends (cable)   358
Bends (in fibre)   58
BER   410
Bi-directional HFC   639
Bi-directional traffic   610
Bidirectional traffic on a single fibre
   strand   254
Binary synchronous communication   706
Biological reactions   101
Bioluminescense   101
Bipolar Junction Transistor   186, 697
Bipolar silicon   395
Birefringence   77, 190
Birefringent "walk-off" block   255
Birefringent material   323
Birefringent materials   248
Birefringent noise   78
Bit error rates   410
BJT   186, 697
BJT operation   699
Blazed FBG   273
Blazed in-fibre bragg grating   206
Block multiplexing   574
Blown fibre   365
Blue end   76
Boron   686
Boron trioxide   37
Bow-Tie fibre   82
Bragg diffraction   316
Bragg effect   317
Bragg grating   144
Bragg reflection   314
Brewster angle   247, 249
Broadband integrated services digital
   network   495

G

Junction diodes   694

K

KDP   327
Kerr effect   93, 306

L

Lambdanet   599
LAN   12, 458, 585
LAN environment   495
Large Effective-Area Fibres   80
Laser   35, 99
Laser chirp   548, 553
Laser drift   519, 548, 553
laser line   125
Laser linewidth   620
Laser noise   563
Laser operation   134
Laser safety   719
Laser selection   404
Laser/receiver cards   616
Lasers   117
Lasers on MM fibre   424
Lasing   121
Lasing threshold   134
Latency   510
Lateral misalignment   352
Lattice momentum   108
Lattice vibrations   317
Layer 1   710, 711
Layer 2   711
Layer 3   711
Layer 4   712
Layer 5   712
Layer 6   712
Layer 7   712
Layered communication architectures   703
LEAF fibre   80
Leaky modes   57
LED   35, 99, 103, 696

Lenses   259
Light detector   169
Light Emitting Diode   103
Light Emitting Diodes   35, 99
Light guiding light   653
Light rays   19
Light sources   99
Light Sources (WDM)   518
Light transmission   32
Lightning protection   359
Lightwave network   569
Line amplifier   628
Line amplifiers (EDFA)   220
Line broadening   133
Linearly polarised (LP) modes   70
Linewidth   125, 133, 392, 518
Linewidth (laser)   589
Link layer   711
Lithium niobate   190, 250, 301, 323, 325, 544
Littrow grating   156, 263, 515, 528
Local area network   12, 571
Local area systems   427
Local communications   570
Local distribution network   572
Local-loop cabling   635
Logic gate   309
LOL   477
Long-period FBG   274
Long-period grating   275
Longitudinal misalignment   352
Loose tube cable   362
Lord Nelson   3
LRC   616
Luciferase   101
Luciferin   101

M

MAC   457, 708
Mach-Zehnder Interferometer   31, 190, 284, 301, 311, 323, 528, 541

N

S